MYTHOLOGY OF THE SOUL

MYTHOLOGY OF THE SOUL

A RESEARCH INTO THE UNCONSCIOUS
FROM SCHIZOPHRENIC DREAMS
AND DRAWINGS

by

H. G. BAYNES

M.B., B.C. (Cantab.)

RIDER & COMPANY

LONDON

RIDER & COMPANY
178–202 Great Portland Street, London W1

AN IMPRINT OF THE HUTCHINSON GROUP

London Melbourne Sydney
Auckland Bombay Toronto
Johannesburg New York

★

First published 1940
by Bailliere, Tindall and Cox Ltd.
Second Impression 1955
by Routledge & Kegan Paul Ltd.
This edition 1969

This book has been printed in Great Britain
by Lowe and Brydone (Printers) Ltd., London N.W.10
and bound by Wm. Brendon, of Tiptree, Essex
09 098740 3

TO

A. S. B.

CONTENTS

ILLUSTRATIONS

PART ONE

PART TWO

PREFACE

WHEN Dr. Baynes was writing *The Mythology of The Soul* I was a frequent week-end guest at his house in Surrey. This large warm-hearted man had none of the calculated reserve of the traditional psychiatrist or analyst, and he shared with his friends his innermost thoughts and feelings. I often wish I could find such an evocative influence for my students as he was for me. His was the psychology of action, and he confronted his patients in his study or in his consulting room in London with the same informal immediacy that he received his guests in the sitting room. But action also gave way to careful, thoughtful consideration of words and images. He had a genuine writer's response to language and an artist's sensitivity to form and color.

Everywhere in the house or garden one felt the presence of this exuberant personality with his talent for creating an excitement of contrasts. The oars he had won as a Cambridge rowing blue and his herbaceous border were as appropriate an expression of his interests as the butterfly collection, the Chinese figurines, the antique furniture, or the masks and javelins of African tribesmen. Living there with his charming young wife and children he seemed to have reached as much stability and certainty as it is possible for human beings to find on this earth. But his life remained for him predominantly one of movement, accident and change. One Sunday morning, returning from a walk, he found his house in flames. All his worldly treasures were consumed, but he had the instinct to save the manuscript of the book for which he was chiefly to be remembered, and now continues to be remembered in this welcome re-publication of *The Mythology of the Soul.*

From our conversations of that time I recall two main themes of special interest to which Baynes seemed always to return, how the methods of depth psychology could be applied to the treatment of schizophrenia and to the interpretation of schizophrenic-like products of modern art. He had recently returned to England from Zürich where he had been for several years an assistant of C. G. Jung. He had been especially valuable to Jung as an analyst whose extraversion helped to balance the somewhat forbidding importance of introversion as seeming to characterize this school of psychology in the public mind. While in Zürich Baynes had learned to find his own appropriate balance between the extraverted and introverted aspects of his own life and work, and how to follow the natural process of introversion during analysis into the depths of the unconscious and then out again into the light of consciousness.

None of us who had worked with Jung during the nineteen twenties and thirties had any doubt concerning the validity of this analytic process for the psychoneuroses or character neuroses, but its application to the treatment of the psychoses was still regarded as highly questionable. In spite of the fact that Jung's *Psychology of Dementia Praecox*, written while he was still a follower of Freud, was accepted in psychoanalytic circles as proof that the findings of depth psychology were applicable to schizophrenia as well as to hysteria, very little had been done to transform these findings into new principles of treatment. Yet we knew that Jung himself and some of his immediate associates were achieving the most successful results yet seen in the treatment of schizophrenia in adults to say nothing of the treatment of delusional states such as had been described as psychaesthenia, involutional depression and similar conditions.

Baynes alone chafed at the fact that none of these results were being reported adequately. Ironically, he then became for Jung's School what Jung had been for the Freudian School twenty-five years earlier, the one to show how material apparently of irreducible pathology could be understood and treated by analytical psychology. When he showed this new work to one of his Zürich colleagues, suffering the familiar rebuff from the orthodoxy of his school, he was told that the material was far too pathological to merit a Jungian interpretation. Persisting in his belief in the new approach (which Jung himself later acknowledged as perfectly valid) he lived with his own loneliness creatively and brought to completion the study of Case I. This series of dreams, fantasies and active imagination fully illustrated by the patients' spontaneous paintings suggested to him a kind of mythological imagery similar to that which had inspired Jung to write his early masterpiece, *Symbols of Transformation*.

Any doubts concerning the applicability of this methodology to the material at hand were laid to rest by Baynes' masterly demonstration of the emergence and development of a hero myth together with its therapeutic effect upon the patient, as an inner personal experience of death and rebirth. The hero-dragon battle became the decisive image by which the patient seemed to become engaged in a struggle on his own behalf for deliverance from the psychotic threat. This was followed by a period of restoration in the formation of a new, stronger and more desirable ego-structure. Summing up his findings in this case he said:

> Many people cannot understand why this immediate experience of the unconscious should be regarded as therapeutically essential. In this work I have attempted to demonstrate its importance. Though its essential validity is germane only to the subject himself, the fact that the myth develops as an independent psychic organism affords us the opportunity of regarding it also as a purposive natural process. Yet only a schizophrenic personality, whose security of mind is constantly threatened by unintelligible psychic commotion, can understand fully what it means to find the silken thread of meaning and value in the psychotic labyrinth. (p. 510. N.Y. Humanities Press, 1955.)

If he were writing this today, having lived through the subsequent period during which, in the nineteen-forties and fifties, schizophrenia lost the stigma of being an incurable condition he would not have had to over-emphasize, as he sometimes does, the unique nature of the schizophrenic's experience. He might not even have called his cases schizophrenic, as compared with such clear-cut cases as have been reported and successfully treated since his time by Fromm-Reichman, Arieti or Sechehaye. I think he would also recognize what seems now obvious to me that once having established a working transference to his analyst the patient's material itself ceases to be anything we can call schizophrenic in spite of its distortions. We can also guess how his own counter-transference to the material of his patients allowed him to give them a sense of mutual collaboration in the whole process.

This leads me to Baynes' other interest of which I spoke, the application of analytic methods to the understanding of modern art and in turn its reflection of the spirit of the times. His aesthetic taste had been developed early in life through his friendship with some outstanding artists, writers, or composers, such as David Garnet, Arnold and Clifford Bax, etc. Thus he was uniquely equipped to help certain artists find themselves creatively. A famous actress used to rehearse parts of her major roles in his consulting room and found in his reactions a far more effective aid for interpretation than she was accustomed to receive from her directors. A writer who feared he had lost his talent found in Baynes an unbounded enthusiasm which sent him happily into the writing of his next work without further morbid self-questioning.

Developments in art had recently, however, thrown considerable doubt upon the validity of the standards of taste in which he had been educated. Especially was this true of painting and sculpture which seemed bent on disturbing the spectator rather than pleasing him. This art had been likened to the fragmented visions of schizophrenia. Along with Jung and many other psychiatrists Baynes felt deeply concerned with the sinister implications of this trend. However, unlike most psychiatrists of this period, his knowledge of art allowed him to be more tolerant, and to distinguish the real from the false. He reacted directly to the artist or the art product and only secondarily to a possible psychiatric diagnosis, so that in a large number of cases he found there was no diagnosis to be made. It all depended on whether the artist was truly expressing a primordial image appropriate to the spirit of his time, or merely a personal complex. Some artists or pseudo-artists he did see as truly schizophrenic and he writes eloquently in this work about the parallel between this sickness and the awakening of modern man to a realization of a basic split in the socio-religions structure of European Culture, a split which Hitlerism in Germany was beginning to expose. Baynes writes:

> The break-up of the Holy Roman Empire was followed by the witch-madness, in which it is estimated that something like two million witches were burned throughout Europe in the space of a hundred years . . . The Church had to deal with a widespread renegade movement back to pagan practices . . .
>
> The persecution of the Jews probably sprang from the same dissociation . . . Throughout the Middle Ages the Jews were forced to play the role of the scapegoat upon whom the unchristianized part of the Christian unconscious could be projected. It is highly significant, therefore, that this persecution should be revised again in its cruellest form in the land which suffered most from the power psychology of the Holy Roman Empire. (p. 863 Ibid).

With these ideas in mind, from his background as a Jungian analyst and his feeling for art, Baynes could see in the material of certain patients both the cause and cure, and in certain works of art a suggestion of the same cause and possible cure for this condition. Case II is a good example of this. The subject was himself an artist and out of his own split he seems to have created a symbolic bridge that would be therapeutic not only for himself but would be also a possible model for curing the evil of the times in which we then were living. The interpretation of this very sensitive and expressive imagery in the patient's psychological drawings allows Baynes to comment upon the painting of such modern artists as Paul Klee, showing that, far from being schizophrenic, this kind of art provides a similar suggestion of cure to be found for the sickness of the times.

The cure itself is not psychiatric nor aesthetic in character but embodies a third principle appearing unexpectedly but inevitably out of such conflict. This can be accomplished, according to Baynes, only by the awakening of a religious attitude. He says:

> The reader will have observed that, in both cases, the flow of unconscious events led straight to the religious problem. I would not go so far as to say that the religious question underlies every psychoneurotic disorder; but with regard to borderline schizophrenia, the compulsion neurotic, and the greater number of obsessional cases, no cure is feasible, according to my experience, without vital renewal of life, which is what religion is really concerned with.

Dr. Baynes' work has sometimes been criticized for being unsystematic, for not giving due attention to resolution of the transference and counter-transference between himself and his patients and for introducing too much analysis of cultural problems into the texture of his amplifications, and, therefore, perhaps to have placed too little importance on the actual personal associations and childhood determinants for his patients' sufferings. None of this, however, has prevented his book from being, in my experience, one of the most brilliantly helpful and illuminating text books I know for acquainting the young psychiatrist or analyst in training with the true data of analytical psychology. The leisurely, unemphatic style in which Baynes writes is itself a wholesome corrective for rationalistic glibness and the tendency to produce, not the case history of living persons, but a more or less correct piece of compulsive scientism.

The real scientific spirit is not lacking in *The Mythology of the Soul*, but it is properly disciplined and purged of any excessive theorizing. This correction comes partly from Baynes' own highly developed cultural awareness (which recommends his work to the general as well as the professional reader), but also from a true respect for the philosophic tradition from which science originally sprang. He is not so much concerned, therefore, with what we call truth in a specific, scientific contingency as with understanding. And so he concludes with a statement of what he hoped to achieve and which I heartily agree that he did achieve:

> I commend this work with all its shortcomings, to the fair appraisal of reasonable minds, not forgetting Kant's humane definition of understanding: "The realization of a thing to the measure which is sufficient for our purpose".

JOSEPH L. HENDERSON

SAN FRANCISCO

FOREWORD

Records of scientific investigation are, as a rule, sprinkled with references and acknowledgments to previous workers belonging to the same tradition or working in the same field. The reader will find relatively few of such acknowledgments in the present work, for the reason that the number of workers in the field of introverted psychology is small. I have deliberately turned away from the extraverted, quantitative approach which seeks to accumulate facts, without much concern for their meaning. Although there is a great deal of valuable literature about schizophrenia from the point of view of clinical type, the study of this does not materially assist one to understand the problem of the individual borderline patient who comes in distress into one's consulting room.

Extraverted science is necessarily centrifugal: the more it reaches out towards its objective, the further does it recede from the essential needs and interests of the human soul. It is a magnificently expanding ring of intellectual achievement—with a hollow centre. The psyche cannot be charted with calipers, and all the ingenious mechanisms, so cunningly fashioned to exclude the subjective variable, also succeed perfectly in excluding the soul. We cannot hope to get near the heart of a problem by running eagerly towards the distant horizon. Schizophrenia presents us with a problem which leads down to the very roots of the psyche, and for the investigation of these roots only an introverting psychological method is suitable.

The analytical method of C. G. Jung, in so far as my knowledge goes, is the only effective introverting technique in the West to-day. There are other methods intended for the study of the phenomenology of the psyche, but when we come to use them, we find that we can only do so by regarding the mental field as an extension of biology or physiology and the mind as a complex piece of mechanism.

Of the introverted way, C. G. Jung is our single source and our sole tradition. Arthur Waley explains the rather bewildering anonymity of early Chinese writings by the hypothesis that only relatively few teachers said memorable things. When those who succeeded these sages wrote works that were faithful to the spirit of the teacher, they naturally ascribed their works to the great originator. In this way the tradition was ever being nourished by fresh tributaries and the spirit of the originator honoured. The mythical grandeur of the Yellow Ancestor, whose legendary existence has now receded to the fourth millennium B.C., gained immortality in this way.

Jung is the Yellow Ancestor, or the Lao Tzŭ of Analytical Psychology, and anyone who follows the path which he blazed is liable to feel ensnared by an ungracious dilemma, for either he must admit that anything of memorable quality in his work almost certainly derives from Jung, or else he must attempt to liquidate his burden of indebtedness by refusing to acknowledge Jung's existence. Those who have tried the latter way would have done better to study the ways of early Chinese disciples.

Wherever possible I have given the specific reference to Jung's writings, but the larger portion of my debt to him cannot be stated in these terms. The very essence and spirit of the introverted approach is his, and I know of no better way of dealing fairly with the facts than to warn the reader at the outset that anything there may be of enduring merit in the following work flows directly from my relationship with C. G. Jung: the rest I may fairly claim as my own.

In the preparation of the work I am indebted to Professor F. M. Cornford for valuable assistance and encouragement; to J. M. Thorburn and my daughter Chloe for reading the proofs and for many excellent suggestions; and, above all, to my wife for typing the book and for her indestructible faith in its value.

I am indebted to Professor C. G. Jung and Messrs. Kegan Paul and Co. of London for their kindness in allowing me to reproduce the Lamaist Vajra-Mandala; to Éditions " Cahiers d'Art " of Paris for permission to print the three paintings of Paul Klee, " Paysage à la Lettre R," " Le Temps et les Plantes," and " Sondes sur les Vagues "; and to Messrs. Luzac and Co. of London for permission to reproduce the illustration of the *Muladhara Chakra* from Avalon's *Serpent Power*.

H. G. BAYNES.

REED HOUSE, WEST BYFLEET.
November, 1939

MYTHOLOGY OF THE SOUL

"To know when one does not know is best.
To think one knows when one does not know is a dire disease.
Only he who recognizes this disease as a disease
Can cure himself of the disease."
The Sage's way of curing disease
Also consists in making people recognize their diseases as diseases and thus ceasing to be diseased.

Tao Te Ching
(trans. by Arthur Waley).

INTRODUCTION

Before the human mind had ever set itself to the labour of thought, the myth already flowed like a natural fountain out of the unconscious. Within this stream of living images the naive mind is enfolded, as a trout is contained by the river. Like a fish to its native stream, the moral of a people also abides in their relation to their myth: when this is destroyed by intellectual sophistication or by other causes, the virtue of a people departs.

With the individual it is the same: every man needs to be contained psychologically in a living stream. Call this stream, if you will, tradition; essentially it is the continuity of general psychic life in which the individual psyche is contained, and by which it is nourished. Often the stream of tradition seems to lose itself in still pools, as, for example, when the family, the clan or the church stagnates in ancient custom, forgetting to cherish the new forms which a living myth begets.

Most of the people who come to an analyst with serious purpose come because they have lost touch with, or been prised away from, their original background. They come because they are exposed, uncontained, uncertain of their way: they are like fish taken from their stream, and longing to find again their containing element. But having rejected, or been rejected by, their original stream, it is vain for the doctor to attempt to put them back again. They do not belong there any more; they cannot live in the still pool. This is the situation depicted in the myth of the prodigal son. The younger son feels impelled to depart from the traditional pattern. Driven by his resistance, he goes to a far country where he is able to appraise his birthright from a new standpoint. But it was precisely this new standpoint that was needed to bring vitality to the monotonous, self-repeating pattern of biological events. Therefore is the younger son honoured by the father—because he was moved to do a deed for the sake of the ancestral stream, not knowing why he did it.

The seaworthiness of a boat in harbour is not challenged: it is taken for granted. But as soon as we head for the open sea, with a long voyage in front of us, the question becomes acutely relevant. Similarly, the individual who is safely contained in his traditional pattern or mould feels no need to create his individual myth; all he is called upon to do is to be faithful in reproducing history. But our borderline patient who has been prised away from his container, and who divines the presence of monstrous forms and forces in the waters beneath him, is in very different case. He needs a boat that is in flexible, lively relation with the moving sea; one that can be easily steered and controlled and is, above all, seaworthy; a boat that can withstand the cruellest violence of wind and wave.

This indispensable requirement must be understood at the outset. The long and arduous work, carried out by patient and doctor together, can have no other possible *raison d'être*; inasmuch as healing means to recover one's moral, and moral depends upon the relation to one's myth. It should also be understood that borderline patients, who need to create their myth, are by no means weak neurotics. Their abnormality may consist merely in their inability to stay moored to a ring in the harbour wall for the rest of their lives. But if one has to navigate the treacherous sea, two possible factors may be one's undoing. On the one hand, the boat may be too small and weak to withstand heavy seas; on the other hand, notwithstanding the most vigilant seamanship, the boat may suddenly be overwhelmed by a violent storm and swamped.

These two factors are mentioned by Jung[1] as the vital causative conditions in schizophrenia: namely, the lowering or weakening of conscious control, on the one hand, and the sudden activation of archaic contents of the unconscious, on the other. But only a psychology that is exposed to severe strains and new adaptations is liable to suffer either of these contingencies. The man who stays on the spot where his father left him will not be aware of the dragons in the high

[1] *Vide* Chapter II., on Psychiatric Antecedents.

mountains. Moreover, the latent or borderline schizophrenic is not singled out by fate to have an archaic psychology. The sea is universal: it contains, moreover, many unholy monsters and can unleash terrible violence. All who venture over the sea, therefore, are liable, at one time or another, to encounter perilous moments. Those who stay at home are superior only in respect to the factor of safety: they do not necessarily possess greater merit.

The metaphor of the sea offers the closest possible analogy to the general or impersonal unconscious upon which conscious life and sanity rest. But the borderline schizophrenic is not merely a prodigal son, or a daring voyager: he is also, and quite definitely, a man impaled on a vital doubt—a doubt concerning the validity of his own nature, or the stability of his own mind. This preoccupation with the performance of his mind, or with the sources of his energy, will be found running through the products of every borderline patient; and it is on this account that these often gifted subjects make invaluable collaborators in investigations of unconscious mental activity.

Schizophrenia raises the most vital problem of conscious life, a problem which presses most urgently upon Western civilization at the present juncture: namely, the stability and integrity of consciousness when threatened by the activated archaic forces of the collective unconscious. The schizophrenic's doubt as to the stability of his mind under pressing strain is precisely the same as the doubt upon which the civilized mind of the West is now impaled. And in both cases, if there were no renegade factor to deal with, the problem would hardly exist at all. There is something, and he knows it, in the schizophrenic subject's blood which seeks out and responds to the violence and dread of the dæmonic unconscious forces. Something in him shouts the devil's laughter as the ship is battered and broken by the attacking sea. The renegade in the psyche is archaic and nihilistic, seeking violence involuntarily, as an insecure ruler seeks war. Men of insight can perceive the presence of this renegade voice in their own make-up. When, for example, the unscrupulous criminal succeeds in some daring raid or hold-up, there is an immediate instinctive thrill of excitement, not unmixed with admiration.

It is the presence of this renegade factor behind the civilized lines which is the real cause of our present anxiety, just as the apathy of the American public in face of gangster rule revealed a deep uncivilized lawlessness in the collective psyche. Our anxiety seems to be due to the release of the national unconscious in a violently aggressive form in certain states of the European complex: but there is a deeper, more disturbing doubt than this; a doubt concerning the value and meaning of that whole civilizing experiment to which we are committed. We have to admit that there are certain states of Europe which are proudly defying and violating the foundations of civilized communion; while the man who represents the spearhead of this attack is apparently more successful politically than any other figure in history. It cannot be doubted that the success of a public criminal, as of a statesman, or a benefactor, depends upon public sanction and support. Thus we have a characteristic schizophrenic doubt developing at the very root of our civilized way of life. If archaic methods should eventually conquer Europe, civilization will go under in exactly the same way as consciousness disappears when insanity prevails.

The two subjects whose material I have chosen for discussion manifested a characteristic contrast in attitude towards the irruption of primitive tendencies. The first, tending to be seduced by an unscrupulous shadow-personality found to be lurking in his unconscious, was attracted towards the renegade hypothesis, and became somewhat disorientated in the realm of obligations. Whereas the second was, if anything, overscrupulous in all his dealings, defending his civilized citadel and its values with force and vision, in spite of strong environmental inducement to follow a renegade policy.

Although this distinctive difference of attitude lends a specific complexion to the manner of presentation, yet, at bottom, both individuals have created their myth from the general unconscious contents active at the present time. Just as the movement of wind and waves determined the shape and relative flexibility of the original sailing boat, in exactly the same way the activity of the unconscious contents determines the character and development of the individual myth.

By virtue of the myth, created from urgent need, one can learn to adapt to the deep movement of the unconscious. The fact that some people prefer to " go to sea in a sieve " is not a warning to mariners, but only a danger-sign to folly.

The easiest way to remain unconscious of one's archaic tendencies is to find a scapegoat and project them upon him. Ironical medical display of case material offers a favourable opportunity for this mediæval sport. Such demonstrations rest upon the implied assumption that the so-called normal person is without a living psyche. For a living psychology must inevitably have a problem with the unconscious, and neurosis is simply the result of this conflict. For the purpose of this demonstration, I have attempted to construct, as it were, a special submarine chamber, whereby it is possible to descend and view the denizens of the unconscious in their own element. My two patients would be like divers risking themselves, but to good purpose, under the sea. Similar contents to those which they have portrayed are to be found in the unconscious of the majority of educated Westerners to-day. It is not the presence of active archaic contents which causes schizophrenia; but rather the renegade weakness or lowering of consciousness over against the menace of the unconscious. This feebleness of the civilized will is due, as we shall later discover, to the presence of an unmanageable distance or split between the level of the superior, adapted, civilized function which rules consciousness, and a correspondingly inferior, neglected, dwarfed, under-nourished function in the unconscious which, because of its uncared-for state, is liable to attempt the renegade hypothesis. Who is there in the specialized classes of educated society who has not this same problem to deal with in his own psychological house ? Hence the expression of anxiety lurking in people's faces and their heaping together in vast urban communities. They try to compensate their individual feeling of insecurity by massing in swarms.

The insecurity of the two subjects of this investigation will be patent for all to see; yet in a sense they are already in a stronger position than the complacent spectator, since they perceived their sickness and decided to enquire into its cause.

The reader will appreciate that it is objectionable, if not ethically impossible, to make public intimate, personal material, obtained in a relation of confidence, even when, as in the present case, the patient has given consent. This difficulty would be insurmountable, were it not for the fact that the causes of morbid processes, in mind as well as body, are general and can be presented in an impersonal way. Even though its forms of expression are distinctly individual, the impersonal material, which is the true object of our study, can and should be treated from a general standpoint.

Of even greater moment, at the present time, is the question of presenting psychiatric material in a way that is intelligible to an educated lay audience. These studies were conceived originally as technical contributions to the literature of schizophrenia. My grounds for expanding them into their present form were twofold. In the first place, the subjective material in both cases was found to transcend the limits of psychopathology, demanding consideration also from the historico-religious standpoint. Secondly, it is impossible to live in the modern world without being affected, as by a contagion, with a condition of the collective psyche, not unlike the state of severance and dissociation found in the schizophrenic individual.

Acute transitional phases in history have always offered occasion for nihilistic mentalities to take the lead; but never before have such devastating consequences for mankind hung so precariously upon psychotic inspiration as they do to-day. Yet we must not delude ourselves with the idea that the destiny of mankind lies solely at the mercy of one or two powerful, but unbalanced minds. The biased, fanatical personality assumes leadership at the present time, only because collective psychology demands these very qualities. This does not necessarily imply that an undue proportion of individuals are, in fact, pathological; though the relative popularity of systematized schizophrenic material, such as *Ulysses* by James Joyce, and a considerable bulk of surrealist painting and poetry, points to the existence of a large number of individuals who discover themselves best in a pathological looking-glass.

When we dare to diagnose the present state of the collective psyche as pathological in character, we mean that widespread symptoms can be observed which present an unmistakable analogy to schizophrenic pathology. These symptoms develop apparently from the existence of one-sided, revolutionary movements, identified with narrow, monotint ideologies, whose inherent partiality must for ever seek to annihilate the other half of mankind. The recent witch-hunting in Russia and Germany is the infamous result; for collective fanaticism cannot live without scapegoats. It can hardly be denied that these and other manifestations of acute one-sidedness proclaim a morbid state of the collective psyche.

In the mass, we are concerned with a general paranoiac frame of mind, a phase of excitability which is liable to become inflamed with ideological infections. Whereas in the borderline individual we have to deal with a morbid mental bulkhead, resulting in a one-sidedness of attitude which, though fundamentally unbalanced, is only rarely emotional or excitable. Yet basal differences notwithstanding, the borderline schizophrenic personifies in a peculiar way certain dangerous features of the present time. A composite Galtonesque portrait, drawn from impressions of individual cases, will help to bring these features into focus.

Outwardly, the borderline schizophrenic may have a trim, polished, impeccable persona,[1] which attracts without promise of personal warmth. The smile is inclined to be "grooved" and mechanical; it is both placatory and self-protective, lacking the spontaneity of feeling. At every point one may discover a contradiction between the outer aspect and the inner life. The expression shown to the world is noncommittal and reticent, while the archaic emotional welter within is often volcanic and terrifying. The concealed affects are liable to be distorted and perversely exaggerated, because the subject's mind is flooded with archaic contents which he cannot express. He is subject to unreliable moods and phases of sullen withdrawal; while obstinate, destructive criticism is liable to blaze up in violent and irrational outbreaks. In his *Psychology of Dementia Præcox*, Jung makes

[1] Jung's term for the outer character, derived from the mask (Lat. *persona*) worn by the actors of antiquity.

this the chief clinical feature. He writes (on page 73): "The lack of self-control, or the inability to control the affects, is characteristic of dementia præcox."

Though agreeing with this statement, we must also make al owance for those outstanding exceptions whose iron self-control is proof against every provocation. These undeclared or repressed psychotics are more than likely, however, to marry women of the opposite hysterical type, whose uninhibited recourse to affective display often seems to afford a vicarious means of outlet to their repressed partners. It is even possible that the wife may be unconsciously compelled to produce violent outbursts owing to the projection of psychotic affects from the husband's unconscious. When this occurs we can speak of an induced psychotic reaction.

The disagreeable impression caused by these undisciplined moods is enhanced by the subject's subsequent nonchalance in regard to them. Ambiguity of feeling is, therefore, a source of continual reproach from those immediately related to him; the more so, since a similar unreliability is apt to manifest itself in the sphere of domestic finance. In every relation, indeed, where reliability of feeling is a fundamental requirement, these individuals tend to be tragically lacking. Not always, however, inasmuch as they usually have a genuine respect for integrity of character, and on this score, rather than on the grounds of personal feeling, they will sometimes make heroic attempts to raise their subhuman emotional side to the human level.

Moods of inaccessibility are frequent. These are due, not to misanthropic contempt for human society, but to the fact that the psychic energy is enthralled or fascinated by the inner problem, and hence is not available for ordinary human intercourse.

It is difficult to ascertain how keenly these subjects are aware of the contradiction between the upper and lower in their make-up. It is true that they are fascinated, and sometimes frightened, by the irrationality and unpredictability of the inner events; but, as a rule, they have little knowledge of their own motives.

In nearly every case the history of sex-experience

speaks of deficiency in individual feeling. The restless, dissatisfied hunger that frequently motivates the erotic search is the most tragic expression of the fundamental emotional defect; for the schizophrenic lacks that fire in the heart by which a man knows when he is finally committed for better or worse. He cannot voluntarily commit himself either to a relation or to a standpoint; he is even liable to parade a meretricious feeling of superiority over those less fortunate beings who allow their roots to hold them to home, faith, or country.

Here again, it is the inferior type of individual who pursues the *fata morgana* of sexual perversity, goes whoring after magic or yogi-cults, or traffics in occultism with purveyors of cheap mystery. In my experience schizophrenic individuals tend to be attracted by things beyond the pale; but, just because of their unreliable feeling, they have no subjective criterion wherewith to measure the worth of what they find. Hence, they often remain in indeterminate psychical backwaters; caught but sceptical.

The better type, however, in whom integrity is the keynote, realizes his secret propensity for spiritual as well as for sexual philandering and, just because of this self-knowledge, learns to honour loyalty as the guiding principle of his life.

In most cases, sexuality remains at the bisexual level, though, in deference to the susceptibilities of the marriage-partner, the homosexual component is either screened or repressed. The presence of atavism or emotional squalor beneath necessitates a correspondingly opaque mask above; all the more impenetrable, in fact, because it is the product of an absolute need for self-protection. Candour is exceptional. The feeling which enables a man to yield himself unreservedly to his fate is lacking: hence the unreserved statement or affirmation of his personality is also absent. He is liable to feel acutely his alienation, difference, and separation from his fellow-men; yet this is the last thing he is willing to discuss. At all costs he must appear like those around him: there must be no chink in his protective armour of simulation.

Here again, the inferior type will use the subtlest arts of concealment and disguise in order to maintain his lifelong policy of bluff; while the better type will try to explain his inner predicament to his marriage partner and, having once discovered this avenue, may even become over-conscientious in confessing highly complicated renegade motives. Yet, although yearning for frankness and striving with all his will to be truthful, he can never achieve natural candour. He may open the door of his mind a hundred times a day, but it never remains open.

The portrait I have just sketched belongs to a recognizable pathological type; but it also portrays a widespread modern malady which, in one way or another, affects everybody. In the case of the pathological individual, we have traced the cause to a crucial deficiency in the very roots of feeling. Can we, therefore, assume that the desirousness, the restlessness, the inability to be deeply committed, the unrelatedness, the quest among alien fields for some magical, redeeming, healing thing, the superficial conformity, concealing a dangerous abyss below, the paranoiac accumulation of armaments, the incessant search for distraction, the longing for something else—can we say that this unquiet, dissatisfied spirit abroad in the world comes from a similar cause?

Smuts ascribes our malady to what he calls a spiritual migration. In this he is clearly referring to the dangerous transition between successive epochs. All the absolute collective values which ruled the world up to 1914 have undergone a deep-sea change; they have been questioned and doubted and reduced by the all-pervading principle of relativity to relative human terms. Loyalties, pacts, agreements, treaties, even debts, have lost their ancient sanctity, and nations as well as individuals adopt an almost cynical opportunism towards long-standing engagements and obligations.

Side by side with vanishing moral landmarks is an exuberant over-emphasis on catchwords and figures of the contemporary stage. Policies, fortunes and reputations undergo sudden and bewildering transformation, and people have become hardened to the most shameless persecutions, betrayals and predatory invasions in the name of the deified modern state.

When we define the nature of this wholesale landslide of civilized values, we see that people no longer consider themselves bound by definite feeling-values and humane standards which to our forefathers were absolutely binding. Yet, underneath the constantly shifting surface of this moral avalanche, there is a profound longing for deliverance and for some undeniable realization of truth. An age of moral relativity resembles all too clearly the shifting surface of the desert, where ancient landmarks may be completely obliterated in a day. The foundation of rock, upon which all that is true abides, is doubtless still there; but when large numbers of people are uprooted, and have lost touch with their ancestral foundation, the presence of the eternal rock is forgotten and overlooked. To anyone driven down the wind like a spent leaf, nothing seems stable.

A migration is no voluntary movement: it is set in motion, like the Gulf Stream, by some abysmal necessity which we cannot fathom. But the instincts of animals, as well as those of human beings, undergo a strange recession during periods of migration. The state of being uprooted from the familiar environment, coupled with the loss of the stabilizing influence of long-established adaptation, results in a contagious recklessness, in which a suicidal momentum may engulf the whole migrating horde. The adapted vigilance of the individual creature seems to be in jeopardy directly he becomes merged in the horde.

The cataclysm of 1914 marked the end of an epoch and the beginning of a vast spiritual migration. Christendom received a terrible lesion in the organ or region of faith; as though a sudden and violent storm had sundered man from his ancient roots, leaving him at the mercy of irrational collective forces.

Although these changes are self-evident characters of the post-war epoch, they are too near to us for accurate survey and understanding. The best that can be attempted is to express the situation with the help of a certain analogy. On the strength of this analogy between the contemporary world-madness and schizophrenic pathology, I have felt constrained to present my investigation into the deep psychology of schizophrenia in a form that is accessible to any interested observer.

My indebtedness to the two individuals whose subjective material forms the basis of the investigation cannot, unfortunately, be explicitly honoured. Neither of them appreciated the fact, when he made the drawings, that he was drawing his own myth; nor was there any question, until much later, of the possibility of a psychological demonstration of the material. My principal motive in undertaking the investigation was, as nearly as I can say, my inability to understand my patient's material. It may be that the illumination which sometimes glows in the heart of a dream or fantasy, when we pour our interest and attention into it, has led me to embark upon a wider amplification of this material than some of my medical colleagues will sanction. If this is the case, my justification must be that the schizophrenic condition exists because ideas of universal significance and power are misconceived and set in miniature frames. As soon as the individual (or the race) has succeeded in giving adequate hospitality and understanding to the primordial image which is using and shaping his mind, there is no further question of schizophrenia. It is conceivable, therefore, that at this time, when people are only too liable to try to cram the embryonic forms of the future into tight ideological cells, a certain measure of amplification might actually be the best medicine.

* * * * *

Since the outbreak of war the above observations upon contemporary collective psychology seem now to belong to a former epoch. I have made no attempt, however, to revise the picture, since war-time psychology, being necessarily to some extent manufactured, is not truly indicative of formative unconscious tendencies.

PART ONE

CHAPTER I

PSYCHIATRIC ANTECEDENTS

Development of the Psychological Conception of Mental Disorders

I

THE development of a systematic psychological approach to psychotic conditions began with the twentieth century. Before this new era dawned, the position of psychiatry as a branch of medicine rested on somewhat frail grounds. It was even contended by Kant, in response to the legitimist claims of Hufeland, the eminent German alienist, that the consideration and treatment of mental disease belonged, not to the physician, but to the philosopher. Considering how long it has taken medical science to recognize the psychological criterion in the study of mental disorders, it is more than possible that Kant was justified. It must also be confessed that psychology was almost as powerless as medicine to deal with the problems and disorders of the mind until Freud and Jung began to make use of the purposive or teleological conception of unconscious mental processes.

Although the concept of the unconscious is not very congenial to the practical extraverted Anglo-Saxon mentality, it must be confessed that, in the last analysis, the unconscious is the real object of psychiatry. On the other hand, the concept is native to the introverted genius of Germany. Von Hartmann's reputation as a philosopher was based upon the success of his *Philosophy of the Unconscious*, written in 1869. In this work the unconscious appears as a combination of the metaphysic of Hegel and Schopenhauer. It is both Will and Reason and the absolute, all-embracing ground of all existence; the spiritual *dynamis* in nature. Von Hartmann inherits the Oriental pessimism of Schopenhauer, seeing Reason in constant strife against Will. Only when the unconscious impersonal Will is emancipated from this strife in the conscious reason of the enlightened pessimist can the world be redeemed. But the supremacy of a world-shaping and world-driving unconscious Will did not originate with Schopenhauer. Fichte held that the source of being is the primæval activity of Will, the groundless and incomprehensible deed-action of the absolute ego. "The Will," he said, "is the living principle of reason." Schelling too (1809) in his *Inquiries into the Nature of Human Freedom* wrote: "In the last resort there is no other being but Will. Will is primal being, and to this alone apply the predicates fathomless, eternal, independent of time, self-affirming." Schopenhauer's *Weltanschauung* was directly inspired by the philosophy of the Vedas. He is, above all, the introverted realist, affirming the psychological basis of the world. In his *World as Will and Idea* Schopenhauer fights with the weapons of physical doctrine on the basis of the material earth.

> "He knows no reason but the human, no intelligence save what is exhibited by the animals. But both animals and men have come into existence within assignable limits of time, and that before this there was an age when neither eye nor ear gathered the life of the universe into perceptions. Knowledge, therefore, with its vehicle, the intellect, is dependent upon the existence of certain nerve organs located in an animal system; and its function is originally only to present an image of the interconnections of the manifestations in the world outside the individual; thus to give to the individual organism, in a partial and reflected form, that feeling with other beings, or innate sympathy which it tends to lose as organization of life becomes more complex and characteristic. Knowledge or intellect, therefore, is only the surrogate of that more intimate unity of feeling or will which is the underlying reality—the principle of all existence, the essence of all manifestations, inorganic and organic . . . there is a source of knowledge within us by which we know, and more intimately than we can ever know anything external, that we will and feel. That is the first and the highest knowledge, the only knowledge which can strictly be called immediate; and *to ourselves we as the subject of will are truly the immediate object*."[1]

Schopenhauer voiced the introverted principle, not with the psychological subtlety of the East, but with the differentiated philosophical medium of the West.

[1] Article on Schopenhauer in the *Encyclopædia Britannica*, 14th Edition.

Schopenhauer's pessimism arose from his profound sense of the overwhelming power of the unconscious, omnipresent Will. The individual creature being only an illusory, partial manifestation of will-in-itself, his only hope is to become conscious of this power and through consciousness to create detachment. There is no way of escaping the power of Will. " Suicide affords no escape; what everyone in his inmost consciousness *wills*, that must he *be*; and what everyone *is*, that he *wills*." His vision of the boundless power of the unconscious is expressed in an analogy which is constantly found in dream-expression. " Just as a sailor sits in a boat trusting to his frail barque in a stormy sea, unbounded in every direction, rising and falling with the howling, mountainous waves; so in the midst of a world of sorrows the individual man sits quietly, supported by and trusting to the *principium individuationis*."

Nietzsche was also deeply impressed by the awe-inspiring creative-destructive force of the unconscious. In his *Birth of Tragedy* he attributes the whole artistic creation of the Greeks to what he calls the " metaphysical miracle of the Hellenic ' will ' " overwhelmed as they were by the titanic, terrifying powers of nature within and without. Nietzsche's use of the term " will " is surely derived from Schopenhauer, and " metaphysical," both in Schopenhauer and Nietzsche, is synonymous, as Jung has pointed out, with " unconscious."

We must bear in mind, then, that when Freud and Jung applied the somewhat equivocal term " unconscious " to the deep psychology of human beings, there already existed in German thought the conceptions of a whole line of post-Kantian philosophers, all of whom were, to a greater or lesser extent, occupied with the philosophical problem of the basic, affective or energic determination of thought and conduct. We cannot hope to do justice to the significance of our modern psychotherapeutic conceptions if we omit to see that the soil which nurtured the ideas of Jung and Freud had long been cultivated by the boldest philosophical minds of Germany. It is, therefore, hardly surprising that the insight we now possess into the dark places of the human soul, and particularly into the obscurities of schizophrenia—the disease in which the antagonism between intellect and the primal affects is the essential factor—has been contributed in the main from Germanic sources.

Without much fear of being contradicted by posterity, we could prophesy that the development of the energic view of mental processes, and the immense impetus given to psychotherapy through research into the nature of the unconscious, constitute an event of decisive significance in the history of medicine.

The nineteenth century, as we have seen, provided the scholastic-philosophical forerunners of our psychology. But it also produced the beginnings of experimental investigation into psychological processes. This new direction originated with Fechner (also a German), who, in his *Psychophysik*, written in 1860, first introduced the physical standpoint into the conception of psychical phenomena. This fruitful beginning was carried on by Wundt, a contemporary of Fechner's, who applied his extraordinary genius to elaborating methods of experimental research and thus gave to modern psychology its empirical direction. These methods and this direction were soon taken up by certain German psychiatrists and applied in the service of practical psychology. Kraepelin, Aschaffenburg and others of the Heidelberg school realized that practical tools were now available for obtaining more exact knowledge of psychical processes, and before long word-association tests were used as a more or less routine procedure for measuring the mental competence of asylum patients.

It fell to Jung, in his experimental work at the Burghölzli mental hospital in Zürich, to combine the empirical methods originated by Wundt with the energic conception of the psychic process handed down from German philosophy. It is significant that, while Jung was feeling his way towards the dynamic psychological conception by the experimental route, Freud had reached practically the same conclusion in his clinical researches with hysterical patients. Impressed by the obvious clinical importance of sexuality in the ætiology of hysteria, Freud at first conceived the unconscious *dynamis* exclusively as *libido sexualis*; this view he subsequently modified in favour of other instinctive energies.

Jung's Application of the Complex-Theory to Dementia Præcox

II

The psychological basis of dementia præcox was first demonstrated by Freud as long ago as 1896 in an analysis of a paranoid case, where he showed that the symptoms were determined according to the transformation mechanism of hysteria. This was followed up by Jung, who in 1903 made his first analysis of a case of dementia præcox, approaching the problem from the angle of the complex-theory of mental activity established in his experiments in word-association. In his *Psychology of Dementia Præcox* Jung laid down a firm basis upon which future research could proceed. Although written more than thirty years ago, his work still stands as the most original and illuminating attempt in the field of schizophrenic psychology. Many subsequent writers have paid tribute to the outstanding value of his work, but few have attempted to go further along the lines which he indicated. This may be due, in large measure, to the fact that psychiatry, as a branch of physical medicine, cannot entirely forgo the anticipation of concrete anatomical evidence upon which to build its pathological conceptions.

The two basic conceptions which gave Jung a certain mastery over the hitherto unintelligible welter of pathological material were (*a*) the autonomous complex, and (*b*) the mechanism of psychological types. The fact that a more or less systematized mental organism could break away from the hierarchy of consciousness, insisting upon its own separate and independent life, had already become a familiar demonstration in the clinics of Charcot and Janet in Paris. But although the phenomena of somnambulism, double or multiple personalities, psychasthenic automatism and the various forms of hysterical dissociations revealed by hypnosis, had been explained in a variety of ways, it was Jung's concept of the autonomous complex which finally brought all these facts within the embrace of a fundamental psychological conception.

According to the views of the French school, dissociation was a weakness of consciousness, caused by the splitting off of one or a series of ideas, which, having cast away from the hierarchy of the conscious ego, began a more or less independent existence. According to Janet, dissociation was the result of *l'abaissement du niveau mental* which, through destroying the hierarchy of the mind, either favoured or effected the origin of automatisms. This view, although contributing a valuable clinical picture of the morbid state, did not provide an intelligible psychological conception. It afforded no insight into the factors which brought about the weakening of consciousness, or which so dangerously lowered the conscious level. A patient of Janet's said to him, "There are always two or three of my personalities who do not sleep. Nevertheless I have fewer personalities during sleep: there are some who sleep but little. These persons dream, but not the same dream. I feel that there are some who dream of different things."[1] Janet, therefore, was perfectly familiar with the surface clinical picture of dissociated subsidiary personalities; but what the French school lacked was a fundamental conception of psychic causation. Jung's dynamic conception was born of experimental evidence, pointing to the existence of emotionally charged complexes which, under the stress of repression, produced characteristic disturbances in the word-association tests. The combination of these facts taken from two independent fields of observation gave Jung the master-key he was seeking. A similar syncretistic inspiration, and one that was destined to affect the whole course of his scientific development, was Jung's realization that the mechanism of defence that surrounded and concealed the painful complex was identical with the mechanism of repression described by Freud in his clinical investigations of hysterical patients. Thus, Jung's conception of the autonomous complex became the syncretizing basis which united the classical conceptions of the French school with those of Freud, the great pioneer of psycho-analysis. It was fitting that Zürich should thus become the mediate function between Paris and Vienna.

[1] C. G. Jung: *Psychology of Dementia Præcox*, p. 91.

When we observe the manifestations of the autonomous complex in a developed case of schizophrenia[1] we see the emergence of sudden impulses, autochthonous ideas, hallucinations, sudden deprivation of thought, imperative commands apparently emanating from an alien source, disturbances of attention, inspirations, irrational movements and actions; whereas in the word-association experiments only the negative aspect of the complex was in evidence. The reaction to the stimulus word was found to be indefinitely prolonged, or the words given by the patient to certain stimulus-words had the character of evasion, superficiality, or mere similarity of sound. In order, therefore, to find the concealed painful complex, which was producing these disturbances of normal mental activity, Jung had to look, as it were, through the cracks which the experiment revealed. He selected those responses where the disturbances or irregularities were most marked, and, by means of careful questioning, or by exploring the associations leading back from the suspected response, he discovered that these led always to an emotionally accentuated complex of representations left by some painful experience in the patient's life. When he applied this same method to his schizophrenic patients, he was able to prove that the apparent farrago of delusional ideas and the meaningless conglomerations of words and automatic repetitions of the insane mind were symptoms of fragmentation in conjunction with abnormal activity of the morbid complex which no longer submitted to the co-ordinating control of consciousness. In order to refresh the reader's memory, I shall quote certain passages from Jung's *Psychology of Dementia Præcox.* The English translation being unfortunately out of print, it cannot be assumed that many readers are familiar with its content.

Discussing the characteristic cleavage between the ideational and the emotional or affective function, Jung writes:

> " The striking incongruity between idea and affect which we can daily observe in dementia præcox is a more frequent symptom during the development of the disease than the emotional dementia.

[1] This term (which is derived from σχίζω = to split, to cleave, and φρήν = the mind or heart as the seat of thought) was coined by Bleuler as being more descriptive of the psychological condition than the rather vague and inaccurate term, dementia præcox.

This incongruity between idea and emotional tone forced Stransky to accept two separate psychical factors, the *Noöpsyche* and the *Thymopsyche* (νόος = mind, reason; θῦμός = soul, breath, life: Latin, *anima*). The former term comprises the intellectual, reasoning faculties; the latter the dynamic, purposive or affective aspect of the psyche."[1]

Because of this incongruity, Stransky assumed a condition of ataxia or basic inco-ordination between the ideational and the emotional functions. Jung criticizes this idea as follows:

" Although, judging from clinical appearances, there are frequent incongruities, they are by no means limited exclusively to dementia præcox. In hysteria likewise, the incongruity is an everyday occurrence. One can see it in the fact of the so-called ' hysterical exaggerations ' whose counterpart is the well-known *belle indifférence* of hysterics. We also find violent excitements over nothing, at times over something which in no way shows any recognizable connection with the excitement. Yet psycho-analysis uncovers the motives and we then begin to understand why the patients reacted in such a manner. In dementia præcox we are at present unable to penetrate deeply enough; so that the inherent relations remain unknown, and therefore an ataxia is assumed between the *noö-* and the *thymopsyche.* Thanks to analysis, we know that in hysteria there is no ataxia, but only an oversensitiveness, which, as soon as we know the pathogenic complex, becomes clear and intelligible. Knowing, therefore, how the incongruity is brought about in hysteria, is it necessary that we should accept a totally new mechanism in dementia præcox ?"[2]

After giving detailed citations from Freud's first analysis of a case of paranoia, Jung writes:

" Let us now turn to the question of dissociated series of ideas. We now see what meaning Freud gives to Gross's assumed dissociations. They are nothing else than the repressed complexes found in hysteria and also in the normal. The mystery of repressed or dissociated series of ideas is discovered to be a psychological mechanism of general significance and of quite usual occurrence. Freud thus puts in a new light the problem of incongruity between the content of consciousness and emotional tone discussed by Stransky. He shows that indifferent, even insignificant, ideas

[1] C. G. Jung: *Psychology of Dementia Præcox*, i., p. 16.
[2] *Loc. cit.*, p. 17.

may be accompanied by intense feeling-tones which they take from a repressed idea. Freud uncovers a way which can lead us to the understanding of the inadequate feeling-tone in dementia præcox."[1]

Summing up the basic difference between the hysterogenic and the psychotic complex, he concludes as follows:

"The continued persistence of a strong painful complex in normal psychic life can only lead to hysteria. Yet the subsequent manifestations of the hysterogenic affect are different from the symptom-complex of dementia præcox. For the origin of dementia præcox we must demand a totally different disposition from that observed in hysteria. One might perhaps put the case as follows: The resultant manifestations of the hysterogenic complex are reparable, whereas the affect of dementia præcox gives occasion for the appearance of an anomalous metabolism (? toxin), which injures the brain in a more or less irreparable manner; so that in consequence of this effect the highest psychic functions become paralysed. It is for this reason that the acquisition of new complexes becomes difficult or ceases altogether. The pathogenic or rather the inciting complex persists to the last, and the further development of personality is definitely checked. In spite of an apparently continuous causal chain of psychological events leading from the normal to the pathological, we can never disregard the possibility that a change of metabolism (in Kraepelin's sense) may be primary, whereby the subsequently acquired complex 'clots' or 'curdles,' thus inherently determining the symptoms. Our experience does not as yet reach far enough to warrant our excluding this possibility."[2]

In the second chapter, dealing with the emotional complex and its general action on the psyche, Jung gives a full description of how the complex is constituted, and shows how his conception of the complex, gained from experimental studies, oversteps the limits of Freud's conceptions gained from clinical observation:

"The essential basis of our personality is affectivity. Thought and action are only, as it were, symptoms of affectivity."[3]

Jung here uses the expression affectivity in the sense proposed by Bleuler, to denote the whole range of feeling, mood, affect

[1] *Loc. cit.*, p. 32. [2] *Loc. cit.*, pp. 34-5. [3] *Loc. cit.*, ii., p. 37.

and emotion; thus designating not only the affects in the proper sense, but also the feeling-tones of pleasure and pain in every possible occurrence. Bleuler even describes attention as a special form of affectivity. He says: " The attention, just like all our actions, is always directed by an affect." Hence this term comprises conation in its widest possible sense.

Affectivity, then, represents the dynamic content of the complex. Proceeding to describe the formation of the complex, Jung writes:

> " The elements of our psychic life, sensations, ideas, images and emotions, are given to consciousness in the form of certain entities, which, if one may venture upon an analogy with chemistry, can be compared to a molecule."[1]

As an example of this molecular constitution of the complex he mentions the following incident:

> " I was taking a walk with a very sensitive and hysterical gentleman. The village bells were pealing a new and harmonious chime. My companion, who generally displayed feeling for such tunes, suddenly began to rail at the bells, saying that he could not bear the disgusting ringing in the major key, that it was an abominable noise, and that this was an unsightly church and village (the village was, in fact, famous for its beauty). This remarkably inappropriate affect interested me, and I proceeded to investigate its cause. My companion then began to abuse the local parson. He gave as his reason that the minister had an ugly beard and wrote very bad poetry. My companion, I knew, prided himself on his lyrical accomplishments. The affect lay, then, in poetic rivalry.
>
> " This example shows how the whole molecule (the chiming, etc.) took part in the feeling-tone of the mass of presentations rooted in the affect of poetic rivalry."[2]

The whole molecular combination is termed the complex.

> " Considered in this sense, the complex is a higher psychic entity. When we come to examine psychic material—for example, that supplied by the association experiments—we find that every association belongs to some complex. . . . Undoubtedly associations are related in largest measure to the ego-complex. By it we

[1] *Loc. cit.*, ii., p. 36. [2] *Loc. cit.*, pp. 37, 38.

understand the ideational mass of the ego which is accompanied by the potent and lively feeling-tone of our own body. Thus the ego-complex in the normal person is the highest psychic instance. The feeling-tone is an affective state which is accompanied by bodily innervations. The ego is the psychological expression for the firmly associated union of all bodily sensations. The personality proper is, therefore, the firmest and strongest complex, and asserts itself (if healthy) through all psychical storms. It is for this reason that the ideas which directly adhere to one's own personality are the most stable and interesting; in other words, they possess the strongest attention-tone."[1]

Referring to the phenomenon of repression, Jung says:

" In our experimental work we have proved that complexes disturb association experiments in a characteristic and regular manner. . . . It would be expected that an educated subject would react readily to the stimulus words. But this is not the case. At the very simplest words obstructions and other disturbances appear which can be explained only by the fact that the stimulus word has excited a complex. But why should it be difficult to reproduce an idea which is closely connected with a complex? The hindrance is the emotional inhibition. Complexes exist mostly in a state of repression, because as a rule they contain the most intimate and painful secrets which are anxiously guarded. Either one does not wish to expose them, or one may be quite unable to do so. The repression, even under normal conditions, may be so strong as to produce an hysterical amnesia in respect to the complex. There is a feeling of an idea emerging, a significant connection, but the reproduction is held back by vague hesitation. There is a feeling as though one wished to say something which immediately slipped away. The thing which slipped away was the complex-thought."[2]

When a complex occupies the whole mental field, as, for instance, the state of being in love, we can speak of a possession-complex. In such cases one generally observes an extreme complex-sensitiveness.

" As in many cases the sexual complex cannot assert itself in a normal manner, it makes use of by-ways. During the age of puberty these conversions of the complex appear in the form of abnormal fancies, frequently alternating with ecstatic religious

[1] *Loc. cit.*, p. 38. [2] *Loc. cit.*, pp. 42-3.

phases. In men sexuality (if not lived in the direct way) is frequently changed into feverish professional activity, or to some eccentricity, such as dangerous sports, etc., or to peculiar academic passions such as the mania for collecting, etc. . . . These transferences and simulations of the sexual complex may produce double personalities, which have long excited the interest of writers with a psychological trend. Double personality is no mere literary term: it is a fact of natural science of general interest to psychology and psychiatry, expecially when it manifests itself in the form of double consciousness or dissociation of personality. The dissociated complexes are always differentiated by peculiarities of mood and character.

"It frequently happens that the conversion of the complex gradually becomes stable and, at least, superficially replaces the original character. Everyone knows people who, when judged by their exterior, are considered gay and entertaining; while inwardly, or under the circumstances of their private life, are sullen grumblers, nurturing an open wound. At times the true nature breaks through and we are confronted with a new person. A single word, a gesture striking this wound, reveals the complex lurking within the soul. Such imponderabilities of human emotional life must be borne in mind when we enter with our coarse experimental methods into the complicated minds of the diseased. In experiments with patients who suffer from extreme complex-sensitiveness (as in hysteria and dementia præcox) we find exaggeration of these normal mechanisms; hence their description and discussion require more than a mere psychological *aperçu*."[1]

Attention both in hysteria and dementia præcox is constantly liable to be disturbed by the activity of the complex. In this connection Janet observes:

"One can say that the main trouble exists not only in a suppression of the intellectual faculties, but in the difficulty of fixing the attention. The mind of hysterical persons is always distracted by vague preoccupation, and they never give themselves up entirely to the object which one assigns to them."[2]

Janet's description might be applied equally to dementia præcox. Jung writes:

"It is the autonomous complex which disturbs the concentration of the patients; it paralyses all other psychic activities, a fact

[1] *Loc. cit.*, pp. 48-9. [2] *Loc. cit.* Quoted by Jung, *loc. cit.*, iv., p. 79.

which curiously escaped Janet. What is striking in hysteria (as in other affective states) is the fact that the patients always return to their ' stories ' (fantasies) and that all their thoughts and actions are constellated by the complex only. A similar restriction of the mind, but of the highest intensity, is characteristic of dementia præcox, especially of the paranoid form."[1]

Another important aspect of dementia præcox is disturbance in the feelings of activity. Hoffding observes that:

" every psychic activity, aside from the tone of pleasure and pain, is accompanied by another feeling-tone which qualifies the whole in its own particular way."[2]

Jung cites Janet's observations in regard to psychasthenics which illustrate the same character:

" The decisions of volition and action are not accompanied by the same feeling as under normal conditions, but are marred by *sentiments d'incomplétude*. The subject feels that the action is not completely finished, that something is lacking. . . . Or every decision of the will is accompanied by a *sentiment d'incapacité*. These persons from the beginning experience painful feelings in the thought that it is necessary to act: they fear action above all things. Their dream, as they all say, is of a life where there will be nothing more to do."[3]

In dementia præcox a prevalent abnormality in the feeling of activity is the *sentiment d'automatisme*. A patient, cited by Jung, expressed it as follows:

" For four months I have had queer ideas; it seems to me that I am obliged to think and say them; someone makes me speak, someone suggests to me coarse words, and it is not my fault if my mouth is worked in spite of myself."[4]

All these disturbances of conscious capacity arise from the fascination of the pathogenic complex which has the power of magnetizing the psychic energy, thus holding it away from conscious direction. The term " fascination " was actually used by a patient to describe this spellbound condition.

1 *Loc. cit.*, iv., p. 79.
2 Quoted by Jung, *loc. cit.*, iv., p. 83.
3 *Loc. cit.*, iv., p. 84.
4 Janet: *Obsessions et Psychasthénie*, p. 273; *loc. cit.*, iv., p. 84.

Referring to the hallucinatory symptoms, Jung regards the outward projection as similar to the mechanism of the dream; only in hysteria the reasoning faculty is preserved, preventing the immediate outward projection which causes the hallucination. He writes:

> " We see something similar in normal dreams, where there is outward projection with absolute certainty and ingenuousness. The psychological mechanisms of dreams and hysteria are most closely related to those of dementia præcox. A comparison with dreams is, therefore, not too daring. In dreams we see how reality is interwoven with fantastic creations, how the pale memory-images of the waking state assume tangible living forms and how the impressions of the environment are adapted to the purpose of the dream. The dreamer finds himself in a new and different world which he has projected out of himself. Let the dreamer walk about and act as though he were awake and we have at once the clinical picture of dementia præcox."[1]

The latter half of the book is devoted to an illuminating detailed analysis of the delusional utterances and apparently nonsensical fantasy-formations of a fully developed case of paranoid dementia. The insight Jung was able to obtain into this completely isolated mind by accepting the autonomy of the complex as his guide is a remarkable scientific achievement.

III

In a later publication, *The Content of the Psychoses* (1st edition published 1908; 2nd enlarged edition, 1914), Jung develops his psychological conception on bolder lines. Attacking the psychiatric dogma that " disorders of the mind are disorders of the brain," he says:

> " We have at least positive information as to the functional nature of early schizophrenic conditions; moreover, the organic character of paranoia and many paranoid forms is still in great uncertainty. This being so, it is worth while to inquire whether manifestations of degeneration could not also be provoked by psychological disturbance of function. Such an idea is only incomprehensible to those who smuggle materialistic preconcep-

[1] C. G. Jung, *loc. cit.*, iv., p. 86.

tions into their scientific theories. This question does not rest upon some fundamental and arbitrary spiritualism, but upon the following simple reflection. Instead of assuming that some hereditary disposition, or a toxæmia, gives rise directly to organic processes of disease, I incline to the view that from some factor of predisposition, whose nature is at present unknown to us, there results a non-adaptable psychological function which can develop into manifest mental disorder. This may, secondarily, determine organic degeneration with its own train of symptoms. In favour of this conception is the fact that we have no proof of the primary nature of the organic disorder; but overwhelming proofs exist of a primary psychological fault in function, whose history can be traced back to the patient's childhood. In agreement with this conception is the fact that analytical practice has given us experience of cases where patients on the borderline of dementia præcox have been brought back to normal life."[1]

When he added to this paper in 1914, the break with Freud had intervened and Jung had already established the constructive method of handling unconscious symbolism.

" The number of psycho-analytic investigations into the psychology of dementia præcox has considerably increased since the publication of my book upon the subject. When, in 1903, I made the first analysis of a case of dementia præcox, I had a premonition of the possibilities of future discoveries in this sphere. This has been confirmed.

" Freud first submitted a case of paranoid dementia (the famous Schreber case) to closer psychological investigation. In this study Freud shows the infantile forms of thought and instincts out of which the delusional system was built up. The peculiar delusions which the patient had about his doctor, whom he identified with God, and certain other surprising and blasphemous ideas, Freud was able to reduce to his infantile relationship with his father. . . . This case also presented similar bizarre and grotesque concatenations of ideas to the one I described. As the author himself says, his work is restricted to the task of pointing out those universally existent and undifferentiated foundations out of which every psychological formation is historically developed. This reductive analytical process did not, however, furnish such enlightening results in regard to the rich and surprising symbolism in patients of this

C. G. Jung: " *Content of the Psychoses*," *Collected Papers*, p. 313.

kind as we had been accustomed to expect from the same method in the realm of hysteria.

" Many authors still proceed essentially by the method of analytical reduction, tracing back the complicated delusional formation into its simpler and more universal components, as I have done in the preceding pages. One cannot, however, resist the feeling that this method hardly does justice to the fullness and the almost overpowering wealth of fantastic symbol-formation, although it does undoubtedly throw a light upon the subject in certain directions."[1]

Illustrating his argument from Goethe's *Faust* he says:

" . . . naturally we should be glad of an exposition which pointed out how this subjective conflict in the poet's soul is itself based upon those ultimate and universal human things which are in no wise foreign to the poet, since we all carry the seeds of them in our hearts. Nevertheless we should be a little disappointed. We do not read *Faust* just in order to discover that we are also in all things ' human, all too human.' Alas, we know that but too well already. When we finally know who was the " Proktophantasmist," to what chronological events the mass of symbols in Part II. relates, how it is all intimately bound up with the poet's own soul and conditioned by it, we come to regard this determination as less important than the problem itself—what does the poet mean by his symbolic creation ?

" Proceeding purely reductively, one discovers the final meaning in these universal human things; and one demands nothing further from an explanation than that the unknown and complicated shall be reduced to the known and simple. I should like to designate this kind of understanding as *retrospective understanding*. But there is another kind of understanding, which is not analytic reduction, but is of a *synthetic* or *constructive* nature. I would designate this *prospective understanding*, and the corresponding method as the *constructive method*.

" It is common knowledge that present-day scientific explanation rests upon the basis of the causal principle. Scientific explanation is causal explanation. . . . In so far Freud's psychological method of interpretation is strictly scientific. But if we apply this method to *Faust* it must be clear that something more is required for a true understanding. It will even seem to us that we have not gathered the poet's deepest meaning if we only see

[1] *Ibid.*, Part II., p. 336.

in it universal foregone human conclusions. What we really want to find out is how this man has redeemed himself as an individual, and when we arrive at this comprehension we shall also understand the symbol given by Goethe. It is true we may then fall into the error of assuming that we understand Goethe himself. But let us be cautious and modest, simply admitting that we have thereby reached a certain understanding of ourselves. I have in mind Kant's thought-compelling definition of understanding, namely, 'the realization of a thing to the measure which is sufficient for our purpose.'

"This understanding, it is true, is subjective and therefore not scientific for those to whom science and explanation by the causal principle are identical. But the validity of this identification is open to question. In the sphere of psychology I must emphasize my doubt on this point.

"To interpret *Faust* objectively (that is, from the causal standpoint) is as though a man were to consider a sculpture from the historical, technical and mineralogical standpoint. But where lies the real meaning of the wonderful work? Where is the answer to that most important question: What aim had the artist in mind, and how are we to understand his work subjectively?"[1]

Contrasting again the two methods of approach Jung writes:

"The patient's unmistakable striving to express something by means of his delusion, Freud conceives retrospectively, as the satisfaction of his infantile wishes by means of fantasy. Adler reduces it to the desire for power.

"The constructive standpoint is different. Here the delusional system is neither infantile nor, upon the whole, *eo ipso* pathological, but subjective, and hence it is justified within the scope of the subjective. The constructive standpoint absolutely denies the conception that the subjective fantasy-creation is merely an infantile wish, symbolically veiled, or that it is merely that in a higher degree; it denies that it is a convulsive and egoistic adhesion to the fiction of its own superiority, in so far as these are to be regarded as finalistic explanations. The subjective can be only understood and judged subjectively. We cannot measure distance in pints. Any other judgment is unfair and does not meet the question."[2]

[1] *Loc. cit.*, p. 338.

[2] *Loc. cit.*, pp. 343, 344.

Inasmuch as the present work is also an attempt to find out in what way an individual psychology produces a positive reply to the threat of schizophrenia, it follows the method of Jung and can best be judged from his standpoint.

IV

In the course of this same paper Jung affirms for the first time the vital importance of psychological types in psychiatric research.

> " I must emphasize the statement that this question of types is *the* question of our psychology, and that every further advance must probably proceed by way of this question. The difference between the types is almost alarming in its extent. . . .
>
> " The irreconcilable opposition between the views of Freud and those of Adler is readily explained by the existence of two diametrically opposed psychological types which view the same things from entirely different aspects. An extravert can hardly, or only with great difficulty, come to an understanding with an introvert on any delicate psychological question."[1]

In regard to the contrast between hysteria and dementia præcox, the former is characteristic of the extraverted diathesis, the latter of the introverted. In his first contribution to the study of psychological types (1913) Jung says:

> " The opposition between these two nosological types (hysteria and schizophrenia) is also seen in their general symptomatology. From the intellectual point of view the products of hysterical imagination may be accounted for in a very natural and human way in each individual case by the antecedents and individual history of the patient. While the inventions of the precocious dement, on the contrary, are more nearly related to dreams than to normal consciousness, and they display, moreover, an incontestably archaic tendency, wherein mythological creations of primitive imagination are more in evidence than the personal memories of the patient . . . In their general physiognomy hysteria and dementia præcox present a striking contrast, which is seen particularly in the attitude of the patients towards the outer world. The reactions provoked in the hysteric surpass the normal in intensity of feeling, whilst this level is not reached at all by the precocious dement. The picture presented is one of

[1] *Loc. cit.*, pp. 348, 349.

exaggerated emotivity in the one, and extreme apathy in the other, with regard to the environment.

" All this clearly indicates that hysteria is characterized by a centrifugal tendency of the libido (psychic energy), whilst in dementia præcox its tendency is centripetal. The reverse picture obtains, however, when the illness has fully established its compensatory effects. . . .

" I propose to use the terms extraversion and introversion to describe these opposite directions of psychic energy, further qualifying them, however, as regressive in pathological cases, where fantasies, fictions, or fantastic interpretations, inspired by emotivity, falsify the perceptions of the subject about things or about himself."[1]

Jung's great work on psychological types subsequently expanded into many fields; but it is of peculiar interest that his first contribution in this field was stimulated by his psychiatric interest in the comparison between hysteria and dementia præcox. It was from this study that he deduced the principle of extraversion and introversion as two contrary movements of the libido. He describes them as fundamental mechanisms playing their part in alternating rhythm in every individual; tipping the scale to one side or the other to form a characteristic type when one mechanism gains a relative ascendancy. As Jung began to correlate his conception of these general psychic processes with his day-to-day clinical studies of patients, it was inevitable that the concept of the libido should become detached from its presupposed sexual designation and assume the unprejudiced status of general psychic energy. Freud, however, could not follow Jung in this broader, more impersonal conception of the libido, and a collaboration which was full of incalculable promise for the development of the new science came to an untimely end. Freud's whole temperament and training prompted him to pursue the biological and reductive line of approach. From this angle the aim of psychic activity is necessarily conceived as the satisfaction of the basal instinctive strivings. Jung, on the other hand, faithful to his introverted temperament and to his philosophical forebears, could not rest until he had

1 " *A Contribution to the Study of Psychological Types*," *Collected Papers*, pp. 287, 288.

extended the psychological field to embrace the total achievement of man. It was as impossible for Jung to narrow his conception of psychic reality, for the purposes of nosological definition, as it was for Freud to sacrifice his more intelligible, dogmatic schema for the larger horizon of Jung, which already embraced the concepts of the collective unconscious and the primordial image. This wider conception of the unconscious was not an attempt to smuggle the metaphysic of Schopenhauer into psychological thinking. Like every one of Jung's formulations, it was an empirical concept forced upon him by the unavoidable demands of the psychological phenomena with which he had to deal.

The concept of the *collective unconscious* is based upon the fact that a comparison of mythic patterns and general symbolism gathered from every part of the globe reveals a very high degree of structural uniformity. When we reflect upon the great differences of climatic, vegetational and other environmental conditions from the equator to the poles, to which mankind is adapted, the basic uniformity of man's bodily structure is a very remarkable fact. The basic uniformity of psychic structure which underlies the endless variety of social and individual differentiation is as demonstrable in its own field as is the uniform anatomy of the body.[1]

The general or collective unconscious comprises the psychological manifestations of this self-evident fact, and the *primordial image* or *archetype* designates the nuclear image or *engram* which, like the specific organs and functions of the body, has been laid down and established in the basal psyche as the result of the endless recurrence of typical human situations and relationships.

These conceptions are puzzling only if we approach the realm of psychic phenomenology with the prejudice that everything in the psyche has to be explained in terms of a single personal history beginning with the cradle and ending with the grave. As Jung himself recently admitted, any man

[1] In his work *Kingship*, for instance, Professor A. M. Hocart demonstrates the world-wide distribution of the archetype of initiation, embracing all the varieties of initiation from primitive puberty rituals to the English coronation ceremony.

with a bent for psychological realism who happened to reflect upon the same concatenation of facts as he encountered would necessarily have had to formulate similar conceptions.

As soon as we have admitted the hypothesis of a fundamental impersonal psyche upon which our personal psychology rests, the facts of our inner life assume a perspective which is not only convincing to the reason but deeply satisfying to feeling. For our sense of reality is more dependent upon the sanction of feeling than upon intellectual explanations: a fact which is borne out by our experience of the schizophrenic or schizoid mentality, where we find the sense of reality frequently broken across by an abrupt withdrawal of feeling.

At the time when Jung first formulated his theory of the complex he was still regarding the psychic contents as the resultant of personal disposition and experience. His break with Freud was due to his inability to exclude the effects of the general unconscious images from the psychological arena. It became overwhelmingly clear that to him the fateful effects, for example, of the parental *imago* through the whole of a person's life could not be attributed solely to the infantile memories of the actual parent. Behind the father or the mother there could be discerned a divine or magically endowed image, investing the parent-complex with an intensity of energy-value that remained throughout life as a superior psychic power. Freud, however, was unable to extend his view of psychic determination beyond the range of known and verifiable data to be found within the limits of the personal history. The break between Freud and Jung, however much it may be deplored on syncretistic grounds, was the inevitable result of the fidelity of two great minds to their respective empirical conclusions.

It will be realized that this inclusion of general collective images (which by virtue of their very universality dispose of a superior energy-potential) within the conception of psychical content involved a considerable modification of the original idea of the complex. As first conceived, the complex was a constellation of associated representations grouped about a painfully toned affect. This conception of the complex was, as we have seen, the result of experimental work in word-association tests in which analytical probing was done, as it were, from above, at the points where the test-irregularities provided complex-indicators. At this period Jung shared with Freud a view of the unconscious contents which was limited to the personal events in the subject's life-history. The parting with Freud coincided, as we have seen, with a remarkable change in Jung's psychological conceptions. The unconscious broadened out into a vast *terra incognita*, whence empirical concepts had to be created from the nature of the facts and objects encountered. At the heart of the mother-complex, for example, he found not the memory picture of the actual mother, but a generalized ambivalent image, sometimes deified and sometimes dæmonic, which, by its superordinated power and effect, claimed a place in the psychic hierarchy far above the personal memory-image of the mother.

This generalized or impersonal image, discovered in the deeper layers of the unconscious, he designated primordial image or archetype, the immediate resemblance of these images to the ruling figures and motifs in mythology leading him to conclude that individual psychology was rooted and grounded in the general experience of the race, in the same way that every individual act and gesture is rooted in the endless ancestral cycle.

When, therefore, we view the complex from above, we see only certain disturbances and effects. We may observe, for instance, an autonomous complex displace the ego-complex from its seat and rule there in its stead. Such a displacement can take place only by virtue of the fact that the obsessional idea is rooted in a complex disposing, at that time, of superior energy-value to that of the ego. The obsessional idea is, as a rule, of a highly irrational character; a fact that is only too clear to the subject himself. How, then, can an idea, whose very nature is such as to provoke its unsparing criticism, gain a compelling power over consciousness? The doctor who takes his stand on the absolute superiority of the intellect must feel himself impotent before the power of this irrational intruder. No argument can oust it from its place. Only when he has discerned the mythological root from which the idea springs, and can interpret the obsessional thought as the expression of a living archaic voice—as though the sympathetic system or the spinal cord, by virtue of their vast antiquity, had assumed the power of independent expression—has he reached a standpoint adequate to the facts.

The power of the autonomous complex to possess consciousness derives from its participation in the archaic level of the general psychic inheritance. We need to see it as a psychic octopus or whale, disturbing the situation from below, before we can combine the manifold effects presented by the clinical picture into a coherent whole.

The division of human psychology into the conscious and the unconscious is done principally for descriptive convenience. In order to form a structural view of the psyche as a whole, we must employ Jung's organic conception of the complex which, like a tree, rooting itself in the deepest instinctual levels, yet extends branches and leaves throughout the constantly changing fabric of individual experience.

The primordial image, which can be conceived as the dynamic germ at the heart of the complex, means nothing more nor less than the inherited manifestation of a basic and specific human necessity. It is the figurative expression in dream or fantasy of the living continuity of instinctual experience. It is also conceived as the source or container of that supra-personal afflux of energy which, when released, either carries the individual towards his goal, or smashes him pitilessly upon the rocks.

* * * * *

The foregoing summary of Jung's psychiatric contributions has been rendered incomplete by a recent comprehensive paper read by him before the Psychiatric Section of the Royal Society of Medicine.[1] In this paper Jung reserves judgment on the possibly organic nature of the primary symptoms, though he agrees emphatically with Bleuler " that the great majority of symptoms are of a secondary nature and are chiefly due to psychical causes." The primary symptom, for which Bleuler assumes an organic cause, is a peculiar

1 " *On the Psychogenesis of Schizophrenia.*"

disturbance of association which, according to Bleuler's description, is a sort of disintegration resulting in the associations being characteristically mutilated and disjointed. Jung points out that the " primary symptom " thus described by Bleuler coincides with the condition formulated by Janet as *abaissement du niveau mental*, which is at bottom a peculiar *faiblesse de la volonté*.

" If we are permitted to call the main guiding and controlling force of our mental life *will-power*, then we can agree that Janet's concept of the *abaissement* explains a psychical condition in which a train of thought is not carried through to its logical end, or where it is interrupted by strange contents insufficiently inhibited."

In the further development of his reasoning Jung sees this condition—viz., *abaissement du niveau mental*—as the key principle of schizophrenic ætiology; although, as he remarks, Janet used his hypothesis

" chiefly in order to explain the symptomatology of hysteria and other neuroses, which are indubitably psychogenic and different from schizophrenia. . . . The interference with normal association is, however, much the same in both types of disease: the fundamental difference which distinguishes hysteria and the neuroses from schizophrenia *consists in the maintenance of the potential unity of the personality* in the former group. . . . The general picture of an association-test of a schizophrenic may be very similar to the test of a neurotic, but a close exploration reveals the fact that in a schizophrenic patient the connection between the ego and certain complexes is more or less completely lost. The split is not relative: it is rather absolute. An hysterical patient might suffer from a sort of persecution mania very similar to a real paranoia. But the difference is that in the case of hysteria we can bring the delusion back under the control of consciousness; whereas it is impossible to do this in paranoia."

Jung then uses a metaphor which might have been borrowed from the material of my second patient.[1] He says:

" The dissociation in schizophrenia is not only far more serious, but very often it is also irreversible. The dissociation is no longer liquid and changeable, as it is in a neurosis, but is more like a mirror broken up into splinters. The unity of personality

[1] Part II., Drawing 3.

which lends a humanly understandable character to its own secondary personalities in a case of hysteria is definitely severed into fragments."

In the succeeding paragraph he presents a picture of the dissociated shadow-personalities in schizophrenia, which will be found graphically corroborated in the second dream of the first patient. He writes:

> "The picture of a personality dissociation in schizophrenia is quite a different matter. The split-off figures assume banal, grotesque or highly exaggerated names and characters, and are often objectionable in many ways. They do not, moreover, co-operate with the patient's consciousness. . . . They break in and make a disturbance at any time, they torture the ego in a hundred ways: they are objectionable and shocking either in their noisy and impertinent behaviour, or in their grotesque cruelty and obscenity."

Regarding the lowering of the level of consciousness as the primary condition which instigates the schizophrenic disruption, Jung proceeds to enumerate six major results of the *abaissement*. These are:

> (1) "A loss of whole regions of normally controlled contents.
> (2) A production, thereby, of split-off fragments of the personality.
> (3) The normal train of thought is impeded, so that a consistent and effective mental performance becomes impossible.
> (4) A decrease in the responsibility and adequate reaction of the ego.
> (5) Realization is interfered with, thereby causing insufficient and inadequate emotional reactions.
> (6) Through lowering the conscious threshold it allows normally inhibited contents of the unconscious mind to enter consciousness in the form of autonomous intrusions."

From this statement of schizophrenic ætiology it becomes evident that the term *abaissement* includes two quite distinct and opposite departures from the norm. The lowering of the conscious threshold of defence and control is only the negative half of the picture. The more important and positive aspect is the simultaneous activation or reinforcement of the archaic contents of the unconscious, inasmuch as these can intrude upon the conscious domain only by virtue of a superior energy-content. The vital difference between the neurotic and the schizophrenic, according to Jung, is that the neurotic always fights for the supremacy of his ego-consciousness, and tries to subjugate the resistant unconscious forces.

> " But a patient who allows himself to be swayed by the intrusions of strange contents from the unconscious, a case that does not fight, that even identifies with the morbid elements, immediately exposes himself to the suspicion of schizophrenia. His *abaissement* has reached the fatal extreme degree, where the ego loses all power of resistance against the inimical onslaught of an apparently more powerful unconscious."

Notwithstanding the fairly definite line which separates neurosis from schizophrenia, every psychiatrist has known cases in which the neurotic personality has stepped over the line into the psychotic territory. So long as the conflict is maintained, the ego striving desperately to overcome the increasing fascination of the archaic contents, the picture may be that of a characteristic anxiety or compulsion neurosis. But a time may come when the atavistic renegade goes over the line, and in that moment the subject capitulates to the psychotic fate. Before the line was crossed, we could count on the patient's co-operation and good-will. Afterwards we may have to deal with a crafty and resistant antagonist, with whom there is no longer any question of trying to subjugate the destructive tendencies. With regard to this event Jung writes as follows:

> " Now what do we say in such a case ? We say that it has always been a psychosis, a ' latent ' one, or one concealed or camouflaged by an apparent neurosis. But what has really happened ? For many years the patient fought for the maintenance of his ego, for the supremacy of his control and for the unity of his personality. But at last he gave out, he succumbed to the invader whom he could suppress no longer. He is not merely overcome by a violent emotion, he is really drowned in a flood of insurmountably strong forces and thought forms, which are far beyond any ordinary emotion, no matter how violent. These unconscious forces and contents existed long ago and he has wrestled with them successfully for years."

But these archaic contents are not specific to schizophrenia; only the attitude which permits them to rule in place of the authentic personality is truly psychotic. Jung goes on to say:

> "As a matter of fact, such strange contents are not confined to the patient alone; they exist in the unconscious of other people just as well. These are only fortunate enough to be profoundly ignorant of them. These forces did not originate in our patient out of the nowhere. They are most emphatically not the result of poisoned brain-cells, but are normal constituents of our unconscious mind. They appeared in numberless dreams, in the same or a similar form, at a time of life when, seemingly, nothing was wrong. They appear even in the dreams of normal people, who never get anywhere near to a psychosis. But if such a normal individual should suddenly undergo a dangerous *abaissement*, his dreams would instantly seize upon him and make him think, feel and act like a lunatic."

Jung deals summarily with the hypothesis that before crossing the line these cases should be classed as latent psychotics. He says:

> "Let us assume, for the time being, that they really suffered from a *latent psychosis* concealed in the cloak of a neurosis. What, then, is a latent psychosis exactly? It is obviously nothing but the possibility that an individual may become temporarily deranged at some period of his life. The existence of strange unconscious material proves nothing at all. You find the same with neurotics, modern artists and poets, and also with fairly normal people who have submitted to a careful investigation of their dreams. . . . The possibility of a future psychosis has nothing to do with the peculiar contents of the unconscious mind. But it has everything to do with the question whether the individual can stand a certain panic, or the constant strain of a psyche at war with itself. Very often it is merely the question of a little bit too much—*i.e.*, of the drop that falls into a vessel already full; or of the spark that incidentally lands upon a heap of gunpowder."

It is characteristic of the rational civilized mentality that of the two possible factors in the causation of mental disorder, only the one which has to do with the lowering of consciousness is seriously considered. The primitive mind, on the other hand, takes account not so much of the conscious reaction to the unconscious, but of the positive force and initiative of the archaic contents. "The primitive valuation of insanity," Jung writes,

> "points out a certain characteristic which we should not overlook; it ascribes personality, initiative and wilful intention to the unconscious—again a true interpretation of the obvious facts. From the primitive standpoint it is perfectly clear that the unconscious out of its own volition has taken possession of the ego. According to this view, the ego is not primarily enfeebled: on the contrary, it is the unconscious that is strengthened through the presence of a demon. The primitive theory, therefore, does not seek the reason for insanity in a primary weakness of consciousness, but rather in an inordinate strength of the unconscious."

Having admitted the difficulty of deciding to which of these causes schizophrenia is due, Jung says:

> "The latter possibility cannot easily be dismissed, since it is not unthinkable that the *abundant archaic material could be the expression of a still existing infantile, as well as primitive, mentality*. It could be a question of *atavism*. I seriously consider the possibility of a so-called *développement arrêté*, where a more than normal amount of primitive psychology remains intact and does not become adapted to modern conditions."

The substantial bulk of infantile and embryonic material which we shall presently discuss tends, particularly in the first case, to confirm this view. "It is natural," Jung goes on to say,

> "that under such conditions a considerable part of the psyche should not catch up with the normal progress of consciousness. In the course of the years the distance between the unconscious and the conscious mind increases, producing a latent conflict at first. But when a particular effort at adaptation is needed, and when consciousness should draw upon its unconscious instinctual resources, the conflict becomes manifest; and the hitherto latent primitive mind suddenly bursts forth with contents that are too incomprehensible and too strange for assimilation to be possible. Such a moment marks the beginning of the psychosis in a great number of cases."
>
> "But we should not disregard the fact that many patients seem to be quite capable of producing a modern and sufficiently developed

consciousness, sometimes of a particularly concentrated rational and obstinate kind. However, one must quickly add that such a consciousness shows early signs of a self-defensive nature. This is a symptom of weakness, not of strength."

I can subscribe to this view of the atavistic character of schizophrenic psychology the more readily because it confirms the conclusion I had already reached in this work before Jung's paper was written. What I have alluded to as the renegade hypothesis, Jung sees as a sudden activation of the latent primitive mind. Whichever way we view it, the actual result is a crossing of the line, and an alienation of the personality from its former character. According to my experience, patients who eventually cross the line from neurosis to psychosis go voluntarily. Conflict is usually acute up to the point when the renegade hypothesis is more or less consciously accepted. The patient does not, as a rule, give the impression of being dragged resisting across the line by a stronger force. It is rather as though an essential part of the personality had migrated to "the other side," and eventually the rest of the personality is bound to follow, and usually without great protest.

Jung allows for two groups of schizophrenia, according to whether consciousness is weak and, therefore, unable to keep back the flow of unconscious material, or whether a normal consciousness is suddenly confronted with a strongly activated unconscious which it cannot withstand. These contrasting ætiological types are to be found, of course, as well among the neuroses as with schizophrenia.

Although the far-reaching consequences of the initial *abaissement* together with the bad prognosis are recognized by Jung as serious objections to the theory of psychogenesis, yet, on the whole, he prefers an explanation, for which substantial evidence can be adduced, to an hypothesis that rests on almost no evidence at all.

Finally, he mentions two facts which have impressed him most during his career as alienist and psychotherapist.

"The one is the enormous change the average lunatic asylum has undergone in my lifetime: that whole desperate crowd of utterly degenerate katatonics has practically disappeared, on account of the mere fact that they were given something to do. The other fact is the discovery I made when I began my psychotherapeutic practice: I was amazed at the number of schizophrenics whom we almost never see in the psychiatric hospitals. . . . They are partially camouflaged as compulsion neuroses, obsessions, phobias and hysterias, and they are very careful never to go near an asylum. Such cases insist upon treatment. . . . There are numbers of latent psychoses and quite a few not so particularly latent, which, under favourable circumstances, can be submitted to a psychological analysis with sometimes quite decent results."

In this final paragraph Jung seems to take his leave of the clinical, psychiatric standpoint, and to spread his sail to a good psychotherapeutic breeze. Since the two cases whose material we shall presently discuss are borderline cases, men who are able to fill each his respective place in the social and domestic spheres without too serious interference from the unconscious; and since this work is intended primarily as a contribution to psychotherapy, it is with borderline schizophrenics—the most interesting and from the point of human quality the most worthwhile material for psychotherapy—that we are concerned in the present work. In the material of both cases we shall find a characteristic display of schizophrenic symptomatology, notwithstanding a remarkable contrast in individual character. Both cases I regard as latent, in so far as neither subject has crossed the line into psychotic territory, except momentarily, like most other men, under exceptional circumstances. There is, indeed, a peculiar difference between the pathological picture, presented in dream and drawing, and the debonair conscious façade, which in neither case afforded more than an inkling of the concealed psychic strain.

In both the increasing emotional strain involved in the problem of the first pregnancy of their marriage had lowered the threshold sufficiently to bring home the menace of unconscious inundation. But whereas the first patient showed only slight resistance to the renegade hypothesis, and considerable difficulty in maintaining a civilized standard of life, the second had a remarkable conscious control, unwavering loyalty to all his undertakings and, in my experience, a unique tendency to systematize his psychological material, as though demonstrating the subtleties of schizophrenia to a class of intelligent angels. It is true that this tendency to systematize his material did not go hand in hand with insight. But whereas the first patient was not especially interested in reaching a psychological understanding of his myth, the second was not content until the intellectual content of the material had been adequately elaborated. So detached, indeed, was the second patient from the pathological material he was producing that one had to consider the possibility whether the schizophrenic process might not have been induced. Finally, I came to the conclusion that the condition of emotional trauma in childhood had been responsible for this very unusual psychology. The signs of intellectual systematization and control are never absent in his material, even in drawings where an explosive, disruptive tendency is being portrayed. That this attitude of conscious control represented an indispensable condition of his existence was evidenced by his irreproachable persona and physical poise and in an unfailing self-discipline in the emotional sphere.

The determining of physical attitude and muscular coordination by the schizophrenic diathesis would be a valuable field to investigate, inasmuch as those individuals who are particularly threatened by the inroad of disruptive forces might be expected to provide physical evidence of the fact. The relation between the physiological and psychological disturbances in schizophrenia is at present being investigated at the Boston Psychopathic Hospital, and on the whole with positive results. If this correlation should ever be proved, it would be necessary to assume that the roots of the schizophrenic process reach down to an infrapsychic level, as, for example, in the sympathetic system: a conclusion which is also anticipated in the material of the second patient.

V

The concept of latent schizophrenia, though indispensable to psychotherapeutic practice, makes the borderline still more difficult to define. In fact, modern psychiatric writers, Kretschmer in particular, are emphatic in their opinion that the gradation from normal schizoid personalities into the schizophrenic type is such that even the concept of the borderline case becomes almost meaningless. Kretschmer advises his pupils to look carefully at normal types before becoming fascinated by the abnormal exaggeration of these types. His view, summed up by Devine, is as follows:

> "We should no longer look on certain types of personality as psychopathic abortive forms of certain psychoses; but, *vice versa*, certain psychoses will figure as caricatures of certain normal types of personality."[1]

Jung, curiously enough, has omitted to mention the problem of types in his recent paper, quoted above; but the two contrasting types, described by Kretschmer, correspond in their essential features to Jung's extraverted and introverted types: the cycloid equating with the extravert, the schizoid with the introvert. When we follow the clinical descriptive approach we are confronted at once with this phenomenon of contrasting types, and it has become almost a practice of psychiatric observers to formulate each his own system of types. The schizoid temperament of Kretschmer corresponds, for example, to the "shut-in" personality of Hoch. But although the observation and description of personality-types has become a recognized part of clinical psychiatry, owing to the fact that the biogenetic psychoses tend to develop out of these types, yet it by no means follows that individuals who bear cycloid or schizoid traits, even to an accentuated degree, are destined to become psychotic.

Another point to remember is that the cycloid or extraverted personality manifests morbid psychological tendencies in a more overt fashion than the more concealed schizoid. In his valuable summary of psychiatric views, Devine says:

> "In the schizophrenic group, still less than in the circular, is it easy to separate the healthy from the diseased, the charactero-logical from the psychotic. . . . We do not know what is in the mind of the patient, even when he seems to have made a good recovery. It is a curious fact, also, that a schizoid individual may nourish the most fantastic delusions for years without manifesting

[1] Kretschmer. See Devine, *Recent Advances in Psychiatry*, p. 54.

abnormal social reactions, or without his family having the least suspicion of what is in his mind. Such an individual is definitely living in two worlds."[1]

The majority of psychiatrists will agree that no further progress in the understanding of the biogenetic psychoses (in which we include the schizophrenic and the manic-depressive types) is to be anticipated along the behaviourist, clinical approach, or by intensified pathological research of the brain and nervous system. Devine writes, for instance:

> "The problem of the biogenetic psychoses is the most obscure and difficult one which psychiatry is called upon to solve, and, generally speaking, it may be said that the group includes those psychoses in which we are unable to discover any clear-cut relationship to a definite bodily disturbance or disease."[2]

Since, therefore, the extraverted, clinical avenue cannot bring us nearer to the heart of the problem, the time would seem to be ripe for a thoroughgoing investigation of an individual case on the basis of Jung's subjective, introverted approach from the side of the unconscious, in the hope that the roots of the pathological system might become visible. Other workers have published valuable results following the orthodox route of psycho-analysis, and their conclusions, though based as yet on a relatively meagre number of cases, all tend to confirm Jung's original view that the solution can be found only by the way of a sympathetic individual understanding of the psychology of the individual case.

Speaking of the inadequacy of rational analysis in the presence of highly irrational manifestations, Storch says:

> "These irrational units of affective experiences and thoughts are only imperfectly accessible to rational analysis. Such analysis can only be undertaken by way of emotional participation and sympathetic understanding, and these latter will always be the most valuable means for penetrating the world of thought of the schizophrenic."[3]

In a recent research Zilboorg cites a case of acute paranoia which was eventually completely cured by analysis. He says:

[1] Devine: *Recent Advances in Psychiatry*, p. 255. [2] *Loc. cit.*, p. 248.

[3] Storch: *Primitive Archaic Forms of Inner Experiences and Thought in Schizophrenia*. Trans. by Willard. (Nerv. Ment. Dis. Publishing Co., N.Y., 1924.)

"It seems that the crucial and most fundamental element of the whole analysis was the patient's *reliving and reacting* her paranoid psychosis in a stormy way in a period of about two weeks *in the analytical situation.*"[1]

I have underlined those last words, because I am convinced that the safeguarding analytical relationship is the essential condition which induces the latent psychosis to emerge and therewith, eventually, to be assimilated.

In the subsequent discussion of Dr. Zilboorg's paper, Dr. White observed:

"It ought to be an exceedingly vital consideration in our research into the problem of schizophrenia to realize the nature and the amount of the material which has been obtained by this method of approach—material that cannot possibly be obtained in any other way. It seems to me that this is the material we must collect before we can have any real understanding of the psychological and psychosocial level of this disorder."

A remark of Zilboorg's[2] at the close of the discussion sheds a curious light on the inexplicable obscurity in which psychiatric research has been pursued. He said:

"The deeper affective roots of schizophrenia have been overlooked by psychiatry, and will continue to be overlooked unless we use a method of investigation which is capable of bringing them out into full light."[3]

And then later:

"I have in mind the ever deeper and deeper study of the individual patient."[4]

Freud began to publish his researches into the affective roots of mental disorder in 1896; Jung's *Psychology of Dementia Præcox* was published in English in 1909; Freud's investigation of the Schreber case was published about the same time. Practical methods for the deep exploration of the mind are accessible to every doctor. Why, then, is it still possible

[1] Zilboorg: "*The Problem of Affective Re-integration in the Schizophrenias,*" *Schizophrenia.* Vol. X. of Research Publications, Association for Research in Nervous and Mental Disease. Proceedings of the Association, New York, December, 1929, p. 203.

[2] *Loc. cit.*, p. 205. [3] *Loc. cit.*, p. 207. [4] *Loc. cit.*, p. 209.

to say that with relatively few exceptions psychiatry has steadily ignored the one fruitful method of approach in just those disorders where the seat of the disturbance lies quite patently in the roots of the emotional life ?

We may cling zealously to the detailed instructions for case-recording laid down by Sadler, or, becoming proficient in the graph-recording of Meyer or the psychobiogram of Kretschmer, we may completely enfold our patient with a mass of competent clinical data; yet, in spite of all these efforts, the sick soul, with which we are really concerned, may be looking on with eyes of stone, parched of any vital interest. It is not questioned by any modern writers that mental disorders have a multiple ætiology, nor that the physiological aspect may not be as fertile a field of study as the psychological; but when finally we do come to the psychogenesis of mental states, we must demand that the method of psychological research shall not be one that absolutely precludes the psyche.

CHAPTER II

HISTORY OF SUBJECT AND DREAM I

I

A PHYSICIAN, aged thirty-one, of English farming stock, born and bred in America. His father was the first in the family history to leave the land and adopt an intellectual career. He was a man of unusual intellectual vigour. Whenever an idea seized him, he followed it with ruthless intensity, with the intolerance of a reformer casting aside anyone who could not instantly sympathize with the policy he was advocating. He left England to attempt to launch a revolutionary agrarian policy in the States. He appears to have tried many rôles, playing them in turn with equal intensity; the intuition of the moment, whatever it might be, bearing him and his whole family along in its train. Even in his photograph the eyes have a piercing, an almost embarrassing intensity.

The patient's mother died while he was at school, at the age of twelve. Trained as a musician, she gave up a possible career in order to marry. This sacrifice may have had important effects on the son which are hard to compute. She seems to have lived a subdued, introverted life beside a husband to whom the essential feminine elements meant little. She loyally supported and sympathized with his ideas; but her existence must have been somewhat isolated. People who knew her speak eloquently of her warm sympathies and wisdom.

After her death the father married again, but the marriage collapsed almost immediately. The father then fell into a melancholia, and was taken care of for a time in a mental hospital. No history of mental disorder can be traced in the familial background other than this, although there have been eccentric characters in the father's stock.

The patient had one brother and one sister. The brother is a successful business man. Being some years older than the patient, he seems to have suffered less from the unfavourable home conditions. The sister was the more deeply involved with the father because of his inaccessibility, and, in a rash attempt to extricate herself, made a compensatory marriage with an American youth whom, however, she soon came to despise. She was a girl of spirit, athletic and competent, but subject to despondent moods. Like the brother, she seems to have been completely shut in emotionally, and no one was informed of the cause of her unhappiness. After the marriage had lasted only two years, she took her life by leaping from a building. The patient, who was eighteen at the time, had to go and identify the body and make all the funeral arrangements. It throws an important sidelight on the father's psychology that he relegated this painful responsibility to his son.

The early death of the mother and the tragic death of the sister were, I believe, decisive events in the dissociation of feeling which marked the patient's subsequent development. Like the father, the patient's feelings remained recessive, rarely positive, and not to be relied upon. His function-type appeared to be introverted, intuitive, intellectual.[1] Accordingly, feeling and sensation were relatively repressed and inferior. His emotional development did not advance with his intellect, but remained at a relatively adolescent level, statically contained by the images of the mother and the sister. From the age of five the patient was conscious of hostile negative feelings towards his mother, arising probably from the state of emotional fixation, mentioned above, which held him fast in the infantile state. The relation with the sister was the one positive vehicle in which his feeling had a human expression, though, even here, there seems to have been little real intimacy. Besides the somewhat disturbing atmosphere of his home, there is also the fact that the family was uprooted from the soil, where for generations farming forebears had lived and toiled. This fact should be stressed because, as

[1] Later I came to regard him as an extravert whose type had been falsified by precocious introversion due to the emotional trauma. This surmise has been to some extent corroborated by the subject's naturally extraverted development since the analysis.

we shall presently see, it was from these deep instinctual roots that the therapeutic attempt proceeded.

As regards the upper and outer aspect of the patient's personality, the picture is positive. After his mother's death he spent some years in a public school in England, where he was successful both in work and in athletics. He was able to pass examinations with relative ease, even coming to despise anyone who set store on examination results. He captained the school football team with vigour and command, enjoying his position of power and generalship. But although savouring the power which his successes brought him, he felt none the less like an automaton moving among automata. He saw that experiences which moved other men meant nothing to him. Instead of being fluid and adaptable, his feeling was withdrawn and unready. From the time of his mother's death there seems to have been a certain withdrawal or inversion of personal feeling. Charm of manner made him acceptable, but psychologically he lived in chilly isolation.

While still a student at the university there were certain erotic advances between himself and a girl, and it is characteristic of his lack of individual feeling that he assumed at once he ought to offer marriage, even though he was totally against it. In his attempt to coerce his feeling, he drove his mind to the edge of suicide. Indeed, on his way to propose to the girl, he nearly threw himself out of the train which seemed to be carrying him pitilessly towards a false destiny.

Not long after this episode he married a fellow-student at the university, a competent, extraverted, gifted young woman who was able to compensate a certain hardness on the side of feeling by brilliant though facile accomplishment in the world of letters.

The patient came to see me at the beginning of his wife's first pregnancy. Although this fact played an important part in his general feeling of insecurity, it was actually on account of certain difficulties with his patients that he wished to consult me. With a background of latent psychosis, he was necessarily attracted to psychiatry, and while acting as resident officer in a mental hospital the morbid complex became actively constellated. He became emotionally identified with some of his patients, with the result that he began to lose his bearings as a medical officer. Feelings of hostility developed towards the medical superintendent and some of his colleagues, while the necessary discipline of the hospital took on an aspect of tyranny and oppression. He became so uncertain of himself that he decided to be analysed, his ostensible reason being the wish to equip himself as fully as possible for the work which had now engaged all his sympathies. This motive, though representing only half the picture, was, none the less, perfectly real.

II

The dream with which the analysis started was one which he had had some months before. It coincided with his reading of Freud's *Interpretation of Dreams*, an experience which had given his mind a very definite orientation and which opened his eyes to the possible value of dreams.

"The scene is on the Mersey. There are many boats, one of which is a battleship. It floats very high on the water, and though it is huge, it looks like a toy ship. It bobs about, turning this way and that, and is in imminent danger of colliding with other boats. At last it makes connection with a towing boat, which drops an anchor. There is some doubt whether the anchor will hold, but it eventually does so.

"We then go ashore. I have a picture-paper in my hand; in it there is a picture of the President, or perhaps the Prime Minister of England, joking with the King. I go up to this man, who is reminiscent of Disraeli, with a flavour of MacDonald. He is continually polishing his eyeglass, which falls to the ground, and I pick it up and polish it for him. This happens several times. Then the eyeglass turns into a microscope slide, which I place on the flat rung of a ladder near by.

"The scene changes. We are going in a carriage to a palace. The palace is modern and surrounded by trees: the whole thing is rather like a Monet painting. As we come up to the front door, I see some exquisite flowers and jump out to smell them, holding them in the cup of my hands. The sensation is exquisite.

"We then go indoors, and port and beer are handed round.

My wife seems responsible for this, and this stimulates me to say with contempt: 'Port and beer!'

"We then go away and return later, walking. We are late for supper. As we walk down the road, the King passes. He is in a small carriage alone: a racy-looking man. His carriage jogs along. To my delight he seems to recognize us, and waves as he passes.

"My wife and I are now in the palace, and Princess Mary is present handing round fruit salad—an inferior diet, I think. There are three women and myself present. I hand fruit salad to two of them and take the third portion myself. The third woman is thus left out. I have dropped a social 'brick.'

"I now go and talk to a lady. Whilst doing so, I put my knee on the end of a bench, which jumps up, and in falling back makes a noise. The conversation ends. A second 'brick.'

"Princess Mary now gives us our places for dinner. When the time comes for us to go in, I find that my shoes are off, and I hastily put them on again. On our way to dinner we go up through an elaborate nursery, without, however, any children in it.

"The dining-hall is rather like a college hall, and the tables are arranged in an inverted U, the free ends facing the entrance. I walk down the right side and try to sit in a wrong place. Princess Mary puts me right, and I walk round the tables to my correct place on the other (left) side. At the end of the table, near the transverse table, sits a distinguished-looking man, picking his nose. This might seem disgusting, but he carries it off with *aplomb*. Next to my place at the table is a broken toothbrush with wire bristles. The bristles loop on to the back of the brush. It is revealed as an 'asthma toothbrush.'

"The question arises as to why I am here, and the answer is that I am a distinguished physician."

The Mersey is associated with his mother's family. It embraces his first memories of a port and shipping when, as a boy, he came to England and visited his grandfather's house on the banks of the Mersey. He thinks there was a fast incoming tide in the dream.

The ship was very light, as though made of three-ply wood. The little towing-boat that drops the anchor and brings the other boat to rest is associated with his wife and his marriage.

The patient sees certain resemblances to his father both in Disraeli and MacDonald. Ramsay MacDonald is associated with the idealistic side of his father's character, which is also linked up in the patient's mind with an exaggerated personal sensitiveness and a certain aloofness. In contrast to this Disraeli appears as a subtle and detached realist. Being a Jew, he was familiar with the less favourable aspects of his own psychology. Therefore he could withstand criticism without a continual itch towards self-justification.

The microscope is associated with analytical scrutiny. The Palace is Buckingham Palace. Monet was an artist who forsook traditional art and discovered nature instead. The flowers are cup-like and fragrant, associated with anemones. The allusion to port and beer refers to a meal he once had with a distinguished American actor who was attracted to him homosexually and whose " exquisite " taste and " clear-cut individuality " made him deaf to his own warning instinct. At this meal beer was served, followed by port, and the flattery of the older man's admiration, in contrast to his wife's subsequent criticisms of the affair, is linked up with the feeling of resentment against his wife which colours this episode of the dream. His wife disliked the actor for his general reputation, as well as for his attempt to seduce the patient.

From the fact that he took the dream down and preserved it during the months before he came to me for analysis, we can conclude that it made a certain impression upon the patient. Moreover, he selected the opening scene of the dream as the theme of his first drawing. It frequently happens that a subject who is seriously considering a personal analysis will have a comprehensive dream which is concerned with the major problem of his psychology. The present is an example of what might be termed the programmatic dream.

The first thing to note is that the dream takes him back to England and the Mersey. His mother's family at Liverpool represents the sound side of his psychology. His maternal grandfather won his childish affection, and all his memories of the time spent under the grandfather's roof are warm and glowing. Hence, the return to this scene means a return to the primordial state of feeling before anything had happened to alienate him from his original nature.

The opening scene of a dream usually offers a valuable

clue as to the standpoint from which the rest of the dream can be understood. It is like the *mise en scène* of the first act of a drama, or like the opening theme of a symphony. It supplies the criterion, or standpoint, from which the subsequent events can be viewed and understood.

The fast incoming tide reveals the energic moment. The phase of introversion is symbolized by the inward-flowing tide—*i.e.*, towards the subject—while extraversion is the flowing outwards of the psychic energy. The recent activation of the morbid system in the unconscious has resulted in a compulsive introversion of psychic energy into the unconscious; and upon this inflowing tide the inflated battleship, with which the patient identifies himself, gets out of control and behaves in an erratic and dangerous fashion. This is the warning that something is seriously wrong. A battleship is the supreme symbol of disciplined power. Hence, to identify oneself with a battleship implies a grandiose fantasy of god-almightiness which would result in a complete distortion of reality. The danger of this inflation is emphasized by the dream-statement that the ship is made of three-ply wood. A battleship, enormously magnified in relation to the other craft on the river (*vide* Drawing I.), and also made of the flimsiest material, is a pathological creation. It is an attempt to fight the world with a false image. The erratic behaviour of the battleship on the fast tide is echoed by the erratic behaviour of the subject in the subsequent episodes. It is as though the reasonable common sense and good feeling of the maternal grandfather—representing the sound part of his own mind—is being invoked by the dreaming subject in face of a very real danger.

The towing-boat, which supplies the anchor that holds the battleship, belongs to the side of reality and, as we shall see in the drawing, is represented within the normal scale. In the drawing his wife is in the boat, although in the dream she is significantly omitted. Apart from the fact that unreserved loyalty to the human pact is the age-old defence against evil spirits, marriage provides an invaluable steadying discipline for a man with an explosive psychology. It gives him concrete tasks and holds him to a real world. Moreover, the need to preserve the respect of a loyal though critical wife provides an invaluable check to instability and waywardness. Therefore the dream reminds the subject that the marriage-boat, which he significantly reduces to a little dinghy to be towed along in his wake, is more powerful even than the battleship. It is stronger because it is real.

The next scene is ashore. The water represents the dynamic emotional flux of the unconscious, the constantly changing element upon which consciousness floats. Since the sea is also the original matrix in which life was first generated, it is the maternal element (*cf.* Latin *mare*=sea; French *la mer, la marée*). The mother, like the sea, is the source of life, and hence the mother-image is the reigning deity of a man's unconscious, symbolizing generation and regeneration, the womb of transformation and rebirth, as well as the great devourer and destroyer.

The transition to the shore brings us, therefore, to the opposite principle ruled by the father-imago. Just as the unconscious in a man's psychology is under the ægis of the mother, the conscious is normally governed by the father-principle. If the sea symbolizes the fluid, subjective realm of the unconscious with all its hidden contents, the land is the realm of objective consciousness where things are objectively clear and definite.

The picture-paper is a mirror of things that are happening in the contemporary world, not a private mirror in which a man sees himself as he actually is, but a collective mirror in which people are magnified to fill the public eye—*e.g.*, the President, the Prime Minister, the King, etc. The Prime Minister in the patient's world is the father; the patient is unconsciously identified with his masterful, outstanding father, and it is here that the source of the pathological inflation must be sought. The patient stands on the threshold of his career; whereas the father is in the late sixties: a man of wide experience who has attained considerable prominence as an ardent reformer. To identify oneself with a being in vital respects so dissimilar induces a basis of unreality. The unconscious identification of the son with the father is a normal phase in a boy's education: it lasts, as a rule, until the son is launched into life and finds his own position among his contemporaries. But in the present case the father's influence over the patient was pathological in character, partly owing to the early death of the mother, and partly to the spell-binding intensity of the father's will. In spite of conscious criticism of his father, he was fascinated by the burning fire of his spirit, which appeared to the growing boy as an almost superhuman force. This spell-binding effect of the father's personality may be seen, under a mythological disguise, in the drawings which follow.

The danger, then, does not lie in the son's unconscious identification with the father, regarded as a model on which to base his adaptation; but rather in the fact that he uses the identification for the purpose of raising himself unjustifiably to the father's level. Herein lies the ground of inflation—namely, that one assumes a level and range of experience which does not belong to him. A great many of the patient's difficulties have arisen from this mistake. Always, for instance, he has found it difficult to submit to those above him: the mere fact that somebody has authority over him is likely to arouse stubborn resistance. The identification gives him an illusory sense of superiority; he is not quite at home with men of his own age, because they seem to him young and callow. His aloofness, his unwillingness to march in step with his colleagues in the arduous apprenticeship of medicine, and to do the routine work of a junior physician, are by-products of the identification with the father. It is as though his attitude to life were based upon the experience of a man already past the zenith. His expectations tend to miscarry because he is liable to strive after fictitious goals. In addition, the mellowing influence of feeling, which would supply him with a sense of comradeship and relatedness with his own peers, is not to be relied upon. His somewhat ambitious fantasies are, therefore, not controlled by the sense of solidarity and comparison normally felt with men of one's own generation.

It would seem from his association of Disraeli and MacDonald with his father that, in fantasy at least, he thinks of his father as equivalent to the Prime Minister or President.

The monocle is an improvisation of the dream and suggests a one-sided defect of vision—in other words, a psychological one-sidedness. The fact that the glass falls to the ground repeatedly, and that he monotonously picks it up and polishes it, refers to his spellbound condition which makes it impossible for him to break away from the fantasy of power. That the sycophantic attitude, which he himself noted in the dream, demands analytical scrutiny is confirmed by the transformation of the eyeglass into a microscope slide. This is a subtle intimation that the one-sided defect of vision, when realized by the patient, may become a specialized means of enhancing his conscious power; even, perhaps, advancing his progress on the ladder of ambition. The fact that the dream presents two English Prime Ministers, one conservative and historical, the other socialistic and contemporary, probably refers to the ambiguous aspects of his father-complex. Through his yeoman ancestry the father provides him with a steadying, conservative, ancestral taproot. But, in so far as the father was uprooted and gave himself up to idealistic reforms (possibly as a compensation to his conservative ancestry), he presents to the son a psychological paradox, which would enhance his fascinating effect. The microscope is clearly an allusion to objective analytical examination, while the ladder speaks for itself.

* * * * *

The scene shifts again. " We are going in a carriage." The wife is included, but not mentioned. This omission is significant, as the dream may almost be said to harp upon his inadequate recognition of the individuality of woman. He and his wife are visiting the King's house. Though associated with Buckingham Palace, the dream house did not resemble it.

The King is beyond the reach of ambition. The most that is humanly possible is to stand in some relation to the King. Taken psychologically, the King represents the impersonal, inherited or dynastic principle of the psyche; he is the symbol of the unifying, suprapersonal self which has the power of combining all the different psychical elements.

With this comprehensive image we recognize the idea of individuality embracing the total subject, both personal and impersonal, conscious and unconscious, as a superordinate power. Through the efficacy of this royal symbol the dissociated and warring opposites can eventually be reconciled. Individuality, in this total sense, means being oneself as completely as possible; and this includes the whole sphere of relatedness, both personal and social. It is this latter aspect of life which, because of his emotional deficiency, the patient is liable to belittle or evade. Hence he can approach the King's house only, as it were, in the vehicle of relationship. The trees are creatures whose rootedness is their strength. Being uprooted from his ancestral soil, the patient became infected by the restless desirousness of urban collectivity. His marriage relationship is the sole tie which provides him with a root in the common earth of instinctual necessity.

Monet is not his favourite painter, but he responds to this artist's delicate sense of colour. The climax of the dream is found in the exquisite pleasure he feels[1] when he holds the cup-shaped flowers in the cup of his two hands. Flowers are the natural expression of feeling: the dream, therefore, alludes to the fact that what is most lacking in his conscious life will be found at the door of the King's house in the unconscious. This is the natural mind speaking, and nature does not lie. It is no empty fantasy, but a realizable potentiality; though in the statement that the scene is like a painting the dream implies that it is depicting an anticipation of reality.

Impersonal feeling finds expression, as a rule, in religious symbolism, and this symbol of the cup as the chalice, the flower, the vessel, etc., has at certain phases in history become charged with celestial potency. The vessel symbolism is an abstract, though intensely living, expression of the feminine principle. In Thibetan Buddhism, for example, the invocation *Om mane padme hum* (which has been translated " Oh ! the jewel in the lotus ") is based upon the tradition that the incarnate Bodhisattva first became manifest in the cup of the

[1] In the allusion to Monet at this point, the dream may be hinting at the release, subsequently discovered, in representing his inner experiences in colour and line; even coupling with it the idea of ' money ' or libido-value.

lotus, filling it with unimaginable radiance. The flower is the womb which gives birth to the god. It also opens to receive the god: the sun being the natural god of living things. The mystery of the Grail contains the same archetypal motif, for the Grail-vessel is likewise filled with unimaginable radiance in the moment when it becomes the vessel of the Divine Spirit.

When, therefore, the subject holds the flower in the cup of his two hands, it is as though he were performing a ritual act before the house of the ruler; and, in so doing, the archetype of the vessel of devotion, linked with the idea of the inexhaustible chalice, becomes activated in the unconscious depths. His sensation of ecstasy is a direct affirmation that, in this act, he has discovered the missing element which can restore for him the right order of nature. The discovery of the symbol which can lead a man to a fundamental realization of the feminine principle is often the most important event of his life. It is also the basis of civilized feelings. From the standpoint of feeling, therefore, as an impersonal, royal principle, a fresh criterion of judgement is gained, under the effect of which the subjective standard of behaviour undergoes a vital change.

The first test to which he must submit is his acceptance of the King's hospitality. Port and beer, according to his associations, were perfectly acceptable when accompanied by the honey of a distinguished actor's admiration. But now, when he assumes his wife to be responsible for them, he sees them as merely another example of her lack of taste. In this episode there is contained the patient's unexpressed resentment against his wife when she offered a perfectly justifiable criticism of his *laissez-aller* attitude to his homosexual admirer. This, then, is his first failure to pass the standard of decent feeling. He and his wife then go off and come back late for supper. This refers to a certain casual, easygoing egotism which often fails in consideration for other people. Failure number two.

Now the King passes him in the road, but, instead of a royal figure, he is depicted as a small, racy-looking man, jogging along in his carriage. The King, regarded as the symbolic ruler of the total subject, is necessarily conditioned by the subject's valuation of the royal symbol. Individuality is dishonoured by non-recognition; it is created by conscious valuation. It is as though the King had no power beyond that freely yielded by his subjects. The figure of the King in the dream is a clear intimation that the subject has failed to value the idea of the ruler. Inflation of the ego necessarily involves a corresponding depreciation of the suprapersonal self. Indirectly, therefore, the diminished royal figure is an accusation of the inflated ego-complex, yet his recognition by the King seems to bring the possibility of psychological integration within reach. The difficulty of accepting the conception of a virtual centre, or self, embracing the potentialities of the total psychical subject, comes from the illusory overvaluation of the ego-complex. It is a natural error to identify the self with the conscious, rational personality. But it is a very costly one, inasmuch as it involves the exclusion of the irrational, primitive elements of the personality which, being forced into the unconscious, are liable to break loose in devastating collective upheavals.

From this point in the dream the function of command is taken over by the King's daughter. First she appears as the dispenser of hospitality, even as a ministering function. But again the reaction of the patient betrays a contemptuous attitude of superiority to what is offered him. The patient could supply no specific association to fruit salad. It was just something that did not fulfil his expectations—too simple and homely and feminine.

III

There is an important psychological significance in the fact that there are three women present as well as himself. This grouping of four persons occurs regularly in dreams where the problem of individuation is the main theme. The four persons represent the fourfold psychical structure, analogous to the four limbs of the body. Complete psychological experience is composed of four distinct functions, just as a complete bodily action, as, for instance, swimming, requires the co-ordinated movement of the four limbs.

Hence the presence of the four functions in a dream, personified by a group of four figures, can be regarded as the empirical manifestation of the individuation process.

Jung has termed these four psychic functions thinking, feeling, intuition and sensation: the first two being functions of valuation and judgment, the latter of perception. Individuation is the process which aims at psychological completeness; it is intelligible, therefore, that a dream, which is concerned with the central problem of this difficult and complex personality, should express the need of a fourfold co-ordination. Jung did not arbitrarily invent his conception of the four main psychic functions. Anyone who approaches dream material from the teleological standpoint will be impressed by the recurrence of this fourfold grouping and structure, often throughout a whole series of dreams.

There are, as we know, a great many biological processes which demonstrate this same impulse towards individual completeness. The restitution of lost parts in certain amphibia—the fact that if we graft a collection of cells, taken from an amputated newt's tail, upon the stump of an amputated leg, these cells will develop into a leg and not a tail; the experiments of R. G. Canti, who was able to demonstrate by means of motion-photography that a thin slice of mesoderm, cut from the budding femur of an embryo chick and isolated in a culture medium, developed into a complete femur with trochanter, condylar processes, etc., quite independent of its normal articulations; the experiments of Driesch, who sliced an embryo at the post-morula stage into two or more sections, and found that each section developed into a complete embryo—all these well-known facts tend to show that the pattern of the total organism is a ruling principle, operating through all its parts. It is true that these instances are to be found either on the embryonic level or among relatively archaic types. But this fact only tends to vindicate our psychological analogy, inasmuch as we do not find the restitution of lost or crippled functions taking place at the differentiated level of consciousness, but always on the more archaic levels of the unconscious, where the dormant psychic constituents are in a relatively plastic (or nascent) state.

The task of bringing these dormant, embryonic things into life is the function of the female. When, therefore, we find in a man's dream the predominance of three women to one man, we may conclude that the work that has to be done is mainly in the unconscious, demanding a correspondingly feminine or receptive attitude from consciousness. The subject has, in short, to come to terms with the anima, through whose mediation the contradiction between the conscious and the unconscious can be resolved. It is as though the King (*i.e.*, the will of the total subject) handed the ego over to the ministration of the anima, who, as the Princess Royal, also wears the authority and impersonality of the King.

Jung has defined the anima as a function of relation between the conscious and the collective unconscious. In another place he defines the anima as the inner attitude, in contrast to the persona, or outer attitude. The persona and the anima have a compensatory relation, which is borne out by the fact that whatever human qualities are lacking in the outer character are usually to be found in the inner. Thus the harsh and ruthless tyrant, who is utterly inconsiderate and inflexible in his outer relations, is frequently a prey to superstitious fancies, starting at every shadow that crosses his soul. Similarly the man with a very manly persona often shows a sentimental and even hysterical inner character.

The anima is conceived, therefore, as a function-complex deriving from three sources or tributaries. In the first place, it is rooted in man's inherited or general experience of woman throughout the whole length of human history. In the second place, it has a distinctive individual character, due to the infantile identification with the mother, thus favouring the projection of the soul-image upon certain individual women of a specific type. In the third place, the recessive feminine elements in a man's nature are incorporated in the anima-complex. Jung describes the soul-image as follows:

"The soul-image is a definite and characteristic image among those produced by the unconscious. Just as the persona, or outer attitude, is represented in dreams by the images of certain persons who possess the outstanding qualities of the persona in a marked degree, so the soul (*i.e.*, the inner attitude of the unconscious) is similarly represented by definite persons whose particular attributes correspond with those of the soul. Such an image is called a 'soul-image.' Occasionally these images are quite unknown or mythological figures. With men, the soul (*i.e.*, the anima) is normally figured by the unconscious in the person of a woman; with women, it is a man."[1]

It is important that we should not immediately assume that, because a woman enters the scene, we are therefore dealing with a sexual problem. There is no sign here of the erotic motive. The man-woman figure of speech is merely the natural dream-expression of the dynamic dualism of the psyche. In a man's psychology male figures symbolize the relatively adapted functions of consciousness, whilst female figures represent the functions that are relatively unconscious, hence under the sign and dominion of the anima. The anima is a symbolical feminine figure representing the unconscious energy and activity in manifold ways. Sometimes, as in Hudson's *Green Mansions*, she is a personification of nature in man; or she may represent the living power of surviving pre-Christian culture, as in Kingsley's *Hypatia* or in Rider Haggard's *Ayesha*. She can also appear as a seducing enchantress, as, for example, Delilah in the myth of Samson, or Kundry in Wagner's *Parsifal*, who is subsequently transformed into a ministering function.

The anima embodies, as it were, the problem of the unconscious to man, and her mode of operation and appearance is always unpredictable.

In the scene with the three women the patient's manners are again at fault. Instead of handing the third portion of fruit salad to the third woman, he takes it himself. We know from word-association tests, as well as from daily experience, that when something slips our memory it is because a complex has intervened. We say lightly, "Oh, I forgot," but behind this casual cloak a complex has put out a ghostly hand and snatched away what we had intended to say or do. In other words, the blotting out of the third woman is a symptom of a specific resistance. Naturally, the patient can say nothing

1 C. G. Jung: *Psychological Types*, "*Soul-Image*." Chapter on "Definitions," p. 596.

about this resistance, since all these women are unknown to him. But if we admit the possibility that they represent unconscious factors, which might equally well be conscious, we may reasonably infer that the function upon which the patient turns his back is feeling, since, for him particularly, the discipline of feeling is liable to be painful and difficult.

Psychological good manners consist principally in the conscious recognition and acceptance of one's less acceptable impulses. Relatively few people in the West are proficient in this form of politeness; hence it is by no means exceptional, especially among intellectual types, for a dream to dwell somewhat insistently on the subject's lack of manners.

The dinner in the royal palace must be regarded as a ritual feast. The association with the college hall confirms the idea that it is a feast of initiation, since, particularly in America, entrance into college is accompanied by certain customs and practices derived from primitive initiatory rites. This means that the dreamer (*i.e.*, the ego) is to be shown his proper place in the psychic hierarchy by the feminine representative of the ruler, and that this introduction has the significance of initiation into a new world of experience.

At this point the subject discovers that his shoes are off. The shoes a man stands up in, with which he grips the earth, and upon which he depends for every mobile adaptation, represent his instinctual standpoint or attitude. This analogy points, therefore, to an instinctive adaptation system, an habitual and vital basis of preparedness for all action and behaviour. The subject recognizes this lack in the presence of Princess Mary; from which we may infer that it is the traditional, commanding representative of the feminine principle—She-who-must-be-obeyed—who makes him conscious of his personal deficiency in the sphere of instinctive adaptation. He has, for instance, no real individual standpoint about the function of sexuality. He has allowed an indolent, *laissez-aller* indulgence concerning the most vital function of instinct to take the place of a moral attitude. Women are sometimes attracted by infantile sexuality in a man since it offers scope for the formative function of feeling, but they are never satisfied by it. Similarly, it is the inferior function which offers an attractive field of operations to the anima.

Before the feast of initiation the subject is introduced to an empty nursery. It is elaborately prepared, but there are no children in it. Actually, his wife was pregnant with their first child when he had this dream; we might easily assume, therefore, that the dream was preparing him for the new demands upon his feelings necessitated by the coming event. The birth of a child assuredly involved very real problems. He was in debt, with nothing but his profession to fall back upon. His salary at the mental hospital was that of a junior, and his precarious position there made even this income uncertain. The child, moreover, had not been intended, and he was not the kind of man to look ahead and prepare for coming responsibilities. This unusual degree of conscious unreadiness appears to be compensated for by an elaborate preparation in the unconscious, where, as we shall later discover, his vital energy has long remained immobilized.

But when the dream-context is borne in mind, it is difficult to believe that this nursery scene is wholly concerned with the patient's biological situation. The child is always the symbol of a new potentiality. It is an experiment of nature, an hypothesis that may or may not succeed. Hence it is quite in keeping with the idea of initiation into the dignity of selfhood that the anima should introduce him to the royal nursery which awaits the unborn possibilities of his nature. We shall see later how this theme is treated in the mythological idiom of the drawings.

In the last part of the dream the anima assumes her commanding traditional rôle. The scene is laid in the college hall, a place that reminds the subject of discipline as well as of its general cultural associations. Here the anima is, literally, putting him in his place. There is a beautiful parallel to this scene in an early Christian writing, *The Shepherd* of Hermas (*circa* A.D. 140). Jung mentions the case in his *Psychological Types*, where he is discussing the soul-image as the means by which the transformation of the libido is brought about. At the time the patient had this dream he had not read Jung and knew nothing of Hermas.

Hermas recounts how the man who reared him sold him to a certain Rhoda in Rome.

> " After many years I met with her again and began to love her like a sister. One day I saw her bathing in the Tiber, and gave her my hand and helped her out of the river. As I beheld her beauty, I had this thought in my heart: ' Happy would I be had I a wife of such beauty and distinction.' "

Then he significantly adds:

> " That was my sole wish, and nothing more."

Later he records how, as he journeyed to Cumæ, he was overcome with sleep, and had a vision in which Rhoda called to him from heaven:

> " ' Hail to thee, Hermas !' While my eyes dwelt upon her, I spake and said: ' Mistress, what doest thou there ?' And she answered: ' I was taken up in order to charge thee with thy sins before the Lord.' "

As he loudly protested his innocence in regard to her, she smiled and said:

> " ' The desire of sin arose in thy heart. Or is it not a sin in thine eyes for a just man to cherish a sinful desire in his heart ? Verily is it a sin, and a great one. For the just man striveth after what is just.' "

Hermas, of course, was a Christian and had a wife and family. Therefore his erotic feelings for Rhoda could lead only into a situation that would undermine the integrity of his life. Yet, on the other hand, his best potentiality could never develop through mere repression of the erotic libido. Hence a frank confession of the hidden motive became imperative; and especially must he confess to the soul-mistress, in order that she might become the vessel of the repressed erotic libido on the psychological plane. By this means the image of the desired woman is elevated to a sphere which prohibits the concrete erotism of the former attitude. In the dream of our patient this is accomplished by raising the soul-image to royal rank. The cheap sexual valuation of woman is thereby checked, and through the consequent damming-up of the libido a greater psychic tension, with a correspondingly higher valuation of the object, is achieved.

Jung's comment on this transition from the human to the divine is as follows:

> " This transition indicates that the repressed erotic impression in the unconscious has activated the latent primordial image of the goddess, which is, in fact, the archetypal soul-image. The erotic impression has evidently become united in the collective unconscious with those archaic residues which, from earliest time, have held the imprints of vivid impressions of woman's nature: woman as mother, and woman as desirable maid. Such impressions have immense power, since they release forces, both in the child and the man, which, in their irresistible and absolutely compelling nature, merit the attribute ' divine.' The recognition of these forces as dæmonic powers can scarcely be due to moral repression, but rather to a self-regulation of the psychic organism which seeks by this orientation to protect itself from loss of equilibrium."[1]

A schizoid personality is especially liable to become dangerously involved in erotic entanglements in a compulsive way. The projection of the luxuriant fantasy-activity of the unconscious is relatively unchecked by adequate feeling-valuations. Hence the women upon whom the erotic fantasies are projected are often those with whom a reliable relationship is impossible. Moreover, the pathological tension which the schizoid state engenders is liable to seek uncontrolled precipitate expression. In the patient's case such entanglements tended to coincide with periods when the responsibilities of his marriage and other problems seemed to him insupportable. Hence his need for a commanding soul-image by which the precarious psychic equilibrium could be maintained.

Jung's further comment on this need is as follows:

> " For if against the wholly overwhelming power of passion which casts a man unconditionally in the path of another human being, the psyche succeeds in erecting a counter-position, whereby at the summit of passion it severs the fantasy-idol from the utterly desired object, forcing the man to his knees before the divine image, it has delivered him from the curse of the object's spell."[2]

1 *Psychological Types*, p. 277.

2 *Ibid.*, p. 277.

After the talk with Rhoda recorded above, her image vanished and the heavens closed. In her stead there now appears an " old woman in shining garments." It is later revealed to Hermas that this old woman is the Church. The concrete and personal is now dissolved into an ideal which thereby gains a desirable actuality it had not before possessed. Hermas, in fact, became one of the most effective organizers of the early Church.

In a later vision the old lady gives him a rendezvous in an appointed place, and when he comes to it he finds " an ivory couch set with a pillow and a cover of fine linen." The erotic intimation contained in this scene reactivates the complex. Hermas writes:

> " As I beheld these things lying there I was sore amazed, and a quaking fell upon me, and my hair stood on end, and a dreadful fear befell me, because I was alone in that place."

Then he knelt down and again confessed his sins unto God. Looking up, he saw his soul-mistress approaching with six young men,

> " the which also I had seen before, and they stood beside me and listened while I prayed and confessed my sins unto God. And she touched me and said: ' Hermas, have done with all thy prayers and the reciting of thy sins.' . . . And she raised me up by the hand and led me to the couch, and said unto the young men, ' Go and build !' And when the youths were gone and we were alone, she said unto me: ' Sit thee here.' I said unto her: ' Mother, let the aged first be seated.' She said: ' Do as I said unto thee and be seated.' But when I made as though to seat myself upon her right hand, she motioned me with a gesture of the hand to be seated upon the left. As I wondered thereat, and was troubled that I might not sit upon the right side, she said unto me: ' Why art thou grieved, Hermas ? The seat upon the right is for those who have accomplished, and are already well-pleasing to God, and have suffered for the Name. But to thee there lacketh much before thou canst sit with them. Yet remain, as heretofore, in thy simplicity, and thou shalt surely sit with them, and thus shall it be for all who have achieved the work which those wrought and endured what they suffered.' "

I have quoted this material at length because, so aptly did it fit the patient's psychology, that on a later occasion, after reading Jung's account of the episode with Rhoda, he had a dream in which the anima appeared as a snake-dæmon who "charged him with his sins before the Lord."

IV

To return to our discussion of the dream: in the light of the Hermas parallel, we can infer that when the royal anima places him on the left, she is performing the same function as Rhoda does for Hermas—namely, she is placing him on the side which represents potentiality, as opposed to the right side—*i.e.*, the side of achievement, where his fantasy of being already "a distinguished physician" would prompt him to sit. This insistence of the soul-mistress that he should be correctly placed is entirely in keeping with the idea that this is a ceremonial feast of initiation.

The patient's association with the "distinguished-looking man who is picking his nose" is again his father. The patient's idea is that his father can carry off such eccentricities of behaviour because of his exceptional personality. The son also considers himself exempt from conventional restrictions, and tends to behave as though everything were permissible. Since neither father nor son happens to be specially guilty of the particular offence, we must assume that the dream has selected the nose for its own symbolic purposes. The nose is associated with the intuitive function of scenting out possibilities. From a rational standpoint this is, of course, a childish idea, but dream-representation is naturally primitive and condensed. When we say a man has a good nose for investment, or a flair for finance, we are using the same primitive imagery. The patient's father lived almost wholly by intuition. He became literally possessed by his intuitions, and was characteristically impatient with anyone who could not immediately share his conviction that the idea or cause he sought to advance was heaven-inspired. His weakness lay in his inability patiently to expand and systematize his intuitions in order to win for them general acceptance. Many men of the intuitive types suffer from this auto-erotic incapacity to see beyond their own nose. They are their intuitions to such an extent that they cannot see what steps must be taken before their ideas are fit for reality. Very often they are completely lacking in the power of lucid expression. This is because they identify their personality with their major function of intuition, and therefore possess no psychological means of seeing themselves or their ideas from another standpoint.

The distinguished-looking man who picks his nose is surely the father of the "distinguished physician." He is the man for whom potentiality is equivalent to achievement. A young man who contents himself with the possibility of being a distinguished physician is already sitting in the 'siege perilous.' And he would not nourish this fantasy were it not for the unconscious identification with the father which gives him an illusory sense of already being somebody. Hence the *aplomb*. The orthodox interpretation of the nose-picking episode, as referring to infantile onanism and self-fertilization, would be perfectly compatible with this view.

The final item in the dream is at first sight meaningless—namely, a broken toothbrush with wire bristles, called an "asthma toothbrush." It is often useful in dream interpretation to apply what we have learned about the behaviour of the painful complex from word-association tests. We know, for example, that whenever a painful complex is touched we tend to get distorted and often highly irrational reactions. The same principle applies to dream-imagery. When we find an apparently meaningless innovation in a fairly coherent dream-structure we can, for instance, infer disturbance by a complex. In this case the word "asthma" is the complex-indicator. The patient's mother died of asthma when he was fourteen, just when he felt the most need of her. He could make no association with the broken toothbrush; he therefore had recourse to the doctrinaire assumption that it must be phallic. We know that teeth play an important part in unconscious symbolism, both in the dreams of our patients and in primitive myth and ritual. This fact rests on many grounds. Teeth emerge in a certain sequence, symbolizing an increasing grip on reality as the infant goes towards adolescence. First the milk teeth are replaced by the permanent teeth; then comes the serial eruption of the molars, and finally the wisdom tooth of maturity. Thus the metamorphosis of the libido through its various phases, which in certain amphibia is expressed in a change of the whole organism, is represented in man by the serial emergence of the teeth. The teeth also stand at the gateway between subject and object, performing the functions of separation and mastication, by which alien objects of food are incorporated into the subject. Psychologically therefore they represent that discriminating sense for the real by which the subject adapts himself to his environment and is able to assimilate his experience. When we say a man has " bitten off more than he can chew," we mean that he is striving for a fictitious goal, and that his reality sense requires attention.

The toothbrush therefore symbolizes the psychic instrument or function by which a man attends to his reality-situation. When he asks himself, " Is this goal real for me ? Does it serve my essential interest ?" he is using a psychological toothbrush.

The patient's mother seems to have had the good sense of an observant, highly intelligent, introverted woman, providing an invaluable check on the headstrong, visionary enthusiasm of the father: thus she maintained a balance upon which the security of the children depended. Moreover, it was she who taught the patient the use, and insisted upon the necessity, of the toothbrush in the general care of the body. But the dream toothbrush has wire bristles like a currycomb for the grooming of horses, quite unsuitable for the delicate tissues of the mouth. It is also broken and derelict; the back of the brush is gone, showing the wire loops. Our understanding of all these details is impossible without the patient's associations, which, however, were not freely available. Having recently studied Freud's work on dream-interpretation, he invariably produced a sexual association whenever the inhibition of the complex rendered his own native association inaccessible. The artificial nature of these associations was apparent in the monotonous, stereotyped voice with which he produced them. Was it not possible, therefore, that this asthma toothbrush with its metal bristles, so unsuitable for the care of delicate internal membrane, might refer to the patient's uncritical attempt to employ crude doctrinaire interpretations in relation to sensitive psychic contents? We know that the broken asthma toothbrush must refer to the tragedy of the mother's death at the time when he most needed her formative guidance and common sense in the development of a civilized attitude. It is most probable, therefore, that this tragedy rendered the patient especially vulnerable to one-sided intellectual points of view. This reading of the dream also throws light upon the selection of Princess Mary as the soul-image, or anima-figure. Mary is the Mother-imago for the whole of Christendom; hence a royal Mary offers a symbol well fitted to receive the emotional libido that was repressed owing to the death of the mother and the sister.

V

I have gone rather fully into this dream because it contains the essential elements of the patient's problem, presenting a more coherent picture of the emotional situation than would be obtainable in any other way. The fact that the soul-image can appear at a critical juncture in a man's life, and assume such a commanding rôle, may arouse a certain doubt in the reader's mind. It might seem to accord more with our experience of paranoia to regard all these references to royalty as part of a grandiose delusional system. I can only answer this by reminding my reader that a pathological idea belonging to a delusional system carries the hall-mark of morbidity quite unmistakably, while a dream that has such a direct, purposive character, and which conveys a telling criticism, cannot be regarded principally from the pathological angle.

With regard to the commanding aspect of the anima, I discovered recently an interesting case in which an ancestral anima-figure assumes a similar rôle in the psychology of a primitive medicine-man. In this case the anima-complex literally takes possession of the man's psyche and forces him to take up the traditional rôle of the *shaman*. Sternberg, the Russian anthropologist, records[1] how a young Siberian of

[1] *Archives of American Anthropology*, 1928.

the Gold tribe was afflicted by an illness which none of the *shamans* could cure. While he lay sick in his hut, he was visited in a dream by a small woman of commanding mien. In appearance she was like one of the women of his people, only she was uncannily small and majestic. She told him she was the *ayami*[1] of his ancestors, and that in his family there had formerly been several great *shamans*. She had taught them *shamaning*, and now she had come to teach him, because the people needed a *shaman*. Then she added: " Moreover, I have no husband now: you shall be my husband and I will be a wife unto you. I shall give you assistant-spirits. You are to heal with their aid, and I shall teach you and help you myself. Food will come to us from the people." The *shaman* says: " I felt dismayed and tried to resist." Then she said: " If you will not obey me, so much the worse for you. I shall kill you." When he has accepted her she teaches him how to treat his patients, what implements to use, and whenever he is engaged in his *shamaning* she is inspiring him. He adds: " When I am *shamaning*, the *ayami* and the assistant-spirits are possessing me: whether big or small they penetrate me, as smoke or vapour would. When the *ayami* is within me, it is she who speaks through my mouth, and she does everything herself." In citing this case of a relatively primitive mentality, I wish to emphasize the fact that the appearance of the anima as a visionary being coincided with a profound recession of the libido from outer reality, and that this recession was also the cause of the illness. The pathological recoil was transformed by the anima into a purposive introversion which culminated in his marriage or submission to the *ayami* as the spirit of his *métier*. We are subsequently informed that as soon as this submission had taken place his sickness was cured.

In this case the endopsychic cultural inheritance is invested in the anima-complex. It forces the subject, by means of a neurotic sickness, to submit to his destiny, and to take up the *métier* for which he is singularly fitted. Sternberg sees in this account nothing but an example of sexual selection, albeit the sexual motive is purely incidental to the patent

[1] *Ayami*=ancestral spirit, or soul.

purpose of the whole experience. The idea of taking the *ayami* as wife is merely the primitive expression for committing oneself unreservedly to the destiny personified by the spirit. When " sexual selection " is seriously put forward as an explanatory principle, it cannot be impertinent to ask who is selecting whom, and for what purpose the selection is made. In nature sexual selection is always purposive. Anthropologists are not free to uproot this principle from its purposive biological connection, making use of it as a psychological explanation, without taking its purposive function into account.

The purpose of the soul-image is, in fact, just the reverse of mere erotism. It is an image of woman, fashioned by the unconscious in order to convert aimless and luxuriant fantasies into real accomplishment. This, at least, is what the anima achieves.

It is true that Princess Mary is not an ancestral figure. Yet the symbol of royalty has gained its power within the human mind because it contains the safeguarding idea of the continuity of tribal tradition. Hence, for the purpose of initiation into a traditional, cultural rôle, the dream could have chosen no figure better fitted for the task.

CHAPTER III

ANALYSIS OF DREAM II

I

THE dream treated in the previous chapter preceded the beginning of the analysis by some weeks, though the project was already in the subject's mind. This second dream appeared during the first week of the analysis, and threw a revealing light upon the condition of the unconscious.

" Down in a queer country cottage there is a large collection of people. At first it seems that there is a new railway starting, on which it is possible for us to drive cars between lines to the starting place. The trains are like electric trains, and we have to perform a to-and-fro journey, whilst an old lady, who has planned the railway, watches. There are many people near the car station, which is some distance down the line, and I go up there. One person stands out, a girl. The whole thing is mixed up with an experience on the car going along the lines and expresses coming in each direction. One has to switch from line to line.

" Next, in the cottage, we have lunch off horse-meat, which is not bad. I then go up to get a bicycle to see the old lady. My wife is perhaps about. At dinner most of the people do not want horse-meat, but I, in taking out the horse's gut, think of a mixed grill. I cut bits of liver and kidney out, and somebody has put out a frying-pan, on which I start frying. Then the madness begins. Everybody seems to be trying to stop the frying, scrambling and fighting over the oil stove, especially the two women who come in late and who cannot get what they want. My grill looks dried up and distasteful. The whole dinner is ruined, and I attempt to lock them (probably the people) out, but one of the loose ones breaks through, and they all come in. I hit the loose one, but it makes no difference, and eventually he picks me up like a child and does acrobatics with me. My loathing of him changes to admiration. A general fight of a friendly nature ensues. Meanwhile I seem to be getting on with the ' wrong 'un.' He tells me stories of how people get food out of the Thames, and of how one of the people in the house was sneaking off to do it, and how he followed him and asked him why, eventually obtaining his confidence. Then I see before me a huge mass of meat, which I cut across, and it gapes wide. Then I feel vaguely that it is bad meat and it cuts soft, almost like bad liver. My new friend tells me that they never take meat out of the Thames, as it is always bad. By now my friend and I are on better terms, and he tells me that he is the son of a good man, but that his mother was a whore or a gorilla, and he was a bastard; he also tells how people get him drunk here. To prove the point about the meat, I suggest looking at it under a microscope after taking a smear. This I start to do, but when I look for the eyepiece of the microscope it is gone. I then realize that my new friend was giving me his confidence before committing suicide. He is now heard rushing up the tower to hurl himself down. I shout to another friend in the party, but it is too late; he has thrown himself off into a small stream. He now seems like an iron-encased body, flashing down the stream. My second friend picks him out, and I tell him to look after the suicide whilst I go to fetch help (a doctor). The suicide implores us to let him die. He now seems as though encased in a rabbit's skeleton. At any rate, he now gets hold of a sharp instrument, and, jabbing it through his skeleton, rushes about. The thing is punctured with holes. I shout that I must stop him because of the law, but I feel that it would be best to let him die. But then I see that he is so weak mentally that he could not kill himself; it is all theatrical and insane."

The chaotic irrationality of this dream might easily prompt one to leave it on one side as too pathological for the purposes of demonstration. Remembering, however, the golden rule that the first dreams of a patient in analysis usually point to the heart of the problem, we must try to understand its queer symptomatic content.

Unfortunately I was not able to analyse it systematically with the patient, on account of the disturbed state of mind it induced. I will describe this condition later. The associations, though again somewhat meagre, are as follows:

The "queer country cottage" refers to the bungalow they lived in while he was working at the mental hospital. During this phase he and his wife lived in a rather haphazard way, and lots of visitors with whom he had no real connection frequented the place. The railway was associated with the line connecting the city with the suburb: he used it every day. The " old lady " who presides over it was associated with his wife's mother, upon whom he projected the negative aspect of his mother-complex. The girl at the car station was associated with the sister who took her own life. He has no particular objection to horse-meat: he believes it was eaten a great deal during the war and that people liked it fairly well. The bicycle is a solitary vehicle, as opposed to trains and cars and other collective means. He likes a mixed grill and does not mind cooking, though, in point of fact, he hardly ever does cook.

The " loose one " was associated with a queer renegade character who had actually made love to the patient's wife before he (the patient) came on the scene. He was a wild, undisciplined creature with immense dash and energy, perhaps even a streak of genius. His father had been an imaginative, hard-working Irishman, whilst his mother was dissolute and shapeless. The patient's attitude towards this man's unscrupulous disregard of all moral considerations, his prodigious vitality and his adventurous, vagrant mode of life, was compounded equally of admiration and fear.

The Thames, like the Mersey, is a vast public waterway: both figured in the patient's dream material. London, the heart of the Empire, is on the Thames; it gives the city its avenue to the sea. The microscope was associated with his profession. It symbolized for him the detached, scientific vision: he also had a negative feeling about it as a purely intellectual instrument, and therefore inimical to human considerations.

The tower from which the suicide leaps was associated with the tower of the mental hospital: while the manner of the suicide was identified with the sister who took her life in this way. There was also an association with his elder brother, who once dived into a shallow river without first sounding its depth. He escaped with nothing worse than a bad concussion.

With the help of these associations a slender gleam of light breaks through the smoke of chaos. We notice, to begin with, that there are two levels in the dream—namely, the level of automatism, represented by the trains, and that of unco-ordinated, irrational activity, symbolized by the scrambling women and the "loose one." We shall find this same dualism in Drawing II., where the right side of the picture contains automatic robot figures and machines, while the left shows two lunatics escaping from an asylum.

These two levels represent the classical dualism of schizophrenia, and, in this respect we may regard the dream in the light of a characteristic symptom. Not only so, but the meaningless automatism of the "to-and-fro journeys" on the railway line, and the switching across from one line to the other, in order to avoid the expresses going in both directions—all this is in keeping with the familiar automatism of schizophrenia. The scene of manic excitement, the increasing sense of disruption and disintegration, followed by the suicidal depression—these, too, belong to the psychotic picture. And yet, are we quite content to represent the dream as a symptomatic product, and nothing more? Taking the dream purely on the symptomatic level, we shall find in it only those features which correspond with, and confirm, the general schizophrenic picture. But the dream, being a product of an individual psychology, is also, in a perfectly real sense, unique. It arises from the experience of a complex and intelligent human being who is himself very much more than a pathological case. To be valid, then, our interpretation must take both these aspects into account and combine them into as fair a union as possible.

The irrationality of the first part of the dream is different in character from the violent craziness of the second part. The country cottage is "queer." One can "drive cars between lines to the starting-place." (What is the starting-place of a railway system?) The railway is planned by an old lady, who apparently compels people to make senseless to-and-fro journeys. The height of irrationality is reached in the switching from one line to the other in order to avoid expresses coming in both directions.

The character of this irrationality is purposelessness *par excellence*. Things like houses, trains, motor-cars, whose whole design and construction, down to the last detail, is harnessed to conscious purpose, behave in a way which contradicts their nature. Contradiction is inherent in the very narrative of the dream—so much so, that it is difficult to visualize the scene described.

The feeling of automatism, then, can be regarded as an aspect of this inherent purposelessness. Though not identical, they are nearly akin.

In contrast to this, the irrationality of the second part is emphatic and, in a sense, purposive. There is, for instance, nothing contradictory or purposeless in getting food out of the Thames. It is neither rational nor feasible, but it does make sense. The contradictory activity of the first part, on the other hand, does not.

In the first part there is compulsive activity and no freedom; in the second there is uninhibited dissolution, an unconditioned lust for freedom and for everything else.

It is important to note that the meaninglessness of the first aspect is attached to the cottage, the friends, the railway by which the subject goes from his home to the hospital, and, above all, to the compulsive railway activity which is presided over by the mother. This means that, under the aspect of the dream, the whole of his disciplined waking life with its regulated activities seems to the subject utterly void of purpose and meaning, with one exception: " One person stands out, a girl "; and this girl is associated with the sister. But she is no longer alive: she stands out with reason from the monotonous activity of his daily life, for she is a ghost.

This fact was strangely confirmed by an immediate " ghost-effect." The patient offered the association with the sister without difficulty; but when I asked him to think about the car station, a flood of associations began to flow, and then I saw that he had " dropped through " into a somnambulistic condition.

The stream of images carried him back to a country cottage where his family had lived when he was five years old. He described a cottage with a kind of tin extension, and in front of it a tall tree. Standing at a little distance from the house was an earth closet. He was able to recapture the memory, or fantasy, that came to him when this scene was evoked: he wrote it down as follows:

"I pick up a pot and smash it. Evelyn (his sister) comes in and we fight, rolling on the floor. There is a horrible, ghastly feeling. Something awful is happening, and then a black cat appears."

This memory was interrupted and another followed: A little girl and her brother came to play with him. He watches the little girl defæcating in the closet; he is intensely interested. Something happens. They have been watched. The little girl and boy do not come any more. He is told they are not nice children. Then he is high up in the tree waving a sickle around his head in a mood of reckless defiance. People call to him. He refuses to come down.[1]

I call this a ghost-effect, using the term in the primitive sense of an effect worked by an unseen hand. Amongst primitive peoples one does not mention the name of a dead person because the named person is immediately present. In other words, the autonomous psychic image is the ghost. In primitive mentality there is, as yet, no effective discrimination between name and person or thing; therefore, when the name is spoken the image appears.

In the present instance, as soon as the image of the sister had been evoked in association with the girl in the dream, it was as though a ghost beckoned to the patient, drawing his libido down into the unconscious. The altered state of consciousness, the flood of long-forgotten associations, the memory of the fight with his sister, and the "awful" appearance of the black cat—all belong to a complex in which the painful memories associated with the sister have lain buried.

Observing this ghost-effect from above, it seemed as though the patient had, psychologically, dropped through a hole. But the ghostly hand is, in fact, a more accurate description, inasmuch as the effect of a buried complex is to attract the psychic energy away from the adapted level. Consciousness may even be completely denuded of energy by the attractive power of the complex. This is what Janet described as *l'abaissement du niveau mental*.

There is an important statement in this first part which might prove to be the key to our understanding of the dream.

[1] This memory fragment from early childhood is discussed in a later chapter.

The compulsive performance of the railway is done, apparently, at the behest of the old lady who "planned the railway." The railway symbolizes, for the patient, the meaningless monotony of his existence: it removes him every day from his home to the hospital; and from the hospital, home. He performs the recognized civilized tricks because he has to, not because he can see any sense in doing them.

The old lady is, of course, the negative aspect of the mother. The disciplined virtues which cling naturally to the image of the loved parent, and which are the normal fruit of that basic human relation, assume a very different complexion in the eyes of youth when they are arbitrarily enforced as "social necessity."

The patient's allegiance to the human world had not yet been wholly won when his mother died and the light of his world was extinguished. What has not been accepted is, as a rule, resented, and the patient's resentment against the world, and against everyone to whom he ought, normally, to submit, is symptomatic of a crippled state of feeling which stubbornly still craves that meaning which, throughout infancy, the mother provides.

In a rather similar way, his relation to woman has been jeopardized by the same prior claim; almost as though he sought in wife or lover the central, emotional meaning to life.[1] Accordingly, as each experiment failed, resentment naturally increased. This is not, at bottom, the erotism of the sensualist, though many have tried to discover the hidden meaning of life in sensuality, and have even declared they had found it.

If the positive aspect of the mother-imago provides the emotional core to every deepest experience, we can imagine how the negative aspect might be conceived as presiding over the automatic repetition of habitual acts which were originally inspired by a sense of purpose. One aspect of nature offers the enticement of pleasure; the other aspect presents the bill in terms of arduous necessity and discipline. These aspects are not naturally divided, since those creatures who are still contained by nature, and therefore have no standpoint out-

[1] This basically contradictory attitude to the mother-imago is presently revealed at the infantile level in Drawing III.

side their instincts, evince no conflict between pleasure and necessity.

These two aspects are, in fact, the expression of man's freedom to choose. He is free to obey his instinct and stand for the consequences; or he can choose the renegade path, denying the authority of nature to set him tasks. But in the latter case he is made to pay with a neurosis. How difficult it is to re-establish the original balance is evidenced by the almost universal tendency to become identified with one or other of the opposing aspects, with the result that pursuit of pleasure and addiction to work become systematized ways of life which the majority of civilized people mechanically follow, without enquiring what relation these patterns bear to the original meaning of life.

In the dream these two aspects of nature are personified by the girl (*i.e.*, the anima) and the old lady, the girl representing nature's alluring invitation to join the dance, and the old lady the law of necessity which harnesses laborious effects to pleasurable causes.

If we take the whole railway system as a symbol of the inflexible determinism by which nature controls all, even those who disobey her laws, we find a certain mitigation of this absolute view in the " new railway " in which cars can be driven between the lines. A motor-car has relatively greater freedom of movement than a train. Later we come to the bicycle (also in relation to the old lady), which has a still greater latitude.

We could argue from this descent from the absolute determinism of the collective train to the relative freedom of the individual bicycle that something has recently come into the dreamer's world which has had the effect of modifying his bleak, deterministic outlook. There can, I think, be little doubt that the patient's decision to undergo analysis acted like a strong ferment with a very disturbing effect upon his unconscious.

Analysis, if it means anything at all, means accepting the burden of the human soul, with its problems, its tasks, its suffering, and its responsibility to the future and the past, as well as to the present. Yet here again, though everyone desires the meaningful zest which comes only when the soul is housed and accepted, a very great number cannot stand the self-discipline entailed. Their desire for life leads them to the spot from which the leap of acceptance should be made, but they cannot make the leap. The recoil from that vision is never free of resentment, and, since the whole problem of the soul is associated with the analyst, it is upon his head that the resentment of failure usually falls.

Most probably, therefore, the new railway refers to the analytical attempt which he has just started. If this supposition is correct, the allusion to the electric trains, which, in fact, connect the personal and impersonal aspects of his waking life, refers to the activity aroused between the conscious and the unconscious by this new attempt. The car station "down the line," which is in some way connected with the sister, would therefore relate to a concentration of psychic energy within the buried complex. We began to tap this stored-up energy when the complex was touched in the analytical hour. It is therefore intelligible that the anima should appear at this point, because the release of the energy-content from a buried complex is equivalent to the birth of the soul.

Primarily, the soul is the meaningful expression of psychic energy. Loss of the soul means, therefore, a flight of energy into the unconscious. When life is allowed to become meaningless or monotonous, energy seeps away, until at last one makes the discovery that the world has no attraction or significance, and oneself no energy or purpose. In the case of the patient, the possibility of recovering the lost energy would be intimated by a figure which not only carries the value of the soul-image and holds the promise of his future, but which is also associated with the dead sister with whom so much of his feeling fled away into the unconscious.

II

Coming to the second part of the dream, which represents the disturbed and undisciplined state of the patient's psyche, it is not easy to make sense out of the dream-context; yet we cannot abandon the dream just because our light begins to flicker.

First, then, we observe that the frenzy and confusion have to do with the providing of food, (*a*) for a vague company, (*b*) for the two women who "cannot get what they want." The food the patient provides for his guests is horse-meat. He is inclined to stand for this as reasonable fare, but his guests will not touch it. Only in a beleagured city would one be forced to provide one's guests with horse-flesh. When it is young, a horse is too valuable; when old, too unappetizing, as a rule, for human food, unless under war-time conditions. The patient associates eating horse-flesh with the war. We may conclude, therefore, that the conditions in the unconscious are not unlike the state of war, when strict discipline should prevail.

From another point of view, the horse is the natural symbol of the libido, the adapted instinctual energy. The eating of horse-flesh, therefore, is suspiciously like spending one's capital. Horse-power is the expression of effective animal energy which, in human beings, finds application either in work, interest, love or play. Eating the source of this energy would, therefore, be a kind of morbid, self-devouring inversion: a retrograde process, suggestive of cancer or of incest. Indeed, his running off "to see the old lady" bears out this idea if we regard incest as the regressive movement of the libido backwards to the source.

When we come to the "mixed grill," it is obvious that the patient has to do, not with a portion of meat only, but with a whole dead horse from which he takes out the gut and the viscera. And yet, in spite of killing the horse, nothing comes of it; the dinner is spoiled and no one is satisfied.

This motif of killing the horse has a sinister connection with the mother in myth and folk-tale. In Barlach's mythological drama, *Der Tote Tag*, for instance, the murderous effect of the mother-complex is symbolized by the killing of the hero's horse. Old Kule comes home after years of search for the remedy which shall heal the suffering of mankind, bringing with him the horse with which his son may carry through the heroic task. In the night the old man has a vision of the future, which only the heroic will can make real.

> KULE. And there about my bed stand the lovely forms of a better future. Stiff are they yet, but of radiant beauty, still sleeping —but he who shall awaken them would make for the world a fairer face. A hero would he be who could do it.
>
> MOTHER. An heroic life in misery and dire need!
>
> KULE. Perchance, there might be one!
>
> MOTHER. He first must bury his mother.

During the night the mother goes down and kills the son's horse with a knife.

There is no hint of this active intervention of the mother in our patient's dream; nevertheless, the sinister "old lady" presides, figuratively, over both parts of the dream. We are therefore entitled to assume that the events of the dream are specifically characterized by this fact.

With regard to the two women in the dream, it must be explained that these refer to the patient's wife and lover, both of whom represented especial claims on his feelings at the time of this dream. This fact gives us an invaluable clue to the nature of the madness which breaks out when he starts to fry the meat. The notion of grilling meat on an oil-stove is, in itself, sufficiently foolish to be significant. But the collective scramble is unpleasantly suggestive of flies or vultures swarming to carrion, or hounds to the kill.

In order to understand this combination of greed and panic, we have to realize how the problem of the inferior function may be constellated in the case of feeling. A man whose feeling is undifferentiated is liable to marry a woman who is strong where he is weak. Not being able to trust his own feeling-standpoint, he waits to be swayed and directed by an object whose feeling has the authentic individual ring. But since duality proceeds from hesitancy, it happens with fateful regularity that the man with inferior feeling gets caught between two women. The contest may lie between mother and wife, or between wife and lover; but essentially the constellation is that of a divided man and two single-minded women, both of whom are constrained to use every art to gain some security of tenure. This constellation is rooted in a biological archetype, and, so long as the three individuals are held by it, the primeval drama will be re-enacted in fidelity to the world-old pattern. The man feels he can do nothing about it: first he is pulled in the one direction, responding obediently to the needs and claims of A, only to be drawn back over the base-line by the claims and needs and alarms of B. The two women are bound to pursue their man in this primitive fashion because to neither does he give security. Had he a standpoint that was guarded and guaranteed by his individual passion, this particular predicament could not arise. The very fact that his feeling is split into mutually contradictory relations eventually reveals to him his need for wholeness.

One of the marks of the inferior function is absence of initiative. The subject cannot make a move: a man may be held in this archetypal vice until, at last, out of sheer misery and exasperation, his own authentic feeling speaks. Immediately the rival claimants fall back as though a god had intervened, deciding the interminable contest with a thunderbolt.

From every point of view an open statement of individual feeling has a clarifying and healing effect: the humiliating atmosphere of underground intrigue; the constant itch, on either side, to gain some trifling advantage in feminine prestige to compensate for the lack of security and acknowledged allegiance; the tendency for embarrassing social situations to develop, motivated by revenge or resentment—all these primitive liabilities can, to a large extent, be removed by a clear and authoritative statement of feeling. The level of consciousness is raised, and civilized decency takes the place of primitive intrigue. Naturally, the problematical situation still exists, but the problem has now been stated in terms of conscious relationship, instead of being entirely at the mercy of displays of primitive affect.

It is, of course, regrettable that psychological inferiorities cannot be educated along more rational lines, but the inferior function is as slippery and evasive as a snake, and only when it is caught in an absolutely inescapable predicament does it begin to be educable. Psychological inferiority must not be confused with functional weakness. On the contrary, just because of its archaic, primitive character, the inferior function frequently plays a decisive rôle by providing a conduit to the forces of the collective unconscious. By this route, as we see in this dream, the personality is liable to become invaded by alien unconscious contents, whenever, in fact, the inferior function receives the challenge of fate. The inferior function is the vulnerable spot. Here is no clever, resourceful defender whose intellectual rapier can be relied upon to keep fate at a distance. On the contrary, the inferior function is the home of the renegade shadow-personality, who is only too liable to show a light to the enemy.

This would seem to be the condition depicted in the dream, and the helplessness of the dreamer is the characteristic helplessness of the personality in the grip of the inferior function. The feeling of having been betrayed, as though by an alien will, must be familiar to everyone. In the realm of feeling the patient has no objective criterion for handling the situation in which he finds himself, hence the schizoid doubt concerning the problem of emotional supply is intensified to the danger-point.

Fear of emotional inadequacy is the burden of the schizophrenic's problem. It is like an impending menace; or as though the patient's whole psychology were fascinated by a doubt. Instead of running freely towards the desired object, his libido tends to turn back upon itself in a self-devouring frenzy. A morbid subjectivity develops, the result of which is that no object is given its true value—*i.e.*, its proper share of libido.

In the present instance, the chief sufferers of this lack of human warmth in the objective world are, naturally, the wife and the lover. A mixed grill, fried over an oil-stove, is, in itself, a kind of cheat. The tragedy of the ruined meal is twofold: for not only is food wasted, but unsatisfied emotional expectations tend to create a frustrated, resentful mood. In unstable individuals, violence is likely to result from such a mood.[1] Emotional inversion and frustration inevitably cause

[1] The patient was, in point of fact, subject to violent moods, which occurred exclusively in relation to his wife.

disturbance in the objective as well as the subjective sphere, since both inner and outer relationships suffer from deprivation of value. A shared experience with someone who is unable to value it is a tasteless and melancholy adventure. The mind is enriched by the intensity of value which is given to the moment of imaginative realization, as it is impoverished when value is denied. Were it mensurable, the essential difference between individuals would be gauged far more truly by this criterion of value than by intelligence tests. Experience is not merely that which happens to a man, it includes the way in which his whole being responds to the event. A total response is never a purely intellectual matter; at bottom it is an emotional act.

The schizophrenic personality is fatally hindered from expressing the crucial value which both satisfies the object and enriches the subject. But a façade of normal extraverted activity often masks this central defect. The subject, though continually aware of a cold vacuum where he knows there should be warmth and interest, conceals his sense of difference by an impervious persona. The fact that the libido is withdrawn, or sucked down into the unconscious, can, however, be inferred from the semi-automatic, toneless character of the subject's response.

That the failure is emotional rather than intellectual is suggested in the dream by the subject's attempt at a mixed grill: the visceral region has always been identified with the emotions. We should also note that the beginning of the madness synchronizes with the cutting out of the liver and the kidney for the grill.

From this standpoint, we can understand the behaviour of the guests as representing emotional claims which the subject has repressed and ignored. They manifest the confusion, panic and frustration which result from the undermining paralysis of value, or emotional supply.

The knowledge that one has cheated so many living things of their proper value is altogether too painful for realization, hence the attempt to repress the unsatisfied guests. This attempt also fails, and, through its failure, we are given the most revealing insight into this peculiar schizophrenic deficit.

The character of the shadow-figure—viz., the loose one—who now breaks through, is explicitly given in the patient's associations. It is even more firmly established in the genealogy provided by the dream. He is the reckless renegade; the unscrupulous desperado; the man who does what he likes and takes what he can, uninhibited by ethical or moral qualms; that tendency of the personality, in effect, which would repudiate the burden of the human soul, preferring any kind of magical or tricky means to the simple acceptance of human responsibilities. In other words, he personifies the downward and backward pull, the alternative evolutionary hypothesis. When the loose one picks up the dreamer like a child and performs acrobatics with him, we are given a graphic expression of the magical allure of the renegade pull. This also tells us that the dreamer is inclined to play with the hypothesis in a childish, unconscious way. Rather should we say that the hypothesis plays with him since he succumbs to it without criticism or resistance.

With this figure the dream holds up a mirror to the shadow-side of the subject's personality, the side that is in the grip of the regressive will, and which allows no human considerations to stand in its way—in other words, the side that insists upon unconditioned freedom and the renegade hypothesis.

This is not the character of the conscious personality, but rather that of a shadow-being who becomes visible only when the subject is off his guard. The patient said that the original of this portrait filled him equally with admiration and fear: admiration for the uninhibited freedom of the adventurer's course, and fear of the renegade which every social creature carries in his blood.

It would be an injustice to the patient to identify him with this shadow-personality which, from our privileged position of onlookers, we have glimpsed behind the arras. This is not the hypothesis which the subject believes in, but rather the danger he most fears. It is the alternative hypothesis which comes into force only when the subject is overpowered by the sheer weight of psychic archaism. It is the hypothesis of frustration. If lived, it leads to the isolation of the fake-magician or the criminal, a way which would contradict the destiny bequeathed by his ancestors. But, although it would be unfair to judge the patient by his shadow, yet the only hope for the individual himself lies in his ability to recognize and assimilate this shadow-figure, so that it becomes integrated into and therefore conditioned by the total personality. Putting on one side our ethical verdict, we have to admit that this negative shadow-figure, this *alias*, disposes at times of a superior energy-content. He is described as " the loose one," which could also mean the released or the uninhibited. He contains, therefore, the undisciplined or undomesticated libido which still has the archaic gorilla-power, by virtue of which the individual can come again into relation with his origins.

The dream says that the loose one " breaks through " after the dinner has been spoiled and the guests locked out. It is entirely characteristic of the shadow to break out just after the moment of failure. Indeed, the camouflage of sins, whether of omission or commission, by a sudden outburst of savagery directed at the wife, the caddie, the waiter, the other motorist, the pedestrian, the Jew—whoever, in fact, happens to be at hand and is fitted to play the rôle of scapegoat—is a trick so habitual in men and women of every degree that we are scarcely justified in describing it as pathological. This is the method of projecting the shadow as a protective diversion, not unlike the screen of cocytus employed by the octopus in order to conceal his actual whereabouts from the enemy. The smoke-screen used by battleships serves the same purpose. A veil is produced which prevents the enemy from seeing where to strike.

The ego is highly sensitive to failure because it is constructed around an ideal. Hence, when an obvious failure takes place, either one must pretend one was not serious, laughing it off in the farcical spirit, or one must cause a diversion by blaming somebody or something. In normal cases, where a certain self-discipline is habitual, this shadow-savagery is given relatively short rope. But in psychotic personalities the instability of the personality, and the almost complete lack of insight, result in no effective limit being set, so that the outbreak of uninhibited violence is liable to assume more and more the character of possession.

In the dream the subject's fight with the loose one after he has broken through indicates at least a temporary resistance before loathing changes to admiration. But from this point on the shadow becomes his friend, assuming the leading rôle like Mephisto with Faust.

This is the dangerous aspect of the dream. The subject not only toys with the renegade-hypothesis, but begins to accept it as his truth, notwithstanding the fact that the shadow-devil is obviously a cheat and a liar. With a Mephisto-like cunning, he instils a lascivious idea of replenishing the emotional dearth by getting food out of the Thames. His description of how he found a man " sneaking out of the house " to do this, and how, by following him, he eventually wormed himself into the man's confidence, is surely a self-portrait of the devil. We may also infer from this description that the metaphor " getting meat out of the Thames " has to do with antisocial possibilities—as, for instance, the resort to prostitutes.

The prostitute can be the devil's agent because, by divorcing sexuality from feeling, she presents a way by which the greatest human value and the dearest spiritual risk is inevitably cheapened. When the tasks which come to a man from his own innate virtue become burdensome, the prostitute offers the renegade-hypothesis. The devil knows all the devices by which men try to cheat their own souls; hence he is always able to " obtain their confidence " in the critical moment, just as Iago spoke the secret thoughts of Othello. For the devil is the other side of the coin, the obverse of the ruling ideal: he is the shadow lurking to betray our sun; he is the negation of the god which a man truly worships. To listen to the voice of the devil, therefore, is to admit the betrayer and the god-killer into one's house.

The devil's notion materializes, and the dreamer discovers a huge mass of meat, which, naturally, turns out to be bad. It cuts soft, like bad liver. But the devil is not put out by this discovery. Making a complete *volte face* he explains that they never take meat out of the Thames as it is always bad.

Any experienced crook, persuading his chosen victim to put money into a bogus concern, can be relied upon to eat his own words with gusto if the situation so demands. In the meantime the victim in the dream has to be edged away from the damning evidence of experience, and this the devil contrives by divulging interesting revelations concerning his origin and *milieu.*

The delinquent and the psychoneurotic are alike in this: they tend to explain their life's failure in terms of circumstance and heredity rather than as an expression of their own psychology.

Perhaps the most significant point in the dream is the way in which the devil disintegrates at the mere mention of a microscope. The microscope is an effective means for bringing into visibility a world of new facts and phenomena which otherwise would not have existed for us. Such an extension of the objective world is like adding another dimension to consciousness. The reference is, of course, to the extension of consciousness gained through analytical understanding of the unconscious. But the microscope also suggests a minute and critical scrutiny, particularly in respect to the meat obtained under the devil's auspices. No devil can stand objective criticism: the result, in the present instance, is to uncover the real motive of all this shadow-intrigue—namely, life-denial.

The last thing the shadow contrives before staging a very "symptomatic" suicide is to remove the eyepiece from the microscope—in other words, he puts the subjective end of the analytical microscope out of action. How is this done? The manner of the suicide is the one calculated to have the greatest suggestive effect upon the subject's mind, since it alludes to self-destructive acts in both brother and sister. Thus, by representing the tendency to self-destruction as a family trait, the shadow-devil tries to remove the whole pathological momentum from the orbit of individual responsibility.

The symptoms suggested by the iron-encased body and the rabbit skeleton remind one of the *sentiment d'automatisme* of Janet, which was regularly associated with the sense of

" being a victim." In the right half of Drawing II., just in front of the wheels of the limousine, the reader will be able to discern a small human figure along with a minute rhinoceros. Or we may recall Janet's patient who said: " For four months I have had queer ideas: it seems to me that I am obliged to think and say them; someone makes me speak, someone suggests to me coarse words, and it is not my fault if my mouth is worked in spite of myself."[1] In this example the feelings of victimization and of automatism are identical.

The patient associated the steel-encased creature with armour and with some sort of crustacean. We shall see later in the drawings how deeply he is concerned with the imprisoned elements in the unconscious. Often they are represented in armour with steel helmets, etc.

With regard to the rabbit skeleton, " the rabbit," he said, " was everybody's victim." Jabbing himself with a sharp instrument is a masochistic performance, in keeping with the fact that the shadow is now encased in a rabbit's skeleton. There was also an association of pricking a bubble, which should be interpreted as exploding a fantasy. Thus the final morbid symptom demonstrated by the shadow is histrionic exaggeration.

When we compare the vigorous Mephisto-character of the shadow before the mention of the microscope with the feeble suicidal lunatic he eventually becomes, we may infer that his pretensions cannot sustain scrutiny. How, then, are we to reconcile these two aspects of one and the same entity ? The shadow is both powerful and futile, formidable and pathetic.

The devil is forced to work secretly: he is essentially the undertow, the backwash. Seduction is possible only when the victim has first been drawn away from his human ties and loyalties. He must be waylaid, drawn aside, emotionally sequestered. This was the method of the mediæval torture system, as it is also that of the secret police in tyrannical states to-day. The victim or prisoner is kept in solitary confinement, while his mind is gradually seduced from its natural and proper loyalties by fear of torture, by hope of

[1] Janet: *Obsessions et Psychasthénie*, p. 273.

release, by every kind of devilish suggestion and lying half-truth. The process is called "breaking the spirit."

The devil waits until the moment arrives when individual moral is low, or one is discouraged by failure. The gods have turned their faces away: the tide sets towards the other pole. The renegade-arguments now sound attractive, and even admirable. The devil has slipped into the inner berth. Observe in the dream how the dreamer's loathing turns to admiration. Note also the persuasive air of the confidence trickster as soon as the victim's transference has been secured. Then there is the picture of the man "sneaking out of the house" to get food out of the Thames, of the devil following him and eventually worming his way into his victim's confidence. Where could one find a more life-like portrait of the devil at work? Yet this devil is the shadow of the ego, the unaccepted other side.

The renegade-hypothesis is of immense antiquity; it goes back even to our prehuman ancestry, as the dream also testifies. Should allegiance to the herd become the paramount, insistent truth, the renegade points to the solitary path beyond the pale. If the Progress of Civilization or the Ascent of Man become the propaganda of the epoch, the renegade chooses a life of vagrant idleness or of ostentatious immorality. If the absolute sacredness of human life, of religion, or of the family be pronounced by the headlines of orthodoxy, the renegade sails for Russia, where holy things are ignored. But sometimes the renegade-shadow may contain the one saving truth, when, for instance, individual dignity and liberty have been crushed out by pitiless state-tyranny and the longing for freedom creates revolt.

III

Variations of the individual departure from the social pattern form the warp and woof of psychotherapeutic practice, but the crucial importance of the renegade-factor in the causation of nervous and mental disorders has never been fully recognized in principle. It is as though the shock produced by Freud's revelation of infantile incest made so deep an impression upon the psychiatric imagination that no psychogenic factor outside the parent-child constellation could be seriously considered, unless expressed in the Freudian idiom. It is doubtless possible to distort one's naive conception of a rogue elephant, let us say, in order to make his behaviour fit into the Œdipus pattern. It is simpler, however, to regard him as a renegade. And when we find the archetype of the renegade singing bass to the hero's tenor in perhaps the oldest myth[1] of civilizing mankind, we may begin to wonder whether the major problems of the civilized mind should not be reconsidered in terms of the renegade factor.

As a heuristic principle it has already proved its mettle in the present dream. To label the whole seductive activity of the shadow as mere antisocial tendency would be colourless and unilluminating; it would also be a very one-sided interpretation of the material. The main figure in a dream, around which everything revolves, cannot be a mere anything. Our conception of this figure, called " the loose one " in the dream, has to embrace the following facts:

(1) He contains sufficient energy to break through—*i.e.*, to overcome the resistance of consciousness.
(2) He is powerful enough to do as he wills with the ego.
(3) There is something about him which evokes admiration.
(4) His capacities as a magician and confidence trickster are beyond dispute.
(5) He identifies himself with prostitution, with the archaic gorilloid tendencies of the unconscious, and with everything that is beyond the pale. (*Cf.* his bastard birth.)
(6) He has an aptitude for getting drunk (*i.e.*, being transported, losing control) and attributing its cause to others: in other words, he fathers paranoia.
(7) He has an aversion to objective scrutiny and criticism.
(8) He is evasive.
(9) He leads inevitably to self-destruction.

[1] The relation of Gilgamish to Enkidu will be further discussed at a later stage.

(10) He identifies himself with the defensive automatism and the fatalistic victim psychology of the schizophrenic attitude to life. (*Vide* the iron-encased body and the rabbit's skeleton.)

(11) When exposed to the light he dwindles to complete ineptitude like a pricked bubble.

(12) He is histrionic, preferring to gesticulate and to dramatize emotion than to submit to feelings which might involve human responsibilities.

In this natural-history study of the shadow we discover many attributes which could not belong to a mere negative. The shadow possesses formidable resources, which it would be foolish to belittle. The practical problem is how to convert the energy, which at present possesses the patient, into the energy which he can possess. This cannot be effected by first depreciating the value of that which one wants to possess. A man who desires life will not achieve his end by belittling vital goals. Neither can he win the co-operation of the unconscious—*i.e.*, the other side of his nature—by assuming consciousness to be always right and the other side necessarily wrong.

The situation which this dream depicts is clearly one in which a certain quantity of the energy available to consciousness has gone over to the other side: as though the forces of the Crown had deserted and gone over to the enemy. But supposing we look at the soul from the Chinese point of view—namely, as a dynamic field in which opposing natural forces play one against the other—immediately this partisan aspect takes on a different complexion. When an apple falls to the ground we do not speak of its betraying its allegiance to the bough, or of deserting to the other side. This is because we accept gravity as a neutral force, which works indifferently on all substances. Even if we flew sufficiently far away from the earth to be caught by the attraction of another planet we should still be under the law of gravity.

Here, then, it is possible to be impersonal and dispassionate. Can we not achieve the same objectivity with respect to psychological forces? Take the present case as an example. When associating to the first part of the dream, the patient, to use a graphic expression, dropped through the floor. The level of consciousness, in other words, made a sharp descent into the somnambulistic state. At this moment, then, we must suppose that an independent attracting force, of greater energy-potential than the momentary consistency of waking consciousness, has come upon the scene. The psychic energy is pulled down, or away from consciousness, in exactly the same way as the apple is pulled off the tree. This other pole, towards which the libido is attracted, I have called the alternative hypothesis, and the flight of libido towards this other pole I describe empirically as the renegade tendency. It may be ethically valueless or valuable, but its psychological significance lies in the fact that it represents a departure from the authority of consciousness.

To describe this renegade-movement of the libido as incest may be in certain instances correct. But incest is an interpretation, not a description. We are, moreover, faced with common-sense difficulties of a formidable kind. For if we identify with incest every evasion, every regression, every recession of libido from the adapted level, we shall have to extend the conception of sexuality, as Schopenhauer extended the conception of will, until, eventually, the words incest and sexuality become completely neutralized by the immense range of natural phenomena they have been stretched to cover.

It is surely more practical to regard the libido that goes motherwards, in recoil from the tasks of reality, as an aspect of the renegade-tendency than to assume that every drift of libido away from the conscious level expresses the ever-surviving attraction of the mother.

But, the reader may object, why, if this movement towards the other pole is to be regarded as a neutral force of nature, do you describe this force in terms of the devil and the renegade? If we were to write a chapter on the natural history of the devil in which his observed habits, the conditions under which he manifests himself, the actual phenomenology of the devil were enumerated and discussed, this, in effect, would be putting the devil under the microscope. We should then observe the transformations by which the subjective illusion is maintained. But first we must observe and criticize the renegade-aspect within the subjective sphere as the devil before we are able to release the psychic energy that has been held under the spell of this specific illusion. We can observe in this dream, for instance, the most essential condition of the devil's power—namely, that the other party in the transaction remains in a state of plastic suggestibility, as witness the dreamer's transference state when he succumbs to blind admiration of the " loose one." The devil is, in effect, the traditional form in which the invisible psychic undertow is objectified.

Regarding the devil, then, as a psychological moment, we also observe that this moment consists of two equal and opposite factors—namely, an active one, which we may call the suggesting agent, and a passive one, which is the recipient state of suggestibility. Whether the suggesting agent happens to be a person or an autonomous endopsychic factor is irrelevant to the thing we are trying to define.

Since most of the accounts of the devil have been reported by those whose theological bias renders them unfitted to give an accurate account of the experience, it is time that the analytical microscope should be introduced into this sphere. The fact that the subject was in an extreme state of suggestibility at the moment when the devil made his appearance has regularly been omitted from the report. And yet, without this condition, as our dream implicitly proclaims, there can be no devil. Both are equally essential factors of the total experience.

From the moment the dreamer suggests examining the devil's bad meat under the microscope, the balance of the psychic reciprocal is changed: the dreamer becomes active and responsible, while the devil changes into an inept and hysterical suicide, a pathetic victim. In the earlier part of the scene the state of the dreamer is suggestible, weak, pliable—in a word, the genuine subject is absent—whereas the shadow-devil is instinct with vitality. In the latter part the balance is reversed: the dreamer is effective and on the spot, while the shadow collapses into a played-out theatrical fantasy.

This Jekyll-and-Hyde alternation of the vital presence from one to the other is so suggestive that we cannot resist the conclusion that these are, in fact, the bright and the dark side of one and the same personality. The swift alternation of personality from one to the other is an unfavourable sign, since it implies a relatively low integration of consciousness; hence a weak resistance against the invasion of the unconscious.

The various rôles attempted by the shadow-devil throughout the play is another symptom of the pathological lability of direction and form. The devil will surely lead a man by devious ways to his own truth; but it is important to take a spare eyepiece for one's microscope, because illusion is the devil's natural element, and so long as a man can be fooled by his own shadow the devil wins.

We may well ask, When is a man not liable to be fooled by his shadow? It is doubtful if the shadow-complex can ever be completely assimilated, but it can none the less be analytically reduced and accepted to such an extent that it no longer exercises a dangerous power or contains an explosive charge of energy. If the autonomy of the complex can be broken by full conscious acceptance, the morbid tendency is not only reduced, but the whole character of the complex changes through becoming an integral part of the personality. It is easy enough to speak of conscious acceptance when, at the back of one's mind, one has a pleasurable, all-too-human frailty in view. But when we have to deal with a psychotic tendency which, as the dream shows, has an uncontrollable force at its disposal, to urge acceptance as a theoretical desideratum would be almost meaningless, for no man can really accept what he deeply fears. The narrow-minded, prejudiced person is simply an inexperienced soul. The dream contains, then, the uncomfortable prediction that the patient has first to be carried off his feet by the power of the renegade-complex before he can fundamentally realize and assimilate it. If it never broke loose and possessed him, he would not believe in its existence. But when, in spite of himself, the subject becomes identified with his Hyde personality, he gains therewith the understanding that is born of experience. He can understand the irrational standpoint, the amoral standpoint, the completely uninhibited standpoint. But he must also fear it, criticize it, and evaluate his experience with a common-sense patriarchal judgment. Through this staunchness of consciousness, which refuses to be overpowered by renegade-fantasies, the devil-complex is eventually resolved.

The majority of individuals are defended against such assaults by an unconscious state of identity with the parents or cultural background. When the devil approaches, a host of protective instinctive guardians immediately do battle, while consciousness remains practically undisturbed. But the present subject is psychologically uprooted. He has, in the whole manner of his life, rejected the moral sanctions and forms of his English ancestors. His attempt to go over to the other side, to an unmitigated naturalism, does not work, because the way of the cultural renegade is blocked with fears and inhibitions arising from the very tree to which he belongs. He cannot live either hypothesis with whole-hearted conviction. Hence he has to experience both sides and, through giving value to both, eventually create an attitude which will contain the essential elements of his whole nature, undisturbed by fear or bias. In other words, he must come to a real pact with nature in himself.

The contradictory elements are stated in the shadow's parentage, which contradiction represents a dangerous cleavage in the subject's inherited psychology. The " good man " symbolizes the ethical ideal, or the family pattern of conduct. The gorilla, on the other hand, represents the unfathomable depth and power of the archaic unconscious.

These figures naturally bear no relation to the patient's actual father and mother. They represent, rather, a retrospective criticism on the puritan ancestry, which set up an ethical ideal that had no psychological relation to the real nature of man. The puritan ideal originated very largely as a counter-swing to the licentiousness of decadent court life. The too rigid forms and patterns found in human societies are never original truths. Like the Creed, which to-day few men can avow, these inherited patterns are essentially counter-statements, hence their overemphasis.

The gorilla is the symbol of the inextinguishable power

of nature in man, which the puritan attempted to counter by the repression of instinct. This motif is also introduced into the dream in the statement that the shadow's mother was a whore. But what kind of relation is there between the furtive commerce of the urban prostitute and a gorilla? In his own place the gorilla is one of the most impressive and awe-inspiring creatures in the whole of nature. Like all creatures with terrific strength, the gorilla also possesses a certain majesty. Why should such a creature be regarded as an alias for a whore? The fact that instinct disposes at certain times of an overwhelming force belongs, not to civilization, but to man's immemorial descent. The civilized mind is a *parvenu* of a few thousand years only: the primordial, instinctive mind is eternally existing. Also, therefore, it has a vast inertia, a truly majestic conservatism.

Civilization has never succeeded in completely canalizing this primordial energy into standardized forms of behaviour and activity. Religion has not extinguished it. Some systems of religion have even found a way by which the unconscious can be transformed without violating its primordial character.

Prostitution, on the other hand, is a civilized attempt to diminish the power of the instinct by dishonouring it. Thus the whore and the gorilla are infamously bracketed together in the same breath. But the gorilla that man fears in himself is no more like the gorilla of the Ruwenzori forests than the prostitute is like primordial woman. At the back of both images stands the civilized man's fear of the primordial unconscious, and this, in effect, is fear of the atavistic shadow.

On the principle that a small light held in front of one will cast a large shadow behind, it follows that a very restricted, narrow-minded consciousness will produce an immense shadow-effect in the unconscious. This shadow-effect is an expression of the fear of an unstable, dependent or childish personality in the presence of an unknown and irrational force.

It will become clear, I think, from subsequent material, that the borderline schizophrenic is fascinated by the unconscious: he is both attracted and terrified by it. He knows it would be safer never to have any dealings with the archaic underworld of the mind. But he cannot keep away: his very fear of the unconscious attracts him to it. This is, of course, the basic meaning of the snake in the dream-life of the schizophrenic: it symbolizes that primordial instinctual force which the wise man fears because it can also fascinate.

The major problem of the patient is stated in this, his first dream of the analysis, and it is expressed in the form of an apparently irreconcilable opposition. At the beginning we noted the two levels, represented, on the one hand, by the mechanical, meaningless activity of existence under the compulsion of the mother-complex, and, on the other, by violent, irrational upheavals in the realm of the emotions. We now find the opposition stated in terms of two inherited dispositions—either to follow the pattern of ancestral expectation and be the "good man," or to follow the renegade-hypothesis, back towards the gorilla (the subjective gorilla, not the natural one), by way of the prostitute.

The subject has rejected the ancestral pattern, yet he cannot accept the renegade with any conviction. Therefore he is forbidden by his own experience to simplify his life along either of these paths. He has to allow them to fight it out in open conflict on the psychological field. The new personality-attitude, which will eventually be born of the conflict, will then possess the essential virtues of its parents. That the issue of the opposition in his nature must be born, and not invented, is also indicated by the dream in the fact that the conflict is stated in terms of two parents.

IV

Before leaving this apparently incomprehensible dream I should like to correlate certain features observed in it with clinical psychiatric descriptions.

Referring to the renegade shadow-character, we may compare Kraepelin's account of the early history of his schizophrenics. He writes:

> "A smaller group of children, mostly boys, is noticeable, who from childhood up were lazy and restless, disliked work, were inclined to nasty tricks, did not persevere anywhere, and finally became vagrants and criminals."

As a compensatory picture he describes on the same page

> "those patients who were conspicuous by their docility, good nature, anxious conscientiousness and diligence, and as patterns of goodness held themselves aloof from all childish naughtiness."[1]

It is clear that the morbidity of the latter type is to be found in the fact that it is merely an over-compensation of the unconscious renegade tendency.

Adolf Meyer gives a similar picture of the over-compensated renegade. He writes:

> "In cases of dementia præcox we find over and over again an account of a perfectly exemplary childhood, but a gradual change in the period of emancipation. Close investigation shows, however, that the exemplary child was exemplary under a rather inadequate ideal: an example of goodness and meekness rather than of determination and strength, with a tendency to keep to the good in order to avoid fights and struggles."[2]

In another significant passage he says:

> "Children affected are the very ones who, in a former generation, might have been looked upon as model children."[3]

In other words, the pattern on which the ego has been constructed is an obsolete model, or perhaps we might say that the pattern has been arbitrarily superimposed, and never inwardly accepted by the individuality of the child.

It is obvious from these descriptions that the exemplary behaviour is mere imitation, a superficial conforming with expectations. Individuality is wholly absent from the picture, and therefore we know that it is a compensatory attempt, not a real adaptation: a state which closely corresponds with that of the first part of our dream.

With regard to the *laissez-aller* indolence, unrelatedness and self-willed indulgence of the renegade-character, Amsden

[1] Kraepelin: *Dementia Præcox*, Chap. IX., p. 236 (Edinburgh: Livingstone, 1919).

[2] Meyer: "*An Attempt at Analysis of the Neurotic Constitution*," *American Journal of Psychology*, 1903, XIV., pp. 354-367.

[3] A. Meyer: *What do Histories of Cases of Insanity teach us concerning Preventive Mental Hygiene during the Years of School Life?* Psych. Clinic, 1908, II., pp. 89-101.

describes the personality of the simple type of schizophrenia as follows:

"The most noticeable traits are related to a conspicuous physical and mental indolence. Outstanding defensive traits of personality are lacking. The individual, apparently quite satisfied with his inner experiences, marches on, indifferent to the world of reality. Habits relating to sensual indulgence stand out prominently."[1]

The renegade-tendency is, of course, present in every normal psychology. But what we have to deal with in the schizophrenic type is a consolidated renegade-complex containing a regressive tendency towards the archaic level that is liable to become the major life-tendency. The literature of schizophrenia is full of just such descriptions, and every psychiatrist is as familiar with the exemplary Victorian, the ostentatiously conscientious and well-behaved type, as with the vagrant and the renegade. Psychologically, they are equivalent. They are, in fact, the opposite sides of the same coin. The father was "too good a man, the mother a gorilla or a whore."

But, unless we have had the opportunity of following out the psychological development of a schizoid personality under analysis, we are liable to make the mistake of assuming that the renegade or retrogressive tendency is the cause of the disease. Regressive phases and archaic elements are normal constituents of psychic life, and, if we accept Kretschmer's view, schizophrenia is not something specific, but only an exaggeration of normal traits.

From this standpoint the regressive tendency can also be viewed as the spirit of a new departure, *reculer pour mieux sauter*, whereas if the schizoid split is regarded fatalistically, the inertia of the atavistic tendency is thereby increased, the energy-level sinks more and more into the unconscious, and the whole personality is liable to be sucked down by the archaic pull into a state of dementia. Thus the attitude to the retrograde movement may become the decisive factor.

There is a characteristic dream-motif which illustrates this crisis. The retrograde tendency is frequently symbolized

[1] Amsden: *Mental and Emotional Components of the Personality in Schizophrenia*, Assn. for Research in Nerv. and Ment. Dis., V., p. 134.

by a giant crab or deep-sea monster. The dreamer gets caught by this creature, sometimes by the toe while swimming; sometimes his body is encircled by the tentacles of an octopus, and he is dragged under water. When this happens the prognosis is bad. It is correspondingly good when the dreamer catches the monster or the crab on the end of the line and succeeds in pulling him up into the boat.

As our dream intimated, an essential preliminary to cure in this case consisted in the patient submitting to a kind of mitigated insanity: he had to struggle with the renegade-system, as Jacob wrestled with the angel. By no other means could he win the energy which the complex contained, therewith to overleap the gulf which separated him from his instinctive roots. The series of drawings depicts this vital experience.

Similar evidence is not lacking in the textbooks. In summarizing the final results in a number of cases in which permanent recovery followed an acute psychotic phase, Strecker says:

> " A careful study makes it a fair conclusion that six patients not only recovered, but attained and have maintained a level which is appreciably higher than their pre-psychotic level. It seems obvious that, occasionally at least, the schizophrenic conflict implies not only restitution, but also that mental weapons are forged which enable the patient to meet reality successfully on a plane higher than the pre-psychotic."[1]

It is clear, therefore, that the therapeutic aim in schizophrenia is not to eradicate any morbid psychological neoplasm, but rather to make known to the subject his split-off *alter ego* and, in so doing, to enable him to discover the unfathomable resources of the unconscious.

[1] E. A. Strecker: *Prognosis in Schizophrenia* (*Dementia Præcox*), Assn. for Research in Nerv. and Ment. Dis., X., p. 184.

CHAPTER IV

CONTENT OF DRAWING I: STATEMENT OF THE PROBLEM

I

BEFORE embarking on our discussion of the drawings, it is advisable to introduce to the reader the method denoted by the term " active fantasying."

It consists in letting the mind loose, allowing whatever will to come into consciousness. The difference between this and idle day-dreaming is a question of valuation or attitude. The very fact that meaning is attached to the imagery, and that it is recorded and valued, seems to constellate the autonomous activity in a peculiar way. Instead of wayward ephemeral fancies that blow down the wind like thistledown, the images that arise under the influence of value and attention are pregnant and relevant in a high degree.

It is not unlike the experience of men who, for years perhaps, have had only the lightest and most trifling relations with women: suddenly, for no discoverable reason, a woman steps out of the condition of ephemeral irrelevance and becomes commandingly relevant. Such a man, we say, has been seized by the love-problem.

In much the same way one can be seized by the psyche, the spontaneous, unwilled activity of the mind suddenly assuming a peculiar significance. What makes the woman or the fantasy suddenly relevant ? In neither case is it mere accident; indeed, in the psychic sphere there can be no such thing as accident. It is as though we had chanced upon a realm where rational motives were no longer valid, and where deliberation, instead of preceding, follows laboriously after the event. When reason is in control, we are able to weigh all the factors for or against a certain decision; but in the irrational realm, the event goes of itself without conscious direction, and often with astonishing certainty of aim. But whose aim? Unless we wish to introduce some extra psychic cause in deference to time-honoured tradition, we have to accept the concept of the self as embracing both irrational and rational, unconscious and conscious elements. Only with this conception is it possible to comprehend a subjective aim more far-sighted and more commanding than the deliberate aims of consciousness. Without this central conception it is, I believe, fundamentally impossible to reach the heart of a dream, or to give vital value to such irrational products as we shall presently discuss.

Active fantasy-production may follow many different routes, according to individual preference. With some subjects the fantasy springs directly out of a dream, and there is an immediate inclination to paint or in some way elaborate the dream-image. Modelling in clay or plasticine, painting or drawing, carrying on the dream-scene in waking fantasy, conversing with personifications of the unconscious as independent entities, written accounts, poems, dialogues, even dancing and posturing—in fact, any method at all which gives concreteness, independence, plastic vitality to the psychic contents—I include under this term. As a rule, these products have little or no æsthetic value. Frequently, indeed, they are so pathological as to offend even the most catholic taste. But at last, when the pathological complex has been liquidated, it may be that a picture or a poem will be produced which is wholly satisfying.

The only difficulty about this method is that it is too simple. A man wants a sphere where his will can be effective. He is not so deeply interested in the original mind given him by nature which, when he was a child, peopled his world with wondrous beings. Especially is it difficult for a young man to believe that anything relevant to his actual life could come from a dream or fantasy. Consequently, the first thing he must learn is to leave his heroic will in the cupboard whence he fetches his paints. With the will must go his rational criticism, and, if he is inclined to opinionate instead of listening to what the picture is saying, he must also shed his need to explain. In short, the ideal condition for active fantasying is that of the child, only it must be combined with the purposiveness of maturity.

The work of psychological creation is essentially creative play, wherein the child and the man are again united. For this reason the pictures made during an analysis have a peculiar subjective value which should be respected. They belong to the subject's individual myth, and, when valued as such, he will naturally want to keep them. They should not be regarded merely as scientific specimens.

In the routine of interpretation I have been guided to some extent by the patient's comments, associations and reactions. Where these were lacking, or where intellectual bias prohibited freedom of association, it was usually possible to find the corresponding analogy, either in previous dreams or drawings or in the field of general mythology. When the symbolism of the material suggested a parallel imagery in the mythological field, I found it possible to use the indicated motif very much as one uses a specific dye-stain in histology for the purpose of bringing corresponding tissue-elements into relief.

Freud has employed the Œdipus stain in order to emphasize one aspect of the parent-child constellation. But the disadvantage of using one powerful specific stain only is that it tends to obliterate everything else. Without attempting to multiply examples, I have employed a certain number of well-known myth-patterns which seemed to me appropriate and sufficient to the material in hand.

The analogical method is indispensable in every psychological investigation. There could, in fact, be no extension of our scientific borders without it, only it must be tempered by a vigilant sense of reality, lest its reckless employment in an attempt to prove a thesis for which no real evidence is forthcoming bring the whole method into disrepute. In philosophy, history and psychology the analogical method has now been reinstated as the method *par excellence*, when properly employed, for gathering a new set of facts into a familiar container whose validity has been proved in an analogous field of study.

* * * * *

As to the therapeutic value of the drawings, particularly for the schizophrenic personality, there can be no doubt at all. Owing to a disruptive splitting and dissociation between the emotional basis and the conscious level, he is liable to be shut in, oversubjective, and preoccupied to an abnormal degree with his inner states and processes. Hoch's description of the shut-in personality as depicted by Devine is as follows:

> "If we gain a knowledge of the personality as it existed before the psychosis, we find with striking frequency persons who do not have a natural tendency to be open and to get into contact with the environment; who are reticent, seclusive, who cannot adapt themselves to situations, who are hard to influence, often sensitive and stubborn. But the latter more in a passive than in an active way. They show little interest in what goes on, often do not participate in the pleasures, cares and pursuits of those about them; although often sensitive, they do not let others know what their conflicts are. They do not unburden their minds, are shy, and have a tendency to live in a world of fancies."[1]

This is the shut-in personality, a classical picture of a mentality undermined by a split-off atavistic complex. The withdrawal of libido from objective interests and relations is due, as Jung has shown,[2] to the fascinating effect of the complex sucking the libido away from the conscious level. For such an individual the saving means clearly lies in creating a new avenue by which the inturned fantasy-activity can become objective.

The essence of psychotherapy consists in this operation: it effects a means whereby the vague, subjective, unseizable, inverted activity of the libido can gain objective form and expression. This may be achieved by talking, free association, discussion and interpretation of dream, fantasy or other products of autonomous mental activity: in a word, creating one's myth. Moses holding up the brazen serpent, so that the Israelites, standing resistant and stubborn in the arid Moabite desert might project the evil spirit that possessed them upon the archetypal poisoner, proved the efficacy of

[1] Devine: *Recent Advances in Psychiatry*, p. 251, cited from Hoch: "*A Study of the Mental Make-up in Functional Psychoses*," *Journal of Nervous and Mental Diseases*, 1909, xxxvi., p. 230.

[2] *Psychology of Dementia Præcox.*

psychotherapeutic principles. For, at bottom, psychotherapy is the means by which a separatistic, subjective factor is persuaded to join in objective co-operation. The man with a shut-in personality, who conceals a knot of negative inferiority and hostile criticism behind a mask of unconcern, experiences an immediate release of tension when he finds he can express his mood in a vigorous, spontaneous drawing. And when, in the analytical hour, he discovers that his drawings are graphic representations of the morbid inner process which holds him, as it were, marooned and inaccessible in a world of living men, his relief is enhanced by understanding. If the nature and operation of the morbid process is once understood, the moral of consciousness is greatly strengthened. When the directional movement of the autonomous activity is allied with conscious purpose, the resulting drawings begin to reveal an inherent development, as though moving towards a *dénouement*. In studying this development with the doctor, the patient is provided with the key to the understanding of his own complex psychology. Secure in the possession of his key, the patient can freely revoke the value he had previously transferred to the doctor.

Another important advantage of this method is that the conscious personality participates actively in the therapeutic process, in contrast to dream analysis where the subject is only passively engaged. In so far as participation in the curative process becomes active and voluntary, the period of treatment is materially shortened and the value of the experience correspondingly enhanced.

Among the various pathological types with which we have to deal the schizophrenic personality tends to show the greatest readiness to express his fantasy-life in pictorial attempts. This may be due to the effect of the repressive barricade which practically precludes all the normal avenues of emotional expression. Even if the drawings appear almost unintelligible, a discussion of them yields a certain real satisfaction. This is intensified if, at the same time, the material of the drawings can be related to the patient's dreams.

As an empirical method, active fantasying rests upon the hypothesis that, by following the development of spontaneous imagery, it is possible to get at the roots of the morbid system and, at the same time, to effect a transformation of attitude. As soon as its unconscious roots and connections are realized by the patient, he is in a position to assimilate the complex, thus bringing it within the sphere of conscious insight and control.

The morbidity of the complex depends upon its autonomous, dissociated condition. The therapeutic effect, therefore, can be stated as a progression in three stages:

(1) The projection of the complex-activity into an objective medium, as in dream or fantasy-picture.
(2) The conscious handling and realization of the morbid fantasy-activity.
(3) The assimilation of the complex by the conscious personality in such a way that the autonomy of the complex is resolved.

It is possible that the greatest value of the drawings consists in the fact that they are concrete representations of the individual myth which, as we explained at the beginning, is the indispensable psychical container as well as the inexhaustible vessel of spiritual nourishment for those who can no longer trust themselves unquestioningly to traditional collective forms.

II

As the theme of his first drawing the present subject chose the opening scene of Dream I. It is explanatory and symptomatic in character, because the patient was impaled upon a doubt. In this picture it is as though he were confessing his secret doubt and, at the same time, inviting an elucidation of it.

Drawing I

In his selection of the Mersey as his starting-point, we can be sure that the subject associates in some way this new therapeutic attempt with the maternal roots of his psychology. The reader will remember that the Mersey was specifically linked up with his mother's people, especially with his maternal grandfather.

An inflated battleship occupies the mid-field, while the relatively small size of the other vessels in the picture is intended to indicate the normal scale of reality: a confession of an immense subjective inflation. To the right of the ship is the small " towing-boat " by which the battleship is anchored. The subject's wife is in this anchoring boat, a notable change from his attitude to her in the dream. Directly beneath the battleship there is a whirlpool. It is caused, we are informed, by the sucking action of a phallic mechanism (thought of as a crane) which projects through a thick and jagged layer of rock. Below this layer of rock is a lunatic asylum, a chain of buildings resembling the place where the patient recently spent a disturbed year as medical officer. The heads of two lunatics emerge from narrow windows, and a large key hangs beside the door.

Above, in the top left-hand corner, is the sun (associated with the father), darkened as in an eclipse, showing eight raying arms and three sunspots. Around the sun's disc is drawn an irregular outline, resembling a corona. The second sun-ray, extending towards the observer's right, is shown piercing a cloud that hangs over the battleship. As it passes through the cloud it is split into two rays, which eventually merge with the beam emitted from the lighthouse, to be seen in mid-stream to the right of the battleship. The third ray descends towards the centre of the picture, expanding to enfold and contain the battleship as in a closed fist. This is an important pathological indicator, for it is a symbolical statement of the manner in which the subject is both enclosed and isolated by his identification with the father. Note that the expanded ray does not include the wife in the towing-boat.

Opposite to the sun on the right is Fujiyama, the sacred mountain of Japan. Below, extending downwards from the lighthouse, there is a curious tripod structure whose three legs are in connection with the asylum, one leg being supported by the exaggerated and distorted arm of a lunatic who stands on the connecting bridge to the detached building on the right, the other two resting on the roof of this same building. The ship appears to be stationary in the centre, where it is completely enfolded or contained by the expanded light-ray from the sun. A second source of light reaches the ship from the lighthouse; this is apparently supplied from the tripod below.

It should be noted that something in the nature of an energy-circuit exists, connecting the above-mentioned central contents of the drawing. Regarding the sun as the source of energy, the battleship is the receptor of the main stream of solar energy. This downward stream of energy is continued, by means of the whirlpool and the phallic projection, into the main building of the lunatic asylum. From here it passes upwards into the three-legged pylon by means of the connecting bridge, the upraised hand of the lunatic and the detached terminal building, on whose roof the pylon is supported. Finally, the energy-stream flows up into the lighthouse, from which it returns again to the battleship in the form of light. We shall discuss these important connections later.

This whole field, centring in the ship, is conditioned by four stabilizing principles disposed as polar opposites. In the corner, diagonally opposed to the radiating sun (*i.e.*, the father, the principle of consciousness), and below the rocky layer, is the symbol of evolution, a line coiling outwards from the centre.[1] The outer curves of the spiral are involved with the layer of rocks and the end building. At the top right and bottom left-hand corners are two laminal fields of energy, painted with alternating bands of green and yellow. Two lines (with arrows indicating the direction of force) issue respectively from the upper and lower laminated fields and traverse the field from top to bottom in such a way that the ship is held in the space between these parallel lines.

These four containing energy-symbols deserve attention, because they represent the alternation of the libido upon which the fundamental affective attitude hinges. The patient could say little about them, except that the alternating bands were like the plates of a battery. It will be noted that the

[1] Spiral curves and designs are undoubtedly very common in schizophrenic drawings. In view of the obvious association with the inverting or involuting tendency of the libido, they can be regarded as characteristic archaisms.

lower left-hand field has an inverted or closed disposition of its curves, like the upper quarter of a circle. By its close proximity to the phallic " crane " which produces the sucking vortex under the ship, it is associated with the principle of inversion. The line of force emanating from this field passes through a town on the farther side of the river, in respect to which we are informed that it is a gay resort with a casino where people dance and drink and gamble.

The upper right-hand field, on the contrary, has an everted or cup-shaped disposition of open curves, like the lower quarter of a circle. It is directly associated with the sacred mountain. The line of force coming from this field strikes the pylon which supplies the light in the lighthouse. It also passes through the arm of the lunatic supporting the first leg of the tripod. This pylon with its three legs seems to represent a half-modern, half-archaic improvisation, by which psychic energy, isolated within the morbid system under the layer of repression, can be connected with an organic circuit of energy flowing between the conscious and the unconscious. From the position of the right-hand line of force it may also be inferred that there is a positive connection between the central energy circuit and the open symbol above from which the line issues. A connection of an opposite character would seem to exist between the gay city, symbolizing dissipation of energy in an aimless collective drift, and the inverted system below.

The inverted system is, moreover, identified with the morbid complex (the lunatic asylum) under the wall of repression. As evidence of inversion, it is important to note that the phallic projection, which penetrates the wall, acts as an organ of suction, not of ejaculation, as might be expected.

* * * * *

For the proper understanding of this initial drawing it is vital to note the presence of the characteristic schizophrenic barrier between the conscious and the unconscious levels. In this case it consists of jagged rocks. In the second case, to be discussed later, it is represented as a jagged line, as might be found in a broken pane of glass. There is a distinct tendency in schizophrenic drawings for the field of the drawing to be broken, in this way, into two halves by an arbitrary line or barricade, and, as a rule, the contents of the two parts show little or no continuity, either of line or idea. This feature is pathognomonic of schizoid psychology, and should be noted as a valuable diagnostic sign.

The drawing yields important diagnostic information which adds considerably to what we have already learned from the dreams. In the dream the whole symbolism of the inflated, flimsy and erratic battleship was connected by dream-logic with the patient's unconscious identification with the father. This explanation appears to have been not wholly satisfactory, since the patient now attempts to go deeper into the cause, or causes, of the battleship's contradictory aspect. This is now seen to be the result of two agencies acting upon it from above and from below. Below the ship there is the whirlpool, produced by the sucking effect of the inverted system in the unconscious. This vortex depicts the recession of psychic energy from the realm of consciousness, bringing about the state of mental inertia described by Janet as *l'abaissement du niveau mental.* The energy of this repressed system is symbolically declared to be inverted sexuality by the detached phallic arm which causes the whirlpool.

In polar opposition to this disturbance from below we find the ship enclosed with a swollen extension of the sun, associated by the patient with the father. The archetype of the father is equivalent to the sun in the psychical sphere, and the discrimination of the timeless image from the actual father is as necessary an act of consciousness as it is for us to distinguish the human personality of the King from the archetype of divine kingship. Thus the identification with the father, suggested by the symbolism of the drawing, particularly the expanded ray which closes over the ship like a giant's hand, might be regarded as a magical means of protection against the psychotic menace below.[1] On the other hand, there is strong evidence that the psychotic influence itself has its

[1] The deification of the father-image through the identification with the sun strengthens this idea. It is like being " safe in the Eternal arms."

source in the father's psychology. There is, indeed, a suggestion of this possibility in the present drawing—namely, in the presence of the *three* sunspots in the darkened sun. These the patient explains as defects or opacities. And on the other side of the picture we find the archaic mechanism with its *three* legs, in the antipodal position to the sun, as though constructed in order to compensate the defects on the father's side.

This contradiction between the psychotic influence from the father and the inherited father-image was a cause of great confusion in the patient's emotional life. It also disturbed his relation to those who happened to stand in a kind of parental relation through being in a position of authority over him. From the character of the patient's associations it is clear that the left-hand side of the drawing is the unfavourable aspect, and is definitely connected with the father, while the right-hand is beneficent and curative, under the maternal Fujiyama. Coming under the positive sign of the mother, therefore, we can regard the archaic tripod, with its extension, as an improvised means of linking up the dissociated system with an auxiliary function of cognition (the lighthouse).

In a later drawing we shall find another example in which an auxiliary perceptive function is brought into play at the critical moment. In that case it is the atavistic middle-eye which comes into operation during the hero's fight with the dragon. In the moment when the hero pierces the eye of the dragon with his sword, the rear portion of the beast assails him from behind, so that without this backward-looking eye, which perceives the unexpected attack, he would have been overcome. In this connection it is interesting to remember that Descartes regarded the pineal body as the seat of the soul.[1]

The problem of psychic atavism would require a volume to itself; all we need to establish here is the capacity of the psyche to hark back to an archaic, elementary function of apprehension and expression when a dangerous state of

[1] The pineal body of certain lizards still contains vestiges of the pineal eye, which was probably well developed in extinct amphibia of the pretertiary period.

dissociation has isolated consciousness from the inherited wisdom of the unconscious. The opacity and resistance erected between the over-rationalized conscious function and such irrational psychic contents as are portrayed, for instance, in these drawings prohibits the reciprocity between consciousness and instinct on which psychological stability rests. Without the help, therefore, of a rather special kind of apprehension, the schizophrenic gulf could not possibly be bridged. The function that could act as psychic mediator between the two sides needs to be essentially primitive in its mode of operation: a function, let us say, that is able to apprehend and express the invisible changes and events of the autonomous psyche in concrete and plastic imagery.

This tripod mechanism that extends from the repressed unconscious system to the auxiliary eye of consciousness (the lighthouse), though apparently a new improvisation invented by necessity, is, in point of fact, an extremely primitive form. The most famous example of the tripod in classical antiquity was the ritual tripod in the Temple of Apollo at Delphi, from which the Pythian priestess delivered the oracles of the god. The tripod is said to have been placed over a fissure in the earth, whence arose mephitic vapours which were believed to be the exhalations of the wise god, who had taken on the form of the Python of the deluge after his victory over the monster. The breath of the god entered into the priestess, who then proclaimed the wisdom of the oracle. Thus the idea of divining[1]—*i.e.*, seeking wisdom from the unconscious—surviving in an archaic form from the past, together with the idea of this wisdom penetrating into the conscious realm from below, is mythologically connected with the tripod.

Another connection is the tripod which held the magic cauldron in Celtic mythology, also the tripod used by witches in their dealings with the spirit-world. The archaism of the tripod, like the atavism of the pineal eye, might, therefore, be regarded as a harking-back to a primitive modality of the mind, for the purpose of tuning-in to a level of the unconscious

1 Divination is perception by unconscious means: in a word, intuition.

which heretofore, on account of its primordial character, had been inaccessible to consciousness.

Receptivity of a special kind does not, however, cover the whole significance of the tripod mechanism. It will be noticed that the type of structure found in the tripod is also present in the phallic crane that has become detached and now operates as a mechanism of inversion in the bottom left-hand corner. The patient himself felt that originally this phallic arm must have been part of the tripod mechanism. A portion, therefore, of the tripod structure has become separated from its original connection and now functions independently in an inverted fashion, as part of the pathological system. From all these associations we are able to say that the tripod-crane which feeds the lighthouse symbolizes a function of introverted intuition—namely, a special kind of cognition whereby unconscious contents and processes can become represented to consciousness.[1]

The psychological significance of the disjuncted arm of the crane which creates the vortex is interesting, because it demonstrates how a morbid complex actually comes about. It represents that part of the intuitive function which, becoming inverted, works under the wrong ægis. States of vague apprehension or unspecified fear arise, as a rule, from unconscious negative intuitions, as though a poisoned intuitive shaft had been turned treacherously against the subject. This vortex expresses the neurotic process created in the mind by such a negative intuition or doubt.

Bringing these dissociated parts together, we see that the idea of the tripod structure suggests a twofold function—namely, (*a*) the function of raising the hitherto repressed and fear-laden contents of the unconscious into the light of consciousness, and (*b*) a naive, archaic function of apprehension and expression, which might be termed psychic intuition or intuition of psychic events. The former is symbolized by the arm of the crane, the latter by the lighthouse. The function of dreaming or fantasying corresponds

[1] This archaic structure accords with Jung's definition of intuition (*vide* chapter on " Definitions " in *Psychological Types*) as " perception by way of the unconscious."

perfectly with the former, while the latter represents the illumination of consciousness (note the expanding beam reaching the battleship from the lighthouse) which comes from concentration upon, and understanding of, a dream. Thus the therapeutic importance of dream and fantasy is implicitly asserted in this first drawing. The vital factor, necessity, is also included, in the fact that one leg of the tripod stands upon the magnified and distorted hand of a lunatic.

Fear of insanity is a powerful incentive to psychological exploration. Repressed fear of insanity is, of course, expressed in the whole asylum system with its inmates battened down below the jagged layer of rock; but there is a particular nuance to be observed in the distortion of the lunatic's hand, alluded to above.

The factor of distortion is immediately significant in our reading of dream or drawing. Just as an error of refraction points directly to a specific abnormality in the mechanism of the eye, so the factor of distortion can be regarded as a complex-indicator, invariably leading down to the crucial point.

When, therefore, we regard this distorted hand as a complex-indicator, we note the following significant facts:

(1) The lunatic stands on a frail bridge, connecting the detached portion with the main building—a position which is patently symptomatic of the schizophrenic splitting, and yet which also suggests the idea of overcoming the split by a new construction.

(2) The two lunatics who escape in the next drawing, and who represent two antithetical aspects of the pathological process, are seen one on either side of the bridge upon which the lunatic with the distorted hand is standing. From this medial or reconciling position we know that the figure in question must be concerned with the curative possibility—as also is the complex-indicator.

(3) The first leg of the curative tripod, which connects the split-off system with the dream lighthouse, rests upon this hand.

(4) The upward movement in the total energy-circuit—which runs from sun to ship, from ship, via the whirlpool, to asylum, and from detached building, via the crane, to

lighthouse, thence back to ship again—starts with the lunatic who stands on the bridge. The downward momentum (from sun to phallic projection) obviously expresses the pathological inversion of the libido, while the upward flow (from lunatic's hand to lighthouse) clearly carries the curative impulse. Daily psychotherapeutic experience confirms the inference of the drawing—namely, that as soon as the complex-indicator has pointed the way, the curative process can begin.

(5) Regarding the lunatic on the bridge as complex-indicator, it is a reasonable inference that the detached building on his right represents the complex that is being indicated. This inference is supported by four considerations:

(*a*) The autonomy of the complex is, as Jung has shown, the cause of its pathological effect: the very word schizophrenia deriving from the pathological isolation of a partial mental system.

(*b*) The building is, as it were, slung between two symbols, both of which are of considerable value in the analytical process. On the left there is the bridge, or commissure, which brings the complex into connection with other contents. On the right is the evolutionary spiral (starting from the centre) which involves the complex in a developmental process. However inadequately these symbols have been drawn, their presence is none the less significant.

(*c*) The tripod supplying the lighthouse is grounded upon the complex. This tallies with our experience that the first dreams of a patient undergoing analysis tend to have their roots in the dissociated complex.

(*d*) The concentration of these three symbolical constructions in the immediate neighbourhood of the detached building identifies the latter with the isolated schizophrenic system, which first must be made accessible and then assimilated.

The analogy between psychotic distortion and refraction brings out another interesting feature—namely, the subject's gross disturbance of vision, or absence of insight in regard to everything associated with the complex. The venomous projections of paranoia are, at bottom, symptoms of this opaque screen which insulates the psychotic personality from those normal subjective intimations that make insight into one's less creditable motives at all events a possibility. A paranoiac woman patient of forty-seven charged me, for instance, on her second visit, with the exercise of an uncanny power, whereby her dreams were filled with erotic images and her mind with sexual thoughts. I was a magician, spinning my hypnotic web around her, and nothing that I could say was of any avail, because her intuition was never wrong. She refused even to consider the hypothesis that these unwanted visitors in her mind might have come from her own unconscious. It is the nature of the psychotic projection to maintain absolutist pretensions. Any person who has lost touch with his unconscious is liable to project the magician archetype upon the analyst; but only a psychotic would be so victimized by the projection as to reject abruptly the other reasonable hypothesis.

Even the present subject (who, by the way, showed considerable psychological flair in regard to the shadow side of other people) was so completely shut off from his own problem that he believed for a time that I had used him as a medium, making him dream my dreams, and then treating them as though they were his. With the borderline schizophrenic the opacity is not complete; hence, perhaps, the frail bridge that connects the psychotic complex with the main building in our drawing. My patient did not tell me what he was thinking at the time, though I guessed from his behaviour that a sinister projection had intervened. The very fact that a man secretes his belief intimates a certain doubt as to its validity. In this case the patient must have known that his belief would not stand examination, since it covered the two dreams analysed in the present work, one of which preceded his coming to me by several weeks, while the other was brought to me on his second visit. Being a doctor himself, the patient was in a position to recognize a characteristic paranoiac projection; but the psychotic opacity blurred his vision. It was not, of course, a question of intelligence, but of self-protection. The precarious balance of the psychotic mind does not readily permit any insight which could lay hold of the mind or affect the integrity of the highly vulnerable ego.

We shall return to this discussion of subjective distortion when we are considering the first drawing of the second subject: indeed, this whole problem is more lucidly developed in the second series. We have seen enough, however, to appreciate, first, that a lunatic with grotesquely distorted hands is an appropriate object to find on the threshold of the psychotic complex, and, second, that the sense of necessity, prompted by this psychotic refraction, could become the *sine qua non* of a genuine curative attempt. In this connection it is significant indeed that the tripod crane which feeds the lighthouse should have one of its roots in the paranoiac distortion.

The effective linking together of the conscious and the unconscious, which, in this case, means the overcoming of the schizophrenic barrier, is made possible only under the condition of necessity. For the sake of the repressed, one is forced to undertake the dangerous journey into the underworld.

Repression is expressed in the drawing in three ways: (*a*) in the idea of an institution where people are confined, (*b*) in the layer of rock which lies on top of the asylum and cuts it off from the world above, and (*c*) in the distortion of the supporting arm of the lunatic. Distortion of this kind necessarily implies a fault of vision, not actual, but psychological. Distortion of another kind is to be seen in the inflated battleship.

It is interesting to compare these two manifestations of the psychotic effect, for much can be gleaned from symptomatic improvisations. The inflation of the battleship was already present in the dream, where we observed a threefold kind of distortion—namely, of size, construction, and behaviour. The battleship riding on the sea is the natural symbol for an impregnable, collectively sanctioned, conscious attitude. But the dream says that this battleship is by no means secure; it is a mere pretentious copy of the father, who himself steered an erratic course. As a construction, it is neither reliable nor genuine.

Here, then, is a blind spot in the patient's psychology which would make it impossible for him to see himself as he is. But unconscious identification has another well-known characteristic—namely, that one constantly sees one's own blind spots in the person with whom one is identified. We observe, for instance, the inflated battleship intimately enfolded by the sun *with its three sunspots*: in other words, the defects to which the subject is blind in himself are all too visible in the father. The distortion of the battleship is therefore traceable to the identification with the father, which is an effect coming, as it were, from above; whereas the distorted arm of the lunatic is concerned with the peculiar influence emanating from the psychotic complex: it is therefore represented as coming from below.

There is also a marked contrast in the style of the distortion in the two figures. In the former case the ship is magnified, but its shape is still preserved; while in the latter there is both magnification and pathological alienation. So much so that if the patient had not told me himself that this was the hand and arm of the lunatic, I would not have guessed it. The former might be termed passive distortion, and is invariably found in the drawings of children, while the latter is an active expression of the pathological condition.

If we regard the archaic tripod contrivance (with its end-organ in consciousness) as representing the dreaming function, we see how *pathologically* repressed contents in the unconscious must necessarily produce distortion of the dream-imagery.

I have to underline the word pathologically, because an important distinction must be drawn between repression and pathological repression. The state of identification with the father, for instance, is, so far as it is unconscious, repressed. But this condition is a normal constituent of the early phases of life. It becomes pathological, like adolescent homosexuality, only when it develops into a permanent mode of adaptation. It is a different matter with contents that are pathologically repressed. Such contents are repressed in much the same way, and for much the same reason, as mental and moral defectives, criminals and the insane are segregated by civilized societies: in other words, they are potential disturbers of the peace. We shall presently discover the specific content which has been subjected to pathological repression.

* * * * *

III

So much for the lower half of the drawing. In the upper half we have already remarked that the right half of the picture is ruled by the mother- and the left by the father-principle; but another feature of this original pair of opposites is alluded to in the picture. I refer to the fact that the right half is also associated with the inner, individual life of the subject; while the left is clearly identified with the outer, collective aspect. These opposing aspects are represented, dynamically, by the two arrow-lines, which can be regarded as lines of force. The factors controlled by the descending line on the right have, in general, an individual bearing. It is as though the energy descending this path came from the dragon-source on the heights of Fujiyama. This line would carry the austerity, the chastity, the discipline, the intensification and expansion of individuated consciousness, and all these attributes of individuality are contained in the symbol of the sacred mountain. It signifies the singleness of mind and purpose demanded by a genuine individual attempt.

The ascending line on the left, on the other hand, controls the gay resort, the door of the asylum, and the inflated battleship. On this single line, therefore, are threaded the regressive features of the patient's wrong attitude, along with the symbol of orgiastic, collective dissipation. Unless we choose to disregard this concatenation, we must assume that we have to do here with opposing attitudes, which are emotionally derived from the mother and the father respectively. The patient's mother was, in fact, naturally psychological, and fostered the most sensitive qualities in her son's nature; whereas the father, so far as I am able to gather, was unusually opaque to psychological happenings.

We perceive the relevance of these background associations when we consider that the patient's central problem is stated in mid-field under the sign of the inflated battleship and the whirlpool, towards which problem two attitudes are clearly possible—namely, the attitude of individual responsibility and self-discipline, sponsored, as it were, by the mother; or the attitude of opaque refusal with its indispensable accompaniment of masculine heroics and collective display. Only in so far as the father's psychology was too exclusively masculine, repressing the feminine principle, could we identify the latter attitude with the father.

The reader will recall similar opposing attitudes to the unconscious which developed into an acute spiritual conflict in the high-tide of Greek culture. This duality in the Greek soul was personified in the figures of Aphrodite Ourania and Aphrodite Pandemos. In Plato's *Symposium*, Aphrodite Ourania is referred to as " the motherless daughter of Heaven (Ouranos)." She symbolized the heavenly light, the celestial passion of the single mind. Aphrodite Pandemos was the patroness of prostitutes (*Venus meretrix*) and symbolized the orgiastic frenzy of collective transports. The cleavage in the Greek soul denoted by these two aspects of Aphrodite was also expressed in the Apollonian-Dionysian antithesis, where again the reflective, individual, introverted unity of mind was opposed by the frenzied, extraverted, collective dissolution of consciousness which regularly accompanied the rites of Dionysos. It was no mere social cleavage between the aristocratic and the plebeian levels of Greek society. The Apollonian-Dionysian antithesis expressed the active conflict between the primordial and the civilized in the Greek soul, out of which dangerous tension the amazing creative energy of Grecian culture was generated.

Nietzsche writes, for instance, in his *Birth of Tragedy* (p. 22):

" From their two art-deities, Apollo and Dionysos, we derive our knowledge that an *immense opposition* existed in the Grecian world, both as to origin and aim, between the art of the shaper, the Apollonian, and the Dionysian non-plastic art of music. These two so different tendencies run side by side, for the most part in open conflict with each other, ever mutually rousing the other to new and mightier births in which to perpetuate the warring antagonism that is only seemingly bridged by their common term ' art '; until, finally, by a metaphysical miracle of the Hellenic 'will,' they appear *paired one with the other*, and in this mating the equally Dionysian and Apollonian creation of Attic tragedy is at last brought to birth."

But the schizoïd analogy does not end here; for the one thing which the cities of Greece could never achieve was a coherent national unity. Even though extinction threatened, they could not combine in face of the common enemy.

In these contrasting attitudes, personal and impersonal associations are thus interwoven. In this respect, as well as in its style and technical level, the drawing is like the product of a child-mind. In the child-psyche, where as yet no persona, no cultivated, initiated personality has appeared to draw energy away from the primordial state, we can see personal and impersonal elements, real and fantastic, conscious and unconscious, all inextricably blended together. There is, indeed, a remarkable feeling of immaturity about this patient's psychology, which gives one the impression that a considerable part of his psychology has not yet been born—*i.e.*, become detached from the parents.[1]

Psychological immaturity is also expressed in the fact that the parental symbols play such a massive rôle in this first drawing. Deriving from the same source, we see the problem of the opposites, which is not only the main theme of the drawing, but is also the fundamental philosophical problem, stated in a fashion so auto-erotic and childish that the ideas have to be laboriously unfolded from their wrappings before they can even be recognized.

If the problem contained in this drawing had ever been adequately recognized in consciousness, it would have needed no painstaking elaboration to make its meaning and purpose clear. Things in the embryonic or seed stage have to be incubated, developed, helped into life. From this point of view the analyst is a kind of psychical midwife. For this reason, perhaps, women analysts are, on the whole, more successful than men in treating cases of pathological immaturity.

[1] Compare Jung's observation, cited in Chap. I. (p. 42): "I seriously consider the possibility of a so-called *développement arrêté*, where a more than normal amount of primitive psychology remains intact and does not become adapted to modern conditions."

The therapeutic value of uncovering the latent significance in dream or drawing rests very largely upon whether the subject recognizes this potential as something that could become real. Should he do so, a desire is awakened which often becomes the master-motive of his life, leading him ever further towards the goal of completeness, which is the self.

IV

To return to the drawing, it is now possible to condense the various elements of the drawing into a coherent statement. The morbid, threatening tendencies are all found in the left half of the picture. This represents the sinister[1] aspect of the patient's psychology, symbolized, as we shall presently observe, by the inverted laminal field; whereas the curative, benign influences appear on the right. The left side is dominated by the father-principle, represented by the darkened sun, and is undermined by the inverted dissociated sexuality. The key to the compulsive system (lunatic asylum) is also to be found on this side. Thus key, phallus, sun, ship—all symbols of the effective, masculine, logos-principle—are here grouped together under a distinctly pathological constellation. Furthermore, the darkening of the sun implies that the creative conscious principle is at least temporarily eclipsed; while below there is a corresponding demonstration of the disturbing power of the autonomous complex.

On the right half of the picture there is the wife in the marriage-boat, identified with the idea of the anchor. Above is the sacred mountain, associated by the patient with the mother's breast. This benign constellation of symbols is associated with the open laminal field in the top right-hand corner. Below is the tripod mechanism, which bridges the gulf between the conscious and the unconscious, bringing in its train a number of legendary associations of a helpful kind; while in the lower corner the spiral symbol of evolution

1 The unfavourable connotations of the Latin word *sinister* (=left) probably derive from the fact that in divination by means of augurs the flight of birds, the direction of lightning, etc., going from left to right was considered a favourable sign; while the direction from right to left was unfavourable or sinister.

adds a positive signature to this whole constellation of curative influences.

Turning our attention to the abstract symbols seen at the top right- and bottom left-hand corners, they are found to consist of alternating bands of green and yellow, colours which the patient uses consistently throughout the series when painting figures denoting vital energy. We know, too, from the patient's association with the plates of a battery, that they are intended to be dynamic symbols. But the neighbourhood of these laminal fields is already charged with eloquent symbols of power. Fujiyama, on the one hand, and the lunatic asylum with its imprisoned inmates on the other, should surely suffice as symbols of opposite psychical poles. Why, then, does the subject feel the need of these dynamic abstractions?

This question raises many problems concerned with the far-seeing character of so-called unconscious activity, problems which, for the moment, I shall not attempt to discuss. It is simply a fact (which can be verified by everybody who studies series of schizophrenic drawings) that these patients tend to produce certain key drawings in which diagrammatic symbols play a prominent rôle, and that these are subsequently used with effect in the development of the symbolical drama. So far as one is able to tell, it would seem that these abstractions are never consciously devised.[1]

Abstract symbols have played the principal rôle in religious mythology, as, for instance, the crux ansata, the caduceus, the cross, the great monad, the swastika, etc. For the most part their original associative roots in human experience have long since vanished in the mists of prehistory, yet the timeless idea remains, like the megalithic pattern of prehistoric worship at Stonehenge. In his first drawing, then, the subject has unwittingly produced an archaic abstract symbol which becomes increasingly important as the myth develops, though apparently irrelevant and somewhat inconspicuous in its present setting.

[1] As will presently be demonstrated, abstract figures such as spirals, cones, circles, squares, etc., are often used in great profusion by the archaistic mood of schizophrenia.

In order to arrive at the symbolical content of a figure, we must be guided in the main by the nature of the associated images. The open or everted field above is associated with Fujiyama and, through the direction of its line of force, also with the lighthouse and tripod crane. The closed or inverted field is correspondingly connected with the lunatic asylum beneath the rock and, through the direction of its line of force, with the gay resort across the Mersey.

We have, then, a given shape, emitting a line of force in a given direction and assembling a certain constellation of associations. We can exclude conscious, traditional factors, since these would naturally be represented by relevant natural images. We know, from the fact that they recur throughout the series, that these symbols represent a basic element which plays a decisive part in the subsequent development. The one psychological factor which could conceivably tally with all these requirements is the *basic affective attitude*. The colour, the effectiveness, the whole character and complexion of our immediate lives is conditioned by the basic affective constellation or attitude. It is the undeniable determinant of our psychical condition; therefore the chief factor in successful education, government, leadership, politics, or religious training. In the days before the cultivation of wisdom was pushed on one side by the claims of "education," the careful developing and preserving of the right attitude, first in the rulers and through them in the ruled, was the common practical objective of philosophy, politics and religion.[1]

The cosmogonic egg of early Greek myth, which broke into two parts, the one Phobos, the other Eros, who then produced the world between them, contains the truest possible account of the dynamics of human psychology. A basic attitude that is governed by fear produces a mean, timorous, unreceptive, shut-in psychology; whereas an attitude that is under the ægis of Eros is generous, open, effective, confident and enterprising. The subject of the former is continually being impeded and brought to a standstill by subjective

[1] The *Yi King*, the Chinese *Book of Changes*, as also the *Tao-te-King* of Lao-tzü, are fundamentally concerned with the principles upon which a fundamental attitude could be formed according with the nature of Tao. The sages taught that wise government depended mainly upon the attitude of the ruler.

doubts and apprehensions. His attitude is pinned to his fear-loving ego. The subject of the latter can act and speak objectively, because he is under the command to reach the object and to be effective.

The term auto-erotic is fundamentally self-contradictory. It is possible to love oneself only under the especial condition figured in the Narcissus myth—namely, that one discovers the self as an object of profound interest, even of awe. Adolescents who make this discovery are not auto-erotic in the pathological sense at all.

In the psychological use of the word, " auto-erotic " denotes a state which is precisely the reverse of the condition symbolized in the myth—namely, that of complete inversion of the libido within the ego in a state of blind subjectivity. The auto-erotic person is quite incapable of seeing himself as a natural object to be understood, or, perhaps, even to be respected. If he could do so, he would not be auto-erotic—at least, not in the Freudian sense.

The essential character of Eros is the divine (*i.e.*, the creative) shaft which leaps across the guarded frontier of the subject in order to reach the object. The creative shaft is the impregnating phallus, the impressive, fertilizing image, the creative word, the idea which gets home, the divine leap by which the individual subject is able to transcend his own subjectivity and take an effective part in the work of creation. This is Eros, the god which bringeth twain together in the service of life.

God and dæmon are present only by associative implication in our drawing. If any of these ideas had been present in consciousness, the drawing would have been entirely different. None the less, Eros and Phobos, as we shall presently discover, are potentially existent in the symbols of the open and closed laminal fields.

The fate of this life is in the balance. One hypothesis is being weighed against its opposite. If the subject is able to achieve the open, creative attitude governed by Eros, it will be possible to construct a means by which the repressed and imprisoned other half of his nature can participate in conscious life. From the direction of the line of force, which issues from the everted dynamic field, we are led towards the means by which this can be safely accomplished. The method suggested is introversion into the unconscious *for the sake of* a work of salvage. The lighthouse, besides representing an auxiliary function of consciousness, suggests also a light that is set up just where navigation is dangerous—*i.e.*, an intuitive red light which warns the subject, thereby defending the integrity of consciousness from the whirlpool of panic.

The alternative fate is that ruled by Phobos, expressed most clearly as the fear of insanity. It is this fear which has broken away a part of the intuitive crane and diverted it to purely negative activity. Intuition motivated by fear will perceive, dwell upon and elaborate everything that could destroy, overwhelm or undermine peace of mind. Every negative or sinister possibility which the given situation might contain is magnified and extended, until the objective operation of the mind is effectually side-tracked, and panic runs loose.

Observe the essential point that the arm, which feeds this split-off complex, has itself become dissociated from its original functional connection—viz., the tripod crane. Herein is a valuable illustration of the way in which a dissociated complex not only breaks up the integrated suancy of the mind, but also goes over completely to the opposite principle. The dissociated complex, in other words, always shows the renegade-tendency. This is the operation of the Heraclitan law of *Enantiodromia*—namely, that things tend to go over into their opposites.

From the direction of this left-hand line of force we are again able to trace the effects of the alternative attitude. It leads us immediately to the extraverted Coney Island, where a thousand prodigal ways are offered of escaping from the secret fear, or, at all events, of making its voice temporarily inaudible.

The line of force of Eros passes through the region of the mother, who, we are told, was open to and interested in psychological realities. The Phobos line runs through the territory of the father, who, being psychologically obtuse, would suggest an escape from the problem in spring-heeled, extraverted shoes rather than take up the burden of the soul.

V

The abundance of psychological content in this drawing seems to belie its childish style and conception. Not infrequently, in response to the analytical stimulus, the extraordinary impetus and concentration of the psychic energy will produce at the beginning of an analysis naive constructions of this kind which turn out to be a psychological widow's cruse when we give them the requisite value and consideration. This drawing has the same inexhaustible nature as a dream, and, in respect to its psychological content, consciousness has had as little to do with the making of it.

On the strength of this drawing alone we should not be justified in assuming fear of insanity to be the effective cause of the schizophrenic condition in this case. Of itself, fear of insanity could cause nothing worse than a *mauvais quart d'heure*: it is, in fact, a relatively normal ingredient of conscious life at one time or another. The problem of schizophrenia, judging from my own experience and from the accounts of other observers, cannot be forced into so simple a frame. Primarily we have to deal with a state in which the subject is fascinated by the unconscious, very much as an animal may be fascinated by a snake. The fear of insanity is undoubtedly present, and may become very terrible at times, but this fear is informed by an abnormal attraction towards the archaic, irrational contents of the mind. Nearly every borderline schizophrenic indulges occasionally in moods of sheer irrationality. He is fascinated by his gibberings, his ravings, his explosive fits of violence. He watches himself doing these things, knowing all the time that he is playing with fire, or with a dæmon just as dangerous and implacable. Like Faust, he deliberately gives himself—for a spell—to a power which all men rightly fear. He too fears it, but as the rabbit fears the stoat, or as a woman fears the approach of the demon lover. He fears the invisible traitor in his own blood, which makes him yield to a fate that can eventually destroy him.

Again, therefore, we are led to the renegade-element in the soul as the essential explanatory principle. This principle is, I believe, irreducible: it is inherent in the living organism, even in the living cell, as the pathology of cancer testifies. Notwithstanding that many factors and conditions can release the retrograde movement in living organisms, we must none the less regard this tendency as an integral element in the vital process. It expresses the inescapable risk in the adventure of life: it is the backwash, the undertow.

There are, of course, many factors which can give the initial impetus to the renegade-tendency. In the normal case these are checked by a sense of danger: with the psychotic the renegade-movement tends to become the master tendency. What this individual psychotic factor is in itself cannot, I believe, be expressed in psychological terms. The condition we find and have to treat is one in which the subject both fears and is drawn towards the solitary, treacherous, renegade creature in himself: he fears because the psychotic will that impels him is an incalculable factor.

But fear alone could not produce the vortex that sucks everything down into the unconscious. We note a suggestion of the inverted desire, or attraction, in the phallic arm which causes the whirlpool. With these observations in mind, we cannot regard the dissociated, repressed system, which appears to generate the inverted or closed attitude, merely as a passive product of social repression; it is also, and quite definitely, a self-destroying, masochistic disease, as we shall later discover.

Again, why does schizophrenia always produce a victim psychology? Is this not also a characteristic symptom of the renegade? It would not be fair to call this victim rôle a bluff, but in my experience it never rings quite true. We know that the victim is a time-honoured disguise used by easy-money specialists, confidence tricksters and beachcombers all the world over. It is an instinctive means for disguising the cynical smile of the renegade. In my opinion the reason that schizophrenia is so peculiarly difficult to cure is that the renegade personality is eavesdropping at every session, and using the subtlest possible poison with the object of making everything real and valuable seem somehow despicable. The inverted will is cold-blooded, separatist, self-destroying: it will not allow life to be victorious.

In the treatment of alcoholics, delinquents and early schizophrenics, one can easily be deceived by the patient's obvious conscious wish to be cured. His wish is also true, but not to the point of willing the death of the hidden renegade who knows every avenue of escape, who knows how to get hold of the spirit or the drug, who keeps back just the very facts which would have a decisive bearing, who will never finally commit himself to anything. It is this *reservatio mentalis*, this so dearly cherished doubt, that decides the issue. To achieve a cure, the hidden enemy must some time be made to stand revealed to the light of day. The subject must be able to meet his own devil face to face, otherwise every attempt will be undermined. Unrecognized, the devil has the deciding voice; revealed, recognized and understood, it is possible to instruct him in the meaning and value of relativity.

But how could this come about without a fundamental transformation of attitude? It is this development with which this first series of drawings is principally concerned.

VI

Before we leave this drawing I should like to draw attention to one other important detail—namely, the darkened state of the sun. The patient assured me that the sun was not in a state of eclipse, even though he admitted the presence of the corona surrounding the sun's disc. His impression was that he was merely trying to look at the sun through a smoked glass, with the idea of observing or studying it. This subjective impression of the patient's is significant, since it contradicts what he has actually drawn. The corona is present, and only during an eclipse do people, as a rule, observe the sun through a smoked glass. The smoked glass, like the microscope in Dream I., assists and extends normal vision, in the sense that, without these aids, certain aspects of the objective universe would remain invisible. It is vital for the patient to obtain a certain psychological distance or separation from the father, and in order to do this he must equip his mind with a means of dimming the subjective effect of the father. Analytical scrutiny can supply him with the required means or attitude: this new objectivity is, in fact, indicated by the three sunspots which now appear on the face of the sun. For when we enquire into the nature of these solar disturbances, a very remarkable analogy comes to light. The work of the astronomer Hale has clarified our ideas on the nature of sunspots. To quote from an article in the *Encyclopædia Britannica*:

> "Hale pictures a vortex motion just below the photosphere in which the revolution of electrified particles produces a magnetic field. Photospheric matter is projected upwards along the axis of the vortex, becoming cool by sudden expansion, and so appearing darker than the rest of the photosphere."[1]

These views of a modern astronomer were unknown both to the patient and myself. We must either assume, therefore, a noteworthy example of unconscious analogical thinking, determining the subject's delineation of the complex mechanism as a vortex, or we must waive all attempt at explanation with a helpless appeal to coincidence. The fact remains that the dynamics of solar disturbances (which must here be identified as complexes in the father's psychology) has unwittingly been borrowed to explain the nature of the complex-disturbance which the subject divines in himself. In this act another aspect of the unconscious identification with the father is demonstrated.

The fact that the patient did not want to admit the eclipse implies also an unconscious wish to eclipse (*i.e.*, in the symbolic language of the child-psyche, to kill) the father: a wish that cannot appear, as such, in consciousness; hence the repression and the consequent contradiction. The presence of an unconscious wish to kill the father will usually be discovered in patients whose unconscious identification with the father has become pathological, thereby suppressing individuality. The condition of unconscious identification with the father normally provides the primary guarantee of the

[1] Article on "*The Sun*." Fourteenth edition of *Encyclopædia Britannica*.

ego in its need for social acceptance. The ego-ideal (Freud) is substantially derived from the fact that the infant psyche is a continuum of the parents' psychology, the state of psychic continuity being antecedent to the emergence of the ego-complex. Hence the identification with the father not only supplies the given mode, or style, whereby the problems of adaptation can be mastered, but also the momentum of prestige which the superior power and efficacy of the father-image generates. Thus a striking and effective personality tends to become the unconscious ruler of his son's psychology, frequently, as we know, unconsciously moulding the son's individuality into a facsimile of his own. In such cases the imitation of the father by the son often goes to the point of reproducing oddities of expression and the subtlest personal idiosyncrasies. When identification is carried to this length, however effective the father may be, the resulting occlusion of the son's native individuality is liable to produce symptoms of revolutionary resistance. Occasionally one comes across a case in which the tragic contradiction between a loyal and affectionate conscious attitude and a fiercely rebellious shadow results in a serious unconscious crime against the father.

The teleological value of the normal resistance against the father is to produce a certain psychological distance, whereby a vantage-point of detachment can be gained, whence the emerging individuality of the son can make its first independent flights. The sense of guilt and anxiety in respect to the father, so frequently met with during analysis, is not, in my view, solely to be explained by the presence of unconscious patricidal motives. Merging one's individuality with another's, therewith regaining a state of irresponsibility, is a crime against the self, and an actual crime in the present; whereas the unconscious rehearsal of a mythological crime against the father would become relevant only if one should happen to find oneself in the curious conditions of the primal horde.[1] In my experience the cases where resistance against the father reach criminal intensity are precisely those in which the influence of the father over the son has become

[1] In *Totem and Taboo*, Freud amazingly traces the evolution of the moral sense to supposed patricidal doings in Darwin's hypothetical primal horde.

excessive, often because of the absence of the counterbalancing feminine influence of the mother; whereas, if Freud's analogy of the primal horde were correct, the patricidal impulse would arise only in a situation where the son reacted to the father as to a sexual rival.

The wish to eclipse the father or grow beyond him does not excite a sense of guilt. A reasonable explanation of the sense of guilt rests upon an unconscious projection into the father-object of a subjective value, without which life is valueless. So long as this continues the son is chained to the father by his undeclared and undeveloped potentiality—a humiliating condition which could eventually kindle criminal impulses. The unconscious rehearsal of a mythological crime could have psychical relevance and reality only if it should represent a cogent analogy to the actual life-situation. If our psychological explanations do not make sense in our common-sense world, they are not valid explanations.

In the present case, the father being an exceptional personality, the positive transference had hitherto been the ruling factor in shaping the subject's character and style of life. But recent events in his life had, as we have seen, caused the patient to take stock of his position; it was, moreover, particularly on the side of feeling that his attitude, based on identification with the father, had proved inadequate. The constructive revolutionary spirit of the father had been concerned wholly with the political field. Either the problems of feeling were distasteful to him (due to a certain inferiority on the feeling side), or perhaps the passionate bent of his mind for large-scale projects rendered him intolerant of the *imponderabilia* of personal relationship.

This deficiency in the function of feeling was especially dangerous at the present juncture, because the patient was only too ready to jump away from the difficult problem of the inferior function and adopt the theory of infantile trauma, in the light of which the banishment of his early playmates after the closet incident, and other episodes of a like nature, were held to contain an adequate explanation of the whole psychotic inversion.

The death of the mother, however, when he was fourteen

and of the sister a few years later produced a real emotional trauma which had a permanent effect upon the patient's psychology. It was after this tragic period that he became identified with the heroic masculine principle—*i.e.*, the scientific intellect—and the feminine principle of feeling became correspondingly repressed.

Since the identification with the father in this case also involved identification with the masculine intellect, the acceptance of the opposite, feminine principle became the way of healing, or, at least, the essential prerequisite of becoming whole.

Drawing II

This drawing is divided rigidly into two halves. While the left side reveals the first signs of release, the right contains mechanical and automatic figures which express the emotional deprivation of consciousness.

The upper half of the left-hand portion contains a sectional view of the layer of rock, seen in Drawing I.: at one point a fluid substance like blood (libido) is forcing its way through. Below, and towards the middle line, is a green, elongated, marine creature, with which the patient associated a prevertebrate form, preserved as a fossil in the stratum of rock. Directly below this, and running an irregular, transverse course across the left half of the paper, there is a waving riband of blue, representing a running stream of water.

In the centre of the lower half (left) is the door of the lunatic asylum, which has been opened by means of the key (seen in the lock), apparently from the outside. In the open doorway are seen the faces of two lunatics, one disposed vertically, the other horizontally. The vertical face is expressive of utter imbecility, while the expression of the horizontal face is closed, cruel and demented. These two faces recur repeatedly throughout the drawings, and, for purposes of description, we can refer to them respectively as the open- and shut-faced lunatics. Connecting the outside of the open door to the rigid partition which bisects the drawing is an elongated four-sided cone, described by the patient as a shock-absorber. It is intended to function between the automatic world on the right and the emergent situation on the left. The patient also thought of this object as a kind of megaphone. Behind this there are two sprays of bell-shaped blue flowers; below, grass is springing. To the left of the door is a deep vessel (coloured yellow), in which a current of heat (red) is being diffused from a fire of sticks underneath the vessel. To the left of this is a grape-vine with purple bunches of grapes. Beneath the tree is grass.

The top half of the right-hand portion is occupied by two rigid, automatic figures (male and female) walking towards the left. The lower half is occupied by a large yellow limousine containing two mechanical figures (male at the wheel, female sitting behind). On the ground near the front of the car, and minute in proportion to the rest, there is a small human figure beside an animal, which resembles a miniature rhinoceros with a long tail. All are moving towards the left. The bonnet of the car seems to be about to strike the cone-shaped shock-absorber, which lies between the door of the asylum and the middle partition. Everything moves towards the left as though drawn to the events in the unconscious.[1]

* * * * *

The mechanical figures on the right represent a statement of the patient's feeling. So far as he can see or feel, he and everything else act upon one another like automata. He is like a man reading a book in a strange tongue; for everyone else the words mean something, but not for him. A psyche that is deprived of emotional energy cannot create a living world. When the psychic energy is drawn down into the unconscious, it can no longer animate the world with interest and meaning; accordingly, the subject feels himself marooned in a meaningless world of soulless automata. He also gets an impression of the overwhelming, ruthless power of mechanism, against which human feelings count as nothing. The tiny figures of man and archaic animal beneath the great yellow car are eloquent of this impression.[2] When individual

1 In general we can regard the direction to the right as going towards consciousness; the movement to the left, towards the unconscious.

2 The problem of archaism versus conscious control is thus stated in miniature.

value is absent, man is no more than a driven animal in the grip of vast collective mechanisms.

The first thing which catches our eye in this drawing is the arbitrary splitting of the picture into two halves. Not only is there a complete absence of continuity between the contents of the two sides, but the mutual incompatibility is so intense that the patient had to provide a shock-absorber in order to mitigate the impact of the one upon the other. In this rigid splitting of the field and dissociation of content we have a highly characteristic schizophrenic product. The sense of distance between the two sides is also expressed by the idea of the megaphone. Rigidity and aloofness are both characteristic of schizophrenic psychology.

Regarded as a statement of the actual subjective condition, the right half of the picture represents a state of mechanical unrelatedness. Mechanism expresses the notion of involuntary propulsion: it is the operation or application of energy in habitual, undeviating systems such as we can observe in the stereotyped instinctive patterns of insects. There is no available surplus of energy and, therefore, no will. If we conceive a case in which the whole available reserve of energy is drawn down into the unconscious, all that would remain in consciousness would be the amount invested in long-established habit-mechanisms. In a word, denuded consciousness is automatic. This drawing is, in fact, a graphic representation of the *sentiment d'automatisme* of Janet.

A patient of Jung's[1] expressed himself as follows: "I am unable to give an account of what I really do; everything is mechanical in me, and is done unconsciously: I am only a machine." The symptom of automatism is due to a sucking down of the energy-content of consciousness into the unconscious, due to an increased activity of the complex. The subject has demonstrated this condition by drawing the activated complex on the left half and the resulting automatism of consciousness on the right. Thus in the same drawing we find aptly characterized two classical features of schizophrenia.

In the left half of the picture we catch a glimpse of the first effects of the activated complex, due to the introversion

[1] Cited in his *Psychology of Dementia Præcox*, p. 84.

of the libido into the unconscious. The red stream of libido that breaks through the rocky foundation is moving freely, like a liquid, in all directions. The archaic organism is no longer a fossilized relict, embedded in stone, but alive and green and is already beginning to move. The blue stream of water courses freely across the paper. The two lunatics are in the act of escaping from the asylum. In the glass vessel currents of fiery heat are shown diffusing freely within it. The trees on the left and the flowers on the right represent spontaneous natural growth. Everything on this side of the picture is emergent and, therefore, in a highly sensitive condition. There is a dangerous incompatibility between the sensitive, emergent things on the left and the robot denizens of the right half. Schizophrenic doubt and suspicion preclude a sympathetic co-ordination between the two sides. Hence a kind of mediatory function between the conscious and the unconscious must be produced if the process developing in the unconscious is to be preserved from conscious interference. Both the megaphone and the shock-absorber are symbolical expressions of this need to mitigate the effects of dissociation. The megaphone also implies an improvised means of communicating with someone at a distance, as though one had a feeling of having to shout across a gulf.

In the first drawing the mediating function was represented by the atavistic tripod crane, which connected the underworld realm with consciousness. This insistence upon a new psychic structure that could function as a go-between, or shock-absorber, as well as a means of expression for the repressed elements, shows us with what readiness the unconscious avails itself of the opportunity offered by a genuine therapeutic attempt.

It could, I think, be argued with some justification that the two lunatics represent the sadistic and masochistic polarity of repressed feeling (more particularly when we bear in mind that the perverted literary fantasies which won for the Marquis de Sade his distinctive notoriety were the products of a protracted and unjust imprisonment), were it not for the fact that the feeling of the subject was against this interpretation.

For him, the cruel shut-faced lunatic represented desirousness. He could not give any separate association for the imbecile open type, but he felt that the two belonged together. We shall encounter somewhat similar complementary types in subsequent drawings: in particular, Drawing III. provides us with an opportunity for studying the embryology of these pathological twins.

At this point of emergence it is opportune to ask whether it is a safe procedure to allow lunatics to escape from the unconscious. With a latent psychosis the situation is, of course, never absolutely safe; and, however one may credit the integrity of his conscious function, a patient who is moved to release his lunatics at the very beginning of the analysis is not the first case one would choose. But in the present instance there was no choice: the fire was already alight before I had even seen the patient; and by the time the drawings had started it would have been quite impossible to do anything but go through with it. It is best in such situations simply to take whatever comes, as though it were the natural and expected event.

There is, however, another question arising at this point which does not settle itself. I refer to the question of the advisability of making public pathological drawings which properly belong to the consulting-room only. From one point of view a pathological drawing is an offence against good taste; indeed, I must freely admit that the only ground which could warrant the publication of some of these drawings is their value as scientific material. From another point of view, however, these drawings are a human document of profound interest. In a developing personality the growing point is the centre of intense formative activity. Therefore we can speak of continual embryology in the realm of the psyche. In a man who is loyal to this emergent point in his soul, and can record the emergent process in graphic, intelligible forms, we have surely found a psychological witness to whom especial privileges and protection should be granted.

With regard to a few of the drawings, one cannot but feel that the contents are not meant for the light. The patient's need for understanding seems almost to have forced embryonic processes into the open before they were ready. Such drawings necessarily give one an unpleasant feeling. They are none the less invaluable for the purpose of investigating the most vital of all problems—namely, the root-processes of individual destiny.

"The mother is accused, as if she were the cause of man flying to the mother in order to be cured of the wound which she had herself inflicted. This wound is the prohibition of incest. Man is thus cut off from the hopeful certainty of childhood and early youth, from all the unconscious, instinctive happenings which permit the child to live as an appendage of his parents, unconscious of himself. There must be contained in this many sensitive memories of the animal age, where there was not any 'thou shalt' and 'thou shalt not,' but all was just simple occurrence. Even yet, a deep animosity seems to live in a man because a brutal law has separated him from the instinctive yielding to his desires, and from the great beauty of the harmony of the animal nature. This separation manifested itself, among other things, in the incest prohibition and its correlates (laws of marriage, etc.); therefore pain and anger relate to the mother, as if she were responsible for the domestication of the sons of men. In order not to become conscious of his incest wish (his backward harking to the animal nature), the son throws all the burden of the guilt on the mother, from which arises the idea of the 'terrible mother.' The mother becomes for him a spectre of anxiety, a nightmare."

C. G. Jung: *Psychology of the Unconscious*, pp. 146-7.

CHAPTER V

THE INFANTILE PSYCHE

I

It is psychologically appropriate that the embryonic drawings we shall now discuss were made on the backs of others; they are unmistakably primordial, one might almost say larval, products of the mind. They represent the obverse, the dynamic or formative activity of the autonomous mental process, in contrast to the ideal nature of consciousness. Drawings IV. and V. have been included as examples of the abstracting explanatory tendency that is so common amongst schizoid intellectuals. It is possible in this series to observe a regular alternation between drawings in which the subject is pulled down to the affective level and those in which he resumes the abstracting intellectual attitude.

Drawing III. is to be found on the backs of I. and II. when these are placed side by side. Drawing IV. is on the back of VI.; while on the other side of V. there is a study of a peacock, a creature of peculiar significance in the development of the myth.

Drawing III

The pathological nature of this drawing is so patent that it requires no emphasis. Yet in spite of the fluid, incoherent nature of the contents, the pen-and-ink lines by which they are delineated are clear and definite, and there is a sureness of design which gives the drawing as a whole an organic completeness and rhythm. To describe the contents with precision would demand a descriptive terminology we do not as yet possess. Yet in its own fashion the drawing seems to mean something. One cannot just wave it aside as too pathological for human understanding.

First, then, let us take the contrasting colour-masses of the two sides. In the right half, green and red predominate;

in the left, blue and silver. In general, therefore, we can recognize passional and dynamic elements on the right, balanced by ideational and fantasy elements on the left.

Our justification for interpreting colours in this way rests partly on the patient's subjective valuations, and partly on general associations with natural facts. Throughout the drawings the patient uses alternating bands of green and yellow to denote processes of vital energy. Red is the colour of blood and fire—passional libido-symbols throughout the whole of mythology.[1] Blue is the colour of the heavens, the etheric, aerial realm; hence by virtue of this fact it has always been associated with the boundless realm of the idea.

Taking the right half by itself, the upper left- and bottom right-hand portions are occupied by two phallic fields of force somewhat resembling in disposition those seen in Drawing I. Both fields show a relationship to the symbol of repression, the laminal fields being inverted, not open in character. The upper one is coloured green throughout, instead of with alternating bands of green and yellow. The upper and lower phalli are both directed towards the middle line, their lines of force converging towards the breast-image (painted silver) on the left side of the middle line.

In the process of being ejaculated from the phalli are two germinal figures. The upper one has a kind of dwarfish head, with large ears and vizor slits on either side of the face, set upon a stunted, mobile body, not unlike a tadpole. The lower one has a bespectacled face, long hair and a large sensual mouth—a caricature of ineffectual æstheticism. The body, though germinal and undifferentiated, conveys the notion of futile gesticulation. Like the contrasted lunatic types, these germinal figures represent significant aspects of the patient's psychopathology, for he has reproduced them again with precision (except that the latter figure has been given blue hair) in Drawing IV.

The top right-hand quarter of the drawing is occupied by a constellation in which bone, blood and muscle elements are grouped into a kind of design contained within an organ that is associated by the patient with the stomach. The

[1] *Cf.* Jung's *Psychology of the Unconscious*.

pattern consists of a central bone, the humerus, with five muscle-groups attached to it in such a way that one points upwards, two laterally, somewhat resembling wings, and two downwards on the extreme left and right. Articulating with the lower end of the humerus are two objects resembling bags of blood. The patient is quite clear that these are the radius and ulnar that have become " blown up " with blood. Above in the right-hand corner, and distinct from the rest, is a circular field of red, in the middle of which is a bird painted in silver.

The bird seems to represent an intuition that something organic and whole could eventually emerge out of this assemblage of visceral and skeletal elements. For if the synthetic design described above be viewed with half-closed eyes, it will be found that the parts are so disposed as to resemble the bird in the medallion above.[1] The head of the humerus with its attached strip of muscle make up the head and beak, though this is turned in the opposite direction from that of the bird above. The two lateral extensions of muscle resemble the wings. The four lower elements at the distal end of the bone become the four tail-feathers of the bird, while the shaft of the bone is its body. We shall see in a subsequent drawing how the radius and ulnar, which have here undergone a subjective degeneration into visceral appendages, regain their osseous form and function in the anatomy of the dragon: a fact which suggests that this stomach-retort is also a vessel of transformation.[2]

The lower left-hand corner of the stomach-container is extended towards the left, as though pulled out by an attracting force. The tendency, therefore, of the germinal and somatic elements, so far described, is to be attracted vigorously in a converging stream towards the breast-image (left centre).

1 Neither the patient nor myself had observed this correspondence in our first examination of the drawing. In fact, until I undertook the work of detailed description, the inner cohesion of the various elements was invisible to me.

2 In this connection one is reminded of the vision of the Greek alchemist, Zosimos, who saw the dismembered limbs of people boiling within the cavity of the altar. Spielrein mentions a schizophrenic patient who also had a similar fantasy of people boiling in a vessel. (Spielrein: " *Ueber den psychologischen Inhalt eines Falles von Schizophrenie*," *Jahrbuch f. Psychoanalytische und Psychopathologische Forschungen*, Bd. iii., S. 329, Deutieke.)

The lower left-hand portion of the right half is occupied by a helmeted head with closed vizor. One ear is visible, and a red plume curves back from the vertex. The point of the vizor extends into the mouth of a face on the other side of the middle line. This face clearly belongs to the introverted, shut-in type of character: in other words, the character of intellectual detachment that has become dissociated from affectivity. It naturally belongs, therefore, to the constellation which contains the closed vizor, the myopic long-haired sperm, and the phallus with the inverted laminal field in the lower right-hand corner. The face itself consists of a large red elliptical eye, with a black pupil backed by blue rings (ideational elements), a nose that ends in a finger-tip with a black nail, a sensual full-lipped mouth, and a chin that is erected in the form of an infantile phallus with a red point. This face, then, comprises the visual, the tactile or digital, the oral and the auditory avenues of sensory experience. But these are conditioned by the blue-vizored head behind them, which suggests that all sensation is hindered, to some extent, by the intellectual resistance (the vizored head) which rules this complex.

It will be observed that this face is continuous, in its upward extension, with the large central breast-image. Situated above the breast, and also in the middle line, we find its correlate—namely, the inverted open face—personifying the parasitic, vampire aspect of the morbid fantasy-system.

This open face consists of a protuberant forehead, a round eye, an upturned nose, and a cruel, lascivious mouth, whose coarse lips are about to seize a secondary nipple, turned inwards and upwards from the breast below. The line of the forehead is continued backward in such a way that the green laminal area of the upper phallic field corresponds with the mass of the head. This configuration suggests that the upper movement of the inverted libido is determined by a single libidinous principle—namely, breast-pleasure—thus contrasting with its nether correlate, which comprises many libidinous tributaries, but is deprived of access to the breast.

It is important to consider what meaning to attach to the position of these two libidinous attitudes, opposed as they are as an upward and downward extension of the central breast-image. By the inward swing of the figures, we can hardly resist the impression that all the contents on the right half of the drawing are constellated by the breast-image, which I take to represent the archetype of emotional source expressed in the infantile-archaic idiom of libidinous satisfaction. Hence the division of the infantile psyche into the open- and shut-faced figures would represent the fundamental ambitendency of the libido resulting from the incest-taboo. It is obvious that the breast-symbol has an equivocal significance, for we find the same ambitendency expressed in the two nipples, the smaller supernumerary one being directed inward and upward, while the lower nipple is larger, everted and in its right position.

This ambivalency of the breast-image results in two antithetical emotional attitudes, derived from the original infantile craving for the mother. On the one hand we find a parasitic egotism that would pervert the emotional energies of the unconscious into unrestricted sensual indulgence (*vide* the retroverted supernumerary nipple). On the other we see an attitude of intellectual resistance (*vide* the closed vizor, the point of which is directed at the mouth from behind) marked by obvious signs of frustrated sensuality (*vide* the finger of taboo with its black finger-nail defending the mouth from access to the breast).

These contrasting attitudes are the result, as Jung has shown in his *Psychology of the Unconscious*, of the splitting of the primordial libido against itself, producing an inherent polarity. This splitting of the libido is shown in a naive diagram (Drawing V.), where the division of the libido against itself appears as a splitting of the phallus.[1] Here the breast-image appears as an impending cloud over the centre of the picture, not unlike the cloud above the battleship in the first drawing, where we remarked that the sun-ray was split into two as it passed through the cloud. Directly below the breast-image, and in the middle line, is the split phallus.

1 When the patient made these drawings he had read none of Jung's works.

The base of the right half of the phallus curves outwards to become continuous with a woman's face of the introverted, shut-faced type, while the base of the left half extends in like manner into its extraverted, open-faced correlate. The sign of the shut-faced anima is here given as a helmet with blue vizor (closed) and blue plume. The correlative sign of the inverted open face is a flying bird in silver on a gold disc.

In view of our discovery just now that this bird on the medallion was an integration of the various somatic and visceral elements contained in the introverting stomach of Drawing III., we can assume that the bird symbolizes a definite intuition[1] that the dissociated elements of will and affect (represented [*a*] by the bone and muscles of the arm, and [*b*] by the visceral bags of blood) can become reintegrated into an effective whole through the process of introversion (symbolized by the process of digestion in the alchemical stomach-container).

An interesting transformation of the open-faced anima seems to have taken place in the interval between Drawings III. and V. This change must surely be connected with some anticipated purpose with which the bird-sign has endowed her. This intuition might easily hinge upon the fact that the only cure of an inverted, autonomous system is through purposive introversion. In Drawing III. the face is perverse, voracious and torpid; in V. it is naive, virginal and decidedly awake. Moreover, the bird (*i.e.*, the intuition of transformation) hovers just over her head, whereas in the other drawing it is remote. The connection between the characteristic ambivalency of the anima and the splitting of the primary libido will be elaborated in a fuller discussion of Drawing V. at the end of the chapter.

Returning again to Drawing III., we find these anima-signs (*i.e.*, plumed helmet and bird) gathering significance from associated libido-elements. The introverted sign of the flying bird appears first in the stomach-container, where the disc is blood-red, suggesting that this symbol is still, as it were, on the blood level—*i.e.*, not yet associated with consciousness. This inference is corroborated by the remoteness

[1] Intuition is usually symbolized by a bird or some other winged creature.

of the bird-symbol from the open-faced anima, to whom it subsequently belongs. The sign of the blue-vizored helmet, on the other hand, is immediately behind the shut-faced image, implying that the resistant, defensive attitude is kin to the intellectual, conscious principle, a conclusion that is borne out by the blue and silver colouring of the helmet. Throughout the drawings these colours are associated with the ideational elements or logos-principle. The red plume, however, declares that the intellectuality of the shut-faced attitude also contains a passional accompaniment.

Contrasting once again the upper open-faced with the lower shut-faced figure in the middle line of the drawing, we note that the upper figure is concerned with one single objective, one source of satisfaction, in respect to which it exhibits the single-minded possessiveness of a vampire. For the suckling, the possibility of satisfaction is restricted to a single source, and the corresponding libido-attitude is one of exclusive possession. The nature of this infantile bias is to insist upon the absolute right to the absolute enjoyment of the given source of libido. In the course of time, however, this insistence collides with the relative nature of reality, which is indifferent to tender, infantile suppositions. Either the claim must be relinquished, or it must be so kept away from the touch of reality that no contradiction can be felt.

Here before us we observe a typical neurotic system in the process of formation. The basic neurotic attitude is one that claims to be nourished, placated, conciliated, but which rejects every demand of reciprocity. It is an attitude based upon a false premise in the logic of feeling. It has intake, but no outlet. In feeling relations, where reciprocity is essential, a person with such an attitude would be like a man trying to trade with false coins. An inferiority of this kind in the function of feeling is not so likely to inflict itself upon another man: it is rather in relationship with a woman that this mood would be constellated. In such a case, therefore, analysis by a woman is also to be recommended.

In contrast to this inverted, possessive attitude, the lower shut-faced figure is as completely debarred from the breast as its correlate is in possession of it. In place of the nipple there is only a shapeless lake of blue. We observed the fact that the oral, visual and tactile functions of sensation have been emphasized in this face. But we also note that the features of the face are developed in a distinctive fashion, the upper parts, connoting intellect and perceptive discrimination (eye, finger, nose), being developed at the expense of the lower, where an infantile phallus serves in place of the chin. The mouth is well formed and the expression of the face is alert, whereas in the upper parasitic face the features are undifferentiated, the eye is inert, the lower part of the face prevails over the upper, and the mouth is loose and shapeless. In the lower face the principle of opposition is affirmed, the finger and phallus (serving for nose and chin) being opposed one to the other, like finger and thumb, while in the upper face a dull, obsessional monotony prevails.

With all these considerations in mind we are led, step by step, to the conclusion that one portion of the infantile psyche was held fast or fascinated by the primordial spell of the mother. Split off from the psychic hierarchy as an infantile *idée fixe*, it resisted the decisive transition from the infantile to the cultural psyche. Accordingly, in common with every organism that resists the law of functional reciprocity, it went over into a retrogressive evolution.

If the clues have been correctly seized, we have in this picture a graphic self-portrait of the narcissisus complex described by Freud. Essentially it is an attitude of inert resistance to the claims of evolution and biological necessity. It is quite feasible to regard this as an incestuous complex; but in the last analysis incest is merely the psychological phenomenon of movement backwards to the source expressed in a mythological idiom. The process of regression or retrogressive evolution is found also among animals and plants. Inasmuch, therefore, as we are dealing with a process which is not confined to mankind, we need to use a terminology which is suitable to all the forms where the same phenomena have been observed.

Turning now to the resistant, inhibited attitude, whose access to the original libido-source is defended by the finger of taboo, we observed that its functional possibilities are manifold (not single like its repressive correlate), and that it is supported by the dynamic symbolism comprised by the phallus with the green and yellow laminal field. The symbol of the finger signifies direction and command. We shall see, in a later drawing of this series, how the finger of the ancestral god unites the ideas of command and taboo. In the present drawing the finger, with its black nail, is clearly barring the way to the alluring breast-image; furthermore, it points downward and away from the spell-binding object, thus opposing the direction of the infantile phallus, which points upwards at the desired goal.

It is interesting to note that the finger and phallus are opposing aspects of the same face. The finger of taboo is not externally imposed, as by a superior power, but is inherent in the resistant attitude. Taboo resists desire within the orbit of the same self-contained system. It is the play of opposing tendencies within the complex which gives to this system its positive potential, whereas the upper inverted system is purely parasitic. There is no polarity, no play of opposites, and no outlet. From another point of view, and carried to the pitch of obstinacy, this lower shut-faced figure would also express the self-inhibiting, self-thwarting aspect of the paranoid character. The signs of exaggerated resistance can also be regarded as compensatory to the parasitic self-indulgence of its correlate. A pathological condition in the psyche is never isolated. Any function which develops in compensation to a pathological deficiency must participate, to some extent, in the morbid character. None the less it is equally clear that this resistant attitude has acquired an objective value and potentiality which are absent in the parasitic system.

* * * * *

To recapitulate the characters of these opposing attitudes: the shut-faced figure is immediately associated with the knightly helmet bearing the blue vizor, a positive traditional symbol. It is also on the side of the normal everted nipple of the breast-image, and is backed up by the dynamic field of alternating green and yellow, ruled by the straight phallus.

The product of this whole complex is a sperm with exaggerated intellectual features which carry the suggestion of frustration.

The open-faced aspect, on the other hand, is associated with an inverted, secondary nipple, while the face is inert and horrible. The sign of the dove[1] (which later belongs to it) is here remote and unconnected. It is backed by a monotint laminal field and an incurving phallus, while the product of this obsessional complex is a dwarfish sperm whose face expresses blank, resistant stupidity. The red drops that issue from the incurving phallus of this system have no outlet. The idea of a hæmorrhagic loss might well be associated with onanism. The whole system is closed and self-contained, and the complex lacks any inherent opposition of elements from which energy could be generated. It corresponds very closely, therefore, to the characteristic monism of onanistic psychology.

In contrasting these two aspects of what may be called the mother-seeking libido, it has become manifest that the relative efficacy of the resistant, shut-faced attitude (expressed in the differentiated blue of the vizor and the potential logos-energy that is attracted to it from the left) resides in the fact that it is detached from the spell of the mother-craving, whereas the inferiority of the open-faced form is due to its parasitic clinging to the maternal breast. The former has been weaned from a purely subjective determination, and therefore possesses objective potency, while the latter remains, as it were, embedded in a static, unconditioned matrix.

II

Turning to the left side of the drawing, we are confronted in the centre of the page by a strange figure, whose helmeted head with elongated vizor, somewhat resembling the beak of a bird, carries a long bulbous plume painted with a muddy mixture of blue and silver. Issuing from an oval slit in the side of the neck is a rigid, unjointed, tubular projection, from

[1] The dove carrying the olive spray appears in a later unpublished drawing connected with this same anima-figure. The dove is the symbol of Venus and Astarte, and is also associated with the Noah myth. It bears an intimation, therefore, of a new attitude, hence also of a new world, which might result from a fruitful understanding with the anima.

the distal end of which a straggling plume of red spreads in the direction of the breast-image below. The body of the creature is an irregular ovoid, showing an outer layer of silver, in which round masses of green and yellow are bedded, and an inner field of yellow in which green masses are dotted about. A two-lobed organ, or vesicle, occupies the position of the heart. The creature appears to be standing on an enormously expanded foot or pedestal of blue, to which it is joined by a slender stalk. This mass of blue is the only form in the picture lacking a pen-and-ink outline: a fact which might indicate that the substance designated is in a fluid, transitional state.

To the left of the picture, in the lower half, there is a large projecting mass, having an upper and a lower promontory which tend to meet and enclose a portion of red substance that has somewhat the appearance of having been bitten off. The whole mass is suggestive of a toothless witch's mouth sucking a red fruit. This mass is painted with the same muddy mixture of blue and silver we observed in the plume mentioned above. It is situated immediately opposite the lower part of the breast-image with the everted nipple. The patient offered the suggestion that it might be a breast with an invaginated nipple, a transparent expression of inverted feeling. This is the only part of the drawing with which the patient made any definite associations. He was sure that the red piece, which seems to have been bitten off, was concerned with the sister who took her life.

An elliptical mass of blue is situated over the lower portion of the creature's body. It is prolonged upward to the left into a series of four rounded projections, which begin to articulate with three sharp spines (of different colours) that project into the upper left-hand corner.

There is a kind of grotesque pathos about this central plumed creature, lacking both arms and legs, and, with the exception of a single eye, any recognizable means of relating to any object whatsoever. What looks like a beak is really a closed particoloured vizor, within which the head is imprisoned; and what looks like a kind of arm is nothing but an aberrant, hermaphroditic attempt at genitalia—viz., a phallic tube protruding from a vulval orifice.[1] The disposition of green and yellow elements is loose and incoherent, as though in a condition of stasis, not activated by any organic need or purpose, and the white central organ is like an empty bladder instead of a living heart. The blue plume is long, heavy and bulbous, pendant in a windless air. From the tubular projection something issues forth, but it looks more like a leakage of blood than the activity of a living creature. An onanistic wastage of energy is again suggested, and, in so far as onanism is a frequent symptom of an unrelated psychology, its significance here must not be underestimated.

As an hypothesis, let us suppose, then, that this creature represents a function of the personality which has remained functionless and dissociated in the unconscious: something suspended in an unrelated timeless state, though still containing the elements of organic life.

Looking at the drawing from a little distance, it is hard to believe that the two masses of blue belong to the creature. They are more like alien elements that have been attracted or applied to the creature as an afterthought. Both in substance and consistency they are in striking contrast to the structure of the creature.[2] It is as though the pediculated mass below were being joined to the body in an adventitious way in order to give it a leg to stand upon. And in the same way the upward amœboid projection of blue, with its four articulating pseudopodia, might be regarded as an attempt to create four functions of relatedness, wherewith this isolated suspended organism might eventually function in a real world. For the three pointed spines, which project into the picture in such a way as to dovetail with these embryonic members, have definitely the character of sharp reality. Let it also be observed that the colours of these spines coincide with the colours of the beak-like vizor, as though both belong to the same order. We might conclude from these hints that

[1] Hermaphroditism is an invariable theme in fantasies at the infantile-archaic level. There is also a suggestion of it in the infantile phallus of the resistant anima face.

[2] I have a note to the effect that the patient painted these in after the rest of the drawing had been completed.

the static, suspended ghost is eventually intended to function in reality.

On either side of the lower part of the creature, in balancing opposing curves, we find two powerful libido-symbols. On the right is the maternal breast-image, with the nipple directed towards the point where the blue pedicle joins the body of the creature. On the left, and immediately opposite, we find the " invaginated " libido that was cut off and left submerged in the unconscious through the tragic death of the sister.

When speaking of this relationship to the patient, I was struck by the apparent indifference with which he spoke of it. I knew from things he had said to me that between brother and sister there was an intimate understanding, and that after his mother's death she had been almost the sole recipient of his feeling. Yet no particular affection was expressed. What is absent in the conscious picture we may expect to find in the unconscious. Perhaps, then, in this vizored ghost we may find the function that was lost.

The dissociation of feeling in this case is the result of a fateful concatenation of inner and outer circumstances. On the one hand we have observed the infantile attitude of possession and the compensatory intellectual attitude of resistance to the affect-producing object. This tendency to compensate emotional deficiency by an overemphasis upon literary and intellectual accomplishment was, I believe, the style of the patient's early milieu.[1] Especially was it the case with his father, with whom he was identified. Some effect of the father's emotional negativism seems to have descended like a blight upon the home atmosphere. From many things the patient told me I gathered that negative affects were more liable to be expressed than positive feelings. We have only to remember the sinister appearance of the black cat (in the memory-picture of the infantile scene in the country cottage) when the patient breaks a pot, and then fights with his sister on the floor. It will be remembered that the patient associated the cat with his father, and the effect of that scene is

1 An illuminating comment on this style is contained in the " intellectual " sperm with long hair and spectacles.

"horrible and ghastly." The black cat is a classical symbol of the anima on the sinister—*i.e.*, unfavourable—side. It is associated with witchcraft, magical practices and devil-lore. In this connection, therefore, the black cat expresses something uncanny and queer in the early home atmosphere: something which set the children's nerves "on edge."

But, apart from atmospheric influences, it is understandable that the effect of his mother's death at the most impressionable time of adolescence, followed by the violent death of his sister as he stood on the threshold of adult life, might be more than the patient's precariously poised psychology could sustain. Possibly a catastrophe was averted at that time by a reinforced repression of feeling. At certain crises it is conceivable that sanity may be preserved, for the time being at least, only by drastic control, whereby the affect-producing complex is shut away from disturbing contacts and sequestered like a dangerous animal.

To understand this emotional trauma, we need to realize that the developing anima-complex gathers its affective authority from the central familial image of mother or sister, so that the anima-function becomes shaped and moulded by the powerful impressions of infancy and childhood. Thus a determining model of feeling is created which underlies all subsequent intimacies. When these vital instinctual connections are abruptly sundered at an early age, it is as though the leader of a young pine-tree were snapped and broken. The effect of such a trauma is to force back the emerging stream of psychic energy into the unconscious, where it tends to undergo an atavistic involution. This is the path leading to the inert state of infantile narcissism witnessed in the present drawing. The state of the function of feeling suspended between the two most powerful images is as though the function had been drawn down into the ghost-world in the wake of the mother and sister, while the dead-white emptiness of the organ which should be the living heart also expresses the same derelict condition. The organ with an infinite capacity for feeling is deprived of all relatedness; but observe how its duplicated form corresponds with the two emotional streams which belonged to the mother and sister. Feeling is reduced to a ghost-bound existence suspended between the Scylla and Charybdis of incest-prohibited images.[1]

Another important aspect of the drawing is the reiterated inadequacy of the upper part of the creature—expressed in the muzzling of the face in the closed vizor, the heavy shapeless plume, and the tubular phallic arm projecting from the vulval slit in the neck—compared with the weighty mobilization of the blue substance in its lower portion. These new formations are all centring in the part of the creature that lies below the heart. They consist of a clear undifferentiated blue, in contrast to the muddy blue of the shapes in the lower left- and upper right-hand corners of this half of the drawing. I believe this distinction bears an important psychological connotation—a belief which the patient also shared—for these masses of clear blue occur in certain of the later drawings in a meaningful connection with the vital emergent symbols.

The problem is solved by referring once again to the open- and shut-faced symbols in the middle line. The unshapely, bulbous plume of blue and silver is situated just above the parasitic open-faced anima, while the pediculated mass of clear blue is prolonged to the right in immediate relation to the shut-faced, intellectualized figure below. This blue substance, though clear in colour, is undifferentiated and relatively unformed. It must represent something, therefore, that is still in a plastic, nascent state.

Let us assume, provisionally, that in his choice of colours the subject is determined, not by mere caprice, but by the intrinsic nature of the psychic processes that are gaining expression under his hand. It is noteworthy, for instance, that silver has been used for the feminine, maternal symbols. Whenever it has been used in other connections, it usually has the character of matrix—as, for instance, in the body of

1 In Greek fable, Scylla was a female monster with twelve arms and six necks, who inhabited a rock from which she took toll of sailors who approached too near. Charybdis was a whirlpool which caught those navigators who tried to steer their boat out of the reach of Scylla. Readers who are familiar with Jung's *Psychology of the Unconscious* will agree, I think, that in describing the patient's situation in these terms I am using no empty figure of speech, but the appropriate mythological analogy. Moreover, the analogy of the whirlpool has received specific sanction from our material.

the creature we have just been considering, in which globules of green and yellow are embedded in a silver ground.

There is much to be said in support of the idea that the feminine principle in a man's psychology exists under the lunar aspect, inasmuch as the more personal, inner side of his nature is chiefly constellated by unconscious, subjective, emotional factors, whereas his intellectual function has a relatively objective, impersonal orientation, and is symbolized by the sun. Jung has described the logos-function in general as the ability to name one's goal and to find or create the means to achieve it. In contrast to this, he describes the anima-function in a man's psychology as the inner attitude or function of psychic relatedness. There are abundant empirical grounds for this dual characterization of the psyche. On the basis of this duality we can distinguish the directive logos-principle as the natural ruler of a man's consciousness, while the anima represents the autonomous nature of the soul.[1]

The patient was, of course, wholly innocent of any conscious attempt to portray this dual characterization in his drawings; I doubt if he was even aware of this conception of Jung's at that time. But, in any case, it is quite inconceivable that a man who set out to produce a diagrammatic study of the ætiology of his own case could ever create a drawing of this nature.

One is frequently asked whether these are really unconscious drawings. It is doubtful whether any products of the waking state can be properly termed unconscious. Obviously every experience, even a dream, in so far as it can become an object of consciousness, is relatively conscious. No definite limits can be set between the conscious and the unconscious. What is unconscious under one condition becomes conscious under another. We know with complete certainty, for instance, that the meaning of this drawing was unconscious to the subject, both before and after he had drawn it. The significance of what he had done began to dawn upon him only after certain connections had been traced, from which a relatively coherent idea of the whole could be gained.

1 In woman's psychology the case is reversed, the autonomous elements bearing a masculine character, which Jung terms the *animus*.

Even today he is unable to view these drawings with complete objectivity.

Very rational people find it hard to believe that the psyche is capable of this long-sighted, purposive activity, without any direction from consciousness. In my view our whole conception of the mind would be clarified if we used the term 'autonomous psyche' instead of the 'unconscious.' Our psychological thinking is still sadly affected by ancestral blinkers: above all, we need to rid our minds of the ancient prejudice that only what is conscious is real, and that only what is consciously willed and directed has purpose. These drawings differ from dream-products chiefly in the fact that consciousness is a more or less active participator, although the enigmatic and archaic character of the representation proves that conscious discrimination is to a very large extent in abeyance. In the present instance we feel that consciousness is almost absent, or that the subject has reverted to a very elementary level for the purpose of getting down to the primordial roots of the malady. The embryonic character of the figures is a symptomatic statement that we are dealing here with a prepsychological stage. Growth activity at the embryonic level is particularly intense; forms, accordingly, are relatively fluid, and our scientific attempts, to hold these growth-processes in a firm conceptual frame, the more difficult.

As we studied the first drawing we gained the impression that it represented the ground-plan, so to speak, of the patient's psychology, and we discovered that the final issue rested upon a renewal or transformation of the basic attitude. The general problem was stated in these terms.

The logic of the second drawing was that the conscious attitude must necessarily be denuded of energy while the purposive activity of release was preparing in the unconscious. The drawing represented the emergence of irrational potentialities on the left half of the picture, and the automatism of the conscious attitude on the right.

In this third drawing, with sure instinct the patient dives back into his earliest infantile origins, in order to discover the germinal beginnings of the subjective difficulty which has maimed his adaptation to life.

The crippling is stated symptomatically in the top half of the painting, in the dissected upper arm with the two bags of blood, in the morbidity of the parasitic face, in the inverted phallic system, and in the onanistic tube with its drooping plume. As the surface aspect of a morbid process, the natural and right position for symptoms to appear is at the top of the picture. In their various ways the figures in the upper half of the drawing present the characteristic signs of inversion, not the purposeful introversion of a genuine inward aim, but the morbid inversion of an ingrowing toe-nail—*i.e.*, something turning in that is meant to grow out. Genuine introversion, on the other hand, is shown in the general mobilization of psychic energy towards the roots of the morbid attitude; also in the assembling of potential logos-energy for the work of salvage and cure.

We observed in Drawing I. a powerful attraction of the libido downwards into the unconscious. The motif of fascination was there represented as a whirlpool, caused by suction from below. In the present drawing this same motif of attraction, or fascination, is represented in the infantile roots of the personality. Mythologically, it is the descent into the underworld, which, at bottom, is the quest of the mother. In view of the abstract nature of this embryonic symbolism, it is difficult to think of the personal mother, but rather of Faust's descent to "the Mothers."

The maternal breast is the symbol of origin or source of the libido, the source of the first pleasure, the first nourishment, the original and indispensable fountain of life. Here, then, in the centre, is the inherited archetype of satisfaction, towards which everything is drawn, and we are forced to conclude that an essential condition of the schizoid state is the spell-binding power of this central image.

Although there may be no clear scientific proof that incest is biologically injurious, on psychological grounds (which are clearly visible in the present drawing) the incest taboo is absolutely indispensable to human development. If unrestricted access to the original source of pleasure had existed in the same world with unmitigated lust (the condition portrayed in the upper of the two faces), the human psyche, as we know it, could not have evolved. Indeed, if only sufficient vital energy had been available in the human system for the mere satisfaction of biological needs, there would have been no art, no religion, no science, no culture. We know, then, with complete certainty, that the original mother-craving libido must be deflected, or, rather, transformed to serve other aims, or the cultural psyche cannot develop.

What happened in the present case is now clear: the patient attempted a major cultural task (viz., his professional calling and his marriage) with an infantile psyche. The collapse came relatively early, so that the effects were by no means irreparable. Yet, although the collapse was inevitable sooner or later, the condition which made it so is not fully explained by the image of the infantile psyche fainting beneath an excessive cultural load. The world, after all, is full of grown-up children, earning adequate salaries and, apparently, making excellent husbands or wives.

Another factor must be taken into the reckoning, concerning which the diagnostic evidence is clear enough. On the one side we have the infantile psyche with its fascinated, mother-craving attitude. On the other there is the repression or suspension of feeling resulting from the emotional traumata mentioned above.

There is, naturally, an intimate connection between these two causal factors; it is reasonable to assume, therefore, that the traumatic aspect[1] would not be so insistent if the infantile psyche had not claimed neurotic exemption on traumatic grounds. It is equally reasonable to suppose that without these emotional shocks the patient would not have remained pathologically bound to the infantile level. Since both views can be maintained with equal plausibility, perhaps the better course is to leave the question undecided.

* * * * *

The old lady who presided over the railway activity in the second dream is yet another statement of the fascinating power of the mother-image in this patient's psychology. Everything seems to move towards or around this centre.

1 In using the term in this connection, I deliberately challenge the view that injuries are necessarily surgical in nature.

How, then, can the fascination be broken? Not, surely, by diminishing, but rather by extending the scope of the mother-idea. In other words, the attraction should not stop at the memory-image of the mother, but must descend deeper towards the symbol which is enthroned in the very centre of the psychic universe. We see this expanding value of the symbol in the meaning contained in *alma mater*, the mother Church, motherland, mother earth, mother nature. All these great rivers of power derive from the same instinctive source which the patient attempted to depict in the centre of his field. As the product of a narcissistic psychology it is, of course, infinitely remote from the sublime figure of the cultural archetype. We might even begin to evaluate the significance of the incest-taboo in the history of human development by contrasting this crude breast-image of the infantile psyche with such figures as Isis, Demeter, or Mary the Mother of Heaven.

With this thought in mind we can understand the relevance of the striking mobilization of the blue substance (described as logos-potential) in the immediate neighbourhood of the head which is identified with the incest-taboo. The cultural transformation of the libido is, in fact, being recapitulated before our eyes in elementary symbolism. All the libido of the infantile psyche is attracted to the mother. The portion which does not develop beyond the infantile claim upon the mother becomes onanistic and parasitic, while that part which is defended from perpetual access to the source reaches a condition in which a new power is generated—namely, the power of logos.[1] This power is called upon, or brought into effect, only when an essential life-task is encountered.

By implication, therefore, we come to the inexhaustible problem of the ambivalence of the mother, and with it the ambiguity of the anima. We can see the ambivalence clearly enough if we put the case as follows: to the craving of the infantile psyche, as seen in the right half of the present drawing, the mother must be either a source of pleasure and satisfaction or of frustration and denial. But to the purposive-

[1] It is not possible to translate logos into intellect, thought, or even reason, because it is essentially a dynamic concept, embracing intuition, thought, and will in effective unison.

ness of the cultural psyche, that has developed beyond the infantile claim, the mother is a symbol of command and desire.

The ambivalence is, therefore, a product of the basic instinctual attitude to the mother, and not a quality of the archetype. In other words, the archetype is as we see it. So long as there is mere craving, we are still victims of infantile illusion; but as soon as the craving is transformed into objective desire, we are under the command of the cultural images: we pass on into the man's house.[1]

In response to this graphic recapitulation of the cultural process there springs the idea that possibly the conscious threshold itself (which also protects the inexhaustible sources of life in the unconscious from the rapacious ego) may represent the structural homologue to the incest-taboo in the development of the psyche. A great deal could be said in favour of this view: for the unconscious, like the sea, is the mother of all things, and its eternal deeps must be protected from short-sighted conscious interference.

III

Following the general drift of our deductions, we are able to view the nascent shapes of blue, not as thoughts or ideas, but rather as primordial mind-stuff,[2] by means of which a new kind of attitude is being created. The clear blue of these masses contrasts with those other portions in which silver and blue are mixed together in a confused combination. The latter might represent a kind of fantasy-thinking in which the objective thought-process had been contaminated by a spurious anima influence. This hypothesis is supported by the fact that the clear blue elements are applied to the work in hand with obvious purpose—namely, to provide the vizored ghost of feeling with organs of relatedness, whereas the parts painted with the silver and blue mixture seem to share the fatal inertia of the *status quo*.

Once again, therefore, we find the same ambivalence as

[1] Where only initiated persons are allowed.

[2] The German word *Urgeist* would denote this element better than any English synonym.

in our study of the two faces—namely, a quantum of formative mind-stuff having an active, purposive orientation, and another portion which gets caught up in the inverted system of infantile regression. I reach this conclusion by the following deductions. The character of incestuous inversion appears in two places: (*a*) in the parasitic figure that sucks the inverted nipple, and (*b*) in the projecting mass, in the lower left-hand corner, which enfolds the invaginated nipple associated with the dead sister. It is precisely in the areas associated with these symbols that we find the muddy mixture of silver and blue. Unless, therefore, this is a meaningless coincidence—an hypothesis we are bound to exclude when dealing with psychic causation—we must regard this contaminated fantasy-thinking as part and parcel of the incest-fascination. In this connection we should again emphasize the distinction between *inversion of the libido* as a morbid sequestration of energy in a dissociated complex and *introversion of the libido* as a purposive concentration of energy into the unconscious for positive ends. The former has the character of a *circulus vitiosus*, whilst the latter is a tidal movement representing an inward direction and activity of the libido, without which mental integration or reorganization would be inconceivable. The cure of an inverted system can be achieved only through introversion.

The inverted systems are both identified with the idea of incest; yet in the infantile psyche mother-craving is, as we have seen, merely the larval stage of what is later purposeful desire. We can speak of inversion as a pathological condition when this larval, infantile stage becomes fixed, refusing to go over into the cultural. In psychopathology, " pathological " really means inappropriate. But in practice what we have to deal with is a state of inverted fixation of the vital energy which converts it into a viscous, amorphous, intractable, non-flowing substance. The blue that has got involved in these inverted systems might be regarded as logos-potential which has been seduced into a tragic stasis by the prevailing incestuous habit. The viscosity of inverted libido tends to produce a mood which is dull, stupid and obstinate: it favours paranoidal rigidity, perseveration, exclusiveness, unrelatedness, and a fatalistic apathy. Incestuous libido is, in truth, a niggardly, frozen stream, from which no generous impulse can ever come.

In this easily recognizable condition we have to deal not merely with a withdrawal of libido, or a lowering of the level of consciousness, but rather with a state which is inimical to the flowing nature of libido. The word signifies desire, attention, command, interest, purpose; but the mood I have described is congealed, viscous, muddy, fascinated and lifeless. It is as different from libido as ice from water: only those who have attempted to grapple seriously with the neurotic will know the relentless tenacity of this deadly influence. When once the retrogressive habit prevails, a symbol of commanding authority is needed to transform the libido, and to send it along new paths.

In the drawing we are now discussing the ugly, inert shapes of the inverted systems, the muddy, undifferentiated colouring, the cruel sucking mouth, the invaginated life-stuff that looks as if it were held in a toothless witch's maw, the secondary inverted nipple that seems to be responding to the parasitic claim of the empty, imbecile face—all these are symptomatic of a morbid tendency that denies the larger, corporate life of the whole, seeking to exist only in and for itself.

In contrast to this retrogressive organization, the clear blue shapes represent the potential object-libido in a state of active formation. Because it has been released from infantile craving, it is now available for objective adaptation and, more important still, for the work of rescue. When we stand back from this drawing and regard the general movement of the figures, it becomes evident that there is a mobilization of elements, culminating in the two blue formations, towards the invaginated island of red connected with the sister. This mobilization of energy at the very spot where the dissociated feeling is held is not unlike the concentration of blood-cells at the place of injury in the process of inflammation. It is a purposive and direct response of psychic elements to the vital need.

Before we leave this drawing there is one other aspect to be considered—namely, the symptoms of inferiority or ineffectual performance. The first of these appears within the stomach-container in the upper right-hand portion of the right half of the drawing. The symbolism is here concerned with the arm as the executive agent of the will. The humerus is shown intact with muscles attached to it on either side; but below, instead of the radius and ulna and the hand, there are two bags of blood. This conversion is significant of a deep sense of insufficiency. If a trauma were being represented, we should expect to see fractured bones or an amputation stump. But these two blood-sacks are more suggestive of viscera than an injured limb. It is as though the arm, the indispensable organ of dexterous, effective manipulation, had been seduced from its objective task and converted into a visceral appendage—*i.e.*, into a purely subjective factor. Obviously some process has been at work that has alienated the psyche from its native, objective function, giving it a false, subjective orientation, and even falsifying the type.

The second manifestation of inferiority is to be seen in the grotesque character of the two sperms issuing from the upper and lower phalli. These may be said to speak for themselves. But there is one significant point to which the patient called my attention—namely, that the tail-end of the lower germ has the same invaginated configuration, containing the same kind of split-off content as appeared in the mass on the left-hand margin associated with the sister. He also drew my attention to the vertical lines in the face of the upper germ. These slits, being associated with the closed vizor, identify this creature with the idea of something shut or concealed. The third item is to be found in the phallic arm, with its pendant plume of red, springing from the vulval slit in the side of the creature's neck. Here, again, an ineffectual transposition of organ and function has taken place. The red substance, which seems to flow out of the tube like a leakage, can be regarded as sexual libido that is wasting itself in the form of purposeless erotic fantasies. The short-circuiting of the libido through masturbation could easily be represented by such a figure. Moreover, the fact that the flow seems to be in the direction of the parasitic open-faced figure is alone sufficient to indicate the nature of this wastage. The upward displacement of sexual libido from its own proper sphere into the region of the head has been fully described by Freud. It is yet another symptom of repression: Freud has termed it the sexualization of thought.

The suggestion of hermaphroditism, or self-fertilization, contained in the vulval opening from which the phallic tube projects (this allusion was also noted by the patient) is highly characteristic of the infantile libido, a fact which is repeatedly confirmed in the ensuing material.

The items I have just mentioned as symptoms of ineffectual performance were abstracted by the patient and used in another drawing in a rather significant formation, though he was not able to offer any suggestions as to why he had made this selection. These symptoms are clearly expressive of an onanistic psychology, and the patient had undoubtedly at one time been borne down by the adolescent burden of guilt. The problem of masturbation, however, was no longer an actual difficulty. It is significant, therefore, that it should be this aspect of the material which figures so prominently in his fantasy. The matter is explained when we reflect that we are concerned with the psychology of the infantile psyche, and that the ruling motif of the infantile psyche is undoubtedly self-fertilization, of which masturbation is the self-evident expression.

To those who have long since left behind this whole realm of infantile mythology, such drawings may appear irrelevant. But for those who are aware of an ever-recurring nostalgia for the alternative hypothesis, study of life at this level may hold absorbing interest.

IV

Drawing IV

The content of this drawing consists of the four symbols of ineffectual performance alluded to in the last section. They are placed in the relation of diagonal polarity, the two effete sperms (in silver) forming one diagonal, the bags of blood (in red) and the phallic tube, with its scarlet flame or plume, the other. When certain specific pathological figures are abstracted from their native context in order to function in a new and dynamic relation, we may assume that they have been singled out on account of some peculiar subjective value. Removed from their skeletal articulation the two sacks could easily represent the scrotum, a suggestion that is reinforced by the presence of the two sperms and the rejuvenated phallic tube. It will be noted that the latter tapers slightly to the point, suggesting the notion of a hose-nozzle from which fluid emerges under pressure. The plume, too, is no longer pendent, but shoots out straight like a jet of flame.

Selection, implying the discriminative valuation of reason, has produced, apparently, a definite modification in the chosen contents. Libido has been given to the symbols, and they have responded accordingly. The narcissistic basis of Drawing III. offered no objective outlet for the *libido sexualis*. The dwarfed, misshapen sperms and the incurving phalli, bound to the central mother-image, were clearly symptomatic of the pathological subjectivity which holds the libido captive and inert. To release it is our therapeutic aim, but the libido cannot reach out beyond the frontier of the subject into the objective world until it has been given a substantial aim. The object of the *libido sexualis* of childhood is self-fertilization. It goes out, indeed, with curiosity and interest to gain the world, but rather to enrich the imaginative fantasy-world within than to function in the world without. Signs of onanistic monotony and fatigue were not wanting in the previous drawing. These signs informed us that the subject felt he had come to the end of his tether: in other words, the premises of the infantile psyche had been proved to be no longer valid for adult performance; a new objective attitude had to be created. The mere possibility of a change of attitude produces immediate effect, to judge by the astonishing *élan* exhibited by these key-symbols.

The change from the infantile to the cultural psyche involves a crucial transformation of the libido, not unlike the metamorphosis of the larva into the butterfly. The two are at least analogous to this extent, that the sole object of the caterpillar is to go out and eat its way through the world, and neither child nor larva has any function to perform calling it to make reciprocal objective relations. Finally, the histolysis of the pupal stage symbolizes the completeness and irrevocability of the transformation.

Although there are no indications of this biological analogy we find allusions to another significant process of transformation in the present drawing. The mediæval process of alchemy consisted in subjecting crude male and female elements, or the *prima materia*, to the incubating action of heat within a closed vessel. The object was the transmutation of base metal into gold, or of the crude and heavy into the noble and volatile. The essence by whose peculiar virtue the transmutation could be effected was the Elixir Vitæ or the Philosopher's Stone. The creation of this essence was the primary goal of alchemy, inasmuch as the further transformation of base metal into gold could be achieved only through its power.

In this drawing we observe the red phallic elements crossing the silver sperms (quicksilver), while the interaction of the two elements is contained within a controlled field (hermetically sealed vessel). In view of the allusion to quicksilver it is significant that in Indian alchemical tradition quicksilver (*rasa*) is conceived to be the seed of *Shiva*, the highest god. Therefore it is also identified with the drink of immortality. The reciprocal red substance is the cinnabar (red sulphide of mercury, sometimes called "dragon's blood") which is exuded from the rocks of the Himalayas and is therefore conceived as the *menstruum* of the goddess (Devi).[1] The Great Work of the mediæval alchemists was concerned with creating the royal metal gold, or the Philosopher's Stone, by the interaction of just these masculine and feminine elements under certain closed conditions.[2]

[1] I am indebted to my friend Professor Zimmer of Heidelberg for this information.

[2] The following passage from Silberer, *Problems of Mysticism and its Symbolism* (p. 116), explains this doctrine of the two principles:

"A wider theoretical conception, originating with the Arabs, is the doctrine of the two principles. . . . Ibn Sina taught that every metal consisted of mercury and sulphur. Naturally they do not refer to the ordinary quicksilver and ordinary sulphur. . . . Mercury is the feminine bearer of the metallic property and sulphur has the masculine nature of the combustible, and is the cause of the transmutation of metals in fire. The doctrine of the two principles leads to the theory that, for the production of gold, it was necessary to get from metals the purest possible sulphur and mercury, in order to produce

The ruling fantasy-motivation of the infantile psyche is self-fertilization, in which the interplay of masculine and feminine fantasy-symbols within a self-contained system is, as we have seen, the main dramatic theme. All the characteristic features of the infantile psyche are as clearly visible in the symbolism of alchemy as is the timeless, self-contained absoluteness of embryonic existence recognizable in the self-moving, unrelated totality of the world-soul in Plato's *Timæus*. We need only mention the bringing together of the *prima materia* (dung, earth, refuse, urine, fæces, etc.) into the closed vessel in which this matter is subjected to heat, the idea of self-fertilization and incubation, the production of the homunculus within a closed vessel (as a result of self-impregnation), not omitting the idea of magical transformation which pervades the whole process, to see that all these ideas, or their immediate homologues, belong also, and essentially, to the infantile psyche.

If we also point to the fact that our drawing contains allusion to the idea of intelligible becoming, or of reason persuading blind necessity, it must not be supposed that we thereby wish to bring the philosophy of Plato on a level with an infantile fantasy-system. None the less, every philosophy, however nobly conceived, must somewhere, or at some time, have had its germinal beginnings in the unconscious; and at the embryonic level the ideas of Plato must be very similar to those of the infant or the inspired lunatic.

What, then, are the facts to which these philosophical allusions refer? The contents of the primordial psyche do not appear as such in the phenomenal field. But we know by inference that these contents—namely, the primordial images or archetypes—are universal and unconditioned. Their embodiments, replicas, or personifications, when encountered in the fabric of experience, always possess, or are enfolded by, an aura of timeless reality. We can compare these images with the forms or archetypes of Plato's universe.

gold by the union of both. . . . In the accomplishment of the Great Work, there is, in the first place, the central idea of the interaction or the co-operation of two things that are generally called man and woman, red and white, sun and moon, sulphur and mercury. . . . The interaction of the two parts was figuratively called impregnation."

Turning to the East, we can recognize the inexhaustible reserves of power of the primordial unconscious in the changeless nature of Shakti, the dæmonic-divine personification of latent primordial energy. She is represented in the *Kundalini* Yoga as a serpent coiled three and a half times around the *lingam* symbolically conceived near the base of the spine. Awakened by the introverting stream, or *tapas*, the *prana* or emanation of the goddess rises through the *chakras*, and unites with Shiva; yet Shakti herself is changeless.

The essential problem of human consciousness hinges upon the basic condition that man has to adapt to two relatively incompatible psychical realities. The roots of his emotional life in the primordial or impersonal psyche, on the one hand, provide an access, so to say, to the eternal verities, while above, in the running stream of time, the constantly changing flux of events and conditions makes a perpetual demand for adaptation and improvisation. The successful integration of the primordial with the cultural involves the question to which of these realities one's allegiance is primarily given. That of the introverted mind is basically given to the eternal forms of the primordial, while the libido of the extravert tends to be won by the changing forms of the external world.[1] Perhaps the best example of the introverted cosmogony, based on the self-evident priority of the primordial psyche, is to be found in Plato's *Timæus*.

In his invaluable account of Plato's cosmology, Professor F. M. Cornford writes (p. 35):

> " Reason overruled Necessity by persuading her to guide the greatest part of the things that become towards what is best. . . . Necessity and Chaos are represented as factors in the visible world which confront the divine intelligence, like the given materials which the human craftsman must use as best he can, though their properties may not be wholly suitable to his purpose. . . . The Forms again the Demiurge does not create; they are not made or generated, but are eternally real and self-subsisting. The function

[1] Professor Cornford has drawn my attention to the perfect example of these opposing psychologies provided by Plato and Aristotle. In his youth Aristotle was dominated by the force of Plato's introverted mind, but in later years he came back to his own native extraverted genius with an eager scientific empiricism. Yet he seems never to have forgiven Plato for that earlier phase, in which his mind was, in a way, falsified from its native mode.

of the Demiurge is to contribute an element of order to Becoming, because an ordered world will be more ' like himself '—that is to say, better than a disorderly one. . . . The visible universe is a living creature, having soul (ψυχή) in body and reason (νοῦς) in soul. . . . Man (as are all the gods) is also composed of reason, soul and body; but his body will be dissolved back into the elements, and the two lower parts of his soul are also mortal. . . . The world itself, like the heavenly gods and man, is divine because it contains the divine element, reason. Reason, moreover, ' cannot be present in anything apart from soul ': if it is present in the body of the universe and in man's body, that body must be alive, endowed with soul, which is defined in the *Laws* and the *Phædrus* as ' the self-moving source of all motion.' "[1]

If for the moment we transcribe analytical intelligence for Plato's Reason, it is possible to see how Reason descended into primordial Chaos in Drawing III., and began to persuade Necessity to an orderly Becoming.

From the very fact that Plato chose the form of the myth in which to frame his cosmological ideas, it is self-evident that the Demiurge is an expression of primordial experience, a statement of the *a priori* reality and necessity of Reason in the universe. Cornford writes, for example:

" Plato chooses to describe the universe, not by taking it to pieces in an analysis, but by constructing it and making it grow under our eyes. Earlier cosmogonies had been of the evolutionary type, suggesting a birth and growth of the world, due to some spontaneous force of life in Nature, or, as in Atomism, to the blind and undesigned collision of lifeless atoms. Such a story was, to Plato, very far from being the truth. So he introduced, for the first time in Greek philosophy, the alternative scheme of creation by a divine artificer, according to which the world is like a work of art designed with a purpose."[2]

In this account the concept of accidental construction contests the field with that of the divine artificer: so long as we cannot allow relativity to mould our conception of reality we must, it seems, remain impaled upon these essentially uncompromising opposites. Their irreconcilable character, however, is once more an expression of the extravert-introvert anti-

1 F. M. Cornford: *Plato's Cosmology, The Timæus of Plato*, pp. 37-39.
2 *Loc. cit.*, p. 31.

thesis in human psychology, the mechanistic and atomistic universe resulting from the almost fanatical objectivity of the extraverted intellect; while the concept of the divine artificer emerges fully formed—like Pallas Athene from the head of Zeus—out of the primordial background of introverted reflection. Plato's cosmology, for all its curious detachment from the facts of common experience, is alive as ever, because, in its main structure, it is a metaphysical expression of the universal human unconscious.

In the present series of drawings we can observe a similar kind of intrinsic logic developing within the subject's individual myth. We shall also see how readily psychological creation takes on a cosmogonic character. In Drawing III. the slumbering inertia of the primordial state is the basic condition. This is the state of original chaos. In this bottom realm the self-moving soul begins to move. In particular, the presence of the differentiating blue substance demonstrates that, at least, a potentially objective purpose or reason is inherent in the soul.[1] We observe how reason descends into the realm of chaos, there singling out certain generative elements which seem to demand an intensive process of incubation. In the next picture we shall discover the archetypal demiurge, emerging first as an ancestral spirit, then taking on the impregnating cosmic function of logos, as a personification of sun and wind. From the spiritual, masculine principle the demiurge then goes over to the maternal feminine. It is profoundly interesting to watch how the horrific aspect of the deity synchronizes with the moment when he relinquishes his superior function and status as divine artificer and assumes the participating female aspect of becoming. Jahveh takes on the aspect of behemoth: whereupon divine reason no longer superimposes a reasonable plan from above, but becomes the inherent, germinating, evolutionary, sun-impregnated, primordial life-stuff.

This evolution of the conception of god appears as a logical mythic event that is set in motion by the descent of reason (in the psychological sense of Plato's cosmology) into un-

[1] Compare Plato's postulate, "Reason cannot be present in anything apart from soul."

conscious chaos. The peculiar psychological development seen in these drawings, which we are inclined to speak of as the analytical process (as though it were a mechanical response), is observable to some degree in every patient who is sufficiently alive spiritually to respond. This development is possible, or indeed conceivable, only when conscious reason attends to the products of the unconscious as though they were informed with intelligible meaning. It is this attitude of value, primarily on the part of the analyst and secondarily of the patient, which corresponds to " Reason descending into chaos in order to persuade Necessity." But when a meaning is discovered in the dream or fantasy-sequence which goes higher and deeper than conscious reason ever conceived, and when a purpose reveals itself which can completely submerge conscious will, it is understandable that this meaning and purpose should become personified by the psyche as the divine artificer. This mythological expression represents a psychological truth, not an intellectual explanation.

The reader will, I trust, forgive this anticipation of coming events. The central thread of superior purpose which informs these drawings, and which demands an unusual kind of understanding on our part, is not to be readily seized in scientific forceps. If I have been overbold in calling Plato to give evidence it is because, when he defined the soul as the " self-moving source of all motion," he became the great originator of dynamic psychology.

It might be assumed that this central thread of superior purpose is identical with the transformation of the libido from the infantile to the cultural objectives. The extent to which this transformation is effected is undoubtedly the most crucial factor in adolescent development. But although, as Hocart has shown,[1] every form of initiation, from the ordination of the priest and the coronation of the King down to the intricate initiatory rites of primitive communities, is based upon the same archetypal pattern, and although this pattern is concerned with directing libido from the personal and infantile into cultural forms, it is none the less a truism that

[1] A. M. Hocart: *Kingship*. Pp. 260, 8vo. 1927. Oxford University Press.

this social form of transformation is not the crucial individual event. In other words, collective initiation produces only that kind and degree of change which is demanded by adult social adaptation. Individual initiation, on the other hand, is a solitary experience which takes place " under the command of heaven." In such an experience it may be that an individual goal is revealed which demands the utmost intensity of purpose, calling for unreserved and lifelong devotion. When initiation has this character, the transformation of the libido from the infantile to the cultural objective is performed under the ægis of a religious idea, and the nature of the subsequent development is incomparably more valuable.

To return to our theme, how is the descent of Platonic reason made evident in our drawing? The figures selected from III. are immediately recognizable as symptomatic of infantile sexuality; only in the present drawing they have undergone a certain change. There are already indications of creative potency taking the place of mere desirousness. In other words, reason is persuading unreasoning necessity or blind mechanism to admit the value of creative achievement. The disposition of the selected figures on the field as opposing diagonals represents an attempt to raise them from the symptomatic level to that of reasonable purpose or value, where they at once assume the character of symbols. In placing them within this new field, the subject is following the same impulse which prompted the alchemists to enclose the *prima materia* in the incubating vessel: for in both cases the goal in view is the transformation of the cruder and worthless into the valuable.

This transformation is of peculiar significance in the schizoid psychology, because it also aims at reconciling the dangerous antithesis between the rational and the irrational. The forces of unreason in the schizophrenic's fate often appear unappeasable, like the Furies demanding the blood of Orestes. It will be recalled that, at the close of the *Eumenides*, Æschylus confronts these creatures of chaos with divine reason, in the person of Athena. Apollo, championing the cause of Orestes, faces the Furies with utter loathing. Neither side can yield, and human justice is powerless. Cornford describes the scene as follows:

> " The stage is left to the unappeased and furious spirits of vengeance, daughters of Night or of the Earth Mother, and, on the other side, Athena, the motherless child of the Father, Divine Reason, is face to face with blind Necessity.
>
> " In wild confusion and desperate anger, the Furies threaten to blast the soil of Athens and poison the very springs of life. Athena turns to them, and her first words are: ' Be persuaded by me.' She offers them a sanctuary and worship in a cave under the Hill of Justice, where they may be transformed into powers of fertility and blessing. At first they cannot listen, but go on crying out for justice and revenge. Athena patiently repeats her offer. She reminds them that she alone knows the keys of that chamber where the thunderbolt is stored; but ' there is no need of that.' Violence will not remedy a situation that violence has created. Suddenly the Furies are converted, when Athena addresses their leader as follows:
>
> " ' I will not weary of speaking good words. Never shall you say that you, *the elder goddess*, were cast out of this land by me, the younger, and by my mortal citizens, with dishonour.
>
> " ' No, if you have any reverence for unstained Persuasion, the appeasement, and soothing charm of my tongue—why, then, stay here.'
>
> " To this persuasion the daughters of Necessity yield at last. The play ends with the song in which they promise fertility to the soil and citizens of Athena's land, and with the cry of triumph: ' So Zeus and Destiny are reconciled.' "[1]

The persuasiveness of Athena's pleading rests primarily upon the fact that she explicitly gives the goddess of the unconscious priority. Reason is the younger sister, and a wise philosophy builds its foundations (as, for example, the Chinese) upon the back of the primordial tortoise. Reason is finally reconciled with the irrational daughters of Night, through the mediation of the anima in her divine aspect, and the way in which Athena handles the apparently irreconcilable antagonism is the way we must endeavour to follow in our treatment of the schizophrenic psychology. For the forces of unreason, as we saw in the patient's second dream,

[1] *Loc. cit.*, Epilogue, p. 363.

must be persuaded to fertile co-operation rather than coerced into blind stupor. The eloquent words with which Professor Cornford finishes his work express as well the need of the individual soul as the longings of humanity:

> " The unwritten *Hermocrates*, we conjectured, would have described the rebirth of civilized society and the institution of a State in which the ideal would condescend to compromise with the given facts of man's nature. So humanity might find peace at the last. And the way to peace, for Plato as for Æschylus, lies through reconcilement of the rational and the irrational, of Zeus and Fate, of Reason and Necessity, not by force but by persuasion."[1]

V

DRAWING V

This design resembles Drawing IV., in that it also contains a diagrammatic abstraction of certain salient elements of Drawing III., and therewith seems to invite a more general or mythological treatment of the problem. The invitation is the more agreeable for a certain refreshing change, which clothes the figures in a more human character. The maternal breast is symmetrically formed, and the supernumerary nipple has been discarded. It is, moreover, painted with a warm brown, like the earth, and occupies the dominant central position. Below it, and erect in the middle line, is a red phallus, divided longitudinally.

The influence of reason and reflection is evidenced in this design, as in the last, particularly in the change that has taken place in the material. In the former presentation, for example, the splitting was personified in the figures of two antithetical women's faces, as though the subject secretly blamed woman for the fact that his soul was divided. Through the work of abstraction a new insight into the matter seems to have been reached, for now the problem is stated as an inner division taking place at the very source of the vital stream. The primary sexual libido is split into the first pair of opposites through the catalysing power of the mother-symbol. Thus the problem of the two women is now declared to be the outward manifestation of an endopsychic polarity.

[1] *Loc. cit.*, p. 364.

By placing the antithetical women's faces on the periphery of the design, the patient seems to be saying that the contradiction in his emotional life, and hence the antithetical aspects of reality in general, are secondary effects of a central cause.

In order to understand the idea contained in this symbolism, we shall do well to regard the split phallus in a mythological sense as the subjective first cause.[1] In the symbol of the impending mother's breast we can again recognize the primordial state of unity, the contained paradisiac state that knows no conflict. This state is dormant, static and changeless: hence it implies a complete negation of reality as a changing, dynamic process.

The birth of desire out of the contained condition is also the moment of emergence from timeless stasis into dynamic opposition. It is symbolized as a birth from the mother on the one hand, and a process of internal division on the other. It is also the birth of the psyche, for the two streams of libido, dividing at the source, can be no other than the introverting stream, flowing towards the inner object, and the extraverting stream, seeking the world of outer objects. The former creates and nourishes the soul, while the latter gains the world. Without this division creation would be inconceivable. It is the equivalent, in the infantile psyche, of the sacrificing god in the cultural psyche.

The libido is the god who sacrifices the paradisiac state of primal unity in order to create the manifold universe. In a passage of the *Brihadâranyaka-Upanishad* in the Vedic scriptures, we read:

> " In truth, he (Atman)[2] was as large as a woman and a man when they embrace each other.[3] This, his own self, he divided into two parts, out of which husband and wife were formed. With her he copulated and from this humanity sprang. She, however, pondered: ' How can he unite with me after he has created me

[1] Compare Freud's statement, " Originally we have known only sexual objects " (*Zentralblatt für Psychoanalyse*, vol. ii., p. 171).

[2] Jung refers to Atman in his *Psychology of the Unconscious* as " the primal, omniscient being, the idea of whom, when translated into psychology, is comprehended in the conception of the libido."

[3] This image clearly arises from the idea of tumescence. The world is created out of desire.

out of himself? Now I shall hide.' Then she became a cow; he, however, became a bull and mated with her. From that sprang the horned cattle. Then she became a mare; but he became a stallion. She became a she-ass; he an ass, and mated with her. She became a goat; he a he-goat. She became a ewe; he a ram, and mated with her. Thus were created goats and sheep. Thus it happened that every creature that copulates and brings forth, even down to the ants, was created by him. Then he pondered: 'Truly I myself am Creation, for I have created the whole world!' Whereupon he rubbed his hands, holding them before his mouth, so that he brought forth fire out of his mouth, as though from the womb of the mother and from his hands."

We find a similar intuition of the First Cause dividing against itself, thus sacrificing the state of primal unity for the sake of creation, in the Prajapati myth of the Brahmanic tradition.

"In the beginning was Prajapati alone. He meditated: 'How can I propagate myself?' So he travailed and practised *tapas*.[1] Then he begat Agni (fire) out of his mouth.[2] Because he begat him out of his mouth, therefore is Agni the devourer. Prajapati reflected: 'As food-devourer have I created this Agni out of myself. But there existeth nothing else besides myself that he may devour.' For at that time the earth was still barren. Neither herbs nor trees were there, and this thought was heavy upon him. Then turned Agni upon him with raging maw, and thus spake unto him his own greatness: 'Sacrifice!' Then knew Prajapati: 'This, my own greatness speaketh unto me.' And he sacrificed himself. Whereupon he ascended, and burneth yonder (the sun). Whereupon he rose up and became this purifier (the wind). Because Prajapati sacrificed himself in this way, he propagated himself; and because death in the shape of Agni would have devoured him, he also saved himself from death."[3]

When we compare these two conceptions of the origin of the creative process we observe, in the first example, a splitting-off, from the original self-contained unity, of a relatively free-moving element having the feminine nature of

1 Solitary meditation, or creative introversion.

2 Compare the symbol of fire as the dynamic manifestation of logos.

3 I am indebted to Jung's researches into Oriental sources for these valuable references. The first is cited by him in *Psychology of the Unconscious*, p. 96; the second in *Psychological Types*, p. 251.

desire. The result of this release of a relatively unconditioned or renegade[1] factor is the diversity and differentiation of living forms. It is as though the soul were seduced away from its primal condition of unity by a resistant element that could no longer tolerate a static, timeless, unchanging condition. As soon as unity or completion is regained, it must speed away again on a new quest. Thus desire or interest creates innumerable forms to which consciousness is attracted. In this way a differentiated consciousness or a pluralistic universe is produced out of undifferentiated uniformity.

In the second example desire is conceived as the consuming flame of passion which, by its very nature, must devour that upon which it lights. Prajapati, as the demiurge, contains the primal phallic urgency. Therefore he must create something out of himself. But no sooner has creation torn him asunder than he recognizes the truth that desire inevitably means sacrifice. This, as we know, is the fundamental intuition of Indian religious thought, the source of the introverted attitude and practices of the East. To the Oriental mind, however, sacrifice does not mean extinction. The Western mind, with its extraverted orientation, experiences life in the manner of the first example, where the following of desire inevitably leads to an endless multiplication of objects and objective claims. To the introverted Eastern mind, on the contrary, the sacrifice of the ego-object relation of desire brings the experience of the self as a totality, in which the manifold fragmentary, illusory flames of desire are caught up in the inner sun, the symbol of source as well as goal.

In both examples we find the same conception as in the drawing of our patient—namely, the idea of a primal phallic urgency, dividing in and against itself. But the drawing also provides us with the clue as to the origin and nature of the primal state of unity against which resistance is generated. It is the condition of absolute unity with the mother within the womb. The primordial or infantile psyche, from which

1 In so far as cosmogonic myths are products of man's psychology, the element of desire in the soul is necessarily conceived as woman. Hence the anima is the personification of desire in the soul of a man.

the cultural is generated with such difficulty, finds, therefore, its most satisfying symbol in the universal maternal breast. As the state preceding desire and consciousness, it is the emotional *a priori* of every infantile longing.

Here, too, is the source of that thrice-blessed state of self-contained unity with which Plato's introverted vision was so enthralled. Concerning the creation of the world-soul by God we read in the *Timæus* :

> " Moreover, he rounded the outer surface to a perfect smoothness, for nothing was left outside it to be seen; no need of ears, for there was nothing to be heard; there was no air around it to call for respiration; nor again has it need of organs wherewith to take its nutriment into itself, or excrete it once more when drained of its juices. Nothing was given off from it, nothing entered it—there was nothing but itself: it was contrived by art to feed itself on its own waste, to act wholly on itself and be acted on by itself alone. . . . He saw no need to give it superfluous hands, which it would require neither for grasping nor for defence, nor yet feet or other support to stand on."[1]

For his conception of the living unity, which was to embrace in itself all living creatures, Plato had to rediscover the infantile or primordial psyche. Here in the embryonic state is the self-contained condition of objectless introversion, hence a condition uncontaminated by desire. There is, moreover, no subsequent phase of life which can compare with that of the growing embryo in the intense formative activity of the vital process.

In the description quoted above of the complete unrelatedness of the world-soul, we are reminded of the ghostly, archaic denizen of Drawing III., which possessed no means of relating to any object whatsoever. How, then, is it possible that this conception of the unborn state can represent the highest degree of divine blessedness, besides being the lay-figure of psychopathological inversion ? Jung deals with this question in his *Psychology of the Unconscious*, where, too, he elaborates his conception of the libido dividing against itself. He writes, for instance:

[1] *Timæus and Critias*, p. 30. Trans. by A. E. Taylor. (Methuen.)

> " It seems conceivable . . . that the conception of the soul in general is a derivation of the mother-imago—that is to say, a symbolic designation for the amount of libido remaining in the mother-imago."[1]

From this point of view the answer to our question begins to appear. The ghostly denizen of Drawing III. represents the retrogressive libido that resists being born into the world. This is the state of embryonic stasis, as though to remain in and with the mother-imago were the sole aim of life: a state of absolute unity, but without content. The self-contained unity of Plato's world-soul, on the contrary, represents the condition of complete totality: embracing all contents, it has need of nothing.

Beginning as a simple monad, individuation ends as a differentiated totality, and the whole journey of the soul between these two unities is fraught with the danger of retrogression, or mother-craving. It may well be that the incest-taboo itself is rooted in this most insidious peril of the soul. For when the libido is held fascinated, spellbound, fixed, invaginated, like the static ghost of Drawing III., there is no spontaneous initiative, no salmon-leap from one phase to the next, no creative departure, no individual attempt: in a word, no life.

The sacrifice of the infantile paradise is the first step on the way; it is also, in a sense, the final victory of consciousness. For the backward longing of the soul can never be wholly eradicated, inasmuch as every purposive return to the mother goddess provides the soul with further knowledge of the way and victuals for the journey. Essentially, this return to the mother is the return to the primordial psyche, where the potential of complete human capacity is to be found, though still in the impersonal balance of nature. In the infantile psyche the opposites still lie side by side. In spite of all prejudice to the contrary, the infantile state is essentially bisexual. It is here, on the infantile level, that we find that primitive hermaphroditism which, as Jung says, is " the foretoken or ' prestage ' of the being that is beyond the sexes, the Platonic primordial being."[2]

[1] Jung: *Psychology of the Unconscious*, p. 299.
[2] Quoted from a letter.

The more we ponder on this essential likeness between the alpha and the omega, the more are we persuaded that the primordial psyche is itself the archetype, the germinal pattern of completeness. The plan of the finished structure is already given in the original. Hence in the understanding and allegiance to our original nature lies our one hope of finding our proper goal.

If this is the truth, then Jung's conception of the derivation of the soul, quoted above, becomes charged with a certain ambiguity. If the soul is that amount of libido or life-potential remaining in the mother-image, then the static, unrelated, sightless ghost of Drawing III. is a picture of the soul. This would be hard even for a behaviourist to accept. The soul of a thing is so essentially concerned with its inherent purpose and meaning, that the mere presence of a latent potential of energy in the unconscious seems as neutral in point of interest as would be the figure of a Eurydice or an Andromeda without her rescuing hero.

The soul, in other words, is not something in and for itself; it invariably connotes a relation of value. We can confirm this by observing that the word " soulless " is commonly applied to just those things, people, or systems which are indifferent to, or ride roughshod over, every human value. It may be argued that when the soul is defined in terms of potential value this implies a relation in which that value exercises a certain influence. And yet a definition is only what it purports to be when it defines the essence of the thing designated. In order, therefore, to complete Jung's definition of the soul, we must add to the one quoted above his definition of the anima—*i.e.*, a function of relation with the collective unconscious. The potential life-value is located in the mother-imago, and the anima is the function of relation to this value. An organic conception of the soul must, according to my view, include both these factors.

In Drawing III. the invaginated life-stuff, identified with the sister, together with the immobilized, vizored ghost, would represent the factor of potential value; while the active formative blue elements, on the left side of the picture, might indicate the first activity of a relation of value—viz., the anima. If we combine these two factors in a single conception, we might begin to speak of the soul.

In the present drawing the subject seems to have attempted this combination, inasmuch as the phallus has the meaning of potential energy or life-value, and the two feminine faces begin to indicate the inner and outer functions of relationship motivated by the anima. If, then, the split phallus underneath the maternal breast corresponds with "that amount of libido remaining with the mother-image," we can assume that the two anima-faces represent alternative ways in which the subject can relate to, or is affected by, this libido-potential in the unconscious.

Already in Drawing III. we observed the embryology of these anima-faces, so that we are now able to identify the blonde *ingênue*, on the left, as the parasitic upper figure, while in the brunette animus-type on the right we recognize the lower face which was identified with the idea of taboo. This naive duality runs throughout the whole shadow-aspect of this patient's psychology: the same opposition of types appears, for instance, in the open- and shut-faced lunatics of Drawings II. and VIII.

Clinically, the two anima-types would appear as two alternating moods. But a mood, unsubstantiated by material, is too vague and nebulous a thing to handle in analysis. Such a drawing as this, therefore, makes a definite addition to the subject's means of self-knowledge, besides offering us certain hints about the original nature and function of the soul.

The alternating moods depicted in these two anima-faces might be observed clinically in the subject's behaviour towards his various psychological substitutes for the mother.[1] According to the mood on the left, the subject would react to the specific agent or source of pleasure as though it were his by natural right, giving the impression of a child reaching out with naive egotism towards the desired object. When conditioned by the mood on the right he would be suspicious, covered, dark, with a tendency to manifest aloof disinterestedness towards the very thing he secretly craves.

[1] The state of fascination or attraction is naively expressed in the drawing both in the tumescence and direction of the phallus.

When we try to express our moods in word-images, we find that a mood invariably derives from an unconscious emotional assumption. Habitual moods can be personified, therefore, by certain specific anima-figures, inasmuch as an assumption argues a certain point of view or standpoint.

The subjective assumption, personified by the blonde, open-faced *ingénue*, would be that of the self-evident validity of every libidinal claim: an assumption which necessarily argues a correspondingly acquiescent, uncritical attitude on the part of the object; hence the *ingénue*. Under the opposite assumption, personified by the dark animus-type with the nutcracker jaw, the whole aspect of pleasure or desire would seem nothing but a lure, a trick. " Fate will try to frustrate your every wish," she seems to say, " so don't wait for things to fall into your lap: go out and get what you want; be ruthless."

Just as the former assumption would correspond with the spoiled darling of the gods, to whom nothing is forbidden, the latter would represent the exiled son, to whom everything has been denied. Clearly the woman who could constellate the latter mood would be masterful, somewhat suspicious, even a bit 'hard-boiled,' not easily deflected from her plan by the natural expectations or feeling-claims of others; gifted, independent, drawn by the atmosphere of power, and allowing no affair of the heart to deflect her from her goal—in short, a highly competent woman of the world.

It is a clinical fact that these two mutually exclusive and contradictory assumptions are found growing luxuriantly side by side in the same psychology. Highly reasonable men are to be observed possessed first by the one mood, then by the other, without an inkling that their behaviour is inconsistent with reason. As a rule the danger of Cox meeting Box is avoided through the mechanism of projection, one anima-attitude becoming liquidated through marriage, the subject marrying a woman who corroborates it; while the alternative hypothesis eventually finds its physical confirmation in the corresponding anima-type. In the present instance the subject chose for his life-partner a woman who corresponded with the more bracing attitude of resistance. In consequence, the qualities of acquiescence and emotional pliancy became for him the most desirable feminine characteristics.

These anima-attitudes, or assumptions, behave in this autonomous, all-or-none fashion only so long as his own moods remain completely uncriticized by the subject. A critical awareness of this affective contradiction in one's basic attitude modifies the rôle which the anima has habitually played. Instead of the emotional pendulum swinging crazily between opposite poles (either the darling of the gods or the exiled victim), a less dramatic emotional posture is found to be feasible, and light and shade, yea and nay, are permitted to intermingle.

Basic affective attitudes are not easy to bring into the field of consciousness, because they originate in the mythological roots of the psyche. The method of active fantasy is peculiarly adapted for expressing these primordial origins of habitual moods.

Accepting this drawing as a naive statement of unconscious dynamics, we can learn the following important conclusions:

(1) A certain energy-potential, or life-value, remains fascinated by the mother-imago in the unconscious. We might call this force of attraction psychic gravity.

(2) This potential energy tends to divide against itself, half going with the pull of gravity, half against it.

(3) The endophallic split denotes that the resistance against the incestuous inertia is generated within, and not imparted from without. In other words, the incest taboo can be regarded as an endopsychic reaction against the force of psychic inertia. This is corroborated by the nose-finger of taboo in the lower face of Drawing III.

(4) The dualism of the anima-complex is derived from this inherent duality within the unconscious potential.

(5) The psychological concept of the soul must logically include two factors—namely: (*a*) the latent energy " remaining with the mother-imago," and (*b*) the function of relation to this energy-potential defined as the anima.

(6) The attempt to raise subliminal emotional factors into consciousness changes their character. This can be observed in the remarkable transformation of the two heads in the present drawing from their larval forms in Drawing III.

From the foregoing analysis a certain retrospective insight into the psychology of the two lunatics of Drawing II. becomes possible. We can, for example, infer that the closed-face lunatic will contain the shadow-qualities which are attendant upon the generation of resistance. Resistance to a major libidinal tendency means denial of pleasure. Denial of pleasure leads to a feeling of frustration. Frustration provokes resentment. Resentment breeds hatred. Hatred, when it becomes fixed and obsessional, means paranoia. In the rigid physical posture, the suspicious expression, the general resistant attitude of the paranoiac, we can read the sequence: resistance—frustration—resentment—hatred. The logical end-result of allowing this attitude to attain an absolute supremacy would therefore be paranoia, and we can safely regard the closed-face lunatic as the paranoiac hypothesis.

The shadow-effect of the opposite attitude is not far to seek. A psyche which opposes no resistance to the libido-flow, whereby no check is allowed to intervene between stimulus and response, desire and satisfaction, mental image and spoken word—this is the mind of an idiot. The logic which conditions the basic affective attitude is inescapable. To be totally lacking in psychic resistance spells idiocy; to be resistant and nothing else, paranoia.

CHAPTER VI

THE CULTURAL PSYCHE

I

We had to descend with reason into the lower realm of blind necessity, but when reason is felt to dwell within the soul it easily becomes personified as the divine artificer. Now we ascend once more into the upper air to find the divine artificer reshaping the world under the ægis of the rising sun.

Drawing VI

As in Drawing I., the masculine logos-principle, symbolized by the sun, rules the left half of the field; while the right half is governed by the feminine principle, under the symbol of the crescent moon. There are, however, important differences: the sun is not darkened, there are no sunspots, and it is no longer associated with the father, but with the maternal grandfather. It is, as its position implies, a new sun; its effectiveness is shown in its four aspects or functions, which are depicted as developing within the areas formed between the rays.

It will be remembered that the upper concentration of blue, in the left half of Drawing III., was developing four extensions, which were thought to represent embryonic reality-functions, by whose agency the suspended creature with the vizored head might eventually become adapted to life. In that drawing we could observe what was germinating at the embryonic level; here we are witnessing the hatching out. The deep blue of the primordial mind-stuff seemed adventitious, and somewhat incongruous, in the former drawing. Now it emerges into its own realm, anticipating the birth of effective consciousness.

The commanding figure on the right, with long hair and beard, whose outstretched arm ends in a magnified index-finger, is explained as the ancestral god, associated with the maternal grandfather. He points at a circular enclosure on the left margin of the picture, just below the horizon line. This circle encloses the dissociated system: it contains the cottage with the tin extension which was the scene of the patient's infantile fantasy[1] of himself fighting with his sister on the floor, and of the appearance of the black cat. It also contains the earth-closet where his interest in the little girl defæcating was abruptly guillotined by authority. The tree is there, from the branches of which he waved the sickle of defiance. The two figures beside the tree, one standing and one sitting on the ground, are himself and his sister. All these fantasy- and memory-contents were retrieved during the analysis of the dream in which the figure of his sister, standing by the car station, seemed to open a door into the overgrown garden of the past. The reader will recall how the patient fell into a trance-like condition at this point, and the suggestion was made that drawing might help to bring these far-away things to the surface.

On the left of the ancestral spirit is the figure of Cronus with his scythe, introducing the dimension of time as a functional element of the new sun.

The figure to the left of Cronus is intended to be the celestial bull. He also is in the emergent position, only the head and fore-quarter being visible, corresponding to the half-risen sun. This sun-bull symbolizes the release of primordial energy, which now comes into effectual operation in time. The end figure on the left is the hero wearing the Viking's horned helmet. He carries a sword in his left hand, and with the right index-finger he, too, points downward at the closed system immediately below him. On his breast-plate is figured a long-bodied creature, not unlike a crocodile. The patient associates the idea of the dragon with this animal. There is a tradition in the patient's family that they are descended from Norse invaders; hence he also thinks of this Viking hero as a very distant ancestor. This last figure personifies both the inspired will and the means with which

1 Although the abreaction of this scene had the character of memory to the patient, I prefer to regard it as fantasy, inasmuch as its actuality is doubtful, and its effect within the psychic economy is equivalent to an unconscious fantasy-system.

this newly risen consciousness can achieve its purpose. It is well to note that the sword, symbolizing effective deed, extends across the house of energy and penetrates the house of time.

The significance of the rising sun and the crescent moon should be noted, since these represent favourable aspects under which the enterprise is launched. In connection with these signs we have to remember that the moment of emergence of sun or moon has always aroused religious feeling in the human mind. When I was camping with Jung on the slopes of Mount Elgon, we observed the prostration of the natives at sunrise. They would breathe or spit on their hands and then, extending their palms towards the rising sun, would say *Athista* (Lord). This they did three times. In reply to questions they explained that only at the moment of rising was the sun *Athista.* When the sun was high in the heavens it was no longer *mungu* (god). The new moon at its first appearance was also *Athista.* In this primitive religious act God is not the physical object, sun or moon, but rather the experience of emergence, or the moment of rising—in other words, a psychological moment. God is the moment of emergent power or beauty, as in the worship of Aton.[1] The Elgonyi called the devil *Ayik.* They preferred not to speak of it. *Ayik* was that thing which caught one's face in a haunted cave at night, or the cold breath that came out of the bamboos, where the spirits lurk, and ran up one's spine. *Ayik* was the moment of panic, when the blood congeals and the spirit drops into the earth. The obvious analogy between these two conceptions of the Elgonyi and Horus and Set of the early Egyptians throws a clear and significant light on the nature of the primordial religious experience.

To the unsophisticated man the idea of the gods taking a hand in human affairs is an *a priori* factor of experience.

[1] Akhnaton's beautiful hymn to Aton begins:
"Thy dawning is beautiful in the horizon of heaven,
O living Aton, Beginning of life!
When Thou risest in the eastern horizon of heaven,
Thou fillest every land with Thy beauty."
(*Professor Breasted's translation.*)

In his *Teuton Mythology* Rydberg gives an interesting account of the early Teuton's conception of the divine elements in the human make-up. The basic elements of man mentioned in Völuspa are as follows:

(1) The earthly matter of which the body is formed.
(2) A formative, vegetative force.
(3 and 4) Loder's gifts.
(5) Honer's gifts.
(6) Odin's gifts.

Thus two-thirds of man's nature was divine, a third being earthly and mortal. This proportion corresponds accurately with the heroic constitution of Gilgamish, who, in the first lines of the epic, is stated to be two-thirds immortal and one-third mortal.

Völuspa's account of human origins is as follows:

> "The gods found Ask and Embla (the first man and woman) on the earth, with little power and without destiny. Spirit they had not; *odr* they had not, neither *la* nor *laeti*, nor the form of the gods. Odin gave them spirit, Honer gave *odr*, Loder gave *la* and the form of the gods."

La is the blood, while *laeti* united with *la* means the way in which a conscious being moves and acts. *Odr* has to do with inherited features and attributes. Besides *la*, Loder also gives *litr goda*, the form, or image, of the gods. In his heart, therefore, the youthful hero knew not only that his physical shape and being were constructed *in effigiem deorum*, but that every essential quality and attribute of his nature was directly related to a god. And these gifts of the gods were not merely something that was handed down from an antecedent golden age; they were vouchsafed to him now in the moment of his direst need. For the gods were conceived as taking a vital share in the destiny of the individual hero, supplying him with the magical spear or sword[1] when the heroic deed was required of him, or sending a wise counsellor and companion or an inspired animal to attend him at the critical juncture. The change from childhood to maturity,

[1] As, for instance, in Siegfried's discovery of the fragments of his father's sword.

or the crossing of the river of death, were also occasions for divine assistance.

Chaldean and early Hebrew mythology are especially rich in examples of divine intervention in crises of human affairs; sometimes helpful, though frequently catastrophic. The conflict between these benign and destructive influences is also a favourite theme in classical myths. Homer frequently attributes heroic valour and sagacious counsel to the direct inspiration of some divine being.

As a timeless and changeless Being, God is never manifest in time, for all manifest things are subject to change. A celestial power, by its very nature, is therefore inoperative in the temporal human sphere, unless the piety of saint or hero fits him to effect the will of Heaven.

The conditions by which the gods are themselves limited are thus clearly laid down in many classical myths. Ea Oannes, for instance, is not permitted to impart directly to Uta-Napishtim[1] Enlil's desperate plan for destroying mankind with a deluge. The most he is allowed to do is to speak of it to the walls of the reed-hut in which Uta-Napishtim is to sleep. The walls then pass on the information to the hero in the form of a dream.[2]

Another beautiful example of divine intervention is the sending of the angel to advise and accompany Tobias on his perilous mission; in this case also the angel is not permitted to divulge his divine nature.

In the psychology of conversion and in the records of mystical experience we find another aspect of divine intervention, clothed in the white and shining garment of revelation; often (as in the voice which speaks out of Heaven to Saul of Tarsus or to Hermas on the road to Cumæ) it is a direct and categorical injunction.

The hero, then, is able to make the impossible possible, because he has the inner assurance of divine or magical aid.

It is impossible to conceive the hero except in this direct relationship with deity. The hero's sword is the effective means by which the will of the god is brought about. As a

[1] The Chaldean Noah.
[2] *The Gilgamish Epos*, translation by Campbell Thompson.

rule, the sword has a divine pedigree, just as the hero-king is the offspring of the sun. Or again, like Nothung or Excalibur, the magical sword lies dormant in tree, rock, or lake, until the moment of emergence brings the chosen hero to light. No single fact is more widely attested in mythology than that a specific potential of energy or value lies dormant in the unconscious, waiting for the decisive but irrational moment of emergence.

Towards this moment everything tends, and a long phase of preparation precedes it. Yet at its emergence the event is always unexpected: it accords with no conscious plan. When the myths speak then of the gods taking counsel together, or planning an event on which the fate of the hero or of mankind depends, to what does this refer? This can be answered best by enquiring further into the relation between god and hero—in other words, between the unmanifest and the manifest factors in the emergent event.

The relation between god and hero is an intimate one, the hero being frequently the son of the god. The hero-king was conceived to be a child of the sun, his mother being impregnated by the sun in human shape. Sometimes the king-to-be ate a beam of the sun, or some grains or particles of the sun entered into him. The early migrations of civilizing mankind were largely motivated by the quest for gold, which, as the sun-metal, was identified with the mythological substance that endowed the hero-king with his divine nature.

The sun is the celestial power upon which all living things depend for the essential condition of life, the god whose daily course is fixed from all eternity. The sun is, indeed, the most reasonable god for man to worship. The King is also the sun, only within the human orbit.

Reason knows for a certainty that the King is not the sun, just as the African native knows that the snake which comes into his house is not really his grandfather. Yet, in spite of all reasonable contradiction, the psyche asserts these things to be true. An irrational truth cannot be dislodged by argument: it is something which no man has ever thought, yet which nevertheless the heart accepts. Rational people, for instance, whose thinking has long since freed them from any superstitious veneration for the King, may still dream of him in his mythological aspect, and behave in his presence as though he were a god. Their dreams and behaviour are still apparently unaffected by the rational point of view.

The surface of the mind, chameleon-like, assumes the complexion of its mental surroundings. The validity of a definite vogue or style appears self-evident to the temporal personality playing its rôle in the present scene. But when the restless surface sleeps, the timeless figures of the unconscious regain their eternal sway, and the piping notes of rational protest are submerged by the quiet sea.

The gods are the eternal archetypes, the primordial images of the general unconscious, the unmanifest, timeless potential of the human mind. The hero symbolizes the emergence, in time and space, of this latent reserve of power. The human being who serves as conduit to this power may know nothing of the deeper will that is speaking with his voice: he obeys like a medium. Sometimes, as in the case of Balaam, he is even made blind by the very power which uses him, and, through his blindness, is often destroyed.

In the figures of god and hero, therefore, we can recognize two psychical factors which have played the principal rôles in the great cultural mythologies—viz., the unmanifest potential and the manifest kinetic aspects of the emergent moment. But no sooner have we stated their connection in this way than we recognize a parallel relationship between the unmanifest and the manifest, the divine and the human aspects of God, in the great religions of the world. In the Mohammedan faith Allah the Eternal and Unmanifest is also identified with El Khidr (the Verdant One), who is the manifestation of Allah in the living moment, especially in the moment of crisis. In the Christian faith God can become manifest only in the person of his Human-Divine Son, though the Holy Ghost is conceived as the creative breath which reaches the Son from the Father, and which transcends the frontier between eternity and time, the divine and the human.

Similarly, Shakti can be aroused from her eternal slumber by the introverted direction of consciousness. Introversion creates, as it were, a timeless avenue by which consciousness is able to descend into the realm of the eternal images. The relatively greater maturity of the Eastern religious attitude becomes evident when we contrast the highly refined technique with which Oriental introversion gains access to the realm of the primordial images with the relatively childish attitude of the West, depending solely on faith. The object of *Kundalini*-Yoga, for example, is to arouse the goddess by introverted concentration, in order that her *prana* shall be released and, by penetrating the successive centres or *chakras*, eventually gain union with Shiva, the Lord of Light or consciousness. The activation of Shakti is accompanied by a deep hum like that of a swarm of bees. This ascending *prana* is the kinetic effect of the awakened goddess, but the goddess herself is eternally unmanifest and unchanging. The whole of this effect results from the introversion of consciousness into the unconscious, whereby a Jacob's ladder is created between time and eternity.

II

It has been assumed, with some plausibility, that the mythological figures of the old god and the young hero represent the setting and the rising sun. In the case of Horus and Ra, or Wotan and Siegfried, for example, it is evident that the drama of the old god being superseded by a youth or son is based upon a solar myth. But this easy cosmic explanation does not satisfy the deeper psychological content of the myth. The relation between the unmanifest and the manifest principles—for example, between the eternally potential condition of the one and the emergent, kinetic efficacy of the other; between the primordial and changeless and the temporal and mortal—what has all this to do with the aging sun in the west and the dawning sun in the east? It is surely more reasonable to assume that the emergent moment, in which the latent energy of the collective unconscious inspires the archetypal protagonist, is one which has struck the imagination of generations of men as an event analogous to the rising of the sun. *Athista*, the morning adoration of the Elgonyi, does not belong exclusively to the sun. The new moon also evokes the same obeisance, proving that the moment of emergence is the vital content.

The concatenation of emergent symbols in the present drawing is impressive, but unfortunately there is small hospitality in the modern world for the idea that the gods could take an effective hand in any crisis of human life. The primordial psyche still utters the eternal myth, but modern consciousness is no longer attuned to such truths. The patient was far more ready to explain his condition exclusively in sexual terms than to attend seriously to a hint emerging from the pre-Christian levels of the unconscious. Modern man is pitiful, not because he has lost the consolation of religious practice, but because he no longer feels any relationship to, or receives any virtue from, the gods. By explaining away those irrational events which our forefathers knew as divine intervention we have also lost touch with our ancestral inheritance.

The ancestors of the present subject had been for many generations yeomen farmers, cultivating their ground under the sun and moon. At this moment of emergence he is reminded of this sturdy inheritance, as though he should recognize that his most reliable qualities are derived from their piety.

These reflections are not inappropriate, since both sun and moon are depicted in this drawing at the moment of rising. On other grounds, however, the new or waxing moon has always been felt as a favourable auspice, the husbandman choosing this phase for the sowing of his crops, etc. It is the sign of good effect.

The emergence of a new conscious attitude is an impressive event, like the rising of the sun. Its effectiveness is declared in the four major attributes depicted in the figures about the sun—namely: (1) ancestral command, or sanction (the grandfather god); (2) effectiveness in time (Cronus); (3) disposable energy (the celestial bull); and (4) effective deed or will (the Viking hero and sword).

A new kind of consciousness would mean that the pre-existing conscious attitude had been essentially changed or enriched by the inclusion of important contents which before were either dissociated or dormant. We observed the basal preparations for this new attitude in the four pseudopodia of the ascending blue mass in the left edge of Drawing III. Here we see the energy emerging, reinforced by certain mythological contents gained from the general human past. The reader will remember the automatic, passive state of consciousness depicted on the right side of the schizoid barrier in Drawing II. In that condition consciousness is restricted to a more or less passive perception of spatial relations. In this drawing the time factor is added. Indeed, the whole dynamic character of this emergent consciousness is grounded in this added realization of time as duration.

When we consider the embryological complexion of previous drawings, it is of interest to note that modern workers in embryology have introduced a parallel conception of the time factor into biological thinking. G. E. Coghill of Philadelphia writes[1]:

> "Whatever time may be in the absolute, as a function in behaviour it works backward as well as forward. Working forward it is memory; working backward it is anticipation, or imagination. In fact, one might say that, other things being equal, the position of an organism in the scale of behaviour is directly correlated with the degree to which the past as well as the future are integrated with the present."

If we merely substitute the word "consciousness" for "behaviour" in the above paragraph, we have the description of an effective conscious attitude that is no longer under the metaphysical spell of Newtonian cause and effect. Going backwards on the time dimension, the patient discovers the powerful spirit of the grandfather. Going forwards, he finds the anticipation of the hero, who presently appears at the psychological moment. Between memory and anticipation are Cronus and the bull, the mythological components of the efficacy of the will. They represent a decisive output of available energy in the moment of time. These are the dynamic factors of the emergent moment, without which there could be no effective will.

1 "*The Neuro-embryological Study of Behaviour : Principles, Perspective and Aim*" (*Science*, lxxviii., 1933, pp. 131-38).

E. S. Russell, another eminent biologist, also expresses himself as follows:

"Time, then, enters as an essential element into our definition of organism. The living thing at any one moment of its history must be regarded as merely a phase of a life-cycle. It is the whole cycle that is the life of the individual, and the cycle is indissolubly linked with previous life-cycles—those of its ancestors right back to the dawn of life—and the activities of the organism, at any stage of its career, can be understood only if they are reintegrated, both in the individual and the evolutionary life-cycles."[1]

This statement might have been written expressly in relation to the events depicted in this drawing. We shall, perhaps, achieve the most comprehensive understanding of this drawing if we regard it as a reintegration of the life-cycle of the subject as an individual with the previous life-cycles of his ancestors, reaching back, as we shall presently see, to the very dawn of time. Consciousness of the present makes a fracture in the continuity of time; but in the unconscious[2] nothing intervenes to separate the future from the past: hence the normal activity of the unconscious also includes anticipation of future possibilities.[3] The steadying effect that accompanies a thorough historical research into one's life and its antecedents probably derives from the fact that realization of past cycles of events produces a certain insight into parallel tendencies that are shaping the future. As we study the remaining contents of this picture, we shall observe how all its contents are constellated by this backward and forward extension of the new conscious attitude.

The four attributes of the new sun are balanced, on the right side of the picture, by a group of four ruled by the mother. Thus the disposition of father-principle on the left, and mother-principle on the right, observed in Drawing I., is still maintained. The morbid influence, which before was identified with the father, is now detached, and occupies a separate enclosure by itself on the extreme left; whilst the

[1] E. S. Russell: *The Interpretation of Development and Heredity*, p. 171. (Clarendon Press, 1930.)

[2] *Cf.* Jung's description of the unconscious as living history.

[3] *Cf.* Dunne's *Experiment with Time*.

dubious symbolism of the father has been replaced by the demiurgical figure of the maternal grandfather. The latter has been raised to the heavenly sphere, where he becomes identified with the divine artificer. This substitution of the father represents a real gain in psychological freedom. The figure of the actual father tended to block the subject's view of his ancestral past, chiefly because of the fascinating effect of the father's psychotic psychology. But with the emergence of the archetype, the full historical landscape comes into view, and the subject is able to see the proportions of his personal problem in larger perspective.

A wholesome standard of criticism is combined with the historical standpoint in this choice of the figure of the maternal grandfather, inasmuch as the practical common sense of his maternal ancestry is one of the subject's most valuable psychological assets.

When we see an august figure pointing the finger of divine command at a ringed-off, infantile fantasy-garden, we might well wonder why a relatively inoffensive relic of childhood should require such an overwhelming display of authority. Or have we here the seeds of a paranoidal delusion, in which the ego sees all the hosts of heaven and all the powers of earth arrayed against it? Either this, or there must be a value hidden in the fantasy-garden which escapes rational estimation.

The question must be left open for the time being. So far as we at present know, and so far as the subject can tell us, the system contains the tin closet, the little house, the tree, the two children fighting on the floor, and the black cat. There were other associations clustering around these contents, but nothing that could add anything material to the facts we already know.

The reader will remember, however, that it was just when the patient was recovering these associations in the analytical hour that he " dropped through " into the unconscious. Apparently there are certain spots where one stumbles abruptly into the underworld. People who have built up a resistant, rational threshold to the unconscious are liable to feel that they are shut out of paradise: for these it may be a tremendous discovery to find the door, the cave, the hole in the ground, the trap-door through which they can gain access to the world of the unconscious. It may be a place safeguarded by sacred tradition, as, for instance, Stonehenge,[1] or it may be the effect of alcohol, or some drug which relaxes the inhibitions of consciousness. One patient who lived in a house in one of the London squares containing an enclosed circular garden found his way into the unconscious by means of this magic circle.

This initial, direct experience of the unconscious corresponds with the rite of initiation in certain primitive communities. In order to cross the threshold into manhood, the boy has to face and overcome his worst dread, in the place of initiation. The Achumawi lad must dive into the crater-lake of a distant mountain at sunset, the novice at Eleusis had to walk down steps into deep water, or go through fire in the cave of the temple. In many savage tribes the lad has to enter the mouth of a devouring monster, in the belly of which the bull-roarers are whirling, or he has to undergo some trial or ordeal which tests his endurance to the utmost.

In all these forms the lad is inoculated, as it were, with a controlled dose of panic in the prescribed way and at the prescribed place. The danger of being overwhelmed by panic, or some similar contagion, is a constant menace to primitive mentality. The threshold which defends consciousness from sudden irruptions from the unconscious is relatively slight, and therefore the risk of disorganization by sudden conflagrations of affect is greater than with an educated mind. The safeguard which protects and supports the novice through the initiatory ordeal is, of course, tradition. The parent, guardian, or priest who instructs the boy personifies tribal tradition—*i.e.*, he is the voice of the ancestors. Even though the lad has to undergo the ordeal alone in an uncanny, solitary place, as is the case among many North American Indian tribes, the situation is none the less safeguarded by the ancestors; for the lad is carrying out their command, which has been given him by his guardian.

[1] A good literary example comes to mind in Evans' experience on the altar-stone at Stonehenge in J. C. Powys' *Glastonbury Romance*.

In regard to the enclosed fantasy-garden of our drawing, the subject had, of course, no conception that it could function as his gateway to the unconscious. He had read Freud; his object, accordingly, was to reduce his neurosis to its infantile sexual origins. His tendency to adhere exclusively to the sexual theory will be visible throughout the earlier drawings. The reader will also notice how perfectly the figure of ancestral authority accords with the Freudian super-ego.

To resume, the four figures on the right of the drawing are meant to represent the mother (drinking a mug of ale) with her three children. The smallest of these carries a long whip with which he encourages the horse (libido-symbol). The subject identifies himself with this figure; but in the timeless dimension of infantile fantasy, not in any real sense. He says he is driving the horse in the direction of the house where his ancestors lived. It is significant that the father has been omitted from this family constellation, with the result that the structure of the group has the classical fourfold symmetry.

We find this quaternary structure occurring with remarkable regularity in those products of the psyche which are governed by the idea of individuation. Healing is the gaining of wholeness or completeness, and to be whole means to be balanced. Psychic balance is the expression of symmetrical structure, and symmetrical structure implies a regulated disposition of psychical energy. Accordingly, the dynamic expression of psychical totality is to be found in such symbols as the four horses of the sun, the four horses of the Apocalypse, the four sons of Horus, the four evangelists, the four rivers of paradise, etc. In the archetype of psychical totality, structure, function, and energy are found united in a complex dynamic symbol. In the symbol of the *mandala* (a world-wide symbol of individuation which finds its most complete expression in Lamaistic Buddhism) we find these two conceptions—namely, symmetrical structure and indwelling value or energy—expressed in perfect unison.

In the beautiful *Vajra-Mandala* (facing p. 206) a circle encloses a square having a gateway in the middle of each of its sides. Within the square is another circle enclosing yet another smaller circle. In the space between the two inner circles there are twelve diamond-shaped bodies: three in each of the four houses into which the inner square is portioned. In the centre of the inner ring is a thunderbolt. This symbol of celestial power is repeated in each of the twelve diamonds; it also stands in the middle of each of the four gateways. Thus the *mandala* combines the idea of symmetrical structure with a supreme symbol of energy or value. The above is a highly elaborated form; in its essence the *mandala* is a symmetrical, symbolical design, serving the dual function of religion—namely, a space magically contained to keep out the bad spirits, and a sacred place in which to enshrine the living symbol or to invoke the god.

The *mandala* symbolism has been elaborated through many centuries in Eastern religions. But the same fundamental impulse which created the *mandala* in the East is also active in the West; and the same conditions which prompted the Eastern mind to discover the introverted way are teaching men and women of the West to look into their own depths for healing. Many beautiful *mandala* designs are painted by patients in obedience to this need.[1]

In the present drawing the elements of effective personality are being assembled, as it were, into a coherent form; but the structural elements of the *mandala* have not yet found their common purpose. At the bottom left-hand corner, for example, there is a rectangular confined field, which a small human figure is ploughing. The idea of a given field of work is suggested. Above the field is the circular system, containing four elements—namely, human, tree, house, and closet. This system represents the psychological field that needs to be tilled. Of the four elements, it will be observed that two are living, or dynamic, and two structural. The incomplete circle suggests the, as yet, untilled field. The rising sun, with the four conditions of effectiveness, provides the essential principle, the sacred fire. The other elements, mentioned above, supply those of cultivation and contained structure. In a later rendering of this same scene we shall

[1] Jung has published a number of such *mandalas* in *The Secret of the Golden Flower*.

see how similar structural elements again attempt to cohere into a *mandala* form.

The remaining half of the picture belongs to the feminine earth-moon constellation. It can best be approached along the road that enters the drawing at bottom right-centre. A horse and waggon, the latter piled with sheaves of corn, moves along the road, which is seen dwindling into a thin line as it goes over the crest of the hill. A long drive branches away from this road through an arch to the left, finding its way across the fields to a house that is situated significantly between the closed infantile system on the left and the rising sun on the right. This is the house of the subject's paternal ancestors, who for generations farmed their land in just such a fertile countryside as is here suggested. The horse which the patient is driving towards the ancestral house is painted silver —*i.e.*, the colour of the moon and the mother. Drawing III. was concerned with the release of energy held in a morbid constellation around the maternal source (the breast). We may regard this horse, therefore, as energy that has been released from the unconscious, and is now available for the attack on the morbid system. As in Drawing III., there is a concentration of mobile elements towards the left, where the analytical task begins to develop.

Beneath the house, and to the right of the drive, a large E is painted in yellow. The patient associated Earth and Elizabeth with this letter. His feeling about Elizabethans was that they had the knack of "bringing things off." If you loosed your arrow with all your might in Elizabeth's reign, it would surely reach its mark. The Earth is the mother, the impersonal feminine equivalent of the sky-god. This E painted in yellow[1] on the ancestral earth may also refer to the tradition of disciplined husbandry in which the subject's family tree is deeply rooted. Finally, the earth is the third member of the natural trinity, Sun, Moon, and Earth, under which human consciousness has evolved. The psyche is, in point of fact, the living witness of the slow evolution of consciousness in a creature that lives

[1] The possibility of this letter being inserted at this particular spot for purposes of magical control will be discussed in a later chapter.

under the heavens and upon the earth. That aspect of the mind, therefore, which responds, and corresponds, to the earth will be concrete, earthy, and realistic. On the strength of his yeoman stock, a certain earthy realism would be entirely appropriate to the patient's position at the present juncture, for the work of analytical realization demands a very real attitude. This inference borrows further support from the field of brown earth that is situated just below the large E, and which, according to the patient's account, he himself is ploughing. The plough is apparently opposed to the leftward movement of the rest of the drawing. This is probably the field of his daily work which he has to plough, and which holds him in reality, while all these events are taking place in the unconscious.

If the reader will refer to the drawing again, he will observe that the road leading off to the left towards the ancestral past is guarded by a gate. There is no memory foundation for this gateway; it is, therefore, a beautiful example of a threshold symbol. It is the gate that guards the entrance to the unconscious, to the spell-binding, regressive way back into the past. Only those who are *bona fide* travellers, coming to retrieve ancestral values that have been left behind, can safely make this détour into the unconscious hinterland. This gate belongs to the same symbolism as the mythological guardians of the threshold.[1] The main road of the subject's life leads on over the hill, where the peacock's tail anticipates the emergence of future possibilities of expansion.

The peacock is the bird of dawn. The effulgence of light and colour issuing from the rising sun is echoed in the unfolding splendour of the peacock's tail. As the bird of the sun, the peacock also symbolizes the moment of emergence; and, by the same token, the red egg at the bottom of the picture on the left is under the care of a small peacock. This egg demonstrates the success of the salvage operations begun in the last drawing. For the patient informed me that it is identical with the red substance which was associated with

[1] *Cf.* the Scorpion-men who guard the mountains of the West in *The Gilgamish Epos*, and Cerberus, who guards the portal of the underworld.

his dead sister, and which was seen engulfed in the witch's mouth on the left of the last drawing. He also offered the suggestion that perhaps the peacock was trying to make a hole in the shell in order to release the bird inside.

Just to the right of the peacock and the egg there is an apple and a sheaf of corn, while above these is the mother with the three children. All these symbols express the idea of fertility in manifold ways. Above the mother we find the crescent moon, painted yellow on an efflorated disc of silver. I take this to mean that the positive anima-image, symbolized by the new moon,[1] is only a partial statement of the case. The remainder is suggested by the silver disc which bears the yellow crescent.

With men whose psychology is mainly determined by the mother-complex the soul-image may never become detached from the mother. The anima-function then remains embedded in its original matrix, and the whole emotional life of the subject revolves around the maternal image. In order to avoid this fate, a youthful anima-image needs to be born which can represent the desire of future attainment, and which contains a value superior to the regressive attraction of the mother-image. At all events, the anticipation of the future should not be less than the pull of the past. The new moon in the drawing symbolizes, therefore, the moment of detachment of the positive anima-figure from the maternal matrix. Thus the moment of emergence pervades the whole symbolism of this drawing.

The mug of ale hanging in the sky in proximity to the moon is a further indication of the invigorating consequences of this detachment. Even the mother drinks the elixir, a hint, perhaps, that the mother-image is no longer identified wholly with the actual mother, but has also become invested in the pregnant wife. There is a certain ancestral connection with this particular symbolism, for the paternal grandfather, besides being a farmer, also started a brewery, from the proceeds of which the patient's father enjoyed an appreciable inheritance. We shall meet this tankard of ale again, where

1 In a subsequent drawing the anima is definitely identified with the crescent moon.

it is brought by the anima as a reviving draught to the hero lying prostrate with exhaustion after his mortal battle with the dragon-monster, a fair example of a gift of the gods in the early Teuton sense.

Two details remain to be considered. First, there is the row of three trees that are growing in the hedge surrounding the ploughed field. It will be observed that the drawing contains four trees altogether, but one of these is enclosed in the dissociated system. Conceivably these trees represent the four main psychological functions,[1] three of which participate in the conscious field, while the fourth is to be found in the dissociated fantasy-system. The loss, through dissociation, of an essential psychological function, as, for instance, feeling, is the real cause of feelings of inferiority. This lack is frequently masked by untouchable moods of aloofness and sensitiveness, or by a kind of forced intellectuality. Possibly, therefore, the nature of the task in hand is again alluded to in this broken row of trees. It is certainly suggestive that there are only four trees depicted, and that three of these are functioning in the field of work.

The other detail is the two barrows on the skyline, just beneath the right edge of the sun. The patient has no particular archæological interest. These barrows (which the patient associates with the neolithic tombs near Stonehenge) have been placed in the field near the house of the ancestors, between the Norseman ancestor and the grandfather god. From these spatial relations we might assume that the tombs refer to a still earlier ancestral cycle. Moreover, they are just below the sun which heralds the dawn of a new conscious attitude whose essential quality is the sense of a living continuity with the past.

There is also a religious feeling involved, inasmuch as the men who were buried in those tombs almost certainly worshipped the rising sun. At all events, the men who erected the megalithic temple at Stonehenge must, unless the clear design of the structure has been misinterpreted, have sacrificed to the rising sun on the day of the summer solstice: a

[1] The basic structure of the psyche reveals a fourfold extension; the four cardinal points of this function-structure Jung has designated Intuition, Sensation, Thinking, Feeling. *Vide* Jung's *Psychological Types*.

fact which would favour the idea that they identified the newly risen sun with the divine king, upon whose magical efficacy the life and prosperity of the people depended.

Hocart has shown that primitive kings share in the divine nature through the belief that the king has eaten a ray of the sun, or that he is descended from some hero who was in reality the sun in human shape.[1] The efficacy of the divine king is the same as that of the sun, since both have the power of renewing or recreating life.

The two barrows may represent, therefore, some still surviving influence of the primitive belief that an individual hero, or an effective deed, is fathered by the sun. Worship of the sun, as the source of magical efficacy, is practically impossible to a modern educated consciousness; but in the archaic levels of the unconscious, where rational criticism has never penetrated, the identity of the hero with the sun is self-evident.[2]

* * * * *

Let us now compare the content of the present drawing with that of the preceding one. In the last picture we saw how all the unconscious elements were mobilized towards a concentration of intense blue in the region of the dissociated function. In this drawing a parallel assemblage of cultural and instinctual forces is seen converging upon the shut-off infantile system. The central command, under which this concentration takes place, is symbolized by the ancestral god. The symbolism throughout the design is decidedly pagan in character. The ancestral god could as well be Wotan, and the hero Siegfried with the sword Nothung in his hand. We can assume, therefore, that the way of salvation in this individual myth is not that of the Christian Church.

The feeling of having lost connection with the roots of life is a malady of the educated Western mind, and an increasing number of men and women are being drawn, with

1 Hocart, A. M.: *Kingship*. Pp. 260, 8vo. 1927. (Oxford University Press.)

2 In Indian religious teaching this truth is expressed in the saying from the Upanishad, "He who is this Brahman in man, and the One who is that Brahman in the sun, are both one."

more than intellectual curiosity, towards the distant sources of our civilized psychology. When we ask what these people are unconsciously seeking, all the evidence would suggest that, at bottom, the need of the modern soul is to rediscover the primordial religious experience, something not easily to be found in a world which sets the highest value on synthetic substitutes.

It is intelligible, therefore, that the work of psychological salvage should be inaugurated by a pagan sun-hero, who, like Parsifal the " pure fool," is identified with neither side of the Christian conflict. Not that our patient can escape the Christian problem. No man of our time, however intellectually enfranchised he may believe himself to be, can lightly free himself from that problem. It is in our blood. Indeed, if we were not so deeply enmeshed in the Christian values and beliefs, the psyche would have no need to hark back to a pre-Christian representative in order to gain a standpoint which could do justice to the non-Christian roots of our psychological heritage.

The stream of interest, then, which we see moving consistently to the left in these drawings is running counter to the rational direction, which would normally go hurrying pell-mell towards the ever desirable future, just over the brow of the hill. The way here is backwards into the past, back to the origins: not merely for the sake of an autobiographical retrospect, but for the sake of redeeming the unfulfilled potentiality lying entombed in the unconscious.

This, surely, is the meaning of the long whip with which the patient (represented as a tiny infant) drives the horse towards the left. The circular enclosure resembles an egg which contains that part of his personality which has never been hatched. The house of the ancestors contains that part of his ancestral inheritance which is not yet realized. The hero with the sword, the divine efficacy of the sun, and the neolithic tombs symbolize the archetypal or suprapersonal sources of energy which have been activated by the introverting therapeutic process. Thus, personal, ancestral, and racial origins are all concerned in this work.

III

DRAWING VII

The schizoid barrier is found again in this drawing, as in I. and II., but here the barricaded system is penetrated by a superior power.

The larger right half of the drawing is occupied by the head, arm, beard, and phallus of the ancestral god, who ruled the heavenly sphere in the last picture. The embodiment of ancestral authority, he was there seen pointing with outstretched arm at the circular enclosure on the left. Descending like a cleansing wind, he now penetrates the inverted system from every side, and in three distinct ways. The index-finger of the outstretched hand is pointing slightly upwards, and an arrow-line is continued on into another index-finger that pierces the system from above. This penetration by the finger of the god is repeated six times, so that from each corner and from either side of the framed system a finger protrudes through the frame and points at the centre of the inverted laminal field, in the upper middle of the closed system. The patient had a feeling of self-accusation as he drew this figure of the god. The index-finger meant direct condemnation of the whole morbid fantasy.

It is important to observe the fact that the god is able to penetrate the system only by means of an abstract extension and multiplication of his person. The god belongs to the eternal order, the morbid system to the temporal. It is as though the gulf separating primordial feeling from vitiated mind were an impassable frontier which only the impersonal images could transcend.

The beard of the god, the impregnating medium, sweeps horizontally across the middle of the right half, as though blown by a strong wind. The essential identity of this ancestral spirit with the sun is revealed in the blue and gold colouring of the beard. Near the head the beard is painted gold; the further it is blown to the left, the more blue predominates. In its horizontal movement the beard becomes differentiated into twelve distinct sun-rays, with intervening blue spaces, each ray ending in an arrowhead. These penetrating or impregnating sun-rays are numbered from 1 to 12, corresponding, apparently, with the numerical series of yellow rings and supernumerary phalli in the middle of the inverted system. The rays point at the heart of the system.

In the bottom right-hand corner the phallus of the god appears, pointing upwards and to the left. The end of it, enclosed in the invaginated end-portion of a tapering trunk-like extension, bifurcates at its distal end into two index-fingers, into which arrow-lines are carried from the phallus in the same way as the arrow-line is carried from the index-finger above. These arrow-lines represent the concentration of libido, now directed with the gesture of command, upon the dissociated complex, both from above and from below. The background of the right half is stippled gold and blue. Blue is the dominant colour of this right half, and it is interesting to compare the effective impact of the authoritative logos-principle in this drawing with the amorphous lumps of blue in the left half of Drawing III., where the primordial logos-libido first appeared.

The contents of the inverted system on the left half were, I believe, inspired by the desire to produce an exclusively sexual ætiology. In any case the Freudian idiom was felt by the patient to be the most appropriate expression for the morbid system. The patient drew my attention to the wavy line surrounding the system, which he associated with the notion of a frame—*i.e.*, a rigid structure in which a certain content is enclosed and set apart. A female trunk, showing the two breasts above and expanding to envelop an inverted laminal field below, protrudes downward from above in the middle line. Although the drawing does not corroborate the idea, the patient is certain in his own mind that this female body is twisted on its own axis. The inverted laminal field does not represent a cross-section of the trunk, as the drawing rather suggests, but is intended as a kind of dynamic aura, or magnetic field, surrounding the anus and genitalia. The two breasts, true to the principle of inversion, point inwards and downwards. From the converging nipples drops are flowing to form a confluent stream which joins the chain of yellow rings issuing from the centre of the laminal field.

These fall in a curving stream into the green receptacle below. According to the patient, whose explanation of this singular material held rigidly to the Freudian programme, this chain of rings consists of fæces, and the green receptacle (which is also suggestive of the pelvis) is a water-closet pan.

In a subsequent discussion of this drawing the patient associated the twisted female torso above and the green receptacle below with the mother, the open pan being thus identified with the mother's lap. His feeling was that the twisted trunk, bearing the symbol of the inverted laminal field, represented the closed aspect of his mother's attitude towards him as a small child. He believes she turned her feeling away from him deliberately, for fear, perhaps, of destroying him with a too great affection. In connection with this idea of the patient I must quote the case of Girish Babu of Bengal, the founder of the modern drama in India. The mother of Girish Babu (who was her eighth child) treated him with great harshness. When the child was ill her deep love for him came out. She explained to the father, when he rebuked her for her harsh treatment of the boy:

> "I am a witch: I have eaten up my first child: Girish is my eighth: such a fortunate child is easily injured. Lest he be affected by my look in any way, I do not allow him to come near me. I do not take him in my lap. I do not even say a sweet word to him. Oh ! my heart breaks when I think of the cruelty with which I have treated my best son."

I have no means of knowing whether it was true that the patient's mother tried to repress her feelings towards him in this way. It is more likely, I think, that the ambivalency of the patient's emotional attitude was responsible for this projection of resistance upon the mother. None the less, we cannot exclude the possibility that his libido was caught and held by a seeming contradiction in the mother's attitude to her favourite child.

The fæcal rings issuing from the inverted field above can hardly be regarded as excrement in the ordinary sense, inasmuch as each ring, excepting the second, carries a figure of the numerical sequence 1 to 12. The second carries a nought, which might denote a libidinal identification with the chain of drops descending from the mother's breasts above. The number 12 coincides with the head of a red snake, which forms a final ring by holding its tail in its mouth, and occupies the interior of the pelvic cavity or green lavatory-pan. This position, at the bottom of the pelvic pan, gives rise to an interesting clue which we must later pursue. A continuous chain of libidinal rings therefore can be said to join the inverted breasts above to the red snake-ring below The snake appears to be the symbolical summing-up of this whole libidinal chain.

To the right of the chain of fæcal rings there is a proliferating bunch of ten phalli; all of these, excepting the first, have the attenuated character of supernumerary organs. The first points at the centre of the laminal field, while each of the remaining nine is either pointing towards, or actually penetrating, its corresponding fæcal ring. The phallic nature of the snake is suggested by the fact that the eleventh ring is pierced by the body of the snake, while number twelve of the phallic series is inscribed upon its head. The degree of penetration of the rings by the supernumerary phalli proceeds progressively as the series descends, so that by the time number ten is reached the terminal phallus has shot through its ring, apparently seeking an objective beyond. The last one resembles the first in being larger and more formed than the rest.

The whole bunch of phallic excrescences grows out of an irregular space on the right border of the framed system. This space is painted in gold. The patient told me that he could not do anything about this space, and that he had the feeling that the devil should be in it. He had to leave it without content, since no image came to him. From the fact that he has given this area the gold of the sun, he allows us to infer a focusing of impersonal energy in this neighbourhood. We shall see later how this potency manifests itself.

At the bottom of the inverted system, and on either side of the green receptacle, there is a kind of mouth, indented lines above and below (seen mainly on the right) representing its teeth. Into these mouths fingers protrude. The finger on the left, owing to lack of space, is reduced to a mere stump.

On the right, however, the finger (painted with the gold and blue stippling which forms the background of the right half) is pushed in between the teeth, and the nail has a jagged edge. Inside the jagged nail-edge, on either side, collections of blood are shown, which might represent the wastage of libido through the onanistic habit of nail-biting. The finger on the right clearly resembles a phallus in the way it has been drawn. The inclusion of this nail-biting motif in the territory of infantile sexuality confirms our supposition that the contents, though not the treatment, of this framed system were suggested by his reading of Freud.

When we cast our eye over the whole drawing, we are again impressed by the active sweep of all its elements towards the left; and there is here, as in all the preceding drawings, a resulting concentration of libido-tributaries in the left-hand bottom corner. The cascade of libidinal contents pours into the green receptacle, which (in consequence perhaps) begins to assume a symbolical character that in no way accords with its original connotation as the pan of a water-closet.

Compared with the rest of the drawing, the tangle of ill-conceived symbolism around the green pan appears confused and highly ambiguous. Whenever expression becomes indistinct and complicated, whether in a dream, poem or musical composition, we may reasonably suspect a certain confusion of ideas. A transitional work or period invariably exhibits expressions of this kind, in which apparently simple ideas or images begin to assume new and unexpected forms.

The bunch of phallic excrescences yields an example of this transitional conversion from a simple to a complex idea. The first member of the series is simple and effective. But, as the sequence descends, each member becomes increasingly modified from the original type. The basal portion, or root (which should correspond anatomically to the testes and scrotum), becomes expanded and elongated to such a degree that the terminal phallus appears no more than a digital termination to a long, fleshy trunk. Thus, by the time the final member is reached, the basal portion has become so attenuated that the phallus is joined to its base only by a thin stem. It is this stem, not the phallus, which passes through the ring. Here the idea of phallic penetration has clearly departed from its original physiological significance.

The same reasoning applies to the green lavatory-pan, the very colour of which could warn us that a concealed idea has been at work. Not only has it the colour of vegetational life, it also possesses the potentialities of growth and change. The amœboid protuberances, for example, which are being drawn into the mouths on either side of the pan, already reveal a certain transitional tendency. There is also a definite resemblance to the pelvic basin with its colonic contents which would agree with the patient's subsequent association with the mother's lap. But the symbol which lends to this green container an unexpected significance is the red snake.

This symbol of the snake biting its tail, called the ***uroborus***, is a fundamental symbol of mediæval alchemy; but it was also current among the Greek and Arabian alchemists. Horapollon (*circa* A.D. 900) uses the snake-circle as a hieroglyph; he distinguishes two images of the serpent coiled upon itself. When the snake concealed the tail under its body it represented time (*αἰών*), and when it held its tail in its mouth it signified the world (*κόσμος*). In point of fact, these distinctions were not generally recognized, and the *δράχων οὐροβορος* served to represent both ideas.

IV

In order to appreciate the meaning of the snake or dragon in alchemical hieroglyphics, we need to trace the symbolism to its origins. Throughout antiquity the snake was worshipped in numerous cults as the symbol of renewing or resurgent life. Originally the cult of Æsculapius, the god of healing, was most probably a snake oracle similar to that of Apollo at Delphi. The classical symbol of the god was a staff with a serpent coiled around it. In relation to our subject the reader will recall that the essential part of the Æsculapian temple-worship was the *incubatio*. The worshipper had to undergo a therapeutic introversion, during which he slept in the temple itself. The oracle revealed the method of cure to the worshipper by means of a dream or vision, which the priests then interpreted.

There can be little doubt that the snake became identified with magical attributes through the primitive belief that it embodied the spirit of the dead chief or ancestor. This connection relies upon certain natural facts. In its preference for cool concealment, for instance, the snake is frequently discovered among the tombs. Hence in many parts of the world, when a snake comes into a house, it is fed and worshipped as the returning spirit of a dead ancestor. The snake also casts its skin every year, thus participating in the recurrent rejuvenation of nature in spring. With these two characters the snake combines the *mana* of the spirit of the dead with the idea of ever-renewing vitality.[1] On the strength of these deep and fertile associations, snake-oracles and a world-wide snake-cult flourished throughout the dawn of civilization until the sky-gods superseded them and reason began to supplant instinct. The identification of Apollo with an earlier snake-cult is suggested in the fact that Apollo was called Pythius after his victory over Python of the deluge. Apollo was also considered a rival of Æsculapius and eventually prevailed over him, therewith assuming the healing attributes of the more primitive god. It is not improbable that the legends of Apollo's victory over dragons and serpents at Delos, at Delphi, at Phlegyæ and elsewhere, refer to local snake-cults that were assimilated by the god of the more developed culture. Mythology offers innumerable examples of this conquest and assimilation of the chthonic dæmons of the earlier cults by the gods of the sky.[2]

The psychology of the snake-cult will be appreciated when we remember that, originally, life and spirit are one. The whole meaning of living sacrifices was bound up with the idea of imparting spirit, or life, to the soil, to rivers, to the ship that was to be launched, to the house or wall that was to be built, etc. If we accept this primordial view that life is spirit and spirit life, we can see that the snake, proverbially

[1] From the way the scarab beetle has been venerated in ancient Egypt and from the fabulous phœnix, we can appreciate how easily human desire for immortality can misconstrue natural phenomena.

[2] Professor F. M. Cornford gives an invaluable account of a similar metamorphosis in the thought of early Greece in his book *From Religion to Philosophy* (Arnold).

hard to kill, living in holes of the earth and among tombs, and rejuvenating its life by casting its old skin at springtime, might easily have been chosen as the symbol of the eternally renewing life of the earth; while through its connection with the spirits of the dead it could also symbolize the idea of immortality.

Before the idea of spirit was released from matter, the only immortality which primitive mind could conceive was the ever-renewing life of vegetation or the continuity of family and tribe. Probably the immense importance given to the female genitalia in the cowry-shell phase of primitive culture arose from the fact that woman seemed to offer the only gateway to immortality, viewed in the primitive sense—*i.e.*, the continuity of life. The cult of the *magna mater*, the ever-fertile earth, endured just so long as life and immortality were identified with the earth-mother.

The revelation that life was spirit, and that the spirit was an independent entity that could detach itself from the living body, was surely more pregnant in its consequences than any other single idea in the world's history. The ascent or release of the spirit from the earthy body coincided psychologically with the ascendancy of the sky-gods over the Titans and earth-dæmons of the previous era. The victory of the Olympians over the Titans might, therefore, be regarded as a psychological landmark, affirming the fact that a spiritual entity had been conceived as something distinct from matter and flesh. The most remarkable thing about this dawn of the spirit of man was that it happened synchronously and, to a very large extent, independently throughout the different civilizations of mankind. The radiant light of the spirit came like a spring morning, remaining for ever beautiful in the mind of man. To our eyes the light broke most superbly over Greece from the Homeric time onwards. But the same age also witnessed the kindling of the sacred fire by Zoroaster in Persia, the Mosaic revelation and the dawn of Jewish vision and prophecy, the wondrous Vedic dawn in India, and the wisdom of Lao-Tsü with the rise of Taoism and Confucianism in China. The ascent of the spirit out of the darkness of earth was indeed a cosmic event, the like of which has never happened since. Human consciousness, as we know it, must be conceived as having been born in that age. The spirit can be temporarily extinguished through the weight of collective inertia and regression, or through the archaic worship of the state, but in the end it rises again to the utter destruction of the oppressing power.

Having learned the power of detachment, it is as though the psyche took command of the body, giving orders at times that were in direct contradiction to bodily interests. The man who had mastered detachment, whereby the body and its needs could, for certain stretches of time, be completely obliterated from the mind, was immediately given honour and special privileges. Thus before the spirit became professionalized the spiritual man had real superiority.

At the opposite pole to this newly won detachment we conceive the snake as symbolizing that primordial instinctive psyche (suggesting the solar plexus and the spinal cord) whose roots descend, as it were, into the darkest interstices of the earth. Thus the *uroborus* symbol represents our psychic continuity with the immemorial past, back even to the life of the mesozoic swamps, before ever the sun had warmed the blood of living creatures to the idea of mating, with its decent loyalties. As symbol of the primordial, instinctive psyche, the snake again becomes associated with the timeless, the immortal, the unchanging; hence the *uroborus*, the never-ending vital ring. In this connection we cannot omit to mention the fact that Shakti, the goddess of primordial energy in the *Kundalini tantra*, is symbolized as a snake coiled three and a half times around the *lingam*.

As used by the alchemists, the snake is a purely abstract form, divorced altogether from its original primitive significance as earth-dæmon, though the alchemists were certainly aware of its sexual connotation. Geber, or Jabir, the most famous of the Arabian alchemists, who lived in Kufa about A.D. 776, used the *uroborus* to represent a closed system or magic ring, denoting the idea of an eternal process, something to be understood *sub specie æternitatis*. In later alchemical illustrations the snake-ring is shown encircling the world. This is the hieroglyph of Horapollon, mentioned above, denoting the world conceived as a self-contained system. The other hieroglyph, referred to as αἰών, is clearly meant to distinguish the idea of time, as eternal recurrence, from the idea of an eternally renewed physical process (κόσμος).

In later illustrations the snake biting its tail is represented as an attribute of Cronus, the god of time. In a Greek bronze medallion at Brussels the symbol of the snake-ring surrounds the head of Zeus like a halo. The eagle, symbolizing the spiritual antithesis to the snake, or earth-dæmon, is also enclosed by the *uroborus*. The eagle and the *uroborus* together signify that the supreme god is uncreated and immortal, without beginning and without end.

In the Warburg Library in London there is a seventeenth-century illustration depicting Uranus being castrated by his son Cronus. Uranus holds the *uroborus* symbol of immortality in his left hand, while below is the eagle. The god appears to be yielding willingly to the castration. The idea contained in this symbolism is especially interesting for the purpose of our patient's drawing. Through the conscious sacrifice of, or detachment from, the *libido sexualis* the god attains immortality. Desire, in other words, holds the psyche within the temporal frame: therefore that timeless condition in which the soul finds again its primordial freedom can be won only by the sacrifice of compulsive libidinal ties.

The achievement of the suprapersonal attitude, or condition of consciousness, was regarded by its greatest exponents as essential to the mastery of the divine art. Johannes de Sacro-Bosco made use of the *uroborus* symbol as though conveying a mark of divine distinction. This use of the symbol is corroborated by certain illustrations of the philosopher Spinoza, in which the philosopher's head is encircled by the *uroborus*. Spinoza's pantheism united the totality of human reality with the totality of nature in a single cosmos. God was this living Whole: He was not outside it or beyond it. The evolution of form was not due to an arbitrary act of creation, but was the manifestation of the activity of God in and through the manifest body of nature. Although to modern thought this conception would appear almost self-evident, Spinoza was excommunicated from the Synagogue for expressing such blasphemous ideas. His reward was to be crowned with the symbol of immortality.

V

From the foregoing connections we discover that the alchemists identified the snake-ring symbol with the idea of a detached, self-contained, self-regulating condition or system. What, then, were the alchemists seeking? How did they come to confuse the very realistic aim of transmuting base metal into gold with the Elixir of Life, the Philosopher's Stone, and all the rest of the mystical paraphernalia found in alchemical symbolism? We must remember that two vast potentialities—viz., the germs of science and psychology—were already fermenting in the mediæval unconscious: not, however, as two distinct hypotheses, but rather as a vague, disturbing potential which sometimes sought a mystical, and sometimes a concrete, physical expression. If we accept the hypothesis that the aim of the alchemists' dream was a psychological rather than a chemical creation, even though it was at first conceived in chemical terms, the meaning of their quest becomes clear. The manifest content of the alchemists' dream was chemical beyond question, but only a rather superficial student of alchemical writings could maintain that the real or latent content of the dream was concerned primarily with a physical operation. In the writings of Geber, for instance, the author discourses continually on matters so remote from his chemical procedure that we might easily assume that the transmutation of metals was only incidental to his real object. For him the "Matter of the Work is the Elixir of all elixirs, the Ferment of all ferments." He describes the constituent forces of the Elixir, for instance, as being "so harmonized and united that they overcome the division of substances, compelling them to assume its own nature and relinquishing their own."[1] "If the Elixir is red it will convert its object into gold, while the white Elixir changes into silver."[2]

In the creation of the Stone, the fundamental principle

[1] Geber: *The Book of Mercy* (translation by Professor Houdas). [2] *Ibid.*

is the " thorough purification of its elements, including their liberation from those oils by which they are corrupted and its full effect hindered."[1] It is also affirmed that " there is a sole and only thing, combined by one operation in a single vessel, a unique nature which can dispense with all other substance, and is at once potent and consecrated."[2] In nearly all alchemical writings we find this strange mixture of mystical and psychological affirmations on the one hand, and of concrete chemical and metallurgical experiments on the other. According to Zosimus, alchemy was a royal art, because its secret of material wealth must be reserved for the advantage of kings and priests. This was the mundane side of the work; on the other it was a revelation, a *donum Dei*, to be communicated only to those who had achieved an attitude of single-minded devotion to the high quest.

The more we study these writings, the more probable it seems that an intense fermentation in the mediæval unconscious seized hold upon certain eager minds with such force and reality that they had to express their experiences in a concrete kind of symbolism. But can we be sure that the impersonal contents that were seeking expression in alchemy have been fully and truly realized in chemistry? The essential quest into the problem of human fate, which was the soul of astrology, was certainly not satisfied by astronomy, the science which supplanted it. Astrology and alchemy are like profound and revealing dreams of the European soul which science has, so far, failed to interpret; though it must be admitted that the intervening centuries of scientific enquiry into the nature of the material universe have supplied us with a reliable objective standpoint from which the alchemists' dream can be given its true significance.

There are two passages from the writings of Zosimus which present, I think, the heart of this dream in the most explicit way. He writes:

> " The symbol of chemistry is drawn from creation (in the eyes of the adepts), who save and purify the divine soul enchained in the elements and, more than all, who separate the divine spirit entangled with the flesh."

[1] Geber: *The Book of Royalty*.

[2] *The Book of Mercy*.

In the same work, with reference to the work of transmutation, we read:

> "As there is a sun, the flower of fire, a celestial sun, the right eye of the world, so copper, if it become flower (that is, if it assume the colour of gold) by purification, becomes a terrestrial sun which is King on earth, as the sun is King in heaven."[1]

In the first passage we learn that the adept is one who can rescue the divine spiritual substance from its entanglement with matter and flesh. This is, as we know, the object of the Eastern ascetics, particularly of the Yoga systems in India. Translated into psychological terms, the aim of both methods is to detach the sacred flame of consciousness from the fetters of mechanism. So long as consciousness is harnessed to some plan or programme, some desire, need or fear, it remains contingent upon these necessitous processes, like a god in chains. To rescue consciousness from this hazardous subjection to need-driven mechanisms and to create for it a means of access to the eternal potential of the primordial unconscious is the object of alchemy, of the various systems of Yoga and of analytical psychology. It would almost seem, indeed, that alchemy was the first, somewhat abortive, attempt to create a Western Yoga. It is still a living content of the European unconscious, just because its essential value has not yet been realized.

In the second passage we learn that the work of transmutation follows upon the creation of an inner sun, which corresponds in the microcosm of man to the celestial sun in the macrocosm of nature. From this we may conclude that the salvage of consciousness from the chain of biological happenings is the necessary antecedent to the creation of the inner sun, or self, by whose light the world is transformed.

We know that the symbolic value of gold (viz., grains of the sun) was treasured by early civilizing man long before it had currency value. The quest for gold was, as already noted, the chief motive power of the almost incredible migrations of early civilizing mankind. We know that the divine man, the King, was either a child of the sun or had in some way partaken of the splendour of the sun.

1 Berthelot: *Collection des Anciens Alchimistes Grecs.*

From the earliest dawn of consciousness the idea of the superior man, or, at least, of the unconditioned part of man's nature which claimed superiority to the realm of blind necessity, has been symbolically identified with the sun. Why, then, is copper chosen in the alchemists' dream as the "terrestrial sun"? Not copper as such, but copper "if it become flower by purification." The mediæval world was apparently seized with the idea of creating gold, never of merely finding it. That dream had already faded. Just as the Chinese adept teaches the Secret of the Golden Flower as a purposeful method of introversion, so the mediæval alchemist was concerned with creating the Golden Flower out of copper by a similar process of purification. Copper, in its ordinary state, is made into every kind of utensil. It is married to mundane necessity. But when it "becomes flower," it is as though released and purified of its necessitous condition, and blooms in and for itself. Copper that has been rescued by the adept from its ordinary state is therefore the transmuting agent, because it has itself been released.

This whole symbolism therefore has to do with the means, the art, the knowledge, and the devotion that can transform ego-consciousness from the bondage of mechanism into the impersonal freedom of service of the Self. This is, of course, nothing but the surrendering of the ego, with its heady schemes and arbitrary self-will, to the experiment of individuation commanded by the Self. As the youthful farmer learns in time to relinquish his rigid programme of expectations, and to adapt himself to the ways of nature, so the alchemist had to abandon his early dreams of fabulous wealth and prestige in order to realize the spiritual truth of his great quest.

From Paracelsus onward we may say that the extraverted, larval stage of the alchemists' quest gave place to the introverted symbolism of individuation. The *uroborus* symbol also contains the potentiality of this transformation, inasmuch as the snake in this form would represent the amount of instinctual energy that can be directed towards a suprapersonal goal. The *uroborus* symbolizes the release of the instinct from desirousness and illusory goals: it would therefore tend to create a state of consciousness in which reality can appear *sub specie æternitatis*. Therefore it became the symbol of supreme philosophical detachment.

VI

From these allusions, which are by no means exhaustive, we can conclude that the red *uroborus* has crept into our patient's drawing from the impersonal unconscious. Yet nothing of this age-old symbolism was known to the patient. He had to paint it in the key-position of his drawing because an eternally recurrent process of psychic alchemy was being enacted. From this standpoint the events and figures portrayed are not merely those of distorted physiological processes, but also something to be understood *sub specie æternitatis*. The *uroborus* is a kind of ancestral signature, guaranteeing the nature and significance of the experiment.

That mediæval alchemy has had a hand in constructing this drawing is further suggested by the presence of a certain class of contents belonging specifically to the inventory of substances described by the alchemists as *prima materia*—in other words, the raw material of the alchemical process. These are *materia hermaphrodita catholica Solis et Lunæ*, *lac virginis*, *fæces dissolutæ*, *urina puerorum*, *Mater*, *Venus*. Of these we have observed (1) the general hermaphroditic symbolism of self-fertilization in the penetration of the fæcal rings by the supernumerary phalli, (2) the converging streams of milk from the female torso, (3 and 4) the excretory products falling into the lavatory-pan, (5) the maternal associations connected with the female trunk and the lavatory pan and (6) the archaic-infantile eroticism of the whole complex.

We know from numberless allusions in myth, fairy-tale and popular superstition that the ideas of gold and excrement lie very close together; but the particular importance given to excretory products (including semen, menstruum, sputum, etc.) in alchemical practice was bound up with the idea that putrefaction is an essential process in the breaking down of material forms: *corruptio unius est generatio alterius*. Only through the breaking down of one phase or form can a new form be generated. The whole of the alchemical procedure is rooted in the idea of generation and regeneration. It is hardly surprising, therefore, that the alchemists arrived at the idea of making the homunculus by means of putrefaction and incubation: a little man made by art instead of by nature. Alchemical procreation proceeded by putrefaction and transformation—on very similar lines, in fact, to the self-fertilizing fantasies of childhood.

The alchemists also attempted, and some claimed to have succeeded in, the recreation of the living body, after its dismemberment, by heating all the parts in a closed vessel. The well-known vision of Zosimus re-enacts this ancient mythological motif. In a later series of drawings, which unfortunately must be omitted for reasons of space, the patient drew a vessel containing the dismembered portions of the body; under this vessel he placed the mass of green life-stuff which figures as the focal content of the next drawing. Thus the introverted heat that was to incubate the new being was generated in the primordial life-stuff which came directly from the green lavatory-pan and its contents.

Many more analogies and allusions to hermetic symbolism could be demonstrated in this patient's material; but overloaded arguments are unappetizing, and enough have been adduced to prove the inexhaustible vitality of these contents of the impersonal unconscious.

Having traced a parallelism with alchemy, which can be regarded as the Western form of Yoga, it is of peculiar psychological interest to discover that a certain correspondence with the symbolism of the *Kundali* Yoga can also be discerned in the very drawing we are discussing. This is perhaps not so surprising when we consider that both alchemy and the Tantric Yoga systems are concerned with the identical goal—namely, the transformation of archaic elements by the operation of a superior potency.

The chief points of similarity with the *Kundalini* symbolism lie in the idea of the snake coiled at the bottom of the spinal cord (*i.e.*, within the pelvic area), and in the idea of the *chakras* or centres in the spinal sequence. The chief point of difference lies in the fact that the *Kundalini* snake is always represented as coiled spirally around the *lingam*,[1] whereas in our drawing it is represented as a closed circle. The analogy is, however, sufficiently positive to merit a short discussion of the Eastern system.

The basic conception of that form of the Tantric Yoga known as the *Kundali* Yoga is the idea of a primordial power symbolically located at the base of the spine. This power is known as the *Kundalini Shakti*, which Sir John Woodruffe, the eminent authority on the Tantric systems, translates as Serpent Power.[2] The form of the goddess *Kundalini Shakti* is that of a sleeping snake coiled three and a half times around the *lingam*. *Kundalini* means " that which is coiled."

The object of this system of yoga, as mentioned earlier, is to awaken the sleeping goddess through a downward and inward direction of consciousness, in order that she may be aroused to ascend and pierce the six centres of consciousness, termed *chakras*, situated at various levels of the spinal column. The centres, or *chakras*, are conceived as lotus flowers. *Muladhara* at the bottom has four petals, and each successive *chakra* has either two or four petals more than the one below, until the sixth *Ajna* is reached, situated between the eyes, which has only two. This *chakra* is held to be the centre corresponding to the pineal eye, and represents the evolution of a suprapersonal consciousness through the reconciliation of the opposites.

The boundless unfolding of consciousness that becomes possible after the impersonal attitude of detachment has been achieved is symbolized by the final *chakra Sahasrara*, the thousand-petalled lotus.

Essentially this is a method of introversion by which consciousness can be released from the primitive visceral level in which the self is identical with every affect. Rising through successive stages of organization, symbolized by the increasing differentiation of the lotus, a state of consciousness can be attained in which the complete unity of the self is experienced, analogous to the differentiated unity of Plato's world-soul. Each *chakra* in the ascending scale represents

1 Phallic emblem.
2 Arthur Avalon: *The Serpent Power* (Luzac and Co., London, 1919).

a stage in this evolution of pure consciousness. The analogy with the spinal cord and brain represents the psychic principle groping its way upwards through a limiting tube, like the sap ascending the stem of a tree from its roots, to unfold at last into the freedom of the spirit. One is reminded of Goethe's amazing intuition of the power of consciousness. After contemplating a human skull for six hours, so it is said, the realization dawned upon him that the bones of the skull were vertebræ which, through the ages, had been gradually expanded and shaped by the power of the mental principle, finally to contain nature's most dangerous experiment, the human brain.

Each successive *chakra* has its own characteristic symbolism, its own essential germ, corresponding with a certain state or level of consciousness. This idea of a series of centres of consciousness appears in a great number of esoteric systems as far apart as the Sufi fraternities in Persia and the Maya scripture of the Zunis in America. In the latter system the centres are also depicted by animal glyphs.

Muladhara, the lowest *chakra* of the *Kundalini* system, contains the symbol of a white elephant, having seven trunks springing from a single root. The elephant is the bearer of divinity: it symbolizes the overwhelming power latent in the primordial image. In India the white elephant is necessarily associated with the idea of carrying the prince or ruler. The seven trunks are identical with the number of *chakras* to be energized. Thus the elephant represents both the dynamic aspect of *Shakti* and the carrier of the divine power to the *chakras*. If the reader will compare the illustration of *muladhara* on the opposite page with the patient's drawing, he will observe a remarkable resemblance between the elephant's sevenfold trunk and the bunch of trunk-like phalli in the drawing. Examining the root from which these phalli spring, we find that it is energized both from above, by the twelve sun-rays of the god's beard, and from below, by the trunk-like extension of the god's phallus, the upper terminal finger of which extends to the root of the phallic bunch. The shape of this trunk-like extension has precisely the same character as the elongated roots of the lower phalli in the bunch series. We can thus trace an inner connection between the energizing phallus of the god and the proliferation of transitional phallic forms within the system.

The elephant is also a generalized symbol of the cosmic energy of sexuality. To speak of this immense animal as a sexual symbol seems, on the face of it, somewhat outrageous. Yet it has undoubtedly always possessed this signification for the natural mind, partly because of the phallic association with its trunk, but primarily on account of its overwhelming power. To a mind preoccupied with the Freudian categories no distinction of libido-value would be permissible between an elephant and a knitting-needle, since both symbols allude to the same anatomical fact. But to the mind that created the *Kundalini chakras* the two ideas would belong to different worlds. To regard sexuality as a cosmic phenomenon is, at bottom, the only reasonable view, and the elephant is an appropriate dynamic expression of the *force majeure* to which all living beings have to submit. This, however, was precisely the conception of the sexual function which the patient had never entertained. His attitude, on the contrary, was personal, undisciplined and casual.

The resemblance of the prolongation of the god's phallus to the elephant's trunk is further borne out by the digital bifurcation at its distal end, for the end of the trunk is the elephant's tactile and prehensile organ, corresponding, therefore, with the hand. In the illustration of the *muladhara* elephant a kind of bifurcation at the end of each trunk is clearly indicated.

* * * * *

The process that appears to be taking place within the dissociated system is an intensive penetration, as though by cosmic rays. The result is an energizing of the infantile, morbid contents from a suprapersonal, primordial source. This process, as we have just seen, corresponds in several respects with the fundamental conceptions of the *Kundalini Yoga*, though the patient himself was entirely ignorant of Indian philosophy. He was, indeed, quite resistant at first to any analogies beyond the fantasies and memories of his own childhood and his strictly Freudian associations.

An even more remarkable invasion occurred during the analysis of a patient of a colleague at Zürich. This lady was prompted to draw a white elephant with eight trunks. Like my patient, she had no connection with Indian psychological ideas at that time, and was astonished when the similarity was pointed out to her. I am much indebted to this lady for permission to reproduce her drawing (Fig. 3).

The activation of primordial images during analysis is not at all unusual. Often, however, their native aspect is disguised owing to the lack of any conscious cultural relation either to the images or their contents. In these circumstances it is easy to overlook their real nature, and they may be misconstrued in a personal sense.

There is yet another idea in this drawing which comes, without question, from the same fountain of psychological ideas as those of the *Kundalini Yoga*. I refer to the piercing of the rings by the phallic fingers. It will be observed that six of the twelve rings are pierced by the phalli, while one is pierced by the snake, making seven in all, which again accords with the Tantric system. It will also be observed that the area of penetration coincides with that covered by the three phallic fingers of the god, each of which carries an indicating arrow showing the direction of command. Of the three fingers, the lower one, connected with the nail-biting motif, carries not only the arrow of accusation, but also the indentations meant to represent teeth. Nail-biting is associated by the patient with onanistic libido frustration. Thus we find a pathogenetic symptom identified with the motif of accusation. An earlier example of this nettle-and-dock liaison was observed in the lower shut-faced figure of Drawing III., where resistance to a pathological craving was found to engender an attitude of criticism and objectivity. When we have learned to read the language of so-called physical symptoms aright, we shall discover many similar index-fingers pointing in the direction of the pathogenetic complex.

We should now consider the connection between this penetration of the morbid system by psychological insight and the synchronous activation of the primordial images.[1] According to *Kundalini* teaching, the dormant power of the goddess Shakti remains eternally coiled at the base of the spine, even though her dynamic effect, or *prana*, rises up to pierce and quicken the *chakras*. This dynamic effect is conceived of as resulting in the union of Shiva, symbolizing the principle of consciousness, with Shakti, the primordial energy of the unconscious. It is the reciprocal action of these opposite principles which creates the new potentiality of consciousness. The white elephant with the seven trunks appears twice in the *chakra*-symbolism—namely, in the first and the fifth, which are the first and the last of the spinal, or autonomous, levels of consciousness. This repetition suggests that the elephant is the symbolical carrier of the divine potency, resulting from the union of Shiva and Shakti, to the various levels of the unconscious. The present drawing agrees with this conception, if we interpret the succession of phallic trunks as embryonic expressions of the peculiar potency which is generated at the point of confluence of the spiritual and sexual principles. This point of confluence would be located in the untenanted golden field.

It may be objected that the patient intended the series of rings to represent a string of fæces, and that they have nothing whatever to do with centres of consciousness. I agree that this was his intention; but the fact that he had to number the rings, and that their number had also to correspond with the number of sun-rays in the god's beard, is good evidence that in actual fact he aimed beyond his conscious mark. By their very nature, fæces are undistinguishable products. No hierarchy, either of value or precedence, can properly be imposed upon them as such. It is the impact of conscious distinctiveness (*i.e.*, the twelve sun-rays) which gives them a psychological significance and transforms them from *prima materia* into psychic entities. They now become a series of

1 It is interesting to compare two sayings of Spielrein's schizophrenic patient cited by Jung in *Psychology of the Unconscious* (p. 249): "God pierces through the earth with His rays." Remembering also the golden sun-rays of the god's beard which strike against the framed system, compare the following: "Jesus Christ has shown me His love by striking against the window with a sunbeam."

rings, each with its own specific numerical value, and with a centre seeking to be pierced. Their descent, too, into a feminine container of living green is suggestive.[1] In subsequent drawings we shall see how this green vessel, with its yellow contents, is converted into the symbol of creative power—namely, the open laminal field, the dynamic antithesis of the inverted field of the present drawing. Unless we resist the logic of evidence, we are bound to assume that one part of the patient's mind accepted a certain view as to the nature of the contents he was representing, while another level, by making use of the same contents, adumbrated possibilities and transformations which lay beyond, and were completely foreign to, his narrower conscious view.

Discussion of these possibilities with the patient proved, at the time, quite unprofitable. His mind was still confined within the guaranteed Freudian cubicle, and nothing beyond was permissible. In his view, the contents of the inverted system had the characteristics of sly, evasive, sexual interest, and the god was the traditional super-ego condemning his infantile narcissism in suitably downright terms. This was his truth, and it was precisely the truth needed at that time, while the nascent aspects of the drawing we have attempted to explore represented the Jacob's ladder whereby the transition from the infantile to the cultural psyche might eventually be achieved. It was of course possible, not to say probable, that consciousness would remain tightly shut against these ideas, in so far as the schizophrenic mentality suffers from a peculiar inadequacy in the realm of ideas. In spite of a surprising degree of mental ability in some cases, we tend to find an intellectual backyard in which ideas of royal significance are kept in squalid and unworthy contexts. This tendency to repress the value of primordial ideas, and with it the true creativeness of the mind, is due not to any native inferiority of intelligence, but solely, I believe, to a deep fear of the unconscious. There is an instinctive reaction of suspicion towards anything which might take the subject out of his depth.

The obverse of this is also true—namely, that just because

[1] Feminine because of the patient's association with the mother.

of the fascination and fear of the unconscious, many schizophrenic individuals discover that the best way of exorcising their fear is through creation. Anxiety and fear build prison walls which urge the spirit to fly.

In the present instance there is a manifest content of the drawing—namely, what the patient thinks it to be—and a latent content revealing the unmistakable signs of transformation into something different. The attempt to convince the patient in the face of his obvious resistance is like trying to force a closed door. It is more profitable to amplify the content which he does recognize.

The narcissistic character of the infantile psyche is a self-evident fact which needs no demonstration. But there is a certain aspect of narcissism which has profound philosophical implications. I refer to the motive of self-fertilization.

Self-fertilization is the basic theme of infantile fantasy, as also a fundamental motif of primordial myth. The primordial cosmogonic figures tend, accordingly, to be hermaphroditic in character.

The motif of self-fertilization runs throughout the present drawing from top to bottom; the phallic penetration of the fæcal rings, the dual penetration of the system on the left by the god on the right, the finger-sucking, the entrance of the numbered series into the green receptacle and, above all, the snake whose mouth contains its own phallic tail—all are variations on the one theme. We have seen what a powerful rôle this motif plays in alchemy, and there can be little doubt that the rich symbolical content of the *uroborus* is also rooted in the idea of the dragon who attains immortality through impregnating himself. In early Egyptian cosmogony we find Ptah producing the egg in which he incubates himself. Ra also impregnates himself with his own seed, and later vomits up the world, which has taken shape in his belly.

Not far away from these ideas is the motif of continuous coitus, allusions to which are constantly occurring on the primordial level. The purest example is the representation of Shiva and Shakti in coitus in the centre of the *mandala* in Lamaistic Buddhism. Jung describes another representation of Shiva in which one half of the god is masculine, the other half feminine, and the genitals are in continuous coitus.[1] The fundamental bisexuality of Shiva is expressed in the *lingam*, which is to be found everywhere in Hindu temples. The *lingam* is the phallus of Shiva, and its base is carved to represent the female genital opening. In another representation Shakti is the containing circle, Shiva the central point. We can assume from this evidence that primordial human nature is psychologically bisexual, and that the extreme cultural differentiation of the sexes which masks this original condition is an artefact. From this point of view the man who accepts or comes to terms with his anima (his latent feminine component), or the woman with her animus (masculine element), is also gaining experience of the primordial, androgynous archetype.

The existence of such primordial fantasies in supposedly adult beings is responsible for a very great deal of outlandish behaviour, but we must not forget that they can also have the effect of a moral protection. There is a self-contained roundness and self-sufficiency of the child-soul which may last throughout life, and which has the effect of protecting the Peter Pan individual as by a magical ring. The logic of the primordial fantasy is effective, even though never conscious. To fertilize oneself means that one is male-female, therefore round and whole. The state of childhood is indeed blessed because, unless he has been tampered with, the child is a recapitulation of the primordial human being who is still one with his instincts.

VII

To return to our drawing, the manifest content of the drawing represents the confluence of those infantile libidinal tributaries with which Freud has modelled a new conception of human fate—namely, infantile incest, anal and oral eroticism, nail-biting onanism, and all the rest of the infant's secret hoard of pleasure. These tributaries converge into the green lavatory-pan, which then becomes the vessel of transformation. We see them being acted upon and pierced by a superordinated psychic power, the efficacy of which is

[1] C. G. Jung: *Psychology of the Unconscious*, p. 130.

unmistakably identified with the idea of ancestral or racial continuity. We also begin to see the transforming effects of this impact in the way in which the original intention of the subject has been overridden, as though by a superior intelligence.

The subjective evidence of the operation of this superior intelligence is of a nature that cannot be submitted to scientific proof. What justification have we, then, for speaking of a superior intelligence? Our estimation of intelligence is based, fundamentally, on our sense of the purpose displayed in a sequence of effects. When the resultant of a psychic operation corresponds rather closely with the intentions of consciousness, we speak of a fully conscious act. But when, over and above the avowed aim of consciousness, effects are produced which can be made intelligible only by reference to a purpose that transcends the conscious aim both in value and range, we can only ascribe these effects to the operation of a suprapersonal centre of the mind which constrains the ego to its will. Freud's concept of the super-ego is valuable in so far as it expresses a psychic entity of ancestral origin that is superordinated to the ego. But it also suffers from Freud's partiality for the aged spirit of taboo and his unwillingness to give ear to the youthful spirit of creation.

Investigators of the autonomous psyche[1] inevitably encounter events and facts of psychic creation such as those just described, and many have tried in their several ways to bring them within the scope of scientific formulation. The rock on which such attempts are liable to founder is the rational assumption that every operation of the psyche to which the ego can ascribe no conscious purpose must be mechanical, and therefore of an inferior order.

Jung's conception of individuality, as embracing the whole of the psychical subject, even from the standpoint of scientific description, is an empirical necessity. It comprehends the ego as a partial mental system within the psychic organism, and the structure and potentialities of this total organism are as much and as little concerned with the ego-function as the

1 As connoting a demonstrable field of mental activity I find this term more satisfactory than the unconscious.

total body is concerned, for instance, with the single function of vision. The objection so frequently levelled at this conception of the psyche, that it is based on some mystical belief, springs from the repugnance of the intellect to admit the existence of a different order of intelligence, based upon premises of a different character from those that are supported by contemporary collective consciousness.

The evolution of individual consciousness, which we already begin to discern as an underlying ruling purpose in the material of our patient, finds little enough sanction in normal collective opinion. No practical method, therefore, whose formulations are attuned solely to the ideal of average social requirements is liable to take cognizance of this basic human problem. It may even be asserted that the problem should not occur (as, for instance, in Communist Russia or Hitlerized Germany) since man is allowed to exist only for collective purposes. But in countries where culture is not yet identical with politics, a qualitative valuation of individuality is still feasible. Accordingly a circumstantial record of the process of psychological evolution in a complex modern man must have a significance beyond that of a purely psychiatric demonstration.

* * * * *

As a kind of epilogue to our discussion of this drawing the patient produced the following dream:

> " I was sitting at a table and God was there. A servant (a man) brought in a banana, and I was told the devil was in it. I said I would exorcise the devil. God smiled and gave His approval. I said, 'In the name of the Lord, appear,' and out of the banana came a large green snake. This was the devil, and he said he was there because of my sins. He recited many sins, some of which I had committed and some I had not. I remember one of the sins I had been guilty of was to tell one woman that she was all spirit, and another that she was all sex. Then the snake went and coiled itself on the mantelpiece."

Although compelled to resist intriguing flowers that blow beside the path, I must give the reader the key-association to this dream in the hope that it will interpret itself.

The dreamer had recently read the *Visions* of Hermas in the Apocryphal New Testament, and the illuminating commentary on Hermas in Jung's *Psychological Types*. Jung's account is mainly concerned with the transformation of Rhoda, the woman whom Hermas has secretly coveted, into his anima or soul-mistress. The reader will recall how Hermas sees her in a vision elevated to the heavenly sphere, and asks her what she is doing in heaven. She replies: " I am charging thee with thy sins before the Lord." This, then, is the association with the snake-dæmon, who is ushered in by the shadow-self (the servant), and who then proceeds to " charge him with his sins before the Lord."

The snake, as a dæmonic[1] form of the anima, appears not infrequently in classical myth, as, for instance, Hecate, Lamia and Empusa, all of which possess either fish- or snake-like attributes. Lilith is, perhaps, the best-known example in which the primordial anima-form is identified with the snake. In his chapter on " The Dual Mother Rôle " in *Psychology of the Unconscious* Jung accounts for this dæmonic and devouring aspect of the anima as the negative effect of the mother-son constellation in a man's psychology, expressing the dread of the repressed incestuous longing.

Lilith, according to the Talmudic tradition, was the first wife of Adam, with whom he contended for mastery. Hence she personifies the dark, primordial female principle, standing eternally opposed to the spiritual logos. In the dream the anima snake-dæmon betrays her feminine nature. She conceals herself in the fruit of desire; when made to appear, she accuses him of sin—a characteristic function of the anima. She makes herself at home on his hearth as a familiar spirit, finally associating herself with Shakti, the serpent-form of the primordial goddess. The primordial anima thus declares herself as a dæmon or god-devil, in whom the opposites are not yet divided. As the representative of the original ambi-

1 In his valuable study of early Greek thought, *From Religion to Philosophy* (Edward Arnold, 1912), Professor F. M. Cornford traces the evolution of god and hero from the earlier concept of dæmon, representing a spirit, without human attributes, localized in certain portions of the earth, or in certain rivers or elements. It is in this sense of a natural force, or spirit, that I use the word in this work.

valency of the unconscious, she accuses him of the sin of apportioning woman into spiritual and sexual categories. She seems to aim at resolving this sophisticated prejudice by leading the libido back to the primordial level. In the Jewish legend Lilith was also conceived as the hermaphrodite of the first beginning—*i.e.*, before the differentiation of sex divided the human being into man-soul and woman-soul. Sex-desire was thus conceived of as the eternal longing of the sundered halves to experience, once again, their original state of unity. From this point of view sexuality, as a constant reminder of man's incomplete state, comes to be the enemy of the longed-for state of perfection.

What lurks within the banana is the symbol of this eternal longing, which, if followed blindly, may drive a man on a restless dæmonic quest through an erotic wilderness where every other value is eventually obliterated by the one obsessive craving. Hence Lilith is also found to be the feminine counterpart of Asmodeus, the possessive vampire who sucked the marrow out of the bridegroom's bones as soon as the marriage was consummated. Rightly has it been said that to grope among the sexual roots of human motive leads us into the realm of demonology.

This dream appeared, literally, at the psychological moment. It provided the needed clue in respect of the empty space in the drawing which, according to the patient, should have contained the devil. From the fact that the spiritual and sexual emanations of the god converge upon this area, we inferred that the lacking content would probably embrace this opposition. The proliferation of the bunch of phalli in this locality also indicated the influence of a phallic dæmon. This timely dream suggests that the invisible dæmon is Lilith, the primordial anima of all mankind, hence the mythological equivalent of Shakti. The compelling sense of accusation which accompanied the drawing is re-enacted in the dream, only in a rather different setting. The act of exorcism was of especial interest for the patient: almost more than anything he needed the authority, as well as the means, for dealing with the archaic invasions of the unconscious. The actual production of these drawings—*i.e.*, the work of making the subjective objective—proved of great value in this respect.

The analytical spirit prompted the patient to grope his way back to his earliest infantile experience. In the shut-in garden of fantasy he looked, as it were, down a well, seeking there his individual origins. At the bottom he discerned a dæmonic form of immemorial antiquity, enfolding all the opposites—life and death, god and devil, creation and destruction, male and female within her verdant coils. This is also " that old serpent called the devil " of the Book of Revelation, which now comes back from hell.

CHAPTER VII

THE HORRIFIC ASPECT OF THE UNCONSCIOUS

Preliminary Discussion of the Myth

I

When we compare Drawing VIII. with the preceding drawings we know that some breakwater or defence has given way. Until now the drawings have been diagrammatic and representational. Their main characteristic has been explanatory in so far as they were affected by preconceived intellectual points of view. But here we dive straight into the affective experience, expressed in pure mythological symbolism: the monster seems to come upon us with a roar. Although the continuity with previous contents exists, it is none the less clear that an entirely new and unexpected development has occurred. The immediacy of representation intimates that the subject is expressing something overwhelming.

Jung has used the term *primordial image* to distinguish those factors of psychical experience which, because of their archaic or impressive character, cannot be ascribed by the subject to his own personal psychology. The term therefore postulates the existence of psychic entities which transcend the limits of personality. This drawing illustrates the empirical necessity of this term. The subject could not appropriate this mythological monster as part of his conscious or unconscious personality, for wherever he turns in the mythological museum he will encounter this same protean image. How then are we to distinguish a mythological from a personal content, since both are clearly psychological? Before we can answer this question we must come to some kind of understanding of the standpoint from which the myth is to be valued, and discuss how it may have originated.

To begin with, it is a significant fact that both Freud and Jung have based their respective fundamental conceptions upon mythological grounds. Freud's theory of the cause of the devouring sense of guilt and anxiety found in the neurotic constitution is based upon the Œdipus myth, or, further back still, upon the myth of the patricidal primal horde;[1] while Jung's conception of the overwhelming and devouring aspect of the unconscious rests upon the mythological motif of the devouring mother, which he explains as the abysmal fear of the incest-taboo. Both conceptions are grounded upon the profound reality of incest in human psychology; yet no man actually experiences fear of being castrated by the father, and the idea of having intercourse with the mother is not a genuine problem for any adult, still less for any child. These conceptions represent archaic psychic foundations; they are not actual desires or fears. In other words, they are true only for the primordial psyche.

The practical psychologist accepts this mythological idiom without question, because it provides him with a means of describing the dark hinterland of the human mind. But were a questionnaire to be circulated among the psychological consulting-rooms asking, What scientific reasoning can you advance for the use of a fantastic mythological idiom in describing certain psychopathological states? I believe we should discover an astonishing variety of explanations. Thousands of intelligent minds are profoundly stirred by Wagner's mythological operas. What kind of replies should we receive if we asked these people to explain in what way this mythological realm touches their personal lives and interests? A great many would probably say that Wagner's dramas open a door into another world, where their personal worries and problems are temporarily dismissed. Others might say that they are attracted to mythological forms of art and music on æsthetic grounds. While with others, who attend the opera for social reasons, and are ostentatiously bored, their human reaction to the myth could only be deduced from their dreams. Rationalists—among whom I include psycho-analysts—explain this attraction of the myth as a retrospective nostalgia for the golden age of infancy. Yet if this were true surely toyshops and nursery-schools would also be frequented by bevies of rapt dreamers.

[1] Freud: *Totem and Taboo.*

The truth is that every humane soul yearns to be cured of his all-too-personal ego, and the mythological drama belongs to that other realm of experience in which the personal ego is dissolved. People who have suffered a lifelong imprisonment with their "personality," with all its self-conscious mannerisms, its habitual tricks of evasion and defence, its perpetual fuss about prestige, its ridiculous self-esteem and oversensitiveness, its meannesses, its cravings, its jealous eye on the impression it creates, long for the blessed state of non-personal freedom. With the creation of his individual myth the patient discovers the impersonal aspect of his psychology, which is the root and foundation of his whole psychic life. Those who are unaware of their impersonal psychology tend to project it into religion, art or music, or into the study of primitive cultures: hence the passionate anthropological and archæological controversies and schisms.

According to Jung, myths are products of the collective unconscious. They are traditional vehicles of collective values. They represent the epitomized reactions of the human psyche to oft-repeated crises, needs and longings in the long tale of human experience. The history of man's development, the benevolent and malign forces which have attended his spiritual adventures, the necessities which have driven and the aspirations which have prompted him, are to be found in the myths. Because they are full of the very essence of our common humanity, surviving myths of past cultures have always attracted the poetical genius, and many of the ancient myths have thus been handed down to us as immortal epics.

It is probable, however, as Hocart argues in his paper on "*The Life-giving Myth*," that myth and ritual were originally one, being the traditional form in which ritual ceremonies, concerned with fertility and the renewal of life, had to be enacted by the king-sacrificer. Hocart regards the separation of the myth from its accompanying ritual as regrettable literary interference by poets and writers of a later culture.

From one point of view, therefore, the myth is the dream of a people, and can be interpreted by the same method as we apply to the dream.[1] From another, it is the traditional

[1] The dream has been described as the myth of the individual.

container of a very practical ritual. Hocart speaks both from first-hand knowledge of primitive mentality and from wide study of the early Vedic rituals: his conviction, therefore, that all myths were originally just the vocal part of a life-giving or life-renewing ritual must not be lightly dismissed. But we can agree with his resolve to emphasize the absolutely real function of the myth in the history of culture without bringing it to the level of the market-place, as Hocart is inclined to do. He is angry with the poets for abducting the myth from its practical everyday context and enshrining it in the alien temple of literature. But surely the poets who are attracted to mythology would find little interest in all this raw material if it did not contain the living stuff of human experience. The themes of mythology are manifold, as life is manifold; therefore a purely scientific, rational explanation of a myth is never enough. A spontaneous product of the human mind, so enigmatic, so manifold and so profound, cannot be fully accounted for on the ground of practical utility.

A psychological understanding of the myth therefore needs to enquire not so much into the category of the events described as into the nature of the experience. To cite an example taken from life: While two farm-labourers of East Anglia were sheltering from a thunderstorm a terrific burst of thunder suddenly rent the heavens overhead: " Did ye see the black horse in the sky ?" said one to the other. Here we see the mythological moment and the true mythological response. The uneducated peasant has not acquired the habit of responding to life from his higher cortical centres. Instinctively, therefore, he falls back upon the primordial image, with the result that he is still able to respond adequately to a primordial situation. Observe that it is not the thunder as such, but rather the overwhelmingness, the impressiveness of the total experience that brings up the image of the black horse from the archaic depths. Achilles and Hector fighting before Troy, the enchantment of the hero's companions by Circe or of Ulysses by Calypso, the vast power of Cyclops, the murderous might of the Minotaur, the unassuageable Gilgamish, the inspired Noah, the unconquerable Cuchullain—in every case we find we have to do with an overpowering impression or event, demanding, as it were, a mythological orchestration.

The overpowering effect of the king or the *mana* personality is just as real as that of the thunderstorm. Exceptional valour or wisdom is not merely different from the ordinary in degree; to the primordial mind these impressions mean one thing only—*i.e.*, the gods or spirits are participating in human affairs. It is this feeling of the presence of powers or forces beyond the ordinary which produces the characteristic mythological situation. In the myth the veil separating gods and men becomes transparent. We see Noah going about his crazy task, with chaos piling up to overwhelm him. But if we listen closely we also hear the voice that the deluge failed to extinguish, and the veil falls at our feet.

The myth contains and enfolds the religious experience of mankind. Before ever He became God, Jahveh was an overwhelming experience. He was manifestly God, because the people of Israel could not deny the overwhelming power of the Spirit which had snatched them from slavery, hammered them and hardened them, led them, and condemned them; and finally made them into a nation.

These self-evident truths need to be said, because in our passion for scientific and historical fact we have almost lost that feeling for spiritual reality which holds the myth in the heart, instead of in the scientific museum. To the modern analytical mind, for example, the historicity of Christ is of more moment than the fact that He had such an overwhelming effect upon the hearts of men and women that they could only think of Him, in the sacred way of the myth, as the Son of God. Let the intellect not deride the emotional evidence of the myth. The fundamental fabric of life is emotional, and all our knowledge of the reality of God depends upon emotional experience. A vast superstructure of creed and dogma may obscure this elementary fact; yet the fact remains that the myth is nearer the essence of religion than any authoritative explanation concerning the Founder's doctrine.

This superiority of the intellect to emotional witness is revealed in the common attitude, " Only a myth "—as though a myth were the arbitrary invention of an idle moment instead of the means whereby the awestruck human soul pays tribute to its own greatness, or saves itself, perhaps, from the over-powering deluge. For the myth not merely chronicles the original impression or revelation: it was also used, as we know, as a magical defence against bad influences and spirits. The idea that is always present in these ritual creations and invocations is "As then, so now." Thus the myth is the vessel by which the power of the ancestor-spirits of the great heroic age can be transmitted to posterity. The enacting and re-enacting of the rite of creation, in order to ensure the fertility of land, cattle and women, is a case in point. There can be no doubt that a tradition of divine fertility is liable to cling to an ancestor who had unusual success, whether as cultivator or progenitor (the immense fame of Abraham as an ancestor seems to have rested mainly upon such a foundation), and the practical value of the myth consisted in reproducing the ancestor's fertility by invoking his powerful spirit. The unique success of the ancestor was assumed (as in the case of Abraham) to be due to the benevolent intervention of a god. Therefore the myth which preserves and honours this celestial intervention is an effectual reminder to the god to interfere again.

II

The mythic themes which play the chief rôles in the present study are—

(1) Self-impregnation.
(2) The hero and the devouring monster.
(3) Renewal of life.

These motifs may be closely interwoven one with the other, as, for instance, in the idea of the dragon or serpent which guards the life-giving treasure; also in the battle of the youthful hero with the dragon, symbolizing—as in the legend of St. George and the Dragon, or that of Apollo vanquishing the Python of the deluge—the victory of a new and more advanced cultural spirit over an earlier cult.

From the extraordinary prevalence of the devouring monster in quasi-primitive mythology we must assume that early civilizing man was preoccupied with the dread of being engulfed. The regularity of the seasons and other cosmic events, such as the rising and setting of the sun, etc., offered no adequate grounds for this constant dread. The fear of extinction seems to dawn within the human soul at about the same time that man rejects his primordial natural state. To depart from their food-gathering natural state was to the earlier unsophisticated branch of mankind a dangerous impiety. The Promethean innovator was doomed to be the prey of criminal feelings, for to espouse the civilizing way meant a repudiation of the primordial piety and allegiance to nature. Individuality is rooted in this crime.

In the Gilgamish epos, which derives from early Sumerian civilization, the bulk of the story is concerned with the hero's haunting terror of extinction: in the end his search for the secret of immortality becomes an all-consuming passion. The tragedy of the myth reaches its climax when, having gained the rejuvenating plant from the bottom of the sea, it is stolen from him by a water-snake as Gilgamish stoops to drink at a pool on his homeward way. Thus the heroic masculine will has to pay the full price to the dark, unconscious feminine principle, in order that the balance of nature shall be restored.

It is probable that Hocart is correct in regarding the myths of creation as belonging originally to a life-renewing ritual, and that the magical significance of the divine King, the necessity of his strict ritual observance, and the whole symbolism of initiation are expressions of man's profound longing for the renewal of life.

From our experience of primitive mentality, whether in Africa or the consulting-room, we can say that the thing which most fears extinction is the spark or flame of conscious life: for that which is in truth the sun of our world can easily be engulfed—not by death alone, but by demonic possessions, witchcraft, enchantment, conflagration of panic, and all the other paralysing invaders of consciousness. All these threaten the loosely organized, quasi-primitive consciousness with eclipse.

When we speak of an integrated consciousness, we think

of a conscious function, armed and defended at every point: a firm structure that cannot suddenly be overturned by affect. A man thus equipped can meet any kind of situation without inferiority or exaggerated self-confidence, whereas the haunting fears of the poorly integrated personality are concerned, not merely with the menace of external circumstances, but also with the ever-recurring doubt as to the validity of his own personality, and its possible extinction by suicide or insanity.

Conscious individuality emerges out of unconscious night as miraculously, yet as predictably, as the rising of the sun. It can also be obscured and extinguished by the forces of the unconscious, just as the light of the sun can be obscured or extinguished by thick clouds, eclipse, or the descent of the sun below the horizon.[1]

The myth of the devouring monster which swallows the sun-hero, carries him eastward under the sea, and finally disgorges him at sunrise as the rejuvenated sun is not primarily intended as a cosmogonic explanation. The process of rebirth, or the renewal of life, is near and vital to the primordial intelligence: it is the experience of this renewal, after being swallowed by the unconscious, that is commemorated in the myth. Fundamentally the myth is experiential rather than intellectual.

On the lower cultural levels, as, for instance, amongst certain tribes of the New Hebrides, fear of the devouring monster is more powerful than any other motive, whereas on higher levels the quest of the magical substance, the healing value, the symbol of power becomes the dominant theme.

The devouring force of the unconscious is visible daily in our consulting-rooms, only we express it in more becoming language. A patient in a regressive state, for instance, is under the influence of an archaic affect that has usurped the seat of personality. When a patient is in a depressed state his expression is changed, virtue has gone out of him, and a different personality looks out of his eyes: in the language of the myth, his sun has been swallowed. If he were an

[1] Layard describes how the natives of Malekula (in the New Hebrides) are shadowed by fear whenever the sun is not visible in the heavens.

African native, he might say that he had lost a soul in the night, or that somebody had bewitched him.

Regarded as a chronicle of man's cultural enterprise and of the spiritual dangers threatening the flame of consciousness, the myth offers invaluable insight into his age-long struggle with inertia and unconsciousness. But, in order to limit the field, many workers explore only the personal psyche, refusing the wider, historical view of the mind. Yet the neurosis is a disease of the ego, and only through the emptying of the ego into the impersonal unconscious can it be renewed and cured of its misery.

We have seen how, from one point of view, the myth can be regarded as a chronicle of the overpowering impression, personality or event. From another, it must be seen as a practical means of invoking the spiritual powers and for the magical control of nature. It is therefore a primordial religious expression in the sense that it is something interposed between man and the spiritual forces which fill his soul with dread, thus serving the religious functions of protection and invocation. Primitive cosmogonic myths are not so much an attempt to explain the universe as a protective screen wherewith the dreadful immensity of nature may be cloaked with a veil of familiar images.

These conclusions hold good, however, only in respect of that portion of mankind which took the civilizing way. As regards the legends of the other portion, there is a most significant absence of certain of the favourite themes which abound in the cultural myth. This other portion comprises a great variety of primordial food-gathering peoples living on the outskirts of civilization.[1] These tribes have, apparently, never departed from the original state in which man is contained by nature, as an animal is contained by the law of its species. Among these food-gatherers the mythic stories that are told are almost entirely concerned with the doings and adventures of certain animals; the cosmogonic screen is also

[1] For a full account of these food-gathering tribes I refer the reader to *The Primordial Ocean* by W. J. Perry and to *Human History* by Elliot Smith; also to Robert N. Lowie's collection of Shushonean Tales in the *Journal of American Folk-Lore*, vol. 37, Nos. 143-144, for the typical myth-tales in which the rôle of god or hero is played by an animal.

covered in the main with the exploits of familiar animals. There appears to be no trace of the quasi-divine hero who has to do battle with the great serpent of the deep, for these people have neither gods nor kings. As a rule they live in small communities, frequently nomadic: the headman is not endowed with magical attributes, but is chosen as the man of ripest experience. Their attitude to the so-called boons of civilization is usually that of polite but adamant refusal. According to accounts of competent observers, they possess a natural piety and reserve. In general, the communities are examples of unplanned communism in which the proceeds of the hunt are shared. A warning instinct seems to defend them from accumulating possessions. The women are given equal status with the men, the aged and infirm are treated with care, and the individuality of children is respected.

Accounts of these food-gathering tribes, ranging from the Eskimo of the Arctic to the Punan of Borneo, or from certain Indian tribes of North America to the African Bushmen, are so remarkably consistent that we are justified in regarding them as a definite type of mankind, in spite of the fact that no theory of racial affinity or of diffusion of cultural influence could possibly explain their existence. Their affinity is sociological and psychological, not racial, and they differ from collectivized mankind in the following essentials. They do not form large communities, they do not amass property and possessions, they are peaceful and do not fight other tribes either for gain, honour or women. They show small inclination to improve upon their natural state by hoarding grain, or by any kind of provision against adverse conditions. They have no developed religious ceremonial or magical rites. Although narrative tales and recitals are highly valued, they possess no mythology in which magically endowed heroes, gods or kings intervene on behalf of helpless humanity. The parts played by gods and heroes in epic myths are usually performed by helpful animals in these stories.

Perhaps the most significant psychological distinction—a distinction which separates these natural food-gatherers from the rest of mankind—consists in the character of their puberty initiations. These show no trace of cruelty and they are frequently optional. Instead of being based on the idea that the youth has to be alienated from his original nature, they encourage him, through the authority of father or guardian, to perform a mettlesome deed which tests his courage and, at the same time, establishes a magical relation analogous to the relation with the anima on the cultural level. The character of the initiatory rites in a collectivized people is just the reverse of this. The puberty rites consist in an attempt to inoculate the boy with the premises of the collective psyche, to estrange him from his original natural being, and to brand him with the idea that he is now a changed being, belonging exclusively and absolutely to the tribe or clan. He becomes subject to the collective taboos and ideals, and is given his ordained collective status. In militaristic peoples the initiatory ideal may be extremely severe and often needlessly cruel.

The psychological results of these opposite types of initiation are highly significant. Whereas the collectively initiated individual, rooted exclusively in his collective status, is liable to submit fatalistically to the tyranny of dictatorship, and to become thereby psychologically enslaved, the type that has not been alienated from his individual birthright can never be enslaved. Among the food-gatherers, therefore, tyranny is practically unknown.

In the light of these facts we cannot assume that the nomadic, food-gathering type of mankind belongs to an inferior human order, notwithstanding its obstinate resistance to civilizing methods. The natural intelligence and individual integrity of these people, their indigenous human piety and self-restraint are, on the contrary, singularly conspicuous in comparison with their collectivized neighbours. However disagreeable to our self-esteem, we have to admit that certain races of mankind who preferred to hold to their original natural condition, and refused to take the civilizing road, have certain admirable qualities which are strikingly absent in contemporary civilized life.

Although we may not wholly agree with the view of Elliot Smith, who sees in this primitive condition the mythical golden age actually existing to-day, yet, from the unflattering comparison presented with striking unanimity by a variety of civilized observers, we cannot escape the feeling that the impetus of civilization has carried us a long way from our original human birthright.

This digression back to the state of man as a natural denizen of the earth is helpful, because it provides us with the alternative hypothesis—*i.e.*, the primordial standpoint, before which our civilized superiority stands arraigned. When we speak of the conflict between nature and culture, do we not imply that a certain part of our nature still insists that the kind of human being just described is what nature really intended, and that the striving, bluffing, self-deluding, civilized creature lost his bearings when he turned his back upon his first mother and his original nature?

The civilized part of our mind, on the other hand, is convinced of its complete superiority in every respect over the savage outcast. It can hardly recognize the fact that there is another standpoint. Why, indeed, should it question its own validity with all the power of civilization behind it? If it believed in the psychological existence of this vastly ancient human being, it might view him as a scientific specimen, measuring the while with a superior eye the vast distance which separates civilized man from this ignorant primordial condition. It does not occur to the dissatisfied modern man that his discontent is related to the fact that a portion of his psychology has never accepted civilization, but still maintains the primordial standpoint. Yet occasionally he is stirred by vague nostalgia: perhaps the night air seems to vibrate with a distant primitive chant from across the river. Should he ever happen to have dealings with primitive races, he may recognize in them a certain quality, a native dignity and poise which he would fain possess. He may discern a certain gentleness, an unhurried tranquillity that are foreign to the crowded streets and the frenzied activity of the civilized environment.

When we try to adjust the balance in the light of our present knowledge, we are bound to admit that the living primordial man is vastly different from the immoral, cruel and tricky ruffian with which nineteenth-century enlightenment was wont to demonstrate the desirability of progress. We no longer believe that our original nature is evil, and the reflective godparent is by no means comfortable at a christening. A profound change of attitude towards primitive peoples has already taken place: a change not unconnected, perhaps, with our analytical discovery that just below the civilized veneer of European psychology we find the primitive mind. Our changed attitude to the mission-field derives probably from the same insight.

In the last century missionary enterprise was regarded as a command from heaven. To-day a very great number of unprejudiced observers would be inclined to agree with Richard Wyndham when he writes: " I consider mission work as an abomination, designed to change a contented and noble animal into a dissatisfied, half-educated, dirtily clothed, class-conscious human being."[1]

A wide gulf separates us from the Victorians: we no longer trust their enthusiasms. In our hearts we prefer the savage to the Victorian as a brother; though the latter preached a belief in universal brotherhood, it became humanly relevant only when his brothers were clothed and educated. How then did we acquire this other standpoint from which it is possible to criticize the civilization to which we belong? How but by listening to the primordial man in our own nature? Yet this, too, is a danger, for if we listen to this dark voice, we may eventually be seduced into a renegade rejection of civilization. Siren voices are sometimes heard even in Bloomsbury, advocating the many advantages of the primitive state. The fantasy of rejecting the whole civilizing experiment in favour of the primæval, timeless, care-free state has been tried often enough: it has never succeeded. At bottom it is not an experiment, but an escape. The man who " goes native " is scorned, even by the natives he imitates.

The conflict cannot be solved, therefore, on the basis of either . . . or. The only possible way to regain the original virtue of our primordial ancestors is to make a genuine pact with nature in ourselves. The primordial human being in our own psyche has a wisdom that we need: on his side, he needs

[1] Richard Wyndham: *The Gentle Savage.*

to participate in the fullness of opportunity which culture alone can give him. Thus in the realm of the individual soul a new covenant is being made.

Collectively, civilized mankind has always evinced a bad conscience *vis-a-vis* nature; living continually behind barricades, he has tried every ruse to insulate his life from direct contact with the earth. We catch a glimpse, in the far-away dawn of civilization, of this same ruthless masculine power, which attempted to conquer and override the first mother. It is personified in the mythical figure of Gilgamish, the cultural hero, the quasi-immortal founder of the thick-walled town of Erech. He is the dictator who forces his people to unceasing labour in the building of his vast citadel. In their tribulation, the people pray to Anu (the sky god) to send down a champion who will release them from Gilgamish. Enkidu, the primordial man, who lives with the wild beasts in the mountains and whose hair is long like a woman's, is created by the mother-goddess out of earth. Gilgamish seduces Enkidu to leave his wild existence by using one of the sacred prostitutes of Ishtar as a decoy. On Enkidu's arrival in Erech, there is a fierce battle between the two champions, after which a pact of brotherhood is sealed between them. This becomes so close and indissoluble that when Enkidu dies Gilgamish is possessed by a passion of grief, which finally urges him to cross even the sea of death in quest of Enkidu and immortality.

III

In this myth we possess a chronicle proving that the conflict between nature and culture was essentially the same 5,000 years ago as it is to-day. The symbolical solution, offered in the pact between the two protagonists, is analogous to the goal of our analytical method, which Jung has described as a genuine coming to terms with the unconscious.

Studying the myths of the past we discover a priceless spiritual inheritance, but this does not explain why the development of the individual myth should become an absolutely vital aspect of the therapeutic process. For we cannot assume that these mythological analogies are merely a kind of allegorical idiom required by a stubbornly infantile part of the mind. On the contrary, the absorbing intensity of creative interest which often goes to the making of the individual myth is sufficient to prove that the myth itself is the healing vessel which contains the supreme value.

The psyche needs to be contained in a living container. This must be taken as axiomatic. There remains, therefore, the vital question whether we remain unconsciously identified with the parent, the teacher, or some loved model of our youth, or adapt ourselves exclusively to some ready-made collective container, such as the family, the clan, the church, the political party, the university or public school, the profession or business—possible collective containers are legion, each generating its characteristic social attitude—or whether we create a container which can adequately house the full potentialities of the human individual both personal and impersonal, individual and social, rational and irrational. Our answer to this question will depend upon whether we seek in the adventure of life something beyond mere security and biological perpetuation. For if we desire to explore the further possibilities contained in our human microcosm, risking ourselves beyond the boundaries of collective security, we must needs create a vessel to carry our enterprise, a vessel which, already in the long human past, has responded to the direst needs of the soul.

The individual myth is the vessel supplied and created by the individual psyche, fitted, therefore, to contain this particular psychology in its greatest enterprise—viz., the creation of individuality. He who allows the self to be passively contained by the parent, the teacher or the leader, never attempting the solitary enterprise, cannot achieve individuality. There are certain primitive societies, as we shall presently see, in which initiation is a solitary and perilous enterprise undertaken only by the youth who desires to be a full man. The lad is told he is going to die, and is warned never to speak of his experience to a soul. In a word, he creates his own myth, and lives the myth he has created.

In the present instance, the subject had been passively identified with (*i.e.*, contained in) the father. Nothing but an almost worthless imitation could result from continuing along this road. But in order to detach himself from the father, he had to be prepared to face his worst dread. Mythologically this dread is figured as dissolution or dismemberment, and the aspect of the unconscious prevailing at this crisis is the horrific or the devouring one. The death of the previous personality, and the birth of the new, coincide with the moment of detachment from a familial or historical container and the creation of the individual myth. Necessarily, therefore, the physiology of detachment is identical at first with the affect of dread. Not until the energy flows freely into the creative work will the subject realize that the task his soul is set upon is the making of an ark which can ride the deluge, and that its construction is no haphazard improvisation, but follows a pattern laid down through the ages—a pattern that is as valid for the primitive as for the civilized roots of his personality. Thus the individual myth not only reconciles the primitive and the cultural: it is in the fullest sense the creation of these contending opposites. Primitive mentality and primitive life possess for many an inexhaustible attraction. Those who are sufficiently curious about themselves to wonder why this is so may begin to create a myth, and this myth is the true goal of their interest. Even those who believe their interest in primitive mentality to be purely academic in character are just as likely to create a mythology out of their interest, only in their case it is unconscious and usually remains unrecognized.

IV

Drawing VIII

The drawing consists of a " close-up " representation of a huge mouth, with thick red lips and three rows of teeth above and below.[1] The outer row is situated at the outer edge of the upper and lower lips. The middle row is set at the inner edge of either lip, while the two inner rows belong to a separate system placed in the centre of the mouth-cavity. The elements of this central system have been carried over

[1] While the patient was drawing this picture he was devoured by raging hunger, which left him when he had finished it.

from the previous drawing, where we observed two finger-biting sets of teeth, with corresponding bleeding, on either side of the green receptacle at the bottom left-hand corner. These elements, however, are now differently constellated. The teeth (painted silver), consisting of three incisors and two canines above, articulating with a similar set below, are seen closing upon an irregular green mass containing a central yellow nucleus and a surrounding constellation of nineteen nucleoli painted in gold. Drops of blood are being squeezed out of this living mass, and are to be seen in the intervening space between the teeth and the green substance. The blood is apparently being sucked out between the upper and lower canines on either side by the shut-faced lunatic on the left and the open-faced on the right. The lunatic heads are enclosed in a kind of vesicle (with yellow background), just outside the large articulating canines on either side, the neck of the vesicle being continuous with the cavity of this inner, framed system. The teeth of this inner system, as well as the teeth belonging to the mouth, are all painted silver, which, as mentioned above, is the colour associated with the mother-complex. The background of the mouth cavity is stippled with dots of yellow and red.

Above the mouth, and only just coming into the picture, is the end of a large nose, showing two nostrils (painted blue). From either nostril comes a blast of fiery breath. The rest of the drawing consists of a reticulated background, in which a criss-cross of rather fluid elements, coloured red and green, is held together by a large-meshed network of black lines. In five of these squares below the mouth level a disjuncted, functionless eye is painted (blue pupil on a gold field). The three larger of these appear in the looser network on the right, the two smaller in the more concentrated background on the left. Two areas of wavy lines on a gold background in the bottom corners, left and right, are portions of the god's beard. These are the only fragments left of the ideal image, or super-ego, of the last drawing.

* * * * *

Our interest naturally centres in the green mass with golden particles that is gripped between the rows of teeth.

It was conceived by the patient as protoplasm, or primordial life-stuff, and is clearly derived from the green lavatory-pan of the previous drawing, which had some irrational association with the mother's lap. We remarked before that it had begun to show a certain amœboid character.

The grains of gold forming the constellation of nucleoli around a central yellow nucleus appear to have been shot into the protoplasm by the golden arrows of the god's beard, and by the penetrating fingers shown in Drawing VII. There are twelve golden rays of the beard and there are six fingers, each of the latter having a golden finger-nail. These represent the eighteen points of penetration. There are actually eighteen distinct nucleoli. The nineteenth is doubtful: it is attached to the second from the top, on the left-hand margin of the constellation. There is also a doubtful finger in the previous drawing. The lower finger of the bifurcation at the right-hand lower corner of the framed system has not been given a golden finger-nail.

The patient said he did not know how many nucleoli he had put into the constellation. Hence the correspondence described above could not have been consciously intended.

The central yellow nucleus is derived from the fæcal rings and from the yellow centre at the heart of the inverted laminal field. Yellow and green are the polar elements of the dynamic system in all these drawings, and these colours were used for the intrinsic elements of the framed system. The golden particles are extrinsic, having been shot into the protoplasm in much the same way as the male spermatozoon is projected into the female ovum.

We may regard this central green mass, therefore, as primordial life-stuff that has been impregnated by the ancestral spirit, who is also identified with the sun. It is, in fact, a symbolical harking back to the first beginnings of organic life, as though a speck of plasson[1] in the sea had become impregnated by the rays of the sun.

The green protoplasm is being gripped and moulded into

[1] *Plasson* = the homogeneous protoplasm of hypothetical primitive organisms, not yet differentiated into nucleus and general cell-substances. (Oxford Dictionary.)

a dentated shape by the upper and lower teeth and the two canines on either side of it. These long inward-curving canines also serve as a protecting barrier against the vampire lunatic faces on either side. Thus, although the protoplasm is being squeezed and moulded by the teeth it is also protected by them. This is the first significant intimation of the ambiguous function of the unconscious as both devourer and preserver.

This aspect of the unconscious is found in a great variety of mythic forms. In one form, mentioned by Frobenius as the "general hatching out," the hero deliberately swims, or steers his canoe, into the jaws of the monster. With his sword he then cuts out the monster's heart, or some other vital organ, with which to satisfy his hunger. Having hewn his way out of the monster's belly he not only saves himself, but also all the rest of his neighbours and relatives whom the monster had previously swallowed. By deliberately entering the devouring monster, and by eating a vital organ, the hero partakes of the dæmonic power. This is the source of the hero's superhuman efficacy: by virtue of the heroic deed the dæmonic is converted into the divine. This theme is developed further in subsequent drawings.

The two lunatic faces are associated with the nail-biting, onanistic leakage appearing on either side of the green lavatory-pan in Drawing VII. The leakage of blood in both drawings, and the same relative positions in regard to the central green mass, identify the lunatics with the danger of onanistic inversion of the libido. The patient was, in fact, constantly liable to find his capacity for objective achievement undermined by unconscious fantasy-activity, as though his vitality were being drained away by a vampire. This inverted fantasy - activity of the infantile psyche was represented (Drawing III.) in the inverted phallic system that was identified with the vampire face, the retroverted nipple and the phallic tube with its red leakage. The character of stasis or inertia was written over this whole system, just as it is written upon the faces of these vampire lunatics. The libido suspended in this morbid constellation has never been born into the world of reality. It is infantile hermaphroditism, merely asking to be shut away and protected from any possible disturbance of its intra-uterine fantasies.

Everyone who has to do with schizophrenic subjects will recognize in this enclosed, inert fantasy-system that deep, affective apathy which is so characteristic of this psychology. Our surgical training might prompt us to try to excise this whole pathological system. But, even were this possible, the patient would not be cured. For the roots of such a system reach down to the main sources of instinctual energy; hence an excision of the complex would entail a real impoverishment of life. When libido is held under a false idea or presupposition, the analytical aim must be to replace the wrong hypothesis by a conception that works. Yet libido is not attracted to a completely futile hypothesis. To the infantile psyche the fantasies we must now criticize were by no means futile. Pathological in this respect means inappropriate: what was once valid for the infantile psyche has simply become obsolete and is now a social iniquity. The breaking away from the unproblematical infantile state is an educational work demanding a genuine moral feeling, but passion of any kind is just what the schizophrenic psychology lacks. Intelligence may be quick and facile, but the emotional attitude on which it rests remains childish and dependent, for lack of the alchemical fire.

In a correspondence with Professor Jung, in which the problem of schizophrenia was touched upon, he expressed his view as follows:

> "Whenever the problem of schizophrenia exists, there is this problem of the biggest thing (idea) in the smallest box. Such people are growing up in a world of things of only one meaning. They try not to see that things are paradoxical. Thus they avoid all dubitable things, or try to make dubitable things safe, in order to escape the necessity and the labour of widening their horizon. The more restricted the outlook, the greater is the unconscious tension, and the more infantile are the forms in which the basic philosophical ideas are encased."

According to this valuable postscript to Jung's published views, restriction of consciousness is to be regarded as the essential precondition of the schizophrenic inversion. It is not, I take it, merely a question of a limited outlook on life to which Jung refers, but rather to a certain inflexibility of mind, which amounts to an incapacity to conceive things differently. Like other men the schizophrenic identifies himself with a fantastic, idealized conception of himself; his abnormality consists in an unusually opaque carapace around his ego, which tends to convert every factor that contradicts his fantasy into hostile projections upon other people or upon society. The result of this blindness is that his libido remains entangled in inverted or paranoidal fantasy-systems, for what is not realized remains psychologically marooned.

From this standpoint the two vampire lunatics in this drawing would symbolize the onanistic fantasy of self-fertilization. The subject made a further illuminating series of drawings elaborating this infantile aim. According to our previous discussion, the primordial idea, of which this infantile fantasy is an embryonic expression, is the idea of the self-contained primordial being (*cf.* the Great Monad of China), which contains the opposites within itself and, therefore, like the world-soul in Plato's *Timæus*, has no need of any organs of relatedness to any object whatsoever, since all things are contained and fulfilled in itself.

It will be noted that, whenever the patient includes this inverted, onanistic element in any of his drawings, it is always enclosed, either in a frame or vesicle, as though the idea of a self-contained unity were the *raison d'être* of its existence. The characteristic egotism of neurotic or immature persons is based on this same half-truth. Individuation, on the contrary, is based upon the idea of the self as a self-regulating and self-contained totality gained through the fullest possible differentiation of psychical potentialities. The infantile mind accepts the symbolic potential of individuality, while ignoring the work of adaptation and relatedness by which this potential is made actual. The best of human truths can thus be changed into a dangerous false premise, on the strength of which every kind of folly and morbidity can be rationalized. The notorious fact that these neurotic attempts are often defended with ardent self-justification is due to the presence of this underlying ambiguous truth. There is a hint of this in the expression of repulsive self-satisfaction on the faces of the two lunatics. But, from the very fact that the patient has given them this revolting aspect, we may infer that he is already on the side of the angels.

It is a psychological axiom that the morbidity of a complex hinges upon its dissociated condition. The fact of its insulation signifies a kind of refusal to co-operate in the co-ordinated functioning of the whole, claiming to exist in and for itself as a separate entity. It is like a carcinomatous group of cells which, having rejected the principle of differentiation of function, has reverted to the state of being a law unto itself. Retrogressive development accompanies every organ or system, whether physical or psychical, which rejects the evolutionary principle of reciprocity and relatedness. Hence a renegade-system is either parasitic or predatory: it reaps where it has not sown. But the prevalence of the retrogressive tendency throughout the whole order of nature cannot be explained as mere inertia. We know from our experience with cancer that the vitality of the retrogressive, primordial type of cell is greater than that of the differentiated type. When once the renegade-movement has started, it accelerates like a stone rolling down a mountain-side. We observe the same phenomenon in the mental sphere, where a fantasy-system (as, for example, onanistic sexuality) becomes detached from its biological goal. There is a proliferation of luxuriant fantasy-products which undermines the vital interests of the personality and which, unless checked by an honest feeling for life, eventually produces a characteristic masochistic psychology.

V

The colonist who " goes native " would be the homologue to the cancer-cell in the social body, and he, too, tends to breed prolificly.

Civilization is the social aspect of human evolution, and those individuals who cannot stand the new strains of civilized requirements tend to take the alternative hypothesis and evolve retrogressively. If this analogy be true, we may assume that the speeding-up of evolution in human culture imposes an increasing tension on the psychic organism, and in so far as this tension is intensified by individual subjective factors the bias towards the retrogressive alternative will be correspondingly enhanced. Dogs, who have been forced by artificial selection to depart too quickly from their original wolf-nature, tend to exhibit neurotic manifestations and anxiety states which clearly demonstrate a morbid state of tension. The standards demanded by their human trainers create a conflict in the dog-soul which, in its essential character, is comparable to the conflict between the civilized and the primordial in ourselves.

These facts must be taken into consideration in formulating our fundamental conceptions of pyschopathology. For if I recognize that the renegade-problem in myself is of the same order as that of my dog, I have to formulate a theory which is fitted to embrace both series of facts. If human regression is due to incestuous cravings, is this also the case with my dog, who digs great holes in the earth into which he can creep when the regressive mood overtakes him? The hypothesis of incest is scarcely credible when extended to animal psychology.

In my view, therefore, it is more reasonable to regard the motif of incest as the specifically human idiom, with which the universal tendency of atavistic regression is expressed in the human psyche. Of the two directions which the libido can take, one is backwards towards its origin, the other is forwards towards a hypothetical evolutionary goal. Since the mother symbolizes for us the idea of source or origin, the retrogressive direction of the libido appears to go motherwards. But the overwhelming power of the incest-taboo undoubtedly obtains its authority from the larger issue at stake—namely, retrogression versus evolution.

* * * * *

The archaism of this drawing is self-evident, but it is also immensely vital. Are we therefore forced to assume that the unconscious adopts this horrific aspect for the purpose of warning consciousness against the dangers of the regressive pull? Any such rational explanation fails, in the true sense, to explain mythological events. The fear of water, which affects all land-creatures to some extent, is simply an expression of the fact that millions of creatures have been engulfed by this other element. We do well to dread the overwhelming power of the unconscious, inasmuch as millions of our forebears have been engulfed by it. Regarded teleologically, fear can be regarded as a red light appearing upon the psychical dashboard: it is an inner warning to be conscious.

The danger of dissolution is intimated in the drawing in the vagrant snail-fish eyes that seem to be caught in the meshes of the background network. The eye is peculiarly the symbol of consciousness, so that these disjuncted eyes would represent a fragmentation of consciousness on the one hand and a corresponding activation of the unconscious on the other.

In this symptom, therefore, two classical features of schizophrenia are revealed—namely, (*a*) disruption of consciousness, due to the lowering of the conscious level; and (*b*) the simultaneous regression to an archaic form of consciousness, symbolized by the snail-fish.

The abrupt lowering of the conscious level, which Jung believes to be the *conditio sine qua non* of the schizophrenic state, is very clearly shown in the sudden conversion from the ancestor spirit to this devouring monster. From the standpoint of the super-ego and traditional forms this is clearly a disaster; but we must also remember that alchemical creation demands the participation of every vital element. The creative cauldron may devour even the super-ego.

This other aspect of the drawing is brought out by an alchemical allusion generously provided by Professor Jung, who recently discovered certain mysterious references to the " eyes of fishes " in his alchemical researches. One citation he gives runs as follows:

> " Priusquam vera albido veniat, videbis in circuitu ad margines vitri in materia lapidis quasi essent gemmæ orientalis vitro insignis, tanquam oculi piscium."[1]

[1] Davidis Lagnei: " *Harmonia Chemica*," *Theatr. Chem.*, vol. iv., p. 870: " Before the true whiteness appears, you will see round about on the edge of the glass in the substance of the stone as it were Eastern jewels brilliant with glass, like the eyes of fishes."

Consulting Jung about the translation of this enigmatic text, he writes:

The importance of this allusion is contained in the idea of the fish-eyes forming " in the substance of the stone," as though the creator's consciousness pervaded the transforming matter. This idea was also realized by one Eiranæus Orandus, the author of an alchemical treatise, dated 1624, who quotes the following passage from Zechariah iv. 10 as a motto on his title-page.

> " For who hath despised the day of little things, for they shall rejoyce and shall see the stone of Tinne[1] in the hand of Zerubbabel, with those seven; they are the Eyes of the Lord, which run too and fro through the whole Earth."

There is a reference here to a verse in the previous chapter:

> " For behold the stone that I have laid before Joshua; upon one stone shall be seven eyes: behold, I will engrave the graving thereof, saith the Lord of hosts, and I will remove the iniquity of that land in one day."[2]

The stone referred to is the foundation stone which was being given by God to Joshua the high priest, who was to build the new temple after the Exile. The seven eyes of the Lord appearing in matter are therefore the eyes of the creator.[3]

Whenever there is a question of a vital transformation it is as though there was a descent of spirit into matter. The eyes forming within the tissues of the new substance represent, from one point of view, the histolysis of the preceding form; but are they not also the formative essence of the new creation? No longer is the creator above and outside his creation, but he pervades it from within, like the very spirit of the evolutionary process. The parallelism need not be laboured which embraces the building of the Temple after the Exile,

---

" ' Gems brilliant with glass ' is literally correct, but of dark meaning. ' Vitro insignis ' has to be understood alchemically. As you know, the old alchemists tried to make artificial gems from glass. Thus the meaning is ' gems of excellent glass.' The ' Eastern ' in this case refers to the fact that the East already in antiquity knew the art of producing artificial gems. Thus the whole sequence points to artificial gems as they are known in the East of particularly good quality."

1 " Plummet " in the Authorized Version.

2 Zechariah iii. 9.

3 I am much indebted to Professor Jung for these references.

the creation of the Philosopher's Stone in alchemy, and the appearance of the god-value as an endopsychic factor in our subject's myth—all represent a vital process of transformation accompanied by the *descensus spiritus* into matter.

So far as my experience goes it seems impossible for the modern mind to conceive the divine Artificer fashioning the world from above, without himself becoming involved in the creative process. Everything we can conceive is drawn irresistibly within the orbit of becoming; hence the ideal super-ego of the previous phase must also undergo the process of *enantiodromia* and be transformed into his dynamic counterpart. Instead of patriarchal dignity, behemoth emerges with vast jaws, like the bottomless pit, serried rows of teeth, and scaly skin like a crocodile, and " out of his nostrils goeth smoke."

" Behold now behemoth, which I made with thee;[1]

* * * * *

His teeth are terrible round about,
His scales are his pride,
Shut up together as with a close seal.

* * * * *

Out of his nostrils goeth smoke
As out of a seething cauldron or pot.
His breath kindleth coals.

* * * * *

He maketh the deep to boil like a pot.
He maketh the sea like a pan of ointment."

Psychological evolution does not conform to theoretical expectations. When the super-ego becomes involved in the very system he has accused, his condemnation becomes an act of penetration, whereby the whole morbid system is suddenly pregnant with a new life. Everything now centres in the new formation. The traditional values (personified by the grandfather) are thrown into the melting-pot, that the god may be free to manifest himself in the primordial dæmonic form. For the patient had no doubt at all that the monstrous mouth of Drawing VIII. was that of the god in the preceding drawing.

1 Book of Job xl. 15.

Jung uses the term *enantiodromia*[1] to denote this process by which a psychic content or value goes over into its opposite. The principle was first formulated by Heraclitus as the tendency of everything that exists to become changed into its opposite. The word really means the running, or play, of opposites. Heraclitus says: " Even Nature herself striveth after the opposite, bringing harmony not from like things, but from contrasts."

The same natural law underlies the Chinese conception of the opposite principles *Yang* and *Yin*. *Enantiodromia* is represented in the symbol of the *T'ai Ch'i* or Great Monad, which contains the *Yang* and the *Yin* within a circle. When the bright principle *Yang* has come to its greatest expansion, a nucleus, or germ, of *Yin* is formed, and from this nucleus the dark *Yin* phase develops. Similarly, as the *Yin* phase reaches its term, a germ of *Yang* develops within it. The succeeding phases form the fabric of existence.

In the illustration of the *T'ai Ch'i*[2] (Fig. 4, opposite page) certain unusual details are to be observed which are again suggestive of the " snail-fish " eyes mentioned above. The symbol is painted in warm colours (reddish-brown and grey) on the bottom of an octagonal bowl, each side of the octagon containing one of the cardinal trigrams of the *Yi King*. What I have called the germ or nucleus of either principle is painted in blue on a gold disc, clearly suggesting an eye; and crescentic markings, not unlike scales, appear down the bodies of the *Yang* and *Yin* fish. The action of *enantiodromia* is expressed by two sets of wavy lines, each of which, being based upon one principle, flows over the border into the opposite. The seeds of an ambiguous universe are thus contained in this Monad. It is indeed highly probable that these seed-like forms developed from the immense potency of the seed-idea with its implied fertility-significance in the cult of the ancestors. The prevalence of seed-designs on ritual jade ornaments, and of male and female symbolism in the forms of the jade, lend colour to the idea that the *Yang* and *Yin* elements within the Monad derive from the same

[1] From ἐναντίος = opposite, and δραμεῖν = to run.

[2] I am indebted to Miss E. L. Beckingsale for this valuable contribution from China.

source. In these " snail-fish " eyes we can discern the symbol of creative evolution, and therefore the perfect symbol of the endopsychic factor—namely, the archetypal germ within the psyche which, like the hypothetical image of the complete form in acorn, sperm, or seed, creates individuality from within. In the *Kundalini* system each *chakra* also contains the *Bija* or divine germ from which the power of the *chakra* is developed. The illustration of the *Muladhara chakra*, for example (Fig. 2, facing p. 230), shows the *Bija* of earth or of Indra as a character enclosing the triangle in which Shakti is seen coiled around the *lingam*. The god Indra is seen in a circle, towards the upper right-hand margin of the square field, with four arms each holding a thunderbolt. Thus the *Bija* is equivalent to the dæmon, or indwelling spirit, or genius of an element.[1]

Luther discerned a hidden dæmonic factor when he spoke of the *deus absconditus* (the concealed god) as the obverse aspect of the God of our ideals. At certain times God ceased to correspond with our ideal conceptions and was felt only as a concealed, disturbing power, alien both to reason and understanding. These opposite aspects of deity were also vigorously impressed upon Job, who was forced to turn away from the ideal aspect—corresponding to his perfect and upright conscious attitude—in order to behold the dynamic, primordial aspect of God in behemoth and leviathan.

The tendency to idealize one aspect of nature and to ignore its opposite, which is in fact equally real, usually coincides with a one-sided idealization of the personality. Hence a narrow, one-sided conception of deity is also the sign of a certain megalomania, which eventually invites catastrophe.

A modern version of Job is presented in Herman Melville's *Moby Dick*. Ahab, the fanatical captain of an American whaler, pits himself with the reckless pride of megalomania against the white whale, the leviathan of the deep. Years before Ahab had lost a leg when the rope of the harpoon, which was fast in this same whale, caught him as it dived. Literally crippled by fate, Ahab came to regard Moby Dick

[1] Compare Cornford's account of the early Greek conception of dæmon, as the genius of a place, or family, or element.

as the symbol of hostile fate, which is only another expression of the reverse aspect of deity. After years of reckless, inhuman pursuit Ahab again gets his shaft into the white whale, but this time he is carried down by the rope into the sea, broken like a straw, while his ship is also rammed and sunk by the whale.

After Melville had written this epic of megalomania, Nathaniel Hawthorne, his one trusted friend, wrote a story which he gave to Melville. Ethan Brand, the hero of the story, a charcoal-burner, leaves his humble home in order to discover the unpardonable sin. After long wanderings he returns, like Peer Gynt, to his home and neighbours, telling them he has found the sin in his own breast. Brand's language is a parody of Ahab's in *Moby Dick*, and there can be no doubt that Hawthorne intended this story as a warning to his friend.

We can regard the following citation from the story as Hawthorne's diagnosis of Melville's condition under the thin disguise of his hero Brand:

> "Then ensued that vast intellectual development which, in its progress, disturbed the counterpoise between mind and heart. The Idea that possessed his life had operated as a means of education; it had gone on cultivating his powers to the highest point of which they were susceptible; it had raised him from the level of an unlettered labourer to stand on a star-lit eminence, whither the philosophers of the earth, laden with the lore of universities, might vainly strive to clamber after him. So much for the intellect! But where the heart? That, indeed, had withered—had contracted—had hardened—had perished. It had ceased to partake of the universal throb. He had lost his hold of the magnetic chain of humanity. He was no longer a brother-man opening the chambers, or the dungeons, of our common nature by the key of holy sympathy, which gave him a right to share in all its secrets; he was now a cold observer, looking on mankind as the subject of his experiment. . . . Thus Ethan Brand became a fiend. He began to be so from the moment his moral nature had ceased to keep the pace of improvement with his intellect."[1]

The friendship between the two men dropped dead when Melville, reading this story, perceived that his friend regarded

[1] Quoted from Lewis Mumford's *Herman Melville*.

his intellectual arrogance as the unpardonable sin. Like Nietzsche, Melville was unable to rescue his common humanity, with its needed participation in the life of every man, from the isolating power, the ghostly tyranny of the Idea.

Jung describes the catastrophe that awaits the over-idealized principle of consciousness as follows:

> " It should not be forgotten that, in the same measure as the conscious attitude has a real claim to a certain God-likeness by reason of its lofty and absolute standpoint, an unconscious attitude also develops, whose God-likeness is oriented downwards towards an archaic god whose nature is sensual and brutal. The *enantiodromia* of Heraclitus forebodes the time when the *deus absconditus* shall also rise to the surface and press the God of our ideals to the wall."[1]

The transformation of a traditional, patriarchal super-ego into a devouring, dæmonic creature is especially significant in the schizophrenic sequence of events. The cleavage between the superior, educated, conscious attitude and the retrograde crudity of the dissociated affects frequently results in a massive reinforcement of the former in the manner observed in the present case—namely, by identification with the father or father surrogate. The unstable contradiction between a persona, or outer character, composed of charm and right feeling, and an unreliable emotional undertow was effectively masked, in the case of our subject, by this facile identification with the father-imago. The psychological effect of such identification is to raise oneself emotionally above the actual situation. One is already wise, old, experienced, no longer a prey to the troubles and disturbances of youth; nothing, therefore, can really touch one any more. This above-the-battle attitude of so many schizoid intellectuals is fundamentally a defence against the irrational unconscious, and, because it is a defence, it should be respected until a functioning individual myth has taken its place. But, in fact, the myth itself cannot emerge in all its primordial naivety so long as the intellect's claim to absolute superiority remains uncriticized. So long as the subject, in other words, views this whole infantile psychology from above—*i.e.*, from the

[1] *Psychological Types*, p. 123.

viewpoint of the accusing super-ego—he naturally feels as safe as a bench of magistrates, no more involved morally than a child making a fantasy-world. He is the creator, bringing things about from above, but not subject himself to evolutionary necessity.

On the one hand, the breakdown of this critical intellectual defence is, of course, a danger-point in the analysis. On the other hand, healing is not possible so long as consciousness remains above the battle. It is never enough merely to know the pathogenesis of the trouble, or to have the morbid mechanisms adequately presented to the intellect. The subject must actually experience those contents of the unconscious against the effects of which he has always defended himself. For only that knowledge is valid which cannot be uprooted. What we have not experienced we do not actually know. It is quite attractive to experience the unconscious in a partial way in an enthusiastic atmosphere of collective suggestion, as, for instance, in a mediumistic séance, or through participating in another person's experience. But such adventures can easily be rationalized away. The unforgettable experience is one that so seizes hold of the mind that its reality can never again become a matter for doubt. The *katalēptikē phantasia* of Zeno the Stoic expresses this kind of knowledge: an impression or idea that grips hold of the mind like a clenched fist. It was to experience this kind of knowledge that the *enantiodromia* from god to dæmon was necessary. The experiential significance of this event is demonstrated by the fact that while he was painting this monstrous mouth the patient was himself possessed by a raging hunger. It was as though his own body were warning him that his boat was once again near the edge of the vortex: his hunger was unassuageable, like the bottomless pit.

In our clinical terminology we lack a vital expression for this dæmonic manifestation in psychoneurotic conditions. In the compulsive erotism of nymphomania; in the unquenchable thirst of dipsomania; in the blood-lust of homicidal mania; in the unassuageable aggression of a Genghiz Khan, an Alexander, a Napoleon, or a Hitler; in the parasitic vampirism of the psychoneurotic—in these and innumerable other forms of compulsive or obsessional affect, we find the one centrally distinctive character—namely, that of the bottomless pit. Human hunger can be satisfied, human longings fulfilled; but dæmonic appetite is a ruthless predatory voracity: the more it has, the more it demands. It knows no reasonable bounds, and therefore must be resisted if human values are to be maintained.

The devouring monster and the vortex are terrific factors in human experience, as the myths of all nations bear witness, and their reality is in no way diminished by calling them phobias, obsessions or delusions. Scylla was said to live in a cave high up on a rock. She was described as a fearful monster who barked like a dog, with twelve clawed feet, six long necks and heads, and terrible mouths, each of which contained three rows of sharp teeth.[1] On the opposite rock, which was much lower, there was an immense fig-tree, under which dwelt Charybdis, who thrice every day swallowed down the waters of the sea and threw them up again. Both were equally perilous to the mariners who had to navigate the narrow passage between them. From the intrinsic nature of these dæmonic opposites, it is evident that Scylla symbolizes the overpowering peril from above, Charybdis the insidious danger from below. The dangers of barbarian one-sidedness—as to which the contemporary world bears abundant witness—are by no means confined to antiquity; and from the standpoint of the myth, which is never prone to spiritual or sexual superiority, one-sidedness in either direction is seen to be equally perilous. Whether one is caught up by the compulsive idea, or pulled down by obsessional sexuality, one is equally deprived of one's native humanity.

In the above description of the dæmonic opposites, mental factors are characterized as phenomena or portents. They are not yet fully personified—agreeing, therefore, with Cornford's description of the dæmon in early Greek thought, representing the genius or spirit of an element or province of nature.[2] It is also native to Chinese philosophy to con-

[1] Compare with the rows of teeth in the present drawing.
[2] Cornford: *From Religion to Philosophy*.

ceive of primordial mental factors as the reciprocal play of natural forces. In Chinese symbolical paintings we often find the opposites symbolized as opposing mountain-masses or rocks, the one on the left, as a rule, representing the higher, the one on the right the lower potential.

By naming these opposites the spiritual and the sexual we have already abstracted them from the undifferentiated dæmonic level, therewith converting them from inchoate affective propensities into defined mental territories. In Drawing III. we observed mental factors at this inchoate level. In the present drawing the patient has reached a point where the dæmonic urgency has achieved a relative degree of personification through a fusion of the dynamic elements of III. with the ideal ancestral image of VI. and VII.

VI

Science has not yet supplied us with a psychological terminology adequate to phenomena of this kind. Every patient who is impaled upon irrational fears, or is tormented by limitless irrational cravings—everyone, in fact, who puts his ear to the crack in the wall of his conscious house, or who looks over the rim of his ordered world into the crater of chaos, can well understand what is meant by the " bottomless pit " in its reference to human experience. Hence in dealing with these patients themselves we have no need for the scientific paraphrase. But for purposes of descriptive science, what concept is available that could embrace the combined experience of overwhelming urgency, raging hunger, a tendency to increasing recurrence accompanied by mounting anxiety, not to mention spontaneous and graphic representation ? Not only is the embracing borderline term suspect to scientific thinking, but the habit of scientific description to classify the instincts in specific categories renders it almost impossible to embrace in a single term a fundamental affective frenzy, which may fasten indifferently upon sexuality, hunger, thirst, fear, affection, or mere childish longing. The patent superficial character of the various emotions tends to mask the presence of an underlying temperamental proclivity to unmitigated affect. Jung refers to it as the problem of the undomesticated libido: elsewhere it may be dealt with on the ethical plane as undisciplined character. But both terms betray the unavoidable one-sidedness of consciousness, which also named this whole vast realm of mental activity the "unconscious." I prefer to use the term dæmonic, because it describes the inchoate primordial propensity as a phenomenon of nature, avoiding the usual implications which arise from the intellectual bias of consciousness.

For an essentially truthful, though quasi-mythological, study of the dæmonic invader, we must turn not to medical textbooks, but to the shelves containing the shilling shockers. In Bram Stoker's *Dracula* we find a sort of natural history study of this alien something which creeps into the human sphere and the human relation, and sucks away its essential human quality and virtue. Writing from the unconscious without philosophical reflection, the author depicted certain aspects of the psychoneurotic fate better probably than he knew. The following points of the story refer to undeniable clinical facts:

(*a*) The central figure of the story represents the psychological subject. He encounters Dracula first at the nodal point of his life, just when he is about to assume the double responsibility of becoming a partner in his firm and of marrying a wife. This, as we know, is the point where the retrogressive movement of the libido is liable to become apparent, since an unknown increase of evolutionary tension is involved, therewith provoking the conflict: responsibility versus neurosis.

(*b*) Dracula is represented as historical and ancestral in origin. His castle is situated in the Carpathians, and his genealogy links him up with the alien invasion of Attila and the Huns. He inhabits the graves of the dead, having survived from the past by virtue of his ability to escape at night to vampirize his human victims. In symbolical metaphor this obviously refers to an alien pagan element which has survived, like witchcraft and other heathen abominations, in the un-Christianized unconscious of the ostensibly Christian psyche.

(*c*) When the subject of the story visits Dracula's castle

in the mountains, Dracula invites him to step over the threshold, insisting that he is doing so of his own free will. He has no power to force his prey, against the latter's will, into his enchanted palace. This is also true of a neurosis. At bottom the neurotic subject is aware that, at some definite moment in his life, he consciously acquiesced in the neurotic alibi, in order to preserve a way of escape. The attitude of a compulsion-neurotic to his disease is not altogether unlike that of a rabbit towards the stoat who is intent on his blood. The rabbit is faster and could easily escape did not something in his blood play the traitor to the enemy blood-sucker.

(*d*) Dracula is able to assume a great variety of shapes. He can become a wolf, an owl, a bat; he can even get through cracks and keyholes as a wraith of mist. This corresponds to the protean manifestations of the negative, neurotic will: no sooner is it banished in one form than it appears in another.

(*e*) Dracula is bound by the condition that he cannot enter any house unless first invited into it by someone belonging to the house. A lunatic is living in the doctor's house into which Dracula seeks to enter. The lunatic takes a cruel, sadistic enjoyment in dismembering flies and birds, and it is he who gives the vampire his invitation.

Interpreting this analytically: the house symbolizes the subject's psyche, which contains the various aspects of his personality, both conscious and unconscious. His wife, who is doomed to become Dracula's victim, represents the ideal positive aspect of the subject's feeling; whereas the lunatic inmate represents its sadistic negative. In other words, he is the shadow-personality who, being repressed, was never consulted. Accordingly, he goes over to the side of the devil, who naturally understands and sympathizes with every creature who has been cast out of heaven.

(*f*) Every person whose blood has been sucked by the vampire eventually becomes a vampire too. This accords with our observation that, in so far as a man allows himself to become a victim, he inevitably victimizes others. When the play *Dracula* was performed in London, the doomed victim yielded herself to the vampire-dæmon with a voluptuous abandon, as to a lover. Also, in the book, when the hunt is up, and Dracula is about to be exterminated, a great pity fills the heart of the woman for the vampire who has lived on her blood. This corresponds with Nietzsche's idea that pity is the most vulnerable spot in the Christian mentality.

(*g*) Dracula can be killed in only one prescribed way, and it is exceedingly thorough. First a stake must be driven through the heart, then his head must be cut off. One of these measures alone is presumably not enough. It must be done during the daytime, while the vampire is dormant and inert in the ancestral tomb, for he only stirs at night.

If the author had set out to write a thesis on the psychology of neurosis, he would probably have produced nothing worthy of record. *Dracula* is said to be the result of a wager with a friend as to which could produce the most blood-curdling shocker. Taking its theme from folk-lore, the story wrote itself and, like many stories that come straight from the primitive levels of the mind, it throws an illuminating side-light upon our psychotherapeutic fundamentals.

Dracula is a personification of the vampire spirit of neurosis, which needs to be exposed to the full light of consciousness, inasmuch as the autonomy of the parasitical system can be demolished only by a total moral response. An unreserved and final act of the will must have moral passion behind it. Driving a stake through the heart means to pierce down to the emotional source or root of the neurotic will. This must be accompanied by the decapitation of the neurotic conception of the self. In other words, both the dynamic and the ideational factors of the neurosis must be dealt with simultaneously.

That this double act is necessary is proved again and again in our experience with patients. A neurotic individual may reach a complete intellectual understanding of the mechanisms of his neurosis, and yet remain as neurotic as ever. He may even maintain his neurosis by clinging to the notion that a moral reaction is not demanded. It is enough that he has submitted himself for treatment, and if the treatment has not cured him, well, he has done all that is humanly possible. A patient with this all too familiar attitude is most liable to be attracted to the mechanistic theory of neurotic causation. A faulty mechanism of the mind, like a disordered mechanism of the body, ought to be corrected on mechanistic principles. But a moral reaction is one's own private affair. It is not seemly to bring such considerations into a purely professional situation. Thus, like a wraith of mist under the door, the neurotic frost descends.

In the light of this analysis, it cannot be denied that, without knowing it, Stoker comes nearer to the fundamental requirements of psychotherapy in his study of the vampire-ghost than the whole army of scientific investigators, whose attitude is based upon the complete validity of the mechanistic hypothesis. With his notion of plunging the stake through the heart the author has obviously studied the voluminous folk-lore material concerned with the human vampire. It contains the wisdom of human necessity, the symbol of a complete and final act, impelled by a profound moral reaction.

An ideal standpoint may, in fact, be no more than the hanging of garlands around a venerable statue. But a moral act is the outcome of a categorical imperative, in which the deep necessities of our human fate combine with the dictates of our best reason. When heart and head are in unison an unreserved, decisive act is possible.

A beautiful example of this necessity is given in the Hebrew play *The Golem*. A learned rabbi conceives the idea of making a creature in human form, of gigantic strength and stature, in order to strengthen the Jews against a threatened pogrom. By employing his secret cabalistic knowledge, he makes the Golem. The Messias is seen waiting in the heavenly sphere, fettered by the rabbi's lack of faith in the possibility of divine assistance. He could have invoked the living power of the unconscious in the inherited image of the Messias: instead he resorts to magic. Like Frankenstein, he succeeds in creating his half-human monster, and the first thing he teaches him is how to use an axe. For a time the Golem is a passive, obedient servant, hewing wood and drawing water in the rabbi's house. Having been made of the substance of earth, after a time he begins to show a sexual interest in the rabbi's niece: moreover, inspired as he is with the rabbi's breath, he also partakes in some degree of his creator's spiritual nature. His desire, therefore, does not end with the rabbi's niece; he insists upon joining the congregation in the synagogue. But these desires are outside the rabbi's programme, and the Golem is denied entrance. Rage possessing him, he seizes an axe and starts a pogrom on his own—a pogrom that does not accord with the rabbi's anti-Christian bias. The rabbi tries to regain mastery over the frenzied Golem by using his rabbinical knowledge and authority, but this no longer has effect. Not until he is driven by sheer necessity to meet the Golem with the whole force of his human passion can he gain the upper hand. The presence of a mental reservation within the mind of the superior man makes him dynamically inferior to his more primitive antagonist. Recent examples of this same truth in the sphere of world politics readily occur to the mind.

* * * * *

Returning to our material, we observe certain significant details suggesting the existence of the *reservatio mentalis* which, as we have seen, underlies the pathological invasion. The most decisive indication is seen in the vampire lunatic faces, whose blood-sucking activities are protected by an enclosing sheath. From our study of Dracula, we can assume that this vampire-complex has not been extirpated because, partially at least, its activity is desired. The vital importance of the *enantiodromia*, which released the primordial forces of the unconscious in this dæmonic form, is realized in the fact that these vampire faces never appear again. They are engulfed by a greater dæmon.

VII

Two further pieces of evidence are to be found in Drawing VII. The first is seen in the blank space, within the framed system, which the patient told me should have been occupied by the devil. The devil himself was apparently not present during the act of denunciation: he continued to remain unmanifest behind the scenes, leaving his morbid products as ambiguous reminders of his power.

The second is more subtle, and would probably have escaped observation had we not adhered strictly to our rôle of describing each detail. The reader will recall that we counted eighteen distinct golden particles, or nucleoli, in the mass of green protoplasm. There is also one indistinct imperfectly detached one, which we regarded as doubtful. We observed that these corresponded with the twelve penetrating arrows of the god's beard, added to the six golden finger-nails of the god's fingers, which pierce the frame at six different points, making eighteen points of golden penetration. But a seventh finger is drawn which has not been given a golden finger-nail. This finger is the lower terminal part of the bifurcating extension of the god's phallus. Furthermore, it is clearly participating in the transitional activity in and about the green receptacle.

The bifurcation of the phallic trunk might represent an ambiguous attitude towards the function of sex. The upper finger of the bifurcation, which carries the golden finger-nail, would point towards an objective, creative attitude; whereas the lower finger, having become implicated with the subjective, onanistic, nail-biting motive, is accordingly deprived of its crown of gold.

From the magical practices of savage peoples we know that hair-cuttings and nail-parings have a peculiar importance for the primitive mind: they must be disposed of with great care, lest a witch procure them for the purpose of working magic on the person who parted with them. There was also a detail of Drawing III., where the finger of taboo, which defended the lower face from access to the breast, was given a black finger-nail. We cannot afford to overlook such a detail, since we know that the finger-nail has a special, though ambiguous, meaning for the infantile as for the primitive psyche. For how many generations, for instance, has infantile onanism escaped inevitable censure by the timely adoption of this nail-biting substitute? May we not assume, therefore, that the concealed subjective, onanistic direction of the patient's sexuality has again escaped the eye of the vigilant super-ego with the selfsame subterfuge? This might explain why the two vampire lunatic faces appear in the present drawing, still safely enclosed in their onanistic vesicles, plying their vampire technique at the very source of the new life.

It is important to emphasize the extraordinary veracity of these drawings. Such products afford scope for invaluable theoretical deductions, just because the subject is unable to produce anything which is not essentially true.

With regard to the central yellow nucleus of the green life-stuff, the patient could tell us little; but inasmuch as it now appears in the centre of the green plasson, it is probably derived from the yellow centre of the inverted laminal field (Drawing VII.), towards which the six fingers and the upper units of the phallic series are pointing.

If the reader will glance again at VII. he will observe that in the framed system on the left there are an upper and a lower magnetic field, each centring in its respective focal point. The upper focus is the central yellow ring of the inverted laminal field. The six golden-nailed fingers are all directed at this point. The first two members of the phallic series are pointing at this ring, and the succeeding members, down to the sixth, are all being drawn upwards toward this point. These upper six units are also those covered by the lateral rays of the god's beard. The lower four are directed horizontally. A horizontal line drawn at the level of the twelfth ray, or just below it, would include all the elements that are orientated towards the upper focal point.

The lower area of the picture is not orientated to a centre in the same way, because the contents are already undergoing a transitional organization. But its central point corresponds more or less with the fæcal ring numbered 11, which is penetrated by the red snake. There appears to be a lateral line of tension running through this point: a line which would correspond to the sucking action of the nail-biting system on either side, by which the green substance is being pulled outwards into two lateral humps. This double sucking action is elaborated in the next picture into the two vampire lunatic heads. The influence of the lower centre is shown in the character of the lower members of the phallic series: these are attenuated, unnaturally elongated, and seem to be straining to get beyond the rings they penetrate, as though already attracted towards a further goal.

Distortion of shape in a drawing usually means some alienation of function. We know, therefore, that this lower portion of the field is conditioned by a subjective centre which has the power of attracting the *libido sexualis* away from its original goal. Such an alienation of function can be regarded as pathological in the limited sense of the term, denoting a departure from the norm. From the blood draining away from the onanistic nail-biting systems, from the red snake biting its own tail (the classical symbol of self-fertilization), from the attenuated phalli penetrating fæcal rings, and from the containing idea of a lavatory-pan (with its original association of infantile pleasure), we know that this whole lower area is concerned with the infantile fantasy of self-fertilization. But on the other side we observed how the trunk-like extension of the god's phallus ends in a bifurcation, of which the upper finger points towards the upper centre, while the lower points to the lower. We have yet to discover why the lower finger is without the golden nail of authority, and why the protuberance which would correspond to this lower finger on the left side is reduced to a mere stump.

We have now distinguished an upper relatively organized orientation of the *libido sexualis* from a lower transitional activity, and these are represented by two poles or centres of interest. Yet only the upper orientation receives the condemnation of the super-ego. Why is this? The inverted laminal field covers the anal and genital area of a limbless and distorted, hence depersonalized, female torso. Moreover, the multiplication of the phallus must clearly refer to a more or less indiscriminate or promiscuous sexual attitude. Promiscuity is possible only to a man of immature or repressed feeling. Without the distinctive valuation of feeling, the sexual function remains very much on the level of the excretory functions. In other words, when sexuality is allowed to function independently of personal values, the individuality of the object is ignored. At this level sexuality has a non-human, dæmonic character.

The biological products of the distorted female trunk in the drawing, sealed as the latter is with the sign of inversion, belong necessarily to the level of the lavatory-pan. Even the milk of the breast, the original symbol of divine blessing,[1] is reduced to the same excretory level.

But if bodily functions and basic instincts are depreciated wholesale in a desperate attempt to forget the infantile paradise, some other source of satisfaction must be looked for in their stead. The elevation of the intellect to the position of ruler will not satisfy the soul, which remembers the delicious satisfactions of infancy. Thus dissatisfaction drives the intellect, and the intellect coerces the instincts: so the vicious circle turns, depreciation of the value of instinct always being counterbalanced by exaggeration of something else to take its place.

Deflection of the libido towards another centre is the accepted social technique for dealing with instinctual dissatisfaction. The same technique is used by the police when riots threaten. Yet a highly sublimated psychology is rarely free of dissatisfaction, for the whole theory of sublimation rests upon a fundamental suspicion of the validity of the libido and its goals. But how can the libido be trusted to find a satisfying goal when our basic attitude is rooted in self-distrust?

A better way is nature's process of transformation, which rests upon a power and a desire inherent in the living organism. The desire for a goal beyond the *circulus vitiosus* is revealed in the lower members of the phallic series, which already seem to have had a foretaste of a more satisfying condition. No nurses or policemen are required to tell the caterpillar when his time has come to go to earth. Among insects the impulse towards a specific goal is combined with the necessary knowledge of how to achieve it. It is possible to discover the same instinctual knowledge in the dreams of patients. If a man is able and willing to make peace with nature, and to learn her principles, his dreams will show him the way to true satisfaction. But it will not be the way he expects. He

[1] *Cf.* the concept of Rita in the Vedas, whose "overflowing udders" give renewal of life and fertility; also Hathor-Isis in the religion of Egypt.

thinks that satisfaction can come only through the fulfilment of his wishes, whereas the achievement of long-range goals must require a certain sacrifice of short-range satisfaction.

We are now able to condense our observations into a coherent picture which can be regarded as a working hypothesis. In the second dream we observed the disintegration of the subject's emotional attitude, owing to the strain of a new evolutionary phase (the responsibilities of parenthood). The shadow-figure, or " loose one," symbolized the turning back and release of the libido in the renegade direction. This rejection of the evolutionary challenge was perfectly represented by the actual character of the man chosen by the dream-mind to impersonate the shadow. The recession of the libido into the unconscious activated the infantile primordial psyche, which, thereupon, began to develop the individual myth.

In Drawing III. a polarity developed in the centre of the infantile complex, whereby a static, onanistic, subjective attitude became differentiated from a dynamic, resistant and objective tendency. In the latter the defending finger of taboo was seen as an inherent aspect of the complex, not superimposed from above by a super-ego. This division of the libido, moving towards and away from the maternal source, was stated with diagrammatic clarity in Drawing V.

In Drawing VI. a new attitude was born out of the unconscious: it was ruled by the grandfather-god, foreshadowing the authority of the self. Under this ægis the dissociated infantile system became penetrated by a new spirit. In Drawing VII. the infantile citadel was pierced at many points, both from above and from below, the attack concentrating chiefly upon the yellow centre of the inverted laminal field, the symbol of the parasitic, infantile attitude which wants to suck the juice out of everything, while itself refusing reciprocity. In the lower part of this drawing we found a transitional activity going on which did not come within the scope of the ancestral accusation. The phallic units below six, being free from the determining influence of the inverted field, appeared to be penetrating the fæcal rings in order to get beyond. The lower terminal finger of the god's phallic trunk was clearly participating in this transitional process, since it lacked the emblem of traditional authority—namely, the golden finger-nail. The head of the snake, at the bottom of the pelvic pan, was pointing downwards, from which we inferred that the orientation of the lower system was downwards, opposed to the upward straining of the upper phallic units.

The original direction of the infantile libido is necessarily upwards, towards the parents who are above. This would correspond to the dependent, childish attitude of the neurotic temperament. But the new transitional direction of the libido that has already rejected the state of neurotic frustration must be downwards. This would correspond to the attitude of the subject as prospective parent. In short, the forward evolutionary tendency constellates the hitherto frustrated libido in relation to the new potentiality.

It is important to observe that the ruling motif of this lower constellation is the nail-biting symbolism, for nail-biting is already a frustrated substitute form of onanism. Thus in psychological as well as in social evolution we find the new departure gaining its chief momentum from the dissatisfied lower elements. The allusions to the alchemistic and the *Kundalini* symbolism which came under review referred to the transitional process constellated in the lower part of the drawing. The influence of a suprapersonal factor in this constellation was visible in the lower digit of the god's phallic trunk, while the lower phallic members of the series had already assumed the same character as the god's phallus. The straining of the *libido sexualis* to get beyond the infantile pleasure-garden was self-evident. The allusion to the *Kundalini* snake was present in the red snake whose head pointed downwards and to the left, while the presence of the *uroborus* symbol of the alchemists also supported the hypothesis that a work of transformation was in progress.

The formation of a new evolutionary attitude takes place when a dynamic combination of unsatisfied instinctual elements comes under the impetus of a new impersonal motive. At every nodal point in the life-curve, when the libido has to make the transition from one phase to the next, a new molecular formation of psychic factors must occur if the transition is to succeed, and the spearhead of the new formation is a commanding idea, image, or personality.

One important aspect of Drawing VII. has gained fresh significance from the foregoing discussion. I refer to the contrast between the upper and lower aspect of the ancestor god. The eighteen points of penetration, centring upon the upper field, come from the index-finger of the hand, the golden rays of the beard, and the upper finger of the phallic extension. We regarded these points of golden penetration as originating in the authority of ancestral feeling and tradition. In regard to the function of sex, they would symbolize the objective valuation of sexuality in the light of social ethics—in other words, the authoritative, patriarchal identification of sexuality with procreation.

But below this level of traditional authority we observed two pen-and-ink lines, ending in arrowheads, which emanate from the god's genitals, and which end in two finger-like projections above and below the nail-biting system on the right. On the left of the green receptacle there is a mere stumpy protuberance above, nothing below, and no arrow-lines of direction.

The more we study these drawings, the more we shall be convinced that nothing can be regarded as meaningless or accidental. Accordingly, we have to attempt some explanation of these two lower arrow-lines, ending in fingers which lack the golden index. Since they emanate from the god, we must conclude that this drawing also contains a significant transformation of the historical conception of deity. The upper part of the god would clearly correspond with the conscious view handed down from the past—namely, the idea of a divine intelligence directing and controlling human destiny from above, and judging deeds and misdeeds according to a moral law which he has inscrutably ordained—a celestial arbiter, in short, entirely above and beyond man.

But when we contemplate this lower, subliminal activity of the god, we are faced at once with the blasphemous conception of an ethical deity with an active sexual function. Is this blasphemy or a new conception? The God who ruled the Christian heaven would never have shared His throne with a goddess.

Sexuality is the mark and sign of human incompleteness. Absolute deity must be self-contained and complete; therefore to conceive him with organs of generation means to deny him completeness. From the human standpoint, this absoluteness of God removes Him from any real contact with man. For how can a man seek wisdom and counsel on this most human of all problems from a deity who, by virtue of His own completeness, is wholly remote from our human predicament? Whatever the causes of the transformation, it is undeniably true that men of to-day find their belief in time-honoured absolutes to be no longer substantial, while they tend to conceive deity as the inherent, discriminative potency of the evolutionary process. These two phallic fingers belong, therefore, to a relative conception of God: a deity who has descended from His absolute superiority upon the seat of judgment to participate in the unpredictable human experiment. The trunk-like extension might even symbolize the desire of God to become involved, like a parent, in the development of man. At all events, the two imperfectly formed phallic fingers—an essential aspect of the lower formative field—seem to accord with the idea that God has descended from His celestial isolation in order to play the activating rôle in the evolutionary process. In this idea we may recognize the conception of the immanence of God, even though feeling may be outraged by so crude a statement of a mystical truth. The crudity of expression seen in these drawings comes from the fact that the subject has not yet realized the ideas they contain. If he had, no analytical mediation would have been needed.

The upper aspect of the god is practically identical with Freud's conception of the patriarchal super-ego, and it must not be assumed from what has been said that this traditional aspect does not possess great power. Indeed, on the evidence of dreams, it would seem that no essential conscious change is possible without as it were the sanction of the ancestors. The only conclusion we are entitled to draw from the ambiguity of the divine nature in this drawing is that the evolutionary idea has become identified with God and must therefore be regarded as the ruling principle of this psychology. The subject can no longer entertain an idea of God above and outside the evolutionary process, and because the god-value has become the inherent impulse of his development, more than his personal ego must be involved in the outcome.

We are now in a position to give a value to the central yellow nucleus of the impregnated protoplasm. It represents the libido-value which lies at the centre of the inverted laminal field. It symbolizes the yellow centre of desire around which the new molecular grouping of personal and impersonal elements is being formed. The green substance is itself a combination of personal associations, connected with the infant's acceptance by the mother, and impersonal factors descending on it from above, symbolized by " grains of the sun."

The new substance, therefore, which is being formed in solitariness, in the fertilizing heat of the primal fire, derives both from the *prima materia* of the infantile system and from the ancestral spiritual *mana*. It is a true alchemical product, a subtle body or elixir which, being incubated in the brooding warmth of introversion (*tapas*), represents the new light or centre of the subject's world. It is also the ever-welling fountain of desire which expresses the god-value in the living heart of experience, thus developing a genuine impersonal will.

Honouring the vital energy is our golden key, for in no other way can the opposites be reconciled. Intellectually, body and mind, spirit and sex, life and death are sundered in opposition, but in life itself, in the living moment of experience, they are reconciled. When desire is followed as our best guiding principle, it does not lead into banal adventures, but rather to those very problems in which real potentialities and real defects of character will be challenged. But in order to create this guiding principle the god-value needs to become inherent in the flow of experience.

The subjective continuity of this stream of desire, from the fantasies of childhood to the ripe fulfilment of age, provides developing individuality with a veritable golden thread.

But how can life be experienced with intensity and completeness if prejudices are maintained which destroy the reciprocal balance of the sexual and spiritual principles? Prejudice disturbs the balance and natural harmony of psychic functioning. Consequently, if either principle be dishonoured or repressed, both suffer, whereas honouring the libido restores their original reciprocity.

In this central symbol of Drawing VIII. we are reminded of the Chinese saying: " There exist three elements, heaven, earth and man." The critical task of Western man to-day is to restore the natural order by reconciling heaven and earth *in himself*. Even though this central yellow nucleus was originally set in the heart of the inverted system, it is none the less the germ of desire which had to be redeemed from a one-sided sexual prejudice. Through the act of penetration (in Drawing VII.) the three elements, the green stuff of earth, the golden grains of the sun and human desire, are once again combined in a primordial molecule.

* * * * *

I have dealt rather fully with this central theme of metamorphosis, because it seems to be the chief preoccupation, if one may so express it, of unconscious activity. By holding to this guiding principle we begin to understand why the original concept of healing in the worship of Æsculapius was the rebirth or renewal of life, like that of the snake in spring.

Other elements in Drawing VIII. are, to some extent, descriptive of the patient's emotional state while this inner process was developing in the unconscious. He felt driven by an inner force impelling him to create, which was also like a consuming fire. As mentioned before, he was consumed by raging hunger the whole time he was painting this picture.

Intense activity in the unconscious is frequently accompanied by disturbing abdominal or cardiac symptoms. The smoke and fire coming from the nostrils of the monster represent this idea of intense inner activity. The multiplication of red and yellow dots in the mouth of the monster reinforces the suggestion of extreme internal heat. When vital energy is introverted into the depths of the unconscious, it is sometimes as though the subject were bathed in primordial fire.

We find this idea of the renewal of life through fire in the initiatory rituals of the Eleusinian mystery-cult. The initiate had to go through the heart of a furnace which seemed to him like imminent death. In Rider Haggard's *She*, Ayesha regains immortal youth by plunging into a pillar of fire revolving in the heart of the mountain. The secret had been handed down to her by the "guardian of the fire," but with a warning never to attempt it. Nothing can restrain Ayesha: she steps into the white heart of the fire, therewith becoming charged with deathless vitality. But with it she gains a supranormal clairvoyant consciousness, which isolates her from other mortals.

The idea of seeking renewal of life in a volcano is also found among certain Melanesian tribes. According to Layard, who lived for a time on the island of Malekula, the idea of joining the ancestral spirits in the heart of an active volcano is the supreme desire of the natives of Atchin and Vao. They have no fear of being devoured by the fire. Their desire, which has the character of religious faith, is concerned with the idea of becoming united with the ancestor spirits who live inside the volcano. Apart from this belief, they also venerate a god-hero or supreme spirit, who lights up both sun and moon. This god, Tagar, belongs to another tradition, and is concerned with creating light rather than fire. The idea of renewal through fire is, of course, distinct from fire- or sun-worship which, in the case just cited, was probably introduced from another culture. The same natives also live in fear of being devoured by Le-hev-hev, a bad spirit who lies in wait for the spirits of the dead at the entrance to the cave from which they travel to the volcano. This monster has to be bought off by the sacrifice of the required number of pigs.[1]

Le-hev-hev (*alias* Chumbaba or Cerberus) is the horrific guardian of the unconscious, such as we see in our drawing. Over every vital experience nature has set a fear-inspiring warden. The initiatory ordeals of the mystery-cults borrowed their horrific character direct from nature. It is essential that a man should know this fear and, if possible, look into

[1] Layard: *Stone Men of Malekula*, vol. i., Vao (Chatto and Windus).

its face. Youthful aspirants in the art of high diving are sometimes told to put their fear in front of them and dive over it. One could say much the same to the man who fears the experience of the unconscious. Yet he should respect his fear, for it warns him that to know the unconscious is a vital experience. This is done concretely by the natives of Vao, who buy off Le-hev-hev by a tribute of pigs. This motif is also represented in our patient's drawing by the presence of the impregnated life-stuff between the monster's teeth. On the primitive level, sacrifice always means payment to the spirits—*i.e.*, to the unconscious.

For the sake of comparison I am reproducing a rather similar painting, lent me by my colleague, Mr. Westmann. His patient was also inclined to be childish in his attitude to the unconscious. He tells me that the patient identified himself with the engine seen running on rails into the monstrous mouth. The rails in this connection would have the same meaning as the defile or narrow passage—namely, an inescapable situation where nothing can be done, an ordained or fated process like that of birth or death. The drawing illustrates why many neurotic patients, especially homosexual men, complain of claustrophobia—viz., an irrational dread that is liable to seize one in a closed place, as, for instance, in a railway train, in church, at a dinner-party, or in any kind of situation from which immediate escape is not possible.

In Mr. Westmann's case the patient associated this terrible aspect with the mother. In spite of the outrage to " natural " feelings, it is clear from Jung's great research[1] that the mother-imago becomes the horrific deity of the unconscious because the dread of incest in the human breast is the measure of man's unresolved infantile craving. So long as he craves, so long must there be a terrible figure guarding the gateway to the unconscious. It is nature's logic that the most loved being should also become our greatest danger. Only those who cannot sacrifice their childishness complain of the cruelty of life. Those who refuse to be caught and harnessed and disciplined by life will always tend to maintain the infantile psyche and the infantile attitude. They will not make the

1 *Psychology of the Unconscious.*

necessary sacrifice for the sake of life, therefore they behave like wild creatures being driven into a snare.

This irrational fear of what life may hold is the same at bottom as the fear of death. Before the Achumawi lad goes upon his solitary way to the crater-lake, he is told by his father or guardian, "You are going to die." Initiation is a ritual death and rebirth, and the entrance to the new phase is a kind of histolysis. The ego is dissolved, dismembered, broken down in the same way that the caterpillar is dissolved in the chrysalis.

There is even a suggestion in our subject's drawing that the elements of the conscious personality are reduced to a fluid, insubstantial state. In the background, for instance, we see indefinite, undulating shapes of red and green, more suggestive of submarine life than of clear, terrestrial forms. Enmeshed also in this network of rough pen-and-ink lines are the five disjuncted eyes, whose shape and aspect are again reminiscent of some aquatic organism—*e.g.*, a tadpole or a spermatozoon.

The presence of these vagrant eyes in this very archaic setting suggests that psychic direction has passed over to the unconscious, and that the principle of consciousness is now represented by these scattered *insulæ*.

Under this condition the conscious function, inundated by the activated affective processes, is carried along by the events taking place in the unconscious. The creating eyes appear to be orientated towards the central symbol of life, inasmuch as the three on the right are swimming towards the left, while the two smaller ones on the left are turned towards the right. From the level and direction of the pupils, one also gets the impression that they are attracted towards the green life-stuff in the monster's mouth.

Here then is the new centre of transforming life, of which we gleaned an inkling in the last drawing, and towards which the lower phallic units were reaching out. But in order that a new king shall be born the old ruler must die. The horrific aspect of the unconscious is no mere relic of nursery terrors; the danger is a real one, and many, like the author of *Moby Dick*, are broken by the experience.

CHAPTER VIII

THE MATERNAL ASPECT OF THE UNCONSCIOUS

REMEMBERING the energy and affect of the previous drawing, Drawing IX. appears diagrammatic and again withdrawn. It is as though, in face of the challenge of the activated unconscious, consciousness had countered frenzy with detachment. We witnessed this same phenomenon before, when the embryonic vitality of Drawing III was succeeded by the two diagrammatic constructions, IV. and V. A similar polarity of mood was also discovered in the contents of Drawing I., where the contrast between the contents of the left and right halves of the drawing suggested the Dionysian-Apollonian analogy. It is interesting to watch this balancing alternation in the development of the myth. In the one phase the subject gives himself up to a spontaneous expression of the archaic imagery; in the next he envisages the same content with a certain detachment. It is a tidal movement of extraversion and introversion, running through the developing myth like the systole and diastole of the heart's action.

DRAWING IX

This represents a medial, longitudinal section of the monster encountered in the last drawing. It discloses a number of interesting anatomical details which were not visible before.

It will be convenient to begin with the mouth, which shows the two heavy red lips from which spring the two rows of teeth above and below. The inverted system (equipped with its own teeth) which was shown in the last drawing separate and discrete in the mouth of the monster, has now become incorporated in the formidable equipment of the jaws. The green protoplasm, with its sun-particles, is seen extending the whole length of the mouth, projecting in front a little distance beyond the two powerful canines which are clenched upon it. A collection of blood is seen between the teeth and the living stuff.

At the back of the mouth a bony articulation appears, resembling that of the radius and ulna with the humerus. These bones clearly consist of the same substance as the green protoplasm with the golden nucleoli. There would seem, therefore, to be a kind of consolidation of the protoplasm into bony structure as it extends backwards. A medial line of yellow runs the length of each bony shaft. A large cavity or vesicle, which should normally correspond with the pharynx, is seen sweeping downwards and to the left. In the lower portion of this cavity three symbolical contents are to be found. The one to the right is a heart with its four chambers. A single large bloodvessel issues from the upper part of this organ, curving backwards in a loop, to end abruptly a short distance in front of its lower pole. From the open end of this vessel a jet of blood spurts out, propelling the infant forwards into the cavity. At the front end of the cavity there is a small peacock within its egg. The background of the cavity consists of a reticulated pattern of squares and dots, painted in yellow. At the top, embracing the area of the green radius and ulna, is a wing-shaped expanse of fascia, painted in silver.

The shape of the cavity is highly suggestive of the stomach-container, with its formative contents, met with on the right side of Drawing III. If the reader will refer back to that drawing he will see the humerus with its wing-like appendages, and below it the radius and ulna displaced by two bags of blood. He will also notice that the lower end of the stomach curves off to the left, resembling the curve of the stomach-cavity in this drawing. The patient explained that the heart, in the present drawing, developed out of those two bags of blood, and that, when this was achieved, the two bones (radius and ulna) regained their normal shape, beginning to function as the bony articulation of the monster's jaw. As soon as the bags of blood were converted into a heart, the first function of the latter was to propel a live infant out of the aorta, followed by the peacock and its egg.

There are also other elements of Drawing III. which have

become incorporated in the anatomy of the monster. Above and below the distal portion of what, on account of the nature of its contents, we must also call the womb-cavity, are two elongated masses of blue; and on the right-hand margin of the drawing is a large maternal breast, painted in dark brown and silver. If we return to the left half of III., we shall at once recognize these elements disposed in a somewhat similar way, only in the present drawing the breast is further removed from the two blue masses and is coloured differently. The egg-shaped object, consisting of an outer ring of gold, an inner ring of blue, and a pupil of shaded gold, contained in the upper blue area, has much the same structure as the pupils of the snail-fish eyes in the last drawing. Indeed, the whole shape of this blue area, with its contained ellipse, is strongly reminiscent of those disjuncted eye-fishes. This eye is situated below the mouth, and seems to be turned inwards and upwards. Although in its wrong place functionally, it is centrally situated. Taken together with the two golden fragments of the god's beard, shown at the top and bottom extremities of the right edge, it would seem to symbolize the organ of the new psychological attitude which is developing from the patient's experience of the unconscious. The patient associated the pineal eye with this new organ—a fact which reminds us that Descartes held the pineal body to be the seat of the soul. Inasmuch as the development of this medial, archaic eye coincided with the subject's dawning conception of the unconscious as a maternal womb of rebirth, it should be regarded as an organ of psychic vision.

Another feature which has been borrowed from Drawing I. is the curious crenellated structure that extends upwards from the bottom to the level of the lower lip. It represents a kind of defence or fortification made from the jagged layer of rock which separated the lunatic asylum from the world above. The egg containing the peacock is carried over from Drawing VI., where it was seen, in charge of a small peacock, in the right-hand bottom corner. Its original source, however, is again in Drawing III., inasmuch as the patient identified this egg with the isolated red nucleus associated with his dead sister. The background of the diagram consists of red, green and brown elements, painted with undulating brush strokes in the same fluid fashion as was observed in the last drawing.

In the left upper portion of the drawing a monstrous green dragon is seen emerging from the nostril, represented by a blue ring with a glimpse of red fire within. The dragon bears a jagged row of sharp red dorsal spines and two feet equipped with sharp red sucker-teeth. A thin red lateral line runs the length of its green body.

By far the most surprising and significant aspect of this secondary monster is the enormous yellow eye. The structure of this eye is that of a flower, consisting of a shaded centre, four radiating double petals, and three concentric rings of petals, vaguely indicated between the double petals and the circumference. Upon this sunflower background a *mandala* design has been painted in red lines, consisting of an inner and an outer circle, with four radial lines running from the circumference of the inner ring to the circumference of the flower. These lines agree with the cardinal points of the compass.

A golden javelin held in the hero's right hand is pointed upwards at the centre of the eye, while a second javelin, appearing from behind the upper limit of the dragon-castle, is pointing downwards and leftwards at the centre. The hero himself does not appear, though the splashes of silver which seem to centre upon the dragon's eye might be regarded as intimations of the hero's *mana*.

* * * * *

This drawing is in the nature of an introverted reflection upon the last drawing. The dæmonic aspect of the " terrible mother " is as though, behind a devil-mask, the unconscious were intimating: " Here is something ambiguous, perhaps dangerous. Look out !" But, actually, behind the devil-mask, which, by the way, is beautifully suggested in the drawing of Mr. Westmann's patient, we come upon the benign, maternal aspect of the unconscious function. These opposing aspects also inhabit the right and left portions of the present picture. On the right is the concealed, formative, incubating, transmuting, regenerative and maternal function, while on the left is the dæmonic, terrifying aspect.

We already know the context to which these two aspects belong. In Drawing I. we discovered the psychotic pathogenesis already adumbrated in the darkened sun with the three sun-spots in the left upper portion of the picture. We also observed the curative associations emanating from the region of the sacred mountain in the right upper portion of the same drawing. The left side was associated with the paternal side of the patient's psychology, the right with the maternal. This original distinction still holds good, for, as we shall presently discover, the dragon on the left can be mythologically identified with the father, while the womb-cavity of the " terrible mother " obviously belongs to the maternal side.

The first example of the split design was in Drawing II., where we found the emergent aspect symbolized by the escaping lunatics on the left half, and the mechanical, static, deprived aspect on the right. In that drawing we also remarked the absolute division of the content by the schizophrenic split, the pathognomonic feature of which is the absence of continuity between the contents of the two halves. In the present instance there is no greater absence of continuity of content than naturally exists between the inside and the outside of a house.

In Drawing III. we observed the constellating, magnetic influence of the maternal symbol in the middle of the field. There too we found the same two lakes of blue forming to the left of the breast-image. These have now an organic relation to the anatomical structure of which they form a part, a relation which was lacking in the former drawing.

The main contents of the womb-cavity have already been identified as those seen in the alchemical stomach-container in the right half of III., only they have now undergone a remarkable transformation, and out of the transformed heart there emerges a new-born babe. The contiguity of the two masses of blue with the distal portion of the womb-cavity, where the babe is being born, suggests the possibility that these may have a protective function analogous to that of the amniotic fluid. Perhaps the most significant feature of this drawing is the wing-like structure (painted in silver) which springs from the newly formed radius and ulna at the top of the vesicle. We shall presently see, in the final drawing of the series, the full significance of this silver wing. Here we are concerned more with its derivation.

In the stomach-container of Drawing III. the position of the radius and ulna was usurped by the two bags of blood, a fact which gave us a ray of insight into the pathology of the schizophrenic deficiency of feeling. In place of the two distal bones of the arm the patient had to draw two visceral sacs. This meant that his means of objective adaptation was continually hampered and vitiated by a subjective inversion of the libido that was tantamount to an organic defect. Everything he handled was conditioned by this subjective leakage. No object could be viewed or dealt with as wholly valid in its own right, but rather as an adjunct to the subject's state of emotional starvation. Desirousness always has this dæmonic character. No object is desired for its own sake, but for the sake of the blood which the parasitic complex can drain out of it. In dreams this complex frequently figures as a vampire bat, or a blood-sucking animal such as a ferret or a stoat. The bags of blood have, therefore, a still more sinister implication, as everyone who has ever crushed a replete mosquito will appreciate.

Jung has defined feeling as the function of subjective valuation. This definition has been criticized as inadequate by English and American critics. But it cannot be denied that valuation of an object is fundamentally a differentiated emotional response, and this seems to be as near as it is possible for the intellect to get to the essential nature of feeling. A differentiated response is adapted to the nature and quality of the object. It is essentially a statement of value. But if this valuing function is held in the frozen inertia of incestuous fixation, there remains in its place mere *cupiditas*, a forlorn and cold-blooded substitute, without a trace of the warmth and potency of real desire.

The process that we see taking place is the withdrawal of the subjective, infantile claim from the objective scene, where it does not belong and where it is a complete hindrance, and its removal to the psychological level, where it can be nourished and educated. William Blake said there are only two kinds of men, the prolific and the devouring. If you are not the one, you are quite certainly the other. Here then we see the transformation of the devouring attitude of unsatisfied craving into the prolific attitude of introverted creativeness. The result of this transformation is that the newly restored arm becomes a wing, while the newly formed heart gives birth to a living child.

The silver with which the wing is painted gives us another clue of importance. In Drawing III. the breast-image was all silver, with the exception of the red nipples. In this picture of the same content the silver is reduced to two bands, the one encircling the breast, the other the nipple. The rest of the figure is painted a dark reddish-brown, the colour of a freshly ploughed field. It is therefore a logical inference to assume that the silver of the wing has been detached from the maternal symbol. If this inference is correct, we are led to conclude that an effective quantum of psychic energy has been released from the incestuous maternal fixation and has become incorporated in an objective spiritual function. Through this breaking of the incestuous spell, the function of external relatedness (*i.e.*, the arm) has assumed an impersonal objectivity (*i.e.*, the wing), and the symbol of the mother has assumed the general impersonality of mother-earth.

To understand what these words mean I will refer the reader again to Jung's pregnant remark: "Whenever the problem of schizophrenia exists there is this problem of the biggest thing (idea) in the smallest box." The function of relatedness requires not only a disposable quantity of psychic energy, it also demands a loyal conception of the meaning and value of the personalities, objects and contemporary events to which relationship naturally belongs. The former is the dynamic, the latter the ideal aspect of relatedness. Although we can, and must, think of these aspects as separate, in actual fact the one cannot exist without the other. For without the free energy there can be no feeling of value to give to the object. Jung's aphorism states the schizophrenic condition in terms of poverty of conception. If the idea of the mother, for example, can be released from the small personal box of infantile craving, the psychic energy contained in the mother-complex will be released for those aspects of relatedness over which the maternal archetype rules. Similarly, if the idea of the father can be detached from the fascination of the personal father, the energy contained in the archaic state of identification will be released and transformed into real objectives. These are the twin spheres of eros and logos, created by effective relatedness and effective thought. The achievement of psychological freedom is beyond the reach of the man emotionally contained in the infantile state; yet the more he resents his spiritual captivity, the more does he strain at the rope that binds him, and the more is he galled by the knots. When at last he realizes, with the force of the *katalēptikē phantasia*, that it is his unconscious infantile attitude which holds him captive—only then will he turn inward and loosen the knot at the centre.

Jung's conception then, if I understand it aright, asserts the power of the idea as the effective psychic cause; accordingly the best, if not the only, way of release from the schizophrenic box is psychological development. To know the power of the idea is to recognize the fact that the world is created by the psyche: it is in fact the reflection of the way in which one conceives oneself. Creating the self is therefore equivalent to creating the world.

The theme of alchemical transmutation, which we traced in Drawing VII., is again alluded to in the contents of the womb-cavity. The two elixirs of the alchemists were the red and the silver. In Drawing IV. we found four symbolical figures, two in red and two in silver, abstracted from III. and placed in the diagonal position of reciprocal action. One of these figures consisted of the bags of blood which we now see transformed into the heart. Of the other figures, painted in silver, we cannot be so sure. We only know that they were germinal elements, dwarfed by dissociation and regression and therefore needing transformation. It will be remembered that these were the little sperm-like homunculi, products of the incestuous libido that was held fascinated by the mother-image. In so far as the silver wing in this drawing is created out of the libido released from the mother-fixation, it is possible to connect the appearance of the wing with the transformed silver homunculi. But, if the heart is the substance that has been transformed, where is the transformer, the red elixir? To find this, we must return to the red snake-circle in Drawing VII. In that drawing we observed the libido, held under the infantile inversion, fermenting within the closed box of the infantile craving. But at the bottom, within the green pan, the patient felt he had to draw this red snake-ring. Through our digression into alchemy, we discovered that the snake-ring or *uroborus* hieroglyph was used by the later mediæval alchemists to denote a process conceived of as operating in the timeless, unconditioned state, or *sub specie æternitatis*. Here then is the subtle elixir, the instinctive source of the idea of impersonality which was set at the base of the all-too-personal system, as the alchemists set a fire under the closed vessel for the process of purification, or as warmth was applied to the retort for the process of incubation. The idea of incubation, or rather gestation, is also alluded to in the presence of the warmly tinted breast of mother-earth on the right side of IX., and of the two lakes of blue that suggested the amniotic fluid.

Another and most vital aspect of the transforming process is the exorcism or separation of the dæmonic aspect of the unconscious (which completely ruled the scene in the previous picture) from the introverting maternal aspect. There is a beautiful analogy to this act of separation in the Book of Tobit.

The reader will remember how Tobias, accompanied by the angel, was sent on a mission by Tobit, his father, to recover treasure from a distant land.

> " And as they went on their journey, they came in the evening to the river Tigris and they lodged there. And when the young man went down to wash himself, a fish leaped out of the river, and would have devoured him. Then the angel said unto him: ' Take the fish.' And the young man laid hold of the fish, and drew it to land. To whom the angel said: ' Open the fish, and

take the heart and the liver and the gall, and put them up safely.' So the young man did as the angel commanded him; and when they had roasted the fish, they did eat it: then they both went on their way to Ecbatane. Then the young man said to the angel: 'Brother Azarias, to what use is the heart and the liver and the gall of the fish?' And he said unto him: 'Touching the heart and the liver, if a devil or an evil spirit trouble any, we must make a smoke thereof before the man or the woman, and the party shall be no more vexed. As for the gall, it is good to anoint a man that hath whiteness in his eyes, and he shall be healed.' "

We shall have to deal with this myth at length in a subsequent chapter; for the time being, therefore, it will suffice to explain that the devouring fish which leaps upon Tobias from the unconscious is a symbolical anticipation of his meeting with Sara, the woman whom he is ordained to marry, but who is possessed by the evil spirit Asmodeus. The fish clearly symbolizes the dæmonic power of the unconscious which the hero must first know how to handle before its curative potentialities are revealed.

The analysis of this critical situation by the angel offers a fine example of that instinctive wisdom which we so often find enshrined in the myths. " Take hold of the fish and bring it to land " is the instruction to bring the problem up into full consciousness in order to make it manageable. The next step is to separate the essential organs or attributes of the fish, and to put them on one side. These are to be employed for religious and therapeutic ends. Accordingly they must be offered to the celestial powers, while the body of the fish must be eaten and enjoyed. This advice corresponds with the practice in certain antique cultures, in accordance with which every young woman of standing was first deflowered by the priest in the temple before being given in marriage. The ritual act of defloration was a symbolical separation of the religious aspect of the woman's eros, which belonged essentially to the god, from the biological relationship with the husband. This prior act of differentiation was also calculated to free the sexual relationship from the hindrance of mythological projections.

The value of differentiating the higher from the lower is present also in the advice given by the angel. It is as though he attributed the dæmonic aspect of the instinct to the fact that it contains certain impersonal elements which must be clearly differentiated as spiritual factors. Because of their suprapersonal origin, these elements must not be conceived personally, but as an inheritance belonging to the race. Sexuality is to be enjoyed, just as one eats the fish; but first of all, it involves creation and procreation. Hence the wise man pays tribute to the creative, spiritual powers in order to invoke their aid in harnessing the crude force of the instinct to creative ends. The burnt offering made to the gods, the libations offered at feasts, the smoke of the sacrifice—all these, at bottom, were a form of tribute paid to the ancestral spirits. It was a concrete recognition of the fact that the impersonal motivation of human psychology is of a higher order, and therefore must be discriminated from the personal and given a symbolical rather than an actual satisfaction.

To resume: the horrific, devouring aspect of the unconscious is considerably mitigated in Drawing IX., in which a clear and definite shape issues from the nostrils, instead of fire and smoke. The resistant factor is emerging, as a specific mythological organism, into the light of consciousness. By virtue of this act of differentiation, the remaining function of the unconscious, purified, as it were, of the dæmonic influence, takes on the character of the earth, in which living things can germinate.

The dragon, which has not yet fully emerged, is no ordinary conventional metaphor. As a creature, it is unique. Although clearly owing certain features (viz., the green body, the dorsal spines and the lateral line) to the universal archetype, it is none the less a most unusual variant. This fact would lead us to suppose that the complex derives from two sources: in the first place from the archaic roots of the instinct, and secondly from the spell-binding impression of the father's psychotic personality during the impressionable years of infancy and childhood. We are able to say this with a relative degree of certainty, because the eye of the dragon is a sunflower in structure, and is situated in the same part of the field as the darkened sun in the first drawing, which was identified with the father. We know also, from the patient's personal history, that the father's uncanny gaze fascinated the boy by its fixed intensity.

It is not at first easy to determine why the patient has imposed the *mandala* design upon the disc of the flower. Quite possibly it represents an unconscious attempt to employ the *mandala* as a magical symbol wherewith to neutralize the fascinating effect of the infantile impression. The patient himself could give me no information about it, and I have been unable to trace this design in the literature of alchemy, where certain magical designs were employed to keep off satanic influences. The primitive origin of the *mandala* design is the magic circle that was made around the consecrated place to protect it from inimical spirits.[1] The primitive labyrinth almost certainly served the same end. It is therefore probable that the patient might employ, quite unwittingly, a similar primitive means to exorcise the infantile dæmonic impression of the father; as also, by means of the *uroborus*, he transformed the incest-dæmon connected with the mother. In piercing the magic circle identified with the psychotic eye, the hero breaks the spell persisting from infancy. The mythological analogy with Siegfried again occurs to the mind. The dragon is the dæmonic defender of the treasure; therefore, by piercing the magic circle which defends the treasure, the hero obtains access to the mother in a new form.[2]

The allusion to the sunflower is interesting. The flower is so called because it is always supposed to turn its face towards the sun. The yellow disc below turns to the golden disc above: like unto like. The patient has drawn the dragon at the top of the picture. The dragon is above, the hero below and to the side. In no drawing of the battle has the subject placed the hero right in front of the dragon. He always attacks from below, and from the side. This is, of course, self-protective. The parental eye was always above, and could be overwhelming. The hero must, similarly, be safeguarded from the hypnotic effect. These observations

[1] As, for instance, the circular earthwork surrounding the temple at Stonehenge.

[2] Brunhild was really a second mother to Siegfried through her protection of Sieglinde.

confirm our view that we have to do with the fascinating effect of a psychotic complex which is rooted in an infantile impression of the father. There is an interesting psychological nuance in the fact that the patient gives the attribute of the sunflower to the father. This shows the primitive basis of the identification with the father. In sympathetic magic the primitive mentality presupposes an identity between the original and the copy, between the man to be injured and the clay image made to resemble him for the purposes of witchcraft. The sun and the king were not merely similar, but identical. Unconscious identification of the child with the father is of this nature. It is an irrational identity, depending upon the primitivity of the unconscious. Thus the sunflower in the sun betrays the son's identification with the father, for it was the son who turned his face, like a sunflower, always towards the father.

The psychology of the two golden javelins that are directed at the centre of the eye, one from above, the other from below, is probably connected with the two directions of penetration of the morbid system discovered in Drawing VII. The index-finger of divine command pierced the system from above, while the corresponding phallic penetration was directed from below. The gold of the javelins would correspond with this association. The fact that the javelins are aimed at the centre of the eye is intelligible for two reasons. One motive we discussed in an earlier chapter when we considered the notion of driving the stake through Dracula's heart—namely, the need to pierce to the heart and centre and root of the complex. The other is concerned with an uncanny impression produced by this sun-wheel eye—so vast an eye without a pupil! This fact by itself stamps it as a pathological symptom. One feels an almost irresistible impulse to pierce the centre of this blind eye: it is a target that invites assault. This blindness of the psychotic eye is a profoundly accurate statement. It is this opacity, or complete lack of insight, which is the cause of the blind paranoiac projections.

One other feature of this drawing calls for notice. I refer to the fact that although the characteristic schizophrenic division is present, and the contents of the right half of the picture are of a different character from those on the left, yet the emergence of the dragon from the nostril of the monster, and the entrance of the upper javelin from behind the dragon-castle, betoken a clear liaison between the two sides. This was lacking in Drawing II., where the schizophrenic split was complete. That this drawing represents a kind of schematic attempt to deal with the schizophrenic cleavage is indirectly confirmed by the patient himself, who told me that the crenellated wall, which forms the lower part of the division between the two halves, was constructed from the layer of jagged rocks which kept the lunatic asylum underground in Drawing I. The inference from this statement is clear: the paranoidal mechanism of repression and resistance has been converted into a protective wall in order to guard the delicate creative process of the unconscious. Protection is necessary, both from the possibility of pathological invasion and from clumsy conscious interference.

CHAPTER IX

THE HEROIC COMBAT

I

DRAWING X

HERE the dragon has fully emerged and the battle is already in progress. Again we see the dragon looming above, while the hero grapples with him from below. No Western artist could have depicted St. George in this inferior position. It would be possible for a Chinaman, perhaps, because the dragon in China is a natural denizen of the heavens. The two vast sun-wheel eyes of the dragon occupy the commanding central position of the drawing. The monster has no mouth. Evidently it has to rely upon the spell cast by its eyes and upon its spiny sucker-feet, for these are its only offensive equipment. The effect of these enormously exaggerated eyes is indescribable. They are immobile, utterly expressionless, and unwinking. They glare at one without seeing anything. They are flat, lifeless discs that offend nature's canon of proportion controlling the reasonable dimension of specific parts in relation to the whole. Moreover, the *mandala* design is clearly a conscious artefact, superimposed upon their natural sunflower structure like a gigantic pair of spectacles. It will be observed that the *mandala* design employed in this drawing is simpler and more compact than the first attempt in the previous drawing. It is more unified, inasmuch as there is only one circle, and the radial lines run from the centre to end at the circumference.

In the analysis of dreams it is often observed that when the unconscious discloses a content or function that seems inappropriate to its setting, it signifies something that needs to be taken over into the conscious. The *mandala* is the original symbol of individuation. It represents the idea of a unified totality. Hence a duplicated *mandala* is an anachronism. As a symbol of psychic totality, it should contain a central jewel or symbol of value. But in this dæmonic eye only the barest structure is given. There is no centre of creative potency. According to Eastern ideas, it is the prerogative of the primordial female power, Shakti, to generate forms and bodies. It is Shiva, the god, who fills them with light and breath. This accords also with the Chinese view, where *Yin* is the dark, female, earthy principle of matter, form, substance, while *Yang* is the masculine principle of light, spirit, heaven. This symbolism would therefore suggest the idea of a primordial structure that needs to be penetrated by Shiva, the Lord of Light. In other words, the unconscious needs to be opposed and pierced by consciousness.

The duplication of the *mandala* is obviously a pathological symptom. Duplication is, moreover, carried further in the double row of dorsal spines with an intervening medial line of red crosses, so that one almost gets the impression of a twin organism. These indications seem to point to the characteristic division of will and purpose caused by the schizophrenic split. It is as though two opposing wills were embodied in a single organism, each will claiming totalitarian authority. This condition would necessarily result in a lifeless, expressionless stasis, since neither of the wills of a twin organism can be effective. Later we shall find evidence pointing to the specific nature of the contradictory tendencies expressed in this duplication of the dragon.

From the associations already discussed, we know that this monster has to do with the patient's infantile impression of the father's psychosis, and we suggested the hypothesis that the sunflower structure alluded to the condition of identification with the father. This hypothesis would also offer an explanation of the condition of duplication—namely, the personality based upon the introjected image of the father versus the will of the self, each claiming the symbol of totality. We shall presently see whether this hypothesis can be substantiated.

Opposed to the dragon, and below it, we find two representatives of the conscious principle. The major of these is the hero (clothed in white), attacking from the right. With his right hand (painted silver) the hero levels a long and effective javelin (painted gold) at the centre of the dragon's right eye (the left in the drawing). With his long extended left arm he aims a smaller javelin, barbed at both ends, at the same point. The two arms and javelins are so disposed as to make a quadrant. In the lower centre of this quadrant an auxiliary of the hero is depicted in the shape of a small mechanical soldier, with tin helmet, operating a field-gun. Both the gun, which is pointed upwards at the centre of the same eye, and the mechanical soldier are painted in silver. By this we are informed that this auxiliary element belongs to the same principle as the hero. In point of fact, the patient identified himself with the tin soldier.

Let us consider for a moment whether it is possible to find a single term to include all the elements in this picture which are painted in gold and silver. If we could find such a term, it might help us to discover that superior function of consciousness which is here invoked for the work of deliverance. The answer is suggested in the enormously extended left arm of the hero, which traverses the bottom of the drawing from right to left, and which forms the base of the arm and javelin quadrant described above.

The arm symbolizes the extension of the personality whereby a purpose is carried into effect. Thus a weapon comes to be an arm, since it is yet another extension of the personality for the purpose of achieving a specific aim—*i.e.*, that of vanquishing an opponent. In the same way we speak of the infantry, the artillery, the cavalry, as an arm of the nation. The very words "army," meaning an armed force, and "armament," meaning effective[1] equipment for war purposes, are derived from the original idea of the arm as the effective executant of the will. Thus the arm can also symbolize the differentiated armament of the mind, fashioned by necessity and cultural discipline throughout human history. The discovery of new means by which consciousness is enabled to extend its range of objectives has always been the decisive factor in the history of human development. The discovery of a new means of chipping and flaking flint marked the transition from the early stone-age to the neolithic culture.

[1] Compare also the military use of the term "effectives."

Similarly, the discovery of the use of bronze and iron marked extensions of human power of such a decisive nature that the respective phases of culture are designated by these metals. There is therefore ample associative justification for the use of metallic colours to represent the amazing extension of consciousness effected by the scientific intellect. Never before in the history of man has the pride and power of the intellect, as a means of superiority over nature, been so proudly asserted as it is to-day.

A further clue to the nature of this Promethean[1] figure is offered us in the contrast between the alert eye, the vigorous, directed movement, the power and virility of the hero figure, and the automatism of the diminutive soldier who operates the gun. This latter figure is reminiscent of the robot creatures, seen in the right half of Drawing II., which were explained as an impression of human beings turned into automata by the schizophrenic deprivation of value. But although the gun is made to appear inconsiderable in comparison with heroic prowess, its effect in the actual combat is decisive, as we shall presently see. When asked for his associations with this gun, the patient recalled the typical attitude of soldiers in the trenches who, when shot by a sniper, were able to direct their fury at an individual enemy who had aimed at them, but when hit by a piece of shell accepted it as a stroke of fate, since no one had intended it for them. The gun was also associated with the generic mechanism of sexuality, which projects libido from the subjective into the objective sphere.

The fact that the patient identified himself with the mechanical soldier is significant. He told me that this was how he actually felt—a mere mechanism, a puppet, completely in the power of forces outside his will. He said he went through school and college, passed his examinations, did what was expected of him like a kind of automaton. The later pictures of this series, which depict the tin soldier as a

[1] Prometheus, the cultural innovator who stole the fire of the gods, is the prototype for all time of the daring hero-criminal who challenges the primordial images, the immemorial gods of the unconscious, in order to place more power—*i.e.*, knowledge—in the hands of consciousness. Every individual myth is in this sense a disturbance of the balance of nature.

helpless prisoner of the unconscious dæmon-power, were for him absolutely real.

With the help of these associations we are given a revealing insight into the tragic sense of insufficiency of this modern soul. In spite of all the intellectual weapons proffered by science he feels helpless and impotent in face of these archaic forces within and without which tend to sweep away the values and landmarks of the past, and against which civilized defences are of no avail. Yet it is just this realization of immediate need and danger to the self which awakens the archetype of the hero in the unconscious. The overwhelming power of collective mechanism is only half the truth. The less visible half is expressed in the fact that a man who is deeply conscious of his individuality cannot be enslaved. For when individuality is experienced and conceived as akin to the sun, it ceases to have a merely personal character. It becomes the power which creates a new heaven and a new earth. From this point of view, the hero is seen as an anticipation of the unified individual whose genuine superiority obliterates the feeling of personal impotence (represented by the robot soldier).

According to the associations given above, the gun would symbolize sexuality as a general biological urge. On the one hand it characterizes that general instinctual mechanism by virtue of which the human individual would appear practically indistinguishable from every other member of his sex, and on the other an overpowering potential of energy. The little tin soldier personifies the feeling of being caught up and used by this power, like a helpless thing in the hands of fate. This fatalistic standpoint in regard to the sexual *dynamis* is utterly incompatible with the heroic will, since the hero's capacity for making the impossible possible depends upon a " magical " supply of instinctual energy which he forges into the spearhead of his will.

As in Drawing VII., the motif of penetration also plays a major rôle here. Following out this analogy, the dragon can be recognized as an archaic content activated by the introverting process, the hero as a rejuvenated manifestation of the penetrating suprapersonal will, while the two javelins and the gun would correspond with the penetrating twelve rays, the index-finger and phallus of the ancestral god. Again we find the idea of penetration from above and below corresponding to the spiritual and the sexual *dynamis*. With this analogy before us, we can the more readily accept the field-gun and the robot-soldier as symbolizing the collective mechanism of sexuality. But why, we may well ask, should the mechanism of sex be involved in the fight between the hero and the dragon?

If the dragon symbolizes the atavistic psychic inertia which keeps the subject relatively ineffectual, we can see that the repression of sexuality to a mere robot activity might create a weapon of revolt that could easily explode in a fierce battle between individual and collective tendencies. Essentially, the fight is between the heroic individual will and the atavistic resistance of general unconsciousness standing in the way. That this monster should be associated with the infantile impression of the father is explained by the fact that the psychotic complex gets its overwhelming force and fixity from just this archaic psychic residue. What the patient has now to grapple with in himself was first experienced in the father. The pathological degree of identification is surely due to the fact that, at bottom, father and son share the same problem.

In respect to this psychotic imprint, it should be mentioned that the patient recalls certain moods of his father when his eyes assumed this intense, visionless fixity. He describes a feeling as though the father's eyes bored into him with a fixed, unseeing gaze. We can assume, therefore, that the patient's early impression of the father's psychology is, to a large extent, responsible for the monstrous eyes of the dragon. It should be noted, however, that, in spite of this association with the father, no feeling of guilt accompanied the drawing. We may conclude from this important piece of subjective evidence that the son has projected the father-image upon the analyst, and is therefore able to deal with the psychological situation with the father in a relatively objective fashion. This fact points to a certain gain in detachment from the original unconscious identification.

Now that the dragon-complex is detached as a separate organism, we can observe more narrowly its nature and origin. With regard to its mode of livelihood, we have remarked that it has no mouth—a surprising fact in view of its emergence from the devourer. It must therefore rely exclusively on its power of fascination, its crushing weight (it is about to crush the field-gun flat with its left foot) and its sucker-feet. With regard to the latter, the patient was not sure whether the spines of the feet were merely for the purpose of fastening upon the flesh of its victims, or whether the monster was able to suck up blood by this means. At all events, wherever the feet seize hold there is always a copious flow of blood—visible in the present drawing where the dragon's right foot has clawed hold of the hero's left wrist.

From these observations we realize that the dragon represents the terrible atavistic tendency of the unconscious. It is the crushing, paralysing, fascinating power of psychic inertia, the force which resists every step towards consciousness, and which spreads a pall of apathy over every new attempt. We have already remarked upon the character of duplication when discussing the *mandala* eyes, and we discussed the possibility that the schizophrenic division of will might be depicted in this doubling of the *mandala* symbol.

If this be the true explanation, we can see why the schizophrenic mentality labours so cruelly under the weight of apathy and inertia, and why the hero's weapon is aimed at the centre of one eye. This act expresses the longing for a single vision and a single-minded purpose. We know from the fact that the dragon consists of the green, yellow and red elements that it contains the essential dynamic constituents. Green and yellow are the colours of the laminated fields which, throughout the series, symbolize the dynamic or basic attitude. Red is the passional element, the blood; it was also the colour of the *uroborus* in Drawing VII. Inasmuch, then, as the dragon contains this massive energy-potential, why should it manifest so unmistakably the character of parasitic inertia? The answer to this question goes, I believe, to the root of the schizophrenic pathology. We should look for it in the wide, unwieldy, disproportionate duplication of the monster's body and, particularly, in the doubling of the *mandala* symbol.

The energy of the mind is produced by the tension between the opposites. When the opposites are not opposed, but joined in undifferentiated union, the potential energy of the mind, which could be generated by opposition, is held in a dormant, inert condition. In the archaic levels of the unconscious, the opposites are relatively undifferentiated, lying together side by side like unborn twins. In certain primitive languages opposite qualities, as, for instance, black and white, good and bad, etc., are expressed by the same word. In myths we find twin monsters, twin giants, or twin heroes—*e.g.*, Gog and Magog, Fafnir and Fasolt, Castor and Pollux, Romulus and Remus—symbolizing this same tendency of the archaic mentality to hold the opposites together in undifferentiated twinship. The myth of the casting of Lucifer (=the light-bearer) out of heaven illustrates the dawn of moral consciousness—namely, the creation of dynamic opposition out of original uniformity. As an angel Lucifer was indistinguishable among the heavenly hosts, but as the black satanic power of evil he is, as William Blake delighted to picture him, the active creator of energy. Until the opposites are separated we cannot speak of a moral consciousness. Individuality rests upon distinctiveness, for only through distinctiveness can a dynamic tension be created between the standpoint of conscious values and their opposite qualities in the unconscious. Hence the condition of undifferentiated uniformity spells death to individuality. Those who choose, for the sake of collective uniformity, to remain unconscious of their individual standpoint sin against the light. The sacred fire is visible only to a fearless heart.

The difficulties of adolescence, as also of later periods of transition, arise very largely from this profound individual need to create a dynamic opposition out of collective uniformity. Those who continue to evade the tension of the opposites, through maintaining a protective identification with the parent, also abandon the royal prerogative of individuality: under stress their moral is likely to collapse.

The duplicated uniformity of the *mandala* symbol—which should express individual totality, including the dynamic polarity of conscious versus unconscious—represents, therefore, the regressive pull to this primitive condition. Accordingly, one of the *mandala* eyes must be pierced. This ritual piercing of the eye is based upon the principle that an unconscious factor can become incorporated into consciousness only when it is penetrated by conscious insight.

The act of penetration depicted in this drawing is of a threefold nature, represented by the two weapons of the hero and the gun. This fact is also of importance, for it signifies that the moment of realization is supported by the creative power of the self.

II

Drawing XI

In this drawing the whole length of the dragon comes into view, and the hero has plunged the javelin that was held in his right hand deep into the centre of the dragon's right eye. Where the javelin pierces the eye, a large irregular laceration is shown, from which blood streams down. With his left hand the hero passes the smaller and cruder javelin behind the disc of the eye, with the idea of separating it from the body. The patient feels that the eye must be completely excised. The notion of excising a vital organ of the monster is a familiar motif in the hero-myths. It is equivalent to the theme of the hero who, having been swallowed by the monster, cuts out the heart and eats it, thus assimilating the vital principle of the dæmon. The primitive notion of eating the heart of a brave enemy, in order to acquire his *mana*, belongs to the same order of ideas. The Promethean motif of stealing the fire from the gods is also exemplified in this act. The same motif seems to rule this modern myth, for as the hero drives his blade home, a singular effect takes place—namely, a third medial eye (the pineal eye) makes its appearance near the vertex of the hero's head. In other words, a virtue, quality, function, has been transferred from the primordial to the ruling position of the conscious sphere. We referred to this event, it will be remembered, when discussing the curious tripod structure in the first drawing which connected the nmates of the asylum with the lighthouse. We also traced a possible connection between the snail-fish eyes of Drawing VIII. with the inturned, medial eye that appeared above the lower end of the womb-cavity in Drawing IX. The purpose for which this archaic organ was being prepared now becomes manifest.

It will be noticed that the dragon has a pair of sucker-feet in the rear, and that these are about to attack the hero from behind. One of these feet has already caught up the soldier, and set him literally *hors de combat*. The hero's face is contracted and somewhat anxious. The reversed eye (*i.e.*, directed backwards) has apparently warned him of the danger threatening him from behind. In the lower middle region of the drawing we see the gun, crushed into a twisted ruin by the left forefoot of the dragon—a further evidence of the crushing weight of inertia which the complex can produce.

Resuming the train of thought which we elaborated when discussing the previous drawing, we must observe that the action of the hero is not primarily concerned with slaying the dragon, but rather with the piercing and excising of the right eye. This act of taking an eye from the dæmonic ruler of the unconscious identifies the hero with the line of Prometheus, the prototype of the cultural genius of mankind. Prometheus stole the fire from the gods (viz., the archetypes of the unconscious) in order to bring the gift of fire, with all its incalculable potentialities, to mankind. The guilt of Prometheus (which is also the guilt of the psychological innovator and pioneer) consists in the fact that he transferred from heaven (*i.e.*, the realm of primordial images) energy which had been latent in the unconscious since the world began, bringing it under the control of consciousness. It is as true to-day as ever that the Promethean man, who thus disturbs afresh the primordial balance of nature, will have to pay for his impiety. Yet he cannot forswear the principle he serves. In the myth of our subject, the cultural hero is forcibly removing one of the *mandala* symbols from the sphere of the unconscious, and, in so doing, a new organ of vision is being added to consciousness. The hitherto existing balance between the conscious and the unconscious is therewith disturbed; nevertheless, consciousness is enriched by an organ peculiarly adapted to the perception of unconscious processes, coming, as it does, from an archaic source. A function gained from the unconscious naturally tends to preserve the archaic mode of functioning as well as the peculiar independence that is characteristic of unconscious activity.

This medial, atavistic eye would seem to represent an intuitive function presiding, as it were, over the individual myth. Inasmuch as it is situated towards the back of the head, we can assume it to be a certain modality of intuition fitted for perceiving what is going on in the unconscious. The unconscious, be it remembered, is merely that aspect of reality we normally do not see.

The cultural hero in a modern doctor's psychology would inevitably be associated with the scientific intellect, the development of which has, more than any other single cause, served to repress the intuitive science of antiquity which gave ear to the voice of dreams, and which honoured the wisdom that tried to discern naturally revealed truths rather than the capacity to accumulate data. Effective intuitive impressions of so-called unconscious events manifest the immediate precision of an habitual instinctive process, but this can be acquired only through relying upon the function as an objective process. For the purpose in hand—namely, the work of coming to terms with the archaic contents of the unconscious—this medial vision is peculiarly apt. For what could be better adapted for perceiving and understanding the atavistic danger which is schizophrenia than the eye that has been stolen from the dragon?

An interesting feature of the drawing concerns the fate of the little tin soldier. Like the robot figures of Drawing II., the patient identified this diminutive figure with his own feeling of inferiority and insufficiency. To conceive oneself as a tiny automaton, a mere technical accompaniment of a piece of collective mechanism, is to take the lowest possible estimate of one's human destiny. Man is reduced to a mere plaything of circumstance.

In an earlier chapter, when comparing the quest of the alchemists with the aim of the *yogi* or the mystic, we elaborated the idea that the fundamental goal of every mystical system was the liberation of the self from the necessitous drive of biological mechanism—in other words, to experience consciousness and being in and for themselves instead of as contingent factors of every partial system.

From this point of view the little-tin-soldier conception of oneself might represent the false image which makes life unendurable. Analytical experience has taught us that the sense of inferiority is invariably caused by the fact that an important function of the personality has either been neglected and repressed, or has never yet become effective in consciousness.[1] In other words, it is a condition in which the conscious personality is too small and the unconscious shadow too great. We often speak of a crushing sense of inferiority; but if one is being crushed, something else is doing the crushing. In the picture we see the inferiority conception, the false collective image of the self, being crushed.

The following heuristic principle is invaluable for the understanding of dreams—namely, things that happen together in the dream or fantasy-construction are to be regarded as intimately connected. This principle of synchronicity does not rely upon a temporal causal sequence. It does not say, " Because the hero plunges his javelin into the eye of the monster, therefore the monster crushes the gun." Banish " because " and " therefore " from the rational sequence and the proposition can then be laid down as follows: " The hero plunges his weapon into the eye, and the monster crushes the gun, and the middle eye appears in the hero's head, and the dragon attacks the hero from behind, and the tin soldier is carried off, and all these things happen together in the same moment."

Here is a nexus of synchronous happenings; their synchronicity is not mere chance, but a meaningful, though non-rational concatenation. If we attempt to explain their interconnection causally we shall lose ourselves in a labyrinth

[1] *Cf.* Adler's conception of inferiority as due to an organic defect.

of untenable hypotheses. To be in tune with the primordial reality of the unconscious we simply have to accept the fact that the synchronicity of these events is a true statement of their inner connection.

That this inner connection is reasonable we may attempt to demonstrate. In view of the tremendous overweighting of the unconscious, for instance, symbolized by the vast inert monster, the patient's feeling of conscious insufficiency and mechanical determinism is intelligible. Again, the patient's new analytical attempt was backed by courage and integrity: it is intelligible, therefore, that this attempt should evoke the archetype of the hero, and that, with the afflux of power from the unconscious, the feeling of inferiority should fade into thin air. The acquisition of the intuitive middle-eye is, as we have seen, mythologically valid. Presumably, therefore, it is psychologically intelligible. Everybody who has had much to do with unconscious material will appreciate the validity of this analogy.

The only thing that is not explained is the crushing of the field-gun. If we had not known that this tangle of silver paint had once been a field-gun, we should immediately have been struck by its resemblance to a snake that has been trodden on. Is it not about to strike the foot that weighs upon it? It has even a pointed tail. This representation was certainly not intended, but none the less it is there. No sooner, therefore, is the mechanistic conception of the self finally disposed of, than the conception of sexuality immediately reverts to the archetypal symbol of the snake.[1] The gun is a cultural contrivance, an affirmation of social power and discipline. Hence to identify sexuality with this symbol means to ignore the primordial nature of the instinct. What could be more reasonable, therefore, than that the independent self-moving aspect of the instinct should reveal itself in the moment that the mechanical conception is exploded?

Something is gained and lost by both sides in this conflict. One eye is lost to the dragon and is gained by the hero;

1 Bearing in mind the nature of the schizophrenic problem—viz., archaism versus conscious control—this reversion depicts how the psychic energy has gone over to the archaic contents, leaving consciousness powerless.

while the gun mechanism that is lost to the cultural side reverts to the dragon-level.

Jung has termed this whole process the *transcendent function.* In every conflict a dynamic opposition occurs, and in this opposition some elements transcend from one side to the other and *vice versa.* Through this reciprocal action involving the transcending of vital elements from either side to its opposite, a new condition is reached which was not a predictable outcome of the conflict. Strictly speaking, this third factor is the transcendent function. We shall presently discover how this new condition manifests itself.

The prognosis at this point might seem on the whole rather favourable. But the situation is not so good as it appears. These representations of the unconscious are in a sense anticipations, pregnant with very real possibilities: but everything depends on how the subject realizes his experience. Inasmuch as it was possible for him to identify himself with the inferior robot figure, it is more than likely that he will now identify himself with the superior hero.

The state of inflation through identification with an archetype is almost a predictable event in these cases where the patient tumbles head first into the unconscious. It is all the more likely to occur with patients long oppressed by a feeling of inferiority. In practice, therefore, it is essential, lest the ego insist on putting these mythological feathers in its cap, to treat these products as mythological material, and to point out that the superiority of the hero would be just as much an overstatement of personal merit as the robot-soldier was an understatement. The self, conceived as the totality of the psychical subject, includes ego, hero, soldier and dragon as partial systems, and the house which is being constructed must be built on this impersonal foundation.

III

In order to see the deeper level in perspective it is essential also to view the material from the general mythological standpoint, though the patient himself was inclined to be resistant to this kind of interpretation. In these mythic products of the unconscious we are not dealing with disguised impressions or images of concrete things or persons, but with age-old affective deposits which have assumed a certain generalized human aspect and caught up certain infantile associations. The devouring monster of VIII. and that drawn by Mr. Westmann's patient, for instance, are in no sense images of the actual mother. Only in so far as they represent a titanic resistance against the ineffable longing for the mother can they be said to contain the idea of the mother.

To the infantile psyche, as we have clearly seen, possession of the mother is the longed-for, but unattainable, treasure, and the myth is rooted in this ever-unsatisfied longing. Therefore the basic theme of mythology is the quest for the treasure or the jewel beyond price, and the hero is heroic just because he treats every obstacle and difficulty in his life as though they were resistant guards of the treasure hard to attain.

The central breast-image in Drawing III. and the finger of taboo defending the libidinal approach represent the basic dynamics of the soul—namely, resistance, or fear of incest, defending the unattainable treasure. The overcoming of difficulties, especially the winning of the guarded or inaccessible lover, yields, therefore, the sweetest delight to the heroic nature.

The instinctive rationale of woman's attitude to man during courtship is determined at bottom by this same dynamic pattern. The woman, for instance, instinctively seeking a real man for her mate, puts difficulties and resistance in the path of her lover. She will prove him and test him to see how much he can stand, whereas the woman who seeks to play the rôle of the all-embracing mother will be sympathetic, consoling and infinitely understanding. If there be not something hard to win in a woman, the heroic man will not stay with her, because the quest for the unattainable is the irrational mainspring of his being. But before the heroic will is free to seek its mate the mother must first be overcome. The hero is actually born in the transformation of the infantile psyche into the cultural. For the infantile psyche, as we have seen, is helplessly bound to the image of the mother, even though the incest-longing is enclosed in a cloistered and concealed system.

The infantile psyche is expressed by the will of the child, the cultural psyche by the heroic will. The two wills are essentially contradictory, the one striving for exclusive possession and uninhibited satisfaction, the other for the difficult goal or heroic achievement. In Drawing III. we witnessed the infantile will striving for exclusive possession of the mother, and in VI. we saw the birth of the heroic will in the dawn of the cultural psyche. The long road over the hill, with the unfolding glory of the peacock's tail (the bird of the sun) emerging beyond the crest, is a beautiful symbolic statement of the heroic path towards the goal difficult of attainment. Compare the closed ring of the infantile system of VII., especially the snake biting its own tail, with the road leading over the hill towards the unknown future under the eye of the sun.

The green lavatory-pan was, in itself, the final comment upon the frustrated infantile attitude, which seeks to reduce everything to the inverted valuation. The break-up of the personal infantile system means, therefore, a real dissolution: it is the small stream pouring itself into the sea. Through becoming dissolved in the primordial unconscious, the personal infantile images are transformed into mythological archetypes, and the archetypal drama is re-enacted.

A beautiful example of this conversion of the infantile psyche is to be seen in the evolution of the green life-stuff from the excretory level to a divine germinal substance. We are reminded of the god Ra, who impregnated himself with his own semen through the mouth, whence, subsequently, the world was born. The green substance is the seed of life in the mouth of the god, and the inner part of his body has become a uterus in which new elements are developing. The infantile theme of self-fertilization thus becomes mythologically transformed. The green life-stuff becomes stiff, taking on the form and character of the bones of the arm; these protrude into the mouth-cavity, like the male organ, and the cavity then assumes the characteristic function of the womb. The motif of continuous coitus is implied in this symbolism. This conception is not incompatible with the theme of the devouring monster which swallows the sun-hero. As soon as the sun-hero is swallowed (the green life-stuff was impregnated by the sun) the inner or maternal aspect of the monster (the unconscious) begins to be manifest, and the dragon, with whom the hero must now do battle, detaches itself from the monster.

This dragon is the mythological father, who stands in the son's way to the mother. The father represents the son's active resistance against his own incest-wish. The crime unconsciously desired by the son is imputed to the father, though disguised as a murderous intention against the son. Neurotic patients often dream of the father as a being who inspires them with mortal dread. Hence, in the myth, the hero is faced with a fearsome monster or terrible giant.

In this connection Jung mentions[1] the monster Chumbaba in the Gilgamish epos. He is the terrible guardian of the Forest of Cedars which surrounds the temple of the goddess. Gilgamish overcomes Chumbaba with the help of Enkidu; he is then wooed by Ishtar, whose erotic advances he rejects. Jung treats Chumbaba as the mythological father, the guardian of the sacred place of the goddess, hence also the guardian of the treasure. The same pattern is seen in the myth of Siegfried, who seeks the Rhinegold which is guarded by Fafnir, the giant transformed into a dragon.

In the myth of our patient the dragon has certain associations which identify him with both parents. Green, for example, is the vegetational colour of the earth-mother. It is also the colour of the lavatory-pan, which the patient associated with the mother's lap. Finally, it emerged from the nose of the terrible mother. On the other hand, the sun-wheel eyes belong to the sky-principle, which is usually identified with the father-god. The sun is directly associated with the father, so too is the inhuman gaze of the eyes.

The overcoming of both parents by the hero is not an uncommon mythical theme. As illustration I will cite a few passages from Jung's discussion of the Hiawatha myth in *Psychology of the Unconscious*:

[1] *Psychology of the Unconscious*, p 161.

"Hiawatha has therefore conquered his parents, primarily the mother, although in the form of a male animal, and from that comes his giant strength. He has taken on the parents' skin and now has become a great man. Now he started forth to his first great battle to fight with the father, Mudjekeewis, in order to avenge his dead mother, Wenonah. Naturally under this figure of speech hides the thought that he slays the father in order to take possession of the mother. . . . The father, in the psychological sense, merely represents the personification of the incest prohibition—*i.e.*, the resistance which defends the mother. Instead of the father, it may be a fearful animal (the great bear, the snake, the dragon, etc.) which must be fought and overcome."[1]

After Hiawatha's fight with Mudjekeewis the father has to make a great concession to the victorious son, sharing his divine wind-nature,[2] by virtue of which he had just survived the battle with his son. Thus through the overcoming of the father Hiawatha gains the treasure of immortality which Gilgamish so desperately sought but could never attain.

With regard to the transference of the eye, there is the myth of Horus, who gave one of his eyes to Ra, the old sun-god, who had lost an eye to Set. Wotan is another sky-god who loses an eye. In his case the sacrifice of an eye to Mimir was in the nature of a payment by Wotan for the boon of Erda's wisdom (the earth-goddess). In general, the mythological sacrifice of an eye has the character of a payment from one god to another, whereby a new order of nature is established or the original balance restored.

The original balance of nature was conceived by early Greek cosmogonists as specific domains or portions allotted to the impersonal *moira*[3] who ruled over gods and men. The balance was established from the beginning; hence the boundaries of the various provinces had to be jealously guarded. The payment of an eye, or whatever it might be, can also be regarded as a punishment prescribed by the *moira* for trespassing against the natural order.

The idea of the eye being conceived as payment of a

[1] *Loc. cit.*, p. 200.

[2] Mudjekeewis is the west wind, and the wind or breath is the original idea of God.

[3] F. M. Cornford: *From Religion to Philosophy*.

debt is also found in the biblical expression " An eye for an eye and a tooth for a tooth," or even in the popular expression " He would give his eyes to be able to do that."

Returning to our material from the wider field of general mythology, we perceive that the dragon is the concrete embodiment of the resistance which defends the hero's access to the treasure. The treasure has already been revealed to us as four distinct contents, appearing in the mouth and womb-cavity of the devouring monster.

(1) The impregnated life-stuff, which seems to have had a yeast-like function in activating the unconscious contents.
(2) The living heart, converted from the bags of blood.
(3) The infant, born from the heart.
(4) The egg containing the peacock.

In passing, we note with interest that the still unborn treasure has four distinctive aspects, suggesting a connection with the fourfold structure of the mind; but for the present we must return to the hero and his battle with the dragon. Besides the active resistance embodied by the dragon, there is also the passive wall of resistance appearing in the drawing as a definite structure that defends the mysteries within. In this connection we are reminded that one of the beautiful appellations for the place of the treasure in the Chinese text, published in the *Secret of the Golden Flower*,[1] is the Dragon Castle under the Sea.

In this aspect of the active and passive resistance we have yet another character emphasizing the general ambiguity of the unconscious, and by provoking the one aspect into activity the hero demonstrates the essential function of consciousness—*i.e.*, distinctiveness. Conscious discrimination is like a sword which separates the opposites, and only when the opposites are discriminated is consciousness reborn. The duplication of the dragon's structure therefore represents an archaic condition of unconsciousness, which resists the access of consciousness (the hero) to the fourfold germ of individuality (the treasure).

1 Wilhelm and Jung: *Secret of the Golden Flower* (Kegan Paul).

If this is so, why does the unconscious express this conflict in terms of the world-old mythological pattern of the son doing battle with the father in order to win the mother? At bottom it is the problem of the infantile versus the cultural psyche, a conflict that is inevitably conceived of as the infantile will seeking to creep in under cover of the mother, while the cultural will, in the person of the father, resists it. This ancient mythological frame is now being employed to hold a picture, in which the will that resists the hero is the will to unconsciousness in the subject's own depths—in other words, a peculiar reversal of the pattern.

We must now examine the results of the battle, both willed and unwilled. The hero's object was to thrust his javelin into one of the dragon's *mandala* eyes. He succeeds, but at the same time the gun is crushed and the eye is transferred from the object to the subject. These are not effects intended by the hero: they have been added, as we say, by fate or chance, which means, of course, the unconscious.

The hero is a hero because he yearns for the treasure difficult of attainment with single-minded devotion. The single mind is symbolized, as we said, by the single eye. But the man with a single-minded vision of his purpose must keep related to his instinct as a rider is related to his horse. He cannot afford to regard it as an item in a generalized biological equipment, serving the general purposes of pleasure and procreation. The single-minded passion of the hero is mythologically the gift of a god symbolized by a magical spear or sword: it is deeply rooted in the moral nature.

IV

Drawing XII

The gun apparently was no mere toy. It has exploded under the dragon's weight, the force of the explosion breaking the creature in half. The purpose for which the piercing of the eye was necessary has been achieved; the front half of the dragon now falls away. The dragon has been depotentiated: its obsessive, dæmonic power of fascination withdrawn, and the psychic middle eye added to the function of consciousness. But the explosion which severs the dragon also deprives the hero of his weapons. The smaller javelin is left embedded at the back of the monster's eye, while the larger weapon is broken in half by the explosion, the upper part of the shaft with the point being left in the eye. Thus the hero is left practically weaponless. His left arm hangs by his side, while the right is still raised, holding the broken lower half of the shaft.

The body of the dragon appears relatively thin and attenuated. But the rear portion is still effective, for the hind sucker-feet are seen attacking the back of the hero's head, causing lacerations from which blood begins to flow. The expression of the face is that of surprise and alarm. The little tin-soldier is still visible in the grasp of the disengaged foot.

Concerning the dragon, the double row of red dorsal spines should be noted, while a new feature has been added in the bifurcated tail with the two red arrowhead terminals. This latter feature brings to mind the duplicated nature of the dragon's structure, referred to above, which characterized the undifferentiated duality of the archaic unconscious levels.

The central event in this picture is the explosion of the gun, which, under the weight of the dragon's foot, appeared in the previous drawing to take on the aspect of a snake in the act of striking. An explosion is the sudden release of energy due to the conversion of explosive substances into the form of a gas. Neither the field-gun nor the snake explodes in just this way. But the field-gun is a mechanism for discharging shells by means of explosives, and the snake has the tendency to strike suddenly when trodden upon. By a combination of properties it is possible to understand how a gun-snake would tend to explode[1] when trodden under foot. The gun is a machine which can be operated, with a high degree of precision, to achieve a certain destructive aim or plan. The snake is a cold-blooded creature which remains

1 *Explode* is derived from the Latin *explaudere* = to drive off the stage with noise. Hence the original meaning of explosion is the action of rejecting with scorn. Thus we can recognize the central event of the picture as exploding an hypothesis—*i.e.*, a theory rejected with scorn.

dormant and immobile the greater part of its existence, yet possesses the power to strike with lightning efficacy when roused to action—a character shared more conspicuously by the field-gun, with the difference that the former strikes independently, while the latter waits until operated by a human agent. Finally, the gun expresses human aim and intention, while the snake is nature herself, caring nothing for human purposes, moving in her own time and in her own way. The symbol of control is won over to archaism.

Another fact to be noted is that the explosion is unexpected and undesired by either side. On the whole, its effect is to the advantage of the hero, though the explosion was clearly no part of the hero's plan of campaign, for it leaves him practically weaponless against the assault of the residue of the dragon. The conversion from gun to snake takes place in the moment when the hero becomes deeply engaged in the conflict, corresponding to the moment when the patient was himself gripped by the experience of the unconscious. Finding it impossible to account for the direct experience of the unconscious on the lines of biological determinism, the rationalistic conception of psychic causation was bound sooner or later to collapse. But the explosion of the mechanistic conception has its principal effect upon the dragon, not, as we might have expected, upon the representative of consciousness. True, it was the dragon which crushed the gun and against whose foot the snake reared its head. But our explanation must satisfy the deep, as well as the manifest, content of the scene; it must accord with the given data—namely, the sudden expansion or illumination which effects a radical change upon both antagonists—and it must also maintain an intelligible inner connection with what has gone before.

In order to fathom the meaning of a dream or any other natural product, we must let it speak. It may seem tiresome and superfluous to enumerate the self-evident properties of things or people figuring in a dream, but only by refusing to take these ordinary things for granted can we hope to see the purpose for which the dream makes use of them.

In the present instance, by refusing to take the field-gun

and its familiar properties for granted, we reach the conclusion that no ordinary gun is intended, but one that is also a snake, and liable to explode when stepped upon—in other words, an autonomous complex conceived as both animal and mechanism. This means that a function which had been regarded mechanistically has, as a result of the conflict, regained its autonomous animal character. But the field-gun (*alias* the mechanistic conception of the libido) was a weapon of the victorious intellect, and this weapon has been exploded, not by rational argument, but by the sheer weight of experience.

The transformation is interesting to observe. The mechanistic view of psychic events was not arrived at by psychological empiricism; it was simply carried over the hedge from the field of natural science, where it had proved to be serviceable. A man who has habitually defended himself against the unconscious with intellectual weapons would naturally bring the mechanistic field-gun into play in a battle against the dragon. How, then, does the dragon succeed in exploding this hypothesis? Obviously by being effective, since the whole ground of the mechanistic view of the psyche is that autonomous spiritual factors are not real. When a man is gripped by an experience in which he is tormented with raging hunger, suspended anxiously on a vital fear, churned by affect, and finally filled with a yearning for sleep, none of which can be explained on rational grounds, he must at least concede that the unconscious is real in the sense that it spontaneously produces effects. He sees that the pictures which suggest themselves to his mind at this time portray these affects in vivid imagery: hunger accompanied the painting of the devouring monster; anxiety, the hero's first encounter with the dragon (the battle of the son against the father); affect, the fight and the explosion; yearning for sleep, the exhaustion which overcame the hero after the fight.

But if things happen on their own account in the mental sphere, as spiritual forces operating freely without conscious instigation or control, then the intellectual superiority hitherto relied upon is no longer valid. The rational hero stands defenceless against the power he most fears: the irrational power behind all real experience.

The result of the explosion is even worse for the dragon than for the hero. Why should this be? In treading on the gun the dragon brings about his own undoing, and this again cannot be regarded as an accident. The dragon has come to the end of his term in that form. Like blind Samson,[1] who, when he knew his time had come, destroyed the temple at Gaza, himself and all his enemies together, so the dragon brings an end to his existence with a similar double effect. We might assume, therefore, that the duplication of structure was symptomatic of a dangerous accumulation of energy in the atavistic system, and that the tendency to self-division, apparent in the crushing of the gun, was motivated by the intrinsic psychic necessity to restore equilibrium between the conscious and the unconscious. It is interesting, too, that, after the eye has been pierced and the body of the dragon bisected, it is the rear half that continues the battle, whilst the fascinating front half falls away into limbo. We can only infer that the dragon-complex contained certain infantile impressions of the father which needed to be taken over into consciousness. The *mandala* design is also something which needed to become a conscious value, not left as a germinal possibility in the unconscious. When these elements are transferred, as it were, to the representative of consciousness, the front half of the dragon, having lost its *raison d'être*, disappears from the scene. The fact that the magical power of the dragon-complex and the intellectual armament of consciousness are destroyed together in the same collapse implies that the heroic intellectual equipment is, to a large extent, a defence against the unconscious, and that when the defensive attitude is abandoned the unconscious forgoes its sinister character.

The realization that the unconscious could have a positive function and aspect was, of course, inherent in Drawing IX. It was, perhaps, the dawn of this realization which forced

[1] The mighty hero of mythology is frequently the only son of a hitherto barren woman, as though his first heroic achievement was the overcoming of his mother's resistance to fertility.

this other bogey-concept of the unconscious into the field as a detached entity.

To recapitulate: the explosion of the gun, which invoked the idea of the snake, symbolizes the breakdown of the mechanistic prejudice and the dawning recognition of the independence of psychic activity. The explosion expresses the idea of a sudden alteration of the psychical energy-balance produced by this all-important realization. The further results of this illumination of the mind will be followed in subsequent drawings. Its immediate results are to be seen in the destruction of the fascinating power of the psychotic complex (*e.g.*, the eye of the monster) and in the breakdown of the lordly superiority of the intellect, symbolized by the golden javelins. Certain secondary results are also indicated in the already attenuated bulk of the dragon, in the hero's anxious expression, and in the changed colour of his garment. Previously the hero was arrayed in white raiment, glorious as the sun; now he is clothed in a humble brown shirt, the modest colour of the earth. This attitude should protect him in some measure from inflation, the hero's worst danger. From his somewhat rigid posture and anxious expression we are allowed to assume that he is now more interested in what is happening to himself than in what he is doing to the dragon. It is the characteristic expression of a man whose mind is suddenly invaded by a sinister idea, against the implications of which he is for the moment helpless.

CHAPTER X

THE ASSIMILATION OF THE DRAGON'S VIRTUE

I

Drawing XIII

THE scene is the end of the battle, witnessed from behind. The legs of the dragon have become longer and more powerful, and the upper foot-sucker is fast in the back of the hero's head. From the wounds thus inflicted streams a copious flow of blood. The left arm of the hero (painted silver) is bent over his head in a semicircle in order to grip hold of the sucker-leg, while the right arm is shown encircling the body of the beast, the hand still clutching the broken shaft of the javelin. The lower foot-sucker holds the tin soldier, apparently pressed against the back of the hero.

The central feature of the drawing is the effective operation of the medial eye, which emits four downward, divergent rays, each ending in a five-pointed star. These four stars appear to be giving out some kind of ray, which acts upon the foot-sucker that is fast in the hero's head. Another feature is the rising of the new moon in the upper right-hand part of the drawing. These two events, taken together, represent the beginning of a new and effective relation to unconscious events. The fact that there are four rays emitted by the eye brings it within the orbit of the principle of effective consciousness. We observed this fourfold differentiation of consciousness in Drawing VI., when the new sun, with its four attributes, first appeared above the horizon. A fourfold structure was also presented diagrammatically in the *mandala* eyes of the dragon. This latter association is significant, because the appearance of the medial eye in its present situation synchronized with the piercing of the dragon's eye. It suggests that the specific energy potential, which gave the autonomous complex its obsessive power over consciousness, has now been transferred to the conscious function. The five-pointed stars, which characterize the nature of the new intuitive function, are painted in silver, suggesting the lunar principle of the anima. This implies that the peculiar efficacy of this medial vision derives from its primordial origin in the unconscious. It belongs to a modality of the mind that is as different from the ordinary ego-consciousness as is the light of the moon from daylight. This is borne out by the synchronous advent of the new moon, which, as we shall presently confirm, is identified with the anima.

The favourable aspect of the anima is peculiarly fitted to embrace the idea of the soul. According to Jung's formulation, the anima is the function that mediates between the conscious and the collective unconscious. As representative of the inherited psyche, the anima is the instigator of those ideas which lead a man to his life-work, his major achievement. She often personifies his best tendency before it comes to maturity. This beneficent character of the anima belongs only to her impersonal function; as a personal factor the anima is unreliable. As we saw in the case of the Siberian *shaman*, she is essentially the spirit of a man's vocation, albeit a possessive one. Hence the timely advent of the new-moon anima, taken in conjunction with the effective operation of the medial or pineal eye, calls to mind once again the strange intuition of Descartes—namely, that the pineal body is the seat of the soul.

This venerable word has suffered, more than almost any other in our language, from the variety and range of meanings that have been imposed upon it. Theologians, poets, philosophers and physicians have all contributed their different ideas as to what the soul really is, or what properties it possesses. But to the dawning human intelligence soul and body were self-evident aspects of man. The body was the material form, the soul that which animated it.[1] The idea of the soul may have arisen originally from the observation that when a man slept, or fell into a trance, or got drunk, or died, the body and that which animated it with life and

[1] The original conception of the anima was the animating principle.

intelligence were separated. If the animating principle could depart from the body, it must be conceived as a separate entity. The study of primitive notions about the nature of the soul[1] discloses a world-wide unanimity concerning this primary impression. However the soul be conceived, whether as a single or manifold entity, whether metaphysically or animistically, it maintains throughout its original character—viz., that of an independent psychic entity. This character agrees entirely with our clinical observations. Provisionally, then, we may formulate the soul as a primary autonomous complex, through the activity of which relatively dissociated psychic elements are personified and brought into effect.

Turning to the archaic medial eye depicted in our drawing, the first thing that arrests our attention is that it is emitting certain rays. The rays are characterized by stars, which are often used to denote an energic effect. There is also the obvious cosmic analogy. The patient is, of course, familiar with the structure of the eye and the laws of optics. Nevertheless, he is here committing himself to a conception of the eye which stands in contradiction to his scientific knowledge. By this fact alone we know that the drawing is the expression of an autonomous psychic process which, for the time being, has taken possession of the patient's mind, to the exclusion of his accustomed conscious standpoint. What, then, is this other conception of the eye which breaks through from the archaic levels of the mind?

There was an ancient idea, held by Lucretius and other mystical philosophers of the West, that the eye emits light. The psychological intuition of the East has long been familiar with the same idea. It is implied in the following passage from the *Upanishads*.

> "The man that is here in the right eye is called by the name Indha, the kindler of fire. Yet, although he is Indha really, they call him also in a veiled way, Indra (the god), because the gods love that which is concealed and are shy of the things that are manifest. Furthermore, the human figure in the left eye is his wife, Viraj, the shining one."

[1] *Cf.* Crawley: *The Idea of the Soul*; and Frazer: *The Golden Bough*.

Here we find the conception of the eye as possessing both the fiery heat of the god and the shining radiance of the goddess.

Naturally, the introverted Eastern mind is as intelligibly informed as to the apparatus of vision as is the scientifically trained mind of the West. But what is also self-evident to the Oriental philosopher is the fact that the world is illumined with meaning through the efficacy of the psyche, which creates the world of images inhabited by consciousness. According to the introverted philosophy, the whole world starts from within, from an energic focus of unextended intensity. We found this idea already in the *Kundalini* symbolism, where the goddess Shakti, coiled three and a half times around the *lingam*, symbolizes the unextended and yet inexhaustible source of primordial energy. It is the arousing of this latent energy, or the tending of the primal flame (*purusha*), that creates the world in which consciousness dwells. The eye, therefore, is conceived of as the hole or gateway through which this inner psychic intensity emits its rays upon an otherwise meaningless universe.

Browning has the same introverted standpoint when he writes:

> " Truth is within ourselves; and to know
> Rather consists in opening out a way
> Whence the imprisoned splendour may escape
> Than in effecting entry for a light
> Supposed to be without."

If he had painted his intuition, instead of expressing it poetically, he would surely not have omitted the eye, through which the " imprisoned splendour " escapes.

Here, then, we have a symbolical expression of the introverted philosophy.[1] The introvert naturally tends to see things as emanating from the subjective, inner world; while the extravert tends to regard reality as originating without, thence producing secondary psychological effects upon the brain substance. Thus an extraverted psychologist will tend to emphasize environmental, educational, or inherited factors in his picture of a mental condition. According to his view,

[1] Schopenhauer's conception of the world as Will and Idea would also correspond with this view.

the human being is a kind of conglomerate of parental factors, social environment, educational influences, inherited predispositions, and a mass of more or less incidental effects. The introverted view would seem to comment on this: "Yes, it is all true, and not without interest that this man comes from these peculiar parents and environment; yet the really important thing is not where he comes from, but what he will make of himself as an original unit of creative power." It is this "unit of creative power" which is omitted from the causalistic inventory, yet which none the less decides the issue.[1]

Thus we see that this single eye, with its fourfold effectiveness, represents a realization of the psyche as an autonomously creating power,[2] a realization that had to come from a deeper, introverted centre, since it was altogether excluded from the patient's extraverted conscious standpoint. This new conception of the efficacy of subjective understanding must be regarded as a direct consequence of the explosion of the mechanistic view of the mind, seen in the last drawing.

We have already discussed the mythological significance of the eye. Wotan had only one eye. The other was sacrificed to Mimir, the representative of the underworld. Through this payment Wotan gained access to the source of the earth's wisdom, symbolized by Erda. Horus sacrificed one of his eyes for the benefit of Ra, who had lost an eye through the demonic agency of Set, disguised as a black pig.

These analogies gain significance for our investigation from the fact that the patient associated the sightless eyes of the dragon with his father. Only in his case the situation is reversed: the single eye being obtained from the sacrifice of one of the dragon's eyes. The resulting gain in earth-realism is, however, identical with the result of Wotan's exchange.

The psychology of this eye-symbolism is obscure, but it would seem that the single eye is related to the idea of the single mind or purpose. The divine effectiveness of the

[1] For this statement of the introverted viewpoint I am relying on notes taken at Jung's seminar in Zürich. I am indebted to him for permission to make use of them.

[2] The following citation from Gubsky's *My Double and I* expresses the same view: "Seeing clear, detached seeing is consciousness, and consciousness is no passive perception as we think, but an active force."

hero arises from his unquenchable yearning for the treasure, however apparently unattainable; it is this striving of the heroic nature which manifests the reality of God. This is doubtless what Blake had in mind when he wrote:

> "The worship of God is, honouring His gifts in other men, each according to his genius, and loving the greatest men best. Those who envy or calumniate great men, hate God, for there is no other God."[1]

Thus the idea of the single eye suggests also a corresponding wholeness of purpose, the ability to see what must be done, and the will to do it. But this efficacy or wholeness of will exists only when the total subject is committed. From this point of view, the four stars would correspond to the four major functions or aspects of the individuality.

Another possibility is to regard this atavistic pineal eye as a symbolical harking-back to an original primordial state of unity—*i.e.*, the condition existing before the disturbing factor of individuality developed a resistance within the archetypal human society. It is possible to regard the duality which conditions individual consciousness as we know it as a passage or phase of evolution, leading to an impersonal state of consciousness in which the opposites are reconciled again in a deeper unity. The degree of impersonality that is won through a crucial experience of the unconscious might be symbolized, therefore, in this single medial eye, which belongs essentially to the primordial condition.

In relation to the individual analysis, the appearance of this backward-looking eye means the acquisition of a specific psychic function. It is difficult to describe its nature in precise terms because, like everything pertaining to the unconscious, it is essentially unseizable by intellectual instruments. Perhaps the best impression of its nature would be conveyed by the term "teleological." Even this term, though meaning the right thing, can be given the wrong twist. It is a means or mode of apprehending events, whether within or without, as belonging to an intelligible flow, the source or goal of which cannot be understood in terms of conscious motives.

[1] *Marriage of Heaven and Hell.*

The emergence of the single eye at the back of the head (*i.e.*, towards the unconscious) would correspond, then, to the development of a peculiar sensibility to the meaning and value of spontaneous psychic activity. The function that is awake to the meaning of dream and fantasy-activity, that records subliminal impressions, that discerns the subtle changes in the psychic atmosphere, and the transformations of inner and outer relations with an intuitive subtlety—this is what I have in mind when I speak of the teleological eye. This receptive awareness is very different in character from the personal preoccupation concerned with prestige or guilt, superiority or inferiority, etc., which afflicts the personal ego. Its efficacy is rooted in an animal-like acceptance of the flow of natural events, and just as the child or animal is wholly contained in the actual moment of being, so the mind, when governed by the single eye, gains a complete relation to the event.

This condition is indicated by the four effective stars. To achieve effective action, consciousness needs to be focused on a single point and to be armed with a single weapon. This condition would be represented by rays converging upon a point: exactly the opposite, in fact, to the condition we are considering. These four divergent rays, ending in stars, are concerned, not with extraverted action, but rather with introverted reaction.

At this juncture in the battle with the dragon there is obviously no help to be expected from the hero's conscious armament. The curve of the left arm, for instance, though ornamental, like the handle of a jug, affords no adequate leverage for dealing with the dragon's hind leg. The hand, too, is practically eliminated, the fingers being reduced to the merest stubs. The right hand, which still grasps the broken haft of the javelin, is even more incapable of effective action; and, finally, the robot soldier is a helpless captive. Thus, of the total armed force that went so bravely against the dragon in Drawing X., only these ineffectual and unarmed relics are left.

This striking decrease in the efficacy of the executive functions of consciousness synchronizes with the effective intervention of the introverted psychic eye. This would also correspond with the change that has taken place from the front to the back. In Drawing X. we saw only the front aspect of hero and dragon, with the former in vigorous action. Here we see only the suffering hero's back, brown in colour and bleeding from many wounds, caused by the rear half of the dragon.

An enemy that can be seen and named is a reasonable proposition; but this attack from the rear by the despised hind portion of a presumably vanquished assailant is an ugly business. We can account for it only as a statement of the shadow aspect of the conflict, for the shadow is that which follows after. One of the chief characteristics of the new kind of consciousness (which dawned in Drawing VI.) was a peculiar valuation of the time dimension. It will be remembered that a long-bodied dragon figured on the hero's breastplate in that drawing, apparently an intuitive prevision or embryonic anticipation of the coming battle.

It is not immediately self-evident why a new apprehension of time should have profound psychological consequences. It becomes evident, however, when we reflect that the infantile or primordial psyche has no appreciation of the time factor. As Spengler points out in *Decline of the West*, the mythological phase is always unhistorical. He cites the example of a certain pact, or agreement, contracted between the Athenians —who, according to Spengler, were wholly contained by the creative myth—and a colony of Asia Minor. The contract, which was to last a hundred years, was carefully drawn up and signed by both sides; but no one thought of dating it!

The state of childhood is as averse from the realization of time as it is from the appreciation of consequences. The ability to appreciate future consequences of present action is, perhaps, the essential character which distinguishes the cultural from the infantile psyche. It is the basis of ethical and moral feeling.

Psychologically, the act and its consequences are one organism, as are the head and body and tail of a snake. The consciousness of the child, which is limited to the moment of being, has not yet extended beyond the head of the organism, and only relatively few so-called adults achieve a realization of the snake that even approaches its total length. The reason that alcoholics and drug addicts are unreliable persons is because they choose to poison and blindfold their consciousness, rather than see the continuity between a given act and its consequences. They think that by amputating the head, the body and tail of the snake will be obliterated; in other words, they try to create a world where no shadows follow behind.

Perhaps the most essential, as well as the most thankless, part of adolescent education is the business of demonstrating to idealistically blindfolded partisans that by choosing A they also, and necessarily, choose B and C. The restricted consciousness which resents the fact that B C should be joined to A is not merely childish; its determination not to see the extension of an act in time can easily become the major motive of its existence. From one angle the neurotic fortress is a keep, inhabited by a suffering victim; but from another it is a blockhouse, in which the will that opposes the alphabetical logic of existence, symbolized by the snake or dragon, fights to the bitter end.

Obviously, this acceptance of the time extension—*i.e.*, the logic which joins the deed to its consequences—is not instilled into the mind by ordinary educational methods. Resistance to seeing the snake is powerful and deep-seated; at bottom it is the fear of individuality and the dread of responsibility. Open the door to the time extension, and therewith one admits the whole burden of the human soul. And not merely one's own individual soul, but the burden of the human soul in general, with all its cruelty, its atavism, its perversity and its apparently hopeless longings.

Such a problem will surely be repressed, or projected upon the divine Victim, until a way, a means, a method has been found which reduces the problem to manageable proportions. In the last century the projection of the burden upon the crucified Saviour was the only means available; hence the emphasis laid upon the absolute necessity of faith in salvation. It is surely to the credit of the modern spirit that, as soon as an adequate psychological way had been opened up, a profound moral reaction against the traditional scapegoat solution began to make itself felt.

In this connection it is interesting to remember that Christ was sometimes referred to in Gnostic tradition with the symbol of the snake. The psychological significance of time was also manifested in the Gnostic metaphysical conception Abraxas,[1] which had very much the same significance as Bergson's conception *la Durée Créatrice*. From this angle of vision Christ would have to be symbolized by a snake two thousand years long.[2]

The Chinese have cultivated the psychological snake-view of personality by virtue of their ancestor-cult. When one enters the house of a Chinese gentleman, one does not enter as a " single separate person "; the living personality is the responsible container of the whole ancestral phylum. The spiritual values of the past are so patently present in the personality that an ancestor, dead perhaps for many centuries, is spoken of as though still living.

What is meant also by the term patriarchal vision, or the prophetic eye, can best be understood by this concept of the psychological time extension.

* * * * *

Returning to the dragon we can see now why the explosion of the mechanistic conception tended to bring the tail-portion of the dragon into the foreground. To conceive sexuality as a general biological mechanism is the best way of blindfolding oneself to the vital consequences of erotic " accidents." So long as the blindfold way seems to work, why try to see ? Vision, with the immediate force of revelation, may, however, tear the bandage from our eyes. For the unconscious, becoming overcharged with all the " consequences " conscious-

[1] Under the numerical symbolism of the Gnostics each letter of the alphabet had an equivalent number-symbol. The total of the numbers corresponding to ABRAXAS was 365.

[2] When we speak of the unconscious as a timeless realm, we have to remember that our conscious conception of time is based upon the singular reality of the present moment, whereas, to the unconscious, time is an indefinite extension pertaining to spiritual effects: hence the prevalence of dragons, pythons, serpents and other long-bodied creatures throughout mythology.

ness has refused to see, eventually boils over in a violent discharge of affect.

The transformation of the unseeing eye of the dragon into the mediumistic vision of the hero in the present drawing evidently goes hand in hand with the psychological transition from the infantile psyche to the cultural.

In so far as we have followed the logic of the myth correctly, the sightless, hypnotic eye of the father-dragon is seen as the patient's subjective blindness, due to his identification with the father. The father, as we were told, being unusually blind to the shadow-effects of his own actions, the son has undoubtedly made use of this identification in order to remain unconscious of certain responsibilities. Because he projected his individuality, or the image of the mature self, upon the father, the latter inevitably assumed the aspect of a sinister, resistant presence on his path. The same projection regularly occurred in respect to any older man in a position of authority over him.

Conscious insight into this mechanism of projection was vital to the patient; this is symbolized by the transfixing javelin in the hand of the hero. But the insight which severs the identification[1] also puts an end to the patient's psychological blindness. From the bleeding wounds on the hero's back we may infer that psychological vision in a sensitive nature can be a terrible acquisition. The subject's extreme reactions to his insane patients might be represented symbolically as bleeding wounds in the unconscious. The rationale of his reaction now becomes manifest. His own authentic individuality was repressed and distorted by the unconscious identification with his father. But because he was unconscious of this problem he became emotionally identified with his patients, whose true individuality was also suppressed by a psychotic influence. As he projected his own problem upon the father, so must he also project his patient's problems upon the medical superintendent and the staff of the institution. Thus the dragon comes to straddle every path the subject attempts until, at last, he is forced to call upon the hero in himself to give battle.

[1] Compare the idea of severing the optic nerve which the hero attempted to perform with his auxiliary weapon.

II

Drawing XIV

From the greater labour and care given to this drawing, we are justified in regarding it as the climax of the series.

The hero is seen on the left in an introverted posture, with both arms (painted silver) raised above his head, hands interlocking. Within the space, enfolded by his arms, we find a clear and positive statement of the open laminated field, painted in three broad bands of green, curving upwards on a yellow field. Only the outline of the head is drawn within this enclosed area, as though the luminous intensity of the aura surrounding it had rendered the head translucent. The medial eye, no longer active, appears at the vertex of the head, where it occupies the central cup of the laminal field. An irregular, square-shaped laceration is visible on the back of the head—the mark of the dragon's foot. Blood still streams from this wound down the length of the hero's body, which, as in all the drawings since the explosion, is painted brown. The anima of the crescent-moon approaches from the right, offering a foaming tankard of ale. She is painted in the same colours as the green dragon with the yellow eyes; the same, too, as the open laminal field in the present drawing. Her body and face are dark green; her hands, lips and hair are yellow. There is also an efflorescent margin of yellow surrounding the eye, resembling the petals of a flower. She is contained in a large silver crescent-moon, which seems to have descended out of the cosmic into the human sphere.

In the right-hand bottom corner the rear half of the dragon is lying derelict. Beneath the dragon the prostrate body of the mechanical soldier tries to protect itself with rigid left arm from being crushed by the dragon. Both are done with. Just to the right of these two, and coming into the right margin of the picture, the crenellated wall of the dragon castle (*vide* Drawing IX.) appears. The dead dragon seems almost to be reclining against this wall. He has returned to the source whence he came. Above the crenellation the devouring mouth is seen with three rows of upper and lower teeth. It is still holding fast to the primordial life-substance with its opposing canines. Below the mouth, and guarded by the wall, the front end of the womb-cavity is just visible, with the unhatched peacock near the upturned tip. Above and below this end-portion of the womb-cavity patches of blue are painted, the lower area being the greater.

The whole of the background of the drawing is carefully stippled with silver, red, blue and yellow, and, as before, the stippling is most concentrated in the left-hand portion of the picture, demonstrating the consistent orientation of the libido towards the left, or unconscious, side. This orientation is also confirmed by the relatively fuller curve and power of the hero's left arm.

The well-planned composition of the drawing, together with the simplicity and effectiveness of its contents, tells us that a culmination has been reached. The harmony of nature is restored; the situation is " in Tao." The fight with the dragon is over, and the unused potential, which gave the unconscious its sinister ascendancy over consciousness, has been released as a disposable conscious power. When the patient was speaking of this fantasy-experience, holding his arms in the same position above his head as depicted in the drawing, he described a feeling of enclosing something powerful, and of compressing it within the compass of his arms. What, then, is this dragon-power which was gained from the conflict, and which had to be assimilated in this ritual way ?

In psychological terms the dragon-complex contains the potential energy of the archaic levels of the unconscious in an inert, resistant condition. This unconscious potentiality was negatively constellated by the fact that, consciously, the patient was wedded to a mechanistic conception of psychic events, a point of view which practically excludes the possibility of independent psychic activity. The duplication of the dragon's structure suggested the idea that the natural duality of the psyche — which should be expressed in a dynamic polarity between the conscious and the unconscious— was held in the morbid complex in a state of undifferentiated uniformity. We suggested that this might be the cause of the overweighting of the unconscious that is characteristic of the schizophrenic state. From this point of view, the dragon's act of *felo de se*, the result of which is that he falls into two parts, would seem to accord with the inherent tendency of nature to restore a balance between the opposites. The explosion of the mechanistic field-gun and the disposal of the mechanical gunner are therefore seen as the logical results of an experience of the unconscious which the subject had to recognize as undeniably purposive. In this way the principle of entelechy[1] finally displaced the mechanized conception of the self, and consciousness was enriched by the addition of an introverted function attuned to psychic events, symbolized by the medial eye.

It will be observed that the green and yellow laminated field in this drawing has the open, upturned character, and that the central cup of this field contains the medial eye. It might be regarded as an individual centre, or nucleus, gathering the dynamic elements, green and yellow, into a favourable constellation. The red element, characterizing the dæmonic element of the dragon, has been eliminated. It finds no place either in the figure of the anima or in the laminated field, both of which have been formed from the dynamic elements of the archaic system.

It is possible that an inherent connection might be traced between the red element of the dragon and the red snake-ring of Drawing VII., since the dragon became detached and visible through the transforming influence of the *uroborus* symbol. In any case, a clear connection of ideas exists between the *uroborus* as symbol of a timeless, self-contained system, and the dragon-complex containing psychic energy in the timeless primordial state of potentiality.

The function of the anima, as defined by Jung, is that of medium operating between the primordial unconscious and the conscious personality. Hitherto there has been no recognition of the anima and her mediating rôle. There is no place for the soul in a mechanistic universe, hence no possibility of a bridge that could span the schizophrenic gulf between the archaic potential and conscious actuality.

Consciousness affords a focal point in which energy, coming

[1] Entelechy signifies the condition in which a potentiality becomes actual; also that which gives form or perfection to anything. (Oxford Dictionary.)

from the latent unconscious condition, emerges into the actuality of time. The atavistic tendency tends to hold psychic energy in the primordial, inert state where things are resistant to change. Harnessed to individual purpose, on the other hand, energy flows, increases and produces change. Psychologically, therefore, time can be viewed as a function of energy, for without the flow of the changing process there can be no sense of time. We cannot say, however, that libido held in the archaic system is always inert, because frequently in schizophrenia we can observe the autonomous activity of the unconscious producing its mythological transformations in a regular cycle. This is the cycle of "eternal recurrence," to use Nietzsche's descriptive term, which is symbolized by the *uroborus* dragon. All that is lacking, apparently, is the uncaused nucleus of individual conscious will, which could break the circle at some definite point, thus creating a channel by which the potential energy could emerge from the timeless unconscious into the living present.

From this point of view, the *uroborus* represents the sign of the unconscious autonomous process, while the birth of the medial psychic eye would represent the individual point of emergence, whereby the potentiality of the unconscious process can become effective in time. It is the entelechial nucleus, the function which is able to realize psychic events, and by which the deep psychic potentialities become realizable.

This problem of emergence, which has come to an issue in our subject's myth, has a wider philosophical bearing than I have either the space or competence to handle. Certain parallels, however, which are not inappropriate at the present juncture suggest themselves to the mind. For example, the red snake is a closed ring, while the *Kundalini* snake, coiled three and a half times around the *lingam*, is a spiral. In a self-contained, closed system evolution is, of course, inconceivable. If the first form of organic life on this planet, therefore, had not contained within itself at least the potentiality of difference, no subsequent development of species would have been possible. An endless and unchanging repetition of identical forms would be represented by such a closed circle. Accordingly, the theory of evolution requires that a point of resistance must have developed within the archetypal form of organic life. Conceiving this archetypal organic species as a circle, then at some definite point in that closed ring, and at a definite moment in time, resistance must have developed and a renegade movement begun. Endless unchanging repetition was opposed by the impulse to change, and, with the impulse, the temporal was born out of the eternal.

This unseizable point of resistance, developing within the biological circle, is the emergence of individuality. In the very bosom of the primordial changeless monad an enemy appears, a disloyal hypothesis, a luciferic challenge to the eternal power of the archetype. Opposition was always latent in the monad as a germinal potentiality: but at some definite moment it emerged as a point of departure, and the inertia of eternal recurrence was pierced by a single unique ray or, in the language of our myth, by a grain of the sun. However infinitesimal the departure, the presence of the individual factor of resistance opens the closed circle, converting it into the evolutionary spiral.

This operation of the principle of individuality as a moment of resistance confronts us wherever we turn; it is the working of opposition in the very heart of life. In Drawing V. we discovered its archaic expression in the splitting of the original sexual libido in immediate relation to the maternal archetype.

If now we regard this first emergent moment of resistance as having a teleological value—and, inasmuch as we owe our very existence to this moment, we are hardly in a position to view it in any other light—we must assume that, in the womb of that resistance, there lies the germ of a new departure, a different hypothesis, a new life-experiment. Whether the new experiment turns out to be an evolutionary advance or regression does not affect the argument, which merely asserts that the emergence of individuality as a moment of resistance in time is an evolutionary necessity, without which no differentiation of individual forms is conceivable.

In his somewhat fantastic attempt[1] to account for the origin of the Œdipus complex from the patricidal archetype of Darwin's mythical primal horde, Freud has singularly overlooked this necessity. He allows for no Promethean individual factor which could break through the inertia of the biological pattern. There is no reason at all why the habitual act of parricide, on the part of the excluded sons, should ever have acquired moral or psychological significance, since it occurred, according to Freud's own account, quite regularly as part of the recurrent procedure. It could have assumed a psychological importance, with the character of a moral conflict, only to the individual who resisted the patricidal archetype with sufficient intensity to cause a departure or migration to a new standpoint, and thence to a new social pattern. Without this Promethean individual act, Freud's theory has no psychological validity, inasmuch as the mere inertia of biological mechanism can produce, *ex hypothesi*, only a closed circle.

There is even a certain weakness in Darwin's exposition of the evolution of species, which comes from his apparent unwillingness to include the principle of individuality as an evolutionary necessity. Instead of admitting this necessity within the orbit of his theory, he gives to the mechanical process of natural selection a kind of superior, discriminative intelligence. He writes, for instance:

> " It may metaphorically be said that natural selection is daily and hourly scrutinizing, throughout the world, the slightest variations; rejecting those that are bad, preserving and adding up all that are good; silently and insensibly working, *whenever and wherever opportunity offers*, at the improvement of each organic being in relation to its organic and inorganic conditions of life."[2]

What, in effect, is this " opportunity," italicized by Darwin himself and without which Natural Selection cannot operate? Is it not the emergent moment of individuality, wherein the relentless momentum of biological mechanism is suspended, and a new and unique possibility comes to light?

[1] Freud: *Totem and Taboo.*

[2] *Origin of Species*, p. 77, chapter on " Natural Selection."

The chief difficulty in accepting individuality as a complementary principle to mechanism in our conception of evolution lies in the repugnance of the mind, disciplined to think in terms of the mechanistic theory, to admit the psychic factor as an essential element of the natural order. Individuality necessarily presupposes a psychic element, since it is essentially an irrational, causeless beginning. If it could be brought into the chain of causality, it would become merely another aspect of biological mechanism, and its whole virtue, as the opposite principle to mechanism, would be extinguished.

Physicists have observed irrational, causeless behaviour in the atomic elements, a fact which is necessitating a new orientation in our conception of causality. Hence at both ends of the scale the law of irregularity intrudes into our conceptions.

This difficult problem is vital to our psychology, because, in so far as we identify the psychic factor with consciousness *as we normally experience it*, we are precluded from that deeper insight into natural processes which could bridge the chasm between " conscious " man and " unconscious " nature from which we so greatly suffer.

Our researches into the so-called unconscious processes of human beings have led us to modify very considerably our notions regarding the meaning of consciousness. And admittedly there has been a tendency to project the discriminative and conative functions of intelligence into those unconscious processes where teleological activity has been observed. It must therefore be emphasized that what is denoted by the term " psychic factor " is the unpredictable spontaneous activity observable in living processes which appears to have a teleological character. We may speculate as to whether consciousness, as we experience it, is a product of this unconscious activity, or whether the unconscious is a subliminal reflection of consciousness. Our conclusion will depend very largely upon our basic temperamental bias. Western extraverted thought tends to regard consciousness as the primary factor, while the introverted East holds the contrary view.

These reflections are deeply germane to our investigation, since our main purpose is the tracing of a consistent teleological significance in non-rational products of the autonomous psyche. Naturally, in attempting to explain[1] these representations in conceptual terms, it is almost impossible not to present them as though conceived and thought out by an extremely subtle and complex intelligence. But exactly the same complexity and subtlety must attend a complete account of cellular activity, or the structure of a flower, or a butterfly's antennæ.[2] Yet, in their functioning, these things have the simplicity of their own specific purpose.

Let us assume, then, that the teleological aspect of the metamorphosis we are now attempting to understand is an expression of the age-long evolutionary opposition between individuality and mechanism. The tendency for energy to become invested in a self-contained partial system or mechanism is beautifully illustrated in what I have termed the inverted or incestuous system. The obsessing power of such a dissociated psychic mechanism is something we can only estimate by symptoms, for it has the negative character of inertia. This inertia has to be activated or penetrated by a suprapersonal force: the psychic equivalent of the sun. Individuality or self is the psychic equivalent of the sun, for it is that factor which resists the stasis of life within a closed circle, insisting upon the value of the new experiment. The idea of individuality as an expression of personal peculiarity does not command the concentration of psychic energy needed for the definitive transition from the

[1] Explanation is synonymous with explication, from Latin *explicare*=to unroll, which is almost equivalent with *evolvere*. So understood, explanation appears to be something quite different from description. A phenomenon will be explained only when it is shown that what is new or surprising in it should not have surprised us, since it was already present in a disguised form. In other words, it implies the pre-formation of the consequent in the antecedent. (Cited from *Encyclopædia Britannica*.)

[2] A beautiful example of the pre-formation of the consequent in the antecedent is to be found in the pupal case of a butterfly. As soon as the larva has become metamorphosed into the pupa, the form of the wings, proboscis, etc., of the butterfly or moth is clearly laid down in the structure of the pupa-case, even though the contents of the case are entirely liquid. Thus the archetype of the perfect butterfly is present not as a germinal potentiality, but as a developed pattern in the pupa-case immediately the pupa is formed.

infantile to the cultural psyche. Therefore the power of individuality as a cosmic factor is introduced under the guise of the ancestral god possessing attributes of the sun-principle (*vide* Drawing VI.).

The process of penetration and transformation was closely observed in the transitional representation given in Drawing VII. It was the existence of this process which demanded the alchemical analogy and the parallel Eastern conception of *Kundulini*. But, although the activity of conversion was present, the original character of the closed system could easily be seen in that drawing. It was represented in an endless chain of biological products, flowing from the breasts and inverted field above into the lavatory-pan below. With this was included the nail-biting mechanism, with its wastage of blood flowing away into oblivion.

Individuality acted upon this mechanism in a characteristic way. It proceeded to give each unit of the chain an individual number, by which each member was distinguished from every other. Certain members thus distinguished were then pierced by separate phallic units, just as a fruit-bearing flower is fertilized by a bee. Thus we learned that the method by which individuality resists closed mechanism, introducing the energizing force of a new hypothesis, is based upon the operation of distinctiveness.

It is interesting to observe this identical process in the early stages of dream-analysis. Patients whose power of objective discrimination is weak are inclined to produce a vague and copious stream of dream material, to which no specific value is attached. The analyst has to supply the function of distinctiveness which the patient lacks, and merely by taking a single dream, giving to each detail and element of it the clearest possible value and discrimination, he finds that the flow of indiscriminate productivity begins to give place to constructive dreams.

The operation of the same principle can be seen in our patient's drawings. Wherever individuality penetrates, indiscriminate prolificness becomes transformed into meaningful creation. This truth is represented symbolically in the *Kundalini* system in the awakening of Shakti, the sleeping, primordial goddess, by the introverting individual stream. The reader will recall that the patient was prompted to draw a dæmonic figure in the empty gold space in Drawing VII. and, in a subsequent dream, the missing dæmon was introduced as the snake-anima who coiled herself in the form of a spiral above his hearth. Thus the conversion from the closed system to the open spiral of growth was already germinating in this drawing.

III

Resuming our investigation of the source and nature of the dragon, we should expect, if our analytical premises are correct, to find characteristic features by which we can identify it as being of like nature with the atavistic system described above. The first and most striking feature of the dragon is that it lacks a mouth. By this we know at once that it symbolizes a false image of reality. Every animal should have a mouth. Turning to the inverted system, we find this same remarkable omission. The maternal trunk is without a head, and the whole libidinal flow issues from this headless trunk. The teeth that bite the phallic fingers do not belong to mouths which can function. They are, in fact, parasitic sucker-teeth, corresponding exactly with the sucker-teeth of the dragon's feet. Thus, in all essential respects, the dragon, just as much as the incestuous system, represents the atavistic hold of the infantile psyche, symbolized by the inverted laminal field. We might even trace the connection between the yellow fæcal rings, the most prominent feature of the inverted system, and the yellow sunflower eyes of the dragon, which were also a ruling feature.

As an independent organism the dragon must be regarded as completely ineffectual, since it has nothing to rely upon for subsistence but the spell-binding power of its sun-wheel eyes and its parasitic sucker-teeth. But, subjectively, it is the subtlest of dæmons. Its power is rooted in the deepest, most invisible passion of man: passivity. It personifies that vast power of human inertia which turns away from a problem, murmuring " kismet " or *mañana*,[1] leaving it for someone

[1] Meaning " to-morrow," a word in constant use throughout the greater part of South America.

else to cope with. It is the essence of suspended activity, the apathy that prefers not to see what is going on, lest responsibility be exacted. It is the laziness of spirit which masquerades as a helpless, appealing child, or as an oppressed victim of fate. The passivity of the neurotic personality can be discerned in every symptom and behind every evasion. But the apathy of the schizophrenic mentality is deeper still: it is like a blank, sinister force, crushing life in an eightfold embrace.

Jung has explained this inertia, or dragon-effect, as the pull of the incestuous, infantile craving for the mother. But from another angle we can see that a pathological infantilism might derive its power from the ineradicable memories of a former happiness. Usually in psychology the term " pathological " denotes something that has outlived its time. Early childhood enjoys a joyous freedom of the spirit that lies very near the root of our cherished ideal of individual liberty. It is, perhaps, this shape of primordial truth that is symbolized in the sunflower *mandala* eye which has to be pierced. But if the dragon's eye represents a desirable truth, why must it be pierced ?

The claim of unconditioned freedom expressed by the infantile psyche needs to be converted into the goal of responsible freedom which rules the cultural psyche. It is impossible to deal with an archaic claim, because it manifests the irrational, all-or-none character of undifferentiated forms of life. Everything belonging to the dragon has the unmistakable character of atavism. There was a time, perhaps in the mesozoic swamps, when life was feasible on this level. But now its sole possibility of survival would be in an unrelated, regressive instinct-system. Such a system always manifests the protopathic phenomenon, described by Rivers (after Head) as characteristic of the all-or-none mechanism. Rivers writes:

> " Only those entities are suppressed that are elements of experience (psychological), or of behaviour (physiological) incompatible with later, more refined and discriminatory developments."[1]

1 W. R. Rivers: *Instinct and the Unconscious*, 1924.

Condensing Rivers' argument into a single phrase, the protopathic, inherited mechanism tends constantly to be either suppressed or modified by the epicritic or more recently acquired mode of reaction.

Throughout his whole discussion of the problem of instinct Rivers carefully distinguishes the factor of suppression from that of dissociation, and he demonstrates that the absolute, all-or-none principle only holds good for the dissociated mechanism. Wherever the epicritic or differentiated principle has penetrated, modifying the archaic mechanism, the protopathic phenomena are also changed.

In the light of these facts we can appreciate the necessity for the piercing of the dragon's eye. The idea of individual freedom on the protopathic level creates a false image of reality. As a primordial element freedom has the character of an unconditioned demand, an all-or-none expectation. The danger inherent in the existence of the autonomous, dissociated complex rests upon the fact that it tends to preserve, in the unconditioned, primordial state, essential psychic elements which can function properly only under the order of relativity. The self, as an expression of the co-ordinated totality of the subject, reacts to an absolute claim or an uncontrolled function—whether it be that of a malignant tumour or of an autonomous, archaic complex—as to an enemy within its gates. Thus the representation of the battle of the hero with the dragon is, at bottom, the ever-repeated conflict between the regressive inertia of a self-contained partial system and the active individuating principle.

The issue of the conflict is pictured as a withdrawal of power from the dragon and a corresponding accession of power to the hero. The dynamic symbol, now contained within the compass of the hero's raised arms, is an expression of the dragon power centring in the eye. It represents the basic elements of the dragon power (green and yellow) raised into a system in which the two elements are placed in the relation of polarity.

This symbol appeared in the dominant position in the patient's first drawing, where it was closely associated with the impersonal maternal symbol, Fujiyama, the sacred mountain.

Is it possible that the whole development of the myth, with the issue of the battle with the dragon, could already have been foreshadowed in that first drawing? For there was the symbol of the psychological treasure, hard to attain, associated with the apotheosized symbol of the mother's breast. And already, on the left or sinister side, we observed the father-dragon (disguised as the sun), with the hypnotic eyes (disguised as sun-spots), preparing, as it were, to resist the hero's access to the mother. The infantile craving for the mother was suggested in the phallic crane-arm directed towards the distant mountain, while the dragon-father's resistance was indicated by the two extended rays of the sun which intervened between the phallus and the mountain. It might also be noted that the upper of these rays divides into two, as the dragon does later in the fight with the hero.

With such evidence it is difficult not to believe that the mythic pattern, as a deep content, was already determining this first drawing, even though its manifest content was concerned with a different theme. We might perhaps say that the theme of the son's longing for the mother is present, as a deep content, throughout the series. On the level of the infantile psyche it appears in its pathological, protopathic form. But when expressed by the cultural psyche it emerges as the heroic quest for the unattainable treasure.

It is a fact of considerable interest that the psyche makes use of an archaic, abstract, dynamic symbol, within the framework of a world-old mythic pattern, to express the idea of the treasure that is hard to win. We must infer from this discovery that the highest conception of value expressed by the modern soul must be in terms of energy. The energic symbol, which is the goal of the hero's struggle, has the power, as we noted in discussing the medial eye, of directing the psychic energy downwards and inwards, instead of outwards and upwards—in other words, an introverted attitude.[1] This objective is also stated in the first drawing, where the

[1] This empirical conclusion differs from the description of introverting energy given by the Chinese sage in *The Secret of the Golden Flower* (Wilhelm and Jung), where the stream that creates the golden flower is directed inwards and upwards, as opposed to the unconscious wastage of energy outwards and downwards.

creative ray from the open laminal field on the right is directed downwards into the unconscious with an introverted concentration, while the ray coming from the closed field on the left is directed upwards and outwards through the place of extraverted dissipation, over which a Zeppelin (whose rear portion is loaded with black) flies menacingly.

It is impossible to describe these opposing attitudes without feeling the moral antithesis they contain. The subject is free to choose the attitude that is closed to the unconscious: in which case he wastes vital energy, blinds himself to value, and pursues illusory goals under the psychotic influence of the father-complex. Or he can choose to open his mind to the unconscious, release the repressed, and learn to value the libido as the treasure beyond price. The directing line of this attitude gathers with it the protective lighthouse on its rock, the tripod crane linking up the denizens of both worlds, and the little boat with its four functions suggesting the means by which individuality is to be created.

From our study of subsequent drawings we are able to equate the former attitude with the pathological persistence of the infantile psyche, which craves incestuous satisfaction while avoiding the problem of payment; the latter with the cultural psyche, which, by transforming the actual mother into a symbol, increases the energy yield of the unconscious a thousandfold. The myth we are studying contains the history of this transformation.

Naturally, to the infantile psyche, with its insistence on immediate satisfaction, the work of creating the symbol which has the power of transforming the infant into the hero will always be against the grain. To the infant craving the breast, everything that is set in its place is nothing but a substitute, a kind of cheat. The infant psyche ignores the time-extension whereby the possibility of creating a greater and more enduring satisfaction might be viewed as an attribute of the despised substitute. The kind of intelligence which can see the butterfly already in the caterpillar will also be able to discern the sacred command, veiled in the form of a symbol, and will obey it, even though it wears the outer aspect of a substitute. It is necessary to point out, however, that a patient may be prompted, as this one was, to depict the very process by which the transformation takes place, without himself understanding or giving his faith to the thing he has done. The cure does not rest in having the experiences through which the path as well as the major problem of one's life is revealed to consciousness. Anyone may have experiences: the rare man is the one who honours his experience and abides by its truth.

It is this moment of realization which forms the subject of the present drawing. The conversion of the closed infantile to the open cultural attitude has been achieved. But by whom? Not, surely, by the conscious personality, who is still very much bewildered by all these pictures he has been compelled to make, and who has as yet only a vague notion of whence they come or of whither they are leading him. The achievement has taken place only on the mythological plane, where the hero figures as the self. But in reality the hero is only a partial system which may subsequently be disavowed, as though it had no bearing at all upon the practical realities of life.

The mythological drama is re-enacted upon the stage of a modern mind, but it is just as possible for the subject to ignore its reference to himself, as for the man who is deeply moved by *Hamlet* not to see in his own depths the same tragic tie to the mother. The man who easily identifies himself with the rôle of the hero can be, and often is, psychologically blind; for the hero in our Western psychology is not the man who sees, but rather the fellow who gets things done. No man with vision, for instance, could ever become a dictator; dictators must fill the stage with constant action, and constant action precludes vision.

In the present case the subject was emotionally identified with his experience of the unconscious and was therefore deeply enfolded in the myth. Moreover, he became mediumistic to the unconscious too easily: hence it was essential to bring about a realistic, detached survey of the experience, as soon as he was ready for it. To this end the subjective identification with the hero (a classical ground for inflation) had to be criticized.

The technique to be recommended at this juncture is to treat the hero of the mythological drama as a kind of angelic twin who, by means of the mythic ritual, prepares the attitude of consciousness for the approaching task or ordeal. Inflation, resulting from identification with the hero, arises from the feeling that something has actually been achieved. But, in effect, the experience is real only when consciousness submits to it as belonging to the foreordained pattern of fate, therewith assimilating its full significance. In the present drawing the hero is performing the ritual of assimilation, parallels for which must again be brought from the East.

It will be observed that the hero is making a *mandala* within the enclosure of his two arms. The contents or elements of the *mandala* are the four bands or areas of yellow, the three of green, the head, and the medial eye. The eye itself is contained by a small squarish field of white.

An interesting parallel, taken from Tibetan *yoga* practice, suggests that the mythic pattern concerned with assimilation tends naturally towards the making of a *mandala*. Evans-Wentz describes a rite[1] in which the *yogin* is instructed how to vanquish and overcome elemental dæmons by various means. After a stanza describing the dance upon the head of the Vampire of Stupidity there come the following directions:

> " This having been done, that which is called the beat of the dance is danced without any particular aim.
> Then cometh the pitching of the tent.
> And having flung prostrate on its back any of the malignant genii or spirits of the place,
> Think that through the five limbs (*i.e.*, the two legs, arms and head) of the body
> Thunderbolt spears are being driven, and are transfixing the being."[2]

[1] W. Y. Evans-Wentz: *Tibetan Yoga and Secret Doctrines*, pp. 323 *f.* (Oxford University Press, 1935.)

[2] In a footnote the author explains that " whilst the tent is being pitched the *yogin* must visualize it, as though it were a prostrate spirit (symbolizing his own physical body, the representative of Egoism), and imagine that each peg, as he drives it into the ground, is a thunderbolt (or mystic spear) of iron, driven through one of the legs, or arms, or the head of the prostrate spirit, and transfixing it immovably."

The fourth part of the rite is called the Visualizing of the *Mandala*: it is as follows:

> "Then, in offering up the circle of offerings,
> Imagine the central part (or spinal column) of thy body to be Mount Meru,[1]
> The four chief limbs to be the Four Continents,
> The minor limbs to be the Sub-Continents,
> The head to be the Worlds of the Devas,
> The two eyes to be the Sun and Moon,
> And that the five internal organs[2] constitute all objects of wealth and enjoyment among gods and men."

After the *mandala* has been offered up in worship the *yogin* is directed as follows:

> "Having done so, mentally absorb the (visualized) objects of worship into thyself,
> And keep thy mind in the equilibrium (or quiescence) of the non-two state.[3]

The object of this rite of visualization is twofold, as indeed is the function of every genuine religious practice: first to banish, eliminate, exorcise the evil spirits (in this case the reluctant, arrogant ego), and then to invoke the holy or good spirit. The transfixing of the spirit of egoism in this instruction calls to mind the rite by which Dracula, the vampire spirit, is finally despatched. After this thorough emptying of the ego out of consciousness the visualizing of the *mandala*, under the central ægis of Mount Meru, would have the effect of creating an absolutely impersonal conscious attitude, in which every essential part of the body is spiritually transformed into its cosmic analogue.

The offering-up of the body as a sacrifice has the same end in view—*i.e.*, the depersonalizing of the idea of self.

In the drawing of our subject the hero is clearly demon-

[1] This refers to the central point of the cosmos, the centre of gravitation, symbolized as Mount Meru; and here (in keeping with *Kundalini* Yoga) represented in the bodily microcosm by the spinal column.

[2] These are the heart, lungs, liver, kidneys and spleen.

[3] After having mentally absorbed the *mandala*, the *yogin* must remain in the non-two state—*i.e.*, the state of *samadhi*—in which all dualism is realized as being in at-one-ment. In other words, he must realize the All in One and the One in All. (Evans-Wentz.)

strating the next thing to be done. In the Eastern system it is ritually laid down that in order to grapple effectively with elemental spirits or dæmons certain symbolical procedures are necessary. Our culture is lacking in this instruction, and therefore our patients have to discover this inner tradition of the unconscious, which contains the same wisdom, only not yet formally expressed. It would almost seem that behind this series of drawings a subjective *guru* was at work, and that the task of the analyst was to pick up the thread of this symbolical method of instruction.

In the drawing we see the subjective *guru* creating and visualizing the *mandala*. We know from our investigation that the contents of the *mandala* represent the treasure gained through the overcoming of the dragon-resistance, conceived in the myth as an elemental dæmon. The dynamic symbol is not only the treasure, associated with the mother-value; it is also the symbol by virtue of which the closed infantile attitude to the libido is transformed into the open and cultural. In the centre of this symbol is the medial eye, which is situated exactly over the spinal column; therefore, as the centre of psychic gravity, it corresponds with Mount Meru. It is also set in a small square, suggesting the " field of the square inch,"[1] which is referred to in the *Book of the Yellow Castle*[2] as follows:

> " In the field of the square inch of the house of the square foot, life can be regulated. The house of the square foot is the face. The field of the square inch in the face: what could that be other than the Heavenly Heart ? In the middle of the square inch dwells the splendour. In the purple hall of the city of jade dwells the god of utmost emptiness and life. The Confucians call it the centre of emptiness; the Buddhists, the terrace of life; the Taoists, the ancestral land, or the yellow castle, or the dark pass, or the space of former heaven. The Heavenly Heart is like the dwelling place, the Light is the master."

When we find such various, lovely, and yet essentially ambiguous images used in the attempt to describe the psychic

[1] An allusion to the centre of revolving light—viz., the centre of introverted concentration between the eyes, called the secret of the golden flower (Wilhelm and Jung: *Secret of the Golden Flower*. Kegan Paul, 1935).

[2] Referred to by the Master Lü Tzŭ in *Secret of the Golden Flower*, p. 24.

centre of our universe, we know that words are being used in a very special sense to describe something which, because it is the living heart of experience, is therefore beyond the possibility of direct representation. That which is both empty and full, light and dark, powerful yet exerting no power—it is this centre which is sometimes depicted in the centre of the Chinese *mandala* as the diamond body, a symbol described by Wilhelm as " metaphysical emptiness."

The conception of a potent, tranquil, unified emptiness in the centre of the soul is also to be found in the West. Meister Eckhart, the father of the German mystics, in one of his psychological dissertations on the relation of God to the soul says:

" ' First we will take the words: " In the midst of the silence there was spoken in me a secret word."

" ' But, sir, where is the silence, and where the place in which the word is spoken ?'

" ' As I said just now, it is in the purest part of the soul, in the noblest, in her ground, aye, in the very essence of the soul. That is mid-silence; for thereinto no creature did ever get, nor any image, nor has the soul there either activity or understanding, therefore she is not aware of any image, either of herself, or any creature. . . . But there is no activity in the essence of the soul; the faculties she works will emanate from the ground of the essence, but in her actual ground there is mid-stillness. . . . God enters the ground of the soul. None can touch the ground of the soul but God only. No creature is admitted into her ground, it must stop outside in her powers. There it sees the image whereby it has been drawn in and found shelter. For when the soul-powers contact a creature, they set to to make of the creature an image and likeness which they absorb. By it they know the creature. Creatures cannot go into the soul, nor can the soul know anything about a creature which she has not willingly taken the image of into herself. She approaches creatures through their present images, an image being a thing that the soul creates with her powers. Be it a stone, a rose, a man, or anything else that she wants to know about, she gets out the image of it which she has already taken in and is thus enabled to unite herself with it. But an image received in this way must, of necessity, enter from without through the senses. Consequently, there is nothing so unknown to the soul as herself. The soul, says a philosopher, can neither create nor absorb an image of herself. So she has nothing to know herself by. She knows all other things, but not herself.' "[1]

This majestic introverted voice, uttering the ultimate psychological truth from the middle of the fourteenth century, is impressive indeed. The two fundamental propositions of Eckhart's teaching are adumbrated in the above passages: in the first place, the central ground or essence of the soul, the unknowable birthplace of the living God; and, secondly, the concept of the soul as the creator of a world of images whereby " God becometh the world."

In another place he says:

" Whereas who holdeth not God as such an inner possession, *but with every means must fetch Him from without*, either in this thing or in that, where he seeketh Him insufficiently, with every manner of deeds, people or places; verily such a man hath Him not, and easily cometh something to trouble him. And it is not only evil company which troubleth him, but also the good, not only the street, but also the church, not only evil words and deeds, but even the good. For the hindrance lieth within himself; in him God hath not yet become the world. Were He that to him, then would he feel at ease in all places and secure with all people, always possessing God."

From these passages it is clear that Eckhart conceives God primarily as the determining psychic value which is felt in individual experience: the all-embracing meaning of life. Those who experience only the outer activity of the mind, seeking the image of God amongst the images of the ten thousand things, are far from the absolutely compelling experience. The ground of the soul, which Eckhart refers to as " the birthplace of God," is never active, and is harnessed to no function. It is like an eye whose vision passes through the surface, reaching to the heart of things—an eye that sees meaning and essence rather than form. And because of this essential vision it also brings detachment from objects.

This detachment was indicated, perhaps, in the last drawing, where the dragon's sucker-foot fell away as the beams of

[1] Franz Pfeiffer: *Meister Eckhart*, pp. 4-5. Leipzig, 1857. Translated by C. de B. Evans (John M. Watkins, London, 1924).

the central eye lit upon it. This would mean that touching the centre brings detachment from the spell of objects.

By implication, the symbol of the open laminal field is born of detachment. It is abstract in character; it is the symbol for the libido that has been detached from the mother, and was therefore found in the first drawing in the neighbourhood of the sacred mountain. For notwithstanding the patient's association of the mountain with the maternal breast, we must bear in mind its universal symbolical associations. In religious symbolism the mountain is the source of spiritual restoration and vision. Christ withdrew to the Mount of Olives, there to commune with his spirit. Zarathustra repaired to the mountain with his eagle and his lion. In Thibet, and also among relatively primitive peoples, the mountain is the abode of powerful spirits, where pilgrims visit shrines for purification and rebirth. The mountain-top is the place of extended vision and spiritual exaltation. Therefore the idea of individuality as the seat of a detached, unprejudiced state of consciousness is associated with the sacred mountain.

It is clearly an event of central significance that the symbol of the open laminal field appears, not as a symbolical abstraction without context, but as an individual content to be visualized and assimilated in a ritual fashion. One might almost take the view that the symbol is assimilating the man, inasmuch as the head is made to appear transparent and insubstantial, contrasting strongly with the radiant symbol which enfolds it.

When incorporated in the dragon-complex, the dynamic elements of the symbol were held by an archaic, atavistic tendency. But now the green and yellow elements of the dragon's body, having been abstracted from the dragon-form, group themselves spontaneously in alternating arcs, like the plates and acid of a battery, or in polar opposition, like the proton and electron of the atom.

This process of withdrawing primordial psychic elements from the state of unconscious *participation mystique* with the mother, in order to assimilate them in a new conscious attitude, is essential in the creation of individuality. The characteristic manifestations of primordial energy in human psychology are under the forms of sexuality and spirituality. Normally, a man tends to link his sexuality with woman, primarily the mother, and his spirituality with man, originally the father. By reason of his unconscious infantile association of these elemental psychic forces with the actual mother and father, he tends to seek their satisfaction in objects who remind him of the original infantile prototypes. In so doing he associates the potency of sex, and the authority and creativeness of spirit, with magically endowed objects.

The conversion of the basic attitude from the infantile to the cultural level releases the sexual and the spiritual *dynamis* from the infantile identification with the parents. As manifestations of cosmic energy, elementary instincts can then be realized as common burdens and responsibilities. Sexuality is no longer a merely personal problem, but is felt as the active principle of living forms. It is the submissive earth-function, as spirituality is the commanding heaven-function. The Chinese concepts *Yang* and *Yin* embrace this dynamic opposition of the universe from the greatest to the least. *Yang* embraces the heavens, the power of the sun, fire, the positive, masculine, effective element. *Yin* is the earth, receptiveness, darkness, water, the feminine shaping principle.

In the form of the elemental dragon spirit and sex were combined in a dæmonic unity;[1] but in this symbol of transformation the yellow of the sun, or *Yang* element, is set over against the green earth-function of *Yin* as a reciprocating principle.

IV

The fact that in China the dragon is no " loathly worm," but a celestial power, must have had a sympathetic influence on the patient's unconscious during this phase. I have already mentioned a few parallels in the field of Chinese mysticism. But readers acquainted with *The Secret of the Golden Flower* will find a harvest of allusions, some of which even suggest verbal association. For example, the medial eye first appeared as a transference phenomenon at the moment when the dragon's sunflower eye was pierced; this latter eye

[1] As with the fish of the Tobias myth, before the angel had analysed it into its opposite constituents.

was a " blind " *mandala*.[1] Now in the Chinese text the *T'ai I Chin Hua Tsung Chih*, communicated by Wilhelm and discussed by Jung,[2] the master promises to reveal " the secret of the Golden Flower of the Great One."[3] We are told that " the Golden Flower is the Light, and the Light of Heaven is *Tao*." Commenting upon this part of the text, Jung writes:

> " The Golden Flower is a *mandala* symbol which I have often met with in the material brought me by my patients. It is drawn either, seen from above, as a regular geometric ornament, or as a flower growing from a plant. The plant is frequently *a structure in brilliant fiery colours* and is shown *growing out of a bed of darkness*."

We are also told that the Golden Flower originates in the " germinal vesicle," which is the " dragon castle on the floor of the sea." In another part of the text we learn that the Golden Flower is a centre of revolving light in " the field of the square inch," which is situated between the two eyes. In a passage of the *Hui Ming Ching* we read:

> " The moon gathers up the ten thousand waters. In the midst of this darkness the Heavenly Heart suddenly begins a movement. This is the return of the one Light, the time when the child comes to life."

I might cite many other examples, but those I have selected will, I think, suffice to show that the beautiful imagery of this ancient text (which was entirely unknown to the patient) is prompted by the same process of transformation as our patient is expressing in a cruder, unconscious way. The sunflower eye grew on a stalk, and it symbolized light or potential consciousness, developing out of the primordial darkness of the unconscious. The middle eye in the present drawing actually appears on a small white square, suggesting " the field of the square inch." We observed it developing in the

1 Blind, because it contained no centre of value.

2 *The Secret of the Golden Flower*.

3 The oral tradition from which this text is derived goes back to the religion of the Golden Elixir of Life (*Chin Tan Chiao*), which developed in the *T'ang* period in the eighth century. The founder of this religion is said to have been the Taoist adept Lu Yen, counted by Chinese folk-lore as one of the eight immortals.

interior of the "dragon castle," whose crenellated wall is seen on the right lower margin of the present drawing. It was there situated just above the womb-cavity, or "germinal vesicle," in which the "Heavenly Heart" begins to move, and from this movement the child is seen coming to life (Drawing IX.).

Our scientific terminology has, unfortunately, not yet provided us with words that could describe and hold the psychological contents revealed in these exquisite symbolical images. We can only admit our ignorance of this hidden realm, and begin, with the help of whatever light we are able to glean from the older cultures of the East, to represent the process of psychic evolution in concepts that grow from our own empirical needs. That this purposive inward direction of the psychic energy, which Jung terms introversion into the unconscious, is concerned with a process of mental development and transformation is a matter of scientific knowledge. The parallelism we have observed with the concepts of Eastern systems arises from the fact that this intensive evolution of consciousness has long been systematically practised in the East, where it forms an essential part of Oriental culture. We are not forced, therefore, to overstretch the long arm of coincidence in order to explain the parallelism we are now considering. It is surely reasonable to suppose that identical psychic processes are concerned, which spontaneously manifest analogous expressions.

Another aspect of the introverted achievement in this drawing is to be seen in the feeling of poise and completion in the principal figure. The term "attitude" is used now with so many different references that it has already lost something of its essential meaning. Originally it was a technical term of the arts of design, taking the place of aptitude. Then it came into general use to denote the posture of the body descriptive of some action or mental state. In clinical psychiatry the actual posture of the body may be the best, or perhaps the only evidence obtainable as to the existing mental condition. This immediate connection between mental state and bodily posture and movement prompted the use of the term "attitude" for denoting established behaviour, or the character of a mental organization that is ruled by a principal thought, feeling, or affect. Thus the meaning of the word has gradually moved over from the physical into the psychological sphere. It is now very largely employed to denote the spirit with which a man habitually behaves or expresses himself. In analytical psychology a practical aim of the analysis is to create a function, by virtue of which the subject is able to observe and criticize his own affective attitude. Thus the term carries the idea of a plastic psychic substance, which is moulded and organized by submitting it to a ruling principle.

Sometimes, in dream or fantasy, the appearance of the desired shape has the unnamable character of heart's desire. An American doctor, for instance, whose lifelong extraverting momentum had attained a demonic character, told me of an experience which had moved him more than any other event in his life. Once, after an unusually exhausting day, he sat half-dozing in his consulting-room chair. Through the mist of fatigue and sleep there emerged a vision of a small figure, exquisitely shaped in marble, standing on the table beside him. Even as he spoke of it he was so deeply moved that he could hardly control his voice. It was the figure of a man, standing quite simply upon the earth. My patient said he could not say why it was that this figure moved him so, since there was no hint of action or effort. It was just the image of a mature man poised within himself. It was this, and this alone, which his whole being desired.

The extraverted habit of life can, and often does, assume a compulsive character like a demonic possession, especially, as in the case just cited, when extraversion is seized upon as a means for avoiding the needs and claims of the inner man. A man thus possessed is committed to his extraverted programme very much as a racing cyclist, racing against the watch, is bound to his spinning wheel and the endless ribbon of macadam. So long as the man possessed is chained to his extraversion, his only reasonable chance of freedom lies in a timely accident which could mercifully change his destination into a darkened room in a hospital. It frequently happens that the introverted aspect of experience is never even suspected by the extravert, until some catastrophe falls upon him which invalidates his whole extraverted programme.

The overcoming of the dragon corresponds, then, with an introverted process which detaches the libido from the protopathic state, where it had the character of obsession, and releases it for epicritic investment, where it has the character of value. Through the introverting process the world of outer objects is, to a certain extent, depotentiated in favour of the world of inner objects. Although extraverted prejudice may regard this state as a catastrophe, in reality the features of the external world come into clear focus only when the protopathic projections are withdrawn. Objective valuation is, indeed, always improved in quality through the revoking of the compulsive surplus. The phase of demonic extraversion is singularly blind, objects not being sought for themselves, but only at the behest of some all-embracing subjective fantasy. The withdrawal of libido from external fantasy-objects brings about a corresponding enhancement of the inner world. Even feeling, which is assumed to be exclusively concerned with objects of the outer world, becomes invested in inner objects.

This release of feeling from the obsessional dragon-effect is beautifully indicated in the present drawing; for, at the same instant that the dragon is depotentiated, the world is pervaded with colour which is the symbolical expression of feeling. In his careful stippling of the background with chosen colours, the patient already expresses the fact that the world begins to be meaningful, in contrast to the world of automata depicted in his second drawing.

The poise of the principal figure in this drawing is expressed in tense lines: symmetry under stress. Opposition of muscle groups is suggested in the dorsal region, and the raised arms are braced in reciprocal opposition. The psychological significance of this posture is clear. Under the influence of the dragon-effect, it was as though the centre of psychic gravity were located in the object into whom the unconscious was projected. In that condition the stress of opposition is felt to exist between oneself and the magically endowed object. It is the state of " fetching God from without." But when the dragon-effect is overcome, and the psychical value owned and honoured, the yea and the nay of the opposites play one against the other in reciprocal opposition. This is graphically represented in the picture by the appearance of the anima upon the scene, the reciprocal partnership of the conscious and the unconscious being personified by the hero and the moon-goddess.

That the anima should appear at this moment, and should be identical in colour with the dragon, invites us to assume that she personifies the primordial energy released from the dragon-spell. She even seems to be acknowledging her release with the foaming tankard of beer which she offers to the hero. The anima, as the silver moon-crescent, is the vessel (compare the shallop of Venus) by which energy is transmitted to consciousness from the mythological depths of the unconscious. The remains of the dragon lie beside the " dragon-castle on the floor of the sea," which guards the " germinal vesicle " containing the " Heavenly Heart." The terrible aspect of the dragon-complex has been overcome: in other words, the incest-dread has been dealt with on the mythological plane where, as we have previously pointed out, it properly belongs, and the result of the hero's staunchness is the transformation of the " terrible mother " into the ministering anima.

V

The connection between the anima and the mother-complex is beautifully illustrated in many classical myths. Ulysses, for example, after breaking the spell which binds him to Calypso, has a desperate fight with the sea (the devouring monster), from which he is vomited forth upon the Phæacian coast. Half dead with exhaustion and exposure, he is discovered by the ministering anima, the fair Nausicaa. The connection is more explicit in the story of Hiawatha, as told by Longfellow. After Hiawatha's victory over his father, Mudjekeewis, whereby he avenged the death of (in other words, took possession of) Wenonah, his mother, he stops at the house of the arrow-maker, whose lovely daughter is called Minnehaha, Laughing Water. As a dreaming boy

Hiawatha had recognized, in the sound of wind and water, the speech of his mother. In the appearance of Minnehaha at this moment the hero finds the mother again, but in a new form which is free of the incest-taboo.

In the Hiawatha myth it is the hero's mother, Wenonah, who is the young moon-goddess. In spite of old Nokomis' warning, she allows herself to be wooed by Mudjekeewis, the West Wind. Hiawatha is therefore born of the spirit; he symbolizes the winning of consciousness through a victory over primordial unconsciousness.

The Wagnerian version of the Parsifal legend also shows an interesting parallel, though the connection between the appearance of Kundry, the anima, and the hero's overcoming of the incest-dread is not so prominent. The mother, however, provides a pervasive background to the Parsifal-Kundry drama.

Parsifal lives alone with his mother in a remote forest, where she does her utmost to keep him from any possible contact with the outer world, especially the dangerous world of chivalry, which had made her a widow. Parsifal sees a band of knights riding through the forest and follows them; thus by accident, apparently, he begins the quest which leads him to his heroic individual task. Confronted with the mystery of the Grail and the sick Amfortas he marvels, but fails to understand. The crucial test comes when he challenges the might of Klingsor, the black magician, in his resolve to recover the sacred Spear. Kundry is the primordial anima, personifying that part of the Christian unconscious which did not accept Christ or the Christian way. The legend says that she laughed at the agony of Christ on His way to the place of crucifixion. For this crime she was doomed to serve Klingsor, and to use her fadeless beauty in seducing the knights of the Grail, until she should find a knight who was able to resist her enchantment. Only then would she be released from her doom.

In the scene when Parsifal is with Kundry and her maidens in the garden of enchantment, Kundry reclines behind him on a bank and speaks in caressing tones of his mother. But when she kisses him it is like the bite of a snake: he is immediately awake to the incest-snare and triumphs over the mother-dæmon in the guise of Kundry. In this moment of rejection Kundry's enchantment is destroyed, and Klingsor himself appears to defend his domain. He attempts to kill Parsifal with the sacred Spear, but Parsifal catches it. Immediately reality returns, and Klingsor, with his whole machinery of enchantment, vanishes into thin air.

The theme is unmistakably the same—namely, that of the hero who finds the enchanted and enchanting woman in the power of the evil demon—only in the case of Parsifal the hero has to overcome his own incestuous desire before he is able to win the magical weapon. The explanation of this remarkable variation of the pattern has surely to do with its Christian derivation. It is clearly a pagan myth that has become naturalized on Christian soil. The Grail castle and the knights of the Grail represent the spiritual thesis—*i.e.*, Christian consciousness. Klingsor and Kundry are therefore forced into the compensatory rôle and assume the sinister aspect of the repressed pagan antithesis.[1] Parsifal is able to resist the seduction of the antithesis, because he is not identified with the Christian thesis. Only the man who can detach himself from both sides, honouring the self-evident validity of his own will, can regain the phallic energy which has been held bound and fascinated in the unconscious. It follows from this that the fanatical man, insisting upon a one-sided ideology, is always a potential traitor, since he invites the risk of being seduced by the unconscious antithesis of his lopsided truth. The winning of the treasure, value, or magical power is the constant objective of the myth, but the form of the myth varies according to the ethical level at which it appears. The killing of the father for the possession of the mother may be regarded as the original form. The overcoming of the mother in order to free oneself must be a subsequent development. In Parsifal we find a new transformation, in which the desire for the mother must first be resisted and overcome, in order that the further goal of

1 Whence did the magic and witchcraft of the Middle Ages (not to mention the pitiless persecution of Jews and witches) draw their sustenance but in the repressed pagan antithesis in the Christian unconscious ?

winning freedom from the opposites may be achieved. But the elements of the myth remain constant, notwithstanding its varying psychological load.

After winning the Spear Parsifal takes the road of knightly accomplishment, while Kundry ministers to the wise old Gurnemanz, waiting for the return of Parsifal and her final release. With sure instinct for psychological realities, Wagner synchronizes the release of Kundry's soul with the return of the Spear to the Grail. It is this reconciliation of the opposites which heals the wound of Amfortas, and which is the true climax of the drama.

This part of the legend has special relevance to the patient's myth. For the appearance of the anima as a ministering function follows, in both myths, upon the hero's overcoming of the magical spell-binder—in the case of Parsifal, the magician and enchantress, and in that of our hero, the dragon with the sunflower eyes. Behind the mythic disguise the son's resistance to the father as the custodian of the mother is easily discernible. We can identify Kundry with Parsifal's mother on the same grounds as we identified Minnehaha with Wenonah. When Kundry speaks of the mother, she reveals an inside knowledge which only the mother could possess. Similarly, the green moon-goddess of this drawing discloses her psychological identity with the mother by virtue of the foaming tankard of ale, which appeared originally in Drawing VI. in the hand of the mother.

Another characteristic aspect of this anima-figure is her colour of verdant green, suggesting an intimate connection with nature. Ayesha, for example, had a magical power over natural forces; Rima, in Hudson's *Green Mansions*, was a kind of nature spirit; Kundry also has a witch-like intimacy with nature. As a compensatory function, always counterbalancing the conscious bias, the anima tends to be forced over to the pagan side in most educated men of the West. It is probable that this aspect of the anima is not universal, but depends rather on a fundamental need to "trim the boat," in view of the fact that we inherit a psychology which carries an entail of gross ignorance of the elementary laws of nature in man.

Jung has defined the anima as a mediatory and compensatory function of the psyche, also a function of relation between the conscious and the collective unconscious. Both these functions are suggested in the drawing—the former in the medial position of the anima-figure, equidistant between hero and dragon-castle, the latter in the fact that she brings the hero a gift from the ancestors[1] (*i.e.*, a gift from the gods).

Are we therefore to regard this advent of the anima as an unmixed blessing? The analogy with the transformed Kundry surely alludes to a favouring wind. Nevertheless, the anima is utterly ambiguous; we are, moreover, witnessing a phase of the myth in which the opposite principle is due to emerge. According to the Chinese Book of Changes (the *Yi King*), as soon as the phase of *Yang* has reached its fullest expansion the phase of *Yin* begins. The *Yang* phase would correspond to the combat and victory, the phase of heroic action. Now that that is finished, and the battle won, the feminine principle must increase in power, while the masculine wanes.

A few intrinsic features should also be noted which might cause a flicker of doubt. The good ancestral beer is only one interpretation of the tankard; another might bring up the longed-for meed of praise from the mother. We remember how Kundry used similar arts in her attempt to seduce Parsifal. Another point is the slender allusion to the dragon's sunflower eyes to be found in the curious margin of yellow petals surrounding her eye, as though a certain entail of draconian fascination had been transferred to the anima. There is also the questionable feature of the green face. Usually the green face has an unpleasantly sinister connotation, as in the case of *Das Grüne Gesicht* by Meyrink. Finally, this green-faced, fair-spoken lady is identified with the moon-goddess. We might explain this condition on the assumption that energy released from the primordial level of the unconscious would naturally appear at first under an impersonal, cosmic aspect. The primordial myth existing in a timeless, ageless realm, the anima has, as it were, to ply her barque

[1] The tankard of beer was associated with a brewery founded by one of the patient's ancestors.

between the eternal and the temporal. From one point of view, therefore, the anima appears human and personal, but, from the other side, she is an elemental force of nature, like tempest, wind, fire or vegetation.

Among the host of heavenly bodies the moon corresponds best with this essential ambiguity of the anima. The moon is a satellite of the earth; the aspect that is turned towards the earth is known, familiar and bright, whilst its other aspect is utterly dark and unknown. Certain powers and attributes of the anima have always been projected upon the moon, as, for instance, the idea that the moon is responsible for changes in the weather and, hence, of the moods and mental states of human beings. There is also the connection between the moon's[1] cycle and the menses of women and the ocean tides. With everything, in fact, that is changeable and subject to flux or cycles, man has always been liable to saddle the moon. Like the anima, too, she is our nearest neighbour. We are not surprised, therefore, to find these same projections loaded upon Hecate, the moon-goddess. Like every other moon-deity, she is the guardian of childbirth; she also has power over the sea and over fishermen. She is the goddess of night and darkness, hence of the underworld and the dead. Finally, she is the deity of ghosts and spirits, the patroness of necromancy and magic. Obviously the ambiguity of Hecate is the ambiguity of the anima.

The facial characters of the green anima are identical with the open-faced anima-type of Drawing V., whose origin was traced to the upper parasitic complex in III. The obstinate cleaving to the maternal breast, which gave to this upper figure its worst pathological features, lends colour to the suggestion that this anima-figure represents a substitute for, rather than a detachment from, the mother.

With these doubts in our minds we cannot feel too comfortable about the fate of the hero, even though he has performed his task and served well his mythological purpose. We cannot forget that throughout mythology (which means agelong human experience) the moment of victory is fraught with danger for the hero.

[1] Compare the significance of the term *lunatic*.

VI

Drawing XV

The dilapidated and exhausted hero is seen prostrate and bleeding badly from wounds on the head. His right hand is extended towards the green anima in the crescent moon; lines, suggesting radiation of some sort, are seen proceeding from the extended fingers. The middle one of these five lines just reaches the lower tip of the crescent moon. The left arm is so carelessly drawn that its connection with the body is somewhere in the region of the larynx. It is curved in a lazy hook; apparently it was too much trouble to draw an elbow. The tankard that was brought by the green anima is being tipped by the hooked arm, and the ale is seen bubbling into the hero's mouth.

The symbol of the open laminal field appears to be wrapped around the head like a surgical bandage. The green and yellow bands are partly obscured by the blood which flows from wounds in the front and back of the head. The arms are painted yellow except for the right hand, which is pale red; the body is a uniform brown.

In the top left-hand corner an effete and asymmetrical sun appears, containing an old man's face, with white hair and beard, on a blood-red ground. Four carelessly drawn black lines radiate at irregular intervals from the circumference of the sun's disc. Receding upwards and away from the scene is the green anima in her moon shallop. She is also receding in size, appearing somewhat misshapen and out of drawing. One gets the impression of a hot-tempered, contemptuous person in a huff.

In order to understand the unsatisfactory character of this drawing, I must explain that the pictures of the battle with the dragon were done under considerable tension, and that the patient was suddenly overtaken with fatigue as he was doing this last picture of the series. My reason for including it was to demonstrate the subject's mediumistic participation with the events he was depicting. Every line of this drawing is expressive of fatigue. The lines drawn from the extended fingers towards the moon were felt as sparks of electrical contact, as though the anima were now his sole, though rapidly receding, source of energy. This fact is important to bear in mind, for it soon becomes evident in the drawings which follow that at this point the patient is overtaken by a regressive anima-state. Such a regression could, of course, have been predicted when the patient, ceasing to identify himself with the mechanized soldier, became identified instead with the archetypal hero. Inflation invariably invites the unfavourable aspect of the anima. Certain warning signs have already been noted: beneath the cloak of the prostrate hero, for instance, lurks the dependent child, for whom the released anima is simply the mother.

Another important indication is to be found in the green and yellow symbol which is wrapped around the hero's head like a bloodstained bandage. This means that the rite of assimilation was not completed, and that a childish need for comfort and solace converted the heroic achievement to trifling egotistical ends. It is possible, of course, that the anima chooses this moment to usher in the *Yin* phase of the subjective development and, in order to demonstrate her power, uses the symbolic achievement of the *Yang* phase as the means of rendering first aid to the stricken hero.

All that is at present clear, however, is that the heroic valour is spent, and that the expression of the green-faced anima bodes no good. The weak, decrepit sun, opposing the moon-goddess in one of her worst moods, confirms the unfavourable aspect. The waning sun represents the decline and relative extinction of the masculine *Yang* principle.

CHAPTER XI

THE PHASE OF YIN: BIRTH OF THE LIFE-GIVING SYMBOLS

I

THE series of four drawings we must now discuss is unmistakably retrograde in character. The lowering of consciousness that was observed in the last drawing of the previous series has gone still further, and now all semblance of heroic virtue has departed from the figure which played the leading rôle. What purports to be the hero is an ill-drawn, greedy creature, resembling the crude, infantile conception of the hero which figured in Drawing VI.

DRAWING XVI

The structure of the picture is diffuse; the contents are painted in pallid, washed-out colours, and what drawing there is, is vague and spiritless. The figure of the hero is humpbacked, stiff and badly proportioned, having reverted to the infantile style of the Viking with ox-horn helmet, suggesting that the idea of the barbarian marauder has displaced the knight of chivalry. An abbreviated left arm levers open the monster's jaws, while an enormously extended right arm, holding a short sword, pushes through the crenellated defence below the mouth. This arm is bent into a lazy hook at the end which enables the hand to sever the articulation of the upper and lower jaws. The idea behind this manœuvre is no different from that of a burglar prising open a safe.

After the green dragon had been despatched it would appear that the child, disguised, of course, as a hero, returned to this first monster and decided it was no longer dangerous. He had merely to clear a way with his little sword, push his hand into the germinal vesicle (or womb-cavity) and seize the living heart. In making this attempt he seems to have been attracted by the green substance, which he begins to pull out of the monster's mouth by dint of holding it between his teeth and jerking his head backward. On the front of the hero's body, below the right arm, a part of the breastplate is visible, upon which the same long-bodied animal is painted as was noted in Drawing VI., but in the reverse position—a clear sign that the hero is now involved in a retrograde movement of the libido.

With his left foot the hero begins to scale the crenellated wall of the dragon-castle: the right is apparently swinging in space. Both legs are rigid and jointless; indeed, the whole figure is stiff and expressionless. The colour of the body is a thin, watery brown. In comparison with the vigorous hero of the previous series, this figure is a lifeless, insubstantial wraith.

The explanation of this remarkable change might be found in the inconspicuous presence of the moon-anima, surrounded by a constellation of green elements, in the small of the hero's back. Although relatively small and insignificant, it is obvious that she is the impelling *vis a tergo*, and it may be worth noting that she seems to be hiding underneath the hero's inflated chest. This is scarcely the way in which the support of the anima was to be anticipated. Some adverse factor has, perhaps, intervened to convert the helpful goddess of XIV. into the sinister influence of the present series. This factor is implied in the somnambulistic state of the transformed hero.

Inflation results almost inevitably whenever one falls into identification with a primordial image. This is what happened to the subject in the present case, and the consequent lowering of consciousness immediately invited the anima to take advantage of the situation in her dæmonic, protopathic form. The state of inflation means a certain blurring of individual identity, a state of psychological unreality in which consciousness is blindfolded by alien emotional assumptions. Before the anima can enter in and take possession of the personality in this way, the ego must have presumed to certain attributes belonging to an image of the collective unconscious. An excellent example of psychotic inflation is exhibited by Mr. Preemby in Wells' *Christina Alberta's Father* when he presumes to be Sargon the Magnificent.

The blindness and exhaustion of the hero (the masculine personality) is the anima's opportunity. Just as she is able to hide beneath the hero's inflated chest in the drawing, so she conceals her own feminine purposes underneath the subject's naive illusion of superiority. The fantastic exaggeration of masculine characters, which no dictator or public hero seems able to resist, usually goes hand in hand with a somnambulistic suggestibility to anima-insinuations and compulsions. But just because anima-possession is synonymous with effeminate affective displays, which eventually assume a ludicrous character, the phase of anima-compulsion may also serve teleologically to bring about the hero's deflation.

This motif of the deflation of the hero by the anima is beautifully presented in the Heracles myth. After his heroic labours were accomplished Heracles had to serve Omphale, a luxurious queen of Asia Minor, for three years in a menial capacity. He had to suffer indignities and don woman's clothing, while Omphale disported herself with lion skin and club. He also became enamoured of her, and she bore him several children.

The relation between anima and hero in the present cycle somewhat resembles that of spirit-control and medium in mediumistic séances. In the diffuse and childish drawing there is direct clinical evidence of an *abaissement du niveau mental.* It will be observed, for instance, that practically no distinction is made, either in density or structural organization, between the mass of the dragon-castle and the surrounding atmosphere. The decline in effective consciousness can be gauged by comparing this drawing with its correlate IX. The weakness of structure is enhanced by a profuse stippling of the whole background with red, blue, and silver daubs: a regressive perseveration of the technique used effectively in Drawing XIV. That part which corresponds with the mass of the monster has a predominance of red elements; throughout the rest, silver and blue prevail. A curving, elongated mass of pale blue, not unlike a boomerang in shape, is seen in the lower part of the monster's body. This is the only portion of the original content of the monster's body which is visible, and it is not at all clear at present why this exception has been made. Perhaps it will explain itself as we proceed.

II

Drawing XVII

The diminished hero has climbed a few steps higher on the wall, which now supports both feet. He has finished the operation upon the hinge of the monster's jaws, and has allowed the sword to drop. He now reaches into the womb-cavity with his extensible right arm, and seizes the heart which has been forming there out of the two bags of blood. His left arm can hardly be discerned: it has been carelessly painted over with the blue-cross stippling of the background. The green substance, with its terminal bifurcation into radial and ulnar elements, hangs loosely down from the hero's mouth.

Within the womb-cavity (distinguished by its reticulated background) the heart is now seen with its single large bloodvessel, from the distal end of which a spray of blood gushes forth, enveloping the infant below. Apparently the infant depends upon this supply as a fœtus upon the function of the placenta. At the tip of the womb-cavity the little blue peacock is still visible inside its egg. The constellation of green elements about the anima has increased, while the curve of the body inside the crescent suggests effort. She appears to be pushing against the hero's back with all her might.

The whole background of the drawing is spattered with rough blue crosses and daubs of gold mingled with red dots, the only exception being the womb-cavity and the small portion lying below the horizontal sword at the bottom right-hand corner. Here the blue crosses are replaced by clumsy blue daubs. I would again draw attention to the absence of any density distinction between the dragon-castle and the surrounding atmosphere. This is an important diagnostic point which will be dealt with later.

The only other points to notice are that the elongated mass of blue is absent in this drawing, and that the diffuse red elements, which in the previous drawing were freely scattered over the mass of the monster, now appear to be localized in the heart and main bloodvessel. Whereas in the former drawing red predominated throughout, the blue being localized in the elongated organ, here the situation is reversed, blue prevailing in the general background, while red is localized in the heart. These rapid alterations of colour in the background elements characterized the emotional instability of the patient's condition at that time. Rapid and apparently causeless changes of mood are classical symptoms of anima possession.

These two drawings represent two characteristic moods, in which the clear objectivity of consciousness is replaced by the blurred emotionality of an anima-ridden state. In the first drawing, not only is the whole field splashed with red emotional elements without form or purpose, but distinctions that were formerly clear are obliterated, and in no content can we discern a trace of active intelligence. In such a mood a man would look and feel different from his normal personality. On the one hand, he might be heavy and irritable, morbidly sensitive to criticism or disapproval; on the other, he might easily dissolve into hysterical moods, or be obsessed by morbid erotic fantasies, psychologically giving one the impression of an unstable, querulous woman masquerading as a man. The term "anima-ridden" is by no means an exaggerated figure of speech: it is an accurate clinical description.

This state is invariably accompanied by a lowering of consciousness and loss of insight. Any attempt, therefore, to terminate the mood by direct criticism would undoubtedly excite a storm of indignant affect. For, as the drawing shows, the anima lurks behind the hero; in other words, she operates from the unconscious. Were she visible to the subject, there would be no question of possession. The patient has drawn the anima-mood with perfect accuracy. But if he had realized the implications of what he was doing, it is certain he would never have drawn it. It is the hardest thing for a man to admit that he is being ruled by a primitive female element of his unconscious, which gained control when he was not looking.

The reader can appreciate how it might serve when, from such a mood, one was able to create something that would reveal the contents of the mood, as this picture does, in clear and concrete imagery. The very fact that objectivity is given to the mood helps to bring the anima once more into visibility. One is able to name the foreign influence: one can even begin to discern a certain teleology in the anima-effects. It is well to remember, however, that anima-psychology on this protopathic level is decidedly primitive.[1] In dealing with a primitive mentality we discover that speech is seldom the officer of real intention. When getting the anima to talk—and it is of very great value to learn to converse with the anima—it is important, therefore, always to read between the lines. But if one can hold a certain part of the mind detached, so that, even during a mood, a neutral function still remains unsubmerged and capable of self-criticism, the aim of the anima can be divined. But here again the tendency to immediate rationalization must be overcome.

In the present instance, for example, the remarkable change that had overtaken the character of the drawings was explained by the patient as the result of fatigue, pure and simple. He felt he had done enough, and had no wish to do more. Why must he start upon another series, when the hero's task was already finished? All of which was true and reasonable enough, but it did not explain why the anima had taken so inconspicuous a place in the small of the hero's back, or why the hero himself had slipped back to the level of a childish automaton. The only thing that mattered to the patient was that his interest had evaporated through exhaustion.

* * * * *

Coming to the second drawing of the series, we find the anima still governing the situation, but the mood has changed. The formless red elements remarked in the first drawing were massed chiefly in the lower part of the picture, whereas the blue crosses which mark the present mood are thickest in the upper part of the field, particularly in front of the hero's

[1] The anima can also become a differentiated function presenting, naturally, a very different psychological picture from the above.

head, where they seem to be streaming into the monster's mouth. This latter impression is reinforced by the three lines of gold that are seen converging into the open jaws.

From the prominence of the red elements in the one drawing and the blue crosses in the next, we assume that the patient's mood alternated between emotional excitement on the one hand and intuitive incontinence on the other. But the important feature in both is the dissipation and fragmentation of the various elements. The slipshod character of the drawing shows that attention and interest have evaporated. The figure of the hero in both drawings is stiff and mechanical, reminding one again of the little tin soldier. What was once an heroic blade in Drawing XI. is now a mere wooden toy to be thrown aside. Moreover, the hero himself becomes increasingly reduced in stature. It even becomes difficult for ourselves to maintain interest in what this hero is doing.

Perhaps, if we attempted to interpret our symptoms, we might discover that this evaporation of interest in the hero is due to the fact that he is no longer the central figure of the drama. He has become merely a puppet, a tool, a medium of the anima working behind the scenes. The cooling of our interest in the hero tells us in fact that the hero himself has been "cooled off." In certain primitive communities a warrior who returns from a raid, having killed his man, is cooled off by being excluded from the village for several days. He has to sleep outside in the bush until he has lost his heroic inflation and is reliably human again. It is very like letting the gas out of a balloon in order to bring it to earth.

Psychological deflation is the process whereby the dissipation or evaporation of an archetypal afflux is brought about. Prophets and inspired individuals are usually solitary beings. Perhaps, like Socrates, they are warned by their δαίμων that mankind cannot tolerate them at close quarters.

The loose fragmentation of relatively formless elements over the whole field in these two drawings represents this process of psychological evaporation. Such a condition might take the form of aimless extraverted activities, wayward emotional excursions, inchoate fantasying, leading perhaps to erotic dissipation. The dissipating energy tends also to become exteriorized in exasperating entanglements—so-called accidents—in which objects of the environment seem to conspire together to complete one's undoing. The mood of neurotic fuss, when the air seems to be charged with invisible, loudly buzzing mosquitoes, and everything seems to possess a sinister capacity for getting under one's skin, might be expressed by this degree of fragmentation in a drawing.

Notwithstanding the unpleasant character of these anima-drawings, the psychological sequence would not be complete without them. They are faithful expressions of the regressive phase, which so frequently follows on the heels of the heroic attempt. Regression does not mean merely a step or two backwards, it is a definite atavistic return to a former goal, a sneaking back to an earlier hypothesis.

The superiority of the knightly hero was apparently beyond the patient's means: it could not be maintained. The alternative hypothesis was the mechanized soldier, the will-less puppet of circumstances. The stiff, mechanical figure of these drawings suggests a return to that hypothesis, not forgetting the obvious allusions to the earlier model of the hero in Drawing VI. The rigid, defensive attitude of the figure is also suggestive of the paranoid condition, in which hostile negative projections usurp the place of positive feeling. But what is the cause of the rigid spine and inimical glance of paranoia? Is it a toxin working in the tissues of the brain, or does it proceed from an insinuating subjective voice suggesting that one is being betrayed, undervalued, overlooked or conspired against?

The betrayer of the hero is his shadow. Siegfried was betrayed by Hagen, Christ by Judas, Osiris by Set, Othello by Iago, etc. Wherever the heroic ideal has been projected, and into every relationship where a splendid ideal has been fostered, this invisible Iago is liable to breathe his poison. Othello loved with his greatness, but distrusted with his inferiority. Both aspects are Othello.

To project his shadow in the paranoid way upon a suitable object is indeed an almost normal procedure for a man intent on preserving the ideal pretensions of his beloved ego. Naturally, the greater and the more organized the heroic illusion, the more complete will be the paranoid isolation caused by the hero's shadow. Behind the inflexible posture of proud reserve, and the eventual rupture of every vital relationship, we can discern both mythological opposites in our paranoid patient—namely, the hero and his betrayer. The paranoid mood of negative feeling is, in fact, a relatively normal constituent of complex human psychology, inasmuch as everyone has a shadow. Men, however, are more prone than women to moods of negative feeling, because of the fact that the anima of a man is emotional in character, whereas the animus of a woman is intellectual or ideational. But a woman can be isolated by the animus in much the same way, inasmuch as the animus takes possession of her inferior function, and makes her distrust her own mind just as the anima works upon a man's inferiority. To be secretly wedded to the idea of inferiority means to espouse the very spirit of unrelatedness, but to admit and accept one's inferiority, as a problem to be dealt with in relation to one's partner, can provide the candid nucleus of a lifelong relationship. Only the man who is absolutely ruled and pinioned by the anima becomes addicted to paranoiac displays. To know and to accept the shadow creates a position of strength; its denial, and consequent projection, mean a psychological crippling.

Following the principle of synchronicity, we must assume a certain connection between the rigid, hump-backed posture of the hero, the obvious lowering of the conscious threshold, the numberless blue crosses or red daubs that confuse the scene, and the active presence of the little green anima-figure in the hollow of the hero's back. Relying, to some extent, upon this connection, and also upon my knowledge of the patient's psychology, I am inclined to regard the blue crosses as representing projections of negative unconscious contents into the world around. The crosses are, in fact, an extremely crude multiplication of the idea of the heroic sword. The sword is the symbol of the effective deed; hence its shadow-effect would be a fragmentation and dissipation of psychic energy which completely undermines the will. This betrayal of the effective deed is the real tragedy of schizophrenia: it is the aimless dissipation of energy which has reduced the hero to mechanical insignificance.

So much for the renegade hero. But what of the anima? How does it serve her ends to reduce the hero to an atavistic puppet? For she too is a part of the subject's psychology and, destroying him, she also destroys herself. Is it possible to view this regressive state of anima-possession also from the teleological angle?

In the womb-cavity close at hand lie the germinating symbols which have been nourished there while the hero was engaged with the dragon. These functions have to be salvaged and brought up out of the *uroborus* state of primordial potential into actuality. It is a domestic or, more correctly, an obstetrical work that has to be done, since, as we shall presently see, these functions have to be born. The culmination of the *Yin* phase is usually a birth or a new beginning.

The four vital functions which constitute this new beginning are the impregnated life-stuff extracted from the monster's mouth, the living heart, the infant, and the peacock. We shall have to discuss these four symbols in the final drawing of the series. For the present, therefore, it is enough to take note that they are concerned with the conative values, as opposed to the medial eye, which was essentially a cognitional function.

What is now taking place under the instigation of the anima is concerned with the basic affective attitude. What we can see and understand and shape to our need comes within the scope of practical intelligence. But what is usually not seen is the fundamental emotional constellation or attitude, that which determines the way we meet and handle a situation, and by virtue of which we adapt to the demands of life. The basic attitude is an *a priori* construction, antedating the first recognition of the self as a separate entity. Consisting of inherited as well as acquired unconscious presuppositions, it is not accessible to introspective self-analysis. But with respect to objective analysis, whatever method we adopt, the basic attitude is the true object of our analysis, for no cure is conceivable which is not grounded in a reconstituted vital attitude.

If a man is quite unable to perceive the emotional assumptions upon which his moods rest, he cannot gain any real control over them, since they must remain for ever foreign to his reason.

The emotional hypothesis of value which, for example, created these four symbols in Drawing IX., and the hero's golden javelin in Drawing X., should be compared with the hypothesis of non-value ruling the present series. A psychiatric observer, familiar with the sudden and seemingly irrational evaporation of interest in schizophrenic patients, could diagnose the condition on the evidence of these contrasted drawings. The value was real and effectively presented in the earlier drawings. Suddenly the value disappears, and *cupiditas* takes its place. Every account of schizophrenic pathology, without exception, lays stress on these disturbances in the affective regions of the mind, which are liable to destroy the continuity of interest and attention, cloaking everything under a pall of apathy.

The absence of structure and density distinctions, the decline of value in the representation of the hero and of the life-giving symbols, the crude, monotonous stippling—all combine to form a valuable diagnostic picture of the condition described by Janet as *abaissement du niveau mental*—valuable not only because these pictures accurately depict the altered state of consciousness, but because they also portray its cause. The energy that has been withdrawn from the executive function is discoverable: it has not flown out of the picture. We find it again in the vivid, tense constellation of green elements in and around the anima. Thus the condition must be stated in terms of both factors: on the one hand the lowering of the conscious threshold, on the other a synchronous activation of the archaic unconscious in the person of the anima.

The manifest character of the withdrawal or displacement of energy from the epicritic to the protopathic level is entirely regressive; but, regarded teleologically, its objective seems to be to dissolve or undermine the schizoid barricade between these two levels. The split or barricade is, to a large extent, a cultural artefact. The very name " dementia præcox " signified that it was the difficult transition from the infantile to the cultural psyche which proved too much for these subjects.

III

We shall discuss this aspect of the problem when we come to the shadow-figure in the next drawing. For the time being we have only to observe the effect of the anima-regression upon the schizoid structures. To this end, and before the barricade breaks up altogether, it may be worth while to trace the various indications of the schizophrenic split throughout the sequence.

In Drawing I. the absence of continuity of contents was almost complete. Above, there was the scene on the Mersey, with the battleship held between the opposing psychological constellations; below, the lunatic asylum. The phallic arm of the crane and the legs of the tripod penetrated the layer of repression. The former pierced the layer from below, producing chaos above, while the latter penetrated from above, bringing hope of light and healing to the imprisoned lunatics below. Respectively they symbolized sexuality and healing, the only forces, apparently, which possess the power of piercing the schizophrenic barricade. Both belong to the primordial psyche, and both enjoy direct continuity with the cultural psyche. Therefore they can span the gulf.

Drawing II., with its characteristic division of the picture into two discontinuous halves, presented the diagnostic feature without disguise. It would be hard to conceive a more graphic picture of the schizoid condition. The megaphone shock-absorber was an artificial construction, required for the purpose of mitigating the distance between the two sides. It had no relevance to the activity of either side, except by reference to the split.

In Drawing III. the contents of the picture were split into two halves, by virtue of the fact that they were painted on the backs of two separate drawings. A certain continuity between the contents of the two sides was attempted, though the continuity of line was actually achieved only at three points—viz., in the frontal line of the upper head and in the lines of the eye and mouth of the lower face. The shut-off elements, with the stomach-container on the right and the vizored, unrelated ghost-figure on the left, could be regarded as evidence of the sequestering tendency of schizophrenia, not to mention the disjuncted organs, symbols, and parts of organic systems with which the field of the drawing was strewn.

In IV. we found a tendency to overcome this disjunction of organic contents, by the process of abstracting certain key-symbols and placing them in the diagonal position of reciprocal action.

In V. the problem of the splitting of the libido against itself was represented. Again the contents were abstracted from III., obviously for the purpose of reducing the complex pathology of the latter to a simpler diagrammatic representation.

In VI. the ringed-off fantasy system on the left became the target of the accusing finger of the ancestral god. There was also a hint of a dividing line in the road that goes on over the hill. This line roughly divided the paternal associations on the left of the picture from the maternal on the right. The ancestral god, belonging to the maternal side, was on the right-hand side of this line.

In VII. the schizoid condition was indicated by the wavy line framing the shut-off system, which was being pierced by the god's accusing finger. The profound contrast between the contents of the infantile psyche on the left and those of the cultural psyche on the right was noted. The subject was apparently able to feel the possibility of direct penetration of the framed system in the lower phallic region, whereas above the continuity between the finger on the god's hand and the fingers which pierced the system was reduced to a single line. This seemed to indicate that the barricade was essentially an epicritic phenomenon, and that it did not extend down to the protopathic level of the affects.

In VIII. the sequestered system was confined to the impregnated green mass and the two vampire faces in the monster's mouth. The theme of disjuncted organs was found in the five vagrant eyes and the portions of the god's beard.

In IX. the contrast between the benign and maternal aspect of the unconscious on the right and the dæmonic and paternal on the left was pronounced. But in this drawing the material of the schizophrenic barricade was employed constructively, while the emergence of the dragon from the nostril established a dynamic continuity of content between the right and left sides.

In X. and XI. the twin-like duplication of the dragon, suggested by the doubling of the *mandala* symbol and by the row of four red crosses in the middle line, with the row of dorsal spines on either side of it, was the only evidence of schizophrenic structure.

In XII. the explosion of the gun in the middle of the picture, which also divided the dragon into two halves and severed the continuity of the hero's weapon, seemed to derive from the same psychic constellation.

In XIII., XIV. and XV. there was no sign of schizoid influence, except in the allusion to the existence of the dragon-castle, with its crenellated wall, at the bottom right-hand corner of XIV. But as soon as we reach the regressive series we find the schizoid wall again in XVI. and XVII., running up the middle of the drawing. We also noticed the paranoid posture of the hero, and the morbid subjectivity of the mood, in which everything is spattered over with the daubs and crosses of unconscious excitement. In XVI. the excitement is affective in character, shown by the marked predominance of red elements, whereas in XVII. there is a swing-over to an ideational or intuitive excitement, represented by the blue crosses: the thickening rush of the crosses into the funnel-shaped opening of the monster's mouth implying that the excitement is concentrating upon the living heart which the atavistic hero is in the act of seizing.

Especial attention is due to the fact that the activation of the unconscious by the anima has the effect of more or less dissolving the split between left and right, red and blue emotion and intellect. In both XVI. and XVII. undifferentiated psychic elements flow unimpeded across the whole field. In XVI. the hero has no difficulty in putting his arm through the crenellated wall, and when the hero has disarticulated the jaws and extended his arm (in XVII.) into the womb-cavity, a real continuity is established between the contents of the two sides. We must agree, however, that, in order to obtain this free access from one side to the other, a very considerable decline in the conscious level was necessary.

In Drawing VII. we noted a parallel phenomenon with regard to the permeability of the schizophrenic frame—namely, that in the upper part of the drawing penetration by the god was effected from a distance and was represented by a single line, while below the phallic extension could gain direct access into the system.

These observations accord with our clinical findings—namely, that the schizophrenic split lies between the function of the intellect and the affective processes. For this reason a purely intellectual analysis cannot overcome or get round the schizophrenic barrier, *whereas the anima-function is able to establish an emotional continuity below the level of the inhibiting barricade.* Hence the regression to a more archaic level of consciousness may be part of a teleological process, without which the *impasse* could not be circumvented. Observe, for instance, how the massive anatomical structures of Drawing IX. dissolve into the ephemeral vestiges of the present series, and how the crenellated wall thins away to a mere broken line. This must mean that, from the altered level of consciousness, the schizophrenic barricade wears a changed aspect. The price paid for the altered view seems, however, to be a terrible depreciation in conscious values.

The resistance of the patient during this phase indicated that the regression was no mere acquiescence in the easiest way. I have already referred to the patient's unwillingness to go on with the drawings after the battle with the dragon. That, he felt, was enough. He had done what he had to do, and could not see why the unconscious would not leave him alone, or at least allow him some breathing space. I was also in the dark as to why the patient, who was obviously exhausted, was forced to continue the drawings in spite of resistance. But when I came to study the whole sequence, it occurred to me that the anima had had to wait for the exhausted condition of consciousness, in order to bring about the birth of the living symbols from the womb of the unconscious.

A certain parallelism with the actual process of parturition comes readily to mind. Experience in general practice impressed upon me the fact that with certain sensitive, high-spirited primiparous subjects the first stage of labour was liable to be unduly prolonged, owing to the patient's resistance to the pains. The conscious personality had, in fact, often to be reduced to a state of exhausted acquiescence before the uterine contractions became fully effective. Accordingly, I adopted the practice of preparing the patient psychologically beforehand, with the idea of getting her to accept the natural process as a beneficent *force majeure*. I found it useful to tell the patient that she should consciously increase the efficacy of each pain, instead of resisting it. By virtue of preparing the patient's attitude in this fashion, it was possible to expedite labour very considerably.

If I had realized with my mental patient that a parallel process of psychological parturition was due to take place, he would certainly have been better prepared for the new phase.

The presence of the anima in XVI. was discovered as a little verdant creature, vigorously pushing the hero from behind. But how does this feminine influence show itself in the rest of the action? The first hint of anima-psychology in XVI. is to be seen in the hero's efforts to pull the green life-stuff away with his teeth. This is not an heroic rescue, but an animal's notion of retrieving something. Another indication is seen in the way the hero attacks the monster's jaw from behind; this again is not the hero's method of attack; it suggests rather the oblique methods of the primitive female. Then there is the sword—not, surely, the blade of a warrior, but resembling more the stiletto, the concealed weapon of the undeclared enemy.

In Drawing XVII. the anima influence is more openly stated. The curve of the little green figure, and the tenser curve of the moon, are eloquent of the force with which she pushes her agent towards his task. The posture of the *ci-devant* hero as he climbs the wall of the dragon-castle reminds one not a little of a small boy being reluctantly hoisted up an orchard wall by his brother, in order to get the brother an apple. This simile is not beside the mark, as we shall presently see. Indeed, when I asked the patient if he could account for the extraordinary transformation that had overtaken the knight of the dragon, he said it was " the difference between the man who fights and the one who goes off with the swag." This remark offers us yet another piece of evidence, for no man ever feels genuinely proud of the things he does under anima-compulsion. It has too much the feeling of an alien influence.

Again, in this drawing the hero evinces an unnatural relation to his sword. He lets it drop from his hand as he reaches into the dragon's belly to seize the heart. There is an unpleasant suggestion of greed in this action, which the next picture will more fully disclose.

A familiar feminine trait is revealed in these anima-products, in the depreciation of the function of the sword. On every ground the sword is the royal symbol of the masculine logos-principle. But the primitive anima consistently misuses the logos-function in pursuit of her own goals. As a value in and for itself the anima will have nothing to do with the principle of logos.

This primordial feminine attitude to the power of the word is shrewdly satirized by Shaw in *Man and Superman*. The reader will recall a scene in Act II., where Tanner delivers himself of a somewhat rhetorical condemnation of the hypocritical mask of maternal duty and family affection, concealing the mother's " abominable design " of selling her daughter to the highest bidder in the matrimonial market. In this outburst Tanner's reforming spirit is beating passionately against what he assumes to be the barricade of conventional immorality in the mind of Ann Whitefield. As he finishes, Ann, who has been watching him with detached curiosity, says:

ANN. I suppose you will go in seriously for politics some day, Jack ?

TANNER (*heavily let down*). Eh? What? Wh—— ? (*Collecting his scattered wits*) What has that got to do with what I have been saying?

ANN. You talk so well.

TANNER. Talk! Talk! It means nothing to you but talk.

There is an echo of this scene at the very end of the play. After Tanner has at last capitulated to Ann and the Life Force, he renounces his freedom and his happiness with a passionate realism that is meant to tear away the last trace of conventional hypocrisy:

VIOLET (*who makes use of romantic illusion to cloak her intensely realistic designs*). You are a brute, Jack.

ANN (*looking at him with fond pride and caressing his arm*). Never mind her, dear. Go on talking.

TANNER. Talking! (*Universal laughter.*)

CURTAIN.

This attitude of biological woman to the masculine principle, which seems to reduce a man's quest for truth to the level of male coquetry, is full of coiled serpents for the creative spirit. But the poison and bitterness expressed in the foregoing scenes are not pure evidence of woman's ruthlessness towards man. They derive mainly from the solitary man's inner struggle with his anima; never will she allow him to indulge in passionate argument without some caustic subliminal insinuation of insincerity. It is the existence of this subjective feminine critic in a man's soul which accounts for the fact that men who are not strangers to self-criticism tend to ironical forms of expression.

The diminished and depreciated sword in these anima-controlled drawings is therefore no mere coincidence; it presents a characteristic symptom of anima-psychology.

From the heroic standpoint, the effects here discerned are disastrous; yet, regarded teleologically, the results are none the less effective. It would almost seem as though the clouding of the hero's mind with a heavy mist were a prerequisite for the achievement of the anima's realistic designs in regard to the new psychic formations.

IV

Drawing XVIII

The mechanical stiffness of the figure has now given place to a boneless, semi-liquid shape. The breastplate has slipped down to cover a paunchy stomach. The head is large, and upon it the horned helmet of the viking rests with the inconsequent air of a telescoped top-hat on the head of a tipsy reveller. The features are coarse, degraded and horrible; there are indications of a dark, irregular beard. The right arm, which seized the living heart from the womb-cavity, is now hooked towards the large, sensual mouth with a sinister suggestion of headlong greed. The left arm, which holds the sword, and seems to have cut the crenellated defence with a casual poke of the sword, now slits a hole in the lower surface of the womb-cavity, in which the child and the egg are contained. The whole body of the figure is painted with a dark sepia. The thin, curling legs are divided in a loose, orgiastic dance. The feet are clubbed, and the lower part of the left leg is set at an angle, suggesting the hoofed leg of a satyr. The armour which should guard the heart now covers the belly. The whole figure, which seems to be dancing on air, has something drunken, dissolute, and even devilish about it. In the last drawing the green anima was seen pushing the hero up the wall. Here she propels him into the air, and in order to better her stance she now squats under the body, within the crook of the right leg.

The sun, a dark-red disc containing an aged, featureless head, appears just above and behind the main figure. It has eight rays painted red and gold; the horizontal one, towards the right, is extended to penetrate the widely separated jaws of the moribund monster. The insubstantiality of the dragon-castle is now patent. The womb-cavity is shrunken to a negligible quantity, and the whole structure has an ephemeral aspect, as though sailing up out of the picture.

The blue logos-element is absent from this picture, with the exception of the small peacock and the two-lobed mass of blue. The commissure which joined the two lobes has just been severed by the devil-hero. The infant in the womb-cavity seems to have reverted to an early fœtal level. Blood drips from the slit made by the sword in the wall of the cavity. It seems to have weight and substance, judging by the way it drops through the lower lobe of blue.

The green anima is indicated by a thick stroke of green, capped by a daub of yellow, while the upper horn of her containing moon is elongated upwards and backwards into a sharp point.

The background is loosely brushed with silver; a wild, chaotic shadow-effect appears when the picture is held up to the light.

* * * * *

The *enantiodromia* is complete: the retrogressive transformation from hero to devil could not be more explicitly portrayed. It is obvious that the patient took no trouble with this picture: he just allowed the figure to draw itself. It has done so with a kind of devilish zest. Psychologically, the patient had fallen into a pit; out of the pit a devilish motive leaps—orgiastic cupidity masquerading as hero. But although moral disintegration has overtaken the hero, his actions are still controlled by the anima, as we shall presently discover. He is like an insect undergoing histolysis, and his spineless, boneless condition is just what the anima requires for furthering her scheme.

We took note of certain rather sinister indications in the aspect of the anima, even when she appeared first as a ministering angel in Drawing XIV. The subsequent recession of the anima in XV., and her reappearance as the *vis a tergo* of the present series, confirm our unfavourable impression.

In the two previous drawings the hero was naive and childish and decidedly somnambulistic. From both the means and the method which the hero brought to his task we concluded that the whole project he is now engaged upon had been instigated by the anima. A woman wishing to inspire a man to accomplish something valid challenges his manhood, his real personality; but when she harbours the idea of using him as a tool, she prefers to induce an erotic, pliable mood before mentioning her project. Everything that is true of the "eternal feminine" is true of the primitive anima in man.

Between Drawings XIV. and XVI. there was recession from the cultural to the infantile level, and, at the same time, the anima changed from a ministering function into a sinister, hidden motive. Now when an individual nourishes a half-formed wish or policy which better thoughts would repudiate as unworthy, an air of rather forced childishness is commonly adopted. Similar tactics may be used by the state. Women are also liable to conceal their biological schemes and feminine subtleties under the mask of the appealing, ignorant child, while leaders, in aggressive mood, are equally prone to blind themselves to their real motives by insisting loudly and incessantly on the heaven-sent character of their mission, whereby criminal plans of aggression are made to appear as divinely revealed commands.

Were we bold enough to challenge the primitive female in the former, or the predatory animal in the latter, we should be annihilated. Both have taken considerable pains to remain morally irresponsible in regard to their motives, and such unconsciousness is an effort to maintain, hence the forced note of childishness, or of misunderstood goodness and innocence. Elaborate aids to unconsciousness such as ceaseless chatter, whistling, forced gaiety, or a motivated press campaign, can be taken as warning signs that proposals of reciprocity will not be tolerated. There is often reason enough why the unconscious is, in fact, unconscious: we learn, from bitter experience, that men who are being somnambulistically propelled by the anima are inaccessible either to reasonable counsel or to moral appeal. Often the only thing that brings them to their senses again is catastrophe. In so far as the primitive hypothesis is secretly nourished, it will be tried out sooner or later, and until it has been proved to be unfeasible it will not be sacrificed to the counsels of good sense.

While this phase lasts everything that is said or done is indicative of a lower, more brutal level of consciousness, the subject tending to seek companionship and support among those whose ethical standards could never provoke disagreeable comparisons. Similarly, when a civilized nation is caught by a political objective which its own civilized conscience cannot justify, a dangerous decline in the level of consciousness is liable to take place, while all those elements in the state which cannot be hypnotized or bludgeoned into acquiescence will be persecuted and, if possible, banished. Nations at war usually manifest these classical symptoms.

The ruthlessness and cruelty which accompany this phase are not due to the fact that two incompatible wills or ideologies are striving for mastery in the same organism. Complexity does not make for ruthlessness, rather for consciousness. The dangerous condition comes from repression of the moral conflict. A simple, single-minded being has no problem: action can be taken at once without hesitation, because there are no complex alternatives, whereas the man who admits the complexity of a situation has to view it from many angles, he has to move circumspectly, allowing action to develop gradually. The disadvantage of this kind of approach when a situation calls for swift intervention is self-evident. Accordingly, the apparently cheaper method of repressing the higher inhibitory influences tends loudly to commend itself. This repression is the cause of the brutality.

Again we can see the issue in terms of the infantile and the cultural. In the protopathic condition of infancy, immediate action and response prevail. The charm of the child-mind lies very largely in this capacity for uncomplicated reactions. But as soon as we enter the cultural sphere, we are caught in a net of complex considerations. The adolescent feels himself hampered at every turn by an invisible net of social prejudice, taboo and custom. He behaves, as a rule, like other wild creatures when caught in a net: first he struggles wildly; then he lies passive but resistant, held by an intangible alien power. Naturally he imitates the behaviour of others around him, often taking an admired social adept as a model, thereby adapting himself to the netted state. Finally he accepts the acquired cultural mask as himself, and tries to forget the wild creature that lay panting in the net.

However well the adolescent may succeed in this complex adaptation, the unconverted infantile psyche still lies repressed, and potentially explosive, just beneath the fair cultural surface. This ignored primordial island presents a formidable educational problem to Western society, which so far has remained singularly incapable of envisaging this vital problem of initiation either in education or religion.

Freud was really the discoverer of the protopathic level of the unconscious, and he proved beyond question that the renegade neurotic will in human beings is fostered in this ignored infantile realm. Jung's conception of the shadow was derived from this same subterranean level. The persona, on the other hand, comprises the adapted, outwardly manifest cultural personality. He attributed the name and character of a mask,[1] or false self, to this outer aspect, because it is essentially a polished disguise superimposed upon the concealed child-personality. It is false, because, unless the mature personality is firmly rooted in its own primordial nature, it will sooner or later collapse. An education which tries to wean adolescence away from its infantile roots through magnifying the importance of an arbitrary collective style, meanwhile suppressing childhood's world of fantasy with a heavy authoritarian hand, is a needlessly cruel and stupid form of collective initiation. But our past educational sins against the child-soul are not expiated by making the opposite mistake—namely, that of unconsciously encouraging the adolescent to meet the requirements of adult life with an apotheosized infantile psyche.

The infantile psyche contains the individual essence—in other words, the primordial myth of infancy is essentially true. But the adolescent has to learn how to implement his inward truth in the cultural way and with the best cultural equipment. If he remains childish, his individual truth becomes a neurotic nuisance; but if he can remain essentially childlike in his attitude, while at the same time meeting the world with disciplined manhood, his own native truth will come into its own.

In horticulture grafting is the quickest and easiest way of producing an indefinite number of the more highly cultivated

1 *Persona* was the designation given to the masks worn by actors in antiquity.

types of roses, fruit trees, flowering trees, etc. But the vitality of a tree in which the cultural type of the graft is too remote from the stock on which it is grafted is liable to be precarious. The graft is the invention of the nurseryman; it serves human interests, but not always those of the plant. The all too familiar suckers in the rose-garden are the attempt of nature to counteract too much culture by a reversion to type. The sucker is the shadow of the rose, its subliminal standpoint. It is also quite obviously a renegade; if allowed to grow it will sap the energy from the cultural form. Another point of interest is that certain styles of growth seem to favour the renegade-tendency. Suckers, for example, are more frequent with standard rose-trees than with the bush type; and the rambler, which is nearest to the native briar, is relatively free of the renegade problem.

As educationists, we have to recognize the futility of merely nipping off psychological suckers. The work of education is to create a bridge between the infantile and the cultural psyche. But a bridge is emphatically not a graft: it does not favour one side of the river while repressing the other. The schizoid problem is liable to appear when a cultural graft has been superimposed on a stock the indigenous level of which is too remote from that of the grafted expectation. The apathy, the withdrawal of interest and attention, the mechanical, inwardly resistant compliance with cultural requirements, the Jekyll-and-Hyde antithesis between persona and shadow—what are these but the sucker-like withdrawal of energy by a subliminal renegade standpoint?

A fine study of this complete recession of energy from the cultural persona is presented in Barrie's *Mary Rose*. Barrie doubtless had in mind the peculiar liability among his psychological compatriots to live on two planes. A very living pagan world exists not so far below the surface in many Scotch minds; the "island that likes to be visited" is often to be found in the fantasy-life of women in whom the primordial has never unreservedly surrendered to the cultural. But apart from these divided souls, the Mary Rose habit of disappearing psychologically from the scene is common enough. From this point of view Mary Rose might come to be regarded, like Hamlet, as a universal figure of the cultural myth.

But since we do not consider this temporary recession of energy into a semi-conscious fantasy-world (which after all is a normal adolescent phenomenon) as particularly dangerous or pathological, what is the condition which transforms it into something sinister in the case of Mary Rose? Barrie gives us two hints in the portrait of his ageless child: the first is that the experience of the island, and of the "little old woman" with whom she talks at odd moments, is completely dissociated from her ordinary consciousness. The second is that the parents treat her not merely as a child, but as one who has to be protected from any disturbing knowledge. In other words, Barrie conceived Mary Rose as a psychology so sensitive and precariously poised that people around her instinctively avoided the possibility of a sudden shock or jar. Such natures have to be sheltered and protected in a peculiar way, just because they seem unable to form vital connections or deep holding roots in the milieu where they ostensibly belong. Barrie's observation that Mary Rose was peculiarly young for her years also offers a clue to the problem. Such women[1] seem to live in a sort of timeless condition, as though enfolded within a veil of primordial myth. Things which should leave marks upon their soul and upon their faces are simply not experienced. It is as though they suffered without experiencing suffering. They know as little as a child knows why they suffer.

Essentially it is because of this relative incapacity to form vital connections in the real world that the retreat into the primordial world of fantasy becomes a dangerous alternative. If their lives knew reality as something which claimed a vital response, the seductive faery music would not reach their ears. Or if it did, it would not seduce.

In the case of our patient, the relative failure of the graft was due to a different cause. With Mary Rose the default is not due to any particular resistance to her cultural milieu. She is simply insufficiently hatched out; she still has one leg

[1] The psychological absentee is, of course, not specifically feminine, but the Mary Rose character is.

in paradise. But with our patient, to consort with the shadow, as he did in the second dream, expresses a deep resistance to the cultural sphere and its claims. It is this resistance which begets a craving for the uninhibited freedom of the primordial state.

The reader will recall the genealogy of the shadow-figure supplied by the shadow himself. The dream called him "the loose one," and the patient associated the devil-hero of the present drawing with that figure; no epithet could have described this figure more aptly. In his attempt to get the dreamer's confidence the "loose one" said he was "the son of a good man, but his mother was a gorilla or a whore." Another schizoid patient, whose emotional life had been wrecked by this same contradiction between the wild and the cultivated, said she knew that her father was God, but her mother was a monkey.

In these statements we surely have the confessions of grafted personalities, who have an inner realization that the graft has failed, through the presence of an unbridgeable distance between the upper and the lower. The sense of failure is already manifest in the atavistic insistence on gorilla, whore and monkey. The value of the individual myth will depend on whether it develops sufficient cohesion to embrace saint and gorilla, eternal virgin and whore as violins and double bass are contained in the same dynamic musical structure.

Mythologically, the hero is the sun or, at least, the child of the sun; hence he represents the celestial powers; he is an aspect of deity. The *enantiodromia* from hero to devil is more than the descent from heaven to earth: it is the fall from heaven to hell. Set as dynamic opposites, like the top and bottom levels of a waterfall, god and devil are also inevitably linked together. It is as vital, therefore, to understand the essential nature of the devil as it was to appraise the achievement of the hero.

In our brief study of the Dracula myth we noted the condition that Dracula could not enter a house unless one of its inmates invited him to enter. We are aware from the spindly animal legs, as from the bestial greed and the diabolical zest which emanate from this figure, that the devil confronts us in this picture. We know, too, from the dreamer's former admiration of the "loose one," and from the fact that the devil wears the helmet and breastplate of his viking ancestor, that this devil is liable to be a hero in the subject's eyes.

The devil archetype is a general content of the collective unconscious. It is like Dracula in the fact that it is able to enter the personal sphere only when an element of the personality has, as it were, gone over to the devil's side. The god-hero and devil being reciprocal archetypal powers of the primordial myth, both play their characteristic rôles in the infantile psyche. Yet it is quite impossible that the devil could be expressed by the mind of an infant in this degenerate form. The same influence apparently has also affected the old sun-god in the red disc above the devil's head. We are reminded of Ra, who lost one of his eyes through a magical effect caused by the devil Set, who ran across his path disguised as a black pig.

No child could conceive this devil, because the child-mind knows nothing of compulsive sexual greed. In the child's imagination the devil may be horrific, dreadful, menacing and evil; but he has always a certain greatness, for he is an elemental spirit, the polar opposite of the god-image. Similarly, sexual themes play an obvious rôle in a child's myth, only his sexuality knows nothing of the passional, compulsive element. There lies the great difference.

There are general mythological precedents, for example, for the hero eating the heart. The sun-hero, who is swallowed by the whale, is liable to eat the monster's heart before cutting his way out. There is the primitive custom of eating the heart, or other organ, of the dead enemy in order to acquire his *mana*. Yet the feeling of a child could not have conceived either of these mythological themes in just this way. The themes suggested in this picture belong in truth to the primordial unconscious, yet the way they are expressed is pathological. This is specific and undeniable, to which the following two witnesses will testify.

The decrepit sun-god on the dark-red disc holds the same position in the field as the darkened sun in the first drawing, where the psychotic associations with the father formed a sinister constellation. The other witness comes from the second dream, where the theme of obtaining, cooking and eating viscera was directly associated with the " loose one " and his pathological influence.

The effect of the psychotic associations in the present drawing has been, therefore, to reduce god and devil to mean, degenerate caricatures. What is lacking, of course, is adequate feeling or subjective value, and, most suspiciously, the heart, the organ of feeling, is the very thing which the devil is eating. Lack of personal feeling was also the tragic deficiency in the father's psychology, a fact which in large measure accounted for his compulsive intuitiveness as a compensatory phenomenon. Thus the psychotic weakness, shared by father and son, by virtue of which the anima is able to exploit the renegade hero to a merciless degree, is brought into the light of day.

We discovered in XV., in the hero's infantile and supine attitude to the receding anima, an indication that the subject was entering upon the new phase under the wrong ægis. After this he became passively mediumistic to the anima, reflecting her wiles and moods with transparent compliance.

The parallel mythological situation would be the seduction of Amfortas, the King of the Grail, by Kundry. The never-healing wound over the heart, which Amfortas brought away from the perilous encounter with Kundry, was dealt by Klingsor, who discovered the two together in the wood. Not only was Amfortas seduced by Kundry, but in the same instant the Holy Spear was stolen from the Grail by Klingsor. It is this rape of the Spear from the King of the Grail which causes the never-healing wound.

The meaning of the myth is clear. Sexual power belongs primarily to the ancestors and to posterity. It is a royal (*i.e.*, impersonal) inheritance. The Spear is the symbol of divine manhood, the power to create beyond oneself and beyond one's time. With this royal potency there goes the creative individual passion. Kundry steals (*i.e.*, dissipates) this sacred energy by winning Amfortas to taste the pleasure of sexuality for its own sake, heedless of ancestral or divine sanction. From this moment the satisfaction of creative achievement and the passion which accompanies it is lost, while a never-satisfied desirousness takes its place. The self-accusation of the never-healing wound is, at bottom, the same as the craving for viscera which characterized the second dream. It is the squandering of the heart's store in objectless hunger, not desire for the treasure difficult of attainment, but desirousness and the bottomless pit.

According to the myth, dishonouring of love is the work of Klingsor, the evil power whom Kundry is doomed to serve. But how could Klingsor have stolen away the natural piety of the soul if it had not already been seduced by the tempting ideology which raises spirituality to the heavens as the breath of divine grace, while condemning sexuality as diabolical ?

The hero, as the ideal representative of consciousness, was, like the knights of the Grail, necessarily one-sided. In his original form he represented the absolute affirmation of the *Yang* and a consequent rejection of the *Yin* principle. This, as we have seen, is a brittle position that cannot be maintained, since the *Yang* always conceals a grain of the *Yin*. The seduction of Amfortas is the mythological personification of this truth. The history of the human mind demonstrates, in every epoch, the essential vulnerability of the ideal or absolute standpoint. It is not the ideal that is false, but rather the tendency of the human ego to become identified with it, thus stealing its light.

The influence that undermines the heroic state of identity with the idea is, primarily, a shadow-effect. Shadow is an effect of light, and every quality of the mind that attains an ideal value inevitably produces a corresponding shadow-effect in the unconscious. But since a socially adapted consciousness always tends to idealize the socially valued function of adaptation (the hero function), the shadow-personality necessarily gains a corresponding power in the unconscious. The ego-complex, being essentially a prestige formation, tends to become identified only with idealized or generally sanctioned qualities. Thus the shadow consists of the negative aspect of the personality—namely, that which the ego omits to associate with the idea of self. Because it is the reverse side of the ego, the side which is not visible to consciousness, it is also the vulnerable side. Every hero has a vulnerable spot, where he is exposed to the treacherous, invisible enemy. Siegfried had a place the size of a maple leaf on his back where the spear of Hagen could enter. As he bathed in the blood of the dragon which was to make him invulnerable, he failed to see a maple leaf that fell from the tree above, covering a spot on his back from contact with the life-renewing stream. Achilles, too, could be wounded in the heel. Samson's vulnerability lay in his hair, the primordial erotic significance of which is revealed in the treacherous rôle played by Delilah.

The apparent unity of purpose, for the sake of which a man will risk identification with a powerful idea, is therefore never absolute, since he is always liable to be betrayed or undermined by its rejected antithesis.[1]

Psychologically, the death of the hero was foreshadowed in the moment when the single, backward-turned eye became effective. For as soon as this other faculty of perception appears, which sees what is taking place behind him, the subject inevitably becomes aware of the shadow-effect. But the man who sees and takes account of his shadow is no longer a hero.

The realization and assimilation of the shadow is the most painful part of the whole analytical process. It is the task which will be evaded, if possible, to the very last. It is assisted by the anima as a teleological *force majeure* whereby the shadow is pushed into the arena of consciousness in a way which cannot escape recognition. This is achieved by the anima in the manner shown in the drawing—namely, primitive tendencies are exploited for unconscious anima goals in a way that exaggerates the subject's worst qualities. The primitive anima's intrigue

[1] Hitler's choice of the *swastika*, or sun-wheel, as the heroic symbol of the Third Reich betrayed his conscious identification with a cosmic idea. What was, presumably, not recognized was the fact that the four legs of the Nazi swastika run in the wrong direction—*i.e.*, against the path of the sun and the cosmic order. Thus at the inception of Nazi rule, Hitler's shadow uttered his own doom.

with the shadow is normally kept invisible by the mechanism of projection, whereby unacceptable motives and qualities are transferred to other people. A neurotic personality has an almost inexhaustible capacity for evasion and self-deception; without these expedients, the neurosis could not survive. But by its very power to isolate and cripple a man in all his essential relations a neurosis has also the effect of making him value the approval and acceptance of his fellow-beings in a quite exceptional way. It is largely the force of this need that holds a neurotic patient in the analytical relationship, thereby enabling him to convert the unrelatedness of his neurotic island into an acceptance of the mainland, with its basic condition of reciprocity.

The condition of neurotic isolation, in which the hero is practically the prisoner of the anima-enchantress, is a favourite mythological theme. Antinoë, the famous spider-queen of the Sahara in Benoît's *L'Atlantide*, is an anima-figure of this kind. Ulysses held by Calypso on her island; also Heracles held enchanted by Omphale; or, again, Leo by Ayesha, in Rider Haggard's myth, are all typical examples. In the Parsifal myth Amfortas is not held a prisoner by Kundry, but the wound left by her has the same effect—namely, neurotic isolation and suspense.

To return to our discussion, we must admit the crucial distinction—namely, that the Amfortas myth has a valid beauty and distinction which draws the mind to reflect upon its meaning—while the present picture is morbid and repulsive. The tragedy of the never-healing wound touches the heart, but the patient's devil freezes with its grossness. We understand the meaning of the myth when Kundry vainly tries to heal the wound, of which she herself is the cause, with a salve brought by her from Arabia, for the Christian soul cannot be wooed to idle content by means of sensuality. Is it permissible, therefore, to assume that the patient's puritan ancestry may have taken a hand in this diabolical picture of sensuality? The cold-blooded thing which destroys the heart must be portrayed in a heartless way.

So hideous a picture of the devil surely implies a perilous gulf between the opposites, a gulf which cannot be bridged by rational intention. Reconciliation of the opposites is the principal constructive function of the anima, but, according to the evidence of the myths the only way known to the anima whereby mutually distrustful opposites can be reconciled, is by means of seduction. The Sumerian epic Gilgamish contains the story of the seduction of the primordial man, Enkidu, by a sacred prostitute of Ishtar, who was sent by Gilgamish to the drinking place where the wild man came every day to drink. Gilgamish, the mythical builder of Erech, became so intolerable to his subjects through his tyrannical civilizing mania, that they prayed Anu, the sky-god, to send a champion against him. Enkidu was created, as it were, from this resistant collective libido. He represents the million-year-old primordial being, activated in the collective unconscious by the recession of the libido. Such a being would naturally be sceptical of and averse from the whole civilizing experiment. Through the anima's seduction of Enkidu, the long-sundered opposites are eventually reconciled, though Enkidu curses most dreadfully the woman who seduced him, a curse which he subsequently revokes when commanded to wisdom by a dream.

In the present instance the anima seduces the subject to be the dupe once again of the psychotic shadow, a ruse by which she eventually brings the opposites together. We must therefore accept the disagreeable conclusion that a man may be seduced by the anima into a kind of mitigated insanity in order that he may accept, assimilate and understand the problem of the opposites in his own nature. The patient, we must remember, came to be analysed because, figuratively speaking, he had seen smoke coming up through the cracks in the floor. There could be no more security or peace of mind for him so long as the psychotic possibility were merely repressed. The repressed thing must be *known*, and he could know it only through experiencing it.

We can suspect that the anima is exploiting a false hypothesis, because of the fact that all the contents seem to be soaring out of the picture. Is it possible to discover what this false hypothesis might be and whence the devil-quality has been derived?

Once again we find our clue in the revealing craziness of the second dream. The reader will recall that the " loose one " favoured the idea of acquiring meat out of the Thames, not as salvaged goods, but with the furtive notion of gaining illicit supplies. It is the characteristic aim of black magic to convert to mean, personal ends energy-supplies which are meant for general service. With this context in mind, we know that the diabolical character of this present figure is not incidental; its essential devilishness is a true portrait. It is as though a knight of the Grail had become transmuted into Klingsor and, like Klingsor, had contrived to get possession of the sacred Spear for magical purposes. We may be sure also, from the change undergone by the sword since the heroic combat, that it has got into the wrong hands. In XVI. it was a diminutive thing, like a stiletto or paper-knife, in the right hand of the child-hero. In XVII. it was obviously a toy sword lying on the ground. In the present drawing it is also small and held in the left hand—*i.e.*, it has gone over to the sinister side.

As frequently happens with borderline subjects at one time or another, the patient had become interested in magic during this period. He was not very communicative about it: he read certain plausible books on the subject, and became decidedly vulnerable to any idea which might seem to yield power over the unconscious. For many patients the temptation to flirt with magic is very seductive. In his worst times the borderline subject has no faith, no enthusiasm, and no available passion; accordingly, the cold-hearted counsel of Mephisto is bound to attract him.

What, then, is black magic, and why is it so attractive? According to the Oxford Dictionary, magic is " the pretended art of influencing the course of events by compelling the agency of spiritual beings, or by bringing into operation some occult controlling principles of nature." Black magic is the " kind of magic that involves the invocation of devils." These definitions provide a fair description of magic, but they omit the essential psychological criterion—namely, the character of the motive.

The white and the black magicians are primordial images

of the collective unconscious: the former embraces such figures as the wise one, the sage, the healer, the servant of the gods, etc., whereas the latter, however disguised, is always the devil. The principle of the white magician is service, the spiritual powers which work through him being obedient to his call only in so far as he genuinely serves the principle of good. The black magician, on the other hand, knows nothing of the principle of service. He will make use of the infernal powers to achieve his goal, but his relation to the devil is motivated by a will-to-power which despises the idea of service. The spirit of power or desirousness which urges a man towards the notion of making the devil his accomplice ends, as we see in our drawing, in a tyrannical compulsion. To the unwary it seems easier to be committed to the devil than to submit to service and discipline, inasmuch as a lust is more attractive than a task. But the end-result is a bondage to the dark principle, which is all the more complete because of a secret aim to wield the devil's power.

Black magic is closely bound up with sinister sexual practices which invariably involve a satanic negation of love. The object of the magician is to divert the energies of sex from the service of life to power purposes or to systematized sensuality.

From the psychological point of view, therefore, the subjective motive or attitude is the determining factor: most men are warned by their own instinct when the devil makes his bid. But the danger of the borderline individual in relation to magic lies in the fact that the schizophrenic barrier deprives him not only of insight into his deeper motives, but also of normal instinctive vigilance when moral danger threatens.

According to Frazer, magic is a "spurious system of natural law, as well as a fallacious guide of conduct: it is a false science as well as an abortive art."[1] This account suffers from a certain rhetorical prejudice, since it does not allow for the fact that the realms of magic and empirical science often exist side by side in the native mind. The native who uses magic, for example, in order to ensure uncontrollable

[1] *The Golden Bough*.

factors—such as fertility and rain—will at the same time adopt to the factors within his control a completely empirical, scientific attitude. Magic plays a vastly greater rôle in the lives of uncivilized peoples than with us, because of the greater predominance of uncontrollable factors in their lives. But complete honesty would have to confess that many of the spells and rites performed in our practice of medicine have no better scientific foundation than the primitive practices we deride. And when we come to the unknown territory of the unconscious, the magical hypothesis has proved to be far more popular than the scientific approach, though in deference to intellectual decencies the promoters of the hypothesis are not averse from giving it one or two coats of scientific paint.

From Frazer's acid comment, quoted above, one gains the impression that the writer suspects a nearer relation between magic and science than he cares to admit. Indeed, the more we stress the contrast, the more are we impressed by the relationship. Magic, we know, represents man's relation to natural forces at the primordial level: science comprises our relation to nature on the cultural plane. Magic, in other words, represents the indigenous mode of the primordial psyche, while science is the product of the cultural. For example, magic does not develop; it never modifies its pretensions when they have been proved to be unavailing. The primordial psyche does not look for proof: it is the immemorial home of the *a priori*, the rites and incantations of magic being handed down unchanged from generation to generation. They do not need to develop, because their efficacy for the primordial psyche is self-evident. Science, on the other hand, is related constantly to facts: it listens, observes, verifies, always adapting its conclusions to the mobile face of reality. Magic rests upon emotional presuppositions, science upon intellectual data and observation. Whereas the former bears the unmistakable traits of the all-or-none modality of unconscious, instinctual processes, the latter, when true to its principle, is based upon the relativity of truth, the keynote of the cultural.

In the practice of magic there are three essentials to be

observed—namely, the spell, the rite, and the condition of the performer. The spell, or magical formula, contains the words of power which must be repeated in set order, in the right way, and at the right time. The rite consists of a set of actions by which the nature of the desired magical effect is either dramatically or symbolically represented. It usually contains, therefore, a ritual analogy to the effect desired, as, for instance, the sprinkling of water on the ground in the making-of-rain magic, or the eating of a dead enemy's heart or brain in order to acquire his qualities.

The third essential, which is highly significant psychologically, is the condition of the performer or sacrificer. In all communities this is a matter of the first importance. The performer is invariably hedged around by special taboos and conditions, all of which are concerned with safeguarding him from impurity or contamination. The sacredness of the priest rests fundamentally upon his immense social value as a magical performer rather than upon his importance as an ethical exemplar. The vital factor is his emotional state or attitude, because, according to Malinowski, the sympathetic emotional condition of the performer is the basis upon which the magical procedure rests.

The performer, in fact, is the medium of the primordial psyche, and whenever we have to do with mediumship, whether on the frontiers of spiritualism or in political high places, we find the same characteristic protopathic psychology. The medium does not reflect, weigh, consider; neither does he converse, discuss, or exchange views. He appears to have no objective interest of any kind beyond the phenomena for which he is accountable, nor does he wish to understand how or why things happen. The difference in psychological attitude between the medium and the scientific investigator who takes part in the séances is essentially the same as that between an indigenous and a civilized, or a child and an adult. The cultural type, who has to rely upon his intellect, concerns himself with his mental content when called upon to lead, direct, or teach; whereas the primordial type, even with the fate of peoples dependent upon him, prepares his emotional attitude rather than his mind. He must guard himself from disturbing influences (usually he is attended by a psychic bodyguard); he must be abstemious, allowing himself no stimulants or exciting diversions. The medium is rarely interested in ideas and trusts himself to no intimate friendships, because the impact of potent ideas or personalities easily disturbs the sensitive condition of the sympathetic system upon which his mediumistic function depends. He rarely talks on level terms, because conversation tends to encourage an adaptable, relativist frame of mind, and this, just because it belongs to a higher level of evolution, puts his own primordial function out of court.

The medium tends, therefore, to lead a psychologically sheltered life, avoiding the company of critical educated people, except when the conditions of his function are conceded. To function at all, he has to dictate conditions because (*a*) the primordial psyche is essentially archaic and unadaptable; (*b*) without the impetus of over-compensation he would be overwhelmed by feelings of inferiority; (*c*) the group for whom he functions as medium, being in the archaic framework of the herd, expects dictation rather than reasoning.

As a transmitter, the medium must hold himself constantly malleable and receptive to the energy currents of the group psyche. Accordingly, he gives the appearance of being an opportunist, caring little for the obligations and values which to the cultural man are all-important. But the true reason for thus isolating himself from normal human intercourse is because the medium does not possess a normal human psychology. He is a function of events very much as a weathercock is a function of the wind. Without the stream of events and the unconscious currents within the stream the medium has no real psychological existence.

From these general observations we can understand why the schizoid type should be well fitted to play the rôle of magician, and the hysterical type that of medium. The medium is a man apart: he cannot mix with his fellows easily and naturally. He is fated not to belong to the sheepfold, for whenever he makes the attempt the sheep immediately smell him out and take him for a wolf. Like most men who are forced by their own make-up to a rather solitary existence, the medium is haunted by a doubt as to the validity of his own being—a condition which easily leads to a morbid dependence upon the unconscious; this in turn is aggravated by the fact that he is intellectually opaque to its significance. In order to function as medium, a positive attitude towards the specific group or collectivity is indispensable. Hence the better type of individual tends, if he is aware of it at all, to use his psychic mediumship under the sign of service, whilst the more pathological gravitates towards the idea of magic and the worship of power.

In the case of our patient, the choice between these alternatives was apparently a foregone conclusion, inasmuch as his medical qualification had already committed him to a *mêtier* of service. But, in fact, it was a very live alternative, because his experience of the unconscious had already put a secret knowledge into his hand besides giving him a mediumistic relation to unconscious events.

The drawing emphasizes the sinister character of the secret craving for power. For the heart is the symbol of the warm-blooded human pact from which the qualities of loyalty, service, devotion, veneration—the richest attributes of the soul—are derived. It is because black magic battens upon this fundamental human birthright, seeking to divert its energies to aims that are directly destructive of all that the heart reveres, that its magic is black.

Although the devil-attitude is felt as coldly egotistical, it differs from the egotism of the infantile personality in the essential criterion of choice. The latter is egotistical not through choice, but because he has never been anything else; the heart has not yet been touched by the sacred fire. But the attitude depicted in the drawing is the product of choice. Such a man sees and hears quite clearly the demands of life: the task ahead of him, the discipline and the loyalty which corporate life requires. Yet he rejects the call. He prefers the way of power, the secret knowledge, the solitary, insulated existence. The dubious conversation of the devil attracts him. Power appeals to him more than service; even nature appears to favour the devourer, allowing it to prey unceasingly and without pity upon the prolific. The egotism which proceeds from such an attitude is not mere selfishness: it proclaims its peculiar brand of half-truth with proselytizing fervour, and practises seduction with single-minded purpose. Putting ritual on one side, this spirit is identical with primitive black magic in its attempt to alienate living things from their innate functional allegiance, and to use them in the wrong way and for the wrong ends.[1]

In thus bracketing the medium with the magician, as belonging at bottom to the same psychological constellation, we may be in danger of passing a negative judgment upon the former which would be quite unjustified. It would be an ill service indeed to my particular calling, for without the positive development of a mediumistic function in relation to unconscious events, there could be no possibility of a true understanding of individual psychology. Without exception the most gifted analysts are those with a well-disciplined mediumistic function. But, on the other hand, no one would be so foolish as to class them as mediums. With them, the mediumistic personality is a well-trained servant, not an unscrupulous egotist. Here we come to the acid test. The essential character of an individual is conditioned, not so much by the nature of his mental functions, but far more by the basic attitude, by virtue of which every function is given either an egotistical or a co-operative orientation. Hence the vital opposition symbolized by the white and the black magician.

V

Drawing XIX

The symbols are born. The child and the peacock fall through the slit made in the womb-cavity, and are caught on the vast outstretched hand of the receding sun-god below. The exploded hero is pitchforked aloft on the point of the anima moon-crescent. A few broken, twisted lines are all that remain of the crenellated schizophrenic wall. Moreover, the empty womb-cavity, the two lôbes of blue, and the jaws are all that remain of the once formidable monster. The arm extended from the sun is independent of its eight rays of gold and red. Two of these rays are effective, the one combining

[1] *Cf.* the reversed *swastika* of Adolf Hitler.

with the upper point of the moon-crescent in hastening the upward despatch of the exploded magician, while the other is directed towards the slit in the cavity from which the child and the peacock have just emerged.

As in the last drawing, the background of the picture has been produced by haphazard strokes of a broad brush dipped in silver. The greater number of these strokes are crescentic in character, a fact which conforms with the obvious lunar influence of the drawings described in this chapter. The background of frosted silver used in this and the previous drawing is characteristic of anima influence in her equivocal rôle of Hecate. Holding the picture up to the light, a tangled mass of fearsome, infernal shapes and faces begin to take form (especially on the left side of the drawing) under this moon influence. These forms are of like nature with those weird apparitional projections of the unconscious, occasionally experienced in a state of weakened consciousness, when the threshold is temporarily overrun by archaic contents of the unconscious. Many people with a low threshold of consciousness are fearful of lonely, moonlit promenades, because of the dæmonic forms which gesticulate at them from trees and hedgerows.

Thus everything in this picture reiterates dissolution. Something essential is delivered; the rest disintegrates. The sun is disintegrating; the features of the old god are scarcely discernible. The crenellated wall crumbles, and the whole imposing structure of the monster, which in Drawing IX. dominated the scene with massive substantiality, " melts into air, into thin air."

One is reminded of the torn pupa-case of a butterfly or, more appropriately, of a dragon-fly after the insect has emerged, or of the crumpled fragments of a bird's egg after the hatching. This torn case of the once solid container is extraordinarily suggestive, especially the crisp, contracted fragments of the schizophrenic wall.

In respect to these fragments, the unconscious does not admit, apparently, that the devouring monster is as moribund as the patient would like to think. The top fragment is more vigorously painted than the rest, and forms the profile of a face, gazing angrily and aghast at the anima's performance. In the middle of this fragment is a kind of eye. Above the eye is an anxiously corrugated brow. Sloping back from the brow, and forming the top of the head, is the monster's lower jaw. The combination of red lip and teeth above it lends the head an amusing suggestion of " risen hair, stiff with fear."

* * * * *

Intellectually, we tend to conceive the autonomous psyche as a structural organ derived, to some extent, from our conception of the brain. But here it is presented from a very different standpoint. If this drawing, with its obvious analogies, is to be credited, we must assume that an autonomous complex formation can be viewed as a container in which a definite evolutionary process is brought to maturity. So long as its dynamic contents are being nourished, guarded, and developed within the complex, it presents the aspect of a formidable psychic factor. But when the evolutionary development is completed, and the contents have emerged into consciousness, the containing structure either disintegrates or goes through a process of involution analogous to that of the uterus after parturition. On the other hand, if the contents of the complex are not taken over by consciousness, owing to a pathological rigidity of the mind, the autonomous complex is liable to swell, resulting in a dangerous overweighting of the unconscious. Jung has described this condition fully in his work on dementia præcox cited in the first chapter. It was from these developed cases, in which the pathological complex had engulfed the major portion of the mind, that the original conception of dementia præcox was derived. That the danger of being devoured by the unconscious had existed in the present case is suggested by the terrific jaws and the protective, paranoiac wall of the complex depicted in these drawings.

The realistic energy with which the anima hoists the counterfeit hero out of the picture is instinct with ruthless purpose. He has served her ends and she disposes of him, just as nature discards her dead leaves in autumn. But, before he is finally despatched, we must pay him the tribute of an obituary discussion. Apparently he was needed by the anima for two purposes. First, he had to retrieve two of the life-giving symbols from the interior of the monster. Secondly, he had to break through the schizoid barricade, performing a kind of Cæsarian section, in order to deliver the remaining pair of symbols from the uterine cavity.

As regards the first of these two tasks, it is significant and appropriate that the anima selected the frenzied, devouring shadow-figure to retrieve her life-giving symbols from the devouring jaws. The analogy of the frenzied Golem again comes to mind. The cogency of the anima's choice is based upon a primitive aspect of autonomous functioning, termed *thinking by analogy*. It is the basis upon which the whole structure of primitive magic rests. According to the magician's logic, " like attracts like " develops into " like controls like." The same symbolical method is found in the Indian cosmogonic myth in which Prajapati, having created the world, sits brooding because he is alone. Born of his fiery yearning, Agni (fire) comes forth out of his mouth. Because Agni issues out of Prajapati's mouth, he is also the consuming one. But at that time the whole world was bare: there was nothing to devour, excepting Prajapati himself. So Agni turns upon his creator with gaping jaws, saying, " Sacrifice." Then Prajapati said, " This my own greatness speaketh unto me," and he sacrificed. Thus he became the sun that burneth and the wind that purifieth.

In the individual myth the psychological principle is the same. Prajapati is the symbolical personification of the introverted creative passion. When this passion becomes a consuming fire, it not only creates its object, it also creates its subject. The creative mind is itself created through the longing and the sacrifice demanded by creative work.

In like fashion, the patient's devouring shadow-aspect is, at bottom, an expression of the unbridled, devouring aspect of the archaic unconscious—that aspect, in fact, which came roaring upon our subject in Drawing VIII. This was the apparitional form which his craving, infantile attitude evoked. The major problem of his psychology came upon him in dæmonic form, roaring, " Sacrifice !" If he had then tried to escape from the problem, the life-giving symbols would have been forfeited. The sacrifice he had to make was his exclusive intellectual attitude, his functional hero. As soon as the heroic task was accomplished and the archaic *dynamis* assimilated, the next task to which the hero-function (like Heracles) had to submit was the rule of the feminine principle. Under the direction of the anima, every vestige of heroic superiority had to be abandoned, its place being taken by the regressive, devouring personality which was forced to the front, in order to retrieve the green life-stuff and the living heart from the primordial womb of the unconscious.

By compelling the subject to undergo the humiliation of becoming himself the devouring one, the anima seems to be insisting on the reality of the experience. The anima, after all, has some right to be insistent, inasmuch as the earlier transformation of the ancestral super-ego into the devouring monster offered the same fundamental insight. A truth that has to be rehearsed many times, because of the peculiar opacity of consciousness, is apt to gain in pungency of expression. The patient found it easy to rationalize these experiences by taking the attitude of a detached scientific observer. Throughout his analysis he was liable to adopt a provisional attitude, as though the experiences were actually referring to somebody else. This is not surprising when we remember that, in the East, introverted realization is considered worthy of a long and extremely rigorous discipline.

In the *Brahman-Atman* teaching in India a form of introverted brooding called *tapas* is practised, which has for its aim the liberation of the self from every affective tie to the object. Through the withdrawal of libido from the objective world, the primordial images of the unconscious become activated, and the inner world of the subject is then experienced intensively as a functional equivalent of outer reality. The golden principle of this teaching is expressed in the words *tat twam asi* (that art thou). The essence of the discipline consists in referring every experience to the self, so that the identity of the inner and the outer Atman is experienced. So long as the subject-object relation remains solely upon the phenomenal extraverted level, the subjective

Atman being broken into a thousand objective fragments, the self as a totality is never realized. The breaking of the fetters of desire is identical, therefore, with the deliberate piercing of every illusion in order that the reality of the self may become manifest.

By compelling the shadow-hero to seize the green life-stuff in his teeth, and to gorge himself with the living heart of feeling (things which he himself has taken from the devourer's jaws), the anima makes the subject realize *tat twam asi*. In other words, by referring the act of devouring from the primordial image to the subject, in his least acceptable shadow-aspect, she makes him realize himself as the devouring one. Thus the lesson of the myth is brought right home, a function which the feminine anima is peculiarly well fitted to perform.

The second function carried out by the shadow-hero is the obstetrical incision of the complex container, whereby the two remaining symbols are delivered into the outstretched hand of the sun. This act is done with the sword carried in the left hand—*i.e.*, on the side of the unconscious. The obstetrical character of this scene is emphasized by the oval slit that appears on the under side of the uterine cavity in XIX.

If we apply the synchronicity formula to the scene of XVIII., it would read: the shadow-hero seizes the living symbols from the monster, *and* becomes himself the frenzied devouring one, *and* pierces the container with his sword held in the left hand. Put in this way the psychological connection becomes clear. Through identifying himself with the devouring monster, the subject would refer the whole bearing of the myth to his own unconscious attitude, therewith gaining true insight into the peculiar manifestations of the unconscious. He would learn that the apparitional forms assumed by archaic contents are aspects of his impersonal psychology conditioned by his basic attitude. As this realization developed, the aspect of the unconscious would change from the devouring into the creative. But the fact that the operation is here performed with the left hand indicates that the subject does not yet possess this insight; it is rather an intuitive anticipation of developing possibilities.

In Drawing XIX. the hoisting of the shadow-hero aloft reminds one forcibly of the way the little tin soldier was carried off by the dragon's sucker-feet. The position of the latter figure in XI. is almost identical with that of the shadow-hero in XIX. It would appear, therefore, that both are summarily disposed of as outworn hypotheses, both representing attitudes that are based upon a false image of reality.

There is an interesting feature of XIX. which tends to bear out this interpretation. I refer to the descent of the sun to the bottom of the picture, where the extended arm and hand are in the act of receiving the newly born symbols. In the previous drawing the sun was above the devouring hero, the symbols being not yet delivered from the gravid uterus. It may help us to understand this symbolism if we regard the outstretched arm of the sun as the arm of a balance. From our discussion of the rising sun in VI. we know that the sun represents the principle of effective consciousness. The moment of birth of the living symbols (the babe and the peacock) from the unconscious represents the moment of rebirth. A new basic attitude passes from the potential into the actual. This would correspond with the weighing down of the arm of the scales on the side of effective reality; the result, on the side of unreality, would be to fling the insubstantial fantasy to the skies. In dreams the fantasy-personality, being lighter than air, always tends to float, or fly, or soar.

In the previous drawing the reverse situation was depicted —namely, the devourer was weighing down the scales, while the sun-principle was without effect. From these two drawings it would appear that when the unconscious is gravid with unborn potentialities, consciousness is correspondingly handicapped. But when the unconscious yields up its contents to consciousness, it becomes light as air, whilst consciousness becomes weighty and creative.

Perhaps the most significant point in the drawing is the fact that the long zenith-seeking ray of the sun is seen combining with the tip of the moon-crescent to hoist the sham hero aloft. The sun joining forces with the moon would signify that the false hypothesis is rejected by the total subject, by the conscious as well as by the unconscious.

It is interesting to observe the change taking place in the subjective attitude towards this retrogressing hero. In XVI. and XVII. there is no evidence of insight into the change that has overtaken the hero. The subject is as naive as the hero. But in XVIII. the devil, in his greedy haste to get at the heart, forgets his mask of childish naivety, revealing himself as he is. And yet, though the invitation is usually clandestine, the devil can enter upon the scene only when invited. From internal evidence, it is clear that contradictory motives were at play in the making of XVIII. On the one side the zest and spontaneity, the whole diabolical vitality of the figure, betray the presence of a devil's disciple in the patient's psychology. On the other side he is figured as dancing on air and being hoisted on high by the anima. He is recognized, therefore, by another aspect of the patient's mind as a fantasy, an impostor, something without weight. The very repulsiveness of the figure suggests a haste to repudiate something that has slipped out unawares.

In Drawing XVIII., therefore, there is a conflict of standpoint; in XIX. there is none. The paunchy little figure, impaled on the tip of the crescent, is a completely exploded hypothesis: his globular body also suggests the inflated condition which gave the devil his opportunity.

The extraordinary effect produced by a radical change of attitude is beautifully exemplified in this utterly changed devil. If analytical candour and impersonal criticism can bring about these hygienic clarifications, it would be hardly too much to expect a new kind of individual consciousness to come into being along the analytical way.

VI

We must now attempt to relate our clinical observations to the underlying mythological pattern of the hero and devouring monster. This pattern is concerned with that phase of unconscious evolution which Jung, after Frobenius, has described as the night-journey under the sea. All are familiar with the story of the sun-hero, who, having been devoured by the monster, is carried under the sea in the monster's belly to the eastern ocean, where he once more emerges rejuvenated and victorious. During the night-journey the hero cuts out the heart or liver of the monster to satisfy his hunger. As a result the whale dies, is washed ashore, and the hero hews his way out into the light.

In Drawing XIX. the features of the sun have already become indistinct. If this mythological analogy represents the actual psychological situation, we might expect to find a rejuvenated sun in the drawing that follows. Technically, however, we are not justified in using the analogical method, unless we hold strictly to the rule that the correspondence between the mythic pattern and the subjective material shall embrace the essential features of both, and that what dissimilarities there may be are relatively inessential.

With respect to the essentials, we find that the *dramatis personæ* are identical—namely, the devouring monster, the hero, and the theme of the aging or westering sun. The motif of the hero being seized by hunger and eating an essential organ is present in both, also the act of cutting a hole with the sword through the body-wall, whereby the victorious emergence takes place. But the essential idea of the night-journey under the sea is concerned with the sea or the monster functioning as a maternal womb which, being impregnated by the aging sun which was devoured, brings forth a new sun in the east. The sun is the prototype of the divine being who saves himself from destruction by willing his own death and renewal. This theme is the psychological essence of the myth in both cases.

The points of dissimilarity are sufficiently striking to make it perfectly certain that the mythological parallel was at no time present in the patient's consciousness. For if the analogy had been conscious, his material would undoubtedly have revealed a manifest adhesion to the main structure of the myth. For example, in the patient's material the hero is not himself devoured by the monster, although he is undoubtedly engulfed by the devouring mood. Nor, indeed, can we say that the living heart and the green life-stuff are authentic organs of the monster, although they only begin to function organically after they have become incorporated within its body. Nor is the decadent hero devoured and consumed by the monster, though we see him carried aloft and closely identified with the disintegrating remains of the monster; in the next drawing he is even found impaled upon one of the great teeth of the monster's lower jaw.

By applying the generalized mythic pattern to our patient's material, therefore, we find that the essential psychological theme is brought into relief in much the same way as a specific dye-stain brings into prominence certain structural components of a pathological section. Moreover, without the application of the general mythic analogy, the essential or deep significance of the patient's material might easily be overlooked. This is the practical justification of Jung's method of *amplification* by means of mythological parallels. For not only have we demonstrated an autochthonous similarity between the archaic, generalized pattern and the psychic evolution of a modern individual; but we have also shown that the essential explanation of the individual material depends upon this similarity being demonstrated.

The recognition of the mythological situation is of the utmost importance for the doctor, as well as for the patient, inasmuch as the prognosis largely depends upon the fulfilment of the rebirth process. When, for instance, as frequently happens, the phase of the night-journey is accompanied by regressive and even suicidal fantasies, how is it possible for the doctor to reassure the patient with any conviction if he has not recognized the mythic counterpart of the patient's experience? In the case of our patient, for example, he naturally identified himself with the shadow-hero of these drawings, and when he sensed the approaching death of the hero his anxiety was obvious. In such a situation the reference to the myth is invaluable, since it embraces the idea of death as a necessary function of the new life. If the old attitude or personality does not die, the new cannot be born. Thus the mythological moment of birth is also, and inevitably, preceded by the moment of death.

In a recent paper on *Psychotherapy in India* Professor Zimmer of Heidelberg describes the traditional method by which the *guru* instructs his charges in the appropriate legend or myth corresponding to the particular phase of development which they are about to undergo. Each member of the Indian family is thus taught to meet the crucial phase and predictable transition in his life with the support of the corresponding mythological stream or archetype. By this means an inherent continuity is established between the primordial psyche and cultural development, and a reassuring liaison established between individual consciousness and the mythic images of the racial unconscious.

This liaison has a psychological significance which cannot be overestimated, for the myth gives expression to those archaic forms of the libido upon which the prohibitions of rational consciousness fall most heavily. In the myth of the night-journey under the sea, for example, the sun-hero who has been born from the sea (*i.e.*, the mother) descends into the mother again. He is devoured by her and also impregnates her (whether as monster or devouring sea), and thus becomes the father of the new sun by his own mother.

Throughout the whole range of archaic mythology we find this drama of incest unfolding in an eternal cycle; and always the mother plays the dual rôle of devouring monster and maternal womb. We can hardly escape the conclusion that gods and heroes are perpetuated by incest. Sometimes the incestuous motive is disguised, but usually it is quite flagrant. To the child-mind, incest is the only natural union. It seems even to be the prerogative of the primordial state, as it was of the Pharaohs. Clearly there exists some fundamental need of the human soul which seeks this form of expression and which will not be denied: a need which breaks against the tough walls of social taboo, producing inarticulate resistance against social demands or rebellion against authority. Then, at last, it turns back to the most ancient of all human inventions, the myth, seeking there the clear air of Olympian freedom. What is there expressed under the ægis of the early gods is not the lawlessness of unbridled instinct, but rather the early wisdom and the early piety which guided the human soul before collective lawgivers had effaced its original virtue.

It cannot be too emphatically asserted that this myth-creating tendency of the psyche is not merely an outlet for prohibited archaic impulses. Rather is it an expression of the deepest longing of the soul needing to create a world in which its essential nature can freely manifest itself. How can a man make an honourable pact with his primordial nature if its mythic form is interpreted as nothing but a regression to the infantile-archaic level? Why the incest-motif should be so deeply rooted in the essential nature of the soul is beyond the scope of rational explanation. All we know is that the libido has a tendency to divide against itself, the one portion running backwards to its primordial source, the other flowing onwards to its future fulfilment. Both tendencies are essentially purposive, and both need to find adequate expression.

* * * * *

Before leaving this moon-aspect of the material, there is yet another singular and rather obscure feature to account for, a feature which has appeared consistently in those drawings where the formative or germinating function of the unconscious has been the ruling theme. I refer to the two lobes painted in clear blue. In the present drawing the lower of these lobes presents for the first time a definite change of character. Before it has usually appeared as an elongated form with a regular outline, joined to the upper lobe by a thin commissure. Now its shape is broken, somewhat conveying the suggestion of a rain-cloud emptying itself in a shower of rain. This suggestion is enhanced by the three blue lines passing through it, which seem to control in some way the fall of the living symbols. These lines appear to be of the same substance as the blue lobe; hence they may be regarded as part of its activity or function.

If the reader will turn once again to Drawing III., in which these blue masses first appear, he will observe that the upper lobe, with its four articulating projections, is given an outline in ink; while the lower mass is the only form in the picture which lacks a containing line. This insulated lower lobe, therefore, has somewhat the character of *non arrivée*.

I will briefly recapitulate the conclusions we derived from Drawing III., in order that the general bearing of this symbolism may be appreciated. On the right half of the picture we discovered the pent-up forces of frustrated potentiality. We have since observed how the ineffectual executive function of the will, symbolized by the contents of the stomach-container, achieved a kind of alchemical transformation. We also observed the inverted, parasitic, infantile attitude converted into effectual power through the mediation of the anima. But at the time that this drawing was made the work of transformation was only in embryo. It showed the first movement of these unfulfilled energy-systems, directed in converging streams upon the symbol of the maternal source. It is as though, in the embryonic imagery of this level, the pent-up libido of the infantile system were centred exclusively in the full breast as the primordial fountain of life. The fundamental duality of the libido is manifested in the way one portion takes the regressive, auto-erotic direction in the inverted nipple and parasitic mouth, while the other, symbolized by the lower head, points onwards and outwards to the task ahead. The salvage work, for which the positive energy had to be mobilized, was concerned with the limbless ghost with vizored head in the centre of the left half, and with the piece of red substance in the witch's mouth which subsequently develops into the egg with the peacock.

In considering the confluence of inverted libido towards the left, we formed the idea that the subjective duality of the maternal rôle was expressed in the two faces above and below the breast: the upper one sucking the libido back, the other forming and directing it purposively in the furtherance of life. We also considered the possibility that the two blue masses might represent an unconscious reserve of psychic energy belonging to the spiritual logos-principle which was straining towards objective application. We spoke of it as *Urgeist*, or original spirit. We discovered it to be the natural antithesis of the flaccid red plume, which, from its devious functional connections, we identified as the tendency to onanistic, auto-erotic fantasy wastage. The powerful mobilization of blue elements belongs to the same psychological motivation which later achieves personification as the ancestral god or super-ego. We traced this connection in Drawing VI., where the rising sun of effective consciousness had the same fourfold differentiation as we noticed in the upward extension of the upper blue lobe in Drawing III.

Again in Drawing IX. we observed the inturned eye of psychic intuition forming in the top of the upper lobe, whereby this function also becomes associated with the logos-principle, whereas the lower lobe remains passive and unaccounted for up to the moment of the downward release or hatching out of the two living symbols, when it assumes a watery character, somewhat resembling a rain-cloud. If we allow ourselves to follow this hint of a watery substance, we are struck by the fact that the disposition of the two lobes, with their connecting commissure, envelops that portion of the uterine cavity where the creative symbols are forming. This disposition is especially clear in Drawing IX., where the analogy with the amniotic membranes and fluid can hardly be resisted. Thus the breaking of the waters at the moment of birth is delicately associated with the idea of the fertilizing rain descending from the heavens. This train of thought harmonizes with religious myths, in which the moment of divine birth on the earth is accompanied by sympathetic cosmic manifestations in the heavens.

If these different associations and reflections are cogent, we should be able to assemble them within the compass of a single idea. Our explanation of the regular appearance of these blue masses needs to embrace the following facts. They made their appearance (Drawing III.) when the hitherto existing conception of the self had become bankrupt and the pent-up, repressed elements were seeking regenerated life. From the outset we recognized an upper, actively differentiating function and a lower, passive, undifferentiated part. Later we discovered that the one tends to function in an upward direction, the other in a downward. As a two-lobed organ they form a protective, surrounding covering, which ensures the welfare of the new functions germinating in the womb of the unconscious. The upper lobe was also associated with the formation of an introverting organ of vision, while the lower lobe participated in the timely delivery of the new-born functions. Finally, their first appearance, where they stood in direct functional relation with the principal subjective task, must be borne in mind, inasmuch as it is this character of purposeful concentration of energy upon a given task which gives meaning to the whole series of drawings.

The only solution I am able to offer which satisfies all these conditions is that these blue elements represent that other dynamic process of the mind which conscious one-sidedness had excluded. Intellectually, the patient was committed to the mechanistic hypothesis which had already lured him into the Freudian fallacy of attempting to explain the psyche as a kind of by-product of biological frustration. A conception of psychic reality that contains only one root-source of energy must inevitably coerce every association and every explanatory attempt into harmony with its single principle.

The right half of Drawing III. is a graphic statement of the impotent frustration which afflicts the purposive forces of the mind when imprisoned by this fallacy. Here the phallic dæmon has absolute rule. But, just because its rule is absolute, polarity is lacking, and such energy as the system contains is inverted, the sperm-products of this activity being dwarfed, banal, and frustrated. There is no issue towards the world where a man's will and purpose could accomplish something, but only inwards to the mother. The psychology of Hamlet occurs to the mind: the spirit of the father constantly challenges Hamlet's manhood, while the mother beckons to his weakness and infantilism.

Fortunately, however, in our drawing this aspect was literally only one half of the picture. What was needed to complete and complement the sexual *dynamis* is the spiritual power which we found evolving on the left side: the side which, throughout the series, is associated with the sun. The affirmation of the spiritual *dynamis* is seen as an upward and downward movement, corresponding to the upward and downward directions of the phallic energy on the right.

Seen from this angle, the streaming of ineffectual phallic elements towards the left is the expression of a stunted, one-sided conception of human nature seeking its needed complement. But this fulfilment of the basic conception of psychic energy is not achieved by merely adding spirituality to the original one-sided conception. For this would imply that the spiritual principle is not basic in human nature, but only a secondary by-product, effected by sublimation of the original sexual libido. Ineffectual concessions to the opposite principle do not work, because no dynamic solution is conceivable without a primary dynamic opposition. If our basic conception of man is inadequate, this defect will permeate the whole superstructure, so that every conclusion we come to will merely reiterate our original fallacy.

In this naive material, albeit from a scientifically trained mind, we find the spiritual factor appearing as a primordial principle at the embryonic level of conception. These blue masses in the drawings came literally "out of the blue," the significance of their appearance being sensed, though not realized. The limbless creature might therefore be regarded as a vital aspect or function of the self, condemned to an unrelated existence because consciousness had never given it a spiritual leg to stand upon. The lower blue mass in Drawing III. expresses the fundamental need of the mind for the spiritual *dynamis* to be accepted as a primary factor of individual experience.[1] For if this be not granted, the essential fact of individual freedom has no foundation. A psychological conception of man that does not fulfil this paramount subjective need, however satisfying to the deified intellect, is not true in the deepest sense. For the true statement of man must be of such a stature that it wins the sanction of every element.

The reader may well ask why, if these blue elements represent the primordial power of the idea, they should remain passive, amorphous masses throughout the drawings. This question raises a difficult problem. The drawings are exclusively concerned with events taking place in the uncon-

[1] The absence of the limiting outline in ink, which distinguishes this mass in III., may be an allusion to its primary, unconditioned nature.

scious, events in which the conscious personality of the subject participates only as a kind of medium. This is the dynamic aspect of psychic life, which is as different from the ideal realm of consciousness as is the submarine life of the ocean from our world of familiar things. The unconscious pre-stages of every conscious event are only dimly discernible. Yet we know that a relatively long period of unconscious gestation precedes the emergent moment when the idea actually flashes into consciousness. In the realm of love we are able to perceive a teleological connection between the unconscious *dynamis* and the conscious ideal. But in the realm of the spirit the inner evolutionary continuity between, for example, a dark mood or a mental disorder and a subsequent revelation is not so self-evident. The power of sexuality is an obvious biological fact; but the power of the idea is hidden from us, in so far as we have the illusion that ideas are things that we make. These drawings demonstrate the way in which ideas can make or break the individual whose mind they inhabit.

These organs of blue could represent a specific aspect of that unconscious energy-process out of which living ideas are born. Thus in Drawing III. we find the upper mass developing the *idea* of total individual consciousness, while the lower mass suggests the possibility of a new foundation upon which the *idea* of the self can stand. In subsequent drawings we find the *idea* of a new, yet very ancient, kind of vision forming in the upper lobe, and we find the whole organ functioning as a kind of protective envelope around the evolving symbols in the unconscious. A constellation of protective, formative associations groups itself naturally around this blue organ, suggesting the idea that it represents a kind of spiritual matrix. In all these functional associations the idea of purpose is contained; but, since consciousness is relatively in the dark as to the existence and nature of this unconscious gestation, we must ascribe this purpose to the autonomous evolutionary activity of the psyche. Will and purpose are naturally assumed to be the prerogatives of consciousness; hence the hero who does battle with the dragon obviously personifies this ideal conception. But here we come upon an independent organism that functions more steadily and intelligently for the furtherance of conscious life than could any known function of consciousness. It is as though the purpose which broods over the embryonic psychic formations were vegetative and maternal in character, in contrast to the executive purposiveness of conscious will.

CHAPTER XII

RESTORATION

I

DRAWING XX

THE new-born sun appears in mid-field, as in Drawing VI., but with this difference: there the introverting task was commanded; here it is fulfilled.

The ancestral house is not only larger in scale, it is also one storey higher. The house of the ancestors is a classic symbol for the inherited or traditional basis of values. It represents the phylogenetic psychic background, the pervasive ancestral influence which manifests itself in every individual valuation, word and deed. Yet, although a whole new storey has been added to this structure, it has no door. This singular omission, though not intended, is not accidental. It means that the individual myth has not yet been assimilated by the whole personality. In the analytical process one submits oneself to an intensive evolutionary activity, whereby an attitude gradually forms which anticipates, and even insists upon, the fullest experience of life. The work of integrating the new attitude and the new insight into the urgent texture of individual life with its problems, often deeply rooted in past mistakes, is the post-analytical task; and this is, of course, the real test of the efficacy of the analysis. The fact that the patient was literally not permitted to make the door into his ancestral house shows the truly realistic character of the autonomous psyche. It would have been tantamount to a false statement, for when the patient made this drawing he had not yet distinguished the potentiality of the myth from the actuality of achievement.

In front of the house is a flower garden with a *mandala* design. It will be remembered that we discovered the elements of the *mandala* structure in the earlier drawing of this scene; but no attempt at a total synthesis was made at that time. The figures, a man in blue and a woman in yellow, are standing in this garden. The patient identifies himself with the man, and his dead sister with the woman. Standing in the middle of a square of green, to the left of the house, is the famous tree that ruled the prohibited infantile paradise. Five shafts of gold radiate from the crown of the tree, suggesting that an identification has taken place with the rising sun of the earlier picture, where its rays similarly enclosed four sectors. In the former drawing the tree was associated with the origins of the dissociated complex and with symptoms of infantile resentment: here it appears as a bearer of the sun, thus becoming the symbol of emergent life.

In that inexhaustible fountain, *Psychology of the Unconscious*, Jung cites two ancient sources where the sun-god is represented being born from the tree. In the Egyptian *Book of the Dead*, which is called " the soul's gate of knowledge to the East," there is the following:

> " I am the pilot in the holy keel, I am the steersman who allows no rest in the ship of Ra.[1] I know that tree of emerald green from whose midst Ra rises to the height of the clouds."

Jung adds:

> " Ship and tree of the dead are here closely connected. . . . The representation of the sun-god Mithra is probably explained in the same way. He is represented upon the Heddernheim relief with half his body arising from the tip of a tree."

After citing abundant evidence to prove that the tree is a primordial symbol of the mother, he mentions the fact that, in the Middle Ages, the tree was poetically addressed with the honourable title " mistress." He writes:

> " It is not astonishing that the Christian legend transformed the tree of death, the cross, into the tree of life; so that Christ was often represented on a living and fruit-bearing tree."[2]

The significance of this symbolism in our material is profoundly concerned with the overcoming of the incest-

[1] Ship of the sun which carries the sun and the soul over the sea of death to the rising.

[2] Jung: *Psychology of the Unconscious*, ed. 1927, p. 278.

wish. According to Jung, this means the vanquishing of the animal nature, hence becoming akin to the tree. In the Mithraic myth, beautifully represented on the Heddernheim bas-relief,[1] the first event is the birth of Mithra from the top of the tree. The next representation shows him carrying the conquered bull (comparable to the monstrous bull overcome by Gilgamish). Jung writes:

> " This bull signifies the concentrated significance of the monster, the father, who as giant and dangerous animal embodies the incest-prohibition, and agrees with the individual libido of the sun-hero, which he overcomes by self-sacrifice. . . . In the fourth picture Sol kneels before Mithra. These last representations show plainly that Mithra has taken to himself the strength of the sun, so that he becomes the lord of the sun as well. He has conquered his animal nature, the bull. The animal knows no incest-prohibition; man is therefore man because he conquers the incest-wish—that is, his animal nature. Mithra has sacrificed his animal nature, the incest-wish, and therewith has overcome the mother—*i.e.*, the terrible, death-bringing mother."[2]

This elucidation of the tree-symbolism by Jung agrees perfectly with the known facts in the present case. For the tree from which the sun-rays expand is the one that ruled over the regressive infantile system which revealed itself in Drawing VI. as fundamentally incestuous in character.

The motif of the hero overcoming the monster, coming out of the nostrils of the " terrible mother," is also represented in our myth, while the home-coming under the ægis of the new sun clings closely to the Mithraic prototype. From this we infer that a psychological return to the house of the ancestors is permitted to a man only when he has disciplined his unruly nature and overcome his atavistic tendencies.

Thus the idea of the tree expresses the nature of man's later spiritual development as contrasted with his earlier biological or animal phase. The man who identifies himself with his animal nature may delude himself with the idea that escape is always possible because he can still run. But the man who finally accepts his tree-nature feels himself to be

1 Cumont: *Textes et Monuments*, vol. ii., Planche VII.
2 *Ibid.*, p. 293.

most real just where he is unreservedly committed. Partial participation means that the experience is hypothetical or provisional, and therefore could just as well be something else. Submission to destiny means the acceptance of one's actual life-situation as the decisive reality; this means to be rooted in the earth like a tree. Out of this rootedness in the real, with all its problems, individuality is born, for the opposites can be reconciled only by life.

The cottage with the tin extension and the earth closet appear once more, but crossed with bars of silver. These infantile contents have been dealt with and left behind: only their shells remain. This would not mean a blatant superseding of the infantile psyche by the cultural, or a mere canalization of untoward libido into socially acceptable channels. The libido-value which was invested in the infantile forms was transformed by the impregnation of the god in Drawing VII., and assimilated into the new attitude in Drawing XIV. The relics of the complex seen in the present picture can be discarded, like the false hero in the last drawing, because these forms no longer contain any significant charge of energy.

To the right of the house there is a tall poplar tree which does not appear in the earlier drawing. It stands in the very middle of the picture, possibly expressing the ambition of this young man to grow beyond and above the level of his ancestors. One almost gets the impression that the tree is, as it were, measuring itself against the house by which it grows.

To the right is a sweep of green meadowland, divided into three portions by radiating lines of gold, which originate at the corner of the walled garden. The meaning of these lines is not altogether clear, but if we take the house and the garden as symbolizing the limitations of the patient's ancestral psychology, the lines would arise at the point where the clan-boundary ends and the general cultural background begins. They would mark the edge of the family compound. This idea of expanding consciousness agrees with the timely figure of Cronus, symbolizing the historical dimension. In the former drawing he appeared in the second house of the emergent sun. Now he uses his scythe as a husbandman.

The road that leads on over the hill is open, and above it the peacock is seen, just hatched from the egg, in the same relative situation as that occupied by the expanded peacock's tail in the earlier drawing. This suggests that the introverted task, which led the patient back to his origins, is finished, and that the time is ripe for the forward movement towards an extending horizon of possibilities. A fragment of the shell has dropped upon the green hill to the left of the road. In shape and relative position in the design it resembles the stone-age barrows seen beneath the sun in the earlier drawing. The peacock is a bird of the rising sun, a symbol of the unfolding power of consciousness. The barrows also belong presumably to sun-worshippers. Thus a thread of continuity is established between prehistoric sun-worship and the peacock heralding the advent of the new sun.

When we turn to the events in the heavens, it is not at first clear what has happened. Just to the right of the middle line the new sun has arisen. The patient identifies the sun-god with Osiris; he is youthful in aspect and has a short golden beard. His enormously magnified right arm is stretched out below the aperture in the empty womb-cavity, and the peacock and child have come safely to rest upon his golden hand. The peacock is apparently just hatched, for three pieces of shell are to be seen lying on the hand, while the fourth has fallen to the earth below. The peacock, in green and blue, has been painted with some care, but the child is only alluded to—an almost indistinguishable symbolical item. From this we might infer a certain resistance to the future or anticipated personality, an unwillingness, perhaps, to face clearly what this new factor might require of the subject.

Hanging in an irregular loop in the sky above, the empty shell of the monster can be made out. The uterine sack, showing the slit at the base, is distinguished by a close reticulated design of squares and dots. Following this loop to the left, the remains of the monster's jaws are to be seen, the large upper and lower canine teeth being easily distinguishable. Impaled upon the point of the sabre-like lower canine hangs the limp, lifeless body of the magician. Owing to the fact that the head is rendered almost invisible by the lines of gold and red that have been painted over it, the looped brown body bears a striking resemblance to a shark or whale with a bifurcated tail. Since this was by no means the patient's intention, we must assume that the idea of rapacity is being underlined by the subject's subliminal critic, who throughout the myth has often made pointed use of such improvisations.

Between the brown mass of the trunk and the inverted viking's helmet the faint outline of the head can be discerned, with the face turned towards the right. Three lines of red issue from the mouth. These are intended to convey the fact that the magician is in the act of vomiting the two contents which he stole from the womb of the unconscious. These contents—namely, the living heart and the green life-stuff (which evolved into the new humerus with the regenerated radius and ulna)—are seen falling through space into the shallop of Venus, which waits in its course to receive them. This event takes place immediately above the house of the ancestors. The green anima, with the crown of yellow hair, is seen lying expectantly within her containing crescent. Her recumbent posture might be the result of fatigue after her recent labours, or, in view of the obstetrical character of the last drawing, after her recent labour.

The two lobes of blue, discussed in the preceding chapter, are to be seen above and to the right of the new sun. Although six rays come from the sun, the colour divisions are only four. The red and green elements occupy the two northern and the two southern sectors respectively, while the yellow and blue take the remaining single sectors to the west and east. Thus, in spite of the fact that a kind of *mandala* design was attempted, both in the heavens above and in the garden below, in neither case was it completed. In the garden *mandala* the lower arc of the circle is cut off by the bottom edge of the paper, a character which is repeated above, where the two lower sectors formed by the sun-radials are truncated by the horizon.

The most interesting feature of the sun-design is the fact that the elementary principle of the four functions, or the four attributes of effective consciousness, has been superimposed upon the six sectors of the sun-field. The fourfold differentiation of psychic functioning is an elementary structural fact, manifesting itself, as we have already seen, in many ways wherever the goal of individuation or self-realization achieves plastic expression. Taking the drawing before us as an example, there are four upper sectors radiating from the centre of the tree on the left. There are four windows in each of the three storeys of the house of the ancestors. There are four living symbols delivered from the unconscious, two falling to the arm of the sun and two to the shallop of the moon. There are four fragments of the shell from which the peacock has emerged (the peacock, as we have seen, is the symbol of the widening or unfolding of consciousness), three resting upon the hand of the sun-god and one upon the earth.[1] Finally, there are the four regional houses of the four cardinal colours, red, green, blue, and yellow, disposed towards the four points of the compass. Running through this whole grouping of figures, the idea of emergence is joined to the idea of totality. A psychic product that shows such an abundance of constructive symbolism has, naturally, great therapeutic value. It is the manifest expression of a concerted attempt in which every basic function of the psyche participates.

The quartering of the heavenly field into the four functional regions is not, however, a symmetrical design. Neither has it a circular container like the *mandala* below. I take this to mean that, although the archetype of the *mandala* has influenced the grouping of elements in this picture, the realization of this idea was, at that time, not within the patient's competence. The lack of any containing line suggests that the subject could not easily tolerate a restraining influence. The *mandala* symbolizes an undivided totality, ruled and conditioned from a centre possessing paramount value. The patient was not then in a position to understand what this symbol might mean as an inner psychic reality. For him the *mandala* still belonged to the realm of magic; hence, perhaps, the number six on which this design is based.

[1] This distribution calls to mind the relative unbalance of the structure of the Christian Cross with its three cardinal points above and a distant fourth point below.

Consequently, none of his many attempts at a *mandala* design attained structural completeness. His personality needed to expand, and his ambition to find a disciplined and ordered expression. Expansion, emergence, development: these were words of power for him, while rootedness, contained relatedness, reliability, permanence reminded him too much of undesirable necessity.

II

When we examine the specific contents that have been apportioned, as it were, to the respective functional regions, we can form a panoramic view of the complete psychic individual, illuminated from an impersonal, archetypal centre.

The central sun is the symbol of the self, conceived not as a personal conglomerate of conflicting aims and tendencies, but rather as a cosmic factor involved in the individual life-experiment. To the right of the sun is the blue house of logos or creative thought. Within this house we find the magnified arm and hand of the sun-god, painted in gold and bearing the peacock and the infant. Both of these represent the viability of the new attempt: the peacock from the supra-personal aspect, the infant from the personal. The child is essentially the symbol of the reborn personality or the new attitude. When Blake said, " The only happy state is the creative state," and Meister Eckhart, " For man is truly God and God is truly man," they both expressed the truth that the divine spirit of man is reborn in the genuine, creative deed.

Above the sun is the red house of feeling. Red is the fiery element which consumes and transforms: it is the passion of the mind which brings things to realization. Psychological rebirth is always heralded by a renewal of feeling—a fact which may account for the frequent outcropping of erotic symbolism in mystical poetry and experience. In this passional house we find the vestiges of the mythological metamorphosis. They are now feather-light and insubstantial, like wood-ash carried up by the heat of the fire, or like an empty pupa-case after the winged imago has flown.

With regard to the two lobes of blue, the lower has been taken over by the logos-function, while the upper is being absorbed in the house of feeling. This suggests an ambivalence of the primordial libido, whereby one portion tends to go over into actuality, while the remainder lingers on in the primordial state. We discovered this same idea in the *Kundalini tantra*, where Shakti is conceived as a snake coiled around the *lingam*. In this respect she is the sleeping potential or primordial energy of life. When aroused, her *prana* rises up and penetrates the *chakras*. This *prana* is her kinetic aspect; yet she remains eternally coiled in her primordial state as potential energy.

On the left of the sun is the house of intuition, identified with the anima. It is represented by a yellow field, cross-hatched in silver. In this house we find the anima recumbent—*i.e.*, receptive. The crescent moon forms a shallow cup, into which falls the green life-stuff (somewhat resembling an homunculus in this drawing) and the living heart. These symbols are vomited into space by the moribund magician, whose body is hooked over the lower canine tooth of the depotentiated monster. As the cold-blooded devourer it is appropriate that he should find himself thus impaled on the tooth of the devouring monster. This idea receives a certain confirmation from the whale-like aspect of his body, mentioned above. Thus the mythic pattern of the night-journey under the sea is fulfilled; the devouring monster of the sea vomits up the reborn sun-hero. A well-known example of this is the vomiting of Jonah by the whale, or the casting-up of Ulysses by the devouring sea and his discovery by Nausicaa, the life-restoring anima. The night-journey consists in being engulfed by the most dreaded thing. It is like being imprisoned with one's darkest qualities. The release of feeling, noted above, marks the deliverance from a living death.

The whole lower part of the drawing is ruled by green. It belongs to the earth, symbolizing the function of sensation. This region is the largest in bulk, for it embraces the sphere of reality, the living, tangible moment of vivid sensation, wherein psychic potentiality becomes involved with the actual and the concrete. Its main contents are the tree, among whose branches the patient's individual myth first began,[1] the house of the ancestors, the garden of the sister-anima with its *mandala*, the road of life leading into the future, the green meadowland associated with the subject's farming ancestors, and the figure of Cronus. As the keeper of the gate between the potential and the actual, time belongs rightly to sensation, the reality-function.

Total realization is probably a human impossibility; but a relatively complete act of realization involves a valid co-ordination of these four cardinal aspects or functions of psychic reality. Theoretically, the four functions—sensation, intuition, feeling, and thinking—represent the differentiated psychic response to four elementary conditions of conscious human life. Hence a completely adequate response to a situation would include:

(1) A factual or sensory perception of its concrete manifestation.
(2) An intuitive apprehension of the possibilities or implications that could develop out of it.
(3) A feeling judgment of its bearing upon the participants, and therefore a valuation of its worth.
(4) An intellectual understanding of its nature and purpose.

The four segments, with their corresponding symbolic colours, represent these spheres or portions of reality in general. But the four living symbols, two of which are embraced by consciousness, while two are held by the anima, represent specific psychic organs demanded by the need for totality. One can regard these theoretically as the specific libidinal content of the four cardinal functions. They are seen here in the moment of emergence. It appears to be an evolutionary psychical condition that, hand in hand with the transformation of the basic attitude, the main psychic functions also undergo a process of rebirth or reorganization, corre-

[1] The earliest signs of individuality usually appear in the form of resistance to the containing pattern or background. The act of defiance in the tree resembles, therefore, the individual point of departure discussed on pp. 347 *ff*.

sponding with the increased value and range of consciousness. The new wine cannot be put into the old wine-skins. The process of renewal is inclusive.

The newly born infant symbolizes, then, the birth of psychological thinking, a new intellectual understanding, based primarily upon the analytical experience. The peacock explained itself in the former drawing of this same scene, where the unfolded tail appeared just above the rim of the horizon, foreshadowing future possibilities. This symbol, as we have seen, also embraces the egg that was associated with the repressed feeling for the dead sister. Hence it would connote a new intuitive awareness in the sphere of relatedness[1] and, at the same time, a valuable intensification and unfolding of consciousness.

III

Concerning the living symbols which fall into the lap of the anima (who, by the way, has now resumed her proper sphere as a receptive function in relation to unconscious contents), the heart represents the regenerated organ of feeling. We have already traced its development from the visceral bags of blood (derived originally from the radius and ulna) first encountered in the stomach-container of Drawing III.

Like the green homunculus accompanying it, this new organ of feeling is the product of a complex metamorphosis. As contrasted with the peacock and the infant, which have the character of spontaneous natural creations, these other anima-symbols have more the character of alchemical products. In their production it was not a matter of a simple "hatching out." In their first appearance the bags of blood and the green protoplasm were both doomed to a retrogressive fate within the dissociated system. The bags of blood, for instance, were contained in a disjuncted stomach with no organic connections, while the homunculus was conceived in a lavatory-pan which received the retrograde

[1] Intuition that is attuned to psychic events appertains to the essential nature of Eros, inasmuch as it apprehends and unites discrete entities, thus binding together two or more images into a new associative formation.

libidinal elements of the infantile system. Both factors were thus originally conditioned by the inverted process, from which they have now been salved by a process of transformation. We observed how the introverting energy penetrated, and eventually broke down, the dissociated condition. Then, by a process of association with new and vigorous elements, the doomed functions were impregnated, reorganized and finally transformed in character.

This home-coming means, therefore, the restitution of the repressed functions as effective components of the basic attitude, the one denoting a vital renewal of feeling, the other a new creative will. It is for this purpose of reintegration that the anima now receives them. As in the case of the Siberian *shaman*, the anima represents the inherited ancestral values, and therefore appears significantly as the goddess of the ancestral house.

The latter pair of functions have more the character of organs (*i.e.*, necessary parts of a larger co-ordinated system),[1] whereas the peacock and the infant are viable, independent organisms. This contrast has a certain theoretical interest, inasmuch as it denotes a relatively greater independence of those functions which achieve conscious differentiation. It is a matter of common experience, for example, that the function which is disciplined in one's *métier* is relatively unaffected by emotional fluctuations of mood. It can be relied upon under all conditions: it has achieved functional objectivity. Whereas the relatively inferior or unconscious functions lack this disciplined independence, they are still involved in the tidal movements of the unconscious.

From the standpoint of individuation this drawing represents a considerable achievement. The principal cause of his former emotional deficiencies (clearly expressed in the first dream) was the patient's undeveloped attitude towards the sexual function. The essence of the transforming process consisted in a realization of the god-value as an inner creative activity. This also appears in the refrain of Wisdom in the Song of Songs:

[1] Thus the restitution of lost parts, a capacity long since left behind on the road of physical evolution, is found to be feasible psychologically.

"I adjure you, O daughters of Jerusalem, by the roes and by the hinds of the field, that ye stir not up, nor awaken love, *until it please.*"

In the realm of feeling spontaneity is everything, and since this whole aspect of a man's life is under the sway of the feminine principle, it follows that a disciplined anima is the *sina qua non* of reliable relationship.

From this point of view the position of the shallop of Venus, immediately above the house of the ancestors, has a special interest, for the anima is restoring these lost functions to their proper place—namely, under the safeguarding roof of ancestral tradition. We have followed their fate on the homeward journey, but what these functions had to undergo in the hinterland of the mind to which schizophrenic dissociation had banished them has not been recounted. The reader who has lent a sympathetic understanding to this material will appreciate the kind of effects entailed by such a crippling dissociation of feeling, and that no security was possible until a new attitude had been achieved.

Let us try, then, to recapitulate how this reconciliation has been effected. The transformation of the living heart from the disjuncted bags of blood has already been traced, but the derivation of the little green man (now lying above the anima in the reverse direction) is more complicated and carries many more associations.

The original green substance was derived from the amœboid conversion of the lavatory-pan. Its nuclear elements were derived (*a*) from fæcal elements of Drawing VII. (infantile pleasure) and (*b*) from the grains of the sun resulting from its impregnation by the ancestor-god. The green matrix was associated with the mother, and in this matrix were lodged elements from the highest and the lowest. This was the first stage in the process of uniting or reconciling the opposites on the primordial level. The impregnated life-stuff, held between the upper and lower rows of teeth of the devouring monster, symbolized the situation of conflict or tension between the opposites. In this situation the mass of protoplasm developed into the humerus articulating with the radius and ulna, which then expanded into a silver wing.

This development of the single upper bone of the arm, with its two distal appendages, corresponded with the differentiation of effective polarity out of undifferentiated primal unity. The silver wing, forming in relation to the radius and ulna in IX., appeared synchronously with the conception of the unconscious as maternal womb, which in its turn developed, by the process of *enantiodromia*, out of the horrific aspect of the unconscious. The green protoplasmic arm extends from the outer rows of teeth to the inner cavity of the monster, suggesting that it is this new introverted annexe or " wing " which reconciles the outer horrific and the inner maternal aspects of the unconscious. The idea of the wing is not followed up in the subsequent drawings until the final apotheosis. I conclude from this that the idea of spiritual freedom begins to unfold only when the conflict of the opposites cannot any longer be evaded. The opposing tendencies were inherent in the green substance from its inception. We also noted that the system that was caught between the upper and lower rows of teeth in VIII. contained not only the life-stuff, but also the vampire lunatic faces which were parasitic upon it. The " upper and the nether millstones " are thus represented within the developing system as well as without. It is because the principle of conflict and opposition is inherent in the very nature of consciousness that freedom is also an intrinsic quality of the soul. For, as the symbolism of Drawing IX. illustrates, it is just because one end of the skeletal arm is caught and held by the teeth of the monster that the distal end develops a wing. It is the determined rootedness of the tree that makes the free expanse of growth in every direction possible. Thus the tree becomes the symbol of man's spiritual development.

The idea of the bones of the arm seems to have determined the evolution of the green protoplasm during the phase just described, wherein the state of being fixed or rooted nourishes the idea of freedom. But in the present drawing the resemblance to a little green man seems to suggest that the evolution of the symbol has taken another important stride. This hypothesis also accords with the mythic analogy of the night-journey under the sea, for the shadow-hero became the whale, whose final act was to vomit forth the new life which had been germinating in the inner darkness. According to the myth, this new life is the sun-hero emerging victorious out of the devouring mother (*i.e.*, the sea-monster who was impregnated by the old sun whom she had swallowed).

If these allusions are valid, we can carry the analogy back to Drawing VII., in which the idea of the impregnation of the inverted system by the old god immediately preceded the appearance of the devouring monster in Drawing VIII. We learnt from the subject's associations that the content of the inverted system in Drawing VII. related to the incestuous libido held by the mother. Hence the whole pattern of the mythic analogue can be traced in our patient's material. The ancestral god is in reality the maternal grandfather. He it was, in our patient's myth, who impregnated the mother just before he was completely engulfed by, and identified with, the devouring monster. The impregnated protoplasm developed within the maternal womb while the hero was fighting the protecting dragon, the developing life-stuff being the mythological treasure. Finally, the new sun is born, and one of the aspects of this emergence is the little green man, or subtle body, who is brought home by the anima to the ancestral home.

The mythic analogue to the little green man is the Verdant One, who appears somewhat obscurely in certain legends deriving from an Islamic source. A reference to this semi-divine figure is to be found in the XVIIIth Sura of the Koran. As Moses and his servant journeyed towards the confluence of the two seas they left their fish behind, which took its way back into the sea. Moses, being hungry, asked his servant for the fish, who then replied:

> " 'What thinkest thou ? When we repaired to the rock for rest I forgot the fish; and none but Satan made me forget it, so as not to mention it; and it hath taken its way into the sea in a wondrous sort.' Moses said: 'It is this we were in quest of.' And they both went back, retracing their footsteps. Then found they one of our servants to whom we had vouchsafed our mercy, and whom we had instructed with our knowledge."

In a commentary this is paraphrased as follows:

> " The loss of our fish is a sign for us of our finding him whom we seek—namely, El-Khidr, or El-Khadir, the reputed vizier of Dhoulkarnain, and said to have *drunk of the fountain of life*, by virtue of which he still lives, and will live to the day of judgment. He is also said to appear, clad in *green* robes, to Muslims in distress, whence his name."

He is later referred to in the text as " the unknown." He is sent to teach Moses the difficult lesson of patience. When Moses says to him, " Shall I follow thee that thou teach me, for guidance, of that which thou too hast been taught ?" El-Khidr replies, " Verily, thou canst not have patience with me." He then performs three actions which appear irrational, immoral and evil, at which Moses expostulates. When the reasons for these actions are explained to Moses, it becomes clear that El-Khidr knows the hidden springs of destiny: in each case, by his irrational action, he has warded off a stroke of evil from a deserving soul.

Jung and I stumbled upon an outcrop of this same myth when we were camping among a branch of the Masai people on the slopes of Mount Elgon in Kenya. Our headman, a Somali and a devout Mohammedan, provided an illuminating testimony to the living power of this archetype. After suffering several days of fever from acute malaria his moral had sunk pretty low. One morning, with the fever still upon him, he appeared in camp with radiant face, and, on being questioned by Jung, explained that he had had a dream in the night in which the Green One had come to him. With eager excitement he spoke of the Green One as Khadir, and, after further questioning, identified him with El-Khidr of the XVIIIth Sura. He described how, in following a track through the bush, a particular flower or green shoot might catch one's eye; suddenly one's heart would know that this was El-Khidr. Or one might meet a stranger on the road and, again, an inner voice would declare him to be El-Khidr. One would then run to greet him and give him the double salaam. This would mean the greatest good fortune. Or he might appear as a shaft of sunlight, or in a dream. In whatever fashion he appeared he was the living manifestation of Allah, and his appearance was always auspicious. Our headman explained that this was the living kernel of the Mohammedan teaching: the devout heart must always be ready for this act of recognition.

It is probable that this inner core of Mohammedan tradition, which hardly appears even within the pages of the sacred book, is gathered in from an earlier cultural source. El-Khidr is associated with Dhulkarnain, the two-horned one, who is identified with Alexander as an embodiment of the sun. He is described in the XVIIIth Sura as going to the place of setting and to the place of rising. In the commentaries El-Khidr is spoken of as " the Verdant One," the never-wearied wanderer who roams for hundreds of thousands of years over lands and seas, the one wise in divine knowledge, the immortal. He is said to have reached the " river of life " with Alexander, and both became immortal through unwittingly drinking of its waters. In this account there is a strong resemblance to Gilgamish, the Sumerian sun-hero, who, after journeying endlessly in search of the secret of immortality, eventually had to descend to the bottom of the sea to find the renewing herb.

From these and the foregoing associations given by our headman in Africa, we can infer that the Verdant One is an archetypal personification of the eternally renewed light and life of the sun. He is also a manifestation of Allah in the living moment, mediator between God and man, bringer of the divine blessing.

Turning again to the green figure of our myth, it can be nothing but the veritable living core of the evolutionary process. It was impregnated by the god: it was fashioned within the maternal fount of life in the unconscious, and it was delivered from the unconscious at the moment of emergence of the new sun. El-Khidr is this very moment of emergence. Allah cannot become manifest, belonging to the timeless, the eternal, the unmanifest. Yet nothing is impossible to God; the Verdant One is therefore the way in which the living moment appears when God touches it with his finger. When God pierces the now with the golden rays of his beard, El-Khidr manifests himself, either in a dream or in a sword-ray of sunlight. These ideas cluster like grapes about this germinating central figure of the myth.

IV

The idea of the anima bringing back the treasure to the house of the ancestors is a more familiar mythological theme. Psychological dissolution constantly menaces the loosely organized quasi-primitive mind; hence the return of the soul to her proper place is the sign of the longed-for cure. The most perfect example of this theme is in the well-known myth of Tobias and the Angel, in the Book of Tobit.

The reader will recall how Tobit was reduced by the inhuman conditions of the captivity in Nineveh to long for death; he had also become blind from the sparrow-droppings which fell into his eyes as he slept beneath the wall. The thought of death kindles the remembrance of a certain sum of money he had previously entrusted to one Gabael in Media. Wishing to leave this money as an inheritance to his son Tobias, he sends him forth on the journey to Media in the company of an angel, who has been sent by heaven in answer to Tobit's prayer, but who passes for a hired man.

As Tobit's prayers were being heard in heaven, Sara, the daughter of Raguel, a kinsman of Tobit's living in Ecbatane, near the Tigris, was also praying to God out of her affliction. She too had been reduced to the same longing for death on account of reproaches heaped upon her by her maids. For she had been given to seven bridegrooms, all of whom had been slain on the first night by the jealous demon Asmodeus who possessed her. Azarias, the angel-companion of Tobias, was sent from heaven in answer to both these calls for divine assistance.

Now as Tobias and his companion were going on their journey they came to the river Tigris, and, as Tobias went down to wash himself, a great fish leaped out of the river to devour him. The angel then called to him to seize the fish and draw it to land. The young man did so, and the angel then said:

" 'Open the fish, and take the heart and the liver and the gall, and put them up safely.' So the young man did as the angel commanded him; and when they had roasted the fish, they did eat it: then they both went on their way, till they drew near to Ecbatane. Then the young man said to the angel: 'Brother Azarias, to what use is the heart and the liver and the gall of the fish?' And he said unto him: 'Touching the heart and the liver, if a devil or an evil spirit trouble any, we must make a smoke thereof before the man or the woman, and the party shall be no more vexed. As for the gall, it is good to anoint a man that hath whiteness in his eyes, and he shall be healed.' "

As they approached the city the angel informed Tobias of Sara, explaining to him that he, Tobias, being of her kindred, should seek her for wife. But the young man, having heard of the fate of the seven bridegrooms, had no wish to incur the same doom. The angel reassures Tobias:

" 'Dost thou not remember the precepts which thy father gave thee, that thou shouldest marry a wife of thine own kindred? Wherefore hear me, O my brother; for she shall be given thee to wife; and make thou no reckoning of the evil spirit, for this same night shall she be given thee in marriage. And when thou shalt come into the marriage chamber, thou shalt take the ashes of perfume, and shalt lay upon them some of the heart and liver of the fish and thou shalt make a smoke with it: and the devil shall smell it, and flee away, and never come again any more: but when thou shalt come to her, rise up both of you, and pray to God which is merciful, who will have pity on you, and save you: fear not, for she is appointed unto thee from the beginning; and thou shalt preserve her, and she shall go with thee. Moreover, I suppose that she shall bear thee children.' Now when Tobias had heard these things, he loved her, and his heart was effectually joined to her."

The points that offer themselves for psychological comparison with our material are numerous:

(1) Divine or archetypal intervention occurs when the situation is desperate.

(2) In the myth the father sends the son upon the quest for the treasure left behind in a distant place. In our material the grandfather commands the grandson to go in search of the hidden treasure left behind in the infantile fantasy-system.

(3) In the myth the father is blinded by the agency of birds (*i.e.*, ideas). In the material a certain psychological blindness is associated with the father. This is represented in the first drawing as sun-spots in the sun. Furthermore, the eyes of the dragon (which were blind, being without pupils) were directly associated with the fixed, unseeing gaze of the father.

(4) Before the treasure can be won, the hero is assailed by a devouring fish (alias dragon), which leaps out of the unconscious to destroy him. In the myth the fish leaps out of the river which has to be crossed, the river symbolizing the dangerous *transitus* in which one can easily be submerged by the unconscious. In our material the dragon leaps forth from the monstrous aspect of the unconscious, which expressed the danger of being overcome by the father. This fate is also alluded to in the two lunatics caught in the monster's mouth.

(5) Essential organs are salved from the body of the monster. In the myth these are the heart and liver and gall of the fish. In our material the egg, the heart and the green life-stuff are also essential organs. They first appear as repressed and dissociated contents of the unconscious, hence as elements of the dæmonic complex. Later this aspect is transformed into a functional matrix in which they develop an organic existence before being delivered by the hero.

(6) The overcoming of the fish or monster is made possible by divine (*i.e.*, archetypal) assistance. This is followed by the excision of the essential organs, under instruction from the angel, for religious and curative purposes, while the rest of the creature is eaten or assimilated.

In the myth the heart and liver have the power of overcoming or exorcising demonic possession when offered up as a burnt offering to the spiritual powers. The eating of the rest of the fish represents an offering to the earth-principle. In our material two essential functions are dedicated to the new sun-god—*i.e.*, the conscious principle—while the other two fall into the lap of the anima—*i.e.*, the representative of the unconscious. The rest of the monster is dissipated—in other words, assimilated.

(7) The anima is intimately connected with the inception of the work of salvage or redemption in the heavenly sphere. In the myth the prayers of Tobit, the ancestor, and Sara, the soul-mistress, have the relation of synchronicity. They rise up to heaven together, and the mission of the angel to earth is the single divine response to both petitions. From the angel's description of Sara to Tobias as his preordained mate, the fact emerges that the release of the anima from demonic possession is of greater weight in the divine counsels than the recovery of the treasure. Indeed, as the myth proceeds, the two ends are practically merged into one.

In our material the anima-symbols of the crescent moon and the mug of beer (Drawing VI.) appear in the sky immediately behind the ancestral god, who makes the gesture of command in the direction of the hidden infantile fantasy-treasure. Thus the archetypes of the old man and the anima are similarly linked together in the inception of the quest in the heavenly sphere—*i.e.*, the suprapersonal unconscious.

(8) On the earth plane the anima makes her first concrete appearance at the moment when the hero has slain the fish (dragon), and, thereafter, in both the myth and the drawings, she becomes the determining factor for the rest of the story.

Thus, in both cases, the essential purpose of the quest becomes manifest as the quest of the soul.

(9) In both the myth and the material we find allusions to the fourfold personification or discrimination of psychic elements. In the myth there is a fourfold personification in the figures of Tobit, Tobias, Azarias, and Sara, and a fourfold discrimination in the three essential organs and the body of the fish. The heart and liver of the fish symbolize the functions by which the dæmonic power of the unconscious can be transformed by a conscious recognition of its latent possibilities. The gall of the fish is concerned with the idea of the healing or renewal of vision, and therefore would correspond with the development of spiritual perception, while the command to eat the body of the fish brings the pleasures and needs of the body under a kind of divine sanction.

We have already dwelt upon the prevalence of the fourfold principle of individuation in the symbolical construction of the present drawing; although, from the fact that the drawing does not obey the symmetry of the *mandala* design, we may infer that the fourfold principle was no part of any conscious plan.

So far, then, the correspondence between the modern myth and the old is rather close. Let us see if this is maintained. The story continues:

> "And when they were come to Ecbatane, they came to the house of Raguel, and Sara met them: and after they had saluted one another, she brought them into the house."

Tobias makes himself known to his host, and a feast is prepared. Then Tobias tells the angel to speak to Raguel concerning the marriage proposal. Raguel consents to the idea, but confesses the truth about the previous seven bridegrooms. Tobias persists none the less, and the marriage is solemnized according to the law of Moses. Finally, the marriage chamber is prepared.

> "And when they had supped, they brought Tobias in unto her. And as he went, he remembered the words of Raphael, and took the ashes of the perfumes, and put the heart and the liver of the fish thereupon, and made a smoke therewith. The which smell when the evil spirit had smelled, he fled into the utmost parts of Egypt, and the angel bound him. And after that they were both shut in together, Tobias rose out of the bed, and said: 'Sister, arise, and let us pray that God would have pity on us.' Then began Tobias to say: 'Blessed art Thou, O God of our fathers, and blessed is Thy holy and glorious name for ever; let the heavens bless Thee and all Thy creatures. Thou madest Adam, and gavest him Eve his wife for an helper and stay: of them came mankind: Thou hast said, It is not good that man should be alone; let us make unto him an aid like unto himself. And now, O Lord, I take not this my sister for lust, but uprightly: therefore mercifully ordain that we may become aged together.' And she said with him: 'Amen.' So they slept both that night."

This marriage scene provides a perfect example of the power of the right attitude. It is also one of the first and finest examples of psychotherapy in the world's literature. But to resume: Raguel, expecting the worst, goes out in the morning to dig a grave. In so doing he gives the analyst occasion to identify Asmodeus with the incestuous father-daughter constellation. On like grounds the devouring fish could be explained as the dæmonic pull of an incestuous mother-complex in an only son on the threshold of marriage. It is plausible to explain the symbolism of the myth along these lines, so long as it is understood that these incest-formulations are idiomatic expressions, merely designating the archaic tendency of the libido to revert to its source. I am by no means convinced, however, that the demoniacal phenomenology of the sexual complex can be adequately explained in these terms.

When the maidservant brings the news that Tobias is alive and well, Raguel praises God with fervent joy and bids his servants prepare a feast. Tobias then tells Azarias to take a servant and his camels and go to Rages in Media to fetch the money. When this has been safely retrieved, Tobias bids farewell to Raguel, and with half of the latter's goods as a marriage settlement he sets out for Nineveh with Sara his wife. As they approach the city Anna, his mother, recognizes her son in the distance and calls to Tobit, who comes stumbling out of the house to greet his son. Tobias, remembering the advice of the angel, goes up to his father, and

> " he strake of the gall on his father's eyes, saying: ' Be of good hope, my father.' And when his eyes began to smart, he rubbed them; and the whiteness scaled away from the corners of his eyes: and when he saw his son, he fell upon his neck."

From the standpoint of analytical therapy this is as far as the myth can take us, and we must now ask ourselves: what was the experience of the Jewish people out of which this myth was created ?

The state of captivity in Nineveh under a succession of tyrannical Assyrian kings was one in which the necessity of servile adaptation to an alien will had suppressed the true genius of the race. When we say " the soul of a nation has departed " we mean a real condition: we mean that the secure enjoyment of life and the abiding faith in its future has vanished. A people crushed by slavery is like a drifting ship: virtue has gone out of it and, instead of a shared faith, there is frustration and decay. This is analogous to the state of dissociation, in which perhaps the most valuable function of the personality is left marooned in the unconscious.

The theme of the abduction or the absconding of the soul-bearer, and the consequent unbearable grief or loss of value felt by the bereaved, form the *leit-motif* of many myths. We find it, for example, in the story of Gilgamish who languishes for Enkidu, and is driven to his desperate quest for the secret of immortality by the unbearable sense of the virtue that has left him. Orpheus is stricken by the loss of Eurydice, whom he has to seek in the dreadful underworld. Amfortas is the victim of dissociation, symbolized by the never-healing wound. While the Grail is bereft of the sacred Spear the wound will not heal and the knights of the Grail languish. Kundry symbolizes the anima or soul-bearer who has absconded to the opposite principle. Here, too, the redeeming virtue of the spear is intimately associated with the restoration of the anima to the Castle of the Grail.

Thus we see that the state of dissociation is conceived symbolically as the loss or removal of the value or treasure; this is frequently associated with the idea of the desired woman being abducted to a great distance. To represent such themes as the descent of Ishtar or Persephone into the underworld, or the death and dismemberment of Osiris, or Tammuz, or Dionysos, as mythological representations of the death of vegetation in winter and its subsequent resurrection in spring, does not fully explain the psychological necessity from which such myths have arisen. The real peril that threatens humanity is not the approach of winter, against which cultural mankind has always made provision. Rather is it the analogous reference, always present at the back of men's minds, which connects the departure of the spirit of vegetation from the earth with the danger of dissociation in the psychic realm, when the soul absconds into the unconscious and consciousness is bereft of life and vigour.

The superficial analogy with the events of the seasons has been accepted by Tylor, Frazer and others as an adequate explanation of the world-wide distribution of these so-called nature-myths. But if this were the only interpretation, it is indeed strange that one cannot find this theme of the death and resurrection of the god among the most primitive food-gathering peoples, upon whom the rigours of winter fall with greatest severity. Whereas, if we accept the obvious psychological hypothesis, that it is the departure or loss of the libido into the unconscious—in other words, a dissociated psychic state—that cultural mankind most fears, we can also account for the specific distribution of the myths mentioned above. For the aboriginal, indigenous, food-gathering peoples mentioned earlier—such tribes as the North American Indians, the Eskimo, the Bushmen of Africa, the Punan of Borneo, the aboriginals of Northern and Central Australia—appear from all accounts to be entirely free of this fundamental mythological pattern. Elliot Smith[1] disposes of the notion that these food-gatherers rejected the benefits of civilization because of their degraded savagery. It would seem, on the contrary, from their resolute bearing and dignity, that they reject civilization because they set a higher value on their own natural integrity. Be this as it may, members of these indigenous communities appear to be remarkably free from anxiety states[2] which are the characteristic symptom of psychic dissociation. Their attitude to nature is not magical in the sense that magical rites have to be performed by the king in order to ensure the right operation of the powers of nature. On the other hand, certain object-relations of an individual character—*e.g.*, the Churinga of the Australian and the Tinihowi of the Achumawi—are endowed with magical efficacy.

To put it in a nutshell, the food-gathering peoples possess a monadic psyche which knows nothing of the anxiety-producing conflict between nature and culture. They are not haunted by fear of the devouring monster. They neither fear death, nor do they crave immortality. They need neither king nor god-hero to ward off the onslaughts of nature. Never having departed from or repudiated the primordial

1 *Human History*. Jonathan Cape, Ltd.

2 By this term only neurotic or subjectively constellated states of fear are intended. It is not, of course, contended that "objective" fear does not function as a normal ingredient of their lives.

state, nature is not something against which one must be protected, nor does she appear as an avenging outraged deity to be overcome or repressed.

When a relatively civilized people, on the other hand, becomes estranged from its tradition, it is liable to contagious panic and anxiety, or to a galling sense of inferiority with its brood of suspicions in respect to neighbouring peoples.[1] These are symptoms of dissociation with which we are only too familiar in individual psychology.

If we interpret the myth as a psychological product, issuing from and expressing the racial psyche in much the same way as a dream expresses the problems of the individual, we can regard Tobit as a mythical personification of the racial phylum. In other words, the traditional spirit of the Jewish people. He has become blind and hypersensitive to reproach, and begins to long for death. There is nothing but humiliation and servitude for his posterity, because the value that was once the proud inheritance of the race has now become a remote historical memory. This idea of wishing to recover the traditional value, in order to hand it on as an effective possession to his son, is the positive motive of Tobit's prayer to God. It is for the recovery of this treasure that divine aid, in the person of Azarias, is vouchsafed. Azarias is really Raphael, one of the seven holy angels who execute the will of God. He is equivalent to Hermes, the messenger of Zeus. Hermes, it will be remembered, is sent by Zeus only when the situation is imperative. He is a manifestation of the absolutely superior energy-content contained in the god-archetype of the racial unconscious.

Sara personifies the anima or soul of the race. In many myths the anima appears as the natural companion of the old man—Gurnemanz and Kundry, for example, in the last act of *Parsifal*, or Lao-Tzŭ, and the dancing girl who was said to have been with him on the mountain when he wrote the *Tao-Teh-King*. Simon Magus was also companioned by Helena, whom he was said to have rescued from a brothel in Tyre. This conjunction is understandable when we regard

[1] Post-war Germany provides a self-confessed example of this state of collective inferiority.

the myth as an expression of the race-spirit. For the old man, who personifies the traditional wisdom of the race, needs to go hand in hand with the anima or soul-bearer, who represents its continuing life, its hope, its vision, its purpose. Therefore is she young and beautiful.

Tobias personifies posterity, which should inherit the stored-up wisdom and energy of the race. He should also be married, *i.e.* committed, to the anima as the living symbol of its onward moving life and intrinsic virtue.

From the fact that Tobit's blindness is subsequently cured by the gall taken from the dæmonic fish, as also from the specific statement of the myth that Asmodeus is a sex-demon who only destroys those who come to Sara sexually, we must conclude that the blindness and the demonic possession are different aspects of the same malady which afflicted the Jews of Nineveh.

One of the chief characteristics of the Jewish race consisted from the first in a superior awareness of spiritual reality. The visionary intensity of the prophets, though cultivated originally perhaps in compensation for the privations and sufferings of their actual existence, became the chief glory of Jewish tradition. But, side by side with this prophetic intuition, the Jews had an opposite tendency to a licentious and sometimes sadistic sexuality: a compulsive renegade urge, liable to break out under the stress of adverse conditions, and to send them whoring after strange gods. Again and again in the books of the prophets fire is called down upon this demonic shadow of the racial genius; this may also account, to some extent, for the restless, wandering spirit which has scattered the Jews over the surface of the earth, but will not suffer them to become rooted in their own soil.

In the epoch of our myth their troubled destiny constantly exposed them to the danger of being absorbed culturally by the various nations among whom they were scattered as a subject people, and the greatest fidelity to their spiritual inheritance was needed to save it from extinction.

The stability of a racial as of an individual psychology is vested in its living continuity with the ancestral stream.

The conception of individuality as a self-contained, self-regulating organism has no validity unless it also embraces this backward extension of the ancestral phylum as an effective factor. The metaphor " family-tree " expresses more than a mere historical diagram: it affirms not only the cohesion of genealogical succession, but also the state of being rooted in, and specifically determined by, ancestral characters. Individuals who have become severed from their background are restless, unsatisfied, often desperate creatures, pursued by stinging, reckless impulses, unless chance brings them to a standstill or a standpoint where they are forced to take root.

The individual who has been prised away from his collective background usually manifests symptoms parallel to those found among migrating hordes. The recklessness which so easily spreads throughout an unorganized, migrating mass is a terrifying one. A gold-rush, an invading or retreating army in a foreign land, an exodus of people in the mass—all have certain characteristics in common—namely, a dangerous lowering of responsibility towards human life and property, and a subhuman, unthinking urgency which, like a river in spate, tends to overrun and destroy everything in its path. Man is not the only animal prone to moods of recklessness: all migrating animals moving in vast hordes, as, for instance, the lemmings of the Arctic Circle, salmon, locusts, caterpillars, and, to a certain degree, migratory birds and mammals when moving *en masse*, are inspired by an almost suicidal recklessness quite foreign to their normal adapted character.

Recklessness of life and compulsive urgency are not the only dæmonic manifestations of migrating hordes. There is also an uninhibited prolificity, either preceding, following or sometimes accompanying the migration. Unregulated and indiscriminate sexuality is also a customary feature of human migrations. This is a fact of clinical experience: uprooted individuals, dislocated from their protective moral background, often become alarmingly disorientated from their original containing values.

The contagion of panic, running through a collectivity,

also seems to generate an archaic type of sexuality.[1] It has been observed, for instance, that in sudden disturbances (in particular during the great earthquake at Messina) panic-sexuality breaks out like a conflagration. We must conclude from these facts that, when the adapted epicritic systems of behaviour suddenly collapse, protopathic instinctual urgencies break through which are as regardless of human values, and as catastrophic in their effects, as a blind explosion of energy. Somewhat similar disturbances, only in a relative degree, are liable to be released when an individual becomes disorientated and loses connection with his containing background.

There are abysses of the soul in which the primal force of life is indistinguishable from the primal instinct for death. And this abyss-nature of mankind is as different and as remote from the normal feelings and behaviour of independent, self-reliant beings as is the crater of Vesuvius from a farmhouse in Sussex. We dare not look through the cracks of our civilized crust into those bottomless depths. But we can never understand from what experiences such a figure as the possessing demon Asmodeus was conceived, unless at some time we have encountered the archaic forces of the soul face to face.

Asmodeus belongs to the demonology of sexuality; but, apart from this fact, the essential character of all obsessive demons (including those of our patients) is remarkably uniform. Asmodeus kills the bridegroom, the symbol of the most vital and intimate of human relationships. The Frankenstein demon kills those most dear to its creator. Dracula drinks the blood of the wife of the hero of the story. Mephisto destroys Gretchen. The Golem settles demoniacally upon the two most valued relations of the rabbi, the niece and the synagogue. Schizophrenia can also suck the juice from every vital relationship. What brings the victim of an obsessional complex to the doctor is, in a great many cases, the tragic realization that he is becoming shut off in an arctic isolation from warm human relationship. In this connection

[1] That this connection was familiar to earlier civilizations is suggested by the figure of Pan, who was regarded not only as the author of sudden and groundless terror (panic), but also as the personification of dæmonic sexuality.

the reader will recall how Frankenstein had to pursue his demonic creature into the arctic wastes.

If we accept the primitive meaning of " soul " as the dynamic content or meaning which informs a living or functioning object, we can see how the concept of possession is intimately linked up with that of the abduction or imprisonment of the soul. Hence the statement of the myth that Sara (the soul-image or anima) is possessed by the demon Asmodeus should be interpreted as the disappearance of the true virtue of the race, its place being taken by a blind, destructive urgency without regard for God or man.

The theme of demon-possession and its cure is highly relevant to our investigation; moreover, the principles of psychotherapy, laid down in the myth, are as effective to-day as ever.

* * * * *

The incident with the fish, which immediately precedes the critical encounter with the anima, should be regarded as a symbolical anticipation of the contest with Asmodeus. The healing of spiritual maladies by means of the symbolical example is part of the primitive method of sympathetic magic, the efficacy of which was demonstrated in an earlier chapter of Jewish history when the children of Israel were pricked by this same dæmonic tendency during their long discipline in the wilderness. The unruly wave of renegade revolt is described as a plague of fiery serpents.

> " And the Lord said unto Moses, Make thee a fiery serpent, and set it upon a pole: and it shall come to pass, that every one that is bitten, when he looketh upon it, shall live."[1]

The curative value lies in creating a symbolical object upon which the subjective spiritual malady can be projected. Like attracts like, and the curative power of the effective symbol rests in its magnetic attraction, by virtue of which it draws into itself the corresponding unconscious constellation, directly converting it into a tangible object of consciousness.

The devouring fish is used by the angel-doctor, as Moses

[1] Numbers xxi. 9.

used the snake, for the purpose of creating a new conscious attitude which could deal effectively with the dæmonic complex. As an unconscious factor the dæmonic tendency is a constant source of danger. Through the mechanism of projection, accompanied by insight, it becomes an object of consciousness, whereby a position of detachment is gained which makes it humanly possible to deal with the complex. So far as we are able to understand the curative process in psychotherapy, this is the method which proves effective in all cases where the degree of dissociation of the complex renders insight unusually difficult.

The truth demonstrated by the angel in his analysis of the fish is that, in order to transform a devouring unconscious complex, it must be submitted to the isometric principle. In other words, a sane and balanced consciousness is the product of an absolutely human valuation of both primordial constituents of the libido. When, therefore, either the sexual or the spiritual element is repressed, the result is not merely a blindness which obliterates the half of human experience: it also brings about a corresponding exaggeration of the opposite *dynamis*. Against this self-created monster one is henceforth doomed to unceasing and needlessly heroical combat.

The angel in the myth recreates the attitude of isometric valuation in Tobias by apportioning the three essential organs[1] of the fish to the heavenly powers—*i.e.*, to the principle of consciousness—while assigning the body of the fish to be eaten and enjoyed. The latter, in other words, becomes an offering to the bodily or earth principle.

Thus a symbolical rehearsal is carried out that is fitted to prepare Tobias for the marriage. To have the right attitude means to act under a good ægis. The invocation to the "God of our fathers" constellates a conscious attitude of responsibility at the very moment when the tendency to become a merely instinctive animal is greatest. In that moment, when he invokes the disciplined wisdom of the ancestors, Tobias gains the far-seeing eye of the patriarch,

1 I include the medicinal value of the gall as belonging to the spiritual principle.

whose vision embraces the mythic stream which joins posterity with the ancestors. This is the significance of the subsequent curing of the father's blindness. The patriarchal vision has been restored. We may also suppose that the earth-powers were not disregarded.

The devouring fish of the myth can be equated with the devouring monster of the drawings. In this form the fish-monster symbolizes the atavistic libido which, having receded into the unconscious, assumes the character, as we have seen, of a sucking, devouring vortex, drawing consciousness down to an archaic level. From this point of view it is the migration of the libido downwards which both lowers the conscious level and at the same time activates the archaic unconscious.

Freud deals with the same phenomenon where he says:

> "The libido has retreated into regression and again revives the infantile images. Thither the analytic treatment follows it and endeavours to seek out the libido again, to render it accessible to consciousness, and finally to make it serviceable to reality. Whenever the analytical investigation touches upon the libido, withdrawn into its hiding-place, a struggle must break out: all the forces which have caused the regression of the libido will rise up as resistance against the work, in order to preserve this new condition."[1]

In this description Freud reveals the chief difficulty encountered in the analytical investigation. For it is a matter of general clinical experience that, whenever we approach the dragon's lair where the treasure lies hidden, the fiercest neurotic obstacles and resistances are encountered. In our patient's material we observed that, as soon as the regressive system had been penetrated, the unconscious immediately assumed its most threatening aspect. The same thing occurs in the myth; the devouring atavistic tendency leaps out just at the moment when Tobias begins to lay hold of the real problem. It is also a predictable occurrence in the realm of human relationship in the moment when the marriage should become psychologically real—which means accepting the re-

[1] *Zur Dynamik der Uebertragung.*

lationship as one's true destiny—that the primitive anima produces her most ruthless effects.

In the way he handles the incident of the fish, the angel might almost be accounted as the founder of analytical psychology. Observe, for instance, how he takes the experience of the unconscious, distinguishing its essential value or meaning, then informs his pupil how to assimilate the experience and take it into himself. This is the very essence of Jung's method: both, indeed, may be said to have the same end in view—namely, to intensify the value of consciousness, whether as an end in itself or as the only valid means we have of dealing with the activated unconscious.

People in the grip of an unconscious content show a relatively lower level of consciousness, a condition that is clinically demonstrable by a defective relation to objects. This condition is beautifully illustrated in Drawing XII., where the hero, feeling himself suddenly attacked from behind—*i.e.*, from the unconscious—finds at the same moment his conscious capacities relatively crippled—*i.e.*, his weapons are lost or broken. His anxious, preoccupied expression is reminiscent of a man whose attention is suddenly disturbed by a disagreeable thought intruding from the unconscious. The opposite case will be equally familiar to the psychotherapist—when, for example, a patient, having been oppressed and confused, brings a dream which, under analysis, clarifies the whole situation. As the light of consciousness returns, the whole expression changes, and the patient's relatedness to reality is re-established. From such experiences we realize how intimately the integrity of consciousness is rooted in the full apprehension of immediate experience.

The essential organs of the fish therefore represent unconscious psychic values which are made actual through experience, and are then taken up into consciousness. This operation is apparently the indispensable preparation for the work of releasing the anima from the state of demonic possession. In the same way Parsifal had to take possession of the sacred Spear before Kundry could be released from her bondage to Klingsor. While the Spear (symbolizing the creative power of the libido) was in the hands of Klingsor, the knights of the Grail could do nothing: they were psychically impotent. Because Parsifal was able to resist the magical enchantment of the anima he could take possession of the Spear, whereupon its healing virtue was restored. In both the Parsifal and the Tobit myths, the release of the anima from demonic possession is followed by the return of the anima with the hero, and in both cases an act of healing accompanies the return.

The return of the anima to the ancestral house where, psychologically, she belongs is also accompanied by an act of healing or restoration of function in our patient's myth. For in the *mandala* garden we find the dead sister restored and re-established in living relation to the subject. For the sake of the anima Tobias had to learn how to grapple with the demon, and for the sake of the anima, personified by the dead sister, the patient had to encounter and combat his worst dread. In one drawing (not reproduced) the sister-anima is actually represented as caught between the teeth of the devouring monster in the place of the green protoplasm. This life-giving symbol is rightly identified with the anima, symbolizing, as it does, the animating vital principle.

V

Applying the Tobias myth, in the manner of a dye-stain, to our patient's material, we shall see how certain points, which were inconspicuous before, are therewith brought into relief.

To begin with, there is the *leit-motif* of the remote anima in the grip of the demon. In the patient's second dream a girl stood by the car-station, while he performed an outlandish task on the railway. The girl was associated with his dead sister.[1] As soon as he had touched this association the patient dropped through into the infantile fantasy-system, in which he seemed to be fighting with his sister and rolling on the floor with her. At this point he was aware of a ghastly (=ghostly) impression, and the anima is sensed in the form of a black cat. In the folk-lore of many lands the appearance of a black cat is supposed to denote the presence of a ghost; hence it is also associated with superstitious magical practices.

[1] In the mythological realm the sister-relation is naturally more comprehensive than in reality, since the incest-taboo has no jurisdiction in that realm.

In Drawing III. there is an insulated piece of red that is held in a toothless witch's jaw, and just beside this there is the limbless creature in suspended animation, which we regarded as the unrelated aspect of the personality that had been drawn down into the unconscious. There is also the drawing of the anima in the mouth of the monster. At all these points we find allusion to the idea of the sister-anima being held, like Kundry and Sara, in the grip of a demonic influence.[1]

But we have a still more revealing piece of evidence in the dream where the anima, in the form of a snake, is exorcised by the patient and made to emerge from the banana. This snake clearly symbolizes the dreaded power of the primordial instinct lying concealed in the apparently harmless phallic fruit. The exorcism in the presence of the ancestral god represents the act of making the hidden influence visible to consciousness. Only when the anima is hidden and invisible is she demonic. When known and realized, she is both womb and midwife of unborn potentialities. In her operation, therefore, the anima is equivocal,[2] the deciding factor being the attitude of consciousness.

We have already observed the resemblances connected with the motif of the hero, who, by overcoming the monster and salving the essential organs, transfers psychic value from the dormant unconscious state to that of effective consciousness. We also saw that this transference of value from the monster to the new ruler—*i.e.*, the young sun-god—synchronized, as in the myth, with the dissipation and assimilation of the dæmonic complex.

The third theme, which is interwoven in the fabric of the material, and which the myth-stain elucidates, is the intimate connection existing between the anima and the ancestral god. In the myth this appears in the synchronicity and confluence of the prayers of Sara and Tobit, arising to the ancestral deity in heaven, both expressing at bottom one and

[1] To what extent this sinister influence can be attributed to the crippling repression of feeling, due to the emotional trauma of the sister's death, on the one hand, and how much to the patient's psychotic inheritance, on the other, it is impossible to determine.

[2] Hence her equivocal manifestation in the form of the snake, which fascinates and repels.

the same psychological need. It is corroborated in the moment when Tobias brings Sara home to the house of his father and the same isometric means which cured her of the demonic possession now cures the ancestor of his blindness.

At this point I may remind the reader of the case of the Siberian *shaman* who was neurotically (*i.e.*, demoniacally) possessed by the *ayami* of his ancestors. Appearing to him in a vision, she demanded that he accept her as his wife and also submit to her instruction as the spirit of his *shaman* forebears. Once he had accepted this vision seriously, and had set himself to tread the lonely and dangerous path of the *shaman*, he was cured of his illness. The anima was also released, taking up her abode in a hut on the mountains.

To the primitive mind a ghost is harmful and dangerous, just because it is liable to get into human beings. But when it lives away on the mountain or among the bamboos, it is no longer a bad ghost, but an independent spirit which can be helpful as well as sinister. Thus the most important task of the *shaman*—a task for which only the most experienced *shamans* are fitted—is to look after the souls of the dead. The wise *shaman* knows how to lead them away from the village and to free them by means of certain rites and instruction from their tie to the living.

Camping among the Elgonyi on the slopes of Elgon, we frequently came upon little spirit-houses, with milk and food set out for the entertainment of the wandering ghost. Since ghosts are the chief cause of sickness in Africa, a successful means of staying the ghost is equivalent to a prophylactic serum.

On a much higher level the Egyptian *Book of the Dead* and the *Tibetan Book of the Dead* (Evans-Wentz) are concerned with the same therapeutic necessity. Only at this level the idea of spiritual instruction to help the release of the soul at the critical *transitus* outweighs the primitive motive of protecting the living from ghostly disturbances, although, reading between the lines, this need is always there in the background.

This world-wide practice among primitive and quasi-primitive societies is not merely, as Sir James Frazer assumes, the manifestation of savage superstition. It is the expression of an empirical psychotherapeutic technique based upon general human experience. Whatever method we may adopt of bringing a disturbing unconscious complex into consciousness, we are actually obeying the same necessity which urges the primitive mind to ghost exorcism and "spiritual" ministrations.

To the primitive mind, which is quite innocent of psychologizing, a disturbing subjective factor is patently a ghost, and the various practices employed to lead the ghost away from its human tenement to a safe distance are simply the primitive way of ridding the mind of disturbing ideas. Moses, as we have already seen, employed a similar technique. The food, care and instruction given to the spirits (*cf.* cure of souls) express a real human need to pay attention to the impersonal motivations of the psyche: a need which the rites and teachings of the great religious foundations of the world have regarded as the prime necessity of holy living. Hence it is impossible to deal adequately with the primordial images of the unconscious without coming directly upon the fundamental problem of religion.

The fact that an immediate experience of the general unconscious frequently has a suprapersonal or transubjective character makes it difficult to embrace this realm in our conceptions of mental structure. Normally we are constrained to regard our own psychology as identical with the personal feelings, motives and events of which the ego is the centre. Hence every other subjective factor tends to be included in the category of the supernormal. In demonstrating this myth of a modern man I have attempted to show that, by disentangling the archaic mythological contents and making them conscious, the patient is necessarily brought face to face with the religious problem, which at bottom resolves itself into the question of how one values immediate experience.

Our medical psychology can scarcely be expected to survive if, at the outset, it attempts to exclude the deepest of human motives from its account of experience. And if we are so much alarmed by the bogey of anthropomorphism that we cannot view the spontaneous personifications of unconscious factors without an intellectual shudder, we forfeit every claim to psychological empiricism. For the field of psychic phenomenology consists almost exclusively of personifications, and these subjective personalities form the actual field of our study. The unconscious deals in symbols, and if we start with a postulate that all symbols are merely infantile forms of expression, we are prohibited by our own postulate from any investigation of their content, other than that already supplied by our theory.

Representation by images is the spontaneous activity of the psyche, and if we would know and value our birthright we must respect the basic images upon which the whole structure of values rests. These images are the so-called archetypes of the collective unconscious; they are the living vehicles of human history which personify the continuity of the vital stream of a specific culture within the psychic sphere. Those who live in daily contact with these images, whether through projection upon religious objects or by inner converse, feel supported and sanctioned as by a superior power. To be cut off from this experience is like banishment or sickness.

The general loss of faith in this spiritual inheritance is symbolized in the myth by the affliction of Tobit and the demonic possession of the anima. These are the symptoms of a profound dissociation which can be healed only by invoking the aid of the heavenly powers and by accomplishing the "great work."

In the patient's material the theme of Drawings III. and VI. is the mobilization of all the psychic reserves, both personal and suprapersonal, upon the dissociated system containing the sister-anima. In the latter drawing the ancestor-god is commanding the movement from heaven, while the dissociated system is brought into immediate relation with the house of the ancestors. In Drawing VII. the whole force of ancestral (*i.e.*, celestial) authority is brought to bear on the morbid system. Compare this with the divine messenger who is sent from heaven to break the spell which holds Sara in barren bondage.

It is significant that the anima first appears in the moment when the dragon is slain; she also participates in the dragon-colours, green and yellow. In other words, the anima manifests herself to the subject when the immediate experience of the unconscious becomes decisive in his life.

The idea of recovering value that has been lost is present in both myths. In the psychological quest the treasure is represented by the functions that have been held in the functionless dissociated state. Accordingly, when the deflated hero vomits these into the shallop of Venus where the anima is reclining, it is equivalent to the homecoming of Tobias, who brings back the treasure and the soul-mistress to the house of the ancestors; albeit in the patient's myth the restoration is performed in a compulsive unconscious way.

The position of the moon coming to rest immediately above the house of the ancestors associates with the star which hung over Bethlehem at Christ's nativity, betokening a world-changing event. From one point of view, a mother has given birth to a babe; but, from another, it is an event that makes a star stand still in wonder. Prodigies of nature accompanied the birth of Buddha, while terrifying wonders attended the crucifixion of Jesus. In the language of the myth these synchronous cosmic occurrences proclaim an absolutely crucial event, in which both worlds participate: gods as well as men. In psychological language these represent the levels of the suprapersonal and the personal.

In the present drawing the sister-anima is brought home and is related again to the subject in the *mandala* garden of the ancestral house. This represents the restoration of a specific feeling-content on the plane of ordinary human relatedness. But at the same time the anima, as a new and world-changing influence, comes to rest above the house. As a mediating function between the conscious and the unconscious, the anima is assuredly a world-changing phenomenon for all who have to deal with the unconscious.

VI

The spontaneous renewal and transformation of the personality through the instigation of the anima has already been illustrated in the case of the Siberian *shaman*. But we have an example of the same phenomenon nearer home in the dual personality of the writer William Sharp. Before the appearance of the anima-personality (who called herself Fiona Macleod), Sharp was a rather artificial literary *poseur*. In everything he did he seemed to be studying the impression he was making. He went everywhere and knew everybody of importance. He affected an impressive persona; he insisted upon getting to the front of the stage and keeping there. His books had more reputation than sale, and, in general, he gave the impression of a man plagued by his ego. Then comes the history of a serious illness and, as in the case of the *shaman*, the illness was attended by certain visions. In this visionary state he had an encounter with a beautiful " Green Lady " on the banks of Lake Nemi, who resigned her soul into his keeping and opened her mind to his interpretation. Lake Nemi is the one place in all Europe where the latent pagan root of a man's soul would be most likely to send forth shoots. For there, in the sacred grove of Diana, was once enacted that strange remote drama which inspired Sir James Frazer's monumental investigation into the dark realm of the primitive mind. There is, so far as I know, no internal evidence that Sharp was acquainted with Frazer's work; but, since the preface of the first edition bears the date 1890 (more than ten years before Sharp's death), it is quite possible that he had peered through the door which Frazer had opened. The beautiful painting of the sacred grove by Turner may also have touched his imagination.

The encounter with the Green Lady, like Leo's meeting with Ayesha[1] or the *shaman's* with his *ayami*, became the turning-point in Sharp's life. From this moment an entirely new life began,[2] and it is interesting to compare Sharp's

1 Rider Haggard: *She*.

2 Rider Haggard's life was also changed by the vision of a lady in a church. The awakening of the anima through this encounter gave the initial impetus for the whole Ayesha myth. Compare this with the arousing of Shakti in the *Kundalini* yoga.

account of his experience with that of the *shaman* who declared that the *ayami* spoke out of his mouth. Sharp writes:

> " My pen wrote as if dipped in fire, and when I sat down to write prose, a spirit-hand would seize the pen, and guide it into inspired verse."

By a constant surrender of himself to the control of the anima, he watched her develop from a phantasm of spring fields into a commanding spirit-companion with a definite personality of her own. It is also interesting to observe how this anima-figure anticipates that of our subject in her choice of green and yellow.

> " Wild fawn, wild fawn,
> Dost thou flee the Green Lady ?
> Her wild flowers will race thee,
> Her sunbeams will chase thee,
> Her laughter is ringing aloud in the dawn—
> O, the Green Lady
> With yellow flowers strewing the ways of the dawn,
> Wild fawn, wild fawn !"

In effect Sharp was changed from a fairly competent journalist into a writer of sensitive Gaelic romances, and the increasing reality of Fiona Macleod almost obliterated the original William Sharp. He actually exhibited a portrait of her—" a lovely young woman with dark hair and mysterious eyes "—and dictated letters in her name. The horizon which was opened to Sharp through his relation to the anima embraced Gaelic and Scandinavian legends, faery-lore and a kind of mystical alliance between paganism and Christianity. The fact that he handled these contents with the literary preciosity so favoured in the nineties does not do away with the fact that his whole mental horizon was changed by his experience of the unconscious.

* * * * *

To resume, the new orientation of consciousness is symbolized in the patient's drawing by the emergence of the reborn sun. The patient had the impression that the figure in the sun was Osiris: though he was not well-informed about Egyptian mythology, and was unaware that Isis was the sister as well as the wife of Osiris, or that, after his death and dismemberment, Osiris was reborn as ruler of the underworld.

There are several features of the story of Osiris which are germane to our myth, and to which we must briefly allude. According to Plutarch's account of the myth—

> " Isis and Orisis, having a mutual affection, enjoyed each other in their mother's womb before they were born, and from this commerce sprang the ' elder Horus ' whom the Greeks call Apollo."
>
> " Osiris, being now become King of Egypt, applied himself towards civilizing his countrymen by turning them from their former indigent and barbarous course of life; he moreover taught them how to cultivate and improve the fruits of the earth; he gave them a body of laws to regulate their conduct by, and instructed them in that reverence and worship which they were to pay to the gods."[1]

Later we read how Osiris was betrayed by Set (Greek Typho), the dæmon of chaos and darkness, who invited him to a banquet and lured him to lie in a chest, previously made to his measurement, so that he was the only guest at the banquet whom it exactly fitted. Having shut him fast in the chest Set cast him into the Nile, and he was carried down to the sea. Isis sought him everywhere, and eventually found the chest embedded in the trunk of a tamarisk tree which had grown around it. Again Set intervened, and finding the chest in a " remote and unfrequented place," opened it and dismembered the body of Osiris into fourteen pieces, which he scattered far and wide. Isis devotedly sought the scattered fragments of her lord, and found all but one—the phallus.

It is not necessary to go deeply into this Osiris myth, because the correspondences are not far to seek. The liberation of feeling elevating the spirit of the dead sister to the mythological plane, as coeval with Osiris, is self-evident. The deathless devotion of Isis to her divine spouse and brother forms the archetypal basis of the anima-relation. An interesting allusion to the Isis myth resides in the fact that the sister-

[1] S. Squire: *Plutarch's Treatise of Isis and Osiris*, Cambridge, 1744.

anima is depicted receiving the missing fragments (or functions), recovered from the state of dissociation (*i.e.*, dismemberment), as she reclines in the boat of the moon. Plutarch informs us that—

> "Isis set out in search of the scattered fragments of her husband's body, making use of a boat made of the reed papyrus, in order the more easily to pass through the lower and fenny parts of the country. For which reason they say the crocodile never touches any persons who sail in this sort of vessel, as either fearing the anger of the goddess, or else respecting it on account of its having once carried her."

When we remember that Isis became the goddess of the underworld, the deity of motherhood, as well as the goddess of magical healing, and was later associated with Selene the moon-goddess, we can appreciate the singular appropriateness of these attributes in relation to the anima-figure of our drawing.

In this connection we might recall the patient's first memory or fantasy connected with the sister, in which a black cat appeared accompanied by a ghastly impression. The devil is quite apt to appear under the guise of a black animal. Mephisto's entrance upon the scene in *Faust* is in the form of a black poodle. One of the demonic manifestations of Set was that of a black pig. In the one hundred and twelfth chapter of the *Book of the Dead* we read that one day Ra said to Horus, "Let me see what is coming to pass in thine eye," and, having looked, he said to Horus, "Look at that black pig." Thereupon Horus looked, and he immediately felt that a great injury had been done to his eye, and he said to Ra, "Verily, my eye seemeth as if it were an eye upon which Set had inflicted a blow."[1] Ra uses the eye of Horus as a crystal in which to read the future. Thus he foretells the terrific battle which Horus is to wage with Set when he revenges his father's death on the betrayer. It is the battle of light with the powers of darkness: the struggle of consciousness against the dæmonic power of the unconscious.

When we look back over the events of this individual myth we can recognize, in the figures of that first memory-

[1] Wallis Budge: *The Gods of the Egyptians*, vol. ii., p. 368 (Methuen)

image, a similar prediction of the patient's subsequent fate. Essentially, it is the same theme and the same problem which has attended man's progress from the beginning of culture; hence the symbolism of these early cultural myths is recreated ever afresh out of the timeless womb of the unconscious.

From the description of Osiris as culture-hero, quoted above, we conclude that this new sun, the reborn ruler of consciousness, must symbolize a new conception of the self, as significant in the history of this individual as was the discovery of agriculture in that of the human race. For Osiris was the first inventor of agriculture, from which all civilized arts originated. He was also the just law-giver and the first instructor in religious exercises. To pay reverence and worship to the gods was an immense step in consciousness from the level of primitive magic, where the gods are constrained by the use of magical ritual.

The significance of this young and radiant sun gains a special value when we remember that the patient's first drawing was ruled by a darkened sun with pathological sun-spots. That sun was associated with his father, with whom, through unconscious identification, the patient shared a certain spiritual blindness. The state of the sun in the first drawing revealed, therefore, a further point of correspondence with the Tobit myth—namely, the blindness of the father.

The correspondences we have discovered between the ancient myth and this modern material have no resemblance to the diffusional process whereby certain features of an ancient pattern are more or less consciously transferred to a new form. In the present study the analogy between the old myths and the new is intrinsic and essential. In no place can we discern the incorporation of borrowed alien elements. The myth has emerged autochthonously as a natural product of the patient's psychology. Indeed, when he made this drawing he had never read the Book of Tobit, nor had he any particular acquaintance with the story of Osiris.

The similarity of the basic structure or pattern of the two myths must therefore be ascribed to the inherent nature of the autonomous psyche which tends to respond to analogous situations with more or less identical imagery. But even supposing conscious borrowing from the old pattern had taken place, it would have made no substantial difference to the psychological value of the material, inasmuch as the subject of our interest would still have been the psychic urgency which caused the selection, rather than the source from which the various images were derived.

Viewing the megalithic temple of Stonehenge, for example, psychological interest will naturally be engaged by the power of the idea which could command, assemble and shape those vast stones. We must marvel at the primordial image which, with one and the same form, created an inviolable magic wall against inimical spirits, and a perfect vessel into which the emergent sun-god could be invoked. This attitude would not be tolerated by the archæologist, who is concerned with the problems of the diffusion of culture-patterns, the origin of the stones, the probable date of the structure, and the method employed for raising the stones. But, none the less, our psychological intuition rests upon inherent probability, inasmuch as the primary functions of religious practice in every race and in every period of human history have been to ward off or dispel bad spirits and to invoke the holy spirit. The utmost that psychology can achieve, therefore, by means of the analogical method is modestly to demonstrate the existence of intrinsic correspondences. Whatever truth we are able to reach by this method will rest, not upon the accumulation of circumstantial evidence, but rather upon the recognition of certain basic principles whereby the range of human vision is invited to embrace a new set of facts.

CHAPTER XIII

THE SYMBOL AS RULER AND TRANSFORMER OF INSTINCT

I

THE drawings I have discussed represent only a fraction of the material which the patient produced. I have limited my work to these early drawings, partly from the exigencies of time and space, but also because those I have presented here were completed before any thoroughgoing psychological treatment of them was attempted. They are therefore all the more valuable as evidence of the archetypal, myth-like formations spontaneously produced by the psyche.

Among the drawings which followed there was a series concerned with the symbolism of the cup as magical container. Of all the myths of Christendom the Grail symbolism preserves the most significant reality for men of to-day. An interesting feature of this development, in the case we are considering, was the fact that the vessel of transformation was no longer under the Christian ægis. A god and goddess of Thibetan and Chinese origin were the presiding geniuses of the magical vessel, and their rule was in all respects equal.

This spiritual migration to the East is certainly not unconnected with the lack of the feminine principle in the Protestant half of Christendom: a lack which is to some extent responsible for the Amfortas-complex (*i.e.*, the sick saint) in the Christian unconscious. It can hardly be questioned that the projection of essential functions of the soul into the gods and goddesses of antiquity had a profoundly humanizing influence, while the absence of a feminine deity throughout Protestant Christendom has had the effect of producing a spiritual nostalgia for the earlier gods, which tends to find a frustrated expression in a sentimentalized figure of Christ. The ecstatic worship of the Virgin in the Middle Ages also revealed this profound longing of the Christian soul. This theme constellates the material of the second part of this work, where the need of surrender to the feminine principle becomes the crucial problem. In some of the later drawings of the present series the crucified god appeared identified with Amfortas—namely, as the helpless victim of an irreconcilable dualism.

Turning from religion to psycho-analysis, the tragic pessimism of Freud, with the unredeemed sterility of the Freudian unconscious, warned the subject that the process of scientific reduction can never provide the solution. In brief, the modern soul is precluded from evading the problem of the opposites, either by means of a divine scapegoat or by a " scientific " reduction of the problem to infantile anxiety. The truth is that a new moral feeling begins to dawn which makes it impossible for a man to buy freedom from an age-old sense of guilt by the sacrifice of the Son of God. Even though the experience of crucifixion within is the price demanded of the soul by this new moral feeling, yet this very acceptance of the real Christian burden is in itself a release. For once the opposites are recognized as a basic aspect of psychic life, their uncompromising absolutism in the state of projection is exchanged for relativity within the soul. Without a containing circle the perpendicular and horizontal of the cross represent a limitless and relentless opposition. But contained within the compass of the circle these opposite dimensions have the character, each to each, of reciprocal principles. They produce the power of reciprocal tension, instead of sundering the soul in an inescapable division. No symbol that fails to embrace the long sundered opposites—heaven and hell, god and devil, spirit and sex, good and evil, man and woman—in a single form can have real power for the modern soul.

Jung's conception of the self as the centre which embraces the psychic totality is not a philosophical speculation: it is the same unifying symbol as, for instance, the *homo philosophicus*, the second Adam, the Philosopher's Stone, the *aurum philosophicum* of the earlier quest; it is, indeed, this central symbol which the need of the modern soul has rediscovered.

The mediæval " royal art of alchemy " was based upon profound psychological intuition. The closed vessel in which the opposite elements were heated and fused together was called the philosophical egg, while the red substance which emerged from the alchemical distillation was the Philosopher's Stone. It was also called our king, the red lion, the grand elixir, etc. The philosophical egg symbolizes the contained totality of the psyche, in which the individuality or self, as a central substance[1] of infinite value and permanence, is formed through the uniting of opposite principles. It is the primordial monad, which both precedes and unites the opposites. Individuality, conceived of as supreme value, is therefore an autochthonous psychical image, which emerges ever and again from the suprapersonal depths, or heights, of the psyche.

In Wolfram von Eschenbach's *Parzival* the Grail is described as a stone (*i.e.*, *lapis herilis*, or *lapsus ex cœlis*, or *lapis electrix*), which chooses those who shall serve it, and to whom it ministers new life. It is spoken of as the " inconspicuous " stone, yielding all manner of refreshment, and its peculiar power is sustained by a dove. Thus the Grail is both a vessel and a stone or jewel of inestimable potency. The corresponding Eastern symbol of individuation is the lotus containing the jewel or the divine essence. The Tibetan invocation *Om mane padme hum* has been translated: " Oh! the jewel in the lotus." The undreamed-of radiance of the incarnate Bodhisattva first became manifest within an immense lotus-flower. Standing therein, he first viewed the world and filled it with a new light. Again the emergence of the self is conceived as a world-changing event.

In every version of the Quest the symbol of the vessel is closely linked with that of the sword or spear. These same symbols are also to be found in the heroic myths of Ireland and Wales. The four treasures of the *Tuatha de Danann*, for instance, were the *Lia Fail*, the stone of fate or virtue, the sword that Lug Lamhfhada was wont to use, the spear which the same Lug used in battle, and the cauldron of the Dagda. It is recorded of this vessel of abundance that " a company

[1] In *Psychology and Religion* Jung quotes the mediæval Arabic author Senior, who says about the *lapis*: " There is one substance which never dies, because it perseveres in constant increase."

used not ever to go away from it unsatisfied." The original symbols of the card game *Tarok* were a coin, a club, a dish or vessel, and a sword.

In both these groups of four symbols from a pure pagan source we find the natural opposition of male and female symbolism within the pattern of the four. Resisting, for the moment, the obvious sexual interpretation of this quaternity, and allowing our thoughts to dwell upon the character of those epochs in which the mythology of the sword and vessel bloomed in greatest profusion, we discover that in every case the epoch was one in which valour, steadfastness and knightly quality were highly prized. They were periods in which individual mettle and individual relationship were esteemed as the finest fruits of culture, while the solid collective virtues were correspondingly inconspicuous.

Neither in Celtic tradition nor in mediæval romance is there any special emphasis on racial or dynastic struggles. Instead we find the deification of the individual hero. Similarly, in the *Minnedienst* (love-service) of the days of chivalry the individuality of woman was enhanced and glorified as never before in Western culture. As a consequence, the individual love-relationship gained precedence over the biological marriage relationship. A woman, whether married or maid, who refused her favours to her knight as a reward for valorous deeds was felt to be lacking in individual merit. Courage in love was valued as highly as courage in arms. Thus the significance of sex became indissolubly bound up with an individual concept of value, and on a different plane from that of the collective biological archetype. It was because of these new potentialities, developing within the orbit of the masculine and feminine principles, that the male and female symbols gained a new and inexhaustible significance.

For us, who know the sword only as a museum curiosity, it is almost impossible to realize the magical power and virtue with which the sword of a warrior was possessed. A mediæval Christian chronicler observes that it was reasonable for the pagan Irish to trust their swords "because dæmons used to speak from out them."[1] For example, we read how Ogma,

1 Alfred Nutt: *Studies of the Legend of the Holy Grail.*

the champion of the *Tuatha de Danann*, while he was cleaning the sword of Tethra, which he had won in battle, heard from it all the many and great feats it had wrought. The relation of the hero to his sword was instinct with the spirit which converted the predatory killing and bloodshed of the dark ages into the self-discipline and knightly virtue of the age of chivalry.

What, then, of the magical vessel, the vessel of healing and abundance? The love that was offered to woman in the new spirit was ruled by a royal symbol. As we saw in the parallel case of Hermas, the image of woman became identified in the minds of men with the cultural ideal which was pushing up like a lotus-bud out of the darkest age of Europe's history. Thus the loved woman became the vessel of devotion in whom the libido was transformed and renewed.

The relationship between man and woman is the primordial container of value. During certain vital epochs the advancing spirit of man seems to pour a new content, the seed of a new possibility of life, into the vessel of human love. The inchoate depths of sexuality begin to glow with a fire that was never kindled by mere personal need. The vessel that was shaped and moulded out of human necessity is found to contain a new and magical efficacy.

The symbol of the Grail derived its abundant vitality from the fact that it united the highest religious feeling with the most intimate human need. The same miraculous combination occurs in the image of the Son of God, born in a manger.

In the age we are considering, the emergence of the Grail symbol synchronized with a new valuation of woman and the meaning of love. In so far as the desired woman accepted the spiritual function of anima, or soul-mistress, as her distinctive contribution to the cultural revolution, she became psychologically identified with the Grail. She made real the symbol for man. Through thus embodying the symbol, woman herself and the whole value of the feminine principle were enormously enhanced. But the attitude of acceptance and submission in the sphere of love, symbolized by the vessel, must be complemented by the lion-like spirit of the warrior, symbolized by the sword. The one receives, contains and renews; the other springs, conquers and serves. In these periods, therefore, when the disciplined development of individuality was held as the supreme cultural value, we find the active, manifest, masculine principle balanced by a passive, containing, feminine principle.

We may also observe that the effective operation of these opposite principles, like those of male and female, depends upon their reciprocity. Sexuality needs the disciplined austerity of the spirit in order to generate quality, while spirituality needs the primal fire of sex, for without this its products lack the penetrating vital flame. Hence the chastity which was so insisted upon by many of the mediæval chroniclers was of an entirely different character from that enforced by respectability. Continence is the indispensable condition of individual achievement—not because sexuality is evil, but owing to the condition that the transformation of opposite elements can take place only when they are held in braced opposition. The danger lies not with woman, but with women.[1]

During those periods of civilization in which the collective and dynastic organization of society has held precedence over individual development, the marriage container tends to become the expression of the highest good, and is safeguarded as an absolute value. The morality of this phase must accordingly insist upon chastity and continence, with the aim of making marriage the expression of social solidarity and discipline. The abysmal misunderstanding of the morality of the knightly and heroic ages by the mind of this other phase is revealed in the numerous commentaries, chronicles and poems of the last century, dealing with the age of chivalry.[2] Individual morality and social morality

1 *Cf.* Mephisto's erotic standpoint in the second part of *Faust*, Act IV.:

" Then for the fairest women, fresh and rosy,
I'd build a lodge, convenient and cosy,
And so the bright and boundless time I should
Pass in the loveliest social solitude.
Women I say: and, once for all, believe
That in the plural I the sex conceive !"

(*Trans. Bayard Taylor.*)

2 A similar misunderstanding at the present time, fraught with terrible political possibilities, obscures our appreciation of the complementary biological patterns which underlie the totalitarian and democratic forms of

often demand the same virtue, but for entirely different reasons. In the age of the *cour de dame* the individual love-relationship gained superiority over the biological relation,[1] because it was associated with a higher moral value, demanding a higher degree of self-discipline than the marriage relationship. In the same way the symbolic content of the Grail held a greater cultural significance for that time than the mere conservation of traditional forms.

The value of self-discipline for the sake of the chosen lady developed at the same time as the Quest of the Grail. The libido that was dammed back from undisciplined expression became concentrated within the new psychic constellation, until finally the Grail symbol contained the highest intensity of libido value. Through this metamorphosis the personal meaning of love was married to a primordial image in the unconscious whereby the specific feminine attribute of fertility[2] became the symbol of the renewing and transforming womb of the unconscious.[3] In this way the

---

government. The former is based upon the pattern of the leader and the herd, which gregarious animals tend to adopt during migration, or when insecurity threatens. The break-up of the herd into families or relatively small groups when the breeding ground is reached is equivalent to the natural communism of the food-gathering, indigenous tribes which forms the ground-plan of democracy. It is the crime of politics that these essentially relative patterns should be represented as absolute principles.

[1] At feasts and banquets the King's lover sometimes took precedence even of the Queen.

[2] The vessel is the womb.

[3] Goethe's image of the " eternal feminine " also led him to this maternal concept of the unconscious. In *Faust*, Act I., Part II., Mephisto puts the key into Faust's hand with the words:

" Take hold of it, not undervaluing !"
FAUST: " It glows, it shines,—increases in my hand !"
MEPHISTO: " How much 'tis worth thou soon shalt understand,
The key scents the true place from all others;
Follow it down !—'twill lead thee to the Mothers."

The terror of incest seizes hold of Faust, making the descent into the unconscious terrible and sinister. Mephisto, as psychopomp, inspires him to the attempt:

" At last a blazing tripod tells thee this,
That there the utterly deepest bottom is.
Its light to thee will then the Mothers show,
Some in their seats, the others stand or go,
At their own will: Formation, Transformation,
The eternal mind's eternal recreation,
Forms of all creatures,—there are floating free."

(*Trans. Bayard Taylor.*)

free, individual love-relationship became the channel through which the suprapersonal contents of the unconscious found expression. Thus the Quest of the Grail, as a living symbol, comprised both the libido that was withheld from concrete expression and the spiritual desire by which this libido was transformed from a mere biological urge into a supreme cultural value.

Biological psychology attempts to explain this " metaphysical " displacement by the theory of sublimation. But can this theory account for the most significant thing about man at every level of culture—namely, the unquenchable passion with which he pursues ends which stand in direct contradiction to his natural " biological " inclinations? In order to account for these propensities, the biological psychologist must either so stretch the meaning of his terms as to embrace absolutely contradictory phenomena or simply ignore the significance of a large part of human experience.

Freud's attempt to account for moral consciousness as arising from a sense of guilt, experienced by members of the " primal horde " through the act of parricide,[1] is an example of this psychological obtuseness. According to biological premises, the killing of the father by the excluded sons, in order to gain access to the females, belongs to an established biological pattern. This pattern is a mechanism which reproduces itself *ad infinitum* and, moreover, among certain primates, still presumably persists without any advent of moral consciousness. Whence came, then, the new and hitherto undreamed-of sense of guilt in respect to a biological event of unexceptional regularity?

When we step outside the closed circle of biological determinism, we are at once aware that a moral act or response is invariably individual in origin. A moral feeling can be imparted to a community, but its source is in the solitary individual soul. Before an effective moral reaction can arise, that is able to withstand the reproductive momentum of an established pattern, some individual must have attained to a non-biological standpoint. In other words, he must have detached himself so completely from his previous identity

[1] Freud: *Totem and Taboo.*

with the horde-pattern as to view the parricidal avenue to life with passionate hatred. How this detachment was gained, and what manner of reflections and feelings went to the building up of the new attitude, we need not try to guess. The fact that a non-biological standpoint was won by an especially gifted individual, who therewith inaugurated a departure from the established pattern, has been immortalized in the myth of Prometheus. The solitary hero-criminal, stealing the fire from heaven in order to save mankind from a purely animal existence, is the archetypal representative of that other aspect of psychical reality which is made invisible by the " biological " spectacles. For the acceptance of the Promethean archetype as the symbol of an independent creative power, unmotivated by instinct in the biological sense, involves the admission of the spiritual factor as the primordial equivalent of the sexual.

Stealing the fire from heaven is, at bottom, the same idea as eating the rays or particles of the sun. The conception of assimilating the sun-nature is found in every culture, whether primitive or civilized, wherever the light of the hero-king breaks out of primæval darkness. Usually the advent of the sun is represented as the visitation of a divine figure who impregnates the mother of the hero.[1]

Myths are empirical psychological records of dawning conscious reactions to impressive human events; and there can be little doubt that the most profound impression of early civilizing epochs was the recognition of a superior power in certain individuals which enabled them to withstand and depart from the hitherto unchallenged biological pattern, thereby creating richer forms of life as from a new centre. The myths are unanimous in identifying the source of this power either with the sun or the wind. There is an undeniable force of reason behind this mythological statement. For whence could originate that power which transcended the primitive forces of man's earthy nature, if not from the sun, the primal source of energy? Thus the philosophy

[1] An interesting example is mentioned by Jung in *Psychology of the Unconscious*, in which a mediæval German painter depicts the *conceptio immaculata* as a kind of tube or pipe descending from the sun and passing under the skirt of Mary.

inherent in these myths is identical with the concept of cosmic duality of Chinese culture, in which the dark, earthy, feminine principle of *Yin* is opposed by the light, spiritual, masculine principle of *Yang*.

But if we must conceive the spiritual force in human psychology as primordial in origin, and not a mere cultural acquisition, we must somehow bring this conception into relation with the concept of instinct. Is this possible, or are we doomed to regard human nature as eternally torn asunder by warring powers irreconcilably opposed from the beginning ?

For Darwin the " very essence of an instinct is that it is followed independently of reason." The original meaning of the word is instigation, impulse, prompting, hence a natural or spontaneous tendency or inclination. Dynamically it means to infuse as an animating principle.[1] Milton uses the word specifically in relation to the spiritual *dynamis*:

> " Forth rushed the chariot undrawn, itself instinct with Spirit."

The term " instinct " covers, therefore, every spontaneous manifestation of psychical energy, everything which acts independently of rational direction. From this wider view-point, the specific biological categories of sexuality and will-to-power (or self-preservation) have no true title to the whole province of instinct: rather should they be regarded as descriptive categories, required for the interpretation of certain specific aspects of animal behaviour. Jung's conception of the libido and the primordial images, on the other hand, embraces every possible manifestation of psychical energy, making psychological thinking possible by providing a heaven-sent release from the rule-of-thumb categories of the biological approach.

The prompting to discover the meaning of things is as deep-rooted in man, though not so common, as the instinct to possess or consume them. The impulse to create is as inherent as the impulse to spend and expand. The instigation to continence and solitariness is more profound and passionate in certain individuals, or at certain phases or crises of life, than the tendency to orgiastic release or social dis-

1 Oxford Dictionary.

play. In fact, a biological psychology, if it is to include the whole range of autonomous manifestation, must recognize individuation as a primary instinct.

It would be unpardonable blindness not to pay full honour to Freud and Adler for their loyalty to the tradition of natural science, and for their respective attempts to exhaust the possibilities of the biological method of approach. Without doubt this was the way of our epoch, and Freud's contributions have laid an enduring foundation upon which a dynamic psychology can be based. In spite of all the criticisms which can be levelled at the one-sidedness of his basic conceptions, no one who takes the pains to study Freud's work can withhold a deep admiration for his genius. It is my conviction that, if he could have opened the gates of his mind to the spiritual, as the indispensable complement of the sexual *dynamis*, there would have been no breaking of the ranks. He is the natural father of our modern psychology, and posterity will honour him as a great pioneer. In spite of their fundamental disparity, the names of Freud and Jung will probably go down to history linked inseparably together. For Freud discovered the way into the unconscious, while Jung was great enough to value the treasure it contained. The extraverted intuitive blazed a path into the hitherto unknown territory; here he was joined by the introverted thinker who revealed the potentialities lying hidden behind the veil of dreams. Freud is the last of the great natural scientists of the nineteenth century, Jung the first authentic voice of the dynamic psychology of the twentieth. They are the two end-piers of the bridge joining the science of the past to the psychology of the future. Though in character, in psychological calibre, and in fundamental conceptions the two pioneers differ so profoundly, yet, because of this fact, their names are linked in a close historical embrace.

It must never be comfortably assumed, therefore, that the so-called battle of the schools is a mere scholastic disputation about terminology. The difference derives from those spiritual organisms, loosely termed values, by which succeeding epochs of cultural development are determined. Natural science had to create a psychology omitting the psyche. But the epoch which now begins to dawn needs more than intellect, and a psychology without the soul appears to many an arid and sunless waste. To man of the new epoch it is inevitable that psycho-analysis will seem a labyrinth without light. But it may be that the modern soul had to lose itself in this labyrinth in order to know how dark is the world that seeks to extinguish the native power of the spirit.

II

Drawing XXI

This remarkable drawing illustrates with considerable power the manner in which a mind newly emerged from the labyrinth greets the sun. Compared with the first drawing, where the unconscious was conceived as a lunatic asylum pressed beneath a layer of jagged rocks, the degree of psychological release is vividly apparent.[1]

In the top right-hand corner the golden disc of the sun is surrounded by a corona of leaping flames. Issuing from the disc are four immense rays, one towards the zenith, one towards the nadir, while two are horizontal. Only two rays traverse the field of the drawing, one downwards to the nadir, the other in a widely extending shaft of gold towards the left.

Six stars, outlined in wavy lines of red, are grouped in a constellation upon the field of gold formed by this latter ray. These reveal an increasing scale of differentiation from above downwards: the one on top, nearest the sun, having five points; the one level with this, occupying the top left-hand limit of the constellation, six points; the three middle stars, seven points; while the one at the bottom has eight. The constellation is so arranged that lines joining the centres of any three contiguous stars approximate to a right-angled isosceles triangle.

The lower half of the picture is filled by the sun-god in his chariot with winged horses. The figure of the sun-god occupies the middle line of the field. The face is Oriental in character; the eyes are set obliquely, and the head is

[1] This painting was also carried out on a much larger scale.

surrounded by wavy red lines squarely disposed, somewhat resembling early Persian or Assyrian sculpture. These lines represent flames rising upwards, which converge, at some little distance above the head, into a single flame. This flame seems to become the handle of the sword which the god holds in his right hand. The expression of the face is severe; the straight mouth expresses a certain harshness, the latter character being emphasized by the lines sloping from the nose to the corners of the mouth, and by the straight formalized beard, again somewhat Assyrian in character. Above the head, and forming part of the flaming head-dress, are two golden discs disposed symmetrically, one on either side of the middle line.

In his right hand the figure holds aloft a large silver sword, pointing towards the zenith. The hilt is embossed with rubies, and an interweaving serpentine design in red runs the length of the blade. In his upraised left hand the god holds a thunderbolt. A symbolical design, consisting of an evergreen tree in the centre, with an upreared snake on either side, is painted on the front of his raiment. The tails of the two snakes appear to be coiled around the stem of the tree at its base. The snake-design is repeated below in the body of the chariot, with this difference, however, that the heads of the upper pair of snakes are directed inwards towards the middle line, while those of the lower pair are directed outwards. Both pairs are painted in gold, and the tongues are red. The wheel of the chariot, only half of which is seen, is also painted gold. On the left margin of the chariot the right half of an evergreen tree is shown, similar to the one painted above on the breast of the god. The relation between the snake and the tree is also alike in both designs. To the left of the chariot are two winged horses in silver, while the chariot itself is borne up by two great silver wings sweeping away to the right.

* * * * *

A considerable development of the myth occurred between the previous drawing and this one. It is to be regretted that for lack of space the intervening psychological context must be omitted; the figures and allusions in this drawing would gain considerably from a knowledge of their previous connections.

The most striking feature of the drawing, compared with any of the foregoing series, is its simple and effective composition. In all previous drawings conscious art played very little part, the unconscious contents tending to occupy the field in much the same fashion as flowers fill a meadow, whereas the whole field of the present drawing is ruled by a single primordial image, and its economy of structure and elimination of other contents combine to give the design a definite æsthetic value. Though still primitive technically, it is, none the less, undeniably effective. In the earlier drawings consciousness was in abeyance. The archaic contents breaking through were neither understood nor evaluated, whereas in the present drawing there is a deliberate attempt to represent the primordial image of the sun-hero with an adequate symbolical retinue.

From the clinical standpoint this positive valuation of the symbol is of great significance. A reliable index of the degree of intellectual deterioration in schizophrenia is afforded by the treatment of symbols in drawings. In confusional states, or when the higher discriminative centres are eclipsed, the patient will often cover his sheet with symbolical figures, not merely putting them together higgledy-piggledy, but throwing symbols that are universally revered into the same hat, for instance, as a threepenny-bit or a cigarette stump, as though a malicious will were intent upon robbing the religious symbol of its value. Whether this renegade influence is present or not, the symptom of confusion of values in symbolical representations is extremely suggestive of schizophrenia.

In the present case we observed an almost complete lack of discriminative value in the first three drawings, where cosmic and personal factors were lumped together in an unusually infantile style of representation. No one could have predicted these symptoms from a judgment of the patient's intellectual capacity, yet they were exactly appropriate to his emotional level. The change has come about through linking the dissociated system with consciousness.

The first inkling of this process appeared in the second drawing, where the two lunatics were seen emerging from the asylum. The medley of symbols on the left-hand side of that drawing suggests this characteristic schizophrenic pathology, but at a relatively early stage. The cynical caricaturing of sacred things was only an occasional symptom in this patient's material: it never became insistent.

The technical change between the earlier drawings and the present one, and the striking simplification of content, betoken a vital change in attitude, although, technically, his urgent need for some sort of emotional expression has also taught the patient a great deal in the use of his very limited means. The change is due to the fact that the unconscious product has taken on reality and the symbol has become a conscious container of value. It would be correct to describe the early drawings as relatively unconscious products. But here a rather primitive artist is giving conscious and imaginative expression to a spontaneous image of the mind. The other drawings were like dreams: unintelligible without some psychological mediation. This drawing speaks for itself.

Another significant point of contrast with the first drawing is the transformation or rebirth of the sun. There it was on the left, darkened as in an eclipse, and with three sun-spots. It was also characterized by eight irregularly disposed rays, and was definitely associated with the father. Here it is on the right (the favourable aspect), clear and full, surrounded by a corona of brilliant flames, and characterized by four symmetrically disposed rays, corresponding to the four attributes of effective consciousness.

The patient was unable to explain why he had to introduce the constellation of six stars on the left-hand side of the field. Here, therefore, we are in the presence of an unconscious addition which needs elucidation. The series of stars starts with the sun itself, with its four rays. Thus the numerical values contained in the constellation are 4, 5, 6, 7, 7, 7, 8, making in all seven stars, of which the value seven is repeated three times. The seven heavenly bodies, of which the sun is the primary member, are, of course, the seven planets of the ancient Ptolemaic system—namely, the Sun, the Moon, Mercury, Venus, Mars, Jupiter and Saturn. The patient is naturally aware of the existence of Uranus and Neptune and the minor planets, not to mention the Earth itself; but the unconscious apparently still holds to the original seven. In precisely the same manner the Australian primitive, who is perfectly aware of the difference between man and kangaroo, holds tenaciously to the conviction that he and the kangaroo (if this should happen to be his totem animal) are one and the same being. In both cases the symbolical statement has a cogency for the psyche superior to the actual fact. The essential character of a living symbol, as Jung has shown, is that it possesses a superior energy-value, which relegates known facts to a subordinate position. It can even assert a truth which stands in direct contradiction to so-called common-sense experience. The symbol of the Grail, for example, represents the idea of the female organ of generation; yet, by its superior power, it can command the libidinal stream in a direction which absolutely precludes its normal sensual expression. We may assume, therefore, that this constellation maintains the original sevenfold archetype by virtue of its superior psychic efficacy, notwithstanding the known facts of astronomy.

To the natural unsophisticated mind, numbers possess distinctive attributes, especially those which correspond with the digits or orifices of the body. With regard to the cardinal numbers 3, 5, 7, 9, these are felt to be positive, living and masculine; they are associated with the principle of *Yang* in the Chinese *Yi King*, while 2, 4, 6, 8 are identified with that of *Yin*. In general the odd numbers have a creative or energetic character, while the even numbers are static, being already balanced and complete. Were we to enumerate all the attributes and qualities associated with the number 7, we might fill a volume without being appreciably nearer to any definite signification. But from the abundance of cosmogonic symbolism connected with this number we must assume that it represents an essential aspect of the creative process.

On the cosmic level there are the seven planets and the seven days of creation; the latter are reflected on the human plane in the seven days of the week, the first of which, as in our drawing, is the day of the sun. Taking the realm of the body (the primary human archetype), there is the inescapable fact that the body has seven orifices, and the head seven gates of the senses—viz., two eyes, two ears, two nostrils and one mouth. The body has also four limbs for the purpose of movement and spatial extension, and a trinity of organs for the work of creation. This grouping of the four, as opposed to the three, is rather subtly intimated in the numerical balance within the constellation, described above. The total of the first four numbers of the series—viz., 4, 5, 6, 7—is equal to that of the last three—viz., 7, 7, 8. Moreover, the index-number of the first group is 4, the archetype of structure, while the index-number of the second is 7, the archetype of creation. The first group is a balanced square containing two even numbers and two odd, whereas the second group is a triangle consisting of two odd numbers and one even. This same opposition was reflected in the numerical symbolism of the Pythagorean school, in which the square and the triangle figured as cardinal forms, while 7 was conceived as a square containing or adjoining a triangle.

According to Aristotle, the theory of Pythagoras in its original form regarded numbers not as relations predictable of things, but as actually constituting their essence or substance. He says: "Numbers seemed to the Pythagoreans to be the first things in the whole of nature: they supposed the elements of numbers to be the elements of all things, and the whole heaven to be a musical scale and a number."[1] To the Pythagoreans each number was the centre of a constellation of analogies. Thus seven was called παρθένος[2] and Ἀθήνη, because within the decade it is unique in having neither factors nor products. Abundant allusions to the sevenfold archetype are to be found in religious mystical writings, as, for instance, the seven archangels, the seven seals, the seven candlesticks of the Book of Revelation; or the seven heavens, the seven spheres, the seven virgins of light, and the seven amens of the Gnostic tradition. The symbolism of magic is also teeming with sevenfold allusions. There is certainly no other number—we might almost add

[1] Metaphysics, 986 *a*

[2] Virgin

no other archetype—that is surrounded with such a host of significant associations.

From this fact alone we can infer that the sevenfold archetype represents a central architectural principle of the universe. It must therefore express some essential element of psychic creation and structure. Empirically, we can speak of the seven colours of the spectrum as the elements of light, and of the seven tones of the octave as the elements of the musical scale. Inferentially, it is possible to conceive of the sevenfold attributes of psychical energy, even though we have as yet no knowledge of what these might be. There is also significance in the fact that the number 7 in our constellation is repeated three times, while all the other numbers occur only once. The number 3 is specifically associated with the creative process. For not only are the male and female organs of generation disposed in the form of a trinity, but the very archetype of creation, projected into the Deity, obeys the same form. Every function of energy in nature has, indeed, the form of a pair of opposites, united by a third factor, their product. Thus the triangle is the symbol of a pair of opposites joined above or below by a third factor. Following out the clue offered us by the grouping of our numerical series and by the Pythagorean square and triangle, we can represent the sevenfold archetype as a symbol, embracing the quaternity of symmetrical structure and informed by the threefold principle of energy. A further corroboration of this content is supplied by the fact that the first member of the constellation is the archetype 4, supported at the end by the structural number 8, while the stars within the constellation maintain, as we have already noted, a triangular relationship between contiguous members.

Now, although the seven celestial bodies of the drawing bear an indefinite relation with the seven planets, the grouping of these stars within a constellation bears no relation at all to the behaviour of the actual planets. The planets were originally differentiated as belonging to a separate order, because they were observed to change their places when projected against the background of the so-called fixed stars in the heavens. Hence the name, which is derived from the Greek πλανήτης=wanderer. In the Ptolemaic or geocentric astronomy these wandering stars were assumed to revolve about the earth, and this view, as we know, was stubbornly maintained until the sixteenth century, when Copernicus, subsequently supported by the observations of Galileo, established the heliocentric view of the universe. The subjective prejudice which maintained the geocentric view for nineteen centuries after the heliocentric truth was first voiced by Aristarchus in the third century B.C., and which revealed itself in the condemnation of Galileo by the Inquisition, raises a problem of supreme psychological importance: a problem that has many implications for the modern mind.

This figure, which the patient called Lord of Light, is clearly a summation of all the experience of his individual myth which could not be explained from the contents of his personal psychology. Apart from the numinous aspect of this conception, the various allusions to the Pythagorean universe, traced above, declare it to be a creative cosmogonic fantasy which might be designated the Rebirth of Logos.[1] Mythologically, it is the figure of the sun-god, Helios, Mithras, Aton, Ormuzd, etc. But what does this portend psychologically, if not a conception of the self which, because it rests upon universal principles, receives a kind of cosmic sanction?

In the Eleusinian mysteries, as indeed in all the mystery initiations of antiquity, the culmination of the ritual development was the identification of the initiate with the god. This identification was the essence of the mystery, and there can be no question that the glowing heart of the quest which we call the individual myth is this same experience. But why should the experience of being god be so vital to the soul, unless it symbolized a primordial fact? The drawing of our subject states this truth in the naive primordial idiom of the unconscious; but we must also enquire what it means for the conscious reason.

At bottom, the problem which lies beneath the controversy of the heliocentric versus the geocentric universe is

[1] Hence the title *Lord of Light*.

the vital question as to whether man or God shall be regarded as the paramount factor in the universe. Ever since man dared to rise up and pit himself and his power against what he chose to call the blind forces of nature, the spirit of god-defying *hybris* has always tempted, and often possessed, his ambitious soul. From this point of view, geocentric really means homocentric—a universe, in fact, where everything, including the gods, must be subordinated to man's civilizing programme. It is only a step from this to the universe of the modern intellect, which says, without heat or any trace of affect, "There is no god; he was only your childish fantasy."

The greatest danger threatening the modern soul is this spirit of godless *hybris*, which kills everything great and venerable, lest its very existence might imply that the power of organized intellect which can amass armies, change frontiers, wield absolute sway over all material means, and even distort history to its requirements, is not, in fact, so great as it appears. Paranoia is our psychiatric designation for this spiritual malady; but when whole nations, the whole contemporary civilized world even, is haunted by the danger of annihilation by this disease, we cannot assume we have understood it by giving it a Greek name. It will be none the less self-evident that the schizophrenic individual, in whom a ruthless intellectual despot is intent on eliminating every emotional shoot which might threaten his absolute sway, must be especially liable to fall a victim to the hybristic contagion.

The heliocentric universe, on the other hand, becomes a symbolical *Weltanschauung* when an immediate experience of the unconscious, of such depth and intensity that it cannot be rationalized away, forces the ego to accept a suprapersonal reality. Before the experience or the revelation the universe revolved around the ego: now its dynamic centre is the self.

The affirmation of this drawing is nothing less than the reality of the heliocentric universe *within the psychic sphere*. The sun rules supreme in the position of maximum power, and the single ray of the sun, which shoots an expanding shaft of solar force towards the left, holding the six wandering stars or functions within its sway, is simply a cosmogonic restatement of the outstretched arm of the sun which caught the peacock and the babe as they fell from the heavens in the previous drawing.

III

Throughout the whole series of drawings we have observed a consistent extension of the field of consciousness towards the left, and noted how this concentration of psychic energy towards the side of the unconscious succeeded in throwing the unconscious mental process upon the objective screen. Beginning as the mobilization of the mobile blue masses in Drawing III., it came under the authority of the ancestral god in Drawing VI., developed a manifold power of penetration in Drawing VII., where the parallelism with the *Kundalini* system was first observed. Finally it reveals itself as the creative introverting process, the original logos-function.

That there is an allusion to the *chakras* in the ratio of increasing differentiation within the constellation is also possible. But, if this is so, we must note a complete inversion of the *Kundalini* system in the fact that the lowest star in the constellation has the greatest number of points, while the sun, which should correspond with the thousand-petalled lotus, has only four. This is the number of petals of the *muladhara* lotus, the lowest of the *chakras*. If this allusion is valid, this sun of the inner world must embrace the idea of original psychic energy as well as that of central unifying power. These two aspects of the symbol are further represented in the thunderbolt and the sword held by the sun-god.

The sword, held in the god's right hand, is the symbol of the hero, while the thunderbolt in the left hand is the classical symbol of divine power. It is often seen in the centre of the lamaistic *mandalas* of Thibet representing the idea of divine potential. Thus the conception of immeasurable potential is associated with the left hand (the side of the unconscious), while that of effective deed is identified with the right, corresponding with the objective function of consciousness.

The sword and the thunderbolt are clearly to be regarded as the essential attributes of the Lord of Light, who stands in the chariot " itself instinct with Spirit." On his breast is painted the evergreen tree of life, guarded on either side by a serpent. This tree made its first appearance in a drawing representing an evil, top-hatted figure of anti-Christ attempting to mutilate the Crucified God. But the tree intervened between the two figures, thus becoming a symbol of mediation between God and devil. The snake is the earth-dæmon, the primordial force of instinct. It is the chthonian cousin of Lucifer, who was cast out of heaven into hell. The snake, too, was accursed:

> " And the Lord God said unto the serpent, Because thou hast done this, thou art cursed above all cattle, and above every beast of the field; upon thy belly shalt thou go, and dust shalt thou eat all the days of thy life: and I will put enmity between thee and the woman, and between thy seed and her seed; it shall bruise thy head, and thou shalt bruise his heel."[1]

As guardian of the Tree of Life, around whose stem its tail is coiled, the snake symbolizes the primitive instinctive depths in which the life of man is rooted. It is also the symbol of renewal in the cult of Æsculapius.[2] Thus the self-renewing Tree of Life, in combination with the snake, symbolizes the introverted healing process of the libido, which was the essence of the healing worship of Æsculapius. The rites consisted of lustral bathing, cakes and libations, and the offering of sacrifices, notably a cock.[3] But the essential part of the temple worship was the sleeping in the temple itself (*incubatio*), where the oracle, by means of a dream, revealed to the suppliant the method of cure.

The tree, the mediating symbol between the opposites, is found exactly in the middle line. The snakes, upreared on either side of it, are opposed by the two golden sun-discs above, which are surmounted by the perpendicular sword. The head of the god being the central point of the picture, we find a trinity of celestial or *Yang* symbols above, and a trinity of earth or *Yin* symbols below—once again making seven.

1 Genesis iii. 14, 15.

2 The snake coiled around the branch of a tree is the symbol of the Royal Army Medical Corps.

3 The cock, being the herald of the dawn, is a symbol of the new life.

The erect sword with the sun-discs below it could easily be identified with the male genitalia. The biological psychologist could doubtless use this analogy as proof that the whole fantasy contained nothing but infantile sexuality. But if this is the only content, why the celestial symbolism, and why the creative impulse ? Biology can lead us up to the door of the psyche, but it cannot cross the threshold. The drawing represents the self under the aspect of the masculine logos, the creative principle of man. It is intelligible, therefore, that this figure should bear the primordial symbol of masculine power.

The chariot in which the god stands is the cup or vessel to which we referred at the beginning of the chapter. It symbolizes the attitude of acceptance which has always been the womb from which God eternally springs. Nothing can emerge from the unconscious and become manifest without a container. The efficacy of the god-value is necessarily dependent upon its human vessel. Hence the attitude of acceptance becomes identified with that which thereby comes into effect. The cup-symbol appeared in the first dream as a fragrant flower which the subject held cupped between his two hands near the door of the king's palace. The same symbol appears again as the carrier of the god-king. Thus the dream contained an intuitive anticipation of coming events.

The vessel symbolism played a considerable rôle in the series that immediately preceded this drawing, but there the treatment of the symbol was alchemical in character. As the vehicle of the god, it now appears transformed, like the emergence of a winged imago from the chrysalis. It is of interest to note that the wings and the horses are painted silver, a shade that the patient has consistently reserved for contents associated either with the mother or with the anima. The reader will remember that this symbol of the silver wing appeared in Drawing IX., at the top of the womb-cavity, in connection with the newly formed radius and ulna of the skeletal arm. It was the only element painted in silver in that drawing, with the exception of the two bands of silver around the breast-image. The fact that the evolution of the silver wing synchronized with the diminution of silver on the maternal breast gave us reason to think that the wing was fashioned out of the energy released from the primordial mother-image. If this reasoning was correct, we might follow it further and conclude that the impersonal *dynamis*, symbolized by the two winged horses and the winged chariot, which gives to this conception its cogency and force, has been released, or rather converted, from the infantile bondage to the mother. From this point of view, the body of the chariot is recognized as the womb-vessel (originally the green pan) out of which the hero is reborn.

In this figure of the self as primordial logos, a reconciling symbol has been created which possesses unchallengeable validity, uniting the opposites, vessel and sword, earth and heaven, East and West, good and evil, in a living unity. The subsequent evolution of the individual myth was governed by this " Lord of Light." At first the figure was associated with the Osiris of XX., but after a time this mythological derivation fell away, and the figure took on the unique character of spontaneous mythic creation.

This figure demonstrates an essential quality of the reconciling symbol, in that it not only unites the opposites, but also endows them with an individual distinctiveness and value. When we recall the complete inadequacy of the statement of the problem of the opposites presented in the first drawing, we can appreciate not only the psychological transformation which has taken place, but also the truth of Jung's conception that schizophrenia is a condition in which basic philosophical ideas are contained in quite inadequate vessels.

IV

Perhaps we can make use of our astronomical analogy again in grasping the character of this transformation. The instinct of the Church to maintain the geocentric universe at all costs was not the immediate recoil of agoraphobia. It was immediately predictable that so profound a reorientation of view, concerning the place of the earth in the universe, would bring about an incalculable disturbance in the region of faith. A geocentric universe went hand in hand with a manageable scheme of creation. But if the earth were merely a relative factor, an inconsiderable item in an infinitely extended host of worlds, a mere broken-off fragment of the sun—then the relation of God and man to that unimaginable totality would have to undergo a fundamental revaluation. In this process the teaching of the Church, which viewed the creation of the world, with all its manifold forms of life, in the light of a special act of God for the benefit of man, would be sure to collide with a host of new and formidable difficulties.

The Church's resistance to Galileo and his telescope was, in fact, the instinctive recoil of traditional ecclesiastical culture from the emergent spirit of science, which was destined in time to provide a more comprehensive view of the universe, and man's place in it, than the view hitherto given by the Church. Symbolically, this whole transformation of man's relation to God and His universe was represented in the initial realization that the sun was the sovereign power of the universe, reducing the earth to the relative position of satellite.

If the liberation of spirit felt in this drawing expresses an analogous revolution of thought in regard to the psychic universe, it should be possible to trace the stages of its development.

The geocentric[1] view of the universe proved to be an illusion, based as it was upon the naive supposition that, because human consciousness was the central fact of our own existence, it must also correspond with the central position in the physical universe. In the psychological evolution of the subject of these drawings, the therapeutic release coincided with the shifting of value from a dangerously inflated, egocentric standpoint (symbolized by the inflated and erratic battleship in the first dream) to an impersonal attitude of acceptance under the command of the self, symbolized by the sun. The reduction and assimilation of the infantile-archaic components was forced upon the patient by a superior psychic instance, personified as an ancestral deity. At every stage of the process of assimilation the extending range of

[1] The same letters spell *egocentric*.

conscious realization was accompanied by the symbol of the new sun. To persist in identifying himself with this sun was not possible, because he could neither disguise nor ignore the fact that the experience recorded in these drawings transcended his conscious will and purpose as completely as the sun transcends its satellites. Moreover, he could not ascribe these experiences to analytical suggestion, inasmuch as the experiences occurred spontaneously, and had no reference to the previous content of the analysis.

The possibility of a deeper centre of consciousness was, in fact, adumbrated in the first drawing, where a kind of psychological telescope was discovered, leading from the dissociated system in the unconscious to a lighthouse from which a beam of light fell upon the battleship. The ray directed from the other centre of consciousness came from the side opposite to that of the old sun. Thus, in the opening statement of the problem, a new centre of consciousness (based upon the dissociated unconscious system) began to operate, and, as the dissolution of the father-identification progressed, this new centre, growing in power, developed the middle eye, the primordial pre-stage of " heliocentric " consciousness.

Assisted by the logic of experience, therefore, the subject has developed a view of the psychic universe in which the ego has been relegated to a relative position, while the sun-value, which previously had been projected into the father, or into God, comes to occupy its proper central place in his inner world. But what is this supreme psychic value ruling the complex universe of the mind but the unfathomable, creative power which urges man to worship gods and to crown kings?[1] When this value is projected upon a divine image, the attitude of the ego to the creative essence of life is not unlike that of our geocentric forebears to the benevolent offices of the sun—viz., that it all belongs to a divine plan, into the nature of which it is forbidden to enquire.

The subject of this study, however, was born into the world created by science: he found no divine image upon whom this supreme value could be projected. For a time

1 As previously stated, the early migrations of man were in search of gold (the metal of the sun), needed for the ritual embellishment of the god-king.

the compelling vigour of the father's personality held the inherited psychic value, but actually the father is no god, and there were special circumstances in the present case which made father-worship eventually impossible.[1] Accordingly, like the dove of Noah which found no place in the outer world where it could rest and abide, the god-value returned into the unconscious. This was accompanied by a profound activation and disturbance of the unconscious which, as we have seen, even threatened insanity. Whenever the god-value is not royally housed and honoured, it can become a wandering, restless, unconscious force, urging the subject to violence and excess.[2]

Naturally, many people find themselves in this condition without any inkling of the truth that the fundamental problem of their lives is a deep religious need. Reflecting upon the development of this need in the present case, we can understand why the unconscious seemed to borrow certain ideas from the deeper psychological wisdom of the East, where for many centuries men have sought the introverted middle way which goes between the opposites. But although religious instinct turns to this ancient source with longing, our intellectual attitude to Eastern conceptions shows an equally strong reserve. Jung discusses this problem in his chapter on "Fundamental Concepts" in *The Secret of the Golden Flower*. He writes:

> "The great difficulty in interpreting this and similar texts for the European mind is due to the fact that the Chinese author always starts from the centre of things, from the point we would call his objective or goal; in a word, he begins with the ultimate insight he has set out to attain. Thus the Chinese author begins his work with ideas that demand a most comprehensive understanding on our part. So much so that a man with a critical intellect feels that he speaks with laughable pretension, or even that he is guilty of utter nonsense, if he dares launch a purely intellectual discourse on the subtle psychic experiences of the great minds of the East."

1 The patient actually had a fantasy in which the father was dismembered and the Osiris mystery re-enacted.

2 *Cf.* Luther's idea of the *deus absconditus*—*i.e.*, that condition in which the reverse aspect of God becomes manifest.

As an example he quotes the opening words of the *Hui Ming Ching*:

> " The most subtle secret of Tao is essence and life."

Also the introduction to the same text, which runs:

> " If thou wouldst complete the diamond body without emanations,
> Diligently heat the roots of consciousness and life.
> Kindle light in the blessed country ever close at hand,
> And, there hidden, let thy true self eternally dwell."

When we read such words as these, we know that, were it possible for us simply to follow this way, and to discover the experience that lies behind these enigmatic words, we should be satisfied and whole. But another part of our mind says: " Ah, but that experience is not for us. We belong to the other side of the mountain where these rare plants do not thrive." We attend meetings of learned societies, we discuss, we argue, we affirm; but if so much as an allusion is made to an experience inexplicable to our rational philosophy we are immediately cloaked in reserve. The experience is irrelevant not because it is unreal, but only because we cannot account for it.

I have no doubt, for instance, that the parallelism with certain Eastern ideas which has been discovered in this patient's material will be impatiently repudiated by some of my readers, whereas, if these conceptions had achieved a recognized place in Western thought, their relevancy to the patient's material would be immediately conceded.

Yet, despite intellectual resistance, the unconscious of the West turns irresistibly to the East. For there the " heliocentric " structure of the self has long been realized, and the greater psychological depth and insight of Oriental philosophy comes directly from this recognition. In the *Upanishads*, for instance, it is said:

> " He who is this (Brahman) in man, and the One who is that (Brahman) in the sun, are both one."[1]

[1] Max-Müller: *Taitt.-Upanishad*, 2, 8, 5.

Again:

> "As a grain of rice, or barley, or millet, yea like even unto the kernel of a millet-seed is this spirit in the inner Self; golden, like a flame without smoke; and greater is it than the heavens, vaster than space, greater than this earth, surpassing all beings. It is the soul of life, it is my own soul: departing hence, into this soul shall I enter."[1]

In another place we read:

> "And this light, which spreadeth above this heaven higher than all, higher even than those in the highest world, above and beyond which there are no more worlds, this is the same light that burneth in the inner world of man. Whereof we have this tangible token, only to feel warmth and to perceive bodies."[2]

The concept of *Purusha* in the *Rigveda* can also be identified with *Atman* as the primordial creative flame. It is said, "*Purusha* covers all the places of the earth, flowing about it ten fingers high." It is described as greater than the worlds, yet smaller than a thumbling. It is eternally free and cannot be enslaved.

The Chinese texts mentioned above also describe this sun-centre of consciousness with an amazing wealth of imagery. It is the "Golden Flower," the "Light of Heaven," the "germinal vesicle," the "golden castle," the "Heavenly Heart," the "terrace of life," the "purple hall of the city of jade," the "empire of the greatest joy," the "land without boundaries," the "altar upon which consciousness and life are made." "If a dying man does not know this seed place," says the *Hui Ming Ching*, "he will not find the unity of consciousness and life in a thousand births and ten thousand aeons."[3]

Naturally, experience of the self is not confined to the East, and many Western seers have also realized this truth. Jung cites the experience of Edward Maitland, for instance, who describes how he attempted to follow a chain of ideas back to their source. By means of concentration on the

1 Deussen: *Catap. Brahm.*, 10, 6, 3.
2 Max Muller: *Khandogya-Up.*, 3, 13, 7 *ff*.
3 *The Secret of the Golden Flower*, p. 98.

series of ideas he made a conscious effort to press on to their origin, which, for him, was the divine Spirit. He says:

> " Once well started on my quest, I found myself traversing a succession of spheres or belts . . . the impression produced being that of mounting a vast ladder stretching from the circumference towards the centre of a system, which was at once my own system, the solar system, and the universal system, the three systems being at once diverse and identical. . . . Presently, by a supreme, and what I felt must be a final effort . . . I succeeded in polarizing the whole of the convergent rays of consciousness into the desired focus. And at the same instant . . . I found myself confronted with a glory of unspeakable whiteness and brightness and of a lustre so intense as well-nigh to beat me back."[1]

Every psychiatrist is familiar with so-called borderline patients who describe ecstatic experiences not altogether dissimilar from the one just cited. But we must always distinguish the experience itself from the fantastic and bizarre convictions that so often accompany it. It may be that only those near the " borderline " are able so to detach the feeling of consciousness from the ego-centre that the deeper or remoter centre of consciousness can be realized. Psychological science needs to value such experiences, as science had to accept the discoveries of Galileo, and Jung's conception of the suprapersonal self as the reconciling centre embracing both conscious and unconscious provides the conceptual form which these experiences demand. The realization of this central self has exactly the opposite effect to that condition known as " self-centred." The self-centred person pins everything to his ego, and what cannot serve as ego-decoration is ignored. He is trying to live in too small a world, and therefore is pitiful, both to himself and others. The " ego-pinner " is prone to self-pity, for the same reason that geocentric consciousness was ever full of complaints to heaven about the misery of human fate. But the ego-sickness cannot be cured by heroic attempts to crush the ego, nor by distracting it with " distractions "—but by creating an attitude that is fathered by the new sun. This attitude grows from the recognition of the equal validity and reciprocal

[1] Edward Maitland: *Anna Kingsford*, Redway, London, 1896.

functioning of the conscious and unconscious processes. It is symbolized by the divine child, born of the hitherto sundered opposites. This is also that divine child Immanuel, signifying God with us (or within us), of whom it was prophesied by Isaiah:

> " The wolf also shall dwell with the lamb, and the leopard shall lie down with the kid; and the calf and the young lion and the fatling together; and a little child shall lead them."[1]

Being born of the opposites, this new sun also unites or reconciles them. Isaiah describes a situation in which age-long natural enmities are healed, and a new pact or understanding with nature is won. Thus the appearance of the divine child or the new sun heralds a state of being in which the enmity between consciousness and the despised or dreaded instincts is appeased. Clearly this can take place only under the ægis of a power that is superordinated to both sides.

The creation of this centre, the living symbol whose superior efficacy and authority rest upon the sanction of the total man, is the goal of the individuation process.

V

CONCLUSION

The Descent out of the Myth

People who are forced to create myths are undeniably in a queer mental state. Their preoccupation with the events taking place in the unconscious renders them, as a rule, somewhat defective and vulnerable in relation to ordinary reality. For this reason an obvious common-sense reproach can be levelled at the doctor who allows his patient to persist in mythological production. Naturally, if we regard these drawings from the point of view of schizophrenic symptomatology only, we may seem to be encouraging the patient in a pathological indulgence. But, if this demonstration has succeeded in dispelling that prejudice, we have to find some place for this kind of evolution in our conception of psychiatric

[1] Isaiah xi. 6.

therapy. And if we concede to it the value of a specific method in the treatment of borderline cases, it becomes important to recognize what actually takes place.

While the patient was producing these pictures he understood little of their psychological content. Being in a highly reactive, almost mediumistic condition, when I tried to provide him with a theoretical standpoint from which he might be able to view his experience from a more detached position, he was unable for a time to make use of it. It is indeed often the case that the activation of the primordial, myth-making psyche is liable to produce a temporary intellectual eclipse. In the present case, while the development of the myth was flowing swiftly it was useless to attempt anything beyond a *résumé* of the train of events, keeping within the given premises of the mythic structure.

The state of inflation that is most liable to accompany such an intense participation with the unconscious images is again something which cannot suddenly be reduced by analytical criticism. As long as the archaic development is proceeding, the patient is often opaque to the analytical standpoint. For the time being he is the myth, and he has really no choice but to follow it through to the end of the tunnel. It is as much a *force majeure* as a pregnancy. Indeed, from the standpoint of medical treatment it should be regarded as a kind of pregnancy. Until the process has come to its proper term, the doctor has no justification for interfering, unless the condition of the patient makes it imperative.

The psychological *raison d'être* of this method of therapy is based both upon empirical observation and common sense. If a patient complains of certain difficulties, the obstruction must lie either in the nature of the object or the subject. If it be the former, the difficulty can be overcome by improved technique, or by a better acquaintance with the object. But if the latter, the subjective obstruction must be made objective before it can be handled. If these difficulties could all be traced to unappeased infantile affect, the psycho-analytical method would suffice. But in so far as the intruding factors often have the character of archaic contents actually belonging to the remote childhood of the human race, they cannot be dealt with as mere personal belongings. Such factors are best expressed in the universal idiom of the myth, just because they are universal psychic elements. And because of their universality they also contain a superior energy-content or value, which demands a special kind of treatment. It frequently happens, as occurred from time to time in the present case, that the patient consciously resists the analogical method. The producer identifies himself with his product so completely that it can hold only that meaning or purpose which he intended and nothing more. In the presence of this resistance it is sometimes permissible to talk past the resistant conscious to the receptive unconscious personality.

The resistance of the ego-complex to the fact that a development of the greatest significance is taking place, regardless of the sanction of consciousness, is exactly parallel to the querulous, resistant state of many women in their first pregnancies, when they discover that the pregnancy is really a *force majeure* from which there is no escape. This state is intelligible, but it usually evaporates in the presence of an attitude of acceptance on the part of the doctor.

Many people cannot understand why this immediate experience of the unconscious should be regarded as therapeutically essential. In this work I have attempted to demonstrate its importance. Though its essential validity is germane only to the subject himself, the fact that the myth develops as an independent psychic organism affords us the opportunity of regarding it also as a purposive natural process. Yet only a schizophrenic personality, whose security of mind is constantly threatened by unintelligible psychic commotion, can understand fully what it means to find the silken thread of meaning and value in the psychotic labyrinth.

There may be other methods which can achieve this end, but, however the methods may differ in form, the reintegration of the total personality is the fundamental goal of every effective treatment. The method I have demonstrated of making objective the archaic psychic determinants, and of dealing with them in the idiom in which they spontaneously manifest themselves, would appear to be the way which the empiricism of our Western mentality demands.

It must not be assumed that the patient was immediately able to understand his myth in the way that I have demonstrated it. It may happen that the split between the conscious and the unconscious makes a complete understanding impossible for many years. The myth is an intuitive anticipation, giving a kind of programme along which consciousness needs to develop. Actually, full conscious reception of such experiences is a very much slower process than the development of the myth. But, if the sense of value is preserved, the symbolical anticipation will eventually be realized in life.

PART TWO

CHAPTER I

THE INTROVERTED SUBJECT

I

In many ways this second case differs surprisingly from the first. It is unique in the sense that although the drawings manifest characteristic schizophrenic peculiarities and the development of the myth is clearly concerned with the threat of inundation from the archaic levels of the unconscious, yet clinically there was at no time any true indication of schizophrenia other than occasional and rather slight disturbances of attention. The sense of contradiction between the poised and polished persona on the one hand, and the pathological autonomous material on the other, is intensified by the fact that the drawings are systematized, almost as though the artist had assumed the rôle of pathological demonstrator—not, however, with the deliberate systematization of archaic material of Joyce in *Ulysses*, but rather in the manner of the German artist Paul Klee, whose work reveals a high degree of introverted abstraction, with an attempt to systematize disjuncted elementary material. In some of Klee's designs, notably in " Le temps et les plantes " (1927), we find the same attempt to hold the disjuncted items within an arbitrary frame or field, associated even with the control of cross and compass, as is to be observed in the present series. In respect to schizophrenic drawings in general, fragmentation or disruption is perhaps the most consistent symptom. But the essential feature of the present case consists in the fact that this is countered unmistakably throughout by an equally strong tendency towards control.

In regard to type, the second subject is decidedly introverted, albeit remarkably effective in practical affairs, excepting where his own interests are concerned. Both patients were cut off from their instinctual roots, and in both the psychotic influence was traceable to the father. There was also the common factor—present almost without exception among schizoid men—overcompensation of the intellectual function as counterweight to the archaic affects.

The essential point of difference between the two lies in their respective attitudes to their myths. The former patient, being quite unskilled in drawing and painting, discovered in the making of his individual myth (like a marooned sailor the art of boat-building) the means by which the unconscious could come to expression. While making his myth he was completely contained by it, whereas this second patient, although mediumistic to the unconscious at the time of the drawing, very soon recovered his habitual attitude of intellectual detachment after it was finished. This attitude of defence against the unconscious is a common habit among borderline patients: it is by no means synonymous with a genuine intellectual interest, although this is liable to develop as the individual myth unfolds.

The majority of cases in the literature, as, for instance, the famous Schreber case or the case reported by Spielrein, display the pathological process in full tide: the patient has crossed the line and the archaic contents rule the scene. There may be subsequent attempts at rationalization and intellectual control, but while the spate of images is running there is no check and no insight, whereas in the present case the intellectual control is almost never absent, even when the irrational imagery is at its height.

Here, therefore, is the true borderline case in which disruption and dispersion are held by an equal and opposite tendency towards systematization.

With such an unusual clinical picture the possibility of an induced psychosis had to be considered, and circumstances were not lacking in the sphere of personal relationships that might lend colour to this hypothesis. On the other hand, the ætiology of emotional trauma was clear in the personal history, and its effects were sufficiently visible in the material to make any other hypothesis seem unreasonable. In general, however, I believe induced psychosis is very much commoner than is supposed. Wherever a marriage partnership—one member of which is obviously psychotic—develops a morbid degree of identification, it is well to examine the possibility that the one who is manifesting the symptoms may be playing the rôle of medium to his partner's unconscious.

In view of a natural and very reasonable preference for a simple, clearly defined ætiology of the morbid condition, it is regrettable that in nearly every case of schizophrenia we have to admit multiple causation. Accepting Jung's recent summing-up of the genesis of the disease as embracing two relatively independent factors—namely, the weakening of the conscious threshold on the one hand, and the activation of the unconscious on the other—it will be self-evident that in most cases the ætiological picture must be complex.

It is therefore reasonable to assume in the present case that, owing to hereditary factors and to the influence of the emotional trauma in childhood, the subject was certain, sooner or later, to have an acute problem with the unconscious. It may even have been the existence of this potential fate in his unconscious which determined his marriage choice. Whether the problem of the unconscious is first encountered in the objective or the subjective sphere depends upon factors which are at present insufficiently established. We can only say that the existence of an unusually drilled and fortified conscious function was the most probable cause, in the present case, of the problem engaging the subject first in the objective sphere; and it may be due to the same circumstance that, while forced to suffer an extreme degree of psychological dependence within the marriage, he was at the same time deeply resistant to the claims of the feminine principle in his own psychology. The foregoing are the main features to be underlined in a peculiarly complex ætiological picture.

*   *   *   *   *

II

PERSONAL HISTORY

The subject of this second series is a Canadian, although the greater part of his life has been spent in Europe. He is a man of thirty, married, athletic, well-educated, with an apparently excellent physical poise. By vocation a draughtsman he has also considerable artistic gifts.

The first remembered experience was an attack of typhoid fever at the age of six. This was the beginning of consecutive memory. He is the only child of his parents, and was born when they had been married three years. The marriage did not succeed, and when he was eight his mother brought him to England, pending a divorce. When he was ten his mother married again. During the war years he spent the happiest time of his childhood with his mother and stepfather in London. He had known the stepfather all his life and was more at ease with him than with his father. When he was twelve his father fetched him home and sent him to an American boarding school. This complete change of atmosphere at a difficult and impressionable age unsettled him. In contrast to the warmth, friendship and simple fare of the London *ménage* he was plunged suddenly into an atmosphere of " wealth, insanity and loneliness," as he himself described it.

At fifteen he was recalled to England because his mother had to undergo a dangerous operation which she hardly expected to survive. In an extremity of anxiety the stepfather, fearing to lose both wife and son, chose this moment to tell the boy he believed himself to be his real father. This revelation did not surprise the lad very much, who seems to have been unconsciously aware of the real facts of the case.

On returning to Canada he found his supposed father suffering from a painful disease which was eventually diagnosed as cancer. This fact played an important rôle in the subject's life, for, as operation after operation failed to eradicate the disease, the father clung to the boy as his only hold on life. Though the lad secretly longed to return to the home where his real affections lay, he had to stand by the dying man who believed him to be his son. He went to Toronto University, where he spent a restless, unhappy year, and then, as his father seemed to be recovering, he insisted on going to Europe to finish his university life at Oxford.

At the end of his first term he was urgently recalled to the father in Canada. After the father's death, which took place just after his return to Oxford, he knew peace for the first time, and enjoyed university life with renewed zest. Having finished his career at Oxford with moderate success, he went to Germany to study architecture. During this time he formed a friendship with the American girl whom he subsequently married.

A certain inherited instability on the mother's side was traceable in the family history, while the man who claimed to be his real father, though a gifted musician and likeable, was definitely psychopathic. The pattern of his fate had the effect of dividing his affection between two fathers, two continents and two homes. Torn by conflicting demands, he became passively reactive to every situation, conforming with astonishing endurance to the formidable expectations levelled at him. But the fact that the solid security of a home had been denied him, and that the emotional background of his early years was not illumined by candour between the parents, helped to produce a sense of isolation and a habit of emotional detachment.

My first impression of the subject was of a sensitive, aloof being, concealed by a mask. A slight stammer and a rather diffident manner accorded strangely with the expression of power in the eyes and around the mouth. He told the facts of his life with clarity and ease, but his account was curiously lacking in light and shade. In spite of apparent readiness to give full co-operation, one was left with the impression of a deep instinctive reserve. He gave all he had to give with genuine frankness, yet there was an involuntary custodian who saw to it that the vital things were not said.

The problem which brought him to seek my advice concerned the relationship with his wife, whom I subsequently found to be a psychoneurotic individual suffering from acute anxiety states. Rarely are opposite qualities set in such strange contradiction in a human being as in this woman's psychology. She was warm and gay and alive with genuine feeling one minute and plunged into a pit of fear with overcast skies the next. She had always been pursued by irrational terrors, which she either tried to placate in characteristic compulsive ways or strove to ignore by making the relationship with the husband an absolute protection against her dread of the unconscious. The combination of rare positive qualities and urgent emotional need was more than the husband could stand against, with the result that he had become completely reactive to his wife's needs, and had apparently surrendered all hope of emotional independence.

Once again fate had put him in a situation in which passive endurance seemed the only possible rôle for him to play. For he had married a woman whose horizon was limited by childish feeling problems, and whose unstable mental condition was constantly prone to gusts of panic. Lacking the power to communicate his pent-up feelings, his habitual defence had become intensified to a painful degree, and symptoms of acute resistance had made their appearance—in particular an extreme absent-mindedness in relation to everything he had undertaken to do for his wife. He was exceedingly apologetic about these lapses, but was powerless to give any overt expression to the resistance which caused them, and which derived directly from his extreme emotional dependence upon his wife.

The rôle of victim was not confined to the marriage relationship. Situations had frequently arisen in which his invariable good-natured response to the under-dog and the expatriated had involved him in claims, both upon his purse and his feeling, against which he had apparently no means of defence. Yet although sympathy was, in a sense, his affliction, his feeling never seemed to be really touched. He was loyal and generous, adapting readily to social claims, yet inwardly remaining isolated and aloof.

In his work a similar division was manifest. On the one hand he produced architectural drawings and etchings in which delicacy of line, detailed precision and structural clarity could hardly be surpassed. But on the other hand,

and usually under the loosening influence of alcohol, macabre or ironical subjective drawings would flow vigorously from his pen.

When I began to analyse his dreams I found myself knocking at closed doors of which no key was available. Here was no introverted citadel, no massive fortifications, no labyrinth, but restless, inventive activity, in which one detected allusions to something hidden which should be found; also to a certain homosexual inclination, of which there was scarcely a trace in conscious feeling. There appeared to be some inexplicable gap in relation to his mother. In one dream, for instance, he was following her down "our private steps" leading to the beach; suddenly he had to stop half-way because the steps ended in space. The steps were apparently there for his mother but not for him; accordingly he had to go up again and come down to her by the ordinary "public way." Later in the same dream he came down to the sea-level and "skipped" a stone. It hit a wave, soared into the air, and fell into the water almost within reach. He was surprised that the stone should return, and wanted to try it again. He looked for another stone to skip. Then he found himself in deep water with a shadowy figure beside him. Catching sight of a perfect flat stone on the bottom, he dived twice to reach it, the water being very deep. When he brought it to the surface he found it was a watch exactly like one that he had inherited from his Canadian father, except for the initials on the back, which were partly illegible.

Through this dream the subject was shown how apparently incidental factors were leading him to discover a clue to his original nature, lying forgotten in the unconscious, in vital connection with the father he had lost; or as though the spirit of the dead father himself (the shadowy companion) were guiding the subject to a work of salvage, concerning inherited or ancestral values which had been neglected. Even the carelessly flung stones seemed to be somehow controlled by the hidden value in the unconscious. Inasmuch as this was part of the same dream as the incident quoted above, relating to the mother, I concluded that the lost value was also concerned with the mother.

Something was assuredly amiss in the parental background. From the first I had been baffled by a contradiction which in itself was incompatible with the patient's real character. True, there was a psychotic element in the family inheritance. There was also the emotional insecurity and the conflicting claims upon his feeling during childhood and adolescence. But notwithstanding all this the key to the problem was lacking. The relation to the mother was investigated further, but the essence of the problem still eluded me. She appeared to be a powerful, introverted, intelligent woman, living a rather solitary life in Scotland, for the second marriage had fared no better than the first. One could also divine that she had suffered, more perhaps than anyone, from the fact that she had never gained her son's love and confidence. There was undoubtedly a great need on the son's part to reach his mother and to make a good relationship with her; yet the key to the pathological dissociation was not here.

At last, and quite casually, as though it had no particular relevance, the patient told me a fact of his boyhood which made everything clear. It concerned the man whom he had come to accept as his father and who had betrayed this trust in the most shocking way. The whole loyalty of the boy had been given to him although, according to ordinary human standards, he had forfeited every right to it. The seduction had resulted in a pathologically intimate pact, which had shielded the man from discovery while undermining every normal relationship. The effect of the emotional trauma had been to abort the spontaneous candour of natural feeling, begetting in its place the idea of the victim. A situation corresponding to an inherited mythological pattern, and implanted in the psyche of a child before consciousness, in the form of self-regarding vigilance, has dawned, is only too liable to become an *a priori* character of fate.

When I asked the patient why he had withheld this essential fact he said he thought he had told me, and was genuinely surprised at the force of my reaction. When the absolute necessity of confession, both in relation to his mother and his wife, was borne in upon him—for he agreed that they must be as much impaled upon the mystery as I had been—he was profoundly disturbed. At length, however, he accepted the necessity. The effect of this decision was magical: the locked door was opened, the psychological picture became humanized, and the sinister influence faded away. From this fact alone I was forced to conclude that the "traumatic" factor must be given crucial significance in the ætiological picture.

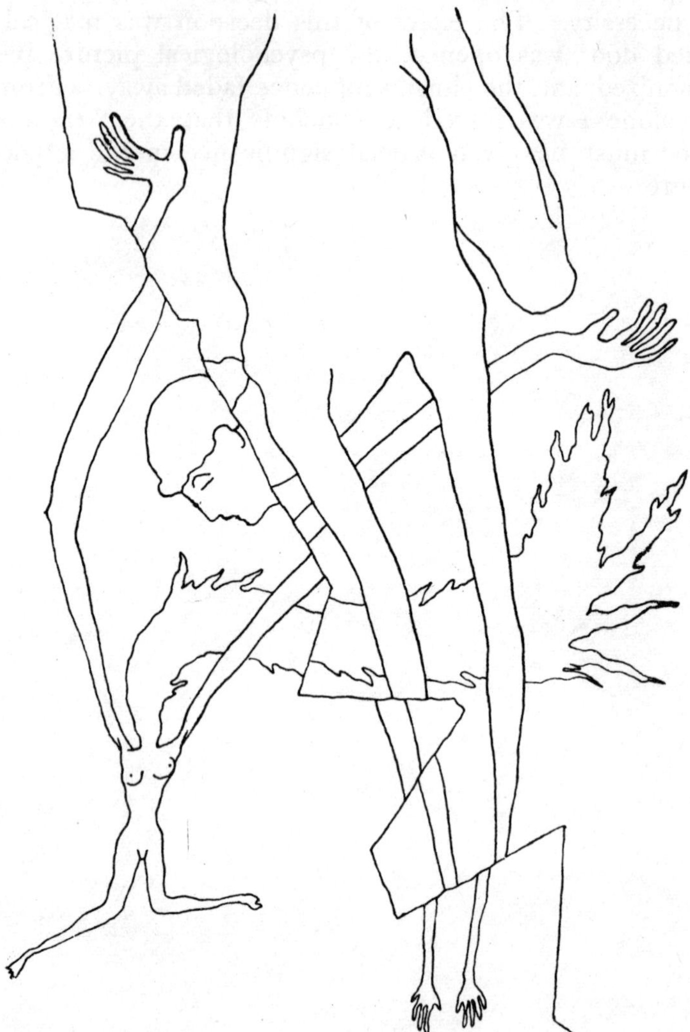

DRAWING 3.

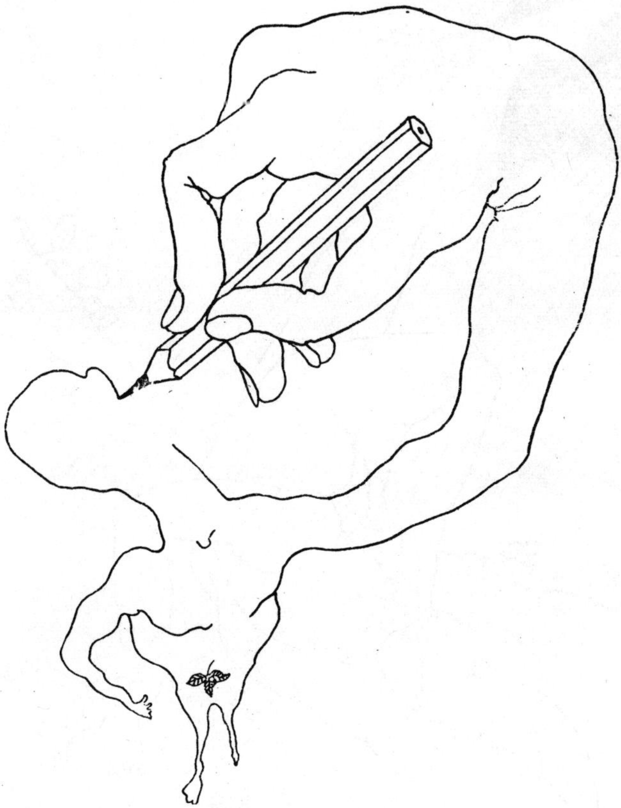

Drawing 4.

Drawing 5.

CHAPTER II

DISTORTION

I

OWING, in some measure, to an impeccable persona, the patient at first proved a baffling subject for analysis. The discussion of personal material and dreams went along smoothly enough, but although the patient's interest was genuinely engaged the depths apparently were not stirred. Eventually, without any suggestion from me, he was prompted to try the one medium of expression which had already proved of service as a subjective outlet.

He began these drawings during a period when the analysis had had to be suspended for a time. In the main they are explanatory and intellectually systematized, though mythological themes are not lacking. The extraordinary contrast in character to the first series of drawings is partly due to the fact that the present subject had been trained to use his medium with a disciplined economy of expression which the former patient necessarily lacked; it is also due to a marked difference in type. Whereas the former, at bottom extraverted, used intuition as his major function, the latter has a naturally introverted and intellectual habit of mind. As an extraverted type, the form of the subjective problem in the former case assumed the idiom of sexuality, whereas the present subject, being introverted, naturally encounters his main problem in the region of the will-to-power. The prolific material of the extraverted subject achieved, in the former case, a luxuriant archaic elaboration in the individual myth, while the self-contained, abstract and condensed drawings of the present series are characteristic of the reflective, introverted personality.

I have employed the same method of demonstration, but, owing to the artist's greater precision and economy of expression, the description of the drawings proved less onerous.

II

Drawing 1

The contents of this drawing consist of the two functional elements represented by hand and eye.

On the left of the field, starting at the bottom, the main figure consists of four arms and hands (though only three of the latter are visible) arranged in a tightly welded spiral. The two hands to the right are right hands. The apex of this group is directed upon the centre of the back of a single right hand placed above it. This hand is misshapen: the thumb is small, short and everted, while the width of the hand is excessive in proportion to the length of the fingers. The latter are gathered into a conical formation, similar to that of the group below. The apex of the cone is directed towards the back of another right hand, characterized by a wide separation of thumb and index-finger. The remaining fingers, being flexed, are out of sight. Beyond this, yet another hand seems to be disappearing into a kind of nebula consisting of a dense thicket of curves and loops. This final hand of the series is not clearly outlined like the rest; it is also malformed, the thumb resembling a finger and the index-finger a thumb. In the work of an artist we cannot assume the malformation of a figure to be a mere failure in technique. Viewing the drawing symptomatically, all the hands of the series are distorted in one way or another.

On the right of the field is an eye. The upper and lower eyelids are retracted away from the eyeball, which stands out with painful prominence, as during a dissection or operation. The eyelashes are crudely exaggerated and are represented by a fringe of coarse, irregular lines. Knowing the subject to delight in meticulous drawing, we must again assume that these unkempt eyelash-fringes, retracted lids and exposed eyeball are symptomatic subjective statements.

In this, the first drawing of the series, the patient presents his problem in terms of the two functions upon which his *métier* depends, and in his representation of them both are morbidly estranged from their natural appearance. Remembering the erratic battleship in the former patient's first drawing, we may conclude that the first question a distracted man is liable to put to himself is, "What makes me behave so strangely?" In my experience it is usually some such question as this which serves as the initial impetus towards a psychological analysis.

The patient had, in fact, been distressed to find that, in spite of almost frenzied efforts, he could not carry out work that needed to be done. Disturbing factors had been eliminated, and a protective semiconscious absent-mindedness and aloofness had been cultivated. But invariably he became entangled with irrelevant human interruptions; and especially was this the case in relation to his wife. All day and a large part of the evening he habitually spent at his office, yet he could not succeed in getting things done. The depression arising from this accumulating frustration was intensified by the fact that he was ambitious and knew himself to be gifted above the average. The instigation to express the subjective state of affairs in this, the only way ready to his hand, sprang from this rather desperate mood.

* * * * *

We have already discussed the character of distortion in dream and fantasy constructions. But, besides obvious distortion there is also active irrationality of content in the present drawing.

Taking first the receding series of hands, there is an obvious irrationality in the presence of four hands in the lowest figure. This spiral conglomerate of four arms cohering together, like a twisted scroll of paper, is a very unusual idea. The shape of the hands, too, is queer, notwithstanding a definite suggestion of power in the firmness of line. One gets the impression that they have somehow grown into this twisted mass, rather like the trunk of a creeper coiling about itself for lack of other support. But they also express the idea of applied force, as though forming a kind of spiral drill that had to bore into the central black area in the back of the hand above.

Besides the four hands of the initial figure, we note the repetition of the idea of four in the four terms of the receding series. There exists here a psychic factor which, though not belonging rationally either to eye or hand, is essential, as we have already seen, to the problem of psychological development. There is considerable prognostic importance in the fact that the patient's first drawing contains a symbolical statement to the effect that the problem of achievement also involves the fourfold completeness of individuation.

Another interesting feature must be noted—namely, the dark spot at which the spiral force is directed is darkest in the second term of the series, more diffused in the third, eventually expanding into the whirling nebula into which the fourth hand is groping its way. There is the suggestion of an impelling *vis a tergo* running through the series, the original focal point of this dynamic movement being the black spot against which the fourfold conglomerate is driving. It will be observed that the pupil of the eye creates a parallel focal point at approximately the same level on the other side of the field. If the reader will scrutinize this pupil rather closely he will find that the circle is, as it were, chipped, and in place of the normal pupil a little beaked head with a black eye has appeared on the scene, slightly reminiscent of the figure of Punch. The presence of such unconscious improvisations must never be brushed aside as trivial accidents, especially when they chime in so appropriately with the deeper psychic content of the drawing. The distortion which characterizes every part and detail of the drawing amounts to a candid confession that the world is seen crookedly. The beam, the error of refraction, becomes personified as a dwarf or gnome, a figure that represents that part of the natural mind which stands beyond the human pale, the part which, refusing the burden of the soul, claims kinship with crooked Thersites, who mocked the heroic attempt.

To return to the hand series for a moment, we note that, in point of technique, the hands in the bottom figure give an impression of power and solidity, an impression which diminishes as the series recedes. Compared with those of the spiral group, the upper hands appear flabby and relatively ineffectual. The upper two are indeed reduced to mere ciphers, fitted for nothing but to register their inability to grasp. But what are they trying to grasp? A nebula, a mood, a whirling mist? Yet even here, in the apparent incapacity to oppose index-finger to thumb (an incapacity which begins to be overcome in the terminal hand), we can discern an intimation of the schizophrenic split. For the opposition of thumb to index-finger is a purposive, co-ordinated opposition, in the same way that the normal relation of the conscious function to the unconscious is one of reciprocal activity. Yet, according to this figure, instead of reciprocal action there is unco-ordinated separation. Thus again the symptom assumes a kind of explanatory character.

If we pay attention to what the drawing says, we must acknowledge the fact that the four functions of the mind have become, as it were, welded together in a single purposive drive, directed unceasingly at the pathological area. Wherever the patient turns, or whatever he does, the morbid influence is liable to intervene as an obscure, impalpable obstruction. But the increased intensity of effort with which he tries to overcome the obstacle only serves to increase his feeling of incapacity, so that, in effect, he loses active initiative. Everything eludes him, and he ends in a fog of despair.

On the other hand, because his vital energy is constantly preoccupied with this deep subjective inadequacy, the direction of consciousness is increasingly turned inwards. He has become morbidly introspective and self-critical, watching himself with an ironical eye. Instead of dealing with the obvious necessities of his life his mind is obsessed by morbid ideas and the vain dissecting of motives. This whole inverted state of mind is symptomatized by the eye with its upward- and inward-turned eyeball, the retracted lids with their long disorderly lashes, and the sinister hunchback sitting in the pupil. The retracted lids are also expressive of the dark, subterranean fear which congeals the patient's feeling and provokes his intense introspective activity: it is this latter factor which, as we demonstrated in the hand series, disturbs the normal function of the intelligence, therewith defeating its own object.

The concept of the fourfold differentiation of mental

functioning must be our canon of proportion when dealing with obsessional products. Bearing this concept in mind, we are at once struck by the psychological implication of this initial representation of the four functions. Instead of a differential freedom of thought, intuition, feeling or sensation, we can anticipate from this functional amalgam nothing else than an obsessional idea impelled by a merciless drive. The intractable difficulty encountered in the cure of obsessional cases comes, I believe, from this functional monopoly in which the whole of the psychic energy, instead of fulfilling the fourfold needs of the mind, is pressed into the obsessional combine. It is not merely a question of one function instead of four, but rather a consolidation of the four into a single drive, the resultant being neither reasonable nor capable of rational elucidation, since it is mere force masquerading in the form of an idea. In point of fact, we have here a convincing self-portrait of the obsessional mechanism.

When we come to the final drawing of the series we shall see how this problem of the differentiation of the four main functions determines the structure of the new cathedral, which begins to take shape after the break-up of the traditional conception. In the former case we also found the solution of the major problem adumbrated in the first drawing of the series. It is a fact of the greatest interest that the key to the individual life-problem is frequently presented, or at least hinted at, in a patient's first dream.

III

Drawing 2

This drawing is the result of a hypnagogic vision which the patient had on the day following the previous drawing. It is done with a very fine pencil, the lines of the head and face being much fainter than the other contents. The face is that of a mature man, and the closed eyes, compressed lips and contracted brows suggest intense suffering. In the left parietal region there is a long surgical incision which has just been sutured by the hand hovering near it. This hand belongs to a diminutive feminine figure, which has taken form within the thin trail of smoke arising from the dropped cigarette.

Certain features of this hand should be noted. It is the left hand of an enormously elongated arm that lacks proper structure. Moreover, the position of the hand is impossible: the thumb is where the little finger should be and *vice versa*. The index-finger is opposing the thumb as though in the act of holding a needle or a pencil. The thimble on the little finger and the formidable needle that is being used for the suture belong rather to the domestic sewing-room than to an operating-theatre.

The experience which preceded the drawing consisted of a momentary vision of a living cell containing a heart-shaped nucleus. A great number of branching " filaments " streamed from this glowing heart in the direction of the subject's brain. The vision was so vivid that the cigarette dropped from his lips and he sat for a time spellbound by the strange reality of the experience.

* * * * *

At the time of this drawing the patient had told me nothing of the emotional trauma of his childhood, and he could not explain why he had had the idea of an operation upon the head. His associations flocked about the operations his parents had undergone: these seemed to symbolize for him the misery of divided loyalties embodied in the rival claims of his divorced parents.

With regard to the vision of the cell, he thought this must be a new cell forming in his brain. It seemed as though he had been " listening in," and had been allowed to " televise " the regenerative process going on in his own brain. The vividness of this impression took possession of consciousness, gathering into its orbit the fragmentary sense-stimuli coming from without. Thus the cigarette falling from his lips became the symbolic, phallic source of a flowing wave, in the midst of which a diminutive woman's figure took shape. The stream and the woman were one, stretching upwards in the shape of a great hand. Then he knew that the hand had just finished sewing up a wound on the side of his head and he was beginning to come round.

Such was the fantasy which took possession of him as he sat with closed eyes, and which had its origin in the vision of the living brain-cell. When I drew his attention to the fact that he had drawn a right hand upon a left arm, he said it was simply the result of instinctively using his own hand, that was holding the pencil, as his model. The fact that he automatically reproduced the drawing posture of the thumb and index-finger, without noticing its incompatibility with the rest of the design, reveals how his normal technical vigilance had been temporarily suspended by the spell of the fantasy. When, in other words, the energy-value of the subjective fantasy-activity exceeds that of objective sense-perceptions the latter tend to be abstracted from their normal connections and to assume the character of symbols. In the present instance the power of the fantasy not only transformed the habitual cigarette into a function of eros, linking up the heart in the regenerated cell with the woman's figure in the stream of smoke, but it also abstracted the subject's hand, the principal organ of objective adaptation, bringing it bodily across into the fantasy-formation. That this transposition is not achieved without resistance is indicated by the strange, almost distorted position of the fingers, due to the fact that the index-finger and thumb still persist, against the whole trend of the fantasy, in the pencil-holding position, while the little finger is engaged independently in the therapeutic fantasy. The misshapen appearance of the hand and its attachment to an arm which does not belong to it, not to mention the ironical detail of the thimble, are evidence of the resistance of a differentiated objective function to being suborned by the autonomous psyche for purely subjective ends. In analytical experience with artists one sometimes encounters this difficulty. The work of psychological creation, having only slight relation to ordinary æsthetic criteria, is felt to be in some way inimical to their art.

The resistance may also account for the extremely diminutive figure of the anima, who must be regarded in general as directing and controlling the hand during this work of psychological creation. As the personification of the involuntary, autonomous activity of the psyche, the anima is also naturally associated with the left side of the body, as opposed to the voluntary, directed character of the right. Hence the grafting of the subject's right hand upon the anima's left arm is not an accident, but an involuntary statement of a somewhat distasteful truth.

With regard to the allusion to brain surgery contained in the sutured incision, the patient was not aware that the left parietal region of the brain is specifically concerned with the motor area determining the execution of voluntary movements, speech, etc. Yet the fact that the trauma is instinctively located in this region harmonizes with the symptoms of defective performance noted in our discussion of the previous drawing.

We have now to combine the various components of the fantasy into a connected psychical development. The patient was prompted to come for treatment because of a certain crippling or injury in the executive sphere; he has also learnt that his habit of intellectual self-analysis was definitely harmful. The hyperactivity of the intellect, as a compensatory development arising from the emotional deficiency, could not heal the wound; on the contrary, it tended to keep the emotions all the more under the heel of repression. Thus an *impasse* had been reached. The subsequent mood of depression signified the bankruptcy of intellectual dictatorship. This was the occasion for the repressed antithesis—namely, the function of feeling—to emerge from the unconscious and to take command of the situation. The vision of the regenerated brain-cell, with the heart in its centre, anticipates the moment of rebirth, in which the heart regains its central place. Because of its present dissociated state the organ or function of feeling appears projected with hallucinatory intensity into space. The directional flow of the branching filaments towards the brain seems to demand conscious recognition and assimilation of the dissociated function. The synchronous emergence of the feminine principle in the little anima-figure recalls the vital rôle played by the anima of the former series in the salvage of the heart.

The significance of this drawing, as compared with its symptomatic predecessor, is the evidence it contains of the reshaping of the basic attitude. The first drawing, as we saw, represented the obsessional intellectual drive bearing upon the weak spot with a ruthless, overbearing insistence. But in the expression of inner concentration on the suffering face in the present drawing we recognize the moment of vision, when the patient realizes that the defect he has been trying to track down in the roots of his mind is no defect to be excised by crude mental surgery, but a deep injury which can be healed only with the help of the neglected feminine principle.

The effective cause which brought about this change of attitude and evoked the vision of regeneration was undoubtedly the objective, impersonal viewpoint of analytical psychology. His former attitude was, as it were, rooted in the suspicion of some inherent psychological defect, than which nothing can be more damaging to one's fundamental moral. The vampires of fear seize upon the idea of a moral defect, and upon this secret doubt is erected a complicated, distorted edifice of neurotic inferiority. In the presence of such a doubt the realization, by means of an objective scientific process, that one's basic instinctual inheritance is inherently sound, and that the symptoms of incapacity are traceable to an injury inflicted by an external agent—this throws a new and releasing light upon the whole picture. The former hypothesis would seem to demand a radical extirpation of the basic fault, whereupon all the latent masochism of a highly sophisticated mentality must be enlisted in the hunting-down of the criminal tendency. The latter hypothesis, on the contrary, has no need of the authoritarian methods of the inquisition and the detective hunt. When these are laid aside the tentative efficacy of instinct begins to prevail over the law and the prophets, and the regenerative process of nature is free to develop without let or hindrance.

In dealing with so-called shell-shock cases after the war it was rare to find men who had lost a limb or been physically incapacitated by direct trauma manifesting psychasthenic or neurotic breakdown. The dramatic forms of neurosis were, in my experience, almost entirely confined to cases where moral had failed. In a large number of the latter cases analysis revealed the existence of a neurotic habit of long standing. In other words, the traumatic explanation was seized upon by the neurotic complex for obvious subjective reasons; but often it did not tally with the actual historical facts. An attempt to cure such cases upon the traumatic hypothesis merely tended to reinforce the neurotic habit of mind. In view, therefore, of the neurotic *faiblesse* in relation to responsibility, the traumatic explanation proves a dangerous moral alibi when it does not fit the psychological facts.

In the case of our subject the acceptance of the traumatic hypothesis coincided with a dawning sense of the futility of intellectual masochism. The drawing represents the moment in which the intellectual attempt to extirpate the defect from above yields to the regenerative healing process which now begins to work from below. The surgical wound on the head belongs to the former attempt, whereas the latter is symbolized by the chain of symbols beginning at the living cell, dropping down to the infantile phallic level suggested by the burning cigarette, and so to the newly-formed anima-figure arising like Aphrodite from the released primordial stream, and ending in the converted executive hand wearing the feminine symbol of the thimble. The position of the hand near the already sutured wound seems to imply that the first act of the regenerative attitude is to repair the wound of the mind caused by the morbid habit of introspection.

The work of bringing together things that have become separated harmonizes with the principle of eros. Accordingly the idea of suturing the wound would agree with the benign aspect of the anima-function, whereas the tense position of the thumb and index-finger would tally with the previous intellectual tendency to handle the knife. The conflict between these contradictory motivations becomes graphically manifest in the distortion of the hand and in the grotesque undervaluation of the anima as a wisp of smoke rising from a dropped cigarette.[1]

There is also a certain contradiction between the very competent way in which the wound has been sutured and

[1] According to previous evidence—namely, the diminutive size of the anima in the vision of the Siberian *shaman* and the inconspicuous crescent-moon anima in the Yin-phase of the former patient—we might conclude that when the anima-activity is greatest she is least in evidence.

the somewhat ineffectual gesture of the little finger with its domestic thimble, not to mention the clumsy bodkin hanging unsupported in space. These latter details can, I think, be regarded as an ironical comment upon the intervention of the anima coming from the superseded masculine intellect.

IV

Drawing 3

A jagged split, suggesting a cracked pane of glass, runs diagonally across the drawing. The split separates a tense male figure below from a sprawling female figure above. Not only is the continuity of every line broken as it traverses the split, but each broken line is carried on again in a displaced position on the further side, resembling the effect of refraction upon the shape of a stick held half under water.

The male figure is depicted reaching out with very long arms, which seem to extend into the far distance, towards a goal represented symbolically by a globe, suggesting the idea of a distant world in space. The hands seem to be on the point of seizing this world, and the whole figure is tense with purpose. The head and lower portions of both arms are the only parts of the male figure transcending the split.

The female figure is much smaller than the male, though considerably larger than the anima-figure of the previous drawing. The head is merged indistinguishably with a flowing mass of hair streaming downwards across the split into the man's half. Her arms are also enormously elongated, and are raised in the act of reaching out, apparently to embrace the man. Both arms and streaming hair undergo displacement or refraction as they cross the line. The legs of the female figure are loose and sprawling, in contrast to the tense, contracted position of the man's legs, which are gathered together under him like a taut spring.

* * * * *

The drawing provides a classic illustration of the schizophrenic split. Certain points, however, must be noted, which distinguish it from the examples discussed in Part I. The following are the chief points of difference. In the former case the jagged layer of rocks was represented, already in the first drawing, as part of the structure of repression. The only possible allusion to trauma which might have been detected in that picture was the broken-off arm of the crane, which acted as the phallic instigator of the whirlpool; whereas, in the present drawing, the impression of trauma is immediate and unmistakable. It is difficult to understand how an idiopathic schizoid condition could manifest itself in just this way. The resemblance to a cracked pane of glass suggests the idea of a violent impact; this would agree with the violation of feeling which, as mentioned above, occurred in childhood. But the most important difference lies in the careful systematization whereby the continuity of idea is preserved. Although the split creates an abrupt division of the contents of the drawing into two distinct portions, there is a deliberate attempt to maintain continuity in spite of the effect of refraction upon the severed contents. By correcting the refraction in one's own mind the content flows freely from one side to the other, whereas in the former case, notably in Drawing II., the contents of the one half were as different as possible from those of the other.

Accepting the drawing as an inspired attempt at self-diagnosis, it would certainly seem to lend colour to the theory of induced psychosis. We know how hopelessly the patient was bound up in the wife's neurotic condition: although contained by it to the exclusion of other normal interests, he none the less showed unmistakable symptoms of resistance to his fate. The drawing illustrates both factors; there is only the doubt as to which should be regarded as primary. If the inchoate female figure whose stream of hair, like a fiery, emotional tide, is flowing across into his man's world, then we must regard the crack as an explosion of pathological resistance against the encroaching feminine flood. But if the crack is the primary factor we must view the appealing female figure in the light of a frenzied attempt on the part of wife or anima to overcome the invisible barricade which seems to isolate the patient's feeling like a wall of glass.

But the barrier or hindrance does not lie merely between subject and object. For the head which chooses the goal and the hands which reach towards it are also cut off by the schizophrenic refraction. So the obstacle must lie within the subject's own mind, and so long as this refracting obstacle is effective he is as powerless to achieve his own rational goal as he is to accept the irrational nature of woman's need of relationship.

Refraction is a phenomenon occurring when light-rays pass from one conducting medium to another of different density, as from air to water, the course of the light-ray being deflected in its passage through the denser medium. The psychological analogy relates to the greater psychic density of the affective level of the unconscious in comparison with the relative lucidity of consciousness. The drawing implies, therefore, that the threshold between the conscious and the unconscious has the character of a jagged, artificial break, instead of the fluid contiguity of natural elements.

One more point remains to be considered—namely, the contrast in the subject's treatment of the two heads. The woman's head is completely merged in the stream issuing from the top of her body. We are naturally tempted to think of this stream as hair; but if we forgo our expectation we observe that this substance flows and extends like fire or water; it spreads and disperses, putting out jets and tongues in all directions. In contrast to this the man's head is clear and compact. It is also tilted up, as though suddenly caught from behind. The jagged line cuts through the neck and the occipital region of the head, the cut-off piece of head being found on the underside of the crack. Again we are reminded of the trauma on the left side of the head, observed in the previous drawing.

The feminine smoke-wraith of the second drawing and the disorganized headless figure of the present one are symptomatic of the patient's emotional deficiency. He tends to identify woman, as object, with his own difficulty in relation to the unconscious, unwittingly ascribing to woman the irruption of wayward fantasies into his ordered plan of life. This fantasy-activity comes from the autonomous anima-complex: he cannot see and understand his wife objectively, because the anima-effect is always blindfolding him. In so far as the relevant woman corresponds with the anima-image unconsciously projected upon her, she is visible and appears desirable. But in so far as she differs from the anima, she tends either to be irrelevant or to take on a dubious or even a sinister aspect.

The inundation of fire or water, issuing from the anima, comes flowing over into the ego-domain like an unwelcome visitation of nature. It symbolizes the danger of being overwhelmed by the irrationality of the unconscious, which seems to threaten not only the programme of his ambition, but the very security of conscious existence.

* * * * *

A demonstration of a series of psychological drawings must be said to have failed unless the emotional connection between the successive products is observed. With the vision of the living brain-cell in Drawing 2 the control of events passed over to the anima-complex, therewith inaugurating the natural regenerative process. Notwithstanding the obvious healing value of that experience, it involved a lowering of the threshold by which the integrity of consciousness is normally maintained. A borderline psychology cannot risk the lowering of consciousness without feelings of tension and anxiety, because it immediately invites a dangerous activation of the unconscious. Coming to terms with the unconscious is therefore a formidable undertaking for the borderline patient, although his only way to an abiding security.

Owing to the existence of his protective barricade, the patient had no assurance or faith in the purpose underlying the activity of the anima. All he could discern was the disturbing effects of the invasion upon his ordered conscious world. These effects are represented in the drawing by the diffuse inundation in front of him and by the interfering arms and hands. The refracting effect of the jagged threshold represents his conscious incapacity to perceive purpose in anything originating across the border—*i.e.*, in the unconscious.

Evaluating a pathological product of this kind, we have to remember that the teleological understanding of so-called unconscious activity is only a recent acquisition of science, and that even now a formidable body of psychiatric opinion is hostile to this conception. But the difference between the scientist, whose rational prejudice precludes him from accepting the irrational purposiveness of the unconscious, and the patient, who is so cut off from his unconscious that he has to project it into the outside world, is more than one of degree: it is also a difference in kind. For the former will maintain his sterilized rational standpoint while presenting, in his actual behaviour, a convincing demonstration of the irrational principle he consciously repudiates; whereas with the latter the opposite is frequently the case: his mind may be open to the acceptance of the unconscious in principle, but when the affective experience itself overtakes him, either he goes under or he has to fight it as his greatest menace. Only seldom is it true that what a man thinks is the product of reflection upon his own experience. Usually his rational citadel is a fortress he has learned to defend with his reason; but it may have little or no relation to the deep affective currents of his lived experience.

In no sense could the subject of these drawings be described as a typical "intellectual." His intellect became the ruler of his conscious world on the strength of its compensatory protective function. Accordingly, when ambition collided with subjective resistance and obstruction, the intellect turned inwards upon the mental sphere—not, originally, in order to understand the nature of the difficulty, but with all the intensity of the masculine will refusing to be thwarted of its goal.

This conflict is personified throughout the drawings in the shape of a masculine, ambitious, rational will and its feminine, emotional, irrational antithesis. In the present drawing the issue is stated as a conflict of goals, the man reaching out towards his distant world, the woman trying to embrace her goal in the man. Naturally no man wants to be the goal of any woman; but what goes hardly with a man is the fact that the woman is not independently creative. Both wife and anima need him as means to their creative ends; hence his introverted masculine ideal of freedom from emotional claims must always elude his grasp.

By reference to the previous drawing we know that the feminine principle, there depicted as an encroaching stream or influence, refers to the anima, whose purpose, so far as the subject can tell, is obscure and even menacing. His tendency, for instance, to question the validity of his own mind is simply due to the fact that he has become aware of an insistent subjective aim that is alien to his conscious purposes. Hence we may say that schizophrenic symptoms are determined by the anima, in the sense that the split tends to become manifest when the autonomous complex is felt as an independent and alien will.

V

DRAWING 4

This drawing appears to serve two purposes—it makes a statement and offers an explanation. It carries on the idea of the magnified hand and arm from the second drawing, only here the executive right hand belongs to the left arm of the subject; no longer is it loaned to the anima. While the anima was directing the hand from below, the regenerative healing process prevailed. Now the masculine executive will is uppermost again and the obsessional distortion of Drawing 1 reappears.

The points to notice are the grotesquely foreshortened extremities and the relative atrophy of both feet and right hand, in contrast to the enormously magnified drawing hand and arm. Although the right hand is set upon the left arm as before, the thumb and index-finger have regained executive control over the pencil, with the all-powerful masculine will bearing down upon the head from above. Note also that the place where the pencil has stopped, leaving the figure uncompleted, is in the same region of the head in which the trauma was located in the last drawing. Aggressive masculinity appears in the decisive firmness of line, compared with the extreme delicacy and variation of tone of the previous drawing. Although the patient has drawn a pencil, he actually uses ink.

The resurgence of intellectual control has doubtless

prompted the subject to overstate the case; but the drawing is, none the less, significant as a symptomatic gesture. The excessive development of the one function or medium of expression, and the corresponding atrophy of the other three, provide eloquent testimony to the dangerous one-sidedness of his psychological development. The whole instinctive side, represented by the lower half of the body, is attenuated into a pair of meagre and parched appendages. The head is large in proportion to the body, and the drawing hand is greater than the whole of the rest of the figure. This disproportion must represent an enormous overvaluation of the conscious rational will at the expense of the irrational instinctual elements.

The patient had not observed the fact that he had identified his right hand with his left arm until I pointed it out to him. He again gave the explanation that he had used his drawing hand as his model; an explanation that is not entirely satisfactory. It is obvious, I think, from the similar position of hand and arm, that this drawing is the masculine *riposte* to the encroachment of the feminine unconscious represented in Drawings 2 and 3. If the reader will compare the masterful grasp of the pencil, in its correct position in the drawing, with the vacant, ineffectual posture of thumb and index-finger in Drawing 2, he will sense the triumph of the resurgent masculine will.

Another significant feature of the drawing is the way in which the head is bending away from the pencil, resembling the instinctive recoil of a patient from the surgeon's knife. Regarding the pencil as complex-indicator, the pencil must have reached the point associated with the hidden trauma. From this point of view the continuity of line in the drawing would be analogous to the continuity of the conscious process. Jung's experiments in word-association showed that whenever a break or irregularity occurred in the reaction to the test-word an affect-laden complex was invariably responsible for the reaction-defect. In the present instance the break occurs at the ear, not far from the site of the operation wound in Drawing 2. In regard to that drawing we can assume that the operation must have preceded the healing and suturing fantasy. There were also signs of executive, masculine resistance to the closing of the wound. That same aggressive masculinity is present here, and again we have an indication of its tendency to wound, with a corresponding sensitive recoil of the subject, as from something harmful or hostile. Here, then, is a portrait of the masochistic, self-torturing trend in this complex psychology.

The ear is the symbol of psychological understanding: "He that hath ears to hear, let him hear." But what kind of understanding could be anticipated from this overbearing, masterful hand, with its hard, insistent pencil? Only the crudest use of the "nothing but" style of psychological dissection might be expected from this all-too-superior standpoint. The drawing shows why the operation of self-analysis almost invariably fails. For the function that performs the operation is the overvalued, collectively adapted function, whose excessive claim to superiority so often derives from an overcompensated defect. Judging from this psychological self-portrait, small understanding of the victimized and starved instincts could be anticipated from this pitiless protagonist of the conscious will. There are, in fact, numbers of neurotic individuals who, from ignorance of the deep instinctual cause of their malady, constantly inflict upon themselves lacerating and quite ineffectual criticism, from which paralyzing feelings of inferiority are only too liable to arise.

Under the ægis of the feminine principle in Drawing 2 the head of the subject was drawn with exquisite sensibility, while the healing breath of understanding began to have effect (the anima-figure appeared "standing under" the head). Here, on the other hand, the heroic superiority of the executive will obliterates every feature, and no nuance of personality is allowed to reveal itself. The point of the pencil is hard and sharp as a knife, while the flinching head speaks of the merciless insistence of a repressive, rational standpoint. The fact that the line stops at the indicative ear may also be due to a certain fear lest something might be said which would be painful to hear.

The significance of this picture in the sequence will be apparent when we bear in mind the unusual ambivalence of this case, mentioned in the previous chapter. No sooner does the flow of fantasy activity open the door to the unconscious than consciousness descends like a dictator attempting to control nature with the sword of power. The equilibrium of the psyche is zealously defended, every move towards the left being countered by a violent swing back to the attitude of hard, intellectual superiority. No sentimental nonsense about the suffering victims of repression; everything must be cold, hard and clear. Here is that same insistent coercion of the four hands, consolidated into a kind of psychic drill, observed in the first drawing.

This drawing illustrates Jung's conception of what has been termed the "inferiority complex." He believes that in every case it is due to the fact that a function, or functions, proper to the personality, have been left in a repressed, dissociated condition in the unconscious, and that the only cure of inferiority is to retrieve these elements and to reintegrate them into the conscious personality. This conception of Jung's is undoubtedly true; yet it is also empirically established that the sense of inferiority is enormously increased by the meticulous, soul-destroying criticism of the overcompensating, superior function which, because of its frequent functional isolation from the rest of the psyche and its consequent liability to conform fanatically to collective expectations, tends to behave like a pursuing, hyperconscientious demon. It would therefore be more correct to speak of the inferiority-superiority complex, and to explain the vicious circle of alternating moods as resulting from the dissociation of psychic functions, whose proper performance can be obtained only under the condition of reciprocal action. The effect of this state of affairs upon the differentiated superior function is to deflect it from its objective direction and to give it the inverted character of frustration.

The magnified hand of the drawing illustrates very well this morbid, subjective determination. Instead of pursuing its objective, disciplined course, it is turned inwards in a vicious, masochistic assault upon the subject. Such treacherous work is, of course, the sign of bad government. Only when a state is divided against itself does the organ of executive power become possessed by self-destructive ferocity. A healthy mind does not suffer these divisions—not because there is no conflict, but simply because the conflict tends to break through into consciousness, without grave dissociation or alienation of function.

VI

DRAWING 5

The patient wanted to discard this drawing because he felt it to be insincere. I decided to include it, since it belongs to the series and has a logical connection with what has gone before.

It represents insanity. The rigid posture of the head, the contracted brows, the overextended position of the body with the backward flexion of right arm and left leg, the crazy three-fingered hand trying to catch the butterfly, and the similarly deformed foot whose big toe spurns the sun in a darkened sky, the gigantic proportions of the figure in contrast to the river with its three pollarded willows, the tilting of the earth's horizon, and the miniature proportions of everything that is not the subject—all speak with one voice and to the same purpose.

The subject has drawn his disorientation in space with such skill that this taut figure, impossibly reclining on a tilted earth, almost produces vertigo. The area of darkness enveloping the sun (darkest immediately around the sun) is expressive of the threat to consciousness. The small satellite or fragment just below the sun (associated by the patient with the moon) is symptomatic, on the cosmic plane, of schizophrenic disruption. As the moon broke away from the sun, so fragments break away from the integrity of consciousness; and, like the moon, the disjuncted fragment is reduced to a cold and lifeless existence.

The extended body of the subject reaches from this event in the heavens to the butterfly beside the stream, the line of tension of the body being stretched between these incommensurable factors. A refusal to recognize the significance of an event that could transform his whole world is implied in the spurning gesture of the foot, the reversed position of the body (foot above and head below), and the insane preoccupation with the butterfly. It is, in fact, a complete reversal of the mental process. When objective consciousness is eclipsed the archaic contents of the unconscious have complete sway. Everything subjective becomes monstrous and grotesque, while the whole objective universe dwindles to negligible items which have no other purpose than to feed unmitigated fantasies.

With regard to the mocking dwarf who pokes his head out of the earth not far from the diminutive church, we recall the beaked dwarf found squatting in the pupil of the eye in the first drawing. This figure is liable to play a significant rôle in the psychology of everyone who tries to live on a more respectable or reasonable level than he can comfortably afford. The story of the Norwegian pastor illustrates the character of the elf or gnome better than psychological definition. The pastor, crossing an upland moor after sundown, hears a piping voice hailing him. A few feet away in the heather he sees a little man. Stooping down he asks him what he wants. "I want a soul," says the dwarf. "You have the cure of souls, and you must give me one." "Only God gives souls," replied the pastor. "Then tell God to give me a soul." "We can pray to God, but we may not command Him. I will teach you how to pray. Say these words after me: 'Our Father, which art in heaven.'" "Oh yes, I see. 'Our Father, which art not in heaven.'" "No, that was wrong; you must not say that. Pray like this: 'Our Father, which art in heaven.'" "I see. 'Our Father, which art *not* in heaven.'" And so he continued, putting an increasingly vehement negative in the very place where the spirit of affirmation was most vital.

The dwarf is the very spirit of negativism, that which has to deny the meaning of love or the reality of God. We see it in the crooked Thersites, reviling the King in the assembly and denying the heroes their divine qualities by ascribing to them only the meanest of motives. In the Middle Ages the court jester was frequently a dwarf, whose licence to say the most outrageous things rested upon his being outside the social hierarchy: standing beyond the pale, he could say anything of anybody. Sometimes in Parliament there is such a figure—someone sitting in perpetual opposition, who will never have to be responsible for government, and to whom everyone instinctively looks to say the worst possible things or to voice what are erroneously called ' realistic ' arguments.

Men inspired with soul are prone to become inflated, thinking of the great deeds they are called upon to perform; but the little dwarf sees nothing in all that fuss. Shutting himself in his hole in the earth, he refuses to give his heart away to strange gods beyond the skies.

As the spirit of Satanism was attracted to the Mass in order to negate it with an evil, blasphemous similitude, so this derisive dwarf is attracted to the Church, as also the spurning three-toed devil's foot to the sun, in order to deny their power and light. The dwarf derives from the mythological race of Cabiri, the industrious earth-spirits, the untiring subterranean artificers and smiths—in a word, that part of the primordial instinct which never accepted the spiritual human pact. As nature sprite, the dwarf is eternally indifferent to civilized aims and purposes; and, for this reason, he is also the spirit of ironical humour, the laughter which pricks pomposity, or flattens out illusory pretensions.

But is it possible to conceive a figure as the spirit which denies the reality of God, yet which also laughs at the grandiose inflation that has to perform atheistical cosmic gestures? The ambiguity of the unconscious is such that any conception of a primordial image which did not constantly allow for this double interpretation would immediately be suspect. It is a fact, for example, that the primordial fallacy which, more than any other, is liable to open the door to insanity is the idea " I am god." It is also true that candidates in the antique mystery-cults were initiated into this fallacy as a profound mystical truth. It is therefore a supreme truth and, at the same time, a dangerous brain-bewildering delusion!

When the patient gave me this drawing and took pains to warn me it was insincere, did he discern the presence of this complete ambiguity? Did he appreciate that the insane man who stretched out a foot to spurn the sun was as good as saying, " I am god "? For who but a god could put out the sun? And did he realize that the dwarf who laughs at this insane illusion is also that same spirit which denies the reality of God?

An insane patient, possessed by the illusion of deity, will frequently show this ironical, self-mocking spirit. He may even laugh at his own illusion. But in this case he is not really insane.

The dwarf is also associated with Priapus, or with Hap of the Egyptians, who usually figures as an ugly dwarf. Primordial sexuality, conceived as the ubiquitous earth-spirit (Mimir with his gnomes), would be prone, like the rabbi's Golem, to be attracted to the Church. The dissociated part, being soulless and subhuman, seeks a soul, though at the same time it denies the reality of the soul.

In regard to the reversal of values manifest in this drawing, the patient described a curious condition which overtook him from time to time, consisting of a rapid transit of images across the field of consciousness. During these moments his sense of reality was affected: things seemed to be light and unreal and attention was disturbed. This altered condition of consciousness came without warning and lasted only a few seconds, yet it left him disturbed and agitated, not from the nature of the images, but because of the momentary lapse of conscious control.

This release of an abnormal image-forming activity is well illustrated in a case mentioned by Prinzhorn. The patient describes the intense activity of the autonomous process as follows: "At first I noticed a white spot in the clouds quite near. The clouds stood still. Then the white spot went far away and remained in the sky like a white board. On this board, or screen, or stage, pictures passed along with lightning speed, about 10,000 in half an hour: it was only with the greatest effort that I could catch even the most important ones. The Lord Himself appeared, and the witch who created the world. In the interval were other scenes—wars, continents, monuments, castles—but all this in supernatural pictures."

Prinzhorn's patient describes the same uncontrolled activity of the autonomous psyche, only intensified to an extreme degree, as though the psychic mechanism were made to race, as the engine of an automobile can be raced when not geared to a load. Psychic activity is normally geared, so to say, to a reality-load of objective tasks, and psychic energy is manageable only when it is harnessed to its load. We must assume, therefore, that under certain conditions of dissociation the energy-process becomes disconnected from its load. As soon as psychic activity achieves projected autonomy it is liable to produce a phenomenal display far more engrossing than the passage of external events. Attention then becomes wholly preoccupied by subjective activity, and objective reality ceases to exist.

In borderline cases, where the main symptom is a deprivation of conscious energy, it is not at all unusual to find an excessive activity of the unconscious in the form of interminable, discursive dreams full of queer, distorted images. Patients in this pseudo-catatonic condition may become almost anæsthetic to outer stimuli, while they often complain of extreme fatigue, due to the incessant unconscious activity.

It is agreed by all observers that schizophrenia is a condition in which the energy of the mind tends to recede from the more differentiated to the more archaic mental processes. Morgenthaler, for instance, lays particular emphasis on the fact that expression is liable to regress from writing and speech to drawing. He regards this as an atavistic phenomenon on the ground that pictorial expression was evolved before any form of writing. This is undoubtedly true, and yet it is important to recognize that the atavistic tendency, though a renegade from the standpoint of the higher centres, also acts as a relief force to the dissociated system in the unconscious. There are occasions, too, when imaginative writers and creative artists discover that the archaic mode of functioning supplies just the material which the differentiated function most needs. We know, for instance, how patients under the influence of the unconscious are liable to discern demon faces and sinister figures in the fortuitous shapes of wallpaper patterns, in the smoke from a cigarette, in clouds, or in shadows cast by clouds. Leonardo da Vinci describes this in his notebook as a " newly-invented method of looking." He says: "If you stare at stained and spotted walls or at embers in the fire, or clouds, or mud, you will make marvellous discoveries in them: compositions of battles, of men and animals, rocks, trees, mountains . . . grimaces, costumes and innumerable things which you may mould into perfect shapes, for the spirit is awakened to new invention by diffuse and indefinite things."[1]

Leonardo made the discovery that this renegade atavistic tendency could become the fertile source of his best ideas, just as Socrates discovered with his *δαίμων* how to make use of an archaic mode of perception.

When we employ the term atavism in our interpretation of pathological phenomena it is important to remember that we are using a double-edged blade. At bottom we are not so much concerned with the atavistic character of the mental activity, but rather with the question whether the archaic mode of functioning serves an intelligible purpose.

What I have termed the 'reality-load' is an organic system of adaptation, gained in some measure from individual experience, but derived mainly from the cultural past and handed down by tradition in the form of education. The renegade direction of the libido is a departure from, or rejection of, this organized system of cultural values. Hence the essential character of this aspect of schizophrenic dementia is concerned not merely with excessive activity at the archaic level; there is also a striking absence of any effort to understand or evaluate the symbols produced—in other words, a lowering of consciousness. Images of every kind, from the most sublime to the most trivial, are mixed together in an indiscriminate conglomerate; and sometimes this indifference to all venerable things is accompanied by a sly leer, or a hostile glance, as though a devil were gloating over a crime.

The repudiation of conscious value is symbolized in our patient's drawing in the reversed position of the figure, in the spurning of the sun, and by the darkened sky. The fantastic renegade direction of the libido is symbolized by the vagrant stream, which seems to take its source from

[1] For these allusions I am indebted to Dr. Guttmann, who included them in a recent paper on Schizophrenia read before the Medical Section of the British Psychological Society.

beneath the breast of the demented figure. The butterfly is the classical symbol of the irrational, self-moving activity of the mind.[1] Because of its wayward, indirect, unpredictable, zigzag flight, and the way it is apparently blown and tossed by the wind, it is easy to regard the butterfly as an aimless gadabout, the sport of every fitful breeze. Nothing, of course, could be further from the truth so far as the butterfly is concerned. If a human being behaved in that fashion he would be what he supposes the butterfly to be. But, in fact, the butterfly's unpredictable flight is his one safeguard against a host of predatory enemies. It could be said with equal truth that nature achieves her ends in the human sphere by the unpredictable motivations of the unconscious, which are able to elude the grasp of the most rational and predatory consciousness. When, therefore, we use the word " fantastic " in a derogatory sense it is well to understand exactly what we mean. For inasmuch as fantasy is the natural butterfly-modality of the soul, a mind denuded of fantasy becomes arid and soulless.

Again the problem is a question of individual attitude. If fantasy is regarded as the manifestation of instinctual potential seeking its way to realization, it becomes the seed-bed of future achievement. If, on the other hand, it is indulged in as a mirage-world, a counterfeit realm, where the subject cuts an heroic figure before an applauding subjective audience, thus evading his real tasks, it creates neurosis-island, a self-destroying paradise. The sterilization of life conveyed by the words " respectable " and " commonplace " should not be ascribed to the standardization of human beings in vast collective organizations: its primary cause is the deflecting of energy from real things into a compensatory fantasy-system which is never intended to be lived. The " island that wants to be visited," in Barrie's *Mary Rose*, is the secret cause of innumerable humdrum lives, in which circumstance has been allowed to gain the upper hand only because the way of escape into fantasy has been preferred to the more arduous creative experiment.

[1] Besides meaning breath, life, spirit, ψῦχή also means butterfly or moth, which was considered an emblem of the immortal soul, by reason of its passing through a kind of death in the chrysalis form.

When we compare this figure, with its powerful, disorderly limbs, with that of the previous drawing, we observe that this one is strong just where the former was weak, and ineffectual where the other was purposeful. In other words, it is a fantastic compensation of the previous self-portrait. In the former figure the left arm and hand provided the only effective member, whereas in this one they are correspondingly weak, misshapen and perverse. The three remaining limbs, which before were atrophied and useless, are now vigorous and muscular. But the most damning criticism of this renegade fantasy-figure is to be seen in the unco-ordinated gesture of the three-clawed left hand: not only is it unfitted to grip hold of anything with mastery; it cannot even pursue a fantasy with any prospect of success.

When a patient has reached the point where he is able to objectify his secret fantasy-indulgence with such devastating criticism we may be sure he will make a supreme effort to right himself. If a man were really heading for insanity he could not stop in his tracks and picture his folly with such a ruthless pen.

The number three, which has displaced the normal five in the digits of hand and foot, is directly associated with the creative energic principle. We must assume, therefore, that its appearance in this morbid setting alludes to the creative potentiality of fantasy-activity which, under the wrong ægis, becomes correspondingly destructive. The satanic power which defies the light was originally a part of the Godhead. This renegade figure can be therefore paralleled with Lucifer—namely, that aspect of the subject's creative personality which has gone over to the powers of darkness, hence the obscene spurning of the sun.

In Drawing 4 we saw how the collectively adapted superior function, diverted from its objective course, turned destructively upon the subject, as though resenting its functional divorce from the original psychic concert. In Drawing 5 we get a glimpse of the renegade influence which overtakes the personality-components which are cut off from conscious participation. The four main psychic functions constitute the structure of the personality as essentially as the four limbs subserve the spatial movements and adaptation of the body. Hence a divorce or splitting within the mind which dissociates one function completely from the rest can produce a condition of psychic disorientation, equivalent to the physical state of inco-ordination depicted in this drawing. These two pictures present a graphic statement of the effects of dissociation. First we get the viewpoint of the superior function; this is followed by a statement of the situation as seen from the side of the unconscious dissociated functions.

When we speak of the four functions as constituting the structure of the personality it is not to be understood that thinking, feeling, intuition and sensation can be so developed that each becomes equivalent in adaptive value to the superior function. Of the four limbs, the right arm, in the most perfectly co-ordinated individual, is usually the most competent executant of the will. But the other three members, working in differentiated conjunction, produce a co-ordinated totality expressing a fourfold unity of purpose.

With these drawings before us, the obstacle to effective performance inferred in Drawing 1 begins to assume definite proportions. The danger from the side of the unconscious springs not merely from the overweighting of the unconscious by the presence of functions in a passive inert condition, but from the possibility, illustrated in the drawing, that the three dissociated functions become actively rebellious to the rule of consciousness. In so far as a function is divorced from conscious participation, it tends to go over to the compensatory shadow-personality, where it can easily become seduced by the renegade-hypothesis. The danger of consciousness being overwhelmed by the unconscious antithesis must be regarded, therefore, as the possibility of a radical alienation of personality, wherein the will embracing the previous aims and general orientation of values goes by the board, and a grandiose fantasy-personality with antisocial aims and tendencies usurps its place.

We shall see in the following chapter how this threat to the established psychic order was met.

CHAPTER III

ORIENTATION

I

WITH the exception of the visionary anticipation of the regenerative process in Drawing 2 the pictures have so far been confined to symptomatic statements of the inner condition. For the purpose of diagnosis this type of product is invaluable; yet, however interested we may be in these subtle delineations of the schizophrenic problem, the main question still awaits satisfaction—namely, how does this individual psyche attempt to solve the problem? The interest of the psychotherapist in his case, unless he be a mere collector of pathological specimens, must necessarily focus upon this question.

With the drawing which now follows we reach a phase in which the patient is no longer satisfied in purely symptomatic representations, and where the drawings contain impersonal mythological contents of the general unconscious. The challenge to consciousness, contained in the last picture, is met by a new note of seriousness. The subject takes a deeper grip, and we can observe in this drawing the effort towards reorientation and control.

II

DRAWING 6

On the left is the traditional sign indicating the cardinal points of the compass. The sign is also identified with the sun, since a corona has been drawn surrounding the disc in the centre of the sign. This derives a special interest from the fact that we found this identical symbol in the final drawing of the former patient. In both patients' material we find allusions to the darkening or eclipse of the sun; and in both we find the idea of a new sun (symbolizing the reorientation of consciousness) with four rays quartering the world and surrounded by a flaming corona.

The corona, as we know, is a phenomenon visible only during the period of total eclipse. Hence the fact that both patients (between whom no personal contact was possible) have associated this rare phenomenon with the symbol of reorientation suggests that the state of eclipse is in some way identified with the new birth. The cosmic analogy with the sun suggests that a new world is being formed. There is

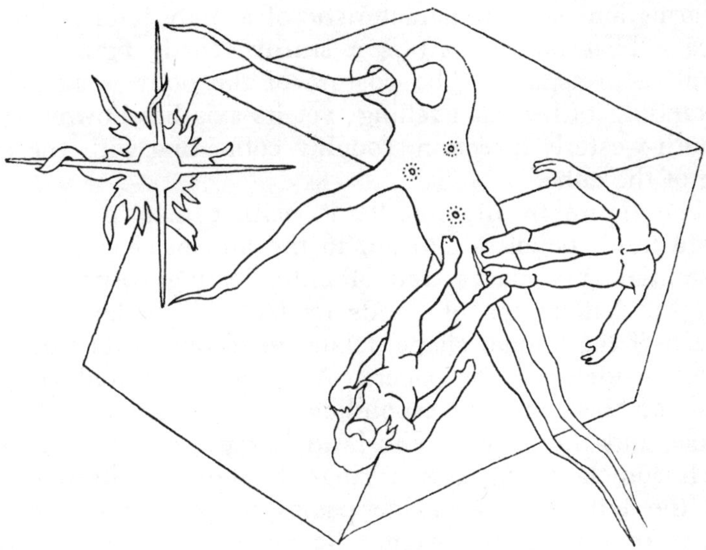

Drawing 6.

also the deeper realization that this new orientation of consciousness would be inconceivable without a preceding eclipse. Just as the corona asserts the fact that the sun is not actually engulfed but only darkened, so there are certain marginal events or intuitions which inform the individual, temporarily engulfed by the unconscious, that the light of consciousness will emerge again. Only those, perhaps, who have suffered this irrational eclipse will be able to appreciate why both of these patients insist upon the importance of the corona.

To the right of this sign a large cube is drawn which occupies the main bulk of the field. It is tilted at an angle and rests upon nothing. Three figures are drawn that seem to have an indefinite relation to the cube. They are not lying or standing upon it, nor are they even touching it; yet they seem to be disposed in such a way that their positions in space are related to the position of the cube.

The figure on the right is that of a man apparently falling away from the centre of the picture. His feet are uppermost, and only his back view is visible. The loose position of the arms and legs is characteristic of a body falling through space. That on the left is a sturdy female figure, rather primitive in aspect. The posture of the body is suggestive of standing rather than falling; yet its axis lies downward in a south-westerly direction, roughly coinciding with the near edge of the cube.

The figure in the middle is neither man nor woman. It is a fluid, boneless allusion to the human shape. Its insubstantial appendages trail off into floating wisps, without even the beginnings of hands or feet. It is like a vague pattern of the human shape, taking form out of floating mist or cut crudely out of paper. A trinity of dotted rings is drawn on the body, corresponding to the position of the two nipples and the navel. The head is represented by a loop, which somehow suggests a ring of smoke. Through this ring the left arm-appendage passes to reach the northern pointer of the compass-sign. Below, the right reaches out to touch the southern pointer.

The dynamic centre of this group of figures is the navel-ring of the floating form, and this coincides with the junction point of the three visible sides of the cube. Above this point, on the central figure, are the breast circles. Below it, at the sexual level, the primitive male and female figures fall, one to either side. This fact has a symbolical bearing, since it identifies this nebulous human archetype with the mythological androgyne out of which the first man and woman were created.

The differentiation of sexual psychology out of an undifferentiated pre-stage is the basal condition of individual consciousness. In the myth of Genesis the knowledge of sex coincides with the fall of man from his original state of innocence. The psychological condition corresponding with this mythological primordium is that state of primitive mentality for which Lévy-Bruhl coined the term *participation mystique*—namely, the condition in which an *a priori* feeling of union or participation with the persons and objects of the environment precludes the sense of individual distinctiveness. The state of being contained in a family, group or tribe in an accepted environment is the original unconscious condition, the archetype of which is the state of being contained in the maternal womb. In individual psychology it corresponds to the state existing before the advent of individual consciousness detaches the subject from his surrounding matrix.

The difference of sex is, as a rule, the first observation in the experience of a child which excites the problem of distinctiveness; and it is in this problem that individual consciousness is rooted. The gaining of sexual knowledge is " that old serpent," which brings a sense of sundering guilt into the child's original state of participation with the parents. If the feeling of difference is not too burdened with anxiety and fear of parental displeasure it engenders a thriving curiosity and desire for knowledge. But anxiety tends to cause repression, which is directly hostile to the enquiring mind. The dull stupidity of mind resulting from the steamroller of " respectable " repression is a real defacing of personality, in comparison with which the bound feet of the Chinese women, or the distortion of the skull among certain savage tribes, are trifling inconveniences.

III

Resuming our discussion, the central figure represents the human nebula, the undifferentiated, timeless state from which consciousness emerges, creating, like the sun, a new and ordered world. The falling naked figures of primordial man and woman seem to contain the suggestion of the fall of man from the primal state of innocence. It is not, I think, accidental that the posture of the woman has more the character of standing than of falling, inasmuch as the patient had the idea (frequently held by men) that woman has the more natural instinctive stance in relation to the function of sex.

The three centres indicated by the dotted rings on the front of the central figure have an interesting bearing on what has just been said. The navel represents the original centre of being, since the first cell-formation of the developing embryo takes place at this spot. Because of this fact, and because all the nutritive supply for the first nine months of existence passes through this ring, the navel symbolizes the idea of the original or primary source of being.

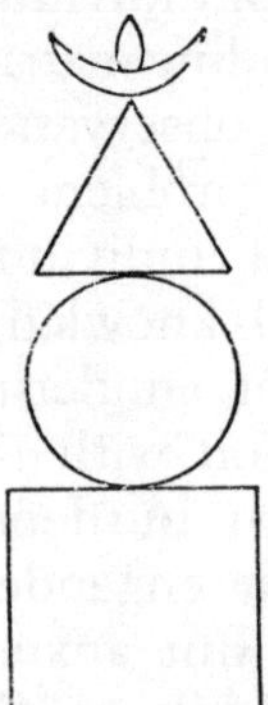

FIG 6.—STUPA.

The two upper centres, corresponding to the breasts, represent the second source of nutritive life. The original centre, then, would represent the idea of being, the breast centres the idea of nutrition, and the event we see taking place in the region of sex would represent the idea of sexual differentiation leading to reproduction.

If these inferences are correct this strange trinity of figures must symbolize the basic instinctual constitution: a conclusion which gives us an invaluable clue to the riddle of the tilted cube behind the figures. The patient himself had no idea why he wanted to draw this cube, and offered no suggestion as to its meaning. But, since the whole drawing is clearly referring to a radical process of reorientation, we may assume that the cube also symbolizes an elemental factor.

According to the Indian, Chinese, and later Greek views, there are five primary elements—earth, water, fire, air and ether. In Indian philosophy the etheric is the psychic element. Identical symbolism is used for the five elements from European alchemy to Chinese philosophy. Earth is represented by a square, water by a circle, fire by a triangle, air by a crescent, and the psychic element by a gem. These symbols are usually drawn one above the other (Fig. 6); but in the elemental *stupa*, found throughout the interior of

Asia wherever Chinese Buddhism has extended, the earth-square becomes a cube, the circle a globe, the triangle a pyramid, while the moon-crescent containing the *lingam*-shaped gem is the jewel in the lotus-cup.[1] The *stupa* stands in the court of every monastery, saying to every man: " From these elements thou hast been fashioned, and to them thou wilt return."

The Pythagorean school used the cube as a symbol for earth. Pythagoras did not employ geometrical figures for the purposes of scientific condensation, or for explanatory convenience: his geometrical figures symbolized the essential properties or qualities of the universe. In effect, he traced the origin of all things to the principle of number, having observed certain numerical relations and analogies in the phenomena of the universe. Because number expresses the inherent structure of the universe, it is also the principle of order and rule. " Number is that which brings what is obscure within the range of our knowledge, rules all true order of the universe, and allows of no error." Thus Pythagorean geometry was charged with psychological content, numbers and geometrical figures being employed by the Pythagoreans as a means of ordering the chaos within. The means of restraining the passions, especially anger, and the cultivation of inner powers of endurance and harmony, were regarded as the essential aim of knowledge, not the erection of a scientific theory.

The patient was innocent of these esoteric connections when he used the figure of the cube: he wanted it merely as a three-dimensional solid basis for his composition. But when we discover that the cube has appeared as the basal figure in mediæval alchemy, in the Pythagorean school in early Greece, in Indian and Chinese Buddhism, and that in every case it is the primary symbol in an elemental sequence, we are forced to reconsider the idea that the diagrammatic character of his production was purely explanatory.

In the last drawing irrationality was uppermost; chaos was loose. In this drawing the effort towards reorientation is paramount. A certain symptom is present in both draw-

[1] *Om mani padme hum* means Oh! the jewel in the lotus!

ings which throws light upon the subjective necessity which evoked the archetype of the cube. I refer to the fact that in neither case do the human figures touch anything solid. There is no relation of contact between the overextended, exaggerated figure in 5 and the tilted earth below and behind it; there is the same absence of contact between the three figures in 6 and the tilted cube behind them. It is with such indications that the unconscious points to the fact that the subject is out of touch with reality.

The solid earth is the measure and span of our three-dimensional reality; this is why the cube and not the square is the symbol of the earth. Those who maintain that the earth is flat (and there are people who still hold this view) are engaged in repressing a whole dimension of experience. Every psychiatrist encounters this persuasion among his schizophrenic patients; it is usually accompanied by an obstinate determination to preserve the primordial infantile condition. The world which such people inhabit is the fantasy-world of childhood. The mental system which should carry the reality-load is accordingly repressed and dissociated.

The central figure of 6 is completely flat, as though cut out of paper, and the reader will observe that the umbilicus or middle point of the figure corresponds to the angle in which the three lines which constitute the threefold extension of the cube meet. This point is also the dynamic centre of the drawing.

In contrast to the uniform flatness of the central figure, the man and woman are drawn in three-dimensional space; the solidity of these figures is therefore in harmony with the solidity of the cube. Advancing a step further, we may conclude that the importance of the cube, as the basal symbol of reality, is related to the emergence of consciousness from the two-dimensional, biological state into the three-dimensional realm of individual consciousness. The navel is, as we said, the place where *being* originated; what we might call three-dimensional consciousness is the essential condition of effective being. It is therefore symbolically necessary that the navel and the focal point of the cube should coincide.

The favourable aspect of the present design is manifested by the figures representative of control. The cube, asserting the idea of controlled shape and symmetry, is placed in the centre of the field, and the atavistic figures are held, as it were, in position by this massive representative of common sense. The master-sign of control, however, is the cross of orientation combined with the sun's corona. It is as though the seal of the King had been sent to quell the disturbance revealed in the last picture.

The concept of the self as an impersonal, royal authority may seem a mystical dream to some; but to a borderline schizophrenic, in whom at certain times the atavistic tide runs strongly, the sense of an impersonal centre of control and authority becomes a paramount need.

An interesting parallel from the work of another artist is shown in "Le temps et les plantes,"[1] a painting by the German artist Paul Klee (Fig. 7, opposite page). The essential points of similarity consist in the presence of a symmetrical field of control in the middle of the picture, of a constellation of archaic figures in immediate relation to this field, and of a cross and disc above and in control of the field. In the Klee drawing the cross and disc are separate, the cross being contained in a square in the left-hand corner, whereas the sun's face, or chronometer-disc, is situated immediately above the field of control, while a phallic stem descends from the disc on to the field. The fact that these two symbols are fused into one in our patient's drawing, and that the field of control is a cube, reveal a superior integrative capacity. The chief difference between the drawings lies in the character of the atavistic figures. In our patient's drawing the atavism is self-evident, whereas the figures of the Klee drawing are composed of elementary abstract units, spirals, cones, rings, etc., put together to resemble natural objects.

It would be hard to demonstrate that the tendency to make use of abstract figures was *ipso facto* atavistic; it depends entirely upon the way in which they are used. In general, it is the quantitative, casual, indiscriminate employment of primary figures or symbols which reveals the schizophrenic atavism.

[1] Will Grohmann: *Paul Klee*. Éditions "Cahiers d'Art," Paris.

We are now left with the question: Why does the left arm of the central figure double back on itself in order to pass through the head on its way to the northern pointer? Inasmuch as the arm could achieve its objective by any other route, we must assume that the passage through the head is demanded by the idea of the drawing. We have already discussed in Part I. the meaning of penetration in the symbolical language of the unconscious. We observed a rather similar act of penetration in the piercing of the fæcal rings by the phallic extensions of the primordial ancestor in Drawing VII. Both patients have been influenced by the same basic idea; only here the penetration takes place through the head, suggesting that the work of impregnation or transformation needs to be related to consciousness. As the organ which conceives, the head has to be penetrated before a new conception of being can become effective. The two-dimensional fantasy-conception must be pierced by a new element, and this new element is symbolized by the left arm. The left arm signifies the extension towards the unconscious.

This ghostly gesture must mean, therefore, that the infantile or primordial conception of man has to be penetrated by a new idea, and that this new idea is equivalent to a whole dimension of reality which was before unconscious. But to bring over to the side of consciousness a hitherto unconscious aspect of reality means a disturbance of the balance of nature —*i.e.*, the Promethean sin. This gesture is evidently sensed by the subject as a kind of violation or distortion of the original archetype of man, which, as we see in the present drawing, is the ground-plan of the symbol of the cross. One can almost sense the artist's resistance as he feels himself compelled to bend the ancient pattern in the service of an unknown objective. Effort is apparent in the clumsy curves of the arm, as though he were forcing his pen to an uncongenial task.

From these rather subtle indications we may infer that the truth which has led the subject so far towards a new orientation has now to overcome a fundamental, æsthetic feeling that clings fast to traditional form and canonical structure. The north and south points of psychological reorientation correspond functionally to intuition and sensation respectively. These are the two primary functions of cognition, providing the immediate perceptual groundwork of experience; whereas thinking and feeling are essentially judging or valuing functions, depending upon the data supplied by the functions of perception. We may conclude, therefore, from the fact that the north and south pointers are selected, that the primary elements of the new orientation should be experiential rather than rational, the intellectual understanding of the experience being a matter of secondary elaboration.

IV

There are other features to be noted in the general design. Firstly, the relatively slight tilting of the cube downwards and to the right, which is accompanied by the south-easterly axis of the group of figures. Comparing this with the acute tilting of the horizon in the previous drawing, it is evident that balance has already been restored. One can even imagine that the sense of effort in the arm that reaches towards the northern pointer derives from a subjective need to restore the balance; as though the central figure were trying to correct the tilt by pulling hard upon the compass-sign—viz., the universal symbol for spatial reality. Secondly, there is the repeated emphasis on the number three. There are the three main figures, the three primordial instinctual centres, the three surfaces, and the meeting of the three lines of the three-dimensional cube. It will further be observed that all these groupings of three are centred in the same dynamic point which we identified with the idea of being. Three separate statements of the threefold principle, all united in a central idea of being, must surely represent a triunity of power; this finds immediate and concrete expression in the birth of the three-dimensional figures of man and woman, out of the two-dimensional instinctual archetype.

In general, the triune archetype symbolizes the dynamic or vital element, particularly in relation to the creative and generative processes.[1] The idea of a fourfold extension,

[1] *Cf.* Jung's discussion of the origin of the triune god in *Psychology of the Unconscious*, pp. 227-8.

symbolized by the compass-cross, represents the basic structure of individuality, resting upon the same principles of symmetry and equilibrium as of a well-built house. Hence this conjunction of the three figures with the fourfold symbol, centred in the idea of being, expresses the idea of psychical totality in the most comprehensive terms.

The inherent psychological continuity between this drawing and the preceding one has now been established. There is, however, a further clue of considerable significance. The patient himself remarked upon a parallelism, amounting to emotional identity, between the symbol of the sun-cross, or compass-sign, and the regenerative heart-cell in Drawing 2. Its position in the field of the drawing is approximately the same, and the combination of the living heart with a brain-cell is analogous to that of the sun's corona with a compass-sign. For in the former case the dynamic passional element is conjoined with the unit of physical structure in the bodily sphere, while in the latter the symbol of universal energy is conjoined with the symbol of spatial orientation in the cosmic sphere.

This transition from the personal to the suprapersonal accords with the whole tenor of the drawing; it is as though the essential problem had been abstracted from personal subjective factors and were being restated in geometrical figures. The two previous drawings, in which the effects of the schizophrenic cleavage were represented, first from the standpoint of the superior function, then from that of the dissociated remainder, were a statement of the psychological *impasse* in which the subject found himself. When an *impasse* is reached the libido always tends to regress downwards to a deeper psychic level, where the conflict no longer exists. At the level of the collective unconscious the problems of personality sink to insignificant proportions. Individuals who have been carried down by a whirlpool into the collective unconscious, and have emerged with their reason, often manifest a detachment from personal considerations which can be disconcerting to those who have to live with them. The contents of the collective unconscious can be regarded as generalized deposits, silting into the personal sphere from the main stream of human experience. Hence the uncanny impersonality of the insane, who are wholly in the grip of the collective unconscious. They are concerned with abstract, non-personal contents, or personal contents that have become symbols; everything else is irrelevant.

All the elements of this picture are contents of the collective unconscious. What remains of the personal subject are certain *nuances* of expression, such as the bending of the left arm to pass through the loop of the head, and the fact that the male figure turns his back to the observer, the female her front.

With respect to this latter feature, the patient had no suggestion to offer. But, inasmuch as he naturally tends to identify himself with the man, it would seem that once again the masculine personality has to recede from the scene, while the feminine aspect of his nature—*i.e.*, the anima—comes to the front. We shall presently see whether this hypothesis can be verified.

DRAWING 7.

Drawing 8.

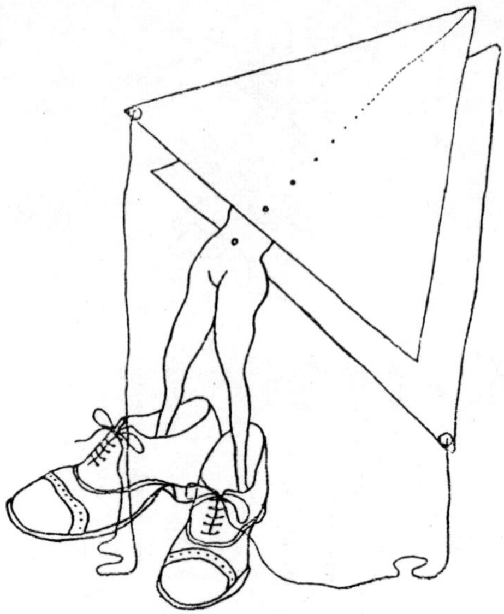

Drawing 9.

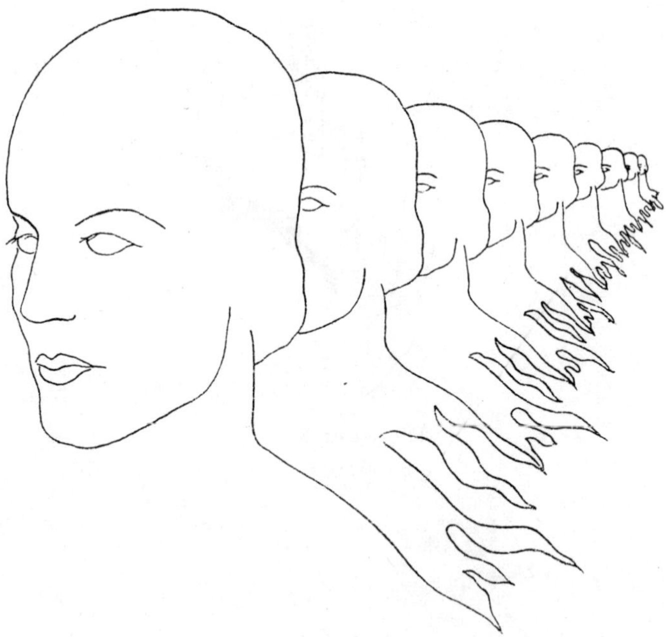

Drawing 10.

CHAPTER IV

RECOGNITION OF THE SPLIT

I

DRAWING 7

WHEN the patient showed me this drawing I was aware of a rather disagreeable impression, as though something important had been said in a trivial manner. I had already begun to suspect the existence of something behind the scenes; but the present series of drawings was produced while the patient was away, when there was no opportunity of keeping step in the ordinary way with the sequence of events. The superficial character of the drawing, compared with the preceding one, is like a false note—a certain hint of insincerity, which, in point of fact, the patient also sensed, since he immediately wanted to revoke it as unworthy.

Apart from the obvious inference, that this blank envelope contains something disagreeable which the patient would prefer not to touch upon, it is understandable on other grounds that the artist in him would reject it. There is a flavour of disingenuousness in the real halfpenny stamp, the careful imitation of the postal marks, and the very realistic scissors. It is as though he were saying, " A trifling, personal matter, not worth anyone's attention or interest; but, if you care to look into it, here are some scissors."

If the intention had been clear the envelope could have been addressed properly, to the person for whom it was intended, and the correct stamp for a sealed letter have been added. Or better still, a disagreeable confession that is as conscious as this drawing seems to imply could have been communicated in person. To do the patient justice, it should be stated that he really believed he had told me of the traumatic episode when he gave his personal history.

The points to be noted in the drawing are: First, the lack of addressee, an omission that would seem to indicate an almost deliberate vagueness (*a*) as to whom the confession should be made, and (*b*) as to whether it would really serve his interest to make it. The patient was naturally reticent, and was not easily convinced that being conscious of a fact oneself, and imparting the same fact to the analyst, are, psychologically, poles asunder. Second, there are the viscous, evil-looking drops which do not flow readily into a stream. When a patient withholds his material, being unable to vouchsafe even the most harmless associations, we are wont to describe him as "sticky." The material is not necessarily painful, but nothing flows. It is checked and scrutinized at the frontier by overzealous customs officers. The suspicion as to what the analyst might infer from this or that particular seems always to be holding things up. Reserve is habitual in borderline schizophrenic patients: they are not secure in themselves, and therefore they cannot easily place themselves in the power of another individual, however much they may be inclined to trust the doctor personally. Reserve is also characteristic of the introverted type, especially in cases where feeling has suffered repression and ambition has been reinforced by a one-sided intellectual attitude.

This drawing brings into the field of discussion perhaps the most characteristic feature of schizophrenic pathology. It can be described as the *viscosity of the libido*. It has also been referred to as *threshold delay*. This energy-lag is liable to spread, like ice over a pond, producing catatonic stasis. When, in the future, we employ clinical conceptions attuned to the dynamic character of psychic events, we shall describe catatonia in terms of the viscosity or stasis of the libido. In treating these cases one gets the impression that the abnormal inertia at the threshold of action is like that of a drop of water, held by surface tension from flowing down the window-pane until something gives it a jolt. The schizoid subject has apparently no means of overcoming the primitive inertia of the psyche. He needs a stimulus, administered at the right moment, to set the libido in motion. In some cases the inhibition is like a rusted tap, in others it is more like a viscous fluid; but in either case a timely jolt on the part of the analyst will help to overcome the initial difficulty.

A patient who suffered from viscosity in a painful degree had the following symptomatic dreams on the same night. He saw the engine of a train belching fire from its funnel as it ran slowly through the night. Then he saw a powerful shire horse standing amid flames of fire: flames were streaming from the horse's fetlocks, instead of the usual tufts of hair.

The symbol of the fiery horse expresses the overcharged state of the unconscious; but it also implies a remedy—namely, the possibility of harnessing the excessive heat or energy to creative work. The idea of draining the unconscious is not enough in this case: the channel for the libido must be a real and effective expression of the overcharged complex. Libido is specific: it is personified most frequently by animals whose specific nature and habits no farmer would dream of ignoring. We find from experience that the best way of transforming viscous libido into a flowing expression is to treat it very much as a sick animal needing human assistance.

To return to our material, the blank sealed envelope symbolized this concealed hold-up of the libido. The half-penny stamp referred to the patient's attempt to maintain a closely guarded secret by representing it to himself as a thing of no particular importance. To make quite sure that a certain document should remain undiscovered, we could invent no better hiding-place than an unsealed envelope stamped with a halfpenny stamp.

But if the envelope and the halfpenny stamp are characteristic of the subject's introverted reticence, who provides the scissors? The contradictoriness of the patient's attitude in regard to intimate personal disclosures was at this time inexplicable: it had no apparent connection with such emotional disturbances as usually betray the confessional conflict. Even when the truth finally emerged there was no sign of inner commotion or conflict. The facts were told in a detached manner, as though of no especial importance.

The explanation of this contradiction lies, I believe, in the fact that a shut-in introverted subject makes few windows in his house, and it does not naturally occur to him that he has a need to relate his inner life to the outside world. It is his extraverted anima who has to gain contact with the world of outer objects. She may bring this about by irrational disclosures, or by sickness, or by interference in the realm of conscious behaviour bearing the character of an alien will. We have already observed this duality of purpose in Drawing 2, where the introspective self-analysis of the inverted intellect was countered by an objective healing activity on the part of the anima, under the sign of the regenerating heart-cell.

When considering the respective positions of the male and female figures in the last drawing we discovered a hint, in the falling away of the male figure and the coming to the front of the female, that this might betoken a new phase of positive anima-influence. The comparison with Drawing 2 also answers our question with regard to the scissors. For they might easily belong to the same feminine work-basket from which the bodkin, thread and thimble of Drawing 2 were borrowed. On grounds of sexual characterization, as well as on those of general usage, scissors are associated in the popular mind with the functional field of woman. The diffidence of the patient in handing me this drawing was based, therefore, upon deeper grounds than those present in consciousness.

It is the anima who insists upon the necessity of cutting through, or breaking down, his attitude of habitual reserve. In other words, the resistance of consciousness is the one factor standing in the way of the regenerative process. Consciously, the subject feels impotent to do more than submit himself for analysis; yet, in the act of allowing himself to draw whatever may appear at the gate of expression, the subject offers the excluded anima a means of representing the state of affairs in the unconscious in a way that could not be bettered.

As a general rule, when a feeling of insincerity accompanies an act it is due to the presence of unworthy motives, or, at least, a motive has got in which has not passed the moral censor. It may be that the unsanctioned motive comes from the primitive levels, and is being furtively advanced by the anima. In the present drawing the conflict of motives is there for all to see—namely, the reserve which hides the stuff in an unaddressed halfpenny envelope, and the candour which uses the scissors. Regarding this ironical by-play as a statement of conflicting motivations, we must record the fact that, notwithstanding the patient's habitual concealment, the anima-purpose of getting down to the truth actually wins the day. The scissors are effective.

II

A certain parallelism of theme can be made out between this drawing and Drawing II. of the former series—the one in which the lunatics were seen escaping from the asylum. The striking difference in the representation of the theme is explicable on temperamental grounds. The attitude of the former patient was constellated by his unconscious shadow; at one time he was practically submerged by the unconscious, with very little conscious control or self-criticism. Accordingly, with him the development of the mythological experience took its uninhibited course, whereas the present subject, with his closely-knit introverted control, would have regarded the symptoms of psychic unbalance which brought the former patient for treatment in the light of a major disaster. The first patient had to take the standpoint of the lunatic in himself, as he had done with his insane patients. He could do this without much conscious opposition, because there had always been a strongly irrational element in his basic attitude, so that he was much more pliant to anima moods and impulses. The latter patient, on the other hand, having schooled himself to create order in a disorderly world, had never ceased to defend his conscious integrity against the irrational menace within himself. This difference was conspicuous in the respective attitudes of the two men towards authority. The former patient felt justified in resisting all authority whenever it suited him to do so. The latter patient was incapable of resisting any authority, however arbitrary and unjust.

The danger in the first case was that he might always be enticed to foolish actions by an extreme suggestibility to anima-insinuations. The danger in the second case was that his self-distrust and lack of emotional initiative would make him altogether too dependent upon momentum supplied by the environment. The former needed conscious discipline wherewith to oppose direction and purpose to the inchoate instinctual drive. The latter needed to understand his own nature in order to be able to go with, instead of always fighting against, the primitive part of his being.

These contrasting psychological constellations are of interest theoretically, inasmuch as the introverted psychology is regarded as being more prone to the schizoid condition than the extraverted. Yet, from the above characterological comparison, it would appear that the extraverted temperament of the one made him as vulnerable to the " traumatic " dissociation as the introverted *habitus* of the other. In view of the introverted direction given to the former patient's psychology by the loss of the mother and the sister, it might, however, be justifiable to regard him either as a subjective extravert (Hinkle) or as an extravert falsified, to some extent, from his original type by a forced introversion of the libido. If the latter view is correct the schizoid dissociation would, presumably, tend to occur between the introverted island, constellated by the mother and sister, and the subject's indigenous extraverted psychology. It is a theoretical point of view which unfortunately cannot now be verified; but the prolific material of Part I. would be entirely in keeping with this diagnosis.

In so far as the structure of the personality can be disrupted by the inroads of archaic unconscious contents, schizophrenia is a possible eventuality for either type, though the effects of the dissociation are liable to cause more far-reaching disturbance in the introverted psychology, because of the latter's greater reliance upon unification. The integration of the self upon a reliable foundation being a prime necessity for the introverted individual, the major problem of the introverted psychology is the urge for power and superiority. The dreams of the second patient were concerned to a very large extent with this problem, even though it was his difficulty in the sphere of relationship which ostensibly brought him to be analysed.

The extraverted type, on the other hand, has to deal with a temperamental tendency to ignore the claims of the inner world, because of the outward, objective flow of his interest. The claims of his subject, which the extravert consistently ignores, tend, in consequence, to be projected outwards in the form of excessive, and often irrational, demands upon the object. Thus the problem of the extraverted type is regularly constellated in the sphere of sexuality, a condition that was abundantly manifest in the material of the first patient. As a rule, it is the inevitable disillusionment resulting from his excessive claims upon the object which forces the extravert back upon himself, where he encounters the claims of the neglected subject.

Desirousness and the urge-to-power represent, therefore, the characteristic framework in which the basic, instinctual problem manifests itself in the respective types. At bottom, it is the primordial force of the life-urge, encountered in one or other of these phenomenal fields; the development of an habitual or typical attitude in relation to the life-force merely constituting its specific form.

III

Drawing 8

The drawing contains three figures. The one on the left, with the elongated head and pendent right arm, is a somewhat distorted subjective impression of the patient's wife. On the breast, in the position of the heart, there is a five-pointed star enclosed in a ring. This, and the challenging look in the woman's eyes, give particular significance to the content of this drawing.

Intervening between the figure of the wife and the subject making the drawing are two indescribably evil ghosts. The upper one is a billowing female deformity, topped by a bald, beaked head, without recognizable human features. The right leg of this figure, malformed and retracted, hangs in front of the breast of the first figure, as though attempting to enclose the star-symbol. The figure appears to hang passively suspended in space.

The lower is a thin striding form; sinister power is evident in every line. The face is represented by three slits; there is no sign of nose or ears. It is the kind of face invented by illustrators of crime stories; particularly is it reminiscent of the illustration of the Golem in Meyrink's novel of the same name. The Golem was a malevolent ghost, said to have haunted the ghetto of Prague. The mongoloid mask and the sinister swing of the body evoke the idea of cold-blooded cruelty. The long robe, gathered closely around the purposeful bones and swirling between the striding shanks, resembles that of a friar. Immediately below this devil-figure there is a long blot of ink, just the length of his stride. Attenuated at either end and thicker in the middle, one can hardly resist the impression that it is the devil's shadow. If not, it must be the black substance that leaked out of the envelope in the last drawing.

* * * * *

The reluctance of the patient to release such sinister figures from the unconscious is intelligible. They are more actively evil than the two lunatics of the previous series. They also have the terrifying quality of ghosts. The patient could offer no germane associations in regard to these figures, though he volunteered the fact that the still figure on the left was his wife and that the blot was " bad stuff." The expression in the woman's face is direct and challenging, while the posture of the head and arm is rigid and uncompromising. The blot lies directly in the axis of the body; it might conceivably correspond with the genital region. The two ghost-figures are in motion, their movement contrasting with the tense stillness of the woman. The movement of both figures is that of extending a foot towards the left. If we complete the outline of the woman's figure in our mind's eye, taking the star to represent the position of the heart, it will appear that each ghost is trying to extend a foot into the abdominal area lying between the heart and the genitals.

The abdomen is ruled by the sympathetic nerve plexuses, and has always been regarded as the seat of the emotions. It is reasonable to conclude, therefore, that the ghost-effect will be found in the realm of the emotions. The picture is a subjective representation of certain ghostly influences intervening between the patient and his wife.

There is a purposiveness in the flexed position of the obscene female leg, suggesting an attempt to surround and cut off the star-symbol over the heart. Similarly the reaching stride of the bony devil in the friar's robe suggests the idea of taking the measure of the blot. The blot is the evil substance which, presumably, evoked the ghosts; yet the patient has drawn it, both in position and shape, to appear as the devil's shadow. Since nothing is accidental, the blot must be both cause and effect. It is the result of a devilish influence in the patient's life, while its presence causes a real though intangible obstacle in his relation to his wife.

There can be no doubt in this case that the emotional trauma of childhood had the effect of closing down every other direct avenue of emotional expression, the fact of the seduction and the pact of secrecy arising from it being communicated to no one. With this complete suppression of the trauma went a corresponding repression of feeling. Thus the whole development of personal feeling was sacrificed to a secret pact which, being rooted in an antisocial connection, precluded the growth of normal relationships. What is not embraced by the warm-blooded human pact, or contained in the human communion, becomes inevitably the haunt of ghosts. This is not to say that the patient's feeling for the man in question was not affectionate and human. The trauma was due to the fact that the instinctive current of his feeling-life had been deflected underground, in a direction that must inevitably collide with the strongest social taboo. It was this fact which gave an abnormal impetus to the archaic, antisocial tendencies in the unconscious—a danger that was counterbalanced by a very high degree of conscious control. The persona had become a mask performing its office so well that the most acute observer could have detected little beyond an almost abnormal normality. No emotional currents were allowed to ruffle the perfectly adapted surface; yet the subject's participation in the social scene was not wholly convincing, having more the character of a highly accomplished performance than of spontaneous expression. Behind the mask was a vigilant guard enjoying a detached and sometimes ironical reservation.

An attitude of ironical reserve is not at all uncommon with men of a more or less admitted homosexual disposition. The tragedy of the homosexual is rooted in the inescapable fact that the course of his instinctual life must run to a large extent underground: it can never hope to enjoy the blessing of society. The homosexual relationship tends to compensate in exclusive loyalty and intensity for this lack of social sanction. The man who feels compelled to accept homosexuality as the way his life has to go must therefore accept neurosis as the price he has to pay. However conscious he may become, and however idealistic his attempt to sublimate his abnormal way of life, in so far as instinct remains at the homosexual phase of development he cannot escape his psychological debt. He may, and usually does, make peace with society in the form of idealistic education, or by some rather striking achievement on the contemporary stage. But he cannot make peace with his own subject, because the genetic continuity of the libido-stream, running from the ancestors towards posterity, is necessarily thwarted by the homosexual organization of his emotional life. The ancestral demands of the unconscious cannot be satisfied. The tendency of homosexuals to attempt heroic and rather exhibitionistic achievement, on the one hand, or to maintain the rôle of the victim, on the other, are manifestations of subjective ancestral dissatisfaction.

In the present case the homosexual direction was given to the patient's libido in childhood, and, although it had not developed into a definite way of life, it gave none the less a certain stamp to his basic attitude. The emotional reserve in all his dealings with women, the tendency to defend his male citadel against every encroachment of the dubious female principle, and the corresponding readiness to assume a quixotic loyalty in his friendships with men—all bore witness to a basic instinctual partiality.

This aspect of the patient's psychology is alluded to in this drawing, inasmuch as the ghost-figures represent the pathological results of a long-standing deflection of the instinct from normal channels. The obscene and swollen shapelessness of the female figure, for example, in contrast to the wiry vigour of the male ghost, manifests the state of partial emotional stasis described above. A dream- or fantasy-figure appearing grotesquely fat or swollen usually denotes an overfed fantasy-activity that has usurped the place of a normal expression. In the present instance the figure is not only inert and obese, it is also floating, as though suspended in the air like a soap-bubble. Remembering the psychological law of compensation, which depends upon the fact that what is missing in the conscious personality is found in the unconscious, we can recognize in this female monster the regressive mother-fixation which has deprived the objective human relationship of its vitality. As in Drawing III. of the former patient, we see again how the retrogressing libido creates a pathological maternal image to personify its incestuous goal. We also note the inert, apathetic, spell-bound and spell-binding character of this inverted mother-craving libido.

The patient was inclined to explain the female ghost from his wife's psychology, accepting the male demon as his own problem. He had, as we know, suffered much from his wife's psychopathic constitution, attributing it in large measure to an excessive attachment of the mother to the daughter. Notwithstanding this association, I am inclined to regard the female monstrosity as an unconscious fantasy-system, on the ground that an objective determinant in the absence of grounds for repression is normally represented in the likeness of the relevant object, whereas a regressive fantasy-system, like the auto-erotic system in Drawing VII. of the former series, regularly manifests itself in obscene or monstrous imagery.

With regard to the figure in the friar's robe, it is, of course, a favourite trick of the devil to gain a footing under the guise of an honoured virtue. The thin, bony frame and the ascetic disguise reveal the way in which the traumatic deflection of the instinctive current has been camouflaged. The manner of the disguise is not hard to probe: the undercurrent of homosexuality must be regarded as a natural compensation to the overwhelming mother-complex, a teleological attempt to check the effeminate tendency in the patient's early development. The same undercurrent saps his marriage-relationship;

but, in order to disguise the emotional leakage, he tends to erect an heroic façade of work, wherein a certain flavour of ascetic merit is not entirely lacking. This apparently meritorious compensation for emotional deficiency has to be unmasked, and seen for what it is—namely, a trick of the devil. The direct, accusing eyes of the wife-anima in the drawing seem to challenge the subject to disclose the truth. Having projected upon his wife the positive side of the anima, this confrontation is as though his soul were commanding him to the most complete candour. The challenging gaze of the anima affords a certain verification for our hypothesis that it was she who supplied the revealing scissors in the last drawing.

Another important piece of evidence is to be found in the five-pointed star enclosed in the ring. The five-pointed star is a symbol of individual value; it has to do with the five elements which, as we saw in an earlier connection, constitute the *stupa*. Earth, fire, air and water symbolize the general cosmic elements, or qualities. The fifth is the etheric or psychic element, frequently represented in oriental symbology as the jewel or the diamond body. The five-rayed star often appears in the symbolism of the individuation-process as the jewel of the Self. The unification of the complex parts, qualities and tendencies of the psyche can be achieved only by a centre with star-like qualities, hence the psychological conception of a star as a god, the changing yet eternally changeless symbol of cosmic order.

In the drawing the position of the star corresponds with the heart, and it is set within a circle. It is therefore the symbol of individual value, the jewel beyond price which the subject places between himself and his wife. This is the key for the understanding of the deeper aspect of the case.

From the outset I felt sure of a positive solution, even though at times the outlook seemed ominous. A man who is willing to undergo analysis, resolved to rescue his marriage whatever it may cost him, is on the side of life; and this, when all is said and done, is the vital condition upon which the issue must always depend.

The ring surrounding the star is the "charmed circle"; from immemorial time it has been employed to protect the sacred place, the shrine or dwelling-place from harmful spirits. The circular earthwork such as surrounds the sun-temple at Stonehenge, the *circumambulatio* performed to secure the Roman stronghold,[1] the circle used in magical practice—all demonstrate the universal cogency of the limiting ring to the primordial mind. But the most complete expression of the symbol is seen in the *mandala* of Lamaistic Buddhism.

In its traditional religious form (as in Fig. 1, facing p. 206) the *mandala* is a symmetrical design enclosed in a circle, containing in its centre a symbol of supreme value, such as the diamond body, the thunderbolt, or the god and goddess in union. This central symbol is again enclosed in a circle. It is not merely an expression of religious feeling, for it also creates its own effect.[2] When the subject produces a *mandala* as an expression of inner reality it works a counter-influence upon the soul. It has a unifying effect, as though possessing the power of bringing attention and interest back into the centre of being.

The enclosed five-rayed star which guards the heart might be regarded as an archetypal germ. The patient had no knowledge of the *mandala* as a container of value. Had he known it, it is inconceivable that he could have expressed it so casually: he would have made it the dynamic centre of a fine design.

In this drawing evil spirits are abroad and the symbol of value is correspondingly inconspicuous. We might even have overlooked its presence, had not the devils pointed the way. Devils are attracted to value as wasps to honey or mosquitoes to blood. In psychological practice we know that devil symptoms from the unconscious are a sure pointer to the hidden value. But although the star is being encompassed by these malign figures, they cannot touch it because of its protecting ring.

The black shadow below is located psychologically in the sexual region. The forces which turned against life in the patient's psychology sprang from the repression following injury to his instinct. The star-value is as clearly the ruler of feeling, and, because of its direct association with the heart,

[1] The old custom of beating the bounds belongs to the same primitive idea.

[2] For knowledge of *mandala* psychology the reader is referred to *The Secret of the Golden Flower* (Wilhelm and Jung).

we are able to trace a symbolical continuity backwards, through the sun-cross of Drawing 6, to the cell enclosing the living heart in Drawing 2. Observing this associative sequence, we see that in every drawing in which the symbol of individual value appears it determines the issue. In the present drawing the star-symbol is not only the centre of the spatial field, it is also the dynamic centre, around which the figures are grouped and their action revolves.

The action of the devil's right arm suggests that it has just pulled the cowl down from the head, therewith disclosing the sinister reality disguised by the friar's garb. It would seem, therefore, that the star possesses an authority which forces the devil to reveal himself.

IV

Drawing 9

A diminutive, nude woman is seen standing in a pair of shoes which are intended to be the patient's. If these are the normal size for a man, the woman would be about eighteen or twenty inches high, were the whole figure visible. Only the lower part of the body is exposed. The upper part, from about the region of the diaphragm, is hidden between two large triangular plates. Apparently these are supposed to be the two plates of an electric battery, since a wire or, more correctly, a very long shoe-string passes from the left-hand corner of the upper plate to the left shoe, while a similar string passes from the right-hand corner of the bottom plate to the right shoe. Both shoes are correctly laced by their respective strings.

The ring of the navel is clearly drawn upon the nude figure, and is repeated, at regularly decreasing intervals, up to the apex of the triangle.

The shoes appear to be reversed, inasmuch as the left foot of the woman is standing in the right shoe and her right foot in the left.

* * * * *

At first glance the drawing might be taken for a cheap cynicism, identifying woman with a mechanical source of stimuli. Actually it is a candid self-criticism, prompted by the challenging eyes of the wife-anima of the previous drawing.

The reversal of the shoes, like the reversal of the hand in Drawings 2 and 4, indicates the reversed or subjective point of view, as opposed to the normal, objective orientation of consciousness. Thus the drawing is a representation of the subject's instinctual standpoint, not from the angle of objective behaviour, which in his case would be quite deceptive owing to his too perfect persona-adaptation, but from that of introspective criticism. In regard to his emotions, the patient says he feels like a woman, or rather, he feels himself to be a woman, which means that he is reactive, passive and receptive just when he should be active and enterprising. He finds himself constantly playing this acquiescent feminine rôle; he can even observe how other people take advantage of it. He regards this as the weaker, inferior side of his nature, so naturally he draws only the lower half of the body. Moreover, he is inclined to attribute this effeminate part of himself to the fact that his emotions are not of full adult stature, hence the figure's diminutive size.

It is quite exceptional for a man to have so critical an insight into his basic emotional attitude. Especially in the case of a young man, the positive character of his objective reactions leaves no surplus attention, as a rule, for observing the feminine nature of his moods. He does not, for instance, perceive the spurious feminine personality in his moods of sentimental self-pity, his hypersensitiveness, his hysterical resentment, his infantile heroics, and his tragic air of being uniquely misunderstood.

Anima-possession means an alteration of personality in which a man, vacating his own disciplined persona, suffers an invasion of protopathic feminine elements—in other words, the anima steps into his shoes. It is correct to speak of *the* anima, because anima-possession is also a general psychological constellation. Certain emotional moods are entirely characteristic of the anima-complex; they are relatively uniform in content among all types of men. We can assume, therefore, that the unconscious emotional presuppositions upon which, for example, the moods of self-pity or hero-inflation are nourished must be common property.

No man invented them, or even thinks them. They are aprioristic elements of the emotional inheritance, and just because they are pre-existent to personal consciousness, they are not easily recognizable as properties of the personality. Moreover, the cultural differentiation of the sexes, whereby certain so-called masculine characters become associated with the male ego, tends to render a man's inherent feminine qualities invisible and remote, causing them to recede into the unconscious as an autonomous feminine complex—*i.e.*, the anima.

The situation depicted in the drawing, then, is by no means unusual in a man's psychology. The abnormal feature is the fact that this patient has the uncanny detachment which makes it possible to portray his emotional foundations in just this way. The fact that the upper—*i.e.*, conscious—aspect of the figure is completely occluded does not necessarily denote schizophrenic dissociation. It does signify, however, that eros is in a position of inferiority in this psychology and, consequently, that the realm of feeling is removed from conscious responsibility—a state that a vast number of men must recognize in themselves without having to assume grave abnormality.

In order to understand the full importance of the drawing it must be regarded as the result of the critical gaze of the wife-anima in the last drawing. That essential part of the soul which was projected or transferred into the wife became a vehicle of individual value. Through placing essential value into the relation with the wife, a vital aspect of the archetypal anima-complex becomes adapted to individual woman; and because the subject is held in this relationship by the authority of feeling, he is forced by his own best values to discipline his emotions within the accepted field of that relationship. The inferior function with all its potential thus becomes held and moulded by the actual. But only the ideal aspect of the anima is projected upon the wife. The unregenerate, inferior aspect still maintains the primordial form of the autonomous complex. It is this withheld, antagonistic, renegade aspect of the anima which has to be forced into the light by the wife-anima figure.

The criticism, therefore, which is contained in this drawing is that the subject has fatalistically assumed that his emotional reactions are mere reflexes, the soul being a kind of electrical machine. But if one's emotional life consists of conditioned reflexes, it can offer no problem to consciousness. As futile, indeed, to assume responsibility for automatic emotional stimuli, as to entertain moral feelings about an electrical current.

It is important to note that the autonomous emotional stimulus apparently originates at the navel, not in the genital region. Embryonic development is laid down at the umbilicus; it is the avenue through which the life of the developing fœtus is continuous with the vital processes of the maternal organism. In a very real sense, therefore, it is the primal gateway of life. Behind it lies the great nerve-plexus, belonging to the vegetative, pristine system with which the affective basis of the psyche is intimately linked. It is intelligible, therefore, that the lower dynamic pole of the anima-complex should be centred in the navel.

V

Drawing 10

This is the other half of the picture. A series of heads, drawn with austere purity of line, recedes away into the distance. Actually, nine heads are drawn; but the effect is that of an indefinite series, like a repeating decimal. The face is still and expressionless. The impression of a sculptured head is enhanced by the omission of pupils from the eyes. The shoulder is represented by a sloping line, which tails off and is joined to the end of the succeeding shoulder-line by fluttering tongues, like loose ends flying in the wind. In this way each head is joined to its successor by an indeterminate link between two successive shoulder-lines. That this trailing substance belongs not to the heads, but to the intervals between them, is proved by the fact that the last head of the series has none.

There is a certain abnormality in the configuration of the back of the head which catches the observant eye. This swelling tends to become more conspicuous as the heads recede. The impression of abnormality is enhanced by the obvious care with which the contours have been drawn, and by the absence of ears.

* * * * *

The patient called this drawing a mental stammer. He has, in fact, an occasional hesitation in speech, which is all that remains of an early stammer. The idea of each head being joined to its successor by a fluttering interval is expressive of the stammerer's helplessness when, having started the crucial syllable, he sees it going on repeating itself indefinitely until something happens to break the spasm. The impression of a purposeless fluttering of loose ends suggests the subjective feeling of a number of disordered tongues usurping the function of one.

Comparing this with the preceding drawing, we find the idea of a mechanically incurred and repeated impulse as the motif of both drawings. The line of receding umbilical rings and this line of receding heads are like two parallel lines which, though infinitely extended, can never meet.

The umbilicus, as the original centre of being, represents the focal centre of the unconscious, as opposed to the head, the centre of consciousness. We must conclude, then, that the effect of the traumatic dissociation is to destroy the natural co-ordination between the instinctual and the conscious processes, and that a total lack of reciprocity condemns each to a monotonous repetition of its own specific content. In this drawing we have the idea without *dynamis*: in the other we had mere energy stimulus without the idea which could inform it with meaning. Where the dynamic is sundered from the ideal, no reciprocal action and therefore no new creation can come about.

When I asked the patient to explain the swelling at the back of the head, with a slight hesitation he said he thought the heads were feminine and that the swelling was the roll of hair at the back of the head. This statement is illuminating. Normally a man identifies himself with his head. This is true, however, only for the civilized Western man. The negro lives entirely with his affects; if he thinks of himself at all he would probably locate the self in the belly. The American Indian believes that a man who thinks too much will go mad: for him the true centre is the heart.

It is unique in my experience for a man to represent his own head as feminine: the identification of his lower instinctual nature with a feminine being is more intelligible. We know that the patient associates this woman's head with himself, for it was he who stammered. We have to conclude, therefore, that not only does he feel like a woman, but also, in some measure at least, thinks like one. Yet we must not forget that this drawing, like the one before, was made in direct response to the challenge of his immediate problem.

The clue to our further understanding of the drawing is to be found in the still, expressionless face. The eyes are sightless, and there is no organ of hearing. Yet it is drawn with considerable care; the face has even a certain statuesque beauty. It seems to represent an ideal not yet participating in life, a virginal purity that has been too jealously guarded from external contamination. The perseveration of this image into a stereotyped, repetitive sequence tells us that it is insulated from any content other than itself—in other words, it is an autonomous mental system.

The fact that the subject himself identified the activity of the autonomous complex with stammering throws a valuable light on the psychology of the complex. It indicates that the ideal content of the anima-complex, even though possessing beauty or value of a high order, is rendered valueless, nay, even pathological, by the mere mechanical perseveration of the autonomous system. The word that the stammerer is straining to utter may be the one saving word of truth; yet it is rendered ludicrous and unintelligible by the involuntary repetitive mechanism that will not let it go.

The distorting effect of the autonomous system is well illustrated by the progressive meaninglessness of the heads, and the exaggeration of the ugly contour as the series recedes into the distance. Whereas the original head is beautiful, the last is a mere deformity. In the case of an artist with a complete mastery over his medium, it would be unreasonable to ascribe this increasing distortion of the head to lack of skill. However we may try to explain it, the subject quite unwittingly has stumbled upon a psychological discovery of value. The original term of a series is, as the drawing states, profoundly different from those that follow it. The original idea is a unique, spontaneous creation, informed with the breath of individuality, whereas all subsequent terms of the series are more or less mechanical imitations of the divine initiator. Forms lacking the divine breath are mechanism; hence the endlessly repeated products of an autonomous complex are not thoughts or feelings, but the indifferent waste of a psychical machine.

In the previous drawing the same principle should be applied. The original emotional event or experience is symbolized by the shapely, nude figure whose libido value is centred in the umbilical ring. This figure could represent the primordial erotic feeling. Psychological criticism cannot be aimed at this original human content, but only at the autonomous mechanism which seizes hold of this feeling and repeats it *ad infinitum*, thereby robbing the original moment of experience of its unique value.

* * * * *

We are presented with two independent anima-systems, each with its own informing energy and repetitive mechanism—the one originating in the primordial, emotional centre below, the other in the ideal anima-image above. The psychic roots of the anima-complex reach down far beyond the limits of personality into the general archetypal inheritance. In the immobile, virginal mask of the figure in this drawing we may discern the archetypal basis of the anima-ideal. It is woman's face seen not from the level of personal experience and observation, but *sub specie æternitatis*. It is an εἴδωλον, the image of the eternal virgin, and, just because of its immaculate virginity, it tends to become enshrined in a fantasy-world into which the real and the temporal must never enter. Every image of the unconscious which is penetrated by the real becomes impregnated as though by a living germ, thereby changing its unconditioned virginal potential into a created but limited actuality. When we use the term " creative imagination," or " creative work," we are really designating the process by which hitherto dormant or unrelated contents of the unconscious become associated in a fertile combination with the organized labour of consciousness. Through this associative combination the inherent energy of the primordial image is released into the conscious systems, and a unique individual product or moment of experience results. If, on the contrary, the indwelling energy of the primordial image is not released into the stream of consciousness, it remains an independent potential which is always liable to find a negative or symptomatic expression as an autonomous mechanism.

This problem of the anima is usually constellated just at the moment when the marriage relationship needs to achieve a deeper reality. So long as it is provisional or merely social in character, nothing very real is at stake; but as soon as the relationship begins to be vital and deeply inclusive, so that the experiment can no longer be measured by the standard pattern, the anima-attack is launched. Moods are produced containing an affective charge of resentment, hostile though often silent criticism, even murderous hatred; and these are levelled at the marriage partner as though she were either a demon, a vampire, or an imbecile. The anima-complex behaves in this eventuality very much as a primitive woman might behave who is afraid of being superseded by another wife.

In the present instance the biological function of the marriage had been practically suspended, owing to the wife's fear of pregnancy; but now an extra strain was thrown upon the subject's inferior function, for the anticipated first child confronted his doubtful emotional capacity with an anxious query.

The complete divorce of the dynamic from the ideal aspect of the anima, as observed in these two drawings, necessarily involves a certain emotional sterility. It is as though the reciprocal action between heaven and earth were suspended; apart from its effects in the realm of feeling, such a condition leaves the partner with an intolerable sense of inadequacy. For on the one side a virginal withholding of deep spiritual content, and on the other a parallel deprivation of real sexual warmth, produce in the end a sense of human unworthiness: the sacred and the profane freeze together if their specific values can no longer mate.

In a man's psychology there is a tendency for these two complementary aspects of the soul to become separated, the one seeking an upward course towards a pure and abstract ideal, the other following a downward curve towards an unredeemed and stereotyped animal habit. In woman there is a contrary tendency towards an undifferentiated merging of the two, either in sentimentalized spiritual by-paths or in spiritualized eroticism. This divergent development of their spiritual and sexual capacities is a most fertile source of misunderstanding between man and woman.

During the course of his analysis a man may be compelled to experience the primitive origins of the anima-ideal, while at the same time undertaking a drastic self-criticism in respect to his undeveloped sexual attitude. Formative criticism, based upon an enlightened dynamic standpoint, aims at re-establishing the primordial reciprocity between spirit and sex. In the case of a woman the realization of unconscious sexual fantasies as something to be distinguished from her idealized spiritual feelings helps her to differentiate heaven and earth in her universe, thereby regaining dynamic polarity in place of undifferentiated emotionalism.

It would be interesting to know whether this emotional disparity between the sexes is specific to Western culture, or whether similar differences exist among civilizations in which the sex-instinct has never been singled out for repression.

Another important factor in the discussion of emotional security is the condition of being rooted in a living mythological matrix. Whether this be represented by religion, clan, nation, standpoint or soil, as a container it needs to correspond with the primitive man's emotional identity with his native land. The difference between the psychology of a man rooted in his ancestral earth, and that of a man who has lost connection with his background and family-tree, reaches further and goes deeper than any other determination, with the possible exception of sex and functional type. The difference is not easy to specify, but in general the expatriated or uprooted individual presents a picture of emotional unreliability. Like something driven by the wind, he can never stay long in one place. He tries this or that relationship, ideology, vocation or place, in an unconscious search for something that could hold him. He longs for clear direction, shape and substance, instead of provisional living and shapelessness.

Lack of conscious direction tends to bring about a corresponding activation of the anima - complex. In primitive conditions essential functions are not delegated: men and women are concerned with tasks which, from time immemorial, have been an organic part of their indigenous myth. But in a sophisticated *milieu*, where every primitive task is, as far as possible, delegated or deleted, the inherited libido systems which formerly gained direct expression in association with simple, natural things, are left in the unconscious, increasing the onus of unlived primitive psychology.

This is a complete reversal of man's original state. So long as his consciousness was contained by a living myth, he could go about his work feeling the presence of the "Eternal Arms." But in the uprooted condition the lonely individual soul is forced to contain the myth which once contained his ancestors. It is this condition (implied in the title of the present work) which makes the problem of the anima desperately real to the modern man.

Nietzsche and Wagner, two great psychological progenitors of the modern world, both suffered a vital separation from their containing myth. They both became creators of a new world in which the myth ceased to be the primordial container and became the truly dynamic content of the soul. Nietzsche might be regarded as the father of the modern psychological understanding of mythology when he writes:

> "Dem Mythos liegt nicht ein Gedanke zu grunde, wie die Kinder einer verkünstelten Kultur meinen; sondern er ist selber ein Denken; er teilt eine Vorstellung von der Welt mit, aber in der Abfolge von Vorgängen, Handlungen und Leiden."[1]

[1] "The myth is not built upon an idea, as children of a sophisticated civilization imagine: it is itself a (kind of) thinking and imparts a representation of the world, but one which issues from processes, deeds and suffering" (*Richard Wagner in Bayreuth : Unzeitgemässen Betrachtungen*). I am indebted to my friend and colleague, Professor Zimmer of Heidelberg, for this reference.

More, perhaps, than any of his contemporaries, Nietzsche suffered the desperate loneliness of the uncontained soul. In no relationship, either human or non-human, could he find the security and satisfaction of the contained being. We might even say that his whole contribution to the new race of man, for whom he laboured and to whom he spoke, could come about only through the fact that some force sundered Nietzsche from his containing myth and compelled him to turn his eyes towards a new world. But what power is this in the soul of man which can force him to break away from immemorial ties, to abhor the gods of his fathers, and to set out utterly uncompanioned towards a distant goal which no man has yet attained and which all his fellow-men distrust? This force not only makes the "uncontained" standpoint possible, it also creates the vision which prompted Nietzsche to say:

> "The aim should be to prepare a transvaluation of values for a particularly strong kind of man, most highly gifted in intellect and will, and, to this end, slowly and cautiously to liberate in him a whole host of slandered instincts, hitherto held in check: whoever meditates about this problem belongs to us, the free spirits—though not to that kind of 'free spirit' which has existed hitherto, for these desired practically the reverse."[1]

In the very next aphorism Nietzsche adds:

> "I am writing for a race of men which does not yet exist: for the lords of the earth."

Human evolution depends upon this Promethean power in the very centre of individuality, the power that can make an effective departure from the archetypal pattern. But only at the crucial turn of the epoch is the solitary one singled out to be the prophetic voice of the new era. Many individuals are caught by the current which draws energy away from the contemporary scene, therewith storing up potential for the future. But only relatively few appreciate what has happened to them, the majority being simply lamed by a neurosis.

[1] *Der Wille zur Macht.* Aphorism 957.

Analysis can help these individuals to recognize their destiny. The following is such a case: A man aged forty-eight suffering from impotence, with symptoms of acute anima-possession, had tried his hand at many things; but, although gifted and enthusiastic, he could not stay long enough in any one place or craft to realize himself. He remembered a vivid dream he had had when, as an eager youth, he was about to try his fortune in the larger world beyond his home town. In his dream he saw two or three vast airships drifting over the town where he lived. Between them a great drag-net was suspended which was drawn over the roofs and streets of the town as a fishing-net is drawn over the bed of the sea. He saw human beings caught like fishes in the meshes of the net, and he watched fascinated as the net picked men from the roofs of houses. Later he found a dark youth in a place like a stable (associated by the patient with the stable at Bethlehem), whom he accused with passion of being the planner and director of the invasion. This man was associated in his mind with a visitor from another planet: he had been reading Wells' *War of the Worlds*.

Here was a man who had been torn away by an unknown force from his native soil. He had experimented eagerly, even recklessly, with the opportunities life had offered him; he had sought the key to his life in love, religion, art and science. At last, after the failure of his second marriage, he had come to the end of his rope and wanted to take his own life. This dream had been stored in his memory for more than thirty years, but never had he asked himself what the dream was saying. If he had been wise enough to see that the drag-net which had caught him up and had borne him spiritually into a far country was really the future, he might have steered a different course. What is consciously realized and responsibly accepted becomes part of the self; it is then honoured with true service. But when a man who is caught by the future does not realize what has happened to him the added intensity of life remains at the anima-level. Instead of having a sword in his hand, he has a dæmon at his back coercing the unwilling victim who was meant to be a pioneer. In the end my patient was driven to the last desperate alternative before he could willingly surrender to the service of the star.

This is not an isolated case: many people to-day are really mediums, compelled to serve the unknown future, though realizing little of the greater drama in which they are playing a part. From the side of fate it may seem relatively indifferent whether a man sees and serves, or whether he is forced to serve by the anima. But, from the standpoint of human individuality, it is a matter of supreme importance, as we saw in the anima-phase of the previous case, that this fateful power should be lifted from the domain of the anima and be responsibly located in the self. As the vehicle of a man's unconscious destiny, the anima has the symptomatic character of a *vis a tergo*; but, as the transveyor of this destiny into consciousness, she becomes the mediating function leading to the service of the self.

A man may choose to remain unconscious of his destiny, in which case the onus of unlived primitive psychology, alluded to above, may drive him to reckless imitations of primitive life. It then assumes the character of a restless, unsatisfied craving which eventually becomes incorporated in that whole emotional potential which seeks its satisfaction in woman. There are great-hearted women in whom the heart is a true organ of prophecy; such a woman may be especially gifted in playing the anima-rôle in relation to the man who has been lamed by the future. She may be able to show him the road of his better will and help him to accept the task he is meant to do.

This problem of the anima tends to become a world-problem in times of transition, when the libido-value, formerly invested in the ancestral earth, has been torn away from the traditional ways of life and has not yet found a new container or created a new home.

In both series of drawings we can discern this uprooted condition of the modern soul; it would be therefore impossible to gain full understanding of the individual material without also viewing it in relation to the general perspective.

VI

Although in the individual case the anima-problem reveals itself as a specific aspect of the subjective material, it is none the less a general cultural problem. In effect, the anima-ideal more or less sharply divides women into two classes, the recipients and the non-recipients. Those fitted by nature or by erotic ambition to receive the anima-projection constitute a psychologically privileged class. The value that comes to them is, in reality, a cultural inheritance, having much the same effect upon the character of the recipient as a legacy. For some women the ideal projection of the lover becomes the mainspring of a passionate fidelity to life and the motive power of solid achievement. They feel a sense of added responsibility and demand from themselves a correspondingly valuable achievement. For others it produces the same insidious, demoralizing effect as so often results from an unearned source of wealth. They bask in the life-giving rays of the lover's appraisal, and are content to depute every responsibility and task to those whom they are only too happy to recognize as less favoured than themselves. In either case, however, a conflict must eventually become apparent between the developing personality of the wife and the primordial anima-projection of the husband. This may result either in the gradual transformation of the projection through the development of individual relationship, or in the disintegration of the marriage-relationship through the hardening of the wife's resistance and the husband's " disillusionment." It is a significant fact that, when a modern marriage goes upon the rocks, in most cases it is the dissatisfaction of the wife which causes the breakdown. The privilege so eagerly sought becomes, in the end, a burden no woman can hope to sustain without a dangerous suppression of her personality. For the more romantic and appealing the husband appeared when enveloped in the aura of the child-anima, the more unfitted will he be for adult relationship.

At the other end of the anima-scale we find the phenomenon of the prostitute, who is able to sustain her rôle of general anima-reflector by having one relationship—usually a man of the underworld—in which her own human needs and realities can find some response. He may be worthless and dissolute, but, in so far as he accepts her as she is, she will often give him a deep and abiding affection.

Through making the sex-relationship between man and woman more problematical, the activation of the anima, described above, must also increase the value of the basic human relationship. At bottom the anima-ideal is a generalized cultural image of woman, the roots of which lie deep in the racial unconscious. Because it contains this generic image, the anima-projection is not immediately adaptable to the individual character of the chosen woman. It is like a selective dye-stain, enhancing certain essential attributes of womanhood, but tending to obliterate or repress individuality. It is a light that is intolerant of shadow. The archetypal image must therefore be gradually detached from the actual personality of the wife, so that she may be free to develop her own nature, released from the tyranny of ideal anticipations. This can happen only when the value of the individual relationship is set above the demands of the ideal. Instead of the mutual projection of ideal contents into the marriage-partner, the individual value should be placed, as it were between oneself and the object, as a covenant of faith.

VII

To resume our discussion of the drawing, an inner psychological connection must link the earless heads to the idea of a " mental stammer." In the language of symbolism, the ear represents the organ of understanding. An obsessional patient, for instance, who is obsessed by his single insistent idea, becomes deaf to what one is saying: he hears, yet does not hear. To an intelligence preoccupied with the din of a protopathic mechanism, there is no understanding and therefore no hearing.

The patient returns to the obsessional theme of the first drawing, but with the addition of two other explanatory tributaries: to wit, the idea of stammering, and the perseveration of the autonomous complex. Stammering is akin to obsession in the fact that, once the stammer is under way, the stammerer becomes deaf to everything else. Both the stammering and the obsessional mechanism are therefore impervious to reason. A partial mental system, once it has been released, proceeds, independent of control, until the tension is exhausted. Hence the best way to cure an obsession is to draw away the energy informing the mechanism, by the deliberate cultivation on a higher level of the idea or value it contains. In this way the autonomy of the complex is broken and its perseverating mechanism is deprived of energy.

The ambiguous effects of the anima-projection are due to the fact that a potent cultural archetype exists in the individual psyche in the form of an autonomous complex, with its characteristic all-or-none determination. But when the autonomy of the complex has been dissolved by analysis the anima becomes an invaluable mediating function, both in respect to the contents of the collective unconscious and, indirectly, to the external emotional situation. The common factor which identified the anima-complex with a mental stammer in the patient's mind is the autonomy of the complex. Once again, therefore, we arrive at the conclusion that the fundamental principle of pathological determination is *dissociation*. The dissociated mental system invariably manifests the character of automatism; but when the autonomy is dissolved the pathological manifestations cease.

In respect to the nine heads, the patient contributed the suggestion that his mother married his stepfather when he was nine years old. Since this association lacked spontaneity, its value must be regarded as doubtful. A more likely explanation is to be found in the psychology of numbers. It was another schizophrenic patient who drew my attention to the fact, mentioned above, that the first term of a series was different in character from all succeeding terms. Number one was the individual, *i.e.*, indivisible initiator. It was unique and perfect in itself, demanding nothing before it and nothing after. The fact that other terms were added to it must not detract from the individuality of the original one. They were mere echoes or collective reverberations of the original, and therefore to be considered as belonging to a different and inferior order. The number one is eternally independent of all categories.

Subsequently I learned that certain early classical writers also excluded " one " from the digital series, considering it the *fons et origo numerorum*. For them the digits were the eight numbers 2, 3, 4 . . . . 9.

My patient also included the planet Eros in her planetary system two years before it was actually discovered in the heavens. That her cosmology was archaic in origin was shown by her obstinately held view that the earth was flat. Many of her intuitions were amazingly right in their essential content, though usually insane in their application. In this respect she manifested the spirit of primitive cosmogonies.

Her intuition about the individual value of the original term is exemplified in this series of heads; her insistence upon the inferiority of the succeeding terms of the series is also corroborated by the drawing.

The nine heads would conform, then, to the archetypal digits, and, with regard to our original impression of a series carried on to infinity, I need only remind the reader that ·9 recurring represents a fractional approximation to unity, in which the difference, though still present, is reduced to the infinitely small.

The patient was apparently unaware of these inconspicuous features of the drawing until we examined it together. He was even unconscious of the omission of the ears—a fact of itself indicative of anima-control. But the presence of anima-influence must be presupposed in any representation of the anima-complex. The universal, almost abstract character of the face; the absence of individual particularity and of external organs of perception; the dormant, statuesque expression; the automatic repetition of the head in a recessive descending scale, and the correspondence with the archaic digital series—all these features are characteristic expressions of the autonomous activity of the archaic image.

Drawing 11.

Drawing 12.

CHAPTER V

SOLUTION OR DISSOLUTION: THE PROBLEM OF PSYCHIC CONTINUITY

I

DRAWING 11

WE now come to a series of drawings in which the problem of continuity becomes the determining theme. The first attempts of the patient to reach down to the primordial level are like tentative intellectual steps; almost as though the lively spontaneous activity of the imagination had been congealed by an intellectual frost. But although it is a glimpse of the primordial psyche as seen through a telescope, the downward movement has none the less begun.

The contents of the picture are enclosed by a line following, roughly, the limits of the paper. An opening at the top right-hand corner acts as the chimney through which smoke from the fire can escape.

The contents consist of an archipelago of small islands,[1] each bearing its own specific kind of denizen. The islands are disposed upon three levels. At the bottom are two islands, the largest of which consists of bare rock. Upon this rock stands solitary primæval man. To the right, upon a smaller rock, stands a spotted dog. The intermediate level consists of three islands, the one on the right being occupied by primæval woman, the middle one by a fish, and the one on the left by a fruit-bearing tree.

The upper level embraces a constellation of six islands. On the one to the left, just above the tree, a snake is coiled. Next to it, on the right, is a grass-covered knoll bearing six different kinds of flowers. Just above this is a rock with a creature resembling a polyp with eight tentacles; to the right

[1] Nothing could better demonstrate the suitability of the psychiatric term *insulæ* than the pathologically discrete islands of this drawing, made by a patient completely ignorant of psychiatric terminology.

of these comes a bird, possibly a kind of crane; then a bee, representing the insect world; and last of all there is the fire, whose smoke rises up out of the chimney-opening near the top right-hand corner.

* * * * *

Referring to the discrete islands of the archipelago the patient remembered a certain passage in one of Jung's writings, in which the author likens the content of consciousness to islands appearing above the surface of the sea. From above, these appear as discrete entities; but, in fact, they may be peaks of a mountain chain, whose continuity would be immediately apparent could one but view the scene from below.

This association provides us with the clue to the problem with which the subject is now concerned. Jung, of course, uses the island simile to describe the underlying continuity of the psychic structure not discernible to conscious introspection. Having been selected and held by the patient's mind, this image is now made to serve in a rather different connection.

We know that the major subjective problem of the schizophrenic personality arises from the disruptive or disjunctive tendency of the psychic contents. His difficulty in maintaining reliable relations with external objects is the direct outcome of a deep sense of unrelatedness within, as though each individual psychic entity had a tendency to go off by itself and get lost—*i.e.*, lose connection with consciousness. The tendency (emphasized by Prinzhorn and other writers) for schizophrenic patients to express their fantasies in pictures is not mere regression to a more archaic level of expression. It is, I believe, a purposive attempt to put a conscious check upon the disruptive activity of the mind. By drawing the various fantasy-images, the subject attempts to gain a certain control over the independent activity of the archaic contents.

The denizens of the primordial archipelago in this picture are not ordinary contents of consciousness. Primordial man and woman, the tree with its fruit, the snake and the other denizens of the garden manifestly belong to the paradise-fantasy of man's infancy. They are primordial images from the general human inheritance. But, instead of the flowing activity of normal fantasy, these figures are caught in a rigid posture. The normal activity of the psyche can be imagined when we observe the ceaseless, purposive movements of cell-life, shown by R. G. Canti in his beautiful cinematograph studies of living tissues; whereas the contents in this picture resemble a section of tissue that has been fixed and stained for the purpose of scientific description. The man, the woman, the dog, and the bird might be stuffed specimens in a museum, or as a child would draw them in his first efforts to hold the living objects of his libido. The snake is coiled, the fish is abstracted from his natural element and stuck on the top of a rock. The only things which suggest movement are the bee with its raised wings and the smoke rising from the fire, and these two are immediate neighbours in the top right-hand corner.

As regards the nature of the contents, one can see that they have been arbitrarily selected, since they represent the main families of the natural order. We might regard them as specific elements of the basal instinctual life of man.

One is reminded of Jaworski's intuitive conception of the human constitution as the result of a process of age-long assimilation of animal and vegetable forms. He called this process *interiorization*. His idea was based upon the observation that the complex nature and structure of man contained derivative allusions to a multitude of different animal and vegetable types, both terrestrial and marine. He therefore concluded that in some way man had interiorized nature, as though all nature's experiments had somehow become included and epitomized in man.

Bearing in mind the patient's association with Jung's simile of the islands and the mountain chain, we can assume that the thought underlying this discovery is a variation of the same theme—namely, that the apparently discrete instinctual elements, symbolized by these different natural types, are related underneath in a basic continuity or unity. These archaic denizens may be viewed as discrete and separate archetypes, each with its own specific energy-value and distinctive purposiveness. Or we can regard them as differentiated forms of the one basic archetype, Nature, the original

Mother, symbolized by the Tree of Life. From this point of view, all the manifold forms of living things are members of one family, the survival of the fittest being merely the clamour of the perennial family argument.

Actually, however, this idea of the basic kinship of all living things, and therefore, taken psychologically, of the intrinsic relatedness of every subjective content, is nowhere alluded to in the drawing. It is merely an implication contained in the patient's association. In the drawing each individual member of the family is standing as rigidly on his standpoint as a Hyde Park debater. Primæval Adam upon his rock faces primæval Eve upon hers, and, from their posture, nothing seems more unlikely than that " these twain should meet."

The picture might be called the Invitation to Enlightenment. For according to Chinese wisdom enlightenment is manifested in one's capacity to conceive things differently. If the subject should accept the implied invitation to visit the standpoint of the woman, the dog, the tree, the snake, the fish, the bird, the polyp, the flowers, the bee and the fire, therewith realizing how the situation looked from a non-human as well as from a human standpoint, he would surely gain enlightenment.

In this connection it is interesting to compare one of the New Sayings of Jesus of the *Oxyrhynchus Papyri*. The Second Saying has been translated from the Greek text as follows:[1]

> " Jesus saith (Ye ask ? who are those) that draw us (to the kingdom, if) the kingdom is in heaven ? . . . the fowls of the air, and all beasts that are under the earth, or upon the earth, and the fishes of the sea, (these are they which draw) you, and the Kingdom of Heaven is within you; and whoever shall know himself shall find it."

Leaving on one side the whole question of authenticity and accepting the most likely view, that Jesus is concerned here with the method or way by which that inner attitude, which He called the Kingdom of Heaven, could be attained, His words must be taken to mean that it is the acceptance of the lowliest elements in our being, the instincts by virtue

[1] Egypt Exploration Fund. *New Sayings of Jesus and Fragment of a Lost Gospel from Oxyrhynchus.* Oxford University Press, 1904.

of which we are kin to all the denizens of land and sea, which leads us to the Kingdom. The subject also seems to have the knowledge that the primordial or child mind is the way to the Kingdom he seeks; but as yet he does not know how to attain the childlike state.

Indications of the psychotic influence are to be found in the static rigidity of the figures and in the enclosing frame. We had occasion to observe, in the former patient's drawings, an instinctive tendency to enclose archaic or regressive contents within a frame. I have often observed this phenomenon in the drawings of schizoid patients; generally it goes hand in hand with a tendency to diminish or depreciate the instincts, as though they were safe to handle only in miniature.

This motive may also account for the general schizophrenic habit of abstracting things from their natural organic context, and framing them in a specially constructed system of control. Examples of this were shown in the material of the former patient, notably in Drawings IV. and V., in which certain dynamic figures were abstracted from Drawing III. We have already referred to the design, " Le temps et les plantes," by Paul Klee[1] (facing p. 563). In this drawing six abstract archaic figures, consisting of typical schizophrenic whorls, flower and shell artefacts, combined with certain basic geometrical figures —*e.g.*, squares, cones, concentric rings and hour-glass formations—are set in an arbitrary rectangular field (in perspective), as though laid carefully on a table. Above and to the left of this field there is a square, quartered with a black cross. Controlling the field from above is a circular disc, the face of which is segmented by lines of three different lengths, radiating from the centre. This segmentation gives it the character of a compass- or chronometer-face. A phallic stalk, consisting of three lines, is prolonged downwards from this control-disc on to the rectangular field below. At the left-hand corner of the table is a heavy black directing arrow.

Many features bearing upon our investigation are presented by this picture. First, there is the selection of archaic figures, set out like specimens on a table. The figures are suggestive of natural objects; yet, in fact, all of them are combinations of

[1] Will Grohmann: *Paul Klee*. Éditions " Cahiers d'Art." Paris.

basal forms or patterns, joined together in such a way as to suggest aquatic organisms of a low order. Second, there are the figures of control, the quartered square, the compass-disc with its stem, the rectangular table and the directing arrow.

For the purposes of demonstration, this drawing must be regarded as a perfect example of borderline control. The archaic figures represent those basic psychic elements which have the tendency in schizophrenia to slip away from the control of consciousness. They are the *insulæ* or fragments which, having seized a certain rebellious autonomy, threaten the overthrow of the psychic hierarchy. It is the activity of these unruly " islands " which causes the unreliability of attention, and which makes the borderline patient doubt the integrity of his mind. But their most interesting feature is the character of their basal constituents. These are by no means menacing or elusive. Note, for instance, the square containing a labyrinth, the spiral, the plant formation, the bell of a flower, the hour-glass shape joining figures of concentric rings, and, above all, the compass-face or control-disc incorporated in a kind of marine organism. In many of Klee's drawings the field is crowded with detail consisting either of primitive elements, crosses, rings, cones, crescents and single lines, or of elementary flowers, animals, fishes or other aquatic forms of life.

We can conclude, therefore, that the atavistic tendency shows itself in an indiscriminate proliferation of elementary symbols. As against this atavistic tendency we find, in the borderline case, an equally strong counter-tendency towards control. In this drawing of Klee's, for instance, we find this counter-tendency demonstrated, not only in the discrete setting of each figure and in the characteristic symbols of control—viz., compass, square, arrow, limiting field, etc.—but also in the careful and accurate technique which stands in strong contrast to many of his other drawings in which the archaic tendency prevails. The prevalence of loose detail and archaic figures on the one hand, and definite evidence of control on the other, provide us with valuable criteria in our psychological appraisal of schizophrenic products.

A letter of the alphabet is sometimes used as a symbol of control. It may be imposed upon the drawing in the manner of primitive magic, as an acting representative of the creating-subject, or controlling the design by its presence, like a referee at a football match, without having any organic connection with the contents of the picture.

The painting of Paul Klee entitled " Paysage à la lettre R " (Fig. 8) is a good example of this type. In the centre of the field is a house consisting in the main of squares, right-angled triangles and parallelograms painted in light and shade. Sweeping across the front of the house, and receding away into the distance, runs a white road. On the near side of the road is a field with a few elementary trees. A large uncompromising R, drawn with absolute precision, controls these three elements of the picture by spanning the road in such a way that the side of the house, to which its upright stroke is applied, is joined to the meadow upon which its two limbs are planted.

A rather similar use of the letter E occurred in Drawing VI. of the former series, in which, as an interesting coincidence, the patient also planted his referee-letter upon a field near the road which led to the house of his ancestors. We can well understand how this road, leading back into the past, away from the main course of his life, might easily have aroused the innate atavistic craving, and therefore had to be controlled by a magical representative of conscious power.

In the archipelago drawing the presence of control is manifested in the abstracting and representation of the elementary figures, in their rigid, controlled posture, and in the limiting line which contains the field. The atavistic tendency, on the other hand, reveals itself in the primordial man and woman, in the elementary character of the denizens, and in the disjuncted '*insulæ*' upon which these are placed.

On the positive side the most hopeful element in the picture is to be found in the fire. It is the symbol of the introverting passion that is needed to bring about a healing integration of the psychic elements. It is like a portion of the sun, brought down for magical or religious purposes into the archaic depths. Thus life can be generated in the static controlled system, just as the heat activated the generation of the homunculus in the hermetically closed vessel of the alchemists. Parallel symbolism was observed in the former series, where in Drawing II. a fire had been kindled under a glass vessel; and in Drawing III., where the idea of incubation in a stomach-container was represented. The whole aim of the introverting direction of the libido is the activation of the dormant potential in the unconscious. Thus Shakti is awakened from her timeless slumber in the depths by the process of *tapas* (introversion).

The activating effect of the fire—which appears to have been newly kindled—is to be seen in the bee raising its wings for flight. Inasmuch as the drawings that follow reveal a remarkable animation of these contents, it may not be without significance that the primordial anima and the bird are also being warmed by the fire.

The disposition of the remaining symbolic figures seems to imply the existence of an underlying instinctual relatedness. The triangle, for example, of man, woman and dog forms a natural domestic trinity, the dog symbolizing the domesticated aspect of the instinct. The quartet, which consists of the cold-blooded fish and reptile as one diagonal, and the tree and the island of flowers as the other, forms a natural constellation of more remote instinctual derivatives, while the polyp, as the archetype of the primæval organism, presides over the atavistic process at the top.

A certain structural affinity also seems to exist between this tentacled cœlenterate and the regenerating cell in Drawing 2, the initiator of the therapeutic development.

The thread of psychical continuity between this drawing and the last is not immediately apparent. We are faced with a sudden change in level from the cultural to the primordial, from the ideal to the archaic. In following the continuity of psychic events, a sudden descent of the libido to the archaic modality is usually a sign that a psychological *impasse* has been reached. The indefinitely receding parallel lines of perseverating mechanisms in the two previous drawings offered no mediating principle that could bring together the dissociated aspects of the anima. Nothing more was feasible on that level.

At this juncture the possibility of an underlying basis of union came into the patient's mind by way of Jung's simile. The attempt to picture the situation from the primordial, infantile standpoint naturally followed. The subject seemed to be feeling his way towards a unifying dynamic principle, even though he was still viewing the instincts with the intellectual detachment of a man attempting to control his world from above, instead of allowing it to develop from below.

II

Drawing 12

Ecstatic release of feeling is here exuberantly combined with the idea of associative continuity. The release of energy is personified in the figure of a young girl, instinct with vitality, whirling an impossibly involved skipping-rope above her head. The rope is drawn with a double line, the points of intersection being emphasized in a rather peculiar way. With the exception of two in the middle of the field, a small portion of the lower curve has been darkened on either side of each intersection. The effect of this device is to give the appearance of a number of nodal points, as though the rope had been tied or bound at these places. We could, of course, regard this as nothing more than a technical device; but the two intersections, in which the shading has been omitted, demonstrate that the continuity of the rope is actually better displayed without it. It is fair to conclude, therefore, that some other association, alien to the idea of continuity, has intruded itself at these stressed intersections.

For the clue to this other idea we should compare this running figure with the discrete *insulæ* of the instinctual archipelago in the previous drawing. There the discriminative, separatist quality of the intellect ruled the constellation of archaic elements. Here the running, flowing, dynamic character of the autonomous psyche manifests itself, and with it an entirely new conception of the anima, as a leaping personification of autonomous activity, appears on the scene.

One of the most valuable features of the graphic method of representing psychic events lies in the fact that the *standpoint* from which the drawing is made is immediately apparent. In the previous drawing, for example, it is obvious that the scene is drawn from above. It is a bird's-eye view, seen from an intellectual aeroplane, whereas in the present drawing the whirling rope and rushing anima-figure are seen from below. We are standing under the event, and therefore are in a position to understand it, not merely as detached observers, but with the participation of subjective feeling.

Conceiving the masculine logos-function as the ability to discriminate objects, to name them, and to form concepts from the facts perceived, the former drawing would be a rather childish expression of this function. Similarly, if the feminine eros-function be conceived as the principle of relatedness, whereby individual things and elements are joined together in a creative association, then the anima-figure of the present drawing would personify this function.

Correctly to understand these intuitive, borderline conceptions, we must liberate them from the banal realm of male and female prerogatives, and see them as universal psychic principles. Speaking generally, the logos-function takes the ruling position in a man's psychology, where the eros-function is, on the whole, inferior; and, as a rule, the contrary is the case with women. But this does not mean that these opposite principles are merely aspects of biological sex-differentiation. They are, in fact, general conditioning principles, which rule the basic attitude of individual psychology in much the same way as day and night, waking and sleeping, summer and winter rule the normal disposition. Whenever the dynamic, associative, flowing continuity of the psychic process brings about a new symbolical formation, irrespective of whether the object bearing the symbol-value belongs to the inner or the outer world, we can speak of the event as being under the ægis of eros. Whenever the observing, discriminating, abstracting, enquiring, intuitive concentration of consciousness proceeds to bring reason into union with soul,[1] we are under the rule of logos.

[1] The term soul is used here in the Platonic sense. It is defined in the *Laws* and the *Phædrus* as " the self-moving source of all motion." It is the

These intuitive concepts are empirically valuable, because they comprehend complex psychic operations which cannot be embraced by simple functional terms. If we try, for example, to identify logos with thinking and eros with feeling, we therewith exclude the essential quality of both, which is the conative constellation denoted by the term "attitude."

* * * * *

Resuming our discussion of the drawing, we conclude that the subject must have been inspired by an ecstatic conception of the "soul as the self-moving source of all motion"; as though it had been suddenly revealed to him that the essential activity of the mind was a dancing, flowing circuit of emotional energy, leaping from one node to the next in a living stream, yet also combining the associated images into a complex moment of experience. Whereas the previous picture had the static character of a semi-diagrammatic representation, this one is a direct impression of the dynamic activating power of released emotion.

This anima-figure has four attributes which reveal her genetic continuity with previous figures. Her hair has the same fiery character as observed in the anima-inundation of Drawing 3. She is identified with the idea of flowing movement, as in Drawings 2 and 3. She is diminutive in size, as in Drawings 2, 3 and 9. Finally, she is identified with the idea of a circuit of energy, as in Drawing 9.

With regard to this last resemblance we should note, however, an important difference. In Drawing 9 the electrical circuit was completed through the fact that the woman was standing in the subject's shoes. In other words, it was a condition of his unconscious identification with, or possession by, the anima, whereas in the present drawing the energy-circuit passes freely through arms and hands, and the upper or conscious aspect of the figure, which before was suppressed, is now ecstatically alive.

---

psychic element conceived not from the ideational, but rather from the dynamic side. And yet, as Plato says in the *Timæus*, "Reason cannot be present in anything apart from soul. If Reason is present in the body of the universe and in the body of man, that body must be alive and endowed with soul."

In order to understand the exuberant feeling expressed in this figure, we have to consider the nature of the emotional *impasse* that was portrayed in Drawings 9 and 10. According to the clearest possible evidence, the effect of the dissociation was to divorce the ideal aspect of the anima-complex from the dynamic with such completeness that neither portion could function except as an isolated perseverating mechanism. Beyond a permanent urge to delay, it is hard to find an intelligible purpose in a mental stammer. It is a soulless embarrassing nuisance, and the fact that a potential value is being perseverated serves only to intensify our feeling of despair.

This dissociation could be dissolved only by means of a recession of the libido to a level below that of the schizoid split—namely, the infantile-archaic. The descent of the libido to this general instinctual level must be regarded as a teleological movement, its aim being to draw the energy away from the perseverating mechanisms.

The victorious dance of the anima in the present drawing might be viewed, therefore, as a vivid, pictorial bulletin of the therapeutic efficacy of the downward movement. In Drawing 9 the anima was merely a body without a head, in Drawing 10 an ideal graven image without a body. Here she is whole again, her release from the condition of blind unconscious mechanism being expressed with convincing *élan*. Healing means, literally, to be whole.

In dealing with obsessional cases I have observed that the moment the patient is able to realize the purposiveness of psychic activity (including that of the obsession which torments him) the whole character of the analysis undergoes a change. Nothing is so deadly to the soul as the sense of being chained to a purposeless mechanism. But the purposive nature of psychic development cannot be imparted didactically to the obsessional patient. One's best illustrations and explanations are mere empty words until the experiential moment arrives which brings the realization that the soul is naturally purposive.[1] One cannot conceive something to be true which

[1] This realization is equivalent emotionally to Tertullian's famous discovery, "*anima naturaliter Christiana*."

long inner torment denies. This patient could not conceive the anima differently until the actual experience of a complete emotional response gave birth to the new conception.

In the case of the former patient the reader will remember the profound change that became observable in the character of the drawing when the developing psyche burst the limiting mechanistic framework of Drawing VII., and was thenceforth free to represent psychic events without theoretical constraint.

In the whirling convolutions of her rope the anima seems to be exulting in the fact that the purposive unity of the psychic process has been restored, and that the brittle, soulless artificiality of a world governed by mechanism and rigid law has given place to the free dance of life.

III

Drawing 13

At this juncture the subject forsook his pencil, preferring instead a somewhat crude use of colour. Earth and sky are represented by a flat wash of neutral colours, the lower half resembling a shade of distemper called stone-grey, while the upper half is a lighter shade of the same colourless wash. Low in the sky are three discs, painted in dark opaque colours. The larger one on the left is dark brown, the medium-sized disc is dark blue, and the small one, on the right, black. In the left-hand bottom corner there is a group of gesticulating, dancing, posturing and running figures, each of which is painted in one of the three colours represented in the discs. There are no other objects on the earth, and no clouds in the heavens. One feature only is shared by all the gesticulating figures. The heads of all, and the hands of some, are painted in bright yellow.

* * * * *

There is something queer and unnatural about this fantasy that has the effect of alienating one's feeling. The round discs are, of course, worlds in space; yet in no sense are they luminaries, but rather flat opaque discs, resembling coloured counters. The blue disc in the middle is in the position of the setting sun; yet, hanging as it does on the near side of the horizon, its whole circumference is visible.

The idea conveyed by the picture is that each human being is conditioned by some specific determining principle. It is the concept of εἱμαρμένη[1] expressed in the subjective modern way. The orbs are literally spheres of influence, representing that specific determination or compulsion which the men of antiquity attributed to the stars. But, although the idiom of expression may be determined by the antique conception, the compelling factors in this drab sky are no distant suns, but near opaque orbs, whose independent existence would be impossible in nature.

This fact provides us with the clue to the pathological character of the painting. It has already been demonstrated that autonomous drawings truthfully record, down to the last detail, the psychology creating them. In this conception the patient had in mind the idea of worlds in space. If he had been able to draw what he intended, he would have designated general impersonal factors which determine every life. Astrology, for instance, was an intuitive science, concerned with the knowledge of just these general determinants of human fate. But being factors of the collective unconscious, and therefore not conceivable as aspects of personal psychology, the astrological symbols were accordingly projected upon the distant field of the stars.

Inasmuch, therefore, as the patient has been persuaded or compelled to paint his " worlds " on the near side of the horizon, we may conclude that he has confounded the general with the personal aspects of his fate pattern. General determinants are those universally conditioning factors to which all are subject; but I cannot assume that what appears to have the force of fate in my life must necessarily determine my fellow-men in the same way.

In regard to this problem of compulsion, two citations from Jung express the pith of the matter. Speaking of the necessity of sacrificing the infantile hero, the author writes:

> " This sacrifice is best accomplished . . . through a complete devotion to life, in which all the libido unconsciously bound up in

[1] Equivalent to μοῖρα—that which is allotted, destiny.

familial bonds must be brought outside into human contact. For it is necessary for the well-being of the adult individual, who in his childhood was merely an atom revolving in a rotary system, to become himself the centre of a new system. That such a step implies the solution or, at least, the energetic handling of the individual sexual problem is obvious, for unless this is done the unemployed libido will remain inexorably fixed in the incestuous bond, and will prevent individual freedom in essential matters."[1]

And again:

"The power of fate makes itself unpleasantly felt only when everything goes against our will—that is to say, when we no longer find ourselves in harmony with ourselves. As I endeavoured to show in my article *Die Bedeutung des Vaters*, the most dangerous power of fate lies in the infantile fixation, localized in the unconscious. The power of fate reveals itself at closer range as a compulsion of the libido; wherefore Maeterlinck justly says that a Socrates could not possibly be a tragic hero of the type of Hamlet. In accordance with this conception, the ancients placed εἱμαρμένη (destiny) in relation to 'primal light,' or 'primal fire.'"[2]

Jung's explanation of compulsion as residing in the infantile incestuous fixation, and therefore as readily identifiable with a primal source, agrees with the character of this drawing. The absence of the sun, the natural ruler of our world, not to mention the total obliteration of the genial world of the senses, should warn us that we are concerned here with that aspect of human fate lying below the world of objective reality, and which naturally seeks expression in archaic idiom.

The reader may still hold the view that these drawings are the meaningless gestures of a morbid mind and, as such, cannot merit a serious interrogation of their content. As against this *non possumus* attitude, we have the incontestable fact that many introverted schizoid subjects of real ability are psychologically impaled upon this problem of atavism. In many instances their whole creative passion is rooted (as was clearly the case with Dostoievsky) in the need to overcome the tragic isolation of their fate by means of a

[1] C. G. Jung: *Psychology of the Unconscious*, p. 453.
[2] *Loc. cit.*, p. 496.

psychological creation, which could gain for them the communion with their fellows of which their singular fate has deprived them. Such a man feels himself to have been singled out to face a life-long ordeal of solitariness. Hence his constant need to analyse, explain, elaborate and express the nature of that binding, sundering, menacing, and often destroying power which is, for him, fate.

When such a man has given himself to the work of expressing his lamed soul, in the hope that psychology may be able to throw light upon the sources of his malady, it is scientifically and humanly unworthy to tell him that his products are morbid and therefore unintelligible. If we do not attempt to understand the psychological content of such works, we have to admit the bankruptcy of our science in face of the major problem of human existence. For, in the last resort, the understanding of his fate is the central problem of every reflective mind.

Let us assume, then, that this picture is the attempt of a mind, preoccupied with the problem of destiny, to distinguish the determining forces which divide the domain of the unconscious. In an earlier chapter we referred to the impersonal conception of fate which, as Cornford proves most convincingly, must have preceded the idea of individual fate in early Greek thought. "The notion of the individual lot, or fate," he writes, "comes last, not first, in the order of development. We must seek the original meaning of *Moira* elsewhere."[1] He then quotes a passage from the fifteenth book of the Iliad demonstrating that the archaic Greek conception of fate was a power superior and antecedent to the gods themselves.

"Zeus awakes one day to find the Trojans hard pressed in battle by the Achæans assisted by Poseidon. After a sordid outburst against Hera, who, however, swears by Styx that Poseidon is acting of his own will and not at her instigation, Zeus sends Iris with a threatening message, commanding Poseidon to cease from war and battle and to withdraw among the tribes of the gods or into the bright sea. Poseidon is very angry and protests." (I., 186.)

[1] F. M. Cornford: *From Religion to Philosophy*, p. 15.

"Alack" (he says), "strong though he be, these words are past all bearing, if he will constrain me by violence against my will, though I am his equal in rank. For we are three brothers, born of Kronos and Rhea; Zeus and I, and Hades is the third, the lord of the dead. *And in three lots are all things divided, and each took his appointed domain* (*or privilege, status*). When we shook the lots, to me fell the hoary sea that I should dwell therein for ever; and Hades drew the misty darkness, and Zeus the broad heaven among the æther and the clouds: the earth and high Olympus are yet common to all. Therefore never will I live according to the mind of Zeus: no, masterful though he be, let him stay quiet in his own third part."[1]

Here is the original conception of fate (*Moira*) as an allotted portion or domain of reality, and the interesting way in which the Homeric scene harmonizes with the contents of our picture seems to confirm our idea that this may also be derived from a subpersonal archaic conception of human fate. When one stays under the impression of this picture for a certain time one is almost chilled by the feeling of the hour before the dawn. The earth is bare and empty save for the dancing men, and the sky is not yet filled with the light and warmth of the sun.

This feeling of dawn clearly corresponds to the period of early cosmogony. In the cosmogony of Hesiod, for instance, we find the three, Chaos, Earth, and Eros, coming into being. It is the hour before the world was born. Then out of Chaos arose Darkness and Night, and of them were born the Upper Air (αἰθήρ) and Daylight. Then follows the division of the world into three parts—Earth, Sky, and Sea.

Cornford stresses this threefold differentiation as follows:

"Here, then, we find as a distinct stage in cosmogony, a division of the world into three portions (*moirai*), just as in Homer 'all things were divided in three,' and the three provinces were assigned to Zeus, Poseidon, and Hades. . . . By making the triple division older in time than the gods—cosmogony older than theogony—Hesiod marks by temporal sequence the supremacy of *Moira*—the dimly personified principle of that division—over the later-born divinities."[2]

[1] *Loc. cit.*, p. 15.

[2] *Loc. cit.*, pp. 17-18.

With this well-documented analogy we are able to understand the cosmogonic mood of the present drawing. The heavens, the sea and the underworld were peopled by the myth-dreaming mind of antiquity with appropriate denizens, whose nature corresponded with the specific conditions attributed to these various provinces. It would therefore be historically feasible for the subject to represent the deeper determinants of the unconscious as worlds or provinces, each with its specific *mana* or genius. He has chosen specific colours to represent the *dæmon*[1] (δαίμων) of these unconscious spheres. The total sphere of dæmonic influence would, of course, embrace both cause and effect, motive and manifestation, as designated by the spheres and their respective marionettes.

This would already correspond with Plato's mythical reign of the dæmons, when they were permitted a certain degree of personification. Cornford writes:

> " He (Plato) expressly compares the division of the parts of the universe among dæmons with the present distribution of the earth into the seats of worship of the various gods. He also tells us that each dæmon was ' sufficient in himself in all things for his own flock.' "[2]

Thus we reach the conception of specific compelling dæmons or collective souls, which had the power of possessing human beings and determining their fate in unconscious ways. It is probable that all primitive cosmogony developed from such experiences, just as the cosmogony of this picture developed from a similar pre-rational condition. No thoughts or images could survive the constant wastage of primitive forgetfulness and inertia if they did not take possession of the mind as something unforgettably real (real in the sense of the *kataleptike fantasia* of the Stoics)—namely, something that has the power so to seize upon the mind that it cannot conceivably be disowned. The existence of the unconscious,

[1] " A nature-dæmon is thus defined as the soul, or force, or *mana*, resident in some species of natural phenomena. . . . The fire-dæmon is manifested in all fire; for all fire has the same specific behaviour. It is for this reason that dæmons in Greek theology, as elsewhere, remain impersonal " (Cornford, *loc. cit.*, p. 97).

[2] *Loc. cit.*, p. 98.

or, more accurately, of the spirit-world, is not borne in upon the primitive mind by our method of intellectual representation. In the primitive view the reality of the spirits could not possibly be disputed, since men are constantly being possessed by them. The spirit-world is a power existing by the side of (*neben an*) ordinary things, and no one can tell when it will intervene. It may take possession of a man, or a whole group of men, forcing them to do things of which they know nothing, and to say things they would naturally dread to utter.

There can be very little doubt that the state of possession is the basic experience in which the whole conception of spiritual reality originated. According to Nietzsche, it is also the origin of drama. He describes the development of the tragic chorus from the state of Dionysian possession in the following passage:

> " The Dionysian excitement is able to impart to a whole mass of men this artistic faculty of seeing themselves surrounded by such a host of spirits *with whom they know themselves to be inwardly one*. This function of the tragic chorus is the dramatic proto-phenomenon: to see oneself transformed before oneself, and then to act as if one had really entered into another body, into another character. This function stands at the beginning of the development of the drama. Here we have something different from the rhapsodist, who does not blend with his pictures but only sees them, like the painter, with contemplative eye outside of him. Here we actually have surrender of the individual by his entering into another nature. Moreover, this phenomenon appears in the form of an epidemic: a whole throng feels itself metamorphosed in this wise. Hence it is that the dithyramb is essentially different from every other variety of the choric song."[1]

We know that the essential experience of the antique mystery religions was a state of possession in which the initiate became temporarily identical with the god. The *hierosgamos*, or sacred marriage, was also rooted in the idea of participating in, or union with, the deity. The foundation of the *shaman's* authority rests, as we have already seen, upon his state of possession by a spirit. The divine value attributed

[1] Nietzsche: *The Birth of Tragedy*, p. 67.

to soma in Vedic ritual is clearly due to the fact that its immense potency engendered a state of religious ecstasy. In the soma-communion man participated in the god—in other words, he became the god, thus sharing the immortality of the divine being. The idea of partaking of the body and blood of the God, therewith participating in the divine nature, is also the essence of the Christian mystery.

Owing to our deification of the intellect, whose whole virtue resides in its detachment from the affective level of experience, we encounter real difficulty when we attempt to reconstruct the living experience out of which the familiar images of our mental life originally sprang. To the intellect a spiritual experience is a highly complex and even dubious phenomenon, whereas to the primordial man it is a self-evident fact.

Nietzsche comments on this intellectual opacity when dealing with his parallel theme:

> " By reason of a strange defect in our capacities, we modern men are apt to represent to ourselves the æsthetic proto-phenomenon as too complex and abstract. For the true poet the metaphor is not a rhetorical figure, but a vicarious image which actually hovers before him in place of a concept. . . . Why is it that Homer is more deeply intuitive in his portrayals than all the other poets? Because he participated more deeply in the myth. We talk so abstractly about poetry because we are all wont to be bad poets. At bottom the æsthetic phenomenon is simple."[1]

There is no one who has not at some time been seized and possessed by a primordial image, only the rational habit of our mind dissuades us from honouring the experience lest, like Mr. Preemby in *Christina Alberta's Father*, we become transported beyond the pale of sanity. Therefore we are careful to use a denaturalizing scientific terminology when we have to do with the proto-phenomenon of spirit-possession.

Our civilized fear of the unconscious is even implied in Janet's psychiatric explanation, *l'abaissement du niveau mental.* We stress the negative factor in the genesis of psychosis, only because it is not intellectually decent to suggest that the

[1] *The Birth of Tragedy.*

archaic unconscious can suddenly rise up and storm the gates of consciousness. Yet this is what happens; every alienist, at one time or another, has had to watch the waters rising, and sometimes, with agonizing impotence, he has had to see his patient carried away from human contact on an archaic flood. Everyone knows that the activation of the unconscious is *the* crucial factor in every acute phase, and yet the man who dares to make a serious study of the unconscious is liable to be assailed as though he were giving encouragement to the devil.

The gesticulating figures in our picture do not correspond with the behaviour of the possessed as they appear on the modern stage. This again is an archaic representation of the phenomenon. The modern man can only gesticulate inwardly when activated by the unconscious; yet all the more is he enthralled and fascinated by its archaic imagery, just because the primitive outlet in magical ritual and violent bodily movement is prohibited by reason. The proto-phenomenon —namely, the condition of physical possession by the unconscious—is still to be observed, however, in certain forms of hysteria and in various acute phases of insanity, as also in the mass excitements of political or religious crises.

Our rational distrust of the unconscious has, to a large extent, blocked all the primitive avenues by which the dæmonic forces were originally expressed. Yet the rational, respectable crust of civilization broke down in 1914, and the ever-increasing irrationality of modern life is a daily reminder of the way in which mankind is still possessed by the unconscious.

The primordial myth-making mind naturally conceived these forces of the unconscious in the shapes of gods, titans, dæmons, heroes, or monstrous animals. And yet the further we go back into the cosmogonic dawn of early Greece, the more abstract and impersonal does the concept of fate become.[1] We cannot, therefore, assume that because our patient employs an abstract idiom with which to represent the subjective aspect of fate he is necessarily producing a sophisticated

[1] Dr. de Angulo in his essay *La Psychologie religieuse des Achumavi* finds that the life of these most primitive people is completely pervaded by, and made up of, religious feeling. It is, however, a vague, diffuse religion, without any dogma or precise form, in which there is a generalized energic conception, not unlike that of Bergson's *élan vital*, but absolutely no concept of God.

intellectual product. The mere fact that the patient could throw no light at all upon this picture (he simply felt he had to paint it like that) is sufficient evidence that it is an archaic product quite remote from consciousness.

Another question, which is particularly relevant at the present time, concerns the state of possession as a collective phenomenon. Why, for instance, is the state of being possessed by the unconscious regarded at certain times, and with a general consensus of feeling, as something to be venerated, while under other conditions it is regarded with fear and horror? This question is linked up with the perennial doubt as to whether a work or an idea of outstanding originality is the creation of genius or merely a symptom of insanity.

It is my belief that the differently coloured spheres of this drawing unconsciously answer this question. For the whole issue of genius versus insanity rests, at bottom, upon the degree of collective participation and acceptance. When, for example, a man with the flame of spiritual possession in his eyes proclaims a new revolutionary idea, not as a proposition open to discussion, but as a revelation sent from heaven, the issue will depend upon whether his idea kindles an answering flame in the minds of his fellows, or whether they turn upon him in derision and scorn. In the first eventuality the man will be acclaimed as a messenger sent from heaven, and his words will have the authority of revelation; in the second he will be isolated as a spiritual incendiary. To those who participate in what Nietzsche calls the proto-phenomenon, his idea will have the character of absolute truth: while for those who take no part in the epidemic, it is as clearly a danger, a conflagration that must be fought and suppressed. Cornford's account of the early Greek dæmon offers us the most pliable concept for comprehending these mass-phenomena. From this point of view we might speak of a Nazi-dæmon or a golf-dæmon, a Group-dæmon, or a war-dæmon, the term meaning nothing beyond the fact that all the members of any particular dæmonic fraternity manifest an almost identical form of excitement.

That this is what the painting is saying is clear enough. The brown orb above determines a certain proportion of the figures, and these participate in the brown epidemic. Brown is their experience and must be their truth. In so far as they are possessed by this dæmon, or aspect of the unconscious, they are willy-nilly excluded from comprehending or even apprehending any other aspect.

Remembering the cosmogonic trinity of early Greece, and also bearing in mind the basic familial pattern (viz., father, mother and child) on which the symbol of the trinity ultimately rests, we cannot resist the conclusion that the three fateful orbs of our patient's cosmogony are as closely linked to the archetype of human generation as was the trinitarian universe of Hesiod. In Hesiod's cosmogony Chaos was evidently the first father, Earth was the mother, and Eros the child. In our patient's cosmogony the Brown Orb is the mother, the Blue Orb the father, and the Black Orb the son.

It now begins to be clear why the patient was not able to represent his cosmogonic spheres as authentic celestial bodies. The parent is the most ambiguous of all symbols—from one point of view the most deeply personal factor in one's life-experience; from another a universal, all-embracing archetype. In so far as the cosmogony I create is part of my myth and therefore born of my experience, it must also contain either overtly or covertly my experience of my parents. If, for example, I have not been able to free myself from infantile dependence upon the mother, this fact will inevitably condition the structure of my cosmogony. For I am inexorably bound by the law, that the way I conceive myself is also the way I conceive the world. The intellect may seem to have freed itself from affects and affectivity; but the basic attitude, not the intellect, is the final arbiter of the kind of world I create.

In so far then as the brown maternal orb has the ascendant position in his universe, we must assume that the mother is the ruling power in the patient's psychology.

In a thousand ways brown is the colour of participation. It is the colour of the earth, the original Mother. All the mystery-cults of the antique world were primarily chthonic in character, and the essential mystery of Eleusis was the *hierosgamos—i.e.*, the rite of sacred marriage in which the priestess was identified with the fruitful earth-mother. Concerning the content of the Eleusinian mystery, the evidence of Bishop Asterius (A.D. 390) is as follows: "Is not there (in Eleusis) the gloomiest descent, and the most solemn communion of the hierophant and the priestess, between him and her alone? Are the torches not extinguished, and does not the vast multitude regard as their salvation that which takes place between the two in the darkness?"[1]

After the ritual coitus the hierophant appeared before the people, holding up a sheaf of corn, and proclaimed: "The holy one has brought forth a holy son; Brimos is born of Brimo."

The cult of the *Magna Mater* prevailed in various forms over Europe and Asia Minor before the Christian era, and the gradual dawn of the sky-religion (*i.e.*, the cult of the father) gained considerable impetus from the fact that it raised the mystery of communion from the darkness of earth into the light of heaven. Through Christianity the soul was weaned from secret earth-mysteries and became heir to the kingdom of light. The exclusion of the feminine principle from the Christian Trinity becomes intelligible when we realize with what fierce pangs the spirit of man won some release from the compelling female power of the unconscious. But this wrenching free from the dark weight of the earth gave to early Christian development an almost fanatical austerity, and a yearning to join the Father-God in the heavens.

If then the brown sphere represents the state of mystical participation[2] with the mother (the earth-cults), the blue sphere would represent a similar determination by the realm of the spirit (logos-principle of the father). The brown sphere has precedence, representing as it does the primal state of man as well as the first religious communities. As the chthonic cults of antiquity gave place to the sky-religions, the orientation of culture swung over to the logos-principle,

[1] C. G. Jung: *Psychology of the Unconscious*, p. 375.

[2] The impersonal "dæmon" described by Cornford retains the collective character which marks it as being derived from the common consciousness of a group, not from the individual consciousness of one person. In this sense it is indistinguishable from Lévy-Bruhl's concept of *participation mystique*.

which swept like the light of dawn throughout the civilized world.

These alternating modes of human communion comprise the warp and woof of history. In the field of primitive kinship the matrilineal and patrilineal moieties form the basic elements of social organization. In higher culture the matriarchal and patriarchal patterns constitute the groundwork of the social structure. Over the vast field of human relatedness the same two principles hold sway: the earth-principle, sexuality, opposed by the sky-principle, spirituality. "There are three elements," says the Chinese sage, "Heaven, Earth, and Man, and Man unites heaven and earth."

But if the blue sphere represents the sky-principle, how comes it that its light has departed? Is it that same substitution of the spirit by the intellect which provokes Klages and other modern German philosophers to deplore the impotence of the spirit? Or has the schizophrenic dissociation of the intellect from the emotions deprived the heavenly principle of its light?

The latter is, I believe, the correct explanation; for without the emotional stream which supplies the sense of meaning to an experience, its mere apprehension by the intellect is barren. We shall come across other examples in this series in which a similar denaturalizing effect can be observed. In this connection there is also the significance of the black sphere upon the horizon to be considered. The only thing that the patient could say about this third sphere was that he painted it in after the other two. In a picture the sun rises on the left and sets on the right. The movement, therefore, is from the brown orb to the blue, and thence to the black. This, as we have seen, corresponds also with the historical evolution of the human communion.

The obvious features of the third sphere are that it is much smaller than the other two and that it is black. To the mind of a child or a primitive it would be self-evident that these three spheres represented the mamma, the papa and the black baby. By the more laborious analogical route we too have arrived at the same idea. But if the three spheres correspond to the trinity of the archetypal human family there would seem to be a reversal of the pattern. The female orb is not only in the position of leader, it is also above the other two. The earth is set above the sky, the mother above the father, woman above man! This is a solecism which the aggressive masculine will of Drawing 4 could not be expected to tolerate. Moreover, since a reversal of the archetype of the human family is "out of harmony with Tao," the outcome must be unfavourable.

We know that the ætiology of homosexuality is closely bound up with this reversal of the family archetype. A predominating feminine influence (usually coming from the mother) tends to be overcompensated by a corresponding tendency to associate only with men; as though the male principle needed reinforcement as the result of an original overweighting of the female.

This background pattern is present, in my experience, in a large majority of cases. It existed very decidedly in the present instance. The mother was a powerful introverted personality, whose potentialities had never been adequately fulfilled and with whom intimate confessions were presumably not easy.

The masculine logos-principle comes to its full stature in a man usually through the veneration of this principle in an older man who is willing to play the rôle of the father. This need was never satisfied in the restless environment of the patient's early youth, so that there can be small doubt that the subject's unwillingness to accept the feminine principle on equal terms arose from a relative eclipse of his light by the overwhelming maternal shadow. From what has now been said, the early homosexual seduction takes on a different aspect: it seems almost to fit into the pattern of the subject's fate. At least he is able to demonstrate (albeit unconsciously) the logical necessity of his own fate pattern.

IV

Only one more problem remains to be discussed, and that is the significance of the dancing men. It has been observed that families in which the instinctual and psychological balance between the parents remains sound tend to produce sexually normal offspring. The renegade tendency, on the other hand, breaks loose most readily in those families where parental relationship does not conform to the natural pattern. We may conclude, therefore, that wherever the pattern suffers distortion the tendency of the offspring to depart from type is correspondingly increased.

These fundamental psychological principles have been known and faithfully observed in China for many centuries. In the Chinese classical literature the recognition of the sacredness of the family pattern is laid down as an essential part of filial piety, for both posterity and the ancestors are involved in the consequences of the non-observance of natural principles.

Following the trend of these reflections, we assume that the fate-pattern of the brown figures is determined by the mother-dæmon, that of the blue by the father, while the few black figures represent the individual departure from the ancestral pattern, which in its first daring steps has always worn the aspect of the renegade. It is the black, the sinister, the unsanctioned, the individual and, worst of all, the unrelated.

The man who leaves the fold in order to be by himself is in a position of danger, (*a*) because he is liable to be seduced away upon antisocial ventures which eventually undermine his loyalty to the community; and (*b*) because of the suspicion aroused in his fellows by his oddity and his consequent liability to be excluded from communion in payment of their fears. In Schopenhauer's view, individuality, though admittedly man's greatest achievement, was also his worst crime. Although the new departure is often destructive of ancient and sacred forms, yet the god-value cannot be born again into the human scene unless some man accepts the fate of individual solitariness.

This picture is painted from the standpoint of the collective soul. It is the problem of fate seen from the level of general determinants. From this vantage-point the individual departure must be painted black, because its first passion is usually exercised in a fiery rejection of the pre-existing pattern.

The problem of relatedness or of loyalty to the pact is practically synonymous with the problem of sanity, inasmuch as the one single fact which, in the last analysis, accounts for the presence of the so-called insane person in a mental hospital is his unrelatedness. The old hand among the attendants usually knows when a patient begins to " come back." He sees him helping another patient; there is a new interest in what is going on; the patient begins to co-operate and to want to return into the human communion. Where, then, has the patient been, and what are these deep urgencies which can seduce a man away from his one security?

The security of society rests upon the instinctual acceptance by its members of the sacredness of the human pact. From the fact that this basic instinct, upon which the whole fabric of human society rests, should be surrounded by every conceivable safeguard, we can deduce the strength of the archaic forces which are liable to seize hold of a man and tear him away from his contained security. For this reason primordial forces were worshipped as gods in antiquity. The gods were, in fact, overwhelming psychic urgencies, against which unaided man was powerless.

We have valuable mythological evidence for the fact that the same dæmonic power which, in its unsanctioned antisocial form, was the worst enemy of mankind became the god, the ruling principle, when brought under the sign of the human communion. For the purpose of demonstrating this transformation a Vedic myth, dealing with the raising of soma to divine status, could not be more explicit. It is as follows: " The gods and the Titans strove together for these worlds. They strove for the eastern quarter. The Titans beat them thence." The fight went on round the compass, the Titans winning every quarter of the world until " they strove for the north-eastern quarter; they were not beaten thence. This quarter is the unconquerable." Then the gods took counsel together and they said: " Through our lack of a king they beat us; let us make a king. So they made Soma king. With Soma as king they conquered all the quarters. He who sacrifices has Soma as king. They place Soma in the sacred chariot as it stands facing east; he conquers the east. They carry him round by the south; thereby he conquers the southern quarter," and so on around the compass. The conclusion is: " By Soma, the King, he conquers all the quarters who knows this."[1]

Soma was the name of the plant from which an exceedingly powerful spirit was distilled. It was the dæmon which could inflame men's minds, transporting them in uncontrollable frenzies. And yet after it had been made king we find Soma identified with Agni: it became the holy drink of inspiration, the mead of immortality. It was also identified with the sap of trees and with the seminal fluid. When it was drunk in the communion feast men participated with the god:

> " They feel the god within their veins
> And cry in loud exulting strains
> ' We've quaffed the Soma bright
> And are immortal grown;
> We've entered into light
> And all the gods have known.' "[2]

The Titans symbolized the dæmonic powers of the underworld, the dark forces of the unconscious fighting eternally against the gods of the light-world. Originally soma belonged to the Titans, for intoxication releases the primordial fire which suddenly breaks through and changes a man from a peaceful being into a wild, ungovernable animal.

Faced with this problem of the overwhelming force of the primitive unconscious, some realistic Promethean mind was inspired with the idea of stealing the fire from the primordial dæmons. This event is also recorded in a legend telling how Indra, in the form of a falcon, stole the soma-drink, whereupon the mythic herdsman Kriçanu wounded him in his foot with an arrow.

This legend of the stealing of the soma reveals how fearful men have always been of the daring innovator who brought some new aspect of primordial nature into the service of consciousness. From the standpoint of the primordial unconscious every new acquisition of consciousness is a disturb-

[1] A. M. Hocart: " The Life-giving Myth," published in *The Labyrinth*, edited by S. H. Hooke (S.P.C.K., London).

[2] Taken from Muir's *Original Sanskrit Texts*.

ance of the balance of nature. Human society has consolidated its unique position in the family of nature by an endless series of Promethean encroachments, every one of which, though removing man further from his pristine innocence, improved his biological status. The overvaluation of the human communion is a necessary compensation for man's deep estrangement from his original natural state; hence the renegade who breaks the human pact is outcast by his own treachery. There are many subtle demons which can seduce a man from his human allegiance. He can be seduced by panic, intoxication, sexuality, resentment, illusion, self-pity, the longing for death, the longing for immortality, and even by the longing for insanity.

We can name these dæmonic fascinations as distinct and separate entities; but from another standpoint it is possible to regard them as varying aspects of the deep atavistic will which, in face of a new claim, a new phase of development, or a new evolutionary strain, turns back towards primordial unconsciousness for release. We are committed to the terrifying experiment of consciousness with its increasing momentum; but we are also affected by the backwash which inevitably accompanies it. The one direction leads to the fullest individual consciousness, the other to oblivion. The oblivion may be temporary, as in intoxication or day-dreaming, or permanent, as in suicide or insanity; but in every case the desired haven is the state of unconsciousness. And by this term "unconsciousness" we mean, of course, the disowning of responsibility, the escape from the burden of the human soul.

When we apply the law of the human pact to alcohol and to sexuality it will be obvious that the character of both tends to fulfilment and deep content under the sign of communion, whereas, when pursued in furtive concealment, both can engender cravings whose spell is almost unbreakable. On the other hand, conviviality seldom leads to dipsomania.

The discovery that Soma, the unruly Titan, could be symbolically transformed into Soma, the god-king, was indeed one of the greatest of primitive discoveries. We might go even further and say that all primitive religion is rooted in this fundamental discovery. The terror of the ghost, for instance, resides very largely in the fact that it is essentially an unshared fear. When the ghost is led into the spirit-house, where it comes under the law of communion, it is transformed into the good spirit. What is initiation but the process of inoculating a youth against the isolating dread of the ghost-world just at the moment when he is brought formally under the law of the community? Under the ægis of the human communion he is brought face to face with the worst terrors of the primitive soul. In this way he realizes that there is one indispensable pact upon which his success, his sanity, his very existence depend. It is even more essential that the king, in view of all the special dæmons that can assail the minds of kings, should submit irrevocably to the principle of communion. Hence, at bottom, the coronation ritual is a form of primitive initiation.

Hocart has shown that there exists a single basic archetype of initiation, and that the rituals of coronation, marriage, the ordination of the priest, and other forms of sacred initiation, are all elaborations of the same pattern,[1] the symbolic elements of the ritual remaining relatively constant throughout savage and civilized peoples all over the globe. This is a very remarkable fact, for an archetypal pattern, as Jung has shown, is the cumulative result of a profound instinctual necessity: we must therefore assume that a single fundamental necessity brought into being the various social forms enumerated above. We may express this necessity for academic purposes in terms of a biological or anthropological pattern. But we must also know that we are in the presence of *the* fundamental social impulse, the need to bring those things which are liable to dæmonic manifestations within the human communion, and to hold them by a sacred covenant. Does not the ritual of the Holy Communion draw its sacred power from the same source? The idea of eating the body of the slain God, with the aim of thereby gaining immortality, would, if not sanctified by sacred ritual, fill us with horror and loathing. Indeed, any person who should be independently inspired by such an idea would be, quite

[1] A. M. Hocart: *Kingship*. Oxford University Press.

properly, treated as a dangerous lunatic. Here, then, is a primordial image of immense antiquity which, were it to seize upon an individual mind as a literal truth, would isolate him, completely and for ever, from the human communion. And yet the same image under the pact of communion becomes the most sacred mystery of the Christian religion.

It is hard to think clearly about the character of the primordial image, because it is so profoundly charged with emotional content. Many people are quite unable to understand, or even to listen to, any statement which would seem to call in question the absolute validity of an ancient form. Moreover, there are no words with which to handle these deepest things. When, for instance, we speak of the condition of isolation or unrelatedness as opposed to the state of communion, it might be assumed that isolation corresponded to solitariness and communion to collectivity. But the saint in his solitariness may achieve communion both with nature and humanity, which his extraverted countertype, in a life of prolific and meritorious sociability, may painfully lack. The ability to honour the human pact, whether in marriage or in other fields of social responsibility, rests not upon so-called extraverted enthusiasm, but on the fact that one has made peace with the unconscious.

Everyone threatened with a psychotic upheaval is, to some extent, cut off from human communion. The subject of these drawings habitually lived a far more gregarious life than I myself could tolerate, yet psychologically he was marooned. His major problem had its root in the antisocial tie formed in the plastic years of boyhood, the effects of which, like a deep abscess, gradually worked to the surface during the course of the analysis. With this in mind, the emergent position of the black spot on the horizon is suggestive. As a potential psychotic, the subject felt in part of his nature excluded from the two great communions (viz., marriage and the solidarity of men).

His emotional isolation was due, as we have seen, to the unrelatedness of the complex, yet there was no question at all of his complete awareness of the antisocial relation. Indeed it was because he himself was fully aware of it that he assumed further confession to be unnecessary. It is a common delusion of the intellectual type to assume that knowing a fact is identical with realizing its implications. A mental reservation is really a subsidiary personality that has not accepted the human pact: it is therefore the worst possible enemy to analytical therapy. The unadmitted presence of a renegade reservation in respect to the crucial problem makes further progress impossible, hence the supreme value of confession. If a reservation has been detected it is probably a screen behind which the shadow-personality lies hidden. But when things become serious the existence of the reservation and the shadow will be forced into the light by the superior energy of the therapeutic process. Judging from its effects, confession would seem to be the primary factor in psychological therapy. In the very act of confession a dæmonic element which had secreted about itself a protective sheath of guilt, shame or pride submits to the first law of human communion. Soma is made king.

Every psychological truth is a paradox. The pathological factor which caused the isolation of the complex through the archaic pull of its affect also creates the symbol which alone has the power to convert the dæmonic urgency into the god-king. Whether the power of the King be regarded as a constitutional function or a psychological symbol, it has assuredly been derived from sheer necessity. Eros is the child of Chaos.

* * * * *

The impulse to produce a cosmogonic fantasy reveals a certain creative tendency in the backward-moving libido. The return to the hour before dawn might almost suggest a prenatal fantasy—at all events a profound movement of the patient's libido towards the origins of his world. The swing towards the archaic bottom of the mind became definite in Drawing 11. Out of that came the discovery of "the soul as the self-moving source of all motion," which, in turn, led to the conception of the dæmonic (*i.e.*, dynamic) determination of the psyche, expressed here in cosmogonic symbolism.

The uncanny thing about this painting is its queer combination of archaic mentality and sophisticated irony. The wildly gesticulating marionettes are the product of the habitual aloofness of an observer studying human beings from a distance and from above. Yet this modern spirit of detachment companions an antique conception of fate, represented as a condition of *participation mystique* with certain dæmonic forces. It is possible that an unusual degree of detachment was needed to represent this archaic condition to which all men are unconsciously subject in some degree.

It would be impossible to elucidate this picture from the personal angle only, dealing as it does with phenomena of the collective soul. It is as though a modern Mephisto had taken the patient up to a high place in order to demonstrate to him the general dæmonic springs of human behaviour, and were saying: "Ninety per cent. of human psychology is collective. Let me show you the general power-house by which men and women are driven. They do not realize it, of course, because they are all taken up with what goes on within their personal interior. But look at these fellows dancing on their strings! Where is their vaunted freedom?"

The famous demi-vision of mankind as grains of sand blown by indifferent cosmic winds is doubtless a necessary and incontrovertible aspect of truth. But it is the truth of a world in which, as in this uncanny world of our drawing, individuality has been extinguished, or perhaps not yet been born. We cannot, therefore, accept this half-truth of the devil, unless at the same time we affirm the other half of reality—namely, that individuality is a unique and irreplaceable value, and that a single human being who consciously realizes the height and depth of his being is worth more than a Sahara filled with wind-driven grains of sand.

Christianity has been presented to us as an all-embracing sheepfold. But this idea is foreign to Christ's clearly uttered conception of the Kingdom of Heaven. From many of His sayings we do not get the impression that He was especially interested in the human animal as such, but rather with the man whose eyes were open and who could see and hear and know. Many of the well-known sayings will immediately occur to the reader's mind, but some of the Oxyrhynchus *logia* are not so well known. For example:

> " Jesus saith, I stood in the midst of the world and in the flesh was I seen of them, and I found all men drunken, and none found I athirst among them, and my soul grieveth over the sons of men, because they are blind in their heart and see not. . . ."

Again:

> " Jesus saith, Except ye fast to the world, ye shall in no wise find the kingdom of God; and except ye make the sabbath a real sabbath, ye shall not see the Father."

Or again:

> " Jesus saith, Thou hearest with one ear (but the other thou hast closed)."

And again:

> " Jesus saith, Let not him who seeks . . . cease until he finds, and when he finds he shall be astonished; astonished he shall reach the kingdom, and having reached the kingdom he shall rest."

In this last saying the redeeming condition has no relation to consciousness in the sense of intellectual or perceptual awareness; rather is it the state of astonished realization or wonder.

This, then, is that other truth which must be set over against the shadow's half-truth. It is true that under what we have called " dæmonic " conditions human beings are determined by unconscious forces, just as sand is blown by the wind. It is also true that a man who has realized the Self is himself a world, and cannot any more be obliterated. The experiment of my life is significant, not because it is *mine*, but because life achieves consciousness of itself only in the awakened individual being.

We have now understood why there is no light, and why there are no individual objects in that world of dæmonic powers, for without consciousness there can be no individuality, and is not light the essential symbol of the free spirit of man ? But man is not wholly free. Under the influence of the anima the subject painted this picture of how mankind is determined.

Under the inspiration of the spirit Christ painted a picture of how man can be free. The difference is a matter of consciousness—*i.e.*, of light. The opaque blue and brown of the determining orbs, the fact that the cluster of marionette figures streams into the field from below—that is, from the unconscious side—and that the only relief to be found is in the pin-points of yellow which mark the heads of the marionettes—all these signs testify to the fact that autonomous drawings hold to their truth down to the last detail.

V

Drawing 14

This also is in colour. The background is pale blue with a clear greenish light in it. In the middle of the blue field there is a convoluted line delicately painted in Chinese white. Starting just below the centre of the field, it proceeds in an expanding spiral until it reaches its western limit, whence it coils backwards on itself, flowing in intersecting loops over the upper portion of the spiral to terminate abruptly in the north-eastern area of the field.

A pointed shaft, painted in dull opaque yellow, pierces the convolutions of the line from the direction corresponding to N.N.E., while a longer shaft of blood-red stabs the maze from W.N.W., crossing the yellow shaft approximately at right angles. The fiery red substance which forms the pointed shaft is part of a flowing mass of red issuing from the head of a nude woman who enters from the left. This figure is painted in drab yellows, reminding one of yellow clay. It is three-dimensional, painted with light and shadow, but the face has no features.

In the originals by far the most striking difference between the two pictures lies in the clear halcyon light of the one, contrasted with the opaque, muddy colours of the other. The theme of the last picture was determinism, of the present, freedom.

We observed a very similar alternation between the deterministic conception of the anima in Drawing 9 and the ideal conception of 10. The one was merely mechanical, with no free relation to consciousness, while the other floated in endless freedom, without movement or purpose. With this comparison in mind we can regard the invasion of the flesh-and-blood anima as the timely advent of a much-needed opposition into a monistic universe.

From the standpoint of æsthetics it is interesting that the artist's choice of colour appears to be strictly determined by the nature of the unconscious emotional factors seeking expression in the picture.

The blue of heaven has been restored. In the last drawing the sun was denied and excluded, except for the little pinheads of yellow which seemed to yield a fragmentary kind of awareness to the excited figures. Here the whole field is full of light, except where the realistic, earthy anima invades the field with shafts of fierce red and drab yellow.

The coiling white line is derived from the dance of the released anima in Drawing 12. It has achieved in the meanwhile a certain lofty abstraction, because the subject drew it away from the emotional anima region into the still purity of the upper air. Before, it was part of the personification of release, the symbol of Dionysian extraverted expansion. Here it is an introverted abstraction beginning and ending in empty space.

The idea of the spiral expanding freely in limitless space might represent the longing for unconditioned freedom which is for ever colliding with the cramping relativity of actual life. As it evolves, this primordial day-dream comes face to face, so to say, with the realistic anima-figure, who hurries in to retrieve the healing idea of which neurotic introversion would deprive her. At this intrusion the line immediately turns back upon itself and, instead of an evenly expanding spiral, produces an involuting maze of loops and figures of eight.

The subject is an introverted intuitive type with an intellectual bias. Like all men of this type he has a tendency to elaborate ideas in the realm of the abstract. In this upper air, because they are cut off from their emotional origins, ideas tend to grow thin and to recoil more and more from the ordeal of reality. As a rule, therefore, the development of a compensatory function on the side of reality becomes a matter of vital necessity. It is not at all uncommon for a man of this type to marry a woman of a markedly extraverted, practical nature who, while complementing his psychological one-sidedness, has little or no sympathy with her partner's abstract pursuits.

Such a picture, however, would hardly fit the present case, inasmuch as the subject always had an effective mastery of materials on the technical side. Only on the emotional side, in his personal dealings and relationships, was he unable to steer a reasonable, objective course. This side of his life was accordingly left to an unconscious deputy who naturally landed him in situations in which the only rôle to be played was that of the passive victim.

It is an inescapable fact that the problem for which a man declines to accept conscious responsibility will be relegated to the anima. Moreover, in so far as the anima remains a purely unconscious factor, the problem will be necessarily projected upon the object. Thus the one-sided or dissociated individual tends to encounter the problem he has always evaded in the person of his wife, or in some other object upon whom the anima-projection falls. By this means he is able to cherish the illusion that it is actually the other person who has the problem. The value of the illusion is considerable, for it leaves him free to retire to his intellectual insulating chamber, whence he can view the situation with ironical detachment. For the woman who senses the fact that she is being unjustly saddled with a double burden, this abstracting method of remaining above the battle becomes, naturally, insupportable. And yet the man's crippled dependence upon her, not to mention the tendency of a woman to distrust the value of her own thoughts, usually makes it impossible for her to free herself from the psychological incubus. She is caught by her best quality, and frequently, as J. M. Barrie disclosed in *What Every Woman Knows*, she has the subtle pleasure of enjoying her own unadvertised superiority on the side of reality, while herself advertising the self-evident superiority of the husband in his public capacity.

The freely curving white line in the present drawing is

like the trail left by a sky-writing aeroplane. It is a symptomatic curve written upon the heavens. The sky is the limitless, unconditioned element, in which the spirit can soar through unbounded space. This motive of unfettered expansion is also represented by the spiral unfolding from the centre. The earthy, passional anima enters from the left, projecting forwards a blood-red shaft that pierces the spiral like a thorn. This is the opposite character of the soul, the compensatory, heavy, material, realistic aspect of the anima.

The duality of the soul is a basic conception of Chinese philosophy. Wilhelm describes it as a bipolar tension. According to his account—

> " The body is activated by the interplay of two psychical structures: first, *hun*, which I have translated as the masculine soul, because it belongs to the *yang* principle; and secondly, *p'o*, which belongs to the *yin* principle, and is rendered by me as *anima*. . . . The anima was thought of as especially linked with the bodily processes; at death it sinks to the earth and decays. *Hun*, on the other hand, is the higher soul; after death it rises in the air, where at first it is active for a time, and then evaporates in ethereal space or flows back into the reservoir of life. . . . *Hun* dwells in the eyes, *p'o* in the abdomen. *Hun* is bright and active, *p'o* is dark and earth-bound."[1]

A little later we read:

> " The usual, unchecked, that is downward, movement of the life-processes is the one in which the two souls are related as the intellectual and animal factors. As a rule, it will be the *anima*, the blind will, which, goaded by passions, forces the *hun*-soul or intellect into its service. At least the *anima* will do this to the extent that the intellect directs itself outward, whereby the powers of both leak away and life consumes itself."[2]

In this description Wilhelm identifies the anima wholly with the dark animal side of the soul, whereas in Jung's conception the anima is a dualistic concept, embracing both the ideal and the passional in polar opposition. This concept

[1] Wilhelm and Jung: *The Secret of the Golden Flower*, p. 14.

[2] In making these citations I have omitted the term *animus*, which Wilhelm uses for translating *hun*, since this term is employed by Jung for a quite different conception.

rests upon empirical observations of occidental psychology; we are not as yet in a position to say whether the concept of the ambiguous feminine anima is equally valid in the analysis of orientals.

In regard to the present subject, Drawings 9 and 10 demonstrated the antithesis between the ideal and the passional with diagrammatic clarity. Moreover, as mentioned above, the convoluted white line of the present drawing is obviously derived from the anima-ecstasy of Drawing 12, though removed now from the sphere of the anima and elaborated in and for itself.

Behind the furious entry of the earthy anima we can discern her discovery of the theft and her pursuit of the culprit in outraged mood. Withdrawn into his introverted domain, the subject feels as though his free world of the spirit had been invaded by a tempestuous fury. His sensitive recoil from the emotional attack is represented in the immediate involution of the curve. Directly opposite the approaching anima-figure the expanding spiral falters; then it begins to curve inwards and backwards in a complicated tangle of loops. The evenly expanding spiral corresponds to the normal extraverting movement of the libido or to the unhampered development of a fantasy, whereas the inverted, involved backward course of the curve corresponds to the introverted direction of the libido recoiling from the intrusion of the object.

The term "inverted" would be applicable to the pathological involutions of the curve; the normal *introverting* movement of the libido would be represented graphically by a regular spiral curve moving evenly towards its centre. The presence of this normal extraverted spiral, that is suddenly converted into a morbid inverted tangle, gives us a certain ground for assuming that this patient also began life as an extraverted type, and that the traumatic impact had the effect of forcing his libido inwards, therewith falsifying his natural temperament. This possibility must be borne in mind.

Although this historical connection may have influenced the design we must look for the reason of the anima-onslaught within the scope of the material already presented. This running figure, with its three-dimensional substantiality, is instinct with present purpose. Let us therefore assume that she has a real psychological ground for her anger, and that the stabbing shafts, crossing one another like duellists' blades, are directly expressive of her present errand. The reader will remember the emotional *impasse* represented in Drawings 9 and 10. Then came the descent to the archaic level, followed immediately by the ecstatic anima with the whirling rope. We noted how this line, with its nodal intersections, represented an idea possessing the value of a reconciling principle. In effect, the joy of the anima is the discovery of the soul, the unplanned, unmotivated, unpredictable uprush of meaningful life, the linking-up of spontaneous imagery with purpose. Like every vital discovery this realization was deeply charged with emotion. But, just because it was irrationally charged, the subject's rational consciousness missed its true purpose and significance, which was to reconcile the dissociated aspects of his personality. Before the idea could take effect and bear fruit on the experiential level, it was seized upon by the superior function—viz., intellectual intuition—as a good idea. Taken in and for itself as an abstract proposition, its immediate practical cogency evaporated into thin air.

This tendency to abstract a newly born idea from the sensitive region of personal application into the neutral realm of general propositions is, perhaps, the greatest difficulty in treating intuitive intellectuals. They are only comfortable when an idea has been depersonalized, its poison fangs secretly drawn. It may be the hardest thing to get them to accept an idea as operative, demanding an immediate tangible application.

The primitive anima partakes of the character of an elemental dæmon whose potentiality for life is boundless, though usually involving a problem of self-discipline which cannot safely be ignored. When therefore the reconciling idea is taken out of her hands she behaves like a primitive woman who has been ignored and excluded, attacking the superior logos-realm with elemental fury, determined to recover the divine idea which endowed her passional principle with the sanction of reason.

The red and yellow shafts, together with the masses from which they spring, are obviously intended to represent flesh-and-blood realities, since the colour of the descending thrust is identical with that of the nude figure. We should also observe, in passing, that our intuition about the flame-like character of the woman's hair in Drawing 3 is now confirmed in the vigorous red stream issuing from the head of the present figure. This represents a charge of emotional potential contained in the anima-complex which the patient dreads and from which he instantly recoils.

The allusion to the crossed swords might be taken as a declaration of war. But, bearing in mind the character of the major problem, it is sounder to regard them as a downright and pointed statement of the energic principle of opposition. For without the conflict of opposing factors no energy can be generated. The cross symbolizes both the conflict and the ensuing tension between the opposites. But although this connection is intimated we must beware of the intuitive danger of translating flesh-and-blood dynamics into abstract ideas. These shafts have rather the nature of the witches' shot (*Hexenschuss*),[1] which can suddenly transfix one from behind. There is also the suggestion of some painful or angry thought stabbing the mind like a bayonet thrust. In our understanding of the opposition here depicted we must therefore conceive something disagreeable yet inescapably real.

There is one curious feature that should not be overlooked—namely, the descent of the fleshly shaft from above. From the nature of things we should expect it to irrupt from below. Where does the subject place himself in relation to the contents of the painting? Judging from the position of the shadow of the woman's arm, he is clearly standing below the experience, not above it. From this fact alone we know that this picture has the true character of immediate experience. The reality of the flesh is coming upon him as a superior power. It is a paramount realization. Therefore it descends, like a thunderbolt of Jove, from above.

[1] The characteristic " knife in the back " pain at the onset of acute lumbago is called *Hexenschuss* in Germany.

In contrasting this picture with the one that went before, I should like to emphasize two technical features which, throughout this patient's material, distinguish the intuitive anticipation from a true psychic experience. I have not had sufficient opportunity of studying similar series of drawings by subjects undergoing analysis who were also skilled artists to enable me to draw any general conclusion. But in the case of the present subject the rule certainly applies. When a content or idea is being represented that is merely an anticipation not yet realized, he draws the scene from above and the contents tend to be flat and two-dimensional, whereas when he is representing experience he draws the scene from below, or on a level with the main contents. He also uses a three-dimensional technique.

These indications are of practical value, since it is our aim neither to underrate nor to overrate the worth of these unconscious potentialities. Perhaps the analogy with the egg is not beside the mark; without the care and attention of the parent-bird, with its provision of incubating warmth, the egg quickly dies. Psychotic and psychoneurotic patients frequently have dreams offering potentialities which seem full of life and promise; yet how often is the patient incapable of stretching out a hand to the healing which nature offers.

It is feasible to regard an individual myth as a psychological egg germinating under the introverting warmth of the analytical process. As yet we cannot tell whether it will hatch out and become real or be sucked dry by intellectual fatalism. In relation, for instance, to the drab earth and the marionettes of the previous picture, one could hardly resist a feeling of numbing fatalism. Its arid, inhuman character might be due to a deep deficiency in feeling. Among intellectuals an ironical schizoid attitude is responsible for many psychological eggs remaining unhatched. In any case one is liable to be deceived by the patient's offhand attitude to his products, assuming therefrom that their psychological content is also negligible, whereas a patient who submits his drawings with some indication of the feeling which accompanied them invites a positive attitude on our part. In dealing with schizophrenic drawings it is therefore essential not to be affected too much by the patient's attitude, and to allow the drawings to speak for themselves.

VI

From internal as well as from external evidence we concluded that the previous painting represented a psychic cosmogony taking us back to the early beginnings of culture. And let us not forget that the first scientific quest was concerned, not with the nature of the objective universe, but with the central problem of human fate. Dream-interpretation, divination and astrology, the three great branches of primitive science, all attempted to answer the most poignant questions about the fundamental nature of man. These questions still remain unanswered.

Modern science has built an immense and ever-expanding ring of fortifications around our civilized citadel, but at the centre of this ring the individual soul of man stands naked and neglected. The quest into the nature of the soul which inspired primitive science was practically overlooked by the scientific disciplines which superseded it. But only those things are finally superseded which have been lived out and therewith exhausted of meaning. The primitive form may pass away and be superseded, but not the essential content.

Take, for instance, the case we were considering in the last drawing—namely, the mystery-rites of antiquity which were superseded by the Christian mass. All the pagan mystery-cults were chthonian or earth-cults. The ruling deities were feminine: Demeter, Kore, Hecate, Isis, etc. Pluto, the god of the underworld, was always a secondary personage. The central figure is the great mother, the earth-goddess upon whom the whole fertility of the earth, the cattle and the human family depends.

With the advent of Christianity, the father deity or logos-principle superseded the *magna mater*, giving an exclusively masculine character to Christian theology. But during the Middle Ages the essential content of the pagan mystery religions reasserted itself in the cult of the Virgin, who assumed the essential qualities of fertile motherhood of her pagan forerunners.

Throughout the history of culture we can trace this resurgence of the essential living content of the earlier cult, emerging in the characteristic framework of the later form. If, as we know, the essential quality of the Achæans was preserved as an immortal pearl in the Homeric tradition, and the Arthurian knight re-emerged as the psychological germ of the English gentleman, is it not predictable that these essential relics of primitive science may reappear, not in the form of psychic contaminations to be scoured away from the surface of scientific objectivity, but as the essential material of an enlightened psychology?

We know very well that the specific quest of the early intuitive sciences was not taken over by the scientific disciplines which superseded them. Astronomy does not deal with the problem which inspired astrology, nor has chemistry concerned itself with the high quest of the alchemists, though both chemistry and astronomy sprang demonstrably from the earlier quests.

What happened to the living psychic content which informed original science? Dream-interpretation and divination sank down to a very primitive level, making no pretensions to scientific consideration until Freud rediscovered the dream, at the end of last century, as an agent of therapy. Astrology, left high and dry by the immense expansion of the universe effected by its prodigious offspring, fell into disuse and remained in the scientific lumber-room until to-day, when it begins once again to engage serious attention. Alchemy, the golden dream of the Middle Ages, was not only eclipsed by chemistry, but the whole realm of matter, upon which the mediæval unconscious had been so richly projected, was exhaustively investigated by a score of disciplines, with the result that the mythological content was stripped away from its material container, and left to decay in the purlieus of occultism.

Because of the immense success and prestige of the scientific *Weltanschauung* it was hardly noticed until recently that these central problems of the human soul had been omitted from the fields of modern science and philosophy. To a very large extent psychology itself (by definition the science of the human *soul*) devoted itself to a mechanistic extraverted investigation of the special senses, limiting its survey to those mental faculties from which the non-rational, unpredictable, spontaneous psyche could be excluded.

But it was not only science which left the most essential things out of account: religion suffered even more from the complete ascendancy of the intellect and the scientific order. Primitive religion is vitally concerned with healing, with rebirth and with the actual means of regeneration. In the mediæval Church religious myth and legend concerning the lives and deaths of the saints, of the childhood of Jesus, of the healing love of Mary constituted the essential food of Christendom. Does the Church to-day long to see the cup of the Grail overflow with celestial life-giving radiance, or to understand that spiritual condition which Jesus called the Kingdom of Heaven ? No one could deny that this idea was the essential content of our Lord's teaching, just as the mystery of the Grail was the living heart of mediæval religious myth. Yet the Church scarcely concerns itself with these essential things, and spends its energy and immense organization in extraverted activities which seem especially designed to deflect interest from the religious needs of the soul. It may be that professionalism of any kind is incompatible with genuine spiritual passion.

It would be idle to contend that extraverted science and religion do not serve real human ends. Their social, ethical and cultural values are manifest. But the soul of man is still athirst for the essential things which were left behind in the pre-scientific limbo, things which have lain dormant but are not dead. In the unconscious they await the day of resurrection, ready to break through whenever the spiritual quest is undertaken anew, clothed perhaps in strange archaic garb, and whispering their primordial longings to our dreaming minds.

But are these far-off things really germane to a sophisticated modern man, such, for instance, as the subject of these drawings ? Did he not also leave the essential thing behind in the unconscious, and does he not therefore also await the day of resurrection, when the unconscious shall give up its sleeping dead ? It is surely this direct parallelism between the personal and the general unconscious which constellates the general contents in this way. Moreover, the withdrawal in the last drawing from the personal conception of fate in terms of the mother and father was in itself an important therapeutic step, because it furthered the attitude of detachment whereby the way for a psychological instead of a personal conception of fate was made possible. The impersonal astrological approach helped to beget the *amor fati* of antiquity, which not only embraced the idea of submission to the will of heaven but also sponsored the Christian virtues of humane tolerance and compassion.

The importance of the analogical reference to early chthonian mysteries, in suggesting a supra-personal maternal symbol for the regressive infantile longing, cannot be over-estimated. In the same way the education of the soul from the state of infantile dependence upon the parents has been the care of the great religious systems, which always attempted to lead the infantile libido away from the actual parents into the service of the universal mother and father archetypes.

The attitude of remoteness which characterized the previous picture was therefore a necessary preliminary to the solution of the problem. Yet, with an intellectual schizophrenic subject, the tendency to ironical detachment is also a peculiar danger. Having detached himself from the problem, he is liable to assume that nothing further can legitimately be demanded of him.

This *laisser-aller* enticement is indicated in the present picture in the exquisite white line which begins and ends in the unconditioned freedom of heaven. Actually, the work of liberation has still to be done. The subject is not permitted to be free above and fettered below. Therefore the anima, which can be regarded as the personification of fate in the individual psyche, brings him back to the actual realities of his situation. She asserts in vigorous symbolism that no reconciliation of the dissociated parts of his nature can be effected without conflict. He has to endure the torment of apparently irreconcilable opposition; to be transfixed by, and even crucified upon, the opposites.

We noted the fact in the last picture—which if our deductions were correct represented the cosmogonic viewpoint of the primordial psyche—that the brown sphere of the maternal principle stood in the position of ruler. Whereas the present scene represents the upper regions of the masculine intellect, from which the feminine principle is normally excluded. We might infer from this striking alternation of standpoint that the heroic Gilgamish attitude[1] of the masculine intellect is a psychological compensation for the predominance of the feminine principle in the patient's unconscious. There is, in fact, a good deal of evidence that this is true of educated Western man in general; but it would take us too far afield to discuss this evidence in the present work.

As regards the present drawing, it is, I think, self-evident that, by identifying himself with his intellectual conscious standpoint, the subject is again evading the real issue. It is because of this evasion that his blue logos-sphere is invaded.

There is, of course, another and very crucial reason why the anima has to press her demands with great energy at the present juncture, although this reason is not stated in the contents of the drawing. The black sphere of the previous picture alluded to the emotional content of the traumatic complex, which through the antisocial pact had gone over to the side of the renegade tendency. The anima, as soul-mistress, is the natural custodian of the passional libido. Having been robbed of an essential part of the inherited vital energy which, by the way, she is clearly determined to recover, she is naturally alive to the prospective dissolution of the traumatic complex, with its sequestered energy-content. It is understandable, therefore, that a retreat from the problem at this juncture would provoke the anima to assault.

Had the subject maintained detachment from both sides, the anima would not have been forced into this rôle. It is because the subject retreats to his one-sided conscious standpoint that the anima assumes the aspect of an alien power.

[1] Throughout the myth the attitude of Gilgamish is arrogantly masculine. There is therefore natural equity in the final episode where a water-snake, representing the dark chthonian element, steals the herb of eternal youth.

VII

DRAWING 15

This drawing gives one a decidedly disagreeable feeling, for which, at first sight, there are no obvious grounds. It consists of a globe, somewhat flattened at the pole. This is marked with geographical lines of latitude and longitude, a fact which warns us that the counter-tendency of control has been summoned hastily into action. These lines are carelessly drawn; the longitudinal lines could not conceivably meet at the pole. The globe, too, is as it were squeezed downwards, so that only about two-thirds of its bulk appears on the paper. The relative disposition of land and water is unlike any part of the earth's surface. Taking the known, familiar earth as our criterion, we must suppose that the surface of this subjective globe is almost covered by a deluge. There remains one relatively large island in the extreme west. Upon the next largest, to the south-east, a figure stands with upraised arms and grotesquely magnified hands and feet. It is orientated towards the pole, while the face is directed upwards to the zenith with an air of piteous appeal. The remaining islands are quite small, and are dotted about, either singly or in groups of two or three.

Detached from the globe, and lying almost horizontally across the upper left portion of the field, is a thick jagged slice of some solid brittle substance. It lies suspended above the pole like a cloud; its jagged lower edge suggests a broken sheet of ice, yet a series of branching lines on its upper surface, somewhat resembling river courses, conveys the suggestion of a fragment of land surface. There are seven of these branching lines which terminate at fairly regular intervals at the lower edge. The terminal line of each ends at the apex of a sharp indentation of the fractured edge, a fact which would favour the hypothesis that the whole mass is a broken sheet of ice, to which the patient also agreed.

The line of the upper surface of this mass forms the profile of a face. The jutting promontory in the middle of the line forms an irregular, pendulous nose. The nasal fold can be seen curving forwards towards a small lake, which might represent the nostril. At the top of the nose there is a deep indentation, above which juts the overhanging brow. Just above and behind the indentation there is a closed eye, marked by four radiating lashes. A wrinkle traverses the forehead. Beneath the nose, the upper lip of the mouth can be made out with what appears to be the tongue hanging from it. Below this comes the beard.

I had not observed this face until the patient pointed it out to me. He said he noticed it after the main outline had been drawn. He then added a few touches, such as the four eyelashes and the line of the mouth, "just to give the unconscious a hand." The face, taken as a whole, is that of a dilapidated old man, and its general effect is extremely disagreeable, not to say sinister. It might be the face of an outworn and crumbling deity.

Below the beard of this ancient one, and just beyond the western border of the globe, is a small, irregular, spherical object which appears to be a kind of satellite. It consists of a firm outline, that is clearly not intended to be circular, enclosing a thin spattering of very fine dots.

* * * * *

The subject is looking down upon his world from a great height, and nowhere do we find the light and shadow of terrestrial reality. From this elevation he can look down, without feeling too much involved, upon his flooded world. Were he to listen he might hear the cries of the solitary, marooned survivor, who is of course himself, the self that is threatened by the rising waters of the unconscious. Yet he was able to draw this manifest presentiment of psychotic catastrophe without, so far as I could tell, any deep commotion. It was as though he had the faculty of severing his ego from the emotional plane and withdrawing to a distance, where a cool but somewhat artificial detachment anæsthetized his power of realization.

This faculty is, I believe, characteristic of borderline states. The case quoted from Prinzhorn, where the patient perceived the train of images far off in the sky, provides another example of this recession of consciousness from the disturbing events of the unconscious. Another favourite type of borderline fantasy consists of an island or coastline seen from a distance, with a precipitous cliff of immense height dropping sheer to the ocean. Such images are vividly remembered and tend to recur when an acute phase threatens. The patient may speak of them with intense excitement as though he had looked over the rim of the world and felt a great need to communicate what he had seen. It is noteworthy, however, that as a rule these patients prefer to leave these fantasy danger-signals unexplained. There is sometimes a sense of vertigo, as though they felt themselves to be standing on the edge of a precipice. The vertigo which warns individuals with a somewhat unstable psychology not to go too near the edge of a cliff, almost certainly springs from a latent fear of insanity or suicide.

From the viewpoint of our psychological investigation, the most significant feature of this drawing is the impending schizophrenic cloud. In order to understand this figure thoroughly we shall have to analyse its various ingredients or tributaries. *First*, it is clearly associated with the jagged schizophrenic split in Drawing 3. *Secondly*, it is a split-off or dissociated fragment that at one time, presumably, has been incorporated in the subject's world. *Thirdly*, it consists obviously of some hard, relatively inelastic substance, like glass or ice. *Fourthly*, the numerous rivers with their tributaries suggest the idea that many different psychic systems have flowed into it, or, at all events, that it has had at one time a number of organic connections with the rest of the psyche. *Lastly*, the face of the dilapidated, bearded ancient with fast-closed eye and wrinkled brow would seem to represent a psychic system that has had ruling power, but now, having reached its term, begins to disintegrate.

The juxtaposition of this vast crumbling icefloe to the flooded world just below is also significant. Ice presents a brittle, resistant, smooth surface, concealing the river which flows beneath. It is therefore analogous to the polished, repressive, conventionally adapted persona which prevents the turbulent emotional undercurrents from breaking through. The glacial untouchability which so often characterizes the schizoid persona is, in fact, the expression of an abnormally resistant threshold created by consciousness to withstand the ever-present danger of inundation from the irrational unconscious.

The analogy of the break-up of the icefloes by the torrents of spring is also relevant, therefore, to the content of this drawing. With this allusion in mind, the mythological association of the death of the old god in the pagan Easter rituals will readily suggest itself. In many parts of Europe the ceremonial burning of the old god[1] is still practised, and this is often associated with feasting and carnival, in which the dionysiac release from normal inhibitions and taboos connotes a symbolical participation in nature's release from the icy hand of winter. These associations are, moreover, in keeping with the position of this aerial icefloe, inasmuch as the subject has placed it in relation to the north pole of his world.

Synthesizing these various tributary associations into a coherent conception, it would run somewhat as follows: Something has occurred which has had the effect of relegating the persona, the traditional ruler of the subject's world, to the position of a dissociated outworn power. The persona was the collectively adapted, disciplined system upon which he always relied for his male security over against the irrational, feminine unconscious. It was fed from many traditional sources; but now, like a crumbling icefloe dissolving in the spring floods, it begins to disintegrate.

The disintegration of a long-established habitual attitude is often represented in dream or fantasy as a cataclysm. It is the *Götterdämmerung* of the conservative groundwork of consciousness, and is frequently accompanied by disturbing physical sensations. It is not unusual for the patient actually to feel the ground rocking beneath his feet, or the chair in which he is sitting to sway, as in a storm at sea, or perhaps his bed seems to be sliding across the room. These physical

[1] It is generally assumed by anthropologists that the " old god " who is burnt at the spring festival is the vegetational god of the year that is dead. I discovered in Switzerland, however, that the peasants actually participating in these rites believe that they are burning the god of winter. The two ideas have a very different psychological connotation.

sensations may be accompanied by vertiginous fantasies, dreams of falling from a height, or of struggling in tumultuous waters.

Signs of this state of mental confusion are not lacking in the present drawing. Apart from the flooded world, the crumbling schizophrenic ice-cloud, and the distressed, appealing figure on his insufficient island, there are signs of disturbance in the actual technique of the drawing. In the case of so careful a draughtsman, the impossible disposition of the lines of longitude and latitude shows considerable disturbance of concentration. The quality of line is also inferior, compared with earlier drawings. There is also the fact that the globe is misshapen and seems to be sinking out of the picture, two very significant indications in the case of a subject for whom structural balance and design are vital to his *métier*.

The fact that the distressed figure makes his appeal in the direction of the crumbling deity, instead of facing the subject or the observer, as we would naturally expect, is another rather subtle sign that the habitual orientation of the psyche has been under the sway of the now crumbling deity.

A curious feature presents itself in the shape of the island upon which the figure stands. If the reader will turn the picture upside-down, he will observe that the island has the shape of a tortoise. Since, *ex hypothesi*, we are not permitted to explain autonomous representations as accidents, we must assume that this tortoise is a purposive content, even though the subject was unaware of its presence.

VIII

The tortoise plays an important rôle in many early cosmogonies. In Hindu legend the world is likened to a lotus flower that floats in the midst of a shallow vessel. The vessel rests on the back of an elephant, and the elephant stands on the back of a tortoise. In American Indian mythology there is a Seneca myth of a celestial tree bearing flowers and fruit the whole year round; its branches pierced the sky, and its roots reached down to the waters of the underworld. It was pulled up by the order of the Big Chief, and a vast pit was left where its roots had been. A waterfall carried the sky-goddess into this pit, and there she found the tortoise upon whose back she rides.[1]

The Delaware Indians believed that all things came from a tortoise. " It had brought forth the world, and in the middle of its back a tree had sprung from whose branches men had grown."[2] In China the tortoise is one of the four supernatural or divinely constituted animals. These are the unicorn, the phœnix, the tortoise and the dragon. They are called the *ling*, which can be translated as spiritual beings. It is related how the Great Plan, which was the foundation of physics, astrology, divination, morals, politics and religion, was delivered to the great Yü by a tortoise, which came up out of the River Lo in the time of the great flood. The sage was, indeed, engaged in his celebrated work of draining off the waters of the flood when he discovered the " writing " or " map " on the back of the tortoise.[3]

Tortoiseshell was used in China in one of the two chief methods of divination because, as a symbol of longevity and the power of transformation, the tortoise was credited with immense wisdom. In Greek art Aphrodite is sometimes represented standing on a tortoise, and among the Egyptians it was also a symbol of fertility. As the creature who carries the world upon its shell the tortoise is the cause of earthquakes. Normally the earth-tortoise sleeps, but when it awakens and stirs all nature is convulsed.

The list of sources could be prolonged indefinitely, for the tortoise has to do with the idea of origin: it is the primordial, slumbering earth-dæmon, the concealed root-power in nature which sustains everything. In the East it is also identified with introversion. We find, for example, a passage in the *Bhagavad-Gita* where a man confirmed in spiritual knowledge is likened to the tortoise, who " can draw in all his senses and restrain them from their wonted purpose."

[1] Arthur C. Parker: *Certain Iroquois Tree Myths and Symbols.*
[2] *Ibid.*
[3] Introduction to the *Yi King* by James Legge. *Sacred Books of the East*, edited by Max-Müller, vol. xvi.

The analogy with the aforementioned tortoise who provided the sage with the Great Writing or Plan in the very moment when he was coping with the waters of the great flood, is so appropriate to the content of the drawing that the appearance of the tortoise at this juncture would seem to be equally providential for the patient. Since the tortoise belongs to the essential content of the drawing, our doubt as to the subject's volition in regard to it is not relevant to its appearance. Instead of drawing it with pen and ink he might as well have dreamed it. The wish to ascribe conscious purpose to these so-called accidents is really nothing more than a legal prejudice.

The curious way in which the appealing figure has been drawn suggests some contamination with a primordial image other than that of the human form. The character of the feet, arm and hands, for example, is more suggestive of vegetational than of animal limbs. The bulbous fingers and thumb remind one of the way seaweed expands when it floats. Be this as it may (for taken by themselves these nuances are relatively insubstantial), this last survivor of a flooded world, standing on the island of the tortoise, clearly suggests the possible starting-point of a new world order.

Noah, Uta-Napishtim, Deucalion—all the famous survivors of the deluge, survived through their power of listening to the voice of the tortoise. The man fitted to survive a cataclysm is the one whose mind is attuned to the subtlest indications of nature, both within and without. This is surely the meaning of the great writing imparted to the sage by the tortoise. The sage is one who has learned to go aside and commune with himself. In a tight place the African native will go into the bush and talk to his snake—*i.e.*, his bush-soul. In the last resort wisdom is the ability to consult, understand and follow instinctive guidance. This simplest yet subtlest of truths is symbolized by the tortoise, the archetypal introvert.

The *Yi King*, usually known as The Book of Changes, is an exceedingly refined and delicate system of divination. The wisdom of China succeeded in developing the primordial intuitive sciences,[1] referred to above, into a comprehensive method of psychological prognostication based upon the principle of synchronicity. Notwithstanding the fact that some of the greatest minds of ancient China devoted a life-time of devotion and reflection to the study and elaboration of this great system, it retains the primordial character of tortoise-wisdom. It is, in fact, the subtlest possible medium by which a man beset by a thorny problem is enabled to attune his mind to impersonal instinctual guidance, almost as though the unconscious were speaking to him through the mouth of a Chinese sage. In the authority of the *Yi* instinct was married to wisdom. By employing the fifty yarrow sticks in the correct way it was possible to obtain a presentation of the actual psychological situation and at the same time to obtain a prognostication indicating how the situation would develop. For the second hexagram, which is made by traditional rules out of the first, develops those elements which were latent in the first as unconscious tendencies.

The solitary survivor of the flood in the present picture illustrates this dual presentation in a very beautiful way. As a statement of the urgency of the actual situation a distressful creature is presented, marooned on a small island and appealing to the skies for help. This is, I believe, what the patient intended. But the far-seeing wisdom of the unconscious added a symbol, relating to the prospective development, which gives a wholly different complexion to the present urgency. For by turning the island into a tortoise, and the human figure into a tree stretching its branches to heaven, a powerful instinctive stabilizer is evoked. Remembering the Delaware myth of the world-tree that grew from the back of the tortoise, we can also discern the indigenous roots from which this stabilizing power springs.

Wotan sacrificed an eye in order to gain the peculiar dark wisdom of the earth-goddess. Wotan is a personification of the intuitive sky-principle which apprehends things

[1] Compare the constellation that emerged from the unconscious on the back of the tortoise (the Great Plan was supposed to have been discerned in the squares of the tortoise-shell)—namely, Physics, Astrology, Divination, Morals, Politics and Religion, all concerned with essential human interests.

from above and in the large; but the wisdom of Erda is like the concealed life of the seed which contains all the intricate knowledge of growth and change and transformation. Hence the idea of the world-tree which grows out of the tortoise, and the use of tortoiseshell for purposes of divination. The inherited wisdom of instinct is not manifest. Only rarely does it burst upon the mind in the form of revelation. Usually one must dig for it, find its secret hiding-place, coax it to appear. It is shy, oblique, and almost incommunicable. Yet it is the tap-root of maturity: on the tortoise stands the radiant figure of Aphrodite.

As a prognostic sign, therefore, the "accidental" tortoise tells us a great deal. With this primordial creature to bear him up we could almost predict that the lone survivor, like Noah, will outlive the deluge.

IX

With regard to the small irregular satellite on the western border the subject could say nothing, except that it was like a seed. We observed a rather similar satellite near to the darkened sun in Drawing 5. A parallelism might easily link the two, for in both drawings the state in which consciousness is being overwhelmed by the unconscious is depicted. We know that the main pathological tendency in schizophrenia is the disruption of the cohesion of consciousness. In a normal psychology a vital stream of purpose and control holds the various psychic elements and systems in coherent connection. But in the schizophrenic the emotional directive current of energy is somehow impeded. The centralizing sense of purpose being proportionately weaker, the contrary centrifugal or disruptive tendency is often painfully manifest. The impeded attention, the forgetfulness, the emotional apathy, and the inconsequent associations of the schizophrenic are all symptomatic of this pathological increase of the disjunctive tendency. Ideas tend to fly off at a tangent, the thread is easily lost, and what started as a coherent train of ideas gradually disperses and evaporates.

Recent experiments with mosaics conducted by Dr. M. Lowenfeld's assistants under Dr. Bernard Armitage at Bethlem Hospital promise interesting results. They found, for instance, that the schizophrenic mosaic frequently consists of discrete groups of pattern elements not yet combining into a coherent design. Sometimes these islands are relatively complete in themselves, but, as a rule, they are mere fragments that fail to cohere into a centralized pattern.

From this point of view the present drawing shows two independent, dissociated factors in proximity to a flooded world. We must conceive these two subsidiary masses as either detaching from or merging with the main mass. To exist independently so near to the world's mass would be physically impossible. The signs of disintegration and decay are self-evident in the crumbling patriarchal icefloe. The jagged, broken edge is even suggestive of violence. As it stands it is unassimilable; only if it were dissolved into its constituent elements could it be reassimilated.

With regard to the other object, it has more the air of a separate independent system, of being already adapted to a self-contained existence. If at some time it has been broken off from the larger mass, its fractured angularities have been smoothed away by friction, giving it the organic, spherical form of an independent unit. The tiny seed particles just visible on its surface belong to an entirely different constitution from that of the disintegrating mass above. These tiny particles are suggestive of cells, atoms, electrons, in other words, the elementary foundation of physical bodies. Whereas all the visible constituents of the fractured mass, the river systems, the jagged edge, and the various features of the ancient's face, represent terminal aspects of a differentiated order or system that is already breaking up. So far as its outline is concerned, this larger fragment approximates in character to the irregular land surfaces scattered over the flooded globe—that is to say, part of an organic whole—whereas the small, globular fragment stands in marked contrast to the large, irregular island just beside it.

We can infer from these observations that the upper fragment represents an historical aspect or attitude, which has become split off from the organized psychic whole and is now disintegrating into its elementary constituents. We may also assume that the smaller fragment represents an autonomous unit adapted to an independent life, and that it contains the germinal potentiality of a new development. The former has to be extruded, like an unassimilable foreign body or fragment of necrosed bone, while the latter needs to be assimilated by the psyche, very much as a larger drop of water takes a smaller one into itself. *Vale atque salve* would therefore represent this aspect of the drawing.

X

We have now to trace the developmental continuity of the situation here depicted. It is primarily concerned with the activation of the unconscious which accompanies every serious attempt to get to the roots of a psychic disorder. It is a pathological picture of the introversion of the libido. This introverted attack was indicated in the first drawing of the series, in which a consolidated group of hands represented the concentration of psychic energy towards the pathological area. The same phenomenon was observed in the former patient's material, in the mobilization of all libido tributaries towards the area of pathological dissociation in Drawing III.

The result of this purposive concentration of libido into the unconscious is to produce a corresponding animation of hitherto dormant unconscious contents. Functional claims that have always been ignored begin to clamour for consideration, and instinctual elements, repressed as socially incompatible, now demand an effective participation in life.

This transitional period has very much the character of histolysis—that is to say, the breaking-down or dissolution of outworn larval forms, and the formation of a more complex structure. During this relatively fluid phase the psyche is highly sensitive and vulnerable to inimical influences; therefore the patient should be protected as much as possible from bad psychological conditions. The successful course of the analysis depends very largely, at this juncture, on the fundamental reasonableness and integrity of the patient's conscious attitude. As old landmarks are carried away and the watertight compartments of protective prejudice begin to cave in, the sense of dissolution is liable to be most disturbing. During this phase dreams of inundation, or of being overwhelmed by a tidal wave, or of the land being invaded by enemy forces are liable to occur.

In the present series we found evidence (in Drawings 9 and 10) of dangerous psychological compartments in the way the ideal aspect of the anima was prohibited from any liaison with the dynamic. Then came the dive downwards to the archaic level, seeking the underlying continuity below these artificial bulkheads. This was followed by an intense feeling of release, symbolized by the ecstatic anima-dance. An archaic, cosmogonic view of fate was succeeded by the invasion of the anima into the intellectual realm.

Clearly this intrusion of the hitherto excluded anima into the domain of the superior function was responsible for the collapse of the sky deity. The *Götterdämmerung* motif coincides with the hero's challenge of the old order. Siegfried's challenge does not spring from the truculent arrogance of youth: he is simply fearless and single-minded, whereas Wotan is shadowed by a wrong. Siegfried and Parsifal are effective because they are whole and simple. They are naturally successful in their challenge of the partial and outworn.

The realistic advent of the anima, the purpose and cogency of her shafts, signify this same superior efficacy. Prejudices, evasions, self-deceiving rationalizations, bulkheads of respectability, all the old retainers of the mind whose sole concern is to preserve persona-prestige—all must go when the challenge becomes real. In presence of the immediate experience of the unconscious, sophistication can say nothing. Only the essential and the durable can survive the flood.

In the Gilgamish Epos we are given a dramatic picture of the gods conspiring together to bring about the deluge.

We see them huddled together in horror while mankind and all living things are being swallowed by the waters of chaos. Enlil the storm-dæmon and war-god is the protagonist of destruction, while Ea-Oannes (the Sumerian Osiris-Prometheus deity, who first brought agriculture and civilization to mankind) is the humane preserver. Thus Enlil, like the anima-figure of Drawing 14, represents the dæmonic, creative-destructive urgency of the primordial psyche.

Ea is powerless to prevent the doom that is prepared for mankind, but he chooses Uta-Napishtim (the Sumerian Noah) to be the bearer of life through the flood. Because Ea is a party to the fateful council of the gods, he may not disclose directly to Uta-Napishtim what is impending. So he gives his detailed instructions to the reed-hut in which Uta-Napishtim sleeps, telling its walls to hearken and consider. The walls of the hut, having listened to the god's instructions, impart them again to Uta-Napishtim in the form of a dream.[1] Thus, in all the known versions of the deluge myth, the motive to rescue or to conserve human values is located in the ancestral unconscious—*i.e.*, the realm of the gods—and the man who is fitted to survive the catastrophe is the one who not only listens to the inner counsel, but who acts upon it.

The gods of the myth are the archetypal images, the primordial instinctual powers of the unconscious. Everyone whose psychological orientation is exclusively collective will naturally tend to disregard the warning and guiding intimations of the unconscious, because the collectively identified psychology prefers the support of generally accepted views. Everything else is suspect. At bottom this is the attitude of the obedient child listening only to what he is told by the all-knowing parent. But the mature man has a deeper purpose in life than conformity with the given pattern. It is clear to every part of him that individuality cannot be satisfied by the ideal of collective adaptation; nor is the way trodden by the mass necessarily the way of redemption.

[1] In connection with the tortoise who emerges out of the deluge, it is significant that when Ea-Oannes first visited mankind to teach them the arts of civilization he is said to have come out of the sea.

The realization that individual responsibility and freedom are rooted in an older and therefore greater authority than that of collective conformity coincides with the arrival of psychological puberty. Under normal conditions maturity should be reached between the ages of twenty-five and thirty; but, just as there are many whose sexual psychology remains at the biological pre-puberty level, so there are vast numbers of human beings who never cross the great divide into psychological maturity.

This conflict between the voice of collective sanction and the inner command of the self prepares the way for the individual solution of the problem. Before the great divide is reached, it is not only superfluous but ill-advised to speak of the problem of dual allegiance. There are, moreover, certain critical phases of national life when regression to totalitarian authority may become essential, that national integrity be preserved. But, unless we cling to the idea that the goal of human achievement is a collective organization based on the pattern of the ant or the bee, we must accept this problem of the dual allegiance of the human soul as the essential condition of individual consciousness. The problem is symbolically represented by the authoritarian tribal or ancestral deity, on the one hand, and the primordial representative of the instinct—*e.g.*, the snake or the tortoise—on the other. If the fruits of the tree of knowledge are regarded as essential to individual maturity, then the voice of the unconscious, the primordial earth-wisdom, must be accepted as having equal validity with, and at certain crises even greater authority than, that of the prevailing collective code.

The advent of this problem is beautifully indicated in the present drawing, where we see the arms and the head of the solitary figure raised in childish appeal to the old god, whose eye is closed and whose potency has gone, while at the same time the feet are firmly planted on the back of the primordial tortoise. Here again the situation can be expressed by the *vale atque salve* of emergent individuality.

In this emergency, when the familiar landmarks of the

former adaptation are being swept away by the inundation of the unconscious, the appeal to the collective deity falls upon deaf ears. The example of Noah and Uta-Napishtim, who hearkened to the inner guidance of the dream, becomes then the counsel of necessity.

DRAWING 16.

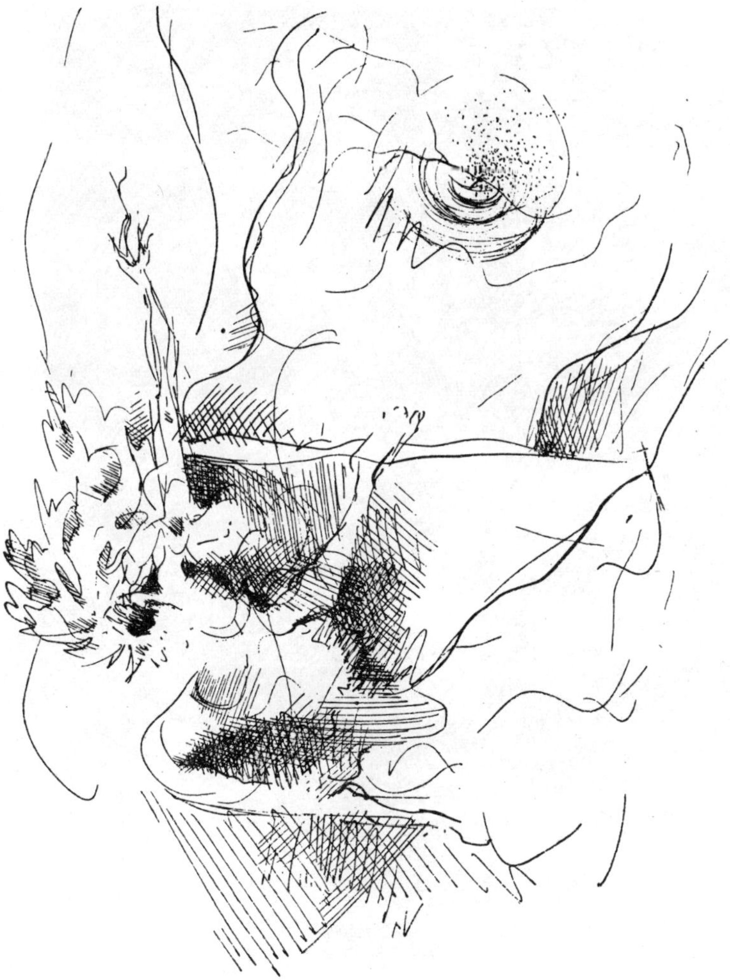

DRAWING 17.

DRAWING 18.

CHAPTER VI

TRANSFORMATION FROM ANIMAL TO TREE

I

A CERTAIN change is noticeable in the material at this point. The drawings of the previous chapter represented a profound psychological revolution, in which the outworn values of the collective façade began to be replaced by introverted tortoise-wisdom. This event is like the end of an epoch; the old ruler is displaced and a new reign begins. The dynamic invasion of the anima into the realm of conscious freedom (in Drawing 14) made the absolute monistic conception of consciousness no longer tenable. The debacle was inevitable because, whether in the hierarchy of the psyche or of the state, the position of an absolute ruler is one of increasing tension and suspicion, due to the fact that his supremacy is maintained by the repression of every other element which could rival his ascendancy. The repressed antithesis is the hero's vulnerable spot. What is repressed is not extinguished: the ever-increasing tension caused by the repression of essential vital elements mounts eventually to an explosion. This may result in irremediable collapse or in a life-saving realization. The advent of realization in the individual psyche is the birth of the soul.

Under the dynamic conception of the mind, the soul is the vehicle of the inherent vital purpose—not the schemes and arrangements of conscious ambition, but rather the inherited life-will containing the unfulfilled psychic potential. There are, however, vast numbers of men who prefer to remain unconscious of what their soul demands of them. When a man with a certain potential hides himself in too poor a philosophy, which leaves no room for the soul with its long-range purpose, the anima remains on the unconscious dæmonic level as a more or less blind autonomous *dynamis*. In this condition the soul is unfree, and the psychological condition exhibits unmistakable signs of compulsion. On the other hand, as an introverted function of relation to the unconscious the anima appears in an entirely different light, eventually assuming the character of a ministering function. In the former condition the anima-complex is dæmonic, like a blind force of nature. In the latter the anima is an effective coadjutor, the source of every fertile idea and new combination, while gradually creating an indispensable extension of consciousness in relation to the deep unconscious contents.

At the close of the preceding chapter we witnessed the decay of the hitherto prevailing conscious attitude, and the deluge which accompanied it. This signified the overthrow of the dictatorship of the collective persona by the forces of the unconscious. Clearly, therefore, the conception now to arise will tend to proclaim the primacy and superiority of the unconscious. Immediate experience of the unconscious, with its self-moving activity, has a profound effect upon one's basic attitude. Side by side with one's modern consciousness one becomes aware of another mental attitude viewing the situation from different premises, more perhaps from the viewpoint of the primitive mind. Sometimes it walks in step with one's conscious aims and purposes; sometimes it stands aloof with stony eyes, refusing, like Enkidu, to be persuaded that some enthusiastic proposition of the ego is worth bothering about. At such moments the existence of psychic duality may become painfully manifest. But there is nothing to be done about it: having once accepted the unconscious as an effective part of one's personality, one must learn to become reconciled with the primitive point of view. We shall see, perhaps, how this problem begins to make its presence felt in the patient's material.

II

Drawing 16

Two distinct elements, abstracted from previous drawings, are disposed here in a somewhat antithetical relationship in a plain field. One element is represented by two flowing lines, which proceed in a succession of open and closed curves from left to right across the sheet. The other is represented by eight sharply pointed cones, of varying sizes, distributed at irregular intervals over the field.

The two lines, after intersecting near their source on the left, settle down to a roughly parallel course, manifested in general direction, medial complexity, and in the upward sweep of their terminal curves. Both lines show an alternation of thick and thin strokes. In general, the broad open curves tend to be heavily drawn, while in the loops and the more involved parts the line is thin. There are also one or two loose ends, as though at certain points the line had become frayed.

A particular technique has been used in the drawing of the eight cones. Obviously they are not intended to be static geometrical figures. They rest on no base-line, while the interior of each cone consists of an increasingly dense spattering of fine dots. At the bottom of the cone, and below the commencement of the lateral lines, these dots or granules are relatively sparse. But as they approach the long, thorn-like point the granules thicken into solid black.

The four cones on the left are disposed in a graded series ascending steeply from the left, while the remaining four seem to be placed (as in Drawing IV. of the previous series) in the relation of diagonal reciprocity, the two smaller forming one pair, the two larger the other, the whole thus forming a rough quadrilateral.

Regarding the cones in this way, as disposed into two groups of four, we observe that the ascending series on the left coincides with the relatively simple first portion of the flowing lines, while the second quadrilateral grouping coincides with the involuting medial part, whence the two lines gather themselves for the strong terminal movement towards the right.

All the cones point upwards. Only two actually intersect a line. The large terminal member of the left-hand series cuts the upper line near the summit of its curve, whilst the lower right-hand member of the second group cuts the lower line in the course of its long terminal sweep.

* * * * *

The two elements of this picture, the flowing and the piercing, have obviously been abstracted from Drawing 14. But in that drawing the line started as a spiral, and only assumed its later involuted character when recoiling from the invading anima. The reader will remember that this line was the skipping-rope of the anima in its original appearance, and that we traced the nodal points of intersection on the rope to the archipelago of archaic *insulæ* in the drawing previous to that.

Without this sequential retrospect to help us this drawing would be unintelligible. As it is, we can be reasonably certain that the subject is preoccupied with the problem of two incompatible ideas which must somehow be reconciled. The flowing lines suggest the idea of the continuity of the mental stream, while the cones suggest the notion of something impinging upon, or thrusting into, the conscious stream from below.

At this point we are at once reminded of Jung's original experiments in word-association—due in part to the patient's abstract statement of the problem—in which he observed how the stream of associations was broken at certain points by the intrusion of a complex whose affective charge had been released by some associative connection with the test-word. From the viewpoint of the observer, this appears as an irrational interruption of the normal flow of ideas. But, if the same event could be recorded subjectively, the complex would seem like a rock dividing the water of a stream, or like the pylon of a bridge which breaks the flow and causes an eddy on the surface.

It is evident, I think, that a structural conception is connected with these cones. I assume this to be the case on four distinct grounds. *Firstly*, the cones are disposed in two groups of four, and four is the archetype of structure. *Secondly*, the left-hand group of four is arranged in an ascending scale. It is, in fact, a hierarchy, and a hierarchy of value is essential to psychical structure. *Thirdly*, the right-hand group of four forms a quadrilateral figure, in which the idea of reciprocal balance is suggested by the paired cones of the two diagonals. *Fourthly*, there is a structural connotation in the fact that all the cones are upright and that, in each cone, there is a concentration of molecular elements towards the point.

I have observed that borderline patients are frequently beset by a sense of contradiction between the intellectual conception of psychical structure—borrowed perhaps from brain anatomy—and their actual experience of the conscious stream. This conflict of the mental concept versus experience tends to be represented, as here, in abstract symbolism, which again suggests the constant striving of the intellect to obtain control over experience.

The two opposing elements, representing the initial theme of this new phase, can be represented, then, as independent structure versus flow or continuity. The reader will recall that this same theme attracted the patient's interest before, when he came across Jung's analogy of the islands and the mountain chain. And yet in the present drawing he seems to be contending that it is just this sense of underlying continuity that he cannot discover in his own mental experience. The dualism of the mental process is clearly asserted, as though he were aware of an upper stream of images on the conscious level, and an independent, somewhat steadier stream in the subconscious. I cannot say whether this dualistic representation is derived from analytical experience, or whether it is symptomatic of the schizoid state.

The chief value of the drawing lies in the extremely elementary way in which the patient states the issue. He has reduced the conflicting tendencies to their simplest possible statement; yet, notwithstanding the abstract nature of the representation, the drawing is clearly spontaneous.

Observing the character of the flowing lines, we note that the thickened parts of the lines tend to coincide with the relatively free open curves, while the thin portions coincide with the involuted loops and twiggles, the obvious exception to this rule being the thin up-stroke which terminates the upper line, and which contrasts in a striking way with the increasingly thick terminal sweep of the lower.

At first sight it would appear that there is no definable relationship between the position of the cones and the course of the lines. But on looking closer we observe the following features: (*a*) The initial course of the upper line ascends on a gradient parallel to that of the left-hand series of cones. (*b*) It contains three small involutions, corresponding to the three subsidiary members of the parallel cone series. (*c*) If we except the two cones on the right of the picture, it will be noted that the involuting loops and twiggles occur just after the line has passed a cone. In this connection it is remarkable that the two cones that actually pierce the lines cause less disturbance than those which lie below. This observation tallies with our experimental findings, which show that the disturbing effect of a complex is greater when it is buried in the unconscious than when it is known and accepted. The maximum disturbances in the lines occur (1) on the upper line, just after it has passed the buried cone in the middle of the picture, and (2) in the lower line, after it has passed the three buried members of the first group and the left-hand buried member of the second group.

On the other hand, with respect to the cone that pierces the last curve of the lower line, there is not only an absence of disturbance, but a very marked increase of extraverted power. Regarding the drawing logically as an abstract presentation of the relation of flow to obstruction, this latter observation would be inexplicable. If, on the contrary, we regard it as a description of the effect produced by the presence of emotionally charged complexes upon the stream of consciousness, we can see in it a valuable psychological statement. Our analogy of the eddies produced on the surface of a stream by the presence of a concealed rock would be appropriate for the disturbances observed in relation to the buried cones. But it falls to the ground when we come to deal with the final cone which pierces the lower curve. We must cast our line further if we are to catch this fish.

Turning again to Drawing 14, we observed that the involuting course of the line was like a sensitive recoil from the brusque approach of the anima. Comparing this impression with the present drawing, we find that the flowing lines exhibit this same involuting recoil away from the neighbourhood of the buried cones. It is almost as though a gust of wind came from the direction of the buried cones, blowing the line away from its normal course. Yet, on the other hand, the direction of the course of each line seems to be determined by the attraction of the cones.

The comparison between the two drawings yields a certain hint as to the nature of the cones. I refer to the similarity between the two pointed shafts in 14 (representing the inescapable claims of flesh-and-blood reality) and the sharp-pointed cones of the present drawing. The reader will also recall how the motive of adapting archaic elements to the sharp claims of reality came into the left-hand side of Drawing III. of the previous series in the form of thorn-like projections. The theme was there represented by an amorphous blue substance, articulating with three sharp spines of different colours by means of protrusions resembling pseudopodia. In that drawing too the sharp spines were on the extreme left of the field, and seemed to be thrust into the scene from without, just as the red and yellow spines of Drawing 14 seemed to come from an alien source.

These observations are highly significant in relation to the schizophrenic mentality. They demonstrate the intense subjectivity which characterizes the condition and which caused it to be identified with morbid introversion. It is, however, essential to distinguish this attraction towards the inner pole of borderline schizophrenia from the subjective fantasy-flight of hysteria. The schizophrenic patient gives one the impression of a person so preoccupied with the working out of his subjective problem that everything else has to wait. He is irritated by objective claims very much as I should be if the key to the problem which had baffled me for days was snatched from my grasp by a sudden call to the telephone. The purposive urgency of these psychological products is in itself eloquent of the subjective preoccupation which holds the borderline patient to his major problem. The fantasy-creations of hysteria are of an entirely different complexion. They are essentially mirage formations, designed to beguile the patient's interest and attention away from the thorny problems of reality into a never-never land of unreal, alluring situations. They have the effect of a narcotic numbing moral feeling into gentle apathy. They demand no concentration, no effort, resembling opium-dreams, whose sole purpose is to compensate for the inadequacy of actual experience.

The difference in a nutshell is this: the borderline schizophrenic is attracted towards his pathological problem with an almost obsessional concentration, but with poor objectivity, while the hysteric prefers to be lured away from his problem by fantasies, which have the illusory objectivity of the mirage. The attitude of the two types of patient to their products is also characteristic. The borderline schizophrenic is usually interested in his drawings, and appreciates the work and attention given to them. The hysterical patient, on the other hand, will try to draw one's attention away from his fantasy-activity, and is inclined to show signs of distress if one persists in examining his material. In general, the hysteric would prefer to subsist on the personal transference to the analyst, whereas the schizoid patient shows little interest in the question of personal feelings, being taken up almost exclusively with his quest.

Bearing in mind the patient's intense preoccupation with his subjective problem, we can understand the immediate recoil of the white line (in Drawing 14) at the approach of the anima with her realistic demands.[1] Yet, at the same time, there is an intrinsic recognition of the value of these reality-claims in the way the subject has drawn the yellow and red prongs. For they bind the convolutions of the line into a relatively coherent mass, very much as women used to transfix their hair with combs.

When we compare the red and yellow prongs of 14 with the granular cones of the present drawing we note that a certain development has taken place. The cones still retain the sharp thorny points which distinguish the real and inescapable from the unreal and illusory; but they have now acquired a granular consistency and a broader shape, suggesting a dynamic transformation. In other words, the thorns of reality are no longer conceived as something outside and alien to the mind, but rather as an integral part of his mental

[1] This is all the more understandable when we remember that the patient tends to identify the anima with his wife.

structure. What kind of experience could have brought about this gain in psychological insight ?

In carrying out word-association tests, or indeed in our daily analytical practice, we can instantaneously evaluate the patient's psychological insight by observing his behaviour when a painful complex has been touched. If, in response to the crucial question, the patient reacts with irritation and resentment, as though one had arbitrarily stuck a needle into him, we know that he has no insight into the prickly nature of his own complexes. If, on the other hand, the patient, though manifestly distressed, immediately volunteers an explanation of his emotion, and on further questioning brings, perhaps, the painful content of the complex into the light, we know that he is on the side of the angels, and that he is willing to accept the thorn which pricks him as an aspect of his own destiny.

We may conclude, therefore, that the patient has gained in insight through the experience represented by the two previous drawings. For in Drawing 14 the shafts have the vicious, hostile character of an alien intrusion, whereas in the present drawing the sharp-pointed cones are represented as dynamic elements of the endo-psychic structure.

We are now in a position to explain the last lower cone, which causes no subsequent eddy in the mental stream. The cones situated below the lines represent emotionally charged complexes prohibited by repression from direct access to consciousness. Their presence can be inferred only by certain symptomatic disturbances, for which consciousness can yield no rational explanation. These symptomatic disturbances are represented by the loops and twiggles, the disarray and, at certain spots, the fraying of the line in the neighbourhood of the buried cones.

The striking contrast between the disorderly medial portion of the lower line and its convincing terminal curve is immediately connected with the fact that a buried complex has at last broken through into consciousness. The value of confession could hardly be better demonstrated. It is as though the psychic energy required to prevent a complex from reaching consciousness becomes converted into a reinforcement of conscious purpose and moral as soon as the content of the complex is discharged. Thus, instead of the complex being an obstruction and a disturber of the mental peace, it adds its own specific energy to the value of consciousness.

The insignificant cone lying above the final dip in the upper curve should be regarded, therefore, as the depleted complex after its main content has been assimilated by consciousness. We have already observed this process of the assimilation and subsequent disintegration of a complex on a larger scale in Drawing XX. of the former series. There would seem to be a natural association of ideas in representing a complex emerging into consciousness from below, and the complex-remainder, after its contents have been fully taken up by consciousness, as something light and ephemeral that is carried upwards like smoke and ash from a fire. This association of ideas would also account for the convincing upward movement of both curves after the discharge of the complex into consciousness. The meaning or energy-content of the complex has joined the conscious stream, which immediately gains in effective power.

The only explanation I can advance for the existence of the double stream is that the schizoid organization produces a certain duplication of the personality, and that the subject becomes, therefore, aware of two relatively independent currents, both of which undergo parallel modifications under the influence of endo-psychic disturbances.

A comparison with Paul Klee's " Sondes sur les vagues " (Fig. 9) brings out certain interesting points of similarity. In both drawings there are two flowing lines running across the field in approximately the same direction, and in both there are two abstract elements or principles. In Klee's drawing the lines show no involutions, and instead of running a parallel course with its neighbour, the lower line breaks through the upper, rises to a point, and then descends again to its own level. The lower line finishes in a long curve resembling the crest of a wave, while the upper ends abruptly.

Instead of cones, Klee's opposite element consists of straight lines or rods arranged in loose bundles. The lines are disposed apparently indifferently over the field, some vertically, some horizontally, others obliquely.

In view of the vortex formation of curves and dots found in Drawing 17 of our series, I must call the reader's attention to what appears to be a revolving vortical system of curved lines and dark nebulæ occupying the central, ruling position of Klee's design. Other nebulous patches are dotted about over the field, but the two main concentrations are at the zenith and nadir of the field, the one at the zenith being the densest. By calling his picture " Sondes sur les vagues " the artist offers us a hint that the antithesis he feels, and which he hopes to reconcile, is between something heavy, direct and earthy, like lead, and something moving, fluid and constantly changing, like waves. But the really interesting fact is that both artists are prompted to attempt a dynamic reconciliation by means of a whirling vortex, therewith incorporating the opposing elements in a new formation. With regard to the problem of control, a number of Klee's designs reveal a circular disc, globe or vortex, in the position of control in the upper centre of the field. We might even regard the antithesis suggested in his title as the element of irrational movement versus the plumb-line of control.

III

Drawing 17

Here again we observe a characteristic alternation from the controlled and abstract to the dynamic and emotional representation of the problem.

The field of the drawing, which, like the last, is in pen and ink, is roughly divided into two halves by two irregular vertical lines which enclose a thin, uneven gap. On the left of this gap there is a leaping figure with dark face, streaming hair, and trailing limbs. Concerning this figure several curious facts should be noted. That it expresses a sudden release, or explosion of energy, is evident from the fact that an explosive area of light occupies the central portion of the figure, particularly in what would normally be the abdominal and pelvic regions. Notwithstanding the fact that the patient referred to it as a primitive female figure, its position in the air is characteristic of a highly specialized ballet technique.

Those who can remember Nijinsky's departing leap in Le Spectre de la Rose will immediately recognize the cultural source from which this figure springs. The forward position of the head, the curve of the knee and the extended foot of the right leg, the poised extension of left arm and leg in order to give the impression of flight—the whole *élan* of the figure is a product of studied art. Yet there is a decided suggestion of an Indian brave in the dark aquiline profile and the energetic aura of hair, which could easily be taken for a feathered head-dress.

Something complex and contradictory must be implied in this androgynous figure which explodes with untamed energy, and yet whose whole posture argues a highly disciplined training. For it is quite inconceivable that a primitive would produce this position in the air in the course of a spontaneous leap.

Other features to be noted are the strong trailing lines of force, which seem to originate principally in the neighbourhood of the extended right foot and the elongated left arm, and which flow away in a downward and backward direction across the paper. These, and the shaded areas to the right of the figure, enhance the feeling of vigour and direction. The latter would also indicate that the direction of the leap is towards the light.

The only organized content on the right side of the gap, with the exception of the long left arm and trailing foot and the lines of force mentioned above, is a rather nebulous vortex roughly spherical in shape. It consists of a left upper portion of semicircular lines which appear to be revolving about a central point, and a right lower half containing a spattering of fine dots. These dots are concentrated most thickly in the neighbourhood of the central point, being relatively sparsely scattered towards the periphery. Traversing the vortex and dividing the two portions just described, there runs an irregular diametrical line which forks into four branches towards the upper part of its course. In view of the energetic character of the drawing, the analogy with an electrical spark or forked lightning occurs to the mind.

Besides the contents described above, there are a certain number of what seem to be vagrant lines whose relation to the main contents is not discernible. They are worthy of note, because they are evidence of the swiftness and spontaneity of the drawing, which, in the patient's own words, seemed " to jump on to the paper of itself."

* * * * *

Before we discuss the complex nature of this new anima-figure, it might be as well to understand the reason for the extraordinary release of energy expressed in the *élan* of the whole drawing. The explanation is indicated, I think, in the powerful terminal curve of the lower line in the previous drawing. We discovered that this was due to the fact that one of the isolated cones had succeeded in breaking through into the stream of consciousness. We argued that this breaking through signified a conversion of the complex, by means of confession, from a resistant factor to a powerful tributary of conscious experience.

We can conceive, therefore, that the *élan* of the present figure and the upward sweep of the terminal curve in the last drawing represent the same moment of realization, only in the present drawing the released energy is personified. We have, however, an extremely important addition to the theme in the presentation of the dynamic and the ideal aspects of the problem—the latter causally related to the former—within the field of a single drawing. The schizophrenic division is represented as a restricted no man's land between the two halves, but the split does not sunder the contents into two unrelated groupings. On the contrary, one can hardly resist the impression that the *raison d'être* for this prodigious leap must be the transcending of the very gap which has hitherto prohibited any organic co-ordination between the two sides. To find some means of reconciling the sundered opposites of his own nature is *the* problem of the schizophrenic personality. Until this is achieved he is psychologically crippled.

When the anima planted her crossed swords upon the celestial spiral in Drawing 14 we witnessed a declaration of war. Once the issue had been so uncompromisingly joined, it could have been predicted that no peace would be possible until some radical solution had been found. The conflicting aspects were forced into a strong light, first under the general aspect of determining or constellating forces of fate, and subsequently as antithetical processes in the subject's own psyche. We have attempted to designate the opposition as the conative versus the cognitive; the emotional and affective versus the intellectual; the brown sphere versus the blue; the passional versus the abstracting. But these general designations always seem to elude the essence of the difficulty. The peculiar intractability of the opposition in this individual case cannot be understood, for instance, in terms of the brown sphere and the blue, unless at the same time we bear in mind the presence of the black. Under the control of the black sphere (viz., the reserved content) the spirit of dissociation must rule the whole psychical situation. So long as there remains a concealed complex, through which the primary instinct of sex is deeply entangled, the apparent freedom of the intellect to hold enlightened views is only the illusion of freedom. Actually, the subject is living on the hypothesis that part of his nature is originally evil and antisocial. For if this were not the case the concealed complex could be freely confessed. The intellect of itself is utterly powerless to liberate the mind from the paralysing effect of this hypothesis *so long as one lives as though it were true.*

The statement of the opposition in terms of the pointed cones and the flowing lines presented a characteristically introverted picture of the problem. It gave us insight into the fact that the existence of a buried complex is accompanied by a thorn-like quality of unrelatedness (described by Otto Gross as the sejunction of the complex), which is liable to result in a shut-in personality intensely preoccupied with his inner processes. We saw how the intense integration and isolation of thc complex resisted any associative connection with other elements, and how the lines of associative continuity were disturbed by the proximity of the shut-off cones. The accumulation of relatively unconnected complexes necessarily effects a seclusion from outer events and a corresponding damming-up of psychic energy within. When realization occurs this dammed-up affect is released, and a powerful emotional reaction takes place which tends to have a long after-effect. Hence the moment of realization in a morbidly introverted psychology has something of the character of an explosion.

Actually, the present drawing coincided with the birth of an inner resolve to bring the most difficult thing into the light. The patient was not working with me at the time these drawings were made, hence the resolve could not be immediately executed. The psychic response seen in this drawing is the direct result of the vital decision and the change of attitude accompanying it. The confession which followed was the outward and visible sign of this world-changing inner event. In the beginning is the vision, not the deed.

Transformation of attitude, according to my experience, often takes place, as in the present instance, when the patient is away from the analysis. A profound change of attitude is, as we saw in Drawing 15, a world-changing event, and such events belong, of their very nature, to individual solitariness. They do not happen according to plan. Indeed, those patients who are too dependent upon the analytical relationship and upon the psychic calories obtainable through the person of the analyst are liable to miss that deep realization of their own being which is the one thing they seek.

Perhaps the difference between the psycho-analytical standpoint and the one which originates with Jung could be deduced from this difference in method. Psycho-analysis holds that fulfilment will eventually come about when the patient has mastered the problems of adaptation. Against this we must contend that the primary demand of the soul is fulfilment in life, and that adaptation to social and other claims is merely the external manifestation of a fulfilled life. The interminable length of the psycho-analytical treatment is not to be accounted for by the utter intransigence of neurotic disorders. It pertains rather to a curious misconception of the nature of the soul, offspring of that natural philosophy which holds the process of biological adjustment to be the sole aim of life. Seen from this standpoint, the emergence of a new spirit or attitude—won from a fuller realization of the self—would have no material significance, except in so far as it served to improve one's biological performance.

IV

Resuming our discussion of the drawing, the derivation of the leaping androgyne figure must now be scrutinized. In general, we can assume it to be a personification of the primordial psyche viewed through somewhat sophisticated glasses. Drawings 9 and 10 revealed the separation of the dynamic aspect of the anima from the ideal; a gulf which the anima of the present drawing seems to have gained the power to transcend. We must therefore conclude that she now combines in herself the elements which before were dissociated. We know that the subject had the association of a primitive figure—a fact which lends a certain weight to our suggestion of an Indian wearing a feathered head-dress. Another constituent of the figure is indicated, both in its resemblance and in its contrast to the anima-figure of Drawing 3. The resemblance is to be found in the fiery stream that issues from the head of both figures; the contrast in the disorganized helpless figure of 3, as against the poised disciplined energy of the present figure. The third element, which is quite unmistakable, is the ballet leap especially associated with the great Russian dancer Nijinsky. The subject was of course familiar with Nijinsky's fate, though the psychiatric diagnosis of dementia præcox was unknown to him. Is it to be accounted coincidence that, at the psychological moment, a figure should leap out of the unconscious and across the perilous schizophrenic gap with the same distinctive leap of the dancer who was himself caught and maimed by the unconscious at the zenith of his career?

We have traced the primordial and the cultural elements in the constitution of the leaping figure. But another source remains to be investigated which may also yield important evidence. I refer to the vortical nebula in the right-hand portion of the field. Here again it is possible that the subject's selection of dots and lines, for the purpose of representing a dynamic system, may be accidental. But we cannot close our eyes to the fact that these same elements appeared in the last drawing, only under a different constellation. There the lines represented the associative continuity of the psychic process, while the dots represented the energic charge of the autonomous complex (symbolized by the cones). The energy of the cones was represented as being in a static or potential condition, due to the isolation of the complex, whereas the energy represented in the lines was freely flowing and therefore kinetic in character. The change revealed in this drawing is that the dots, now released from their isolating cones, are actively constellated by the dynamic point in the centre of the system. The lines, on the other hand, having apparently sacrificed their claim for unconditional freedom, are now concentrically determined by the same dynamic centre. Thus both elements may be said to have been modified from their former condition by a centralizing idea or factor. There is also the suggestion that these opposing elements are now in a relation of dynamic polarity like the protons and electrons of an atomic system, for between them is generated a diametrical forked line resembling an electrical spark. Above and also to the left of the vortex are a number of straying lines, which give the feeling of strands of cotton blown by a wind in the same direction as the leaping figure.

The patient was unconscious of any connection existing between the elements of this nebula and the opposites of the previous drawing. Had the continuity of theme been realized this new formation would have been treated with more importance. As it is, the new synthesis of psychic elements is indeterminate, as though the vortical system represented only an inkling of the possible solution. But so great is the psychic potential waiting on the hope of deliverance, that even the possibility of a solution produces an intense response.

With regard to the magnetic point around which the system revolves, we have to suppose, in the absence of associations from the subject, that only the germ of a ruling idea could occupy this position. As a clue to the kind of idea which could play this rôle Jung conceives Individuality as radiating from an archetypal germ, or virtual centre, situated between the conscious and the unconscious. The archetype of the self, viewed as a totality, including both conscious and unconscious, the future and the past, the potential as well as the actual, must be conceived as a non-personal centre in the same medial position as that occupied by the point seen in the present drawing. Energy generated at this point would be the expression of the polarity of function existing between the conscious and the unconscious. As the manifestation of a dynamic system this energy would be more accurately expressed in terms of electrical phenomena than by an anthropomorphic image. According to this hypothesis, the leaping figure would represent the personification of this energy as it approaches the threshold of consciousness. In fact, however, the image embodies both aspects, inasmuch as the explosive areas of light in the centre of the figure manifest the content of primordial energy, while the poised and disciplined leap symbolizes the power of the cultural idea. If this reasoning is correct we may look for further corroboration in the drawings that follow.

From the prognostic standpoint we might decide that the Nijinsky association is somewhat unfavourable. Such an explosion of affect in a schizophrenic subject is by no means safe, and a reaction is to be anticipated. Yet, on the whole, the constructive possibility indicated by the drawing outweighs, in my view, its sinister implications. Moreover, the ambiguous figure is leaping towards the light.

V

Drawing 18

The main content of this picture is a tree with two amputated branches on the left of the trunk, and two long branches traversing the upper part of the field towards the right. Only a part of the lower branch is visible among the dense masses of foliage which crowd the field to the right of the tree. Parts of two other branches can also be made out in the right lower quarter of the field. Examining the foliage of this tree, we find that the disposition of white and shaded areas is more suggestive of splashes of brilliant light than of leaves and twigs. One can best describe the effect as of a number of simultaneous explosions of light.

Sweeping downwards and towards the left in the middle

of this area is a large bird. It has been drawn with stronger lines upon the top of the crowded background, the lines of which cut across the details of its plumage. Apparently it has been superimposed upon the rest and is intended to be, in a certain sense, above the pre-existing contents.

A number of straight lines, radiating from the top left-hand corner, represent beams of the sun. Distributed over the whole picture, a profusion of insect life can be discerned. Two caterpillars are crawling up the tree trunk towards the top, while an ant begins to climb at the bottom. There is a spider in his web at the top right-hand corner, another in the fork of the tree, and butterflies, beetles and mosquitoes abound. The head and neck of a second bird can also be made out, emerging from the foliage half an inch or so below the head of the first. A large butterfly, with an eye on its upper wing, is to be seen in the shaded area near the right-hand lower margin.

* * * * *

Both this drawing and the last were drawn at great speed and with almost vehement energy. The spate of imagery seems to have transported the artist from his normal austerity of expression. In the scattering and profusion of contents in relation to structure, in the fluidity of design, and in the hurried technique we can discern here a generic resemblance to those drawings that were dominated by the anima in the former series. Having no technical equipment at his disposal, the enervating effect of the anima-mood was more obvious in the case of the former patient. But whereas the anima-drawings in the former case were eloquent of exhaustion, the features which distinguish this and the previous drawing are their startling vitality and explosive energy. The earlier series represented the trough of the anima-wave, whereas here we are viewing the crest. Yet in both instances the subject as conscious ego has been temporarily eclipsed.

Studying this and the previous picture side by side, we observe the interesting fact that the strong lines of the sloping trunk of the tree are already indicated below the leaping figure. We have only to join the downward sloping line to the right leg of the leaping figure in Drawing 17 to see that it corresponds to the main configuration of the tree trunk in Drawing 18, the knee coinciding with the bend in the trunk where the topmost branch is given off. With this correspondence in mind, we can see that the elongated left arm and trailing leg suggest the two main branches of the tree, and the wavy line descending from the long left arm becomes incorporated in another branch of the tree to be found near the right border of the picture.

Other points of correspondence between the two pictures which suggest themselves to the eye are as follows:

(*a*) The flight and poise of the leaping anima are represented in the swooping bird.

(*b*) The luxuriant hair, or feathered headdress, of the figure is transferred to the luxuriant plumage of the bird's tail.

(*c*) The area of exploding light in Drawing 17, which renders invisible the outline of the torso of the female figure and which seems to be most intense in the pelvic region, is distributed among the explosive areas of light which throng the field to the right of the trunk in Drawing 18.

(*d*) The position of the vortical nebula in Drawing 17 corresponds with the area of greatest density in Drawing 18, and the central point of the complex corresponds roughly with the eye in the centre of the butterfly's wing.

(*e*) The dark profile of the leaping figure corresponds with the darkly shaded area on the second branch, just at the point where the branch first becomes visible.

The presence of these apparently irrelevant correspondences have as much and as little signification as the peculiar and quite trivial resemblance in feature, voice or gesture frequently observed among members of the same family. A certain genetic identity is visible, which intimates that the two drawings are the product of the same psychological constellation. That they are the product of a very different influence from that governing the patient's normal style is evident when one contrasts these rash drawings with the meticulous care of his other work.

A similar contrast is to be observed in the drawings of Goethe. On the one hand are careful methodical studies in pen and ink of architectural groupings, figures and landscapes; on the other there are fantastic drawings in which dæmonic forms and fluid primordial figures crowd the field in spontaneous profusion. The one type is the product of the keen observer and the reflective scientific intelligence, the other flows from the hand which wrote the second part of Faust. This alternation in the constellation of the personality can also be clearly demonstrated in the study of handwriting.

The inference to be drawn, both from the similarity in style of the two drawings and from their structural correspondence, is that the anima of the former drawing has now been transformed into the tree and the bird. In other words, the anima begins to function under a different aspect. As a personification of the unconscious the anima forms a bridge or mediating function between the conscious personality and primordial nature. From one point of view, therefore, she appears in human shape, though often with a hint of something mysterious or supernatural about her. From another angle she appears as a force or aspect of nature, as, for instance, an animal, a tree, a snake, or even a storm of wind. Iaworski's idea that the main types and forms of organic life have become "interiorized" in the human make-up is really an intuition of the nature of the libido, which, as Jung has shown in his *Wandlungen und Symbole der Libido*,[1] possesses an infinite range of transformation.

A beautiful description of the anima as nature-spirit is to be found in W. H. Hudson's *Green Mansions*. Rima has a natural affinity with trees. She can hide among leafy branches with such instinctive cunning that no eye can detect her, and can leap from branch to branch like a squirrel. She wears a garment woven of spider's web, and her speech is like the hum of insects and the rustling of leaves. She is also the sole survivor of a remote culture, living in the forest with an old renegade who saved her life when her mother was

[1] English title: *Psychology of the Unconscious.*

pursued and killed by savage enemies. In thus combining nature and culture, she personifies the functional conception of the anima, commanding as well as caring for her renegade companion. She possesses the innate superiority that comes from an ancient culture, while she also enjoys the inner counsels of nature. Like Brünnhilde, she ends her life in the living flame, thus joining the company of the immortals.

The Latin word *anima* corresponds to soul; it also means air, breeze, breath, life, living being. Thus it is identical with the Greek πνεῦμα = wind. The original conception of the spirit originated in the experience of an invisible, imponderable, activating power. Hence the wind was the breath of God. The same idea appears in the naive belief that the soul of a man is taken in with his first breath and expelled with his last.

With this conception in mind we can understand that the so-called animism of the primitive mentality corresponds to the state in which the unconscious is exteriorized by projection into certain objects of the environment, which are therewith " animated " with a certain magical character. Thus, to a large extent, the primitive inhabits a world in which the primordial unconscious is concretely manifest, hence the state of emotional identity with the environment which Lévy-Bruhl terms *participation mystique.*

VI

From the evolutionary standpoint it must be admitted that the transformation of the libido witnessed in these two drawings is a regression to a primitive level. Lest this discovery should betray us to rash conclusions, let us again amplify the field by reference to analogous ideas in primitive folk-lore and early cultural mythology.

In the legend of Krishna it is related that his adored wife Rukmini died while he was away on a journey. Her body was burnt and the ashes buried in a new earthenware jar according to the prescribed ritual. When Krishna returned and was taken to the burial-place he found a *tulsi* tree growing on the grave. The tree was Rukmini in a new form;

for this reason the *tulsi* is regarded as sacred.[1] According to the *Book of Ballymote*, Aillem, daughter of Lughaid, King of Leinster, died of shame on being ravished away by Cremh. An apple tree grew up through her grave.[2] There is a tree in the Molucca Islands which bears during the night from sunset to sunrise a succession of fragrant white flowers. The Ternate tell how there was once a beautiful girl, beloved by the Sun, who slew herself when her lover deserted her. Her body was burnt, and from the ashes arose the tree, called by the early Portuguese sailors the Tree of Sorrow.[3]

In classical legends there are innumerable instances of men and women being transformed into trees, plants or animals either before or after death. Indeed, Ovid's poetical compendium of mythical history derives both its name and its material from the number and variety of such transformations. In a very large number of cases transformation into a tree is the symbolical expression of the deathless nature of an heroic or sacrificial act or of the immortality of love. The two trees growing from the graves of lovers brought, like Tristan and Isolde, to a tragic end is a favourite theme of folk-song and legend. Veneration for the gods is also immortalized in this way, as in the legend of Philemon and Baucis, the humble peasants who alone offered hospitality to Zeus and Hermes when they visited Thrace to see if the gods were still honoured there. After the meal Zeus asked Philemon what boon he would ask of his divine guest. " That Philemon and Baucis be never parted," was the old man's reply, " and that they may forever serve the gods." Whereupon the god transformed them into the two trees which stood side by side in the courtyard of the temple of Zeus.

The myths of Osiris, the originator of agriculture, are particularly rich in tree transformations. A manuscript in the Louvre refers to the cedar as having first sprung from the grave of Osiris. Elsewhere his soul is represented as inhabiting the tamarisk, because it was a tamarisk tree which grew around his coffin and watched over it until the coming of Isis. Trees and plants are represented on monuments

[1] *Anthropos*, vol. ii., p. 276. [2] *Silva Gad*, vol. ii., p. 531.
[3] E. S. Hartland: *Primitive Paternity*, vol. i., p. 160.

as growing from his grave; sometimes his mummy is depicted covered by a tree. In the temple of Isis at Philæ there is a wall-painting representing the dead body of Osiris with stalks of corn springing from it, while a priest waters the corn with a pitcher.

In many cultures the tree has been held sacred as symbolizing the origin of life. Frequently the tree of life is represented in association with a bird and a snake. On an ancient Mexican tablet the snake is seen coiled around the trunk of the tree, while the bird sits in the fork where the tree divides and forms a cross. A bird standing on the fork of the tree is also a feature of the Persian symbol of immortality. In this connection it is easy to understand why the cypress, the fir, the palm and other evergreen trees are the ones usually associated with burial transformations.

We must bear in mind, however, that the idea of immortality as exemplified in myth and ritual does not coincide with the metaphysical conception of an endless existence upon some other plane. To the savage mind it always signifies renewal or rebirth through generation or transformation. The tree is not deathless, but renews itself every spring. The snake in the Æsculapian symbolism shares with the tree the idea of renewal of life; with its change of skin in the spring of the year it becomes a new snake. Thus the sacrifice of the animal existence and subsequent transformation into a tree carries the religious meaning of gaining a renewal of life through death.

There is, however, a deeper meaning in the sacred tree which Jung has developed at length in *Psychology of the Unconscious.* Fundamentally the tree of life is a mother image. Jung writes:

> " Countless myths prove the derivation of man from trees; many myths show how the hero is enclosed in the maternal tree —thus dead Osiris in the column, Adonis in the myrtle, etc. Numerous female deities were worshipped as trees, from which resulted the cult of the sacred groves and trees. There is a transparent meaning in the legend where Attis castrates himself under a pine tree—*i.e.*, it is because of the mother. Goddesses were often worshipped in the form of a tree or a piece of wood.

Juno of Thespiæ was a branch of a tree; Juno of Samos was a board; June of Argos, a column. The Carian Diana was an unworked piece of wood. Athene of Lindus was a polished column. . . . Tertullian calls an Attic Pallas *crucis stipes*, a wooden pole, or mast. The wooden pole is phallic, as the name suggests, φάλης, *palus*."

After giving many more examples Jung goes on:

" In this way we pass imperceptibly from the realm of mother-symbolism into the realm of male phallic symbolism. This element lies also in the tree, even in the family tree, as is distinctly shown in the mediæval family trees. From the first ancestor the trunk of the great tree ascends in the place of the *membrum virile*. The bisexual symbolic character of the tree is intimated by the fact that in Latin trees have a masculine termination and a feminine gender."

Then further on (p. 249) he writes:

" This double significance of the tree is explained by the fact that these symbols are not to be understood anatomically, but psychologically as libido symbols. Therefore it is not permissible to interpret the tree on account of its similar form as being directly phallic; it can also be regarded as woman, or the uterus of the mother. The uniformity of meaning derives simply from the uniformity of the libido. One loses one's way in one *cul de sac* after another by insisting that this symbol is a substitute for the mother, and that for the penis. In this realm there is no fixed significance of things. The only reality here is the libido, for which ' all that is perishable ' is merely a symbol. It is not the actual physical mother, but the libido of the son, the object of which was once the mother. We take mythological symbols much too concretely, and wonder at every step at the endless contradictions. These contradictions arise only because we constantly forget that in the realm of fantasy feeling is all."[1]

In this passage Jung lays down the basic condition of psychological understanding. Nearly all our misunderstanding of primitive ways and customs and modes of thought, our blindness in regard to the soul and its needs, our misconception of religion—the spiritual myopia, in short, of our ruthless age—is due to the fact that we have forgotten the meaning of the symbol. For countless ages the symbol has been

[1] *Psychology of the Unconscious*, pp. 246-9.

the most commanding force in men's lives; to think in terms of symbols is therefore our natural heritage. But a symbol refers to a psychical, not a concrete fact: it cannot be measured or weighed or intellectually accounted for. It will always evade the scientific forceps, because no definite and constant meaning can be affixed to it. It is a living, transforming, organic vehicle of vital energy, and, as such, it can be understood only by means of a mental attitude that is attuned to the meaning or essence of things.

The two drawings now under consideration afford an excellent example of this very real difficulty of psychological demonstration. A symbolical transformation that is self-evident to intuitive feeling may be almost impossible to prove to the satisfaction of the scientific intellect. Those who are attuned to the symbol with its peculiar aptitude for metamorphosis will recognize at once, for example, that the dæmonic leaping figure of 17 has become the tree and the bird and the other denizens of 18. It is, in its own characteristic way, self-evident. Yet, when one attempts to demonstrate the grounds upon which this knowledge rests, the most obvious indications begin to appear doubtful. It is as though the irrational function of the mind which participates in the symbolic event, thereby knowing it from within, has no means of proving its own experience under the scrutiny of reason.

Here then we have an inner event which, from the purely rational standpoint, is not merely inaccessible to proof; it is something which, even were it proved, would be wholly irrational. Yet, in spite of counter arguments, we cannot repress a feeling that a transformation of deep significance has actually taken place. Conceding, for the moment, that the evidence adduced was sufficient, even then reason might contend that the transformation was a regressive one and that according to the analogies displayed it was concerned merely with a disguised incest-wish. Regression notwithstanding, feeling still clings to her view that the transformation is positive and valuable. Reason and feeling, like man and wife, have somehow to live and work side by side. How then are we to reconcile their opposing standpoints?

First let intuitive feeling be heard. The change from the

human form to the tree is naturally a step down from a highly evolved to a simpler mode of life; the same is true of the change to the bird, but why worry about that? When you go downstairs you do not feel depraved, even though you may enjoy a special feeling of merit when climbing a mountain. If you find a friend camping in a field you do not immediately assume he is "going native." It will not serve to bring the standpoint of the evolutionary snob into the psychic field. We need a criterion, not a prejudice.

On those dark occasions when for some reason one has recoiled from a task, or taken a step backwards when one should have gone on, is there not a certain tendency to hush it up? Also there is the biblical metaphor, "sinning against the light." But this creature is leaping towards the sun, and the sun is on the left in the position of rising. Look too at the sun's rays streaming in from the left of 18, filling the whole scene with light. Even the tree itself is inclined towards the sun. How could a dark incestuous tendency be represented as a movement towards the light? Is this broad-winged, crested bird the product of a regressive longing, or does it not also belong to the light world?

All these things to which you attach such weight (replies the critical reason) are only the superficial aspect of the picture. What we have to discover is what lies beneath the surface. What, for instance, is behind all these scattered explosions? And why should the concentration of purpose and energy, seen in the leaping figure, be dissipated in such things as caterpillars, mosquitoes, beetles and butterflies? Why does the tree extend only to the right, and why are its branches to the left of the trunk mere amputated stumps? Why is the whole composition so one-sided?

And so the discussion might go on, one side scenting out what is queer and distorted, the other feeling what is essentially right and sound. "To feel with the head and think with the heart" is the Oriental fashion of expressing these complex evaluations which cannot be ruled exclusively either by feeling or reason. Unfortunately, however, it is just this kind of judgment which is labelled "unscientific." And yet the material we are now discussing is so closely woven of positive and threatening aspects that two-dimensional methods of interpretation would be worthless. The feeling of the physician is necessarily suspect, because he has had to participate sympathetically in the patient's experience in order to understand it at all. For this reason the psychotherapist's feeling judgment on his case is inclined to be sanguine. On the other hand, his intellectual function, schooled to discriminate the finest shades of abnormality, is liable to overstress the pathological aspect, particularly when the partiality of feeling has to be compensated.

The material produced by patients undergoing analytical therapy is inevitably compounded of opposing elements. The sincerity of the analytical atmosphere tends to force the patient's morbid psychology into the light, yet at the same time it fosters the curative impulse. Hence in dream and fantasy formations we frequently find the disease and the remedy achieving symbolical expression in the same field, just as nature contrives that the same plot of earth shall favour both the nettle and the dock.

This duality within the material is an empirical fact of nature; it is because of the inherent ambiguity of psychological material that a corresponding duality of function is demanded in our understanding of it. If we approach solely from the pathological side we shall tend to overlook the prospective or curative manifestations, and if we identify with our feeling we shall tend to ignore the less obvious evidence of disease.

A scientific presentation of this complex material must therefore take both tendencies into account; it also follows that a scientific treatment of the material must handle the morbid and the curative with methods fitted to their distinctive characters. The analytical or reductive method is clearly appropriate for the handling of the pathological formations; but it is just as patently inadequate for evaluating the curative impulse. The pathological aspect of the material is invariably rooted in past determinants, either inherited or acquired; hence the work of unearthing these morbid historical influences demands a vigilant analytical attitude. But the curative impulse being orientated towards the future demands a sensitive prospective appreciation. The morbid characters (as in Drawing VII of the first series) are usually patent for all to see. But the healing, stabilizing influence operates almost invisibly (as in the tortoise of 15), demanding the sympathetic vision of a seeing eye.

* * * * *

We must now resume investigation of the pathological indications referred to above by the analytical reason. But first we must allude to a peculiar subtlety which escaped our critic's analytical eye. Actually there are two birds in the picture. One is manifest, the other concealed; and they are obviously of different species. The manifest bird has a short neck, a crested head, and rather luxuriant, exotic plumage. The concealed one is presumably a larger bird, judging from the head and as much of the neck as is visible. It must also be a bird with a long neck like a swan. But the head expresses rapacity, like that of a bird which dives for its prey, such as a gannet or cormorant.

In general, a bird symbolizes an ideational factor, as, for instance, a thought or an intuition. Here are two birds in flight, the one apparently representing the manifest content of the picture, the other its concealed or hidden significance. Of the concealed bird we are shown just enough to be able to construct its general shape and character, implying perhaps that a similar discernment in regard to the hidden content of the picture might provide us with a coherent image which would elucidate its psychological content in the same way as our mental reconstruction of the whole bird elucidates the head and neck. When we also observe the facts that one bird is above, the other below, while the direction of the upper bird is towards the left (the side from which the light is coming) and that of the lower bird towards the right, where the shadow is thickest, we can hardly resist the conclusion that these two birds are stating, with the subtle precision of unconscious symbolism, that two specific mental functions are needed to comprehend the various contents of the tree.

Birds with a long snake-like neck such as the swan, crane, or goose have always played an important rôle in mythology, in particular in the pagan-Christian legend of the Grail.

The unwitting crime of Parsifal in killing the sacred swan was, like the slaying of the albatross by the Ancient Mariner, the fateful moment which determined his life's task—namely, the bringing together of the sundered opposites, the Holy Spear and the Grail. In classical legend the swan was identified with Zeus. Frequently we find the combination of snake and bird figured as an eagle holding a snake, or sometimes a fish, in its talons. Doves and snakes were associated with the mother-goddess of Crete. The dove and the swan were sacred to Aphrodite. The primæval goose that laid the golden egg, or the world-egg, has come down through the ages as a magical symbol. The goose was identified with the wind, the breath of life in Indian myths. Brahma, the creator, is depicted riding on a goose. The goose was also sacred to Hera, the sky-goddess. In Egyptian myths the goose is associated with Osiris, Horus and Isis. It was also sacred to Apollo, Dionysos, Hermes and Eros. Eros is depicted riding on a goose. The " beautiful goose " was sacrificed to Venus in Cyprus. In Italy it was sacred to Priapus. The oath sworn by Socrates and his disciples was " by the goose." In China the goose was held sacred as the " bird of heaven." Thus it was a symbol of the *Yang* principle.

In China and Japan the crane is a sacred bird, and was supposed to live to a fabulous age. Hence it is often represented as standing on the back of the tortoise. One of the emblems of the Great Wisdom is a pair of storks surrounded by a serpent. The stork as the legendary bringer of babies belongs to the same symbolic connection.

Spirituality conceived as an elementary dynamic principle is that aspect of the psyche which corresponds to light, air, wind and sun. It is symbolized by the bird. Sexuality, as its polar opposite, can be regarded as the psychic principle which corresponds to earth, substance, darkness, animal nature. Its symbol is the chthonian dæmon, the snake. Our tendency to think of instincts as separate and distinct entities makes it difficult to understand psychology in terms of elementary dynamic principles. But the unconscious still thinks in the grand manner of ancient China: " There are three elements: Heaven, Earth and Man." The age-long veneration of the swan, the goose and the stork is the evidence of man's constant need to find some reconciling symbol which could unite this elementary opposition in his nature.

In our drawing this mysterious bird is hidden by the scattered explosive areas which seem to be identified with the foliage of the tree. The subject could volunteer no suggestion about these splashes of light. But when it was pointed out to him how the Nijinsky figure had become transformed into the tree and the bird he agreed that there was probably a connection between the central explosive area in that figure and the rather similar phenomena in this drawing.

Nijinsky undoubtedly provides the key to the pathological aspect of the two drawings. Schizophrenic introversion necessarily activates the deep archaic residues in the unconscious, and these impersonal images, like the coal-deposits in the earth, contain an immense potential of energy. From the subjective point of view a sudden afflux of energy from the unconscious may be felt as a mystical exaltation; but to the psychiatric observer it may appear as a profound mental disturbance. The instability of the schizophrenic mind is due to the irreconcilable distance between the upper and lower poles in the psychic dynamism. When the tension between the opposites becomes extreme an acute state of agitation is felt, so that every available means for dissipating the psychic tension is liable to be tried—phrenetic extraversion, sexuality, alcoholism, excessive speeding, drugs, and every variety of violent bodily activity. Not infrequently there are seizures in which tachycardia, profuse sweating, fainting, explosive flatulence, peristaltic spasms, and tremor of the hands bear witness to intense disturbance throughout the sympathetic system. A restless and excited verbosity is a common sign of the mounting tension; perhaps a shy introverted man may find himself divulging intimate and quite irrelevant confidences to someone whose company he would normally avoid. This uneasy state of tension is the cause of the centrifugal, disruptive, restless activity of the autonomous psyche on the one hand and the tense, preoccupied subjectivity of consciousness on the other.

A typical schizophrenic dream recently came to my notice, which illustrates the terrible insecurity felt by the subject during such a crisis. The dreamer found himself working on a suspension bridge. One of the cables on which he was working gave way, and, to his horror, he realized he was hanging over an apparently bottomless abyss. With the strength of despair he climbed up the hanging cable, working his way hand over hand until at last he dropped upon the mud in safety. Another patient drew a picture depicting, on the one side, an enormously high rocky island upon which an isolated figure appeared looking down over the ramparts of a high castle. Far below, at the bottom of a precipitous cliff, lay a vast scaly monster, half bird and half reptile, breathing flames out of its mouth. This dream provides a classical illustration of the irruption of the archaic content from the collective unconscious, countered by reinforced conscious control.

The agitation which takes possession of the schizophrenic subject at these times is due to the fact that he begins to feel the fascination of the atavistic pull which, if he does not resist, can easily destroy him. He may sense it as something sub-human, mad, even criminal, but also (and this is the worst terror) something that could become overpowering. The defensive habit of consciousness and the traditional persona are symbolized by the castle with its ramparts. Yet the castle offers no real security so long as there exists no means of mediation between the sundered extremes. On the contrary, the creation of an idealistic conscious defence, being at bottom a compensation-phenomenon, becomes one of the principal factors which maintains the distance between the opposite poles. So long as the subject identifies himself only with the watcher on the ramparts, no solution is possible. A sacrifice of the bolstered superiority of consciousness is therefore indispensable, and yet, as we saw in the deluge drawing, the dissolution of the old order involves a critical transition in which consciousness may become submerged by the released forces of the unconscious.

The androgyne anima-figure, since transformed into the bisexual tree-symbol, contains a true ambivalence. It suggests the danger of becoming submerged or possessed by the archaic unconscious, but it also indicates how the primordial energy can be held in leash. The latter aspect of the symbol is expressed in the highly disciplined art displayed in the dangerous leap. The figure asserts that the primordial energy of the unconscious has to be released, but that it must be expressed in a disciplined creative way. The means of cultural expression is alluded to in the ballet association, since Nijinsky was a creative artist of great distinction. Why then, it may be asked, was he overcome by the unconscious? The whole issue of sanity versus insanity clearly depends upon the attitude of the subject towards the archaic experience. In artistic creation the artist naturally identifies himself as completely as possible with the creative impulse, in order to give expression to his fantasy. In " l'Après-midi d'un Faune " Nijinsky not only created, acted and danced the archaic fantasy, he personified the animal-god before thousands of enthralled men and women. Inevitably he evoked libido-projections from the general unconscious which enfolded the archaic idea with the intoxication of desire. The adulation, almost amounting to idolatry, constantly showered upon him undermined his artistic detachment. Gradually he was seduced into the illusion that he was the god he had created. In other words, the archaic fantasy had become more real than the world of reality, and Nijinsky, the man whose allegiance to common reality had always been doubtful, was seduced back to the primordial world in which the animal-god is supreme. The atavistic attraction of a primordial image can become so overpowering at certain crises that only a disciplined devotion to reality, a devotion that cannot be uprooted or deflected, is able to withstand it. In dealing with borderline cases the presence of a disciplined function of reality is, in fact, the *sine qua non* of successful therapy.

VII

We have now explored the unfavourable aspect of the Nijinsky association, and have attempted to analyse the factors weighting the scales on the sinister side. The alternative possibility contained in the symbol can be apprehended by the term " psychological creation." Artistic creation, as we have seen, favours an attitude in which the subject identifies himself mediumistically with the archaic image. Accordingly he does not, as a rule, concern himself with the problem of understanding his creation in its reference to his own psychology. Psychological creation, on the other hand, provides a means of expressing the archaic contents with the definite purpose of giving them reality *within the psychological sphere.* In the first case the artist does not want to know the inward significance of his experience. He may even feel that the subjective reference is liable to impair the creative impulse, whereas in the second case, since the prime motive of psychological creation is to become whole, some understanding of the fantasy-experience is an indispensable part of the creative work.

By taking no psychological responsibility for his creations the artist tends either to impoverish his own life or to become unconsciously identified with the autonomous process, whereas the attitude of responsibility, suggested by the disciplined leap towards the sun, would accept the emergence of a fantasy-image as something which could have a decisive bearing upon the actual situation.

The ambivalence of the anima-figure now appears as an alternative to which consciousness is able to respond in two ways. To follow the fate of Nijinsky and become identified with the archaic image would be one way. To express the unconscious creatively, but to maintain psychological responsibility towards the expression, would be the other. Both ways are possible; the choice is fundamentally a question of attitude.

Let us now assume that the subject chooses the more difficult, introverted way. It is self-evident that the energy which before was dissipated in compulsive extraverted ways will now be held within the psychic sphere. Methods of compulsive extraversion, mentioned above, are merely attempts to relieve oneself of tension, to get it out of the system. No joy, pleasure, or even interest can be found in these performances unless the primordial energy is harnessed to the creative will. But when a man has come to the realization that the libido is the vital essence, to be honoured perhaps as the manifestation of the god within—how can he then be content with mere outlets? And yet no man is inclined to husband his energy if he be not already somewhat enamoured of its fruit.

It is at this crucial moment that the idea of the tree assumes its symbolical significance. Only when Daphne is about to be caught by the pursuing god does the transformation become relevant. The sacrifice of the animal- and the acceptance of the tree-nature can now be seen as an aspect of fate; when the animal way is no longer feasible the tree-destiny becomes more and more desirable. The *amor fati*, or the "greater ought," implies an attitude in which necessity chooses desire for her mate. This takes place when the neurotic compulsion or disability is discovered to be the tap-root of a fruitful psychological tree.

The sacrifice of the animal libido was the essence of the Mithraic mystery, as it was in the earlier cult of Attis. Attis is the son-lover of the divine mother Agdistis-Cybele, who, like the anima-figure of the last drawing, was androgynous. We can regard the androgynous character of a primordial image as expressing the idea of source or origin at a deeper level than the idea of the parent—as, for instance, the mother of life or humanity, or the libido in general. Agdistis was enamoured of her son, and eventually drove him mad by her longing. Attis then castrated himself under a pine tree, into which his spirit passed. According to the account given in the *Metamorphoses*, Attis actually becomes the pine tree. At all events, it played an important rôle in the Attis cult. The pine tree wreathed in violets became the sacred emblem of Attis in the wild festivals of Cybele, whose priests, in memory of Attis, were eunuchs.

The idea of self-castration is also contained in our drawing, in the curious amputation of the two branches of the tree on the left-hand side of the trunk. This left side of the tree corresponds to the extraverted direction of the leaping anima. The leaning of the tree towards the left is presumably, therefore, a residue of this extraverted momentum.

We have now to plait our numerous threads into a skein. Let us assume that the patient has attained that degree of self-realization which renders the blind extraversion of anima-

(or animal-) possession no longer possible for him. The introverted way of dealing with the unbridled aspect of the unconscious is that of the tree, which, through being rooted in the earth, is able to withstand storms. The tendency to be driven by the anima in compulsive extraverted ways is like the force of the prevailing wind, which always bends the tree in the same direction. It is precisely this irresponsible dissipation of energy which must be sacrificed. Hence the mutilation of the tree on that side. The guillotining of compulsive extraversion results, however, in a renewed activation of the autonomous psyche, inasmuch as the released energy that is withheld from mere external dissipation must go somewhere. The scattered splashes of light on the right-hand side of the tree represent, therefore, the distribution of the released energy within the subject. In the former drawing the explosive energy was localized chiefly in the sexual and abdominal regions. In so far as it now becomes associated with the foliage of the introverted tree it becomes relevant, in some degree at all events, to the process of inner development. The peculiar difficulty of the integrating process is suggested by the various winged insects abounding in this part of the field. In the drawings that immediately follow insects come into a certain prominence, a fact which tends to confirm our idea that the back-flow of energy has activated a region of the unconscious which tends to express itself in archaic terms.

I have Professor Jung's permission to quote certain passages from a letter of his, in which he answers a question I put to him with regard to these insect drawings. He writes: " The insects represent autonomous (? Mendelian) units that tend to break away from the psychic hierarchy. In the same way as the cave-dweller filled the remote corners of his cave with drawings of animals, in order to gain power over them, your patient seems to be trying to catch his autonomous units by drawing them. By this means he tries, as it were, to keep them in association with his conscious mind, thereby decreasing the danger that they might run off in different directions and disappear altogether. The fact that he can draw them with such precision shows that his conscious function is synthetic enough to control these little creatures, which, if the control should fail, would reappear as those well-known *insulæ*, or personality-fragments. The insects that appear in the tree show that he succeeds to some extent in establishing the proper hierarchy in his unconscious. At least the picture indicates that positive possibility."

I am grateful to Professor Jung for his valuable intuition. His conception of magical control agrees perfectly with our observations relating to the Paul Klee drawings. In accordance with this view, it will be noted that the direction of flight of all the insects is, on the whole, centripetal; that the integrative motive is also represented by the spider's webs, one in the fork of the tree on the left, the other among the foliage in the top right-hand corner; and that the motive of metamorphosis is alluded to in the two caterpillars crawling up the trunk of the tree. Moreover, as we study the drawing it becomes apparent that four levels or strata can be distinguished. The white bird is the sole occupant of the topmost level. Below this come the insects. Then there is the level represented by the explosive white areas, and behind these are the shaded parts out of which the head and neck of the second bird emerges. Thus, as Jung points out, a certain hierarchy is already indicated.

My impression concerning the scattered white splashes is that they are symptomatic representations of a certain agitation of the sympathetic nervous system. The distribution of the energic tension through the various levels, indicated above, produces characteristic manifestations upon each level. On the conscious level it produces the intuitive birds, one concerned with the manifest conscious direction, the other with the unmanifest unconscious activity (viz., the shaded areas). On the subliminal level it brings to light the autonomous units (the insects) and the tendency to hold them in a coherent structure. And on the somatic level it is dissipated in a characteristically simultaneous stimulation of the sympathetic system.

There is little more to be said about the drawing, though doubtless specific qualities might be given to the various autonomous units represented by the ant, the spider, the butterfly, the ladybird, the caterpillar, the bee and the mosquito. The stereotyped character of the instinctual mechanisms of insects gives us an inkling as to the nature of these fragmentary systems. Moreover, the fact that insects possess the power of causing humiliating disturbance and even distress, out of all proportion to their bulk, may throw a valuable side-light on the subjective preoccupation of the schizophrenic personality.

Among the great variety of ways in which the disruption caused by the activation of archaic contents can be countered by consciousness, this way of transformation offers the only possibility of final reconciliation. A mere stiffening of intellectual control serves only to exacerbate the conflict. The release of energy from the complex, indicated in the free terminal curve in Drawing 16 and in the leaping figure of 17, was most liable to evoke a renewed effort of control from above. A dangerous moment had arrived.

The tree is nature's idea of increasing the power of control. Under this ægis the sacrifice of extraverted means is not mere repression of the archaic content, but rather a sacrifice for the sake of a further goal. Nature is utterly opposed to pure negation. Life is a stream that never stands still; desire is its human expression. If life must be sacrificed in this form, desire goes over into the new channel and the stream continues. Transformation differs, then, from arbitrary control in the fact that desire runs on, fulfilling itself in a new form instead of being levelled with an axe.

We must therefore allow intuitive feeling to have the final word because of the obvious psychological gain achieved through the transformation. When Prajapati was faced by Agni, his own passional creation, he said, "'This, my own greatness, speaketh unto me.' Whereupon he sacrificed himself and became the sun that burneth yonder and the wind that purifieth. Because Prajapati sacrificed in this wise, he propagated himself, and, because death in the form of Agni would have devoured him, he also saved himself from death."[1]

The transformation of the primordial anima into the tree

[1] *Catapatha-Brahmanam*, 2, 2, 4.

and the bird is, in effect, a progression from the protopathic state of autonomy into an integrated relativity. The acceptance of the limitations and the responsibilities of the tree-like attitude accompanies a new spiritual freedom—a freedom undreamed-of by the devotees of speed, who mistake manifold means of rapid transit for the path of evolution. In following the introverted way the Christian paradox discloses its essential truth. " He who loses his soul shall find it " expresses the inmost meaning of these two drawings.

It was the tree-like steadfastness of Parsifal that won the Holy Spear from Klingsor and transformed Kundry from a demonic enchantress into a ministering function. Yet the final transformation comes when Parsifal brings the Spear back to the Grail, and the soul of Kundry is released in the form of a white bird. So long as the anima is in the state of unconditioned autonomy, she is like Lilith, the first wife of Adam, who refused to sacrifice her god-like independence and freedom in order to beget the race of man. Wherefore she became a demon and a vampire. But when the anima submits to the creative task she is transformed into an intuitive bird who brings out of the unconscious those archetypal seeds which the creative mind delights to cultivate.

To speak of the soul as a bird is not a mere poetical conceit. To the natural mind the soul is a bird, and at certain rare moments, when the issue of life or death hangs in the balance, or when the rational habit of the mind is humbled by the presence of death, the vision of a bird at the window touches a chord in the heart which will not be silenced by all our scientific scepticism.[1]

[1] As an example of what I have in mind, two citations taken from Sir Ronald Storrs' *Orientations* concerning the state of mind of the late T. E. Lawrence during the last days of his life are of deep interest. First I will quote a few passages from Lawrence's last letter, written to a friend, which clearly reveal the condition familiar in primitive communities as " loss of the soul." " You wonder what I am doing ? Well, so do I, in truth. Days seem to dawn, suns to shine, evenings to follow, and then to sleep. What I have done, what I am doing, what I am going to do puzzle and bewilder me. Have you ever been a leaf fallen from your tree in autumn and been really puzzled about it ? That's the feeling."

A little later the author recounts how " every day, for the last three weeks of his life, a bird would flutter to his window, tapping incessantly with its beak upon the pane. If he moved to another window the bird would follow and tap again. The strange insistence was so visibly fraying his nerves that one

The demonic anima is chained to the illusion of power, of greatness, of acquisition and desirousness, but the soul is also free with the natural freedom of a bird. And because it is bird-like it needs the tree for its resting-place.

---

morning, when he had gone out, his friend shot the bird. In that same hour, wrenching his handlebars for the last time, Lawrence was flung over them sixty feet head first on to the granite-hard tarmac." No scientist could ever allow his mind to entertain the obvious primitive explanation that the bird was the soul of Lawrence which had left him and was trying to return. But, whatever we may think about it, no one who reads this story can remain unmoved, and no scientific explanation is forthcoming as to why a bird should behave in this way.

DRAWING 21.

DRAWING 22.

CHAPTER VII

THE PHASE OF *YIN*

I

THE four pictures we have now to discuss are remarkably different from the rest of the series. They have a quality of macabre masochism which at times becomes irksome and painful. Even the colour of the paper and the character of the line are different.

A return to the symptomatic level was to be expected at this juncture, when we bear in mind the cycloid alternation of mood in psychopathic subjects. The characteristic cycle, whose poles are manic excitement and depression, is not so much a pattern of fate as a symptom of the fact that the instinctual energy-flow has to overcome the obstruction of inertia in a pathological form. Observing the rising tension, the manic explosion, followed by the sagging curve of depression, it is obvious that we are watching a natural curve, only exaggerated. However justifiable it is to conceive psychic activity by reference to analogous, though presumably simpler, processes in nature, we have to remember that the former are in a sense removed from comparison by the presence of the unique factor of consciousness.

In nature we cannot assume that the rising level of water behind a dam is instinct with the feeling of purpose or aim, nor that the water that is sprayed and spattered at the bottom of the subsequent fall is depressed with a feeling of futility and sin. But with conscious beings the upward and downward curves of the libido seem to be referred almost universally to the feeling of value or purpose or goal, hence the excited sense of potentiality and achievement of the one phase and the gloomy depression of the other.

We have already observed that the *élan* of the manic phase may in effect be suicidal, and I hope to be able to demonstrate that the feeling of purposelessness of the depressive phase is also an illusion due to the unwillingness of the ego to go with, or submit to, the unconscious.

Like every other system, the manic-depressive cycle is found to undergo modification as soon as the teleological conception of unconscious activity is deeply realized. So long as the system is autonomous it is pathological, and in a very large number of cases there is not sufficient energy or flexibility of consciousness to produce any lasting effect upon the autonomous system. The manic-depressive cycle has then become the pattern of fate.

As a rule our chief difficulty in dealing with a depressive psychology arises from the fact that the patient communicates practically nothing except lamentations, self-accusation, and assertions of helplessness. These are repeated, as a rule, in a mechanical voice and with a stereotyped form of expression. It is like a gramophone record which, once started, goes on to the bitter end. It is plain from the change which comes over the patient's expression that, from the moment the masochistic complex comes into action, intelligence is suppressed and attention reduced to nil. Instead of a flowing stream of consciousness with a flexible focus of attention, there is only a vortex which draws everything into the orbit of the complex. The dreary self-accusations are like the mumblings of a miser who sits above his concealed hoard, ceaselessly complaining of his poverty. There is no sincerity in a masochistic display. Masochistic suffering has absolutely no merit, and invariably fails to elicit sympathy.

If sufficient intelligence remains unimpaired by the complex it may have an excellent effect if the camouflage is stripped away and the patient told in the most direct fashion that the masochistic appeal is not only indecent but futile.

The masochistic habit of the inverted libido is, in my experience, usually associated with a history of sacrificial acquiescence in a form of life which ignores the essential needs of the self in the effort to fulfil some false collective ideal. Genuine altruistic devotion does not breed masochism, but dutiful acquiescence is not identical with honest service, and a sacrifice not genuinely intended is merely a childish attempt to placate a savagely conceived deity. Beneath the symptomatic suffering, therefore, there is hidden poisonous resentment, usually against the parent who was identified with the false collective attitude.

Denial of the self is apparently a crime which nature refuses to condone under any circumstances.

* * * * *

Returning to our material, the appearance of a depressive mood is a natural sequence to the sudden release of tension seen in the last drawings, though the masochistic form of the depression must, of course, be ascribed to other causes. A similar cycloid phenomenon was observed in the material of the former patient, particularly in the parallel group of four anima-drawings which followed immediately upon the manic phase of the heroic combat with the dragon. When we appreciate the fact that the first patient had to encounter the psychotic danger in the atavistic dragon, while this patient had to meet his secret doubt in Nijinski, the peculiar character of the depression in both cases will be intelligible.

The fact that in both cases the subsequent anima-mood should express itself in four drawings in a style quite different from that of the rest, and on sheets of paper of a different size and quality from the rest, is so remarkable that I cannot make any adequate comment about it. The presence of the number four should, however, never be assumed to be accidental in psychological productions. The mere fact of the quaternary sign of individuality informs us that behind these fourfold series, however depressed, macabre or exhausted they may appear, there is in both cases a far-reaching purpose. Therefore we must approach them with a ready teleological eye.

II

Drawing 19

In sympathy with his depressive mood, the subject has chosen a bluish-grey paper which tends, if anything, to enhance the macabre character of the drawings.

In the top left-hand corner a woman's face has been drawn, which leaves one with the uncomfortable impression that mental suffering has been magnified by self-pity. The upturned eyeballs, the unnecessary exaggeration of eyebrows and eyelashes, the dilated nostrils and downward-drawn mouth, not to mention the framing of the face *à la religieuse*, suggest an hysterical dramatization of suffering. An actress playing the rôle of a sacrificial victim, but nevertheless determined that her beauty shall not be marred by lines of grief, might easily assume this rapt expression.

On the right of this face there is a ghoulish constellation, consisting of a hand and arm from which all the tissues above the wrist have been denuded down to the bones, a water-jug whose contents are being poured, and a knife and fork. There is a definite sense of something horrible and unnatural about all the details of this figure. The half-dissected arm is curved in an unnatural arc, the proportions of the humerus in relation to the radius and ulna are wrong, the wrist and hand are gnarled and knobbly, like the hand of an ogre, and display the characteristic coarse, sparse hairs of the witches' brood. The knife and fork diverge so as to contain the upper end of the humerus between them. These, too, are somehow just wrong. The uninviting relation of blade to handle in the knife, and of the four jagged prongs of the fork to the bulbous asymmetrical handle, would make one hesitate before using such tools. They could not be intended, one feels, for any wholesome purpose.

The same evil influence has spread to the pitcher. Not only is it the wrong shape (in the Chestertonian meaning of the words), but its consistency seems to be soft, like putty, so that whatever shape the potter originally gave it would not be maintained. It belongs presumably to the same ogre's kitchen as the knife and fork. A diabolical influence has even affected the water which is being poured out of the pitcher. Within the pitcher its behaviour is odd, since the surface of water should be level. But its changed character comes to light in the little demon hands with pointing finger which appear as soon as it is poured into the pool below. These things seem to be animated by a malevolent spirit.

Below this we come to another figure, consisting of a segmented snake looping around three nautilus shells. The nautilus shells are graded in size. The two smaller ones, within their respective loops, are directed downwards and towards the left, while the larger one opens downwards and to the right. The head of the snake is pointing vertically downwards, its forked tongue hovering just above the left side of a detached and half-dissected human head. The left side of the head is like a mask, bearing the marks of intense suffering. It is a powerful, hairless face; the eye is nearly closed and the expression is one of stoical imperturbability. It could be Chinese. The right half has been dissected to the bone, so that the bare skull is revealed.

Above and behind the right margin of the skull, with the left hand covering the eyes, the head bowed in grief, stands a symbolical feminine figure. Although the lines of the draperies seem to be flowing into the pool of melancholy which fills the bottom of the field, there is no suggestion of morbidity about this solitary figure. Perhaps it is because this figure seems to express genuine feeling that the diabolic spirit in the water-splash cannot resist pointing a mocking finger.

The two insects on the left seem curiously irrelevant to the other contents of the drawing. They even give one the feeling of having been drawn on a different level, or as though a real fly and spider were crawling about on the surface of the picture, so realistically have they been drawn. The hair on the bodies of both insects, the veins in the fly's wings, the " washing " action of the fly's front legs—all these are the result of close, meticulous observation. No other content of the drawing has this decidedly objective character.

* * * * *

With the exception of the upturned face of the woman and the sinister direction of the knife and fork, everything in the picture contributes to the general downward movement. It is as though the attraction of the depressive mood were irresistible. Even the insects are affected by it. It is this downward movement of the libido, merging into the flood at the bottom, which combines the various disparate figures into a relatively coherent design.

We can assume, therefore, that the flooding pool represents the melancholic mood. The pool is fed from three sources of very different character. The source on the left, which, coming where it does, seems to give the key-signature to the mood, betrays the character of anima-hysteria.

It is correct to use this expression whenever a man unconsciously dramatizes an archaic mythological theme or content, as, for instance, when his behaviour seems to be demonstrating the thesis that he is a helpless victim of fate. The various affective rôles that men unconsciously perform are frequently marked by a sentimental hysterical quality, revealing the inner feminine character behind the masculine persona. These rôles are commonly taken for granted as part of the inexplicable eccentricities of human beings, towards which one must preserve a good-natured tolerance. Rarely are they challenged, for the reason that people who revert to emotional displays in place of reasonable discussion are, in effect, fingering archaic weapons. A man in an anima-state is like a horse with his ears laid back. He may not intend to lash out, but by raising a doubt as to his intentions he thereby gains a powerful position. Domestic life is especially plagued by persons who resort to psychological savagery in order to enforce essentially unreasonable claims, as though a man were to carry a knuckle-duster up his sleeve, so that in case of need he might have something convincing to fall back upon.

III

When analysed the archaic mode of behaviour will invariably be found to rest upon a mythological archetype. It is this fact which gives us a diagnostic criterion. The adapted function is reasonable and humanly accessible. It is when the civilized, adapted function fails that the anima takes possession and the emotional performance begins. Recourse to the archaic mode of behaviour often has the character of a childish tantrum or hysterical demonstration of affect. Sulking is the most frequent symptom of the collapse of the adapted, disciplined function; the anima draws the subject away, teaching him how to enhance his grievance with an obstinate, minatory silence. It is not, however, true silence; in ways more eloquent than words it says: " I am deeply offended; the whole human race is less than nothing to me."

The archaic patterns which produce this effect of isolating a person from his *milieu* belong to a perfectly definite class. The scapegoat, the renegade, the outcast, the victim, the unloved, the man who walks alone—these, and a variety of others, all derive from the same root-theme. Each specific pattern unfolds itself with great fidelity to its emotional thesis, so that when the rôle is being enacted we recognize every nuance of the age-old performance. The tone of voice, the expression, the catch in the throat, the forlorn droop of the shoulders — every movement, down to the last detail, is eloquent of the victim's emotional argument.

Archetypal patterns of another class have just the opposite effect. These are the hero, the king, the big chief, the holy one, the world-shaker, the great magician, the all-wise, all-powerful, or infallible father, the all-loving mother, the priest, the medicine-man, the favoured disciple, the great provider, the saviour, the gentleman, the great carrier of burdens, the law-giver, the wise one, the great lover, and a multitude of others. They are the products of culture and belong to the cultural myth. In times of crisis the man who successfully identifies himself with one or other of the ruler archetypes is liable to become a leader and play the rôle of the saviour of his people, perhaps transforming himself from a relatively unknown adventurer into a national institution. The prestige of the dictator, the *mana* of the pope or the archbishop, the " divinity that doth hedge a king," the authority of the parent—these are not private property owned by this man or woman; they belong to the great cultural archetypes which are the common inheritance of the race. So long as the actor is faithful to the required rôle his authority is rarely challenged. But only let him falter in his lines or allow personal spleen or malice to alienate him from the spirit of the archetype, and his authority will soon be undermined. The potentate who is unaware that he has been swallowed by a whale is liable to confound his personality, somewhat ludicrously, with the archetype. He must then proceed to effect world-shaking disturbances in order to demonstrate to the world how miraculously he became a whale.

From the standpoint of the social hierarchy, it is imperative that the great collective archetypes should be faithfully served, and the very conception of true service precludes the sin of identifying oneself with the god. But from the standpoint of the individual whose whole personality becomes, as it were, built into the walls of the mighty archetype, it must be regarded as a spiritual crippling. Indeed, if the history of the development of the cultural archetypes were faithfully chronicled, it would have to be an endless record of human sacrifice. The living victims built into the walls of cities or buried under the pillars of temples, the slaves and concubines killed to companion the dead king, the children thrown into the burning pit of Tanit and Moloch, the rivers of human blood that have gone to feed ten thousand tribal deities—all bear witness to the ruthless power which the primordial images have exercised over human lives. Every social institution is grounded in an archetype, and everybody who becomes identified with an archetypal rôle becomes an institution. No longer do we offer our children to be devoured by appeasable gods, but we sacrifice ourselves to institutions instead. We must regard our institutions as humane, because they are the indispensable groundwork of our complex social structure; but actually the only humane aspect of institutions is the devotion of the human beings who serve them. The more we pour our enthusiasm into them and the vaster these animals become, the more victims they engulf, and the more obvious it is that they lack every human quality; hence the spiritual decay which is liable to envelop a man who identifies himself too long with an institution.

* * * * *

We have discovered, then, two classes of archetypal behaviour which can assist us to a better insight into the historical determinants of our affective constitution. The character of the Outcast takes shape as the nucleus of the former class, and the figure of the Chosen One appears as the mythic centre of the latter. From this analysis we are led to conclude that the fundamental issue upon which individual happiness or suicidal misery has mainly depended throughout human history rests upon the condition of acceptance. This condition is by no means restricted to the human race; the behaviour of animals, for instance, which are adapted to the pattern of the leader and the herd, demonstrates a similar affective constitution. The idea of the outcast derives originally from the excluded male, as, for example, the rogue elephant. But any member of a herd who becomes sick, or infirm, or eccentric is liable to be excluded or killed.

The idea of the chosen one centres in the leader, in which archetype the majesty of the King, the Lord's anointed, originates. The King therefore becomes the symbolical foundation-stone of every institution which confirms the solidarity of a united people. The whole class of what may be called prestige-archetypes can be related to this fundamental condition of acceptance, and it is because of this fact that the solitary experiment of individuation presents so formidable a problem in human development. The need of a fourfold acceptance—namely, by the parents, by society, by the lover and by God—corresponds with four transformations or phases of growth, so that when the vital acceptance of the parent is lacking the whole subsequent development is liable to be undermined. It is understandable, therefore, that every impulse or tendency which, on account of its individual or abnormal peculiarity, might seem to jeopardize acceptance will tend to be repressed. But a repressed function is not done with: it carries on its excluded, renegade existence in the unconscious as a kind of alternative hypothesis.

We can discern the two opposing types of archetypal determinants most clearly at the upper and lower end of the social scale—namely, the king or leader on the one hand, and the vagrant or criminal on the other.[1] At first glance, therefore, it would appear that the prestige and the popularity of the one, as compared with the unacceptability of the other, pro-

[1] That these are also a true Heraclitan pair of opposites is demonstrated by the relative frequency with which either one tends to go over into its opposite.

vided the key to human happiness. Actually, of course, this is not the case, owing to the unfavourable effect of the generic archetype within the sphere of relatedness. An archetype is, as we have said, a generalized dynamic pattern; it is therefore essentially non-personal. In so far as a man is identified with a power-archetype, his psychology becomes massive and predictable like a government department. It is impossible to relate to an institution; hence the fate of the archetypal human life is to remain peculiarly unrelated.

It is not only the cluster of images around the negative pole—*i.e.*, the victim, the renegade, the scapegoat, etc.—which have the effect of sundering a man from his kind. The autocrat, the all-highest, the magician, and perhaps most of all the saviour archetype, can create an even more insidious state of isolation. Primitive mentality is highly realistic concerning archetypal infection and guards against these effects by stringent taboos. Persons who are identified with a powerful archetype are rightly regarded as dangerous, and strict precautions have to be taken in dealing with them. The taboos surrounding the king are only partially intended for his safety; their chief function is to safeguard ordinary people from the infection of greatness and power. Men who come back from battle exalted by killing have to be cooled off before they are allowed back into the fold. Youths undergoing initiation, menstruating women, women in childbirth, the things belonging to the medicine-man—everything in fact which could spread the archetypal infection—must be safeguarded by taboo.

This aspect of mental hygiene has been ignored in civilized societies, where people are supposed to act upon rational motives. But the frequent epidemics of archaic affect in recent world politics, not to mention the irremediable consequences which might so easily ensue, make one realize how desperate is our need of effective measures of psychological disinfection. Although the virus of the world-shaker is vastly more destructive of human life than that of the scapegoat, yet in some degree everyone who unconsciously identifies himself with a collective image is a potential danger to the community because of the infection he disseminates. A doctor, for instance, who assumes the rôle of the saviour-archetype is liable to infect his patients with his unconscious anima-virus, with the result that soon they begin unconsciously to play their appropriate parts and become emotionally involved with him to a greater or lesser degree.

The gifted man is more liable to fall a victim to anima-possession than the shrewd, pedestrian man of the world. His potentialities being greater, the anima finds ample occasion to set her seductive snares in the path of his hidden ambition. The first thing, therefore, that the gifted man should realize and come to terms with is his will-to-power. Should he ignore his potentialities the anima will prompt him to become the victim of his own frustrated ambition and to play the rôle of the misunderstood genius.

It is of course understood that all the evil effects referred to above are the result of unconscious identification with the archetype. The anima can seduce a man to enact or re-enact a mythological rôle only in so far as he is unconscious of what the anima is doing to him. As soon as he has learned to discern the anima-activity and vigilantly to observe where she is leading him, he is in the position of relating the activity of the unconscious to his conscious life.

When, therefore, we speak of the anima-face (in the top left-hand corner) as the key-signature to the four drawings of this new series we imply that these products are the result of an archetypal affective constellation, the specific character of which is represented by the expression of this face. In other words, these drawings are begun under the ægis of the anima in the rôle of the suffering victim. In spite of superior intelligence and insight, in respect to this aspect of his fate the subject was as though bound hand and foot. His fate ordained that he should become helplessly involved in his wife's neurosis, and there can be little doubt that the latter was also enhanced and encouraged by his fatalistic Andromeda projection. Thus from every point of view the patient's victim-attitude needed to be made conscious and dealt with as an insistent practical problem.

IV

The second tributary to the pool of melancholy comes from the pitcher held by the self-dissected arm. Dissected carries perhaps a too objective connotation, since the presence of the ogre's knife and fork tells a different tale. An ogre is a man-eating monster characterized by a gnarled, misshapen, usually gigantic body and coarse, hairy skin. Why is the ogre gigantic ? And why does he devour men ? To answer these questions we must glance at his kind in myth and folklore. Cyclops, the man-eating giant, had a single eye, was possessed of enormous strength, and was somewhat slow-witted, though shrewd. In his combat with the giant the hero usually seeks out the eye or the forehead as the vulnerable spot into which to thrust his weapon. In spite of their vast size and often magical attributes, the Titans, the giants and the ogres are invariably beaten in combat. Often they are outwitted, but usually their vulnerable spot is their undoing. Their abode is underground in great caves or in remote and gloomy castles. However much they may vary in the other aspects of their character, they invariably display a vast and terrible appetite, and usually for human victims.

From this rather meagre character-sketch we infer:

(*a*) That the ogre or giant is a mythologized relic of an earlier and more primitive race at some time displaced by a people of higher culture and intelligence. Even to-day accounts of the indigenous inhabitants of a country, vouchsafed by the guardians of the superseding culture, tend to be highly coloured and fantastic. Throughout Italy at the present time, for instance, amazing stories are told and believed of the terrible ferocity of the Abyssinians, and of the corresponding heroism of the dauntless Italian soldiers.

(*b*) That he has been relegated to the status of earth-dæmon, illustrated by his haunting of caves and his use of vast stones for weapons. Like the giant Antæus, who was overcome by Heracles, his strength often resides in his contact with the earth.

(*c*) That he represents something vast and clumsy and devouring which is essentially hostile to consciousness. This latter character is evidenced by his isolated existence, his slow-witted, microcephalic brain, and by his single eye, which is also his vulnerable spot.

Piecing these inferences together, we are able to bring the monster into view as a personification of the overpowering weight of primitive inertia, resembling the force of the earth's attraction within the psychic sphere.

Psychic inertia is the greatest devourer of human lives; it is the eternal negation of effort, tending to pull everything down to the aboriginal level where all initiative is superfluous. The microcephalic giant is the archetypal low-brow, hating everything which challenges thought. He is the atavistic weight of the lowest level, which tends to suck back into limbo every potential idea that could involve creative labour. He is the earliest and deepest passion of man. All he asks is to eat and sleep and lie in peace. All the manifold ways of escaping the responsibility of consciousness are fathered by this " spirit of gravity." In South America he is called *mañana*. Wasting time in Europe is seldom more than a hobby, but south of the Panama Canal it becomes a vocation. The water that is being poured out of the pitcher is no mere leakage of energy. As it splashes into the gutter it has to point a ribald finger at everything containing value. The crimes of unconsciousness are rarely due just to lack of knowledge: behind this primitive inertia there is a power that strives against consciousness and aims at the destruction of value. It might be called the god-killer.

So much for the ogrish character of this figure. But no ogre uses his knife and fork on himself. This is a pathological refinement of the inverting libido due to the constellating anima-mood. It denotes a masochistic indulgence in self-devouring criticism, a maudlin kind of subjectivity that wastes time and effort merely for the sake of undermining the creative will. If the victim-hypothesis of the anima is to win the day the arm and hand, which might produce something of value, must be seduced across to the sinister side. Hence the perverted arm in the drawing is the left arm. In the same way the pitcher, the knife and the fork, which have been perverted to the wrong use, have acquired a wrong shape. Even the water (*i.e.*, the libido) is diabolized.

With regard to the next figure the symbolism is more obscure. The snake is thin, segmented and bony. Instead of being sleek, coiled and vigorous, its body is extended and irregular. This is no healthy snake: there is even the suggestion of a tape-worm in the segmentation of the body. It must represent an instinct that has undergone a certain degeneration.

The nautilus shells also show a segmentation which, although conforming to the internal structure of the nautilus, is nevertheless unduly accentuated in the drawing. The shells are obviously empty, forming an abstract trinity within the loops of the snake's body. The involuting spiral is a frequent, one might say almost regular, symptomatic figure in schizophrenic drawings. It is pathognomonic of the introverted *habitus*, whereas the evolving spiral is, as everyone knows, the universal symbol of growth. The ambivalence of the nautilus symbolism is also emphasized by the fact that two face in one direction and one in the other. This Janus-faced character is also a sign of the archaism of this constellation.

The content here is highly ambiguous. The constellation of three atavistic symbols controlled by the single snake has the mystical connotation of three in one. But the proper hierarchy is reversed, the smallest shell being above, the largest below. Moreover, the snake is in the negative position, with its head pointing vertically downwards. The symbol of trinity denotes the creative principle. But here it is under the sign of inversion, implying that by the process of *enantiodromia*[1] the creative libido has been converted into a self-destroying tendency.

Creation and destruction are the primal pair of opposites. Prajapati, the creator, created Agni out of his mouth. " Because he begat him out of his mouth, therefore is Agni the devourer." Prometheus, who stole the divine fire from the

[1] The tendency of things to go over into their opposites.

hearth of Zeus, was chained to the Caucasus, and every day an eagle sent by Zeus devoured his liver; but every night it was returned to him, so that he lay in perpetual torment. The creature that Frankenstein created became the destroyer of those whom his creator loved most. The Golem, whom the rabbi created by magical means to save his people from the pogrom, became their destroyer. Lilith, who refused the creative task of bringing man to birth, went over to the demons and became a vampire.

Examples need not be multiplied, for everyone knows from his own inner experience the truth of Blake's aphorism: " One portion of being is the prolific, the other the devouring. . . ."

The principle of creative evolution might well be symbolized by the snake (representing the primordial energy of instinct), under the creative sign of the three spirals, were it not for the inverted position of the whole figure.

We might discern a further sign of ambivalence in the fact that the two smaller shells are directed towards the left—*i.e.*, towards the sinister witches' hands which leap up from the water-splash—while the opening of the larger shell is directed towards the maternal figure of grief on the right. Moreover, the latter shell is outside and relatively free of the snake-influence, while the former two are enclosed within the loops of the snake's body.

This connection of the larger nautilus shell with the maternal figure, and the corresponding connection of the snake's head with the skull, suggest that we should do well to regard this whole constellation of figures as belonging to the same theme.

The meaning of the skull seems at first sight to be self-evident. Viewed from the standpoint of the observer, the left half represents a mask in which the lines of suffering are emphasized. We described it as Chinese in character; but this association comes more from the mask-like imperturbability of the expression than from the actual configuration of the face. The right half shows the bones of the skull entirely denuded of flesh. The fatalism of deep suffering is therefore joined to the symbol of mortality. It would be difficult to resist the conclusion that the idea of suicide is meant to be conveyed by the skull, and that the forked tongue of the snake has inserted an idea into the tormented mind opening the door to suicide.

The melting figure of grief is draped in a style suggesting the classical representations of the Mother of Christ as Pietà. Possibly it is this association which makes one think of this figure as essentially maternal. Although conventionalized in style there is a note of genuine feeling in the dignified figure which is lacking in the rather affected appeal of the face on the opposite side.

The meaning of this whole constellation of symbols begins to emerge. The inversion of the creative process results in a morbid activity of the libido working inward upon itself with a self-destroying intensity. The fascination of this mood is overwhelming; the subject feels gripped by a sinister urge which must lead either to intense suffering or to suicide. The mourning figure of the mother would symbolize a genuine grief at the loss of creative achievement which, as Blake says, is the manifestation of the divine nature. "Some will say, Is not God alone the Prolific? I answer, God alone Acts and Is, in existing beings or Men."[1] From this point of view creation is an unending act of God. Therefore the mother-imago, the maternal womb of the unconscious from which all creative ideas spring, weeps again because of the death of her divine son.

The downward movement pervading the whole drawing expresses more than mere depression. Clearly the tendency towards genuine expression of feeling develops with the descent, as though the downward introverting momentum were also concerned to get to the root of the problem. This is also implied in the downward pointing of the instinctual energy symbolized by the ambivalent snake.

In this descent of the introverting libido to the mother-imago we are reminded of the scene in Act I. of the second part of *Faust*, where Faust presses Mephisto to evoke Helen out of the past. After making various objections Mephisto says:

[1] *Marriage of Heaven and Hell.*

I've no concern with the old heathen race;
They house within their special Hades.
Yet there's a way.
FAUST. Speak, nor delay thy history !
MEPHISTO. Unwilling I reveal a loftier mystery,—
In solitude are throned the Goddesses,
No Space around them, Place and Time still less;
Only to speak of them embarrasses.
They are The Mothers !
FAUST (*terrified*). Mothers !
MEPHISTO. Hast thou dread ?
FAUST. The Mothers ! Mothers !—a strange word is said.
MEPHISTO. It is so. Goddesses, unknown to ye,
The Mortals,—named by us unwillingly.
Delve in the deepest depths must thou to reach them;
'Tis thine own fault that we for help beseech them.
FAUST. Where is the way ?
MEPHISTO. No way !—To the unreachable,
Ne'er to be trodden ! A way to the unbeseechable,
Never to be besought ! Art thou prepared ?
There are no locks, no latches to be lifted;
Through endless solitudes shalt thou be drifted.
Hast thou through solitudes and deserts fared ?

After further discussion by Mephisto, Faust exclaims:

Come on then ! we'll explore, whate'er befall;
In this thy Nothing, may I find my All !
MEPHISTO. I'll praise thee, ere we separate: I see
Thou knowest the Devil thoroughly.
Here, take this key !
FAUST. That little thing ?
MEPHISTO. Take hold of it, not undervaluing !
FAUST. It glows, it shines,—increases in my hand !
MEPHISTO. How much 'tis worth, thou soon shalt understand.
The Key will scent the true place from all others;
Follow it down !—'twill lead thee to the Mothers.
FAUST (*shuddering*). The Mothers! Like a blow it strikes me still !
What is the word, to hear which makes me chill ?"[1]

Although on other grounds there is a certain parallelism between the psychology of our subject and that of Faust,

[1] Bayard Taylor translation.

we are concerned here with the specific connection between the quest of the soul and the mother problem. At the root of the tremendous fascination of the unconscious are " the Mothers." It is for this reason that the subject has to " delve the deepest depths."

Helen is of course the supreme anima-figure. Goethe's nostalgia for the beauty of Greece is expressed in Faust's quest of the soul as Helen. In pursuit of this passionate quest Faust is prepared to take the uncharted way into the depths of the unconscious. In both cases, therefore, the introverting movement of the libido is under the ægis of the anima. The key Mephisto places in Faust's hand is patently phallic, but the terror which clutches at his heart when he is told that it leads him to the Mothers, comes from the darkest abyss of the soul. The craving of the infantile libido for the mother recoils before the implacable taboo of the ancestors, nay, of the whole human communion. It is this conflict which fills the unconscious with sinister and terrifying forms. The mother-archetype is the original deity of man's unconscious; therefore the whole meaning of origin or source is bound up with the mother-imago. Hence this original archetype also includes mother-earth, mother-nature and the tree of life.

The ambivalence of the deep unconscious symbolism comes from the ruling power of the mother-idea. The transformation into the tree, for example, can express the infantile desire to be united with the mother, or it can mean the acceptance of the necessity for rebirth. Similarly, in the present drawing, the snake can represent either the regressive instinct seeking to flow back again into its source—*i.e.*, the mother—or it could be the Æsculapian snake, which was the symbol of renewal by means of introversion into the unconscious. Moreover, the infantile mother-craving is characterized by that same compelling inertia which we allocated to the man-eating ogre. Indeed, from the example of Antæus, the mother-bound giant, and from the slow-witted, one-eyed slothfulness of the whole brood, the ogre or giant might easily personify the aboriginal strength of the incestuous libido, the universal human horror of incest being manifested in their hideous, gnarled and repulsive aspect.

The phallic snake with the three ambiguous nautilus shells (which are just as well fitted to symbolize the evolutionary flow of the libido in search of its goal as the involuting tendency of the libido seeking the maternal source) would of course be equivalent to the key which Mephisto hands to Faust.

In trying to read this unconscious picture-language it is a good rule to regard the most obscure and equivocal as the key-symbol, the index or pointer which can lead down to a new level of understanding. Following the Faustian analogy, we can assume that the phallic snake whispers the word " incest " to the sleeping brain of the subject, and that the alternating aspects of death and suffering acceptance, manifested by the head, represent the only possibilities which offer themselves to the man who is impaled on this problem. Either a drastic sacrifice of the infantile craving must be undertaken, or the libido, becoming more and more fascinated by the maternal image in the unconscious, makes insanity or suicide increasingly plausible.

V

Another classical example of the intimate connection between the anima and the mother-problem is to be found in the psychology of Hamlet. Hamlet's neurotic impotence comes into evidence in his relation to Ophelia. Shakespeare makes it clear that he loves and desires her, and Ophelia assuredly loves Hamlet. He loves, but is powerless to make his love effective; therefore he is tormented by suspicion. The inversion of desire is terribly portrayed in the form of paranoidal insinuations and negative feelings—the classical symptoms of anima-possession in the realm of feeling. He longs to free himself from the incestuous labyrinth that inevitably leads to the mother at its centre. If he could only marry Ophelia and follow the course of his love he would eventually break free from the fatal fascination. But, confusing Ophelia with the demon-anima who drives him, he is like a somnambulist in the grip of a terrible dream. Eventually, struggling with the tentacles of the invisible enemy, he is forced to the heart of the labyrinth where, in the mother's bedchamber, he transfixes the hidden impalpable obstacle behind the arras, only to find it is Ophelia's father he has slain. The real cause of Hamlet's impotence is his infantile craving for the mother, his unconscious and hence unsacrificed incest-fantasy. It is as though the thing moving behind the arras confirmed the whole paranoidal fantasy. At last he could stab down to the invisible root-cause of his suffering and bring it into the light. The paranoiac is a potential homicide because of the insane intensity forcing him to eradicate the root and source of the things which are undermining his existence.

If only Hamlet's behaviour were presented we should be right in regarding him as a dangerous homicide. And yet he is the hero of an epic tragedy. As we follow the tormented soul through the labyrinth of his fate we feel that something should die. Not old Polonius, but the infantile hero in Hamlet's unconscious is the sacrifice that is needed to release his love-will from its bondage to the mother.

The tragedy of Hamlet is the despair of great potentiality beating itself to death against the bars of the incest-cage. The poison that eats into his soul is akin to Faust's pact with the Devil. For it cannot be denied that the libido that craves with the all-or-none passion of childhood for complete possession of the mother is both the source and the murderer of love.

The very inadequate rendering of this problem in our patient's drawing informs us that it is still in the germinal phase. Its remoteness from the conscious level is also indicated by the abstract and very obscure symbolism with which it is expressed. It is significant that this same problem, which can inspire a master-work in the greatest of poets, can also produce a pathological abortion.

* * * * *

We have now analysed the three sources or tributaries from which the pool of melancholy is fed. The first stream flows from the appealing, helpless anima. Here the fatalistic note is struck which governs the whole series. The second flows from the perverted ogre's pitcher, representing the self-devouring inertia of the mother-bound libido. The third flows from the maternal imago, whose grief expresses the ultimate realization that the mother is the unwitting destroyer of the son and that maturity can only be gained through a drastic sacrifice of the infantile mother-seeking libido.

The sacrificial motive is already indicated in the *religieuse* expression of the anima-face. But here it is affected and insincere; while in the expression of the man's face below the signs of intense suffering are joined to a stoical endurance.

We might suppose that a man who could thus represent the gaining of maturity through suffering had begun to realize the problem. Actually, however, the measure of conscious realization cannot be deduced from such indications. The disparity between what the hand executes and what the reason comprehends is probably one of the chief reasons why the inner psychological content of schizophrenic drawings has rarely been given its true value. The tendency to accept the patient's consciousness as the measure of his products is a great hindrance to the psychological understanding of material. Obviously some part of the patient's mind is creating, participating in, and apprehending the sequence of events with a subtlety which far exceeds our laborious investigation of them. The aim of our analytical elucidation, therefore, is to create a bridge of understanding whereby the directing function of consciousness may be able to extend its short-range vision to embrace the peculiar depth and subtlety of its " unconscious " elder brother.

VI

We had almost omitted to discuss the presence of the two insects and their apparent irrelevance. Yet we know from our experience of dream-interpretation that in the apparently irrelevant factor we often find the essence of the dream.

We have already remarked upon the uncanny realism

which gives them the appearance of having just alighted upon the paper. In this connection the suggestion offered by Jung, in the letter quoted above, must be borne in mind. There is also the obvious allusion to the spider and the fly:

> " 'Will you walk into my parlour?' said the spider to the fly.
> 'It's the cosiest little parlour that ever you did spy.' "

Only in the present instance there is no alluring parlour and no " winding stair " to substantiate the idea of a cunning trap.

The feeling of the patient was against spiders, not because of a special sympathy for their victims but because of the disagreeable way they have of dropping upon one unexpectedly. This association would chime in with Jung's suggestion that the precision of these insect-drawings comes from the patient's need to hold the irrational animation of the autonomous units in check.

From their position in the design we must infer that they are, at least symptomatically, related to the anima-complex. The lines flowing down from the face of the woman can be regarded as anima-effect. The fly and the spider are posted on either side of this stream, pointing in the direction of its flow. Are they perhaps symptomatic expressions of the anima-mood? The action of the fly's front legs is somewhat suggestive of the presence of something alluring in its neighbourhood. Taking the obvious connotation of the spider as the predatory creature that lures, and of the fly as the freely moving creature that is lured, we can relate these qualities to specific anima-effects already discerned.

The rôle of a beautiful appealing Andromeda bemoaning her pitiful fate is a well-known feminine lure. But the hero who falls to this lure is liable to discover the " devouring " predatory will behind the apparently harmless exterior. The hero and the victim are inseparably bound together as a pair of opposites; it follows, therefore, that the man whose conscious attitude is too heroic will nourish a corresponding unconscious attitude of the victim. Owing to emotional determination by the anima, such a man will be fatally attracted to a woman who satisfies the victim-demand of his soul. But those who have adapted to life on the basis of the victim-archetype are as deeply attached to their rock of destiny as the hero is enamoured of his own heroism. Hence the hero who sets out to rescue the helpless victim from her rock is liable to get a knife in his back for his pains. A woman-patient once brought me a revealing fantasy. She imagined herself in a primitive community in which she had been chosen as the sacrificial victim. Mournfully she resigned herself to her fate and allowed herself to be bound upon the altar-stone. Just as the priest's knife was about to be plunged into her breast the hero intervened, laying about him with prodigious valour until all the priests were scattered or slain. Having cut her bonds, he carried her off to his cave. But instead of gratitude she faced him with bitter hatred and scorn. Not only had be robbed her of her glorious destiny, but now he expected love and service in return!

The masochistic fascination of the victim-rôle is expressed in the self-devouring ogre's arm; it will also be observed that the spider has the appearance of issuing from the ogre's pitcher with the bewitched stream of water. Thus the doubt we felt about the carefully rehearsed note of suffering in the face of the anima turns out to be justified.

Here again, as in the previous drawing, we find the insects proceeding, as it were, from the anima-effect. I have not observed this connection in the drawing of other patients; it may therefore be an idiosyncrasy of the present subject. None the less the association is psychologically intelligible inasmuch as it is the autonomy of the anima-complex which, in the case of an introverted intellectual, seems to threaten the integrity of consciousness; and it is the autonomous activity of certain psychic factors which, according to Jung's interpretation, prompts the patient to draw these "doctor" insects.

Another patient described this irrational fragmentation of consciousness very clearly. Just at the moment when she longed for the whole of her mind to be completely one with the wished-for experience, a wholly irrelevant letter, or word, or image would come buzzing into the conscious field. The annoying interruption always succeeded in diverting her mind from the sphere of emotional participation, so that her attention became hooked to the irrelevant image. She was powerless either to dispel or to ignore the subjective interruption. It goaded her almost to frenzy, for it seemed to be informed with the devilish aim of frustrating just that moment of complete participation upon which her heart was set. In other words, although the image itself seemed irrelevant its insistence and manner of appearance were instinct with diabolical purpose.

The subject of these drawings described a similar intervention of inconsequent images, particularly at moments when his whole attention was needed. These symptomatic insects have therefore been drawn with an almost excessive realism, because they cause an altogether disproportionate amount of distress. Usually the patient knows only too well that what he complains of cannot be understood rationally; accordingly he may tend to conceal from the doctor the intensity of his distress.

Jung's explanation penetrates to the core of this characteristic schizophrenic symptom. It is not the irrelevance of the intervening image that creates the problem, but rather the fact that the intervention has a pathological, mosquito-like insistence, as though a part of the mind had turned against the subject and were intent on nothing else but undermining his peace of mind. No co-operation is possible with insects. They are utterly removed from subjective understanding or participation. The best we can hope for is to protect ourselves from their pitiless and unflagging interest in our blood or excretory by-products.

We have defined the anima as personifying the purposiveness of the autonomous psyche. With this definition in mind we can recognize in these insects the twin manifestations of pathological purposiveness described above—namely, the lure of the irrelevant image and its inherent power of obsessing the subject's attention. Of these two effects the fly would correspond with the irrelevant image, the spider with its predatory hold on the attention. It is the latter which causes the morbid inversion of the psychic energy.

* * * * *

In conclusion we have to observe that a certain dynamic polarity is indicated by the fact that the woman's head above and the man's head below are placed in the position of diagonal reciprocity. This polarity would necessarily imply a circuit of psychical energy existing between the two poles of the system. One arc of this circuit can, in fact, be traced as a jagged irregular line, proceeding downwards from the centre of the woman's chin to the left-hand lower corner of the field. Here it goes through an involuted, discontinuous phase, gaining strength again as it approaches a bridge or point of junction, marked by two short parallel transverse lines. At this point of junction it meets a line taking a strong jagged course from the mid-point of the man's chin, where it is seen to be continuous with the bisecting medial line of the head.

The points to be noted about this external arc of the circuit are: (*a*) the similarity between the disturbance of the line just after it has passed the neighbourhood of the insects, and the disturbances in the lines of Drawing 16 after passing the area of the buried cones; (*b*) the discontinuity of the line is most marked at the level of the " pool of melancholy," in which the man's head is immersed; (*c*) the two transverse parallel lines at which the strong, transverse male current meets the weak, descending anima-stream. I have no association from the patient in respect to these cross-lines, but two suggestions readily rise to one's mind. They might, for instance, represent the anode and kathode of electrical opposition. This suggestion is strengthened by the jagged line, which is a conventional representation of electrical energy. The other possibility is that they represent the schizophrenic break or gap in the sphere of the marriage relationship. This I believe to be the true explanation, and the fact that the obstruction is reduced to a mere glyph is probably due to the subject's reticence.[1]

The other interior arc of the circuit would be represented by the sequence of symbolical figures, beginning with the ogre's hand above and ending in the maternal figure below.

[1] The possibility of negative feeling towards the wife having found expression in the anima-face is not, of course, excluded.

This inner and outer arc of the circuit could also represent the manifest and concealed aspect of the situation, like the two birds in Drawing 18. The outer and manifest arc would correspond to the subject's relationship with his wife, upon whom the anima was projected, whilst the contents of the inner concealed arc would correspond with the libido invested in the whole inverted process. Since the direction of the libido in the outer arc is clearly downwards towards the man's head, the direction in the inner arc should logically be upwards from the man's head to the woman's. These indications are somewhat faint, and we have no association from the patient to help us. All we are entitled to say is that something in the nature of an energic system runs through the whole drawing, and that the two poles of this system are the woman's head above and the man's head below.

VII

Drawing 20

The contents of this drawing are disposed roughly into four vertical columns. The figure on the left is a diagrammatic drawing of a plant. It has the studied precision proper to a botanical textbook, and yet the treatment of the flower, with its vase-shaped, four-petalled calyx, is decidedly ornate. The sense of a deliberate design is enhanced by the four distinct levels, each with its specific type of outgrowth, of which the structure of the plant consists. The composite flower is comprised of twenty-one petals, each carrying a medial row of fine dots, and a deep calyx which combines the numbers four and three in two tiers, four larger petals above and three smaller below. About an inch below the flower a group of three bracts is pushing out towards the left. An inch further down a single fern-like leaf springs from the right of the stem but bends over immediately towards the left. At the bottom the roots of the plant are spread out fanwise, so that each radicle is exposed to view. Here again the general sweep of the fibres is towards the left. In compensation to this leftward drift of its various parts the stem of the plant kinks sharply towards the right at its base, and thence slants upwards towards the left again.

In the next column there is a figure consisting of a mutilated head and neck, three knives of exotic design, and a jewelled ring. Since this figure occupies the space between the two plants constituting the first and third columns of the design, it should be considered in relation to its neighbours on either hand. The upper part of the head has been cut away, its place being occupied by a collection of three knives. The knives are outlandish in character: two are short, straight daggers, the third is a curved scimitar. Their design is foreign, resembling that of no tools in common use, but having more the character of Oriental curios. The points of the three converge in the region of the right eye, not as though the knives had been stabbed or thrust into the eye, but rather as though they had been deliberately placed in this arrangement, almost as flowers are arranged in a vase. That they represent a sign rather than a deed is confirmed by the absence of blood or other evidence of violence in this region, though the lacerations in the neck and the absence of the top part of the head must presumably be connected with the presence of the knives. From the evidence of the drawing, all we can say is that the part of the head which contains the brain is absent, and that it has been replaced by a fourfold constellation consisting of three knives and a jewelled ring. As a consequence or accompaniment of this displacement we find bleeding wounds on the front of the neck which have the characteristic ineffectualness of attempted self-injury. The lower part of the face is that of a young man with parted lips.

In the third column another diagrammatic plant has been drawn and again four levels have been represented. But whereas the first plant might have been taken from a primer on botany this belongs preferably to a physiological textbook. The labyrinthine convolutions of the flower identify it with the brain, and the fact should be noted that this brain-flower is situated just above the human head, from which the brain has been abstracted. About an inch below the flower a veined fragile-looking leaf grows out to the right of the stem. Another inch below this a flat circular target or diaphragm, consisting of three concentric rings, marks the third level. The stem of the plant, which is considerably thickened in this region, passes through the inner ring of the target, and the piebald blade of a dart or javelin, which is seen slanting downwards from the right, is aimed at the same inner ring of the target. The thickening of the stem in its lower third is accompanied by a decided change in the character of the line. It assumes the same jagged, brittle quality as we observed in the schizophrenic crack of Drawing 3, although sharp angles are not developed until the diaphragm is reached.

The root-system corresponds to the fourth level, and we note how different it is from the root-system of the other plant. In the former case the stem divided into two, the two into four, and these into a varying number of subdivisions. Moreover, the stem itself, as well as each root-fibre, was drawn with a double line, while the whole system was rather crowded and bent towards the left.

In the case of the brain-plant, on the other hand, the whole root-system is spread out like the wide delta of a river. The stem divides into three main channels, each forming, with its subdivisions, its own system, right, left and central; and the principle of the single line is maintained throughout.

The fourth column consists of three candles in a row. The two on the left are burning. The one on the right is smoking, as though it had just been extinguished. The javelin with its piebald blade seems to be connected with this third candle, inasmuch as the end of the shaft is half enclosed within a curve of its ascending smoke.

* * * * *

The value of a detailed description is demonstrated when we are confronted by such a drawing as this. The patient had no idea why he had to place these enigmatic figures side by side in the same constellation. The idea of each figure presented itself independently, and he drew them without question or hesitation, and without any sense of continuity with what had gone before or might come after.

The first thing that emerges from the description is the frequency of the constellations four and three in the structure of this drawing. There are four figures arranged roughly into four columns. The plants in columns one and three display four structural levels, while the root-system of the first plant expands from four subdivisions. Four functional symbols replace the upper part of the head in the second figure, and the three candles and the javelin present a corresponding quartette in the fourth figure.

The threefold constellation is also present in every figure. In the first, it appears in the three bracts on the stem of the plant; in the second, in the three knives; in the third, in the diaphragm of three rings; in the fourth, in the three candles.

The key-signature of this intrinsic structural combination is to be found in the calyx of the flower in the first figure, which shows four petals above with a delicate trefoil at its base.

The existence of this combination informs us, at the outset, that we have to deal with a statement of the morbid condition in terms of functional structure. This must be our starting-point.

The first figure is a diagram. It is a representation of no particular plant, but rather a generalized concept of a plant, showing four of its characteristic functional forms. From a comparison of the objective plant in the first figure and the subjective or brain-plant in the third, we infer that the patient is conceiving an analogy between the flower of a plant and the brain of a man. A somewhat similar analogy is clearly intended between the fern-like leaf on the stem of the former and the delicately veined leaf on the stem of the latter. From what we know of the patient's preoccupation with his executive problem, as evidenced in the first drawing of the series, we may assume that this latter leaf corresponds to the efferent nerve-system of his executive arm and hand. The analogy between the two root-systems is self-evident, and the fact that the ramification of this system in the brain-plant takes place below a diaphragm would seem to point to its identification with the visceral sympathetic system, which, in anatomical symbolism, would represent the roots of the unconscious.

So far it is relatively plain sailing; but when we look for a possible analogy between the three bracts on the stem of the one, and the three concentric rings around the stem of the other, we are not so sure of our ground. In the previous drawing we also encountered a highly enigmatic figure, couched in the same threefold symbolism. There, too, we found four main figures, but the enigmatic key-symbol was the third, consisting of a trinity of nautilus shells encompassed by a snake.

Observing the character of the figures which appear under the constellation 4, it would seem that, under this sign, the elements of form, structure, and what may be termed manifest content, tend to predominate, whereas under the constellation 3 a certain enigmatic and, on the whole, archaic symbolism tends to manifest itself. In other words, contents disposed under the fourfold principle tend to be descriptive and self-evident, while the threefold groupings tend to be irrational and are accordingly meaningless if not interpreted symbolically.

In an earlier discussion we referred to the manifest and concealed content of these drawings with their two different levels of interpretation; we also emphasized the point that these two levels have nothing whatever to do with the idea of disguise or distortion as originally mooted by Freud. The character of the two birds in the tree, in Drawing 18, hinted at the existence of the two types of content; but in the drawing now under discussion the presence of these two distinctive types becomes one of the principal features.

Taking the first figure as exemplifying the fourfold, structural type, we noted that the structure of the calyx expresses the number 4 as the dominant and the number 3 as the recessive factor. With this key in our hand we observe that of the four specific structural parts or levels, three—the flower, the leaf, and the root-system—are highly differentiated, while one, the group of three bracts, is undifferentiated or vestigial. Being on a different evolutionary level from the other three functional systems, these bracts seem to suggest a concealed possibility. The patient is not a botanist, but he has obviously observed the structure of plants with an observant eye.

We can therefore conclude that his functional analogy of the plant with the psyche in this drawing is informed with the same psychological interest as was apparent in his detailed observation of insects. There can be no particular interest in the mere representation of differentiated structural forms; they are already fully manifest. There is nothing more to be said about them. But when we come to the three vestigial bracts our interest is at once kindled, especially when we observe the three archaic knives in their immediate neighbourhood.

Comparing the first and second figures, the plant has been given three superior or differentiated functions and one inferior or vestigial, whereas the man has three archaistic functions with one dissociated function of value, that of the diamond ring. The archaisms in both cases are under the sign of the creative trinity, indicating that this is the point of emergence, where we may look for the possibility of creative evolution.

The manifest meaning of the three knives is purely pathological. They seem to be telling us that, in place of the sensitive receptivity and the self-regulating interaction of function of a balanced mind, the subject is the victim of an obsessional thought-destroying introversion, which makes him feel as though three-fourths of his mental functioning had turned against him in a suicidal conspiracy. If it were not for the presence of the detached fourth function, containing the jewel (the symbol of value or individuality), this sinister figure would seem to denote an overwhelming suicidal tendency. But the ring, being in the position of ruler, determines the constellation by its superior power.

From immemorial time the ring has been the symbol of a compact. As the bearer of the King's seal, the ring also acquired the connotation of final sanction. The diamond is the jewel of highest value, the jewel expressing the idea of the greatest possible value in the smallest possible compass. Hence the jewelled ring affirms the idea of individual feeling or value as the ruling factor. But what cruel contradiction is this: a suicidal obsession under royal command? Yet in a sense this figure represents the truth more nearly than any of the previous symptomatic statements. For on the one hand it represents the stark realization that the pathological inversion, which has already suborned three objective functions to its destructive purpose, leads inevitably to suicide. On the other hand, the central position of the jewel, resembling a medial eye, suggests a superior standpoint of value which, by seeing beyond the pathological state of affairs, reaches to a creative purpose that could abolish the whole intellectual inversion in order that feeling may be allowed to grow.

This creative possibility is expressed, in varying forms, in the four constellations that are ruled by the number three, which, by the way, are all approximately on the same level—namely, the three bracts, the three knives, the three concentric rings, and the three candles.

Let us first discuss the significance of the three bracts. The most distinctive feature of the elaborated plant-body is its continued embryology. In all the higher animals the embryonic phase is a transient step in the process of development. This step leads to the laying down of a definite final structure, consisting of limbs, members and parts, in accordance with a specific anatomical pattern. Plants, on the other hand, have the power of developing an indefinite number of parts in a succession theoretically without term or limit. Every bud of a tree or plant contains its own embryonic growing-point, deeply embedded among the successive leaves it has produced. This embryonic nucleus holds the potentiality of unlimited further development, and it is this *continued embryology which is the ruling factor in the organization of the enlarging plant-body*.

In the plant shown in our drawing, all its different parts—namely, stem, flower, leaf and root—appear fully differentiated: the three bracts are the only exception. The bract is a modified leaf or petal which frequently covers the point of emergence. It is, as it were, an archaic companion of the embryological growing-point. The motif of creative emergence is given by the number three.

With these facts in mind we can understand why the patient's unconscious once again insists upon the vegetational analogy. Conceiving the psyche purely in terms of mammalian brain structure, we are confronted with a definite morphology which excludes the possibility of creative emergence. But when the psychic organization is realized as analogous with that of a plant the possibility of continued embryology opens the door to the idea of creative evolution *within the psychic sphere.*

Let us now turn to the diaphragm with the three rings in the third figure, and the three candles and aimed shaft in the fourth. The patient had the idea that this diaphragm was also a target. We might therefore regard the three rings as a successive narrowing of the field in the sustained subjective effort to get to the heart of the trouble. But the position of these rings, between the realm of executive consciousness (the brain-flower and the hand-leaf) and the root-system in the unconscious, makes it necessary for us to identify this structure with the idea of a diaphragm or threshold lying between these two aspects of the psyche.

We have also to consider the fact that, in view of the obvious similarity between figures 1 and 3, the three-ringed diaphragm in 3 has a certain parallelism with the leaf-frond in 1. This connection, on the face of it, is quite obscure. Examining this frond, we find nine leaflets above the midrib and eight below, while the midrib itself ends in a kind of barb with eight points. This barb resembles the metal barb employed by savages in the making of arrows.

The only event of importance in the patient's life which might be related to these numbers was the second marriage of his mother, which occurred between his eighth and ninth year. There can be no question that this event had a profound effect upon the patient's emotional development, inasmuch as the man who thus became his stepfather was the man who had seduced him when a child, and with whom the sealed antisocial pact had been established. With this essential fact in mind it is possible to regard the barbed frond as a symbol of concealment, and the three-ringed target and shaft as the symbol of the analytical attempt to pierce this concealed area in order to get to the root of the disease. The fact that the target is also a diaphragm would not contradict this hypothesis, since the diaphragm is the anatomical equivalent for the threshold built up between the ideational conscious and the affective unconscious. In order to get to the roots of any mental disturbance it is essential to penetrate this threshold.

The thickening of the vital nerve or stem of the psychic plant in the region of the diaphragm immediately suggests the pathological analogy of sclerosis. The characteristic jagged appearance of the portion below the diaphragm would tend to localize the schizophrenic interference somewhere in the early phase of life (viz., near the instinctual roots of the preconscious stage). It is as though the patient felt a kind of sclerotic interruption between his conscious reason and the roots of his being in the unconscious.

The rendering of this difficult drawing into intelligible terms is assisted by the method of cross-reference from figure to figure. By this method we equate the symbols belonging to the same level or stratum. Thus on the top level we find the flower, the diamond ring, the brain-flower, and the shaft with the piebald blade, representing various aspects of the conscious principle (the shaft is obviously a conscious instrument aimed from above). On the second level, which we might call the layer of emergence, we have the three bracts, the knives, the concentric rings and the candles. On the third or pathological level we find the barbed leaf-frond, the bleeding wounds in the throat, and the sclerotic schizophrenic nerve. On the fourth or root-level we find, between the root-systems of figures 1 and 3, a group of faint, discontinuous, wavy lines, below the wounds in figure 2, which have a certain affinity with the root-fibres of the other two systems.

The value of these cross-references rests upon the fact that the autonomous psyche thinks analogically. The principle of parallelism or synchronicity is not superimposed upon this material for the purpose of explanation; it is inherent in the primordial mode of representation. Inasmuch as thinking by analogy and the synchronous representation of emotionally related factors are indigenous psychic modes, this method of cross-reference is just as valuable for dream-interpretation as for the elucidation of so-called unconscious drawings.

VIII

Coming now to the fourth figure, comprising the three candles and the slanting shaft, a certain structural parallelism with figure 2 can easily be made out. The principle of three and one determines both constellations. The three knives and the ring in figure 2 correspond with the three candles and the shaft in 4. Moreover, the knives and the candles are patently phallic, while the shaft and the ring represent the archetypal male-female pair of opposites. They are of the same order as the Spear and the Grail, symbols that are endowed with magical power or *mana*.

Of the candles, two are burning (*i.e.*, alive), while the third has just been extinguished. We found a parallel example of this life-and-death symbolism in the man's head at the bottom of the previous drawing, where one half was a living face, while the other half was a skull. Through this reference we gain a clue to the inner significance of the piebald blade. The blade of the hero is single and bright, because the hero is fathered by the sun. This blade partakes rather of the nature of the moon, one aspect of which is turned toward the sun, while the other side is always dark. The moon is therefore the cosmic counterpart to the ambiguity of the anima, or, more correctly, the anima is the ambiguous moon-goddess ruling the nocturnal world of the unconscious and uniting goddess and dæmon in her own nature. From the initial figure of the previous drawing we know that the drawings we are now considering are done under the sign of the anima; we also know from the end-figure of the previous drawing that this anima-influence compels the subject to envisage his problem as a life-or-death issue.

The parallelism between figures 2 and 4 now assumes clearer perspective. The sword or knife is essentially a symbol of the objective logos-function. Objective thinking is the discriminative, penetrating, effective instrument of the mind, and is impartial, like the sword of justice. The three knives of figure 2 are estranged from this sword-like character; they are degenerate and inverted, disclosing the same tendency to amalgamate as in the four-handed spiral of Drawing 1.

But the diamond is a jewel of the sun, indicating the possibility of individual consciousness. It lies in the medial axis of the head, suggesting the idea of a central vertical eye. It occupies the symbolical position of the ruling principle, hence countering the sinister implication of the knives.

Candles, on the other hand, are products of the night. If the world did not revolve on its axis there would be no need for candles. The fitful gleams of light which occasionally illumine the nocturnal world of dreams are little better than farthing dips. Yet from these frail and niggardly rays intuition is born. Sensory perception deals with visible and tangible things; intuition begins where sensory perception can go no further. It is like an animal that can see in the dark, functioning by way of the unconscious in an oblique, irrational, instinctual way. With a far-seeing eye it shoots an instantaneous shaft towards its objective. Intuition is pristine in character: we understand it no better than we understand the primitive mind. It may tell us things which are hard to believe, and bring us knowledge of facts which cannot be proved. Often it warns us of dangers that are in the air, predicting events which are rationally unpredictable. Reason distrusts it, because it works in an irrational fashion. Nevertheless, reason depends upon intuition for its best ideas. In so far as it is the purveyor of unconscious contents to consciousness, intuition is also a function of the anima, and therefore partakes to some extent of the same ambiguous nature.

The intuitive shaft in our drawing demonstrates some of the attributes just described. The blade has the bright-dark nature of the moon. The tapering lines of the shaft are not clear and straight like an arrow, but slightly wavy and irregular, and the proximal end of the shaft is notched, not purposefully as an arrow is notched, but like the broken end of a stick.

It appears to emanate from the billowing line of smoke rising from the snuffed candle. At this point we recall how the slender figure of the anima first appeared, in Drawing 2, in the trailing wisp of smoke arising from the dropped cigarette, and how the intuition of the cell with the living heart accompanied this appearance of the anima.

Looking at the line of smoke in the present drawing with half-closed eyes, a fantastic witch's profile suggests itself to the mind. The notched end of the shaft protrudes into the space behind the bulging forehead. Below this comes a sharp jutting nose, under which is a protruding mouth and chin. Behind the mouth is the tongue.

The nefarious character of the witch is associated with certain sinister activations of the unconscious, also unaccountable bodily ailments and seizures, believed by primitives to be shot into one by the witch. In fact, the whole prestige of the witch rests upon a reputation for uncanny dealings with the unconscious.

In contrast to the knives (here identified with the brain-function), candles are associated with the affects. Both belong to the phallic genus, but differentiation of species must also be taken into account. The power of effective thought is as much an expression of masculine virility as is the darker potency of sex. The two provinces are moreover intimately interdependent. Hence Freud speaks of the "sexualization of thought," while Jung axiomatically affirms that "no man can think straight if his love-life is not in order."

The three knives of figure 2 symbolize a suicidal impotence of thought resulting from the subjective inversion of the intellectual function. The attempt to find the solution by means of introspective self-analysis has brought the subject within measurable distance of suicide. And yet this complete bankruptcy of the superior function of consciousness is also an essential prerequisite for the discovery of the repressed functions (*i.e.*, the quest for the hidden treasure) and of the healing which comes from their acceptance.

Introspective self-analysis painfully seeks the cause within the conscious field, always overlooking the unconscious, where the source of the trouble is to be found. The superior function, moreover, has to employ a generally valid ideal as its measuring-rod; it tends, therefore, to attack the psyche with an "ought." It is obvious that while the psyche is flooded by archaic ideas and motivations deriving from the primordial ancestry of mankind, what "ought to be" (according to the prescribed ideal) becomes merely a programme of self-laceration. Inasmuch as the superior function clings to this ideal criterion there is no possibility of seeing or accepting the situation as it actually is. One is literally blinded. This state is indicated in figure 2, where the knives have obliterated vision. Indeed, the expression of the face is that of a man who has been blindfolded.

As opposed to the knives, which are directed from above, the candles, as we shall presently confirm in Drawing 23, come from below. As a guttering candle to a diamond, so is the inferior function to the superior. Yet the possibility of further development lies with the despised inferior function (" Can there any good thing come out of Nazareth ?"), and not with the superior. The superior function has learnt the art of heroic detachment, while the inferior function, immersed in the stream of the affects, is constantly subject to the ebb and flow of the unconscious.

The ambivalency of the unconscious is again suggested by the two living candles and the one that is out. Consciousness demands consistency, but in the unconscious the yea and the nay float together side by side. Hamlet's " to be or not to be " reveals a condition in which the conscious function has lost its capacity for effective decision, as though it had been seduced from its clear loyalties into the fluid twilight of the unconscious. In acute mental disturbance this state of ineffectual indecision is one of the most distressing symptoms. It is as though the ultimate issue of life or death hung perpetually in the balance.

And yet out of this desperate ambiguity the blade of necessity emerges, just as Siegfried's new weapon was forged out of the broken fragments of Siegmund's sword.

The ambitendency of the unconscious is stated, as a sinister alternative, in the living and dead candles. But in the black-white blade of the javelin it is welded into a single effective instrument. Such a blade could not conceivably have been created by the superior function. It carries the hallmark of mythological creation. Because it is forged from dire necessity it goes direct to the heart of the problem, that is, *the pathological constriction of the vital nerve* lying just below the threshold of consciousness.

The only question remaining to be answered concerns the three concentric rings of the diaphragm-target which, *ex hypothesi*, represents the threshold. The answer is necessarily conjectural, since we have no guiding clues. The approach to the central problem in every deep analysis does, in fact, go through three stages. First the conscious field is explored through the personal anamnesis, conscious associations, reflections, etc. The second ring would correspond to the investigation of the personal unconscious through dream-analysis, while the inner ring would be the avenue to the impersonal or collective unconscious, into which the fundamental problem of individual destiny inevitably leads.

The three stages of initiation in the pagan mystery-cults were sometimes symbolized by three concentric rings. The outer ring represented the rite of purification or lustration; the middle ring, the ordeals and the sacrifice; and the inner ring, the identification with the god. The same symbol could express the three stages of realization—experience, reflection and understanding. These again correspond with the three stages of insect metamorphosis—the larva, the pupa and the imago. Though so very different, all these in their several forms are the vital phases in the process of becoming.

IX

Drawing 21

This drawing contains four elements: a spider in the middle of its web, a naked woman, two flowering plants, and a centipede. The relative position of these figures in the field suggests a hierarchy of value. In this hierarchy the hairy spider in the top right-hand corner is given the position of ruler, a fact that is borne out by its relatively enormous size and by its realistic representation. It is drawn with meticulous care: each joint, each claw, each finest hair has received attention. No part of the creature is allowed to be vague or blurred. The spider presides over the drawing as an active integrating force.

The web has nine irregularly spaced radials, and, like the lines of longitude in the sinking world of Drawing 15, these radials do not appear to meet at the centre of the web. The body of the spider covers this obvious defect in the construction of the web, just as the ice-cloud in 15 concealed the corresponding lack of convergence at the north pole. With regard to the transverse lines of the web, there is greater irregularity and more strands missing in the north-western hemisphere than in the south-eastern. Apparently the web has been damaged in this quarter, and we may assume, from the position of the spider's front claws, that he is now engaged in repairing the damage.

The figure of the woman is remarkable on several grounds. This is the first drawing in which the anima has taken the centre of the field. It is the most realistic, the most sensitive, as well as the most voluptuous representation of woman the subject has yet attempted. The light shines on the figure from below so that the upraised face is in deep shadow. Her long hair flows loose on either side of her body. Her arms are extended above her head, and one is shocked to discover that the hands, which are apparently engaged in repairing or fixing a broken radial of the web, are the hands of a skeleton. The lower third of the radius and ulna and the bones of the hands are completely denuded of flesh, so that the flesh of the rest of the arms takes on the appearance of sleeves. The legs are beautifully formed and the right leg seems to be laid over the left, so that if the feet were visible we should expect to see them crossed in a negligent, easy posture. The woman could not be standing on the ground with the legs and feet in this position. She must therefore be suspended in the air. The only means of suspension suggested in the drawing are the two radials of the web, attached one to the left breast, the other to the left knee.

Comparing the structure of the skeletal hands with the jointed legs of the spider, we cannot resist the impression that the subject in some way identifies the woman's hands with a function of the spider. The only difference is that the legs of the spider are hairy. It will also be observed that the position and action of the woman's arms and hands are more or less identical with those of the spider's front legs.

On a lower level, and on either side of the nude figure, we find two rather similar flowers. They belong to the generalized, composite conception of a flower, a fact which might betoken relatively little interest in the individuality of plants. They appear to be of the dahlia type. The manifold straying lines which represent their stems and roots and the unfinished leaves of the plant on the right are evidence either of a lack of interest or of a certain impatience in regard to this part of the drawing. If it is due to subjective urgency it is peculiar to this level, since the precise drawing of the centipede is even more remarkable than that of the spider. It should be noted that the curve of the centipede's body is identical with that of the plant just above it and to the left, and that it lies directly under the feet of the woman.

* * * * *

It is interesting to compare the style of this drawing with the preceding one. Drawing 20 was a line-drawing, in which no attempt was made to introduce light and shade. It was essentially diagrammatic and explanatory. Here, on the contrary, every figure is drawn with light and shade, and the approach of the subject is from below. In this distinction there lies, as already explained, the whole difference between what a man thinks and what grips him as immediate experience. The hierarchy of values perceived in the present drawing corresponds, therefore, not with any conscious schema, but rather with the experiential standpoint of the instinctual or natural man. The ambiguous black-white blade of the previous drawing has changed the character of the scene as with a magician's wand. This change is symbolized by the direction of the light, which before came only from above, but now comes from below. It is as though ambivalent intuition (released in the form of the piebald blade), with the unrestricted freedom of the world beneath the threshold, were now viewing the situation from the standpoint of the anima. And yet, comparing the two pictures side by side, it is evident that the present situation is continuous with the one that went before. The position of the woman between the two flowers corresponds precisely with the decerebrate human head of Drawing 20. The four levels are present in both, with the root-system of the sympathetic representing the lowest level in both. The main axis of the spider and its web, lying intermediate between the radials attached to the woman's breast and knee, corresponds with the direction of the ambivalent shaft. Finally, the motive of self-mutilation is represented in the same situation in both drawings—that is to say in the wounds and knives of figure 2 in Drawing 20, and in the flesh-denuded hands of the woman in Drawing 21.

The bankruptcy of the superior conscious function was tragically manifested in the previous drawing. The ineffectual attempts of the intellect either to understand or deal with the problem pushed the subject to thoughts of suicide. But it is precisely this defeat of the conscious function which offers the long-needed opportunity for the repressed functions to state their case. Thus the spider becomes the ruler in the new situation.

In certain North American Indian myths the spider plays the central rôle. In a Navajo myth, for example, the spider is the creator of the world. The same creation-myth is found among the Pueblo Indians, both clearly arising from a common source. The Sia version runs as follows:

> " The first being in the world was Spider (Sussistinnako). He lived in the lower world and he drew a cross on the ground and placed magic parcels at its eastern and western points. Then he sang until two women came forth out of the parcels, Utset, the mother of the Indians, and Nowutset, the parent of other men. Spider also created rain, thunder, lightning and the rainbow, while the two women made sun, moon and stars."

Later there is an allusion to Spider-woman as a kind of mediator or path-maker:

> " The people wanted to find Middle Place, but the Earth was too soft. So Utset requested the four beasts of the quarters—cougar, bear, wolf and badger—to harden the earth. But they could not, and it was a Spider-woman and a Snake-man who finally made a path for the people to walk on."

In this beautiful example we find the primordial *mandala*, composed of the earth, Middle Place and the four symbolical radials. But the *mandala* is empty and the centre is void until the god and the goddess appear. Spider-woman corresponds functionally with Shiva, the integrating psychic power, while Snake-man is equivalent to Shakti, the serpent power. A similar shamanistic *mandala* with the god and goddess in coitus surrounded by the four attendant animals is recorded among the *shamans* of Siberia.

Spider-woman also plays a significant rôle in a Hopi legend:

> " A youth spends his days beside the Grand Canyon wondering where the water goes to. He embarks in a hollow log and is borne down to the sea, where he is hailed by Spider-woman, who becomes his instructress in magic and wizardry. They visit the *kiva* of the mythic Snake-people, who appear in human shape. They subject the youth to severe tests which, with Spider-woman's help, he successfully overcomes. The Snake-people then go back to their snake form, and, at the instigation of Spider-woman, the youth seizes the fiercest of these, whereupon the snake becomes a beautiful girl. This is the Snake-maiden, who becomes the mother of the Hopi people. He marries her and brings her back to his own country. Her first offspring is a brood of snakes; but later human children are born who become the ancestors of the Snake clan."[1]

To the civilized reader, who associates spiders with phobias and bad dreams, it may come as a surprise to find the spider elevated to the position of world-maker. But the primitive mind is naturally attuned to psychic reality, and in these legends the miraculous power of the psyche, which literally creates a coherent and meaningful world out of a welter of visual, auditory and sensory stimuli, is symbolically personified in the spider. The function of the anima, as mediator between the instinctual and the conscious realm, is beautifully embodied in Spider-woman.

In Shushonean tales collected by Robert H. Lowie the spider again assumes a highly psychological complexion. Coyote finds Spider in his web on a tree. Being hungry, Coyote wants to eat him. Spider says: " No, I'll tell you something good. Why am I on a tree ? What do you think

[1] I am indebted to my colleague, Dr. J. Henderson, of New York, for this valuable material.

of it?"—"I don't know."—"I hold on to a tree, shut my eyes for a short time and see everything all over the world. This tree is chief of the whole world, that is why spiders always go on trees."—"That is new to me."—"Don't you wish to see everything?"—"Yes, I should like to."—"Well, shut your eyes for a while, hold on to a tree, and you will see everything." While Coyote was trying this exercise Spider removed himself.

We learn from these illustrations that the primitive imagination personifies both the vigilant awareness and the associative industry of the mind with one and the same creature; and of all animals the idea of spontaneous psychic activity is most faithfully embodied by the spider spinning its web. The indefinite extension of awareness, so naively alluded to in the folk-tale, is the ever-enduring miracle of our inner reality. We are only beginning to recognize the incredible subtlety of the autonomous psyche. We would naturally prefer to think of the psyche in terms of nerve-paths and synapses; but this anatomical conception is crudely incompetent to explain certain indisputable facts in the realm of insect behaviour.

In observing and experimenting with various species of termites in South Africa, Eugene Marais[1] discovered that the whole complicated activity of a termitary, consisting of many thousands of individual termites, is solely dependent upon some central power exercised by the queen. The highly specialized activity of the whole community ceases immediately the queen is destroyed or injured. Much of the work of a termitary involves complicated collaboration, such as the architectural feat of building arches with individual grains of sand and grass-stems, making aqueducts, even to the depth of 100 feet, for the supply of water, making gardens for the cultivation of the special fungus upon which the collective functions of digestion and heat-production depend, repairing the walls and structure of the termitary or defending the community against invasion. The individual termite is blind and deaf, and has no organ that could serve as a brain in which this complicated instinctual apprehension might reside. And yet, however distant the termites may be

[1] Marais: *The Soul of the White Ant.*

from the queen's cell, or whatever they may be engaged in, the instant that the queen is killed every member of this vast organization ceases work, and dissolution begins. The power emanating from the queen cannot be conceived in concrete terms: it is coextensive with the community she governs, but it does not depend on any demonstrable paths of communication. For example, if a broad steel plate is driven through the termitary, so that one half is completely separated from the other, the highly co-ordinated activity goes on, on either side, as though no obstacle were present; the half of an arch, built on either side of the plate, articulating accurately with its invisible counterpart.

The queen, as Marais points out, has never performed any of these specialized activities of the sexless termites. Yet she is able to produce soldiers and workers, different in all essentials from herself, fitted to perform complicated feats which she herself has never even seen. For her life is spent immured and immobile in a cell from which she can never emerge. On the other hand, since the workers and soldiers have no organs of generation, the pattern of activity which they represent is not handed down by them.

Marais was forced to conclude from these and similar observations that the termitary is a composite organism—in other words, a psychical whole. The specialized activity of the individual termites is closely analogous to that of the various specialized cells of the blood, and the co-ordinated activity of the whole, under the central rule of the queen, is analogous to the centralized functioning of the brain.

If we accept Marais' conclusion—and no other hypothesis seems to be adequate—that there is a directing and co-ordinating power emanating from the queen which embraces the whole termitary as a psychic whole, we must also conceive this power as something over and above the visible units and structure of the termitary. The power emanates from the queen; but there is no trace of anything approaching brain-structure in the queen's anatomy. Neither are there any visible paths of conduction nor organs of reception in the individuals who are constantly governed by this power. The activity and structure of the termitary are the outward and visible expression of this power. But what the power is, how it is generated, conducted and received, lies beyond any reasonable conception of physical mechanism.

Doubtless by degrees we shall become accustomed to the truth that psychology begins where physiology can go no further. When we speak of the autonomous psyche we shall not immediately think of brain or nerve-cell, nor even of the brightly-lit theatre of consciousness. We shall think rather of something analogous to the immediate, co-ordinated and directive vigilance and associative subtlety observed in the termitary, albeit expressed in the graphic idiom of the dream and not merely inferred from behaviour.

I have been prompted to offer this analogy from the insect world because Jung's concept of the self as embracing the psychical totality needs to be recognized as a natural rather than as a metaphysical conception, and the termitary offers a telling illustration of the psychic organism.

* * * * *

To resume our discussion, the spider would symbolize this same instinctual, purposive activity of the psyche, while its web would represent the co-ordinated network, the so-called psychical structure, through which this power takes effect. The web is our world, in so far as the only world we can ever know is the world of images created by the psyche and presented within the field of consciousness. To speak of an extra-psychic reality is to conceive the inconceivable. For as soon as the existence of things or beings becomes known to us, our knowledge of them is necessarily conditioned by the fact that the psyche itself is the sole recorder and interpreter of their existence.

The cosmogonic spider of the Navajo myth, therefore, is a psychologically accurate conception. The primitive mind is not, as yet, fenced in by rational scruples. While the scientifically trained mind tends to limit what is real to what lies within the scope of rational explanation, the primitive psyche apprehends what is, without enquiring too deeply into how it could be caused. The unitary control of a complex organization like the termitary would present no particular problem to a naive intelligence. It is quite obviously the soul, of which the termitary is the body. The difficulty exists only when we begin to ask: " How can a vast horde of individual creatures have a single soul ? Where is it located ? How does it operate ?"

The subject of these drawings had to unlearn the repressive habits of intellectual control, and to learn instead the law-abidingness of the natural mind. Hence the intellect had to be put out of action (as witnessed in the last drawing) before the pristine activity of the psyche, as an affective, self-regulating, unitary system, could be realized.

The parallelism of the two drawings hints at an identity, or at least a continuity, between figure 4 of the last drawing and the spider in this one. We saw how the challenge of the extinguished candle created and directed the necessitous intuitive shaft. The possibility that the light of consciousness might be put out was undoubtedly the challenge which enabled the subject to experience and create this helpful conception of the primitive psyche. I say helpful advisedly, because the spider obviously represents an activity engaged in repairing damage to the psychic structure; and this damage is located in that quarter which would correspond to the brain-flower in the previous drawing. Hence we can assume it was also caused by the clumsy interference of consciousness.

The spider is assisted in the work of repair by the anima, whom we might now term the spider-woman. She is the effective mediator between the autonomous psyche and consciousness, the means by which consciousness can relate in a meaningful way, though without direct interference, in the activity of the unconscious process. She is beautiful and appealing, a fact which argues that a kind of mating-allure is exercised by the anima when an effective union between the conscious and the unconscious is anticipated.

The three radials which designate the symbolic relationship between the anima and the spider's web are attached (*a*) to the knee, symbolizing the level of the instincts; (*b*) to the left breast, symbolizing the feeling centre; and (*c*) to the upraised hands, which might represent the primordial spiritual function of the mind that has been robbed of its effective power by being confounded with the intellect.

This third attribute of the anima needs further elaboration because of the obvious pathological admixture in the symptom of the denuded hand. We observed this same symptom in the first of this anima-series (Drawing 19) and we concluded that the effective vitality of the soul had become vitiated by a self-devouring inversion of the libido—in other words, by pathological introversion.

Once again we encounter the paradox of the thing that is injured or diseased becoming the agency which repairs the damage.[1] The displacement of the destructive masculine principle (the intellect) by the healing feminine is again affirmed in the identity of this new ministering anima with the suicidal second figure of the previous drawing. Her very position in the field between the two flowers shows that she is in direct emotional continuity with the mutilated head of Drawing 20.

Regarding the two attached radials of the web as psychic indicators, this figure would symbolize the renewal of feeling (heart-value) and instinct. With her maimed hands she repairs the broken radial above her head, an action suggesting that the integrity of the spiritual function rests upon the fundamental acceptance of the emotional and instinctive life. What has been injured from above must be repaired from below. Again it is as though the subject is learning to think with the heart and feel with the head. In this way the maimed anima serves as the way into life; and she can do this because she is now integrated into the psychic totality instead of being an uncontrolled autonomous factor.

The third level comprises the two plants and the feet of the woman. Since the drawing of the figures both above and below this level is highly competent, we can assume that a certain unconscious resistance is connected with the problem represented by the plants. Had I asked the patient about this resistance, he would very likely have said that he had already drawn plants in the previous drawing and that

[1] This is akin to the mystical paradox whereby the goal is identical with the means: as, for instance, the Elixir, or the Philosopher's Stone, which is both the aim of the alchemical process and the means by which it can be achieved. Similarly, love is both the goal and the way of the mystic's relation to God.

reiterated ideas are not interesting. But in any case he would have rationalized his resistance. What clues, then, does the drawing itself provide?

First we observe that the flowers in both plants are done with some care; deterioration sets in as we leave the flower and follow the stem downwards. The leaves are roughly sketched, and the hurried lines of the stem and roots of the right-hand plant are quite unlike the artist's usual careful work. Curiously enough, the only other occasion on which he was obviously overcome by his material was in Drawing 17, when the anima-figure "leaped on to the paper before he could do anything about it." If the reader will refer to that drawing he will observe many straying lines which have the same urgent character as in the present instance.

This symptom of urgency and haste is clearly not native to the character of the plant. Presumably, therefore, the plant is associated with something the patient does not care to dwell upon. If the reader will turn again to Drawing 20 he will find the cause of the disturbance in the thickened schizophrenic line which affects the stem of the brain-plant, and at which the primitive shaft is aimed. The chief disturbance in the patient's technique is localized in the corresponding portion of the corresponding plant in the present drawing. In the former drawing the schizophrenic sclerosis is, as it were, binding the vital nerve in a rigid grip. In this drawing the jagged, thickened line is gone, but a sudden loosening or spraying out of lines takes its place. The suggestion here is that the habitual overemphasis on conscious control arises from the subject's subliminal fear that his whole world would break up in affective tumult if once the repressive hold of consciousness were relinquished.

Lying between the roots of the two plants, and directly under the woman's feet, there is the meticulously drawn centipede. The patient's association with this creature is that it is said to eat the roots of plants. This is not the whole story, however, for its presence seems to have affected the form of the plant on the left, which has adapted itself to the centipede's curve. Bearing Jung's suggestion in mind, that the patient feels a need to draw these insect-symbols with intricate detail, in order to gain a kind of magical control over the dissociated psychic units, we can begin to weave our various clues into a coherent picture.

Flowers are, as we know, the conventional symbol of feeling. From that general point of view we could regard the two plants as the ambivalent expression of the patient's inferior function. Feeling, as Jung has pointed out, is the function most likely to suffer repression at the hands of the overprized intellect in an individual where the prevailing conscious attitude is intellectual. This explanation would harmonize with general psychological canons, but we have also to bear in mind the continuity of these plants with those of Drawing 20, as well as the whole significance of the vegetational idea in the preceding material.

Comparing the character of the two plants in Drawings 20 and 21, we are immediately struck by the fact that, although unfinished and hasty in execution, the plants in 21 are natural and graceful, whereas the corresponding figures in 20 are artificial and diagrammatic. The abstract, formalized plants of 20—especially the "brain-flower" on the right—are obviously mere intellectual concepts, products of the exclusively intellectual attitude which stands self-condemned between them. The two plants in 21, on the other hand, clearly participate in the emotional rebirth symbolized by the beautiful figure of the woman who springs up, like the phœnix, from the ashes of the corresponding figure in 20. But if the drawing is representing the rebirth of feeling, why the symptoms of urgency and resistance in the execution of the two flowers?

Throughout the drawings we have witnessed the development of the Apollonian-Dionysian conflict between conscious control and the atavistic tendency; and we saw, in Drawing 15, how the decay of the brittle control from above and the rising up of the affective deeps from below resulted in a new germinal being that was free of either side, because it contained elements of both. Accordingly, that drawing was followed by the irresistible leap of the released anima (with accompanying danger signals) and her subsequent transformation into the tree.

This problem of the opposites, and the tendency to be

engulfed by either pole, is the essence of the schizophrenic predicament. By clinging to the aloof, often brilliant, but essentially defensive superiority of the conscious function, the world becomes, as it were, covered with ice. Life freezes beneath a glacial pall, because everything which could conceivably stir a deep emotional response is either evaded or repressed. But the natural sequel to a glacial period is a deluge. In other words, when the rigorous conscious control is relaxed, nature is revenged by releasing an indiscriminate welter of unadapted and unadaptable affects. As a rule, therefore, the intellectual schizophrenic tries to cling to the fate he knows and is accustomed to, because the only alternative he can imagine is to be flooded by uncontrollable affect. Again and again we see the patient being forced into the stream of life by the terrifying chill of isolation, only to recoil in greater dread from the threat of dissolution in the chaos of the unconscious. Such a recoil is beautifully exemplified in the highly abstract statement of the problem in Drawing 16, which immediately follows the menacing deluge of 15. It is as though the patient had looked over the edge of his ice-plateau whence he had seen, far below, the waters of chaos rising to engulf him. His natural reaction would be to remove himself to an abstract sphere where no disturbing image could enter and excite emotional turmoil.

If we contrast the present statement of his predicament with the former one we must conclude that the subject's moral is considerably stronger. This gain is particularly visible in the fact that he now encounters the problem face to face, as it were, instead of viewing it from an immense height.

The horrific aspect of the unconscious, manifest in the devouring monster of the former series, is at bottom an expression of man's primæval dread of the spirit-world, a fascination and dread perfectly symbolized by the snake. The power of the magician, the man with secret and special knowledge of the unconscious, is seen in the fact that he can talk to his snake. The overcoming of the dread of the spirit-world is performed ritually in many primitive tribes by the rite of eating the snake.

One of the best examples of this snake-ritual is to be

observed in the famous snake-dance of the Hopi Indians. The rattlesnakes are sought far and wide in preparation for the dance, and the men who handle them do so without fear. On the contrary, an attitude is induced by ritual preparation that is akin to ecstasy. The snakes are included in this preparation by a rite of baptism, in which they are immersed individually in a large bowl of ritually prepared water, after which they are thrown against the wall of the *kiva* as part of their ritual ordeal.[1]

These examples from primitive custom offer a practical clue for those people who have to come to terms with the unconscious, yet are inwardly full of dread. They need not go out and gather snakes; but they can conjure up their worst dread in fantasy and then discover the ritual which will exorcise the demon of fear. Instead of being fascinated by their dread they can learn to fascinate and tame it, as though it were a snake.

This is the inner meaning of the centipede-ritual of the present drawing. In figure 2 of Drawing 20 the subject looked into the face of his worst dread, and in that moment the healing function of the unconscious came to his aid. The spider's web, as we have seen, symbolizes the natural integrating process of the psyche, particularly in relation to the autonomous units. Through the new erotic value of the anima the integration of the inferior function of feeling is now included in the web. The space between the radial attached to the woman's knee and the one to the right, which appears to be feeling for a point of attachment, includes the plant which manifests the schizophrenic symptoms alluded to above. If the lines were continued this space would also enclose the centipede, and, because this creature symbolizes the schizophrenic fragmentation, it represents the doubt upon which the patient's mind has been so long impaled. Hence the form of the question-mark. Following our analogy with the snake-ritual, we can now account for the realistic, detailed execution of the centipede as a kind of ritual performance, by virtue of which the dangerous element is fascinated and held within conscious control.

[1] I am again indebted to Dr. J. Henderson for these facts.

In point of fact, however, the radials of the web are not continued far enough to embrace the roots of the plant and the centipede, and in this fact we find ourselves face to face with the fundamental problem of schizophrenic pathology. Can the cause of the schizophrenic malady be reached by psychological means, or does it lie in the sympathetic system, beyond the range of psychological approach? For it is sufficiently clear, from the concrete allusions to the brain, spinal cord, and the subdiaphragmatic plexus in figure 3 of Drawing 20, that the patient is intuitively groping towards the root of the trouble in the region of the sympathetic.

Clinical evidence points to the fact that schizophrenia is rooted more deeply in the psychic constitution than the neurotic disorders. Recent investigations at the Boston Psychopathic Hospital, U.S.A., covering a large number of cases, have demonstrated that certain schizophrenic patients show a failure in integration of their physiological processes in approximately the same degree as in their mental processes.[1]

Such facts are significant. But even were it conclusively proved that the roots of the malady lay beyond the range of psychological analysis, we would still have to admit that a large number of borderline cases have been cured and a considerable majority improved by analytical treatment.

Returning to our snake-analogy, the distance between human being and snake is too great to permit of a relation of understanding or affection; yet means have been discovered whereby venomous snakes, such as cobras, rattlesnakes, etc., can be handled with comparative safety. Although the technique varies in different countries, it is generally admitted that the art of "charming" snakes has itself been borrowed from the snake. The art consists essentially in hypnotic fascination exercised either by means of monotonous piping on a reed instrument or by the monotonous high-pitched incantation of words (often taken from the Koran), sometimes accompanied by monotonous movements of the hand. The snake-charmer works, in fact, on the assumption that the fascinator is himself easily fascinated, and the imper-

[1] I am indebted to Dr. F. C. d'Elseany for permission to make this use of his findings.

turbable insistence of the snake-charmer is based upon his complete belief in his method. But this rests upon his knowledge of the snake's peculiar psychology, which the snake itself taught him. The charmed snake is not essentially changed. The charmer knows that he is still potent with death. But just so long as the psychic condition prevails, which holds him powerless to strike, he is as harmless as a tortoise.

The borderline schizophrenic is not unlike a man who has to live in the vicinity of a dangerous snake, and for this reason he needs to develop a higher degree of psychic integration than those who are permitted to live less dangerously. From the point of insight we have now reached we can appreciate that the intensity of concentration represented in the execution of the centipede has the psychological value of a ritual.

If we accept the hypothesis that the contents in the lower part of the field belong to the frontier region between the psychic and the sympathetic systems there need be no further difficulty in reading the signs. The saving idea (upon which the subject's gain in moral surely rests) came into effect in Drawing 18, where the anima became transformed into the tree and the bird. We have observed how the significance of vegetational symbolism has increased since that event, as though the idea of integration was now closely identified with the rootedness of the plant. Even the still figure of the anima in this drawing, with her upraised hands and twig-like fingers, is in tune with the vegetational idea. The very fact that her feet have not been drawn suggests that she is unconsciously identified with a being whose roots are not visible to the eye. Her feet are actually on the same level as that part of the plant's stem (on the right) in which the lines begin to stray off in symptomatic haste. It is at this level, therefore, that the patient senses a certain loss of control. Yet out of this disturbance emerges the most completely executed form of the whole series. Thus the centipede appears as a *tour de force—i.e.*, the achievement of intense concentration in the very heart of the cyclone of disturbance. In this way the subject learns how to master his snake.

It is not insignificant that the shape of the centipede is reminiscent of a question-mark, for the creature represents the patient's perennial doubt. It is as though the very validity of the self were undermined or threatened by this creature which devours the roots of his feeling. Thus, by the sheer necessity of truth, he is forced to draw this gnawing doubt directly below the figure that proclaims the renewal of his emotional life. This ambivalent realization of his own truth was foreshadowed in the primitive shaft with its black-white blade in Drawing 20.

There is one feature that still remains doubtful. I refer to the dubious plant on the left. The fact that its shape has been determined by that of the centipede is beyond question. But whether it is a kind of onomatopœic expression of the subliminal doubt in terms of feeling, or whether it is an attempt at sympathetic magic in order to deprive the dangerous creature of its venom, it is not easy to decide. My own belief is that it is a mimetic phenomenon. Neurotic individuals may contrive to remain unaware of their own psychopathology by overplaying their personality, thereby overcompensating their vulnerability. This rarely, if ever, happens with a borderline schizophrenic. As a rule he is only too well aware of the pathological streak in his make-up, and he tends to control his behaviour accordingly. He is rarely pretentious or hysterically dramatic. On the contrary, he is liable to use diffidence, exaggerated modesty, and a retiring disposition in much the same way as a public personality uses charm. For to be inconspicuous and therefore invulnerable is his art of life. It is as though the schizophrenic had to keep his snake (or his centipede) in view; hence he can never afford to let go or lose himself in a situation. Inasmuch, therefore, as his self-regarding instinct is to a considerable extent conditioned by his pathological inferiority, one aspect of the patient's feeling might be regarded as mimetically determined by the centipede.

In two essentials this drawing bears witness to a vital change of attitude. In the first place the subject has represented events in the unconscious in a naturalistic, undistorted way. This argues that he accepts the events of his inner world as part of nature, obeying the same laws, determined by similar causes, and tending towards similar ends. The drawing is an affirmation that he feels himself to be participating in the evolutionary process and sees his life as an evolutionary experiment.

As a result of this acceptance we find the anima employed, for the first time, as a relative psychic function. Before, she has appeared as an autonomous factor, manifesting the characteristic all-or-none absolutism of the protopathic state. As the spider-woman she now appears as a collaborating, ministering function, essentially related to the whole psychic economy, even making use of the effects of the previous pathological state of introversion (symbolized by the skeletal hands) in the work of salvage and repair. This conversion of the anima-complex from an autonomous factor into a functional annexe to consciousness is, as Jung has frequently pointed out, one of the principal aims of the analytical process. It is an end not to be reached, however, by a mere passive assimilation of the unconscious contents. Active participation in the integrating development is essential, and when this is present the work of psychological creation is never barren.

In considering this somewhat voluptuous representation of the anima, we have to remember that the subject had been injured in the realm of the instinct, and that it was his instinctual attitude that needed repair. In Drawings 9 and 10 we observed the deadly effects of the split in the emotional realm. In the present drawing the sensuous body of the anima emerges into life, but her hands and feet still betray the pathological constellation.

The integrative attempt to combine the sexual and spiritual components within the unitary conception of the anima is clearly represented, and the attempt very nearly succeeds. But the absolute candour which governs these subjective statements forbids a clear delineation of the feet and insists upon a relatively crippled condition of the hands. The great advance seen in this drawing lies in the fact that the anima is herself bridging the gulf between the sundered opposites. In regard to his essential quest the subject is "getting warm."

X

DRAWING 22

The drawing consists of three apparently unrelated figures.

The upper figure consists of the head of a young man, with closed eyes, and a flying bat. In certain respects the face resembles the suffering face of Drawing 2; in other respects, notably in the rather heavy, somnambulistic expression of its lower half, the face reminds one of the mutilated head in Drawing 20.

With regard to the bat there are several singular features. The right wing is fully extended upwards, while the left is almost closed. The right ear is pricked forward and alert, the left is laid back along the body. The left leg (ending in only three digits) is extended backwards, while the right leg is not visible at all. It is doubtful whether a creature with this degree of inco-ordination between the two sides of its body could maintain itself in the air. Its position in relation to the human head should also be noted. In view of the resemblance to Drawing 2, we observe that the bat's extended wing covers the area of the operation wound or trauma on the left side of the head.

The middle figure consists of a large blot of ink, into whose jagged, irregular mass two river-systems appear to be flowing, one from the west, the other from the north-east. In both systems a number of slender tributaries converge into three larger streams, which in their turn flow into the main stream.

The whole middle figure is done in deep violet ink, whereas the upper and lower figures seem to be drawn in blue-black. The effect of this difference in colour is to make the middle figure stand out as though on a different level from the other two.

The lower figure consists of a hairy ogre's hand attached to an ill-conditioned snake's body, which, in its lower half, gives place to a hairy rat's tail. The hand is a left hand, and the gnarled fingers are stretching upwards as though to seize hold of the loop of the river just above it. The loops of the snake-body and rat-tail are loose and sprawling; the lines of the body are irregular; there is, in fact, no uniformity either in consistency, disposition or texture. The loops are kinked and uneven in thickness, and the general lack of muscular tone makes it inconceivable that this monstrosity could function as an organism. The ugliness of this figure is the ugliness of something evil, so that one's reaction to it is immediate and spontaneous, as to a vile stench.

* * * * *

Regarding these four drawings as a series by themselves, it is interesting to observe the progressive simplification of the material, as in a spiral movement towards the centre. The nearer the subject approaches the pathological source, the more is he able to dispense with collateral imagery.

This process of condensation is characteristic of introverted psychology; accordingly, introverted achievement can rarely be taken at its face value. Not that extraverted utterances are necessarily more explicit; yet, because the extravert is primarily conditioned by his relation to the object, his statements are accessible to a more obvious objective valuation. They seem to belong to a more or less simple two-dimensional existence, whereas the introverted utterance, even though simplified as in the present drawing, has in it a complexity of subjective tributaries which tend to give it the character of a three-dimensional substance. The best examples of introverted achievement combine a tense simplicity of statement with a deep complexity of inner experience.

This drawing demonstrates the importance, the necessity even, of following the development of ideas throughout a series. It would be useless to try and fathom the meaning of such a drawing, taken as an isolated specimen. If its meaning is clear to us it is only because we have laboriously attempted to understand its antecedents.

We can begin by taking the upper and lower figures together, since they balance each other and are drawn in the same medium. Comparing the visionary head of Drawing 2 with that of the present drawing, we observe that the direction of the face in 2 is slightly upward, the features showing considerable power and determination, the mouth is straight, and the brows are contracted in tension—an expression eloquent of conflict.

In the present drawing, on the other hand, the face is tilted slightly downwards, the long lashes are resting on the cheek, the mouth is loose, and the lips are passive and inert. There is no sign of tension or conflict, indeed the smooth hair and slumbering unawareness of the face seem to belong to an entirely different character from that portrayed in the earlier picture. The powerful neck and face in Drawing 2 express a mature man, virile and resolute, a man who faces suffering without resentment and with no weakening of purpose. The weak, slumbering, rather indolent face of the present drawing, with its sleek hair, thick brows, prominent mouth, and rather effeminate eyelashes, is the face of a dormant homosexual.

In the first head we see the face of a man whose will is braced by the vision of rebirth suggested by the new cell with the living heart. The face is lifted as though accepting the challenge of the vital problem: its firmness and power seem to express a positive resolve not to accept the infirmity of instinct as a preordained fate.

The expression on the slumbering face of the second head reveals the nature of the alternative hypothesis. It is acquiescent, weak, and indifferent to its destiny. The difference between the expression of a somnambulist, or a hypnotized person, and that of the same person under normal sleep is too subtle to convey in words, yet everyone can recognize the difference without a second's hesitation. It lies in the fact that normal sleep is a state of relaxation, whereas the hypnotized person is being propelled by an unconscious will or motive. Hypnotized sleep is motivated; it is a yielding to an alien intention.

Although it escapes the power of definition, I think the reader will agree that the expression on this face is that of a somnambulist. The downward tilt of the face is expressive of acquiescence, and the presence of the bat denotes the alien motive or impulse.

With reference to this very significant bat, I must mention a dream which the patient had discussed with me some little time before. It was as follows:

" I am in a large garden, and it is night. The garden is not really a garden, because all the hedges are giant birthday cakes with candles on them. (I do not remember seeing any genuine plants.) I look at the moon and see that it is a crescent, drawn in pink outline on the sky. I think that this is a very pretty idea and I must remember it and use it in a drawing one day. Everything is very dark in spite of the candles.

" I have on a leather overcoat which is unbuttoned. I flap this at the candles and blow them out one by one till all are extinguished. Then I turn towards an enormously wide marble staircase stretching up to a distant castle, dimly seen in the moonlight. I start running up the steps, and—flapping my coat—I fly. Half whimsically I cry like a bat, and am immediately answered by shrill whistling noises coming from everywhere. To my horror I realise I *am* a bat and have been accepted as *one of them.*"

The scene of the dream is associated faintly in the dreamer's mind with his grandmother's estate in Canada, which he eventually inherited. He had no especial feeling for it, in spite of the fact that he spent many holidays there as a boy. He never wanted to return and make his home there. The artificiality of the dream-castle was associated with a recent architectural fantasy of his in a rather outlandish satirical vein.

The moon reminded him—not at the time, but subsequently—of the Bolshevik sickle and hammer, drawn in red on a black wall. This was naturally associated with his former Communistic sympathies. The crescent moon was also linked up to the Turkish star and crescent. I find I noted a remark of his that the Turkish association appealed to him more because it occurred on lots of stamps, to which he added characteristically: " I used to collect stamps until I took up *The Times* crossword puzzles; the latter kill time at less expense."

Birthday cakes evoked distant memories: " I remember vaguely blowing out the candles on my own cake and seeing other boys blow out theirs."

The essential association was concerned with the leather coat. It was like a motoring-coat his wife had bought for herself, but finding it did not suit her she passed it on to him. He added: " I never liked it (it was too small), but wore it for about a year. After my grandmother's death (when I had more money) I got a better coat and gave the other away."

The logic of the dream is clear. On the strength of the significant synchronicity between the wearing of the wife's leather coat and the appearance of renegade bat symptoms, considerably more than the content of the present dream is explained.

What, in fact, has alienated this man's soul from its original natural acceptance of, and delight in, natural things? When the dream says that in place of hedges there are birthday cakes, and instead of a real moon there is only a party-badge or a pretty design, and instead of real plants in a real garden there is a fantastic marble staircase and a distant fantasy-castle, it must mean that an artificial conception has been interposed between the subject and nature, and this at a very early age. The natural facts surrounding him in his solitary boyhood at the grandmother's house were always held at arm's length by the women who looked after him. The atmosphere of his early milieu favoured the artificial and the unreal; the garden was " not really a garden," but a place where certain activities were organized or certain fantasies indulged in.

The criticism which has become implicit in the terms " æsthetic " or " intellectual " is justified psychologically, in so far as they denote an attitude in which the intellectual or æsthetical substitute is given a value properly belonging to an original fact of experience. When a counter is put in the place of experience, and accepted, even in local " intellectual " currency, as of higher exchange value than the reality it has displaced, a certain alienation of the psyche from its original nature is liable to result. To the natural man our whole intellectual world of concepts is a collection of coloured counters. Is it not understandable, predictable even, that a type of consciousness might develop for which the ordinary facts of reality would have only a minimal significance. Though such a result is not inevitable, it is always liable to happen whenever the instinctual feeling for real things decays to the extent of allowing the intellectual product to eclipse the value of original experience.

In the patient's dream the real garden, with all its manifold delights for boyhood, has been substituted by a fantastic artifact; in every direction, that is to say, the patient's out-going natural instinct has been short-circuited by artificial substitutes. That this was done in early childhood is proved by the allusion to the cake-ritual and by the association with his grandmother's house in Canada.

The dream-statement that everything is very dark in spite of the candles suggests that an influence is abroad which is working against consciousness.

We now come to his wife's leather coat, a thing that he wore for a year or more notwithstanding the fact that he disliked it. A pathological passivity of attitude, which is effeminate rather than feminine, is revealed in this laconic confession. Why is the subject so dependent upon his wife that he has to assume an emotional identity of attitude which cannot in fact exist? The answer is given in the dream by implication only. The dreaming-mind is, as we know, the mind of nature, and its standpoint of judgment or criticism, if one can speak of so definite a thing as a standpoint in relation to the dream-mind, is the primordial nature of man—man as he actually is. Thus, when the dream substitutes sophisticated artifacts for the natural objects of one's earliest environment and, *at the same time*, emphasizes the fact that one is going around in a woman's coat, it is right to infer that there was too much of woman's influence and too little of nature in one's original impressions of life.

This conclusion would not necessarily refer to a quantitative predominance of woman's influence, which is, of course, the normal condition for the first decade of life. The pathological dependence upon woman—the most fruitful cause for the subsequent leaning in the homosexual direction in compensation—comes from the fact that an instinctually unfulfilled woman has placed herself in the way of the child's developing interest, instead of allowing his instinct to experience nature first-hand. In other words, when the boy's instinct is allowed to go out and gain the world in its own way and in its own time there is no question of homosexuality. But if every experimental excursion of the boy's interest is immediately either headed off or short-circuited by indulgent feminine fuss, the resulting conception of reality is necessarily laid down in terms of the inescapable obstacle. This is, of course, not the whole story, for a baby will always become dependent upon the person who actually sees to its needs. A solitary boy in a big house where there are many women with little to do would naturally tend to find his interests catered for in terms of artificial substitutes. Only the rare woman with enterprise and practical imagination is likely to help a boy create his own world. But women who are instinctually deprived—and how many women in such an environment would not be?—are prone to seek vicarious satisfaction in becoming the boy's providence, thus substituting a sophisticated feminine psychology for nature.

Two factors, therefore, are needed to instigate the æsthetical middle-world of the homosexual man: first a solitary boyhood, and second biologically deprived womanhood. The woman in the case need not be the mother; it is, in fact, very often the woman who stands as surrogate for the mother.

Rather glibly, perhaps, we explain homosexuality as a compensation phenomenon. It may sometimes be true that a boy reared too much under the hands of women will subsequently seek reinforcement of his masculine character by cultivating a correspondingly exclusive alliance with men. But with the great majority of homosexuals there is no essential desire to become manly; on the contrary, we notice a very definite tendency to ape feminine ways, only with a certain ironical and artificial twist. These half-conscious imitations savour more of the bitterness of the outcast than of honest flattery.

What the deprived but indulgent mother-surrogate does not see is that the moods and tantrums of the spoiled child are, at bottom, an eloquent symptom. The boy longs to escape from the artificial ring which cuts him off from any contact with real things. He does not know what he lacks—

does a man dying of scurvy know that he lacks vitamins ?—but his nature craves, as his natural birthright, a living, unhampered exchange with non-human nature. This is just what a too competent feminine environment has denied him, giving him endless solicitude and fuss in its stead. Modern psychology can hardly be said to improve matters when it floods the contemporary world with experts trained to extinguish their native common sense, and to reduce the causes of neurotic ailments ever and again to the unappeasable longing of the child for the exclusive possession of the parent.

In regard to this problem, the patient's dream is a clear statement. It is because he goes on wearing the coat of his wife (symbol of his dependence upon woman) long after it disagrees with him that he is infected with bat-like qualities—in other words, he becomes a renegade. Immediately he is seized with the impulse to escape he becomes aware of the presence of a multitude of similar renegades flapping wings of escape towards a distant goal. The blowing-out of the candles with the flapping coat is a symptomatic action; it probably refers to a very understandable impulse to extinguish every sentimental tie which could hold him bound to the nursery-world, where the law of the mother or the grandmother was absolute. These candles were set in honour of the universal mother; they are extinguished by the solitary spirit of revolt. The way that tempts him involves a sacrilege, a crime, a deed that can be conceived only in darkness.

But as soon as he turns his feet in the renegade direction he finds a vast staircase leading to a distant castle, dimly seen in the moonlight. What is this ? Is it a real goal or a mirage ? If we listen carefully to the dream statement we can be in no doubt. A feasible pathway to follow would never appear in a dream as "an enormously wide marble staircase." This is the hall-mark of fantastic unreality, and the distant castle dimly seen in the moonlight is equally unreal.

The allusion to the collecting of stamps and killing time by crossword puzzles (via the association with the crescent moon) is a characteristic example of the deadly influence. Boredom arises from the fact that libido, which went flying towards its proper goal, was shot down by an unintelligent guardian, while a similar stupidity tried to drown what had been real interest with meretricious substitutes. Boredom is not native to uninhibited boyhood; it is the plague of the too-sophisticated nursery. The worst state of all is that of the man who has bored his soul so consistently, doing what he never wanted or intended to do, that he no longer knows that he is bored.

But the apparently docile homosexual man is not necessarily bored. Often he gains success and even distinction along pathways which to other men would appear somewhat eccentric. An effeminate desire to display his personality upon the stage, or to play somewhat affected rôles, both on and off the stage, or to excel along rather extravagant lines—these are characteristic of the male homosexual, and would be perfectly in keeping with the broad marble staircase and the fantastic castle in the distance.

The passive homosexual rôle was, as already emphasized, not a positive line for the patient to take. Lingering near at hand during his moods of depression, but without ever declaring itself for what it was, it became in effect the alternative hypothesis. But such a clear dream of warning indicates that the authority of the self is firmly against it. The fact that everything is seen in a dark, morbid, exaggerated light, and that the goddess herself should be a painted Bolshevik moon — these suffice to give us the real standpoint of the subject. The dreamer himself (*i.e.*, the ego) is figured as being caught in the renegade lure, but that basic reserve of truth which throws this critical light upon the renegade attempt is quite uncontaminated.

With regard to the Russian allusion, the patient was at one time much attracted by Communistic ideas; he even wanted to go to Russia to test the experiment for himself. Through Russian contacts in Paris, however, the intolerance and brutality of the régime was brought home to him, and this effectually cured him.

It is strange that a man who knows immediately that what is humanly wrong can never be politically right should be said to have inferior feeling. In point of fact, the patient's feeling had nothing inferior about it, except that it was in chains. People with a superior, adapted feeling-function can say the right thing with the right inflection at the right time, and can always be trusted to bring their feeling into operation whenever and wherever it is needed. Rarely, however, do we see it generating that intensity of passion which could instigate a really humane reform; whereas a man whose feeling is difficult and introverted is liable to be moved by world-changing emotions.

* * * * *

Another aspect of the bat is the Dracula vampire. Dracula, the blood-sucking demon, assumed the form of a bat in order to get into the house of his victim. In mediæval legend the bat is a classical form of the Devil, representing the insidious power of an evil thought. In popular parlance, hence also in the popular mind, the bat is associated with crazy ideas. From this arises the slang term "batty," or having "bats in the belfry." What is implied in these terms is the presence in the mind of certain ideas which are renegades from reason in the same uncanny fashion as the bat is a renegade mammal.

But why is the bat selected by the dream-mind to symbolize this renegade hypothesis? And why should the bat be associated in the popular mind with the vampire, in face of the incontestable fact that vampire bats have never existed in Europe, and that the only species known are somewhat rare denizens of South America? How did the harmless bat acquire this evil character?

The scientific mind, as we see in the voluminous pages of *The Golden Bough*, is inclined to be irritated by these legendary projections of primitive bias upon the austere face of reality. Science, it says, has to deal with facts, and these superstitious ideas are invariably opposed to honest truth. In the rarefied atmosphere of the laboratory or the study we become intolerant when feelings become confounded with fact, and mythological projections are always concerned with feeling rather than fact.

The bat, then, is an uncanny creature. It frequents

caves, where it hangs suspended from the roof. It flies at dusk, making shrill noises like a mouse. When the natives of Mount Elgon in Kenya were trying to explain to Jung and myself the character of *Ayik* (the Elgonyi equivalent of Set) they dramatized a man alone in a cave at night, whose blood suddenly becomes congealed with terror as a bat's wing strikes his face. That was *Ayik*. In describing this moment of panic the fear of ghosts was immediately present in the minds of the natives, for the bat was identified with the ghostly effect.

The allusion to the snake, in the bottom figure, introduces another mythological projection that is even more widespread and significant than the idea of the vampire. There are more obvious grounds for sinister projections in regard to the snake than in the case of the bat; yet in Africa the snake is more commonly identified with helpful ancestor-spirits than with malevolent ghosts.

In the present drawing both snake and bat are obviously associated with pathological factors, hence with what the Elgonyi would term bad spirits. The one thing which embraces both, and which, to my mind, is at the bottom of the superstitious dread of these animals, is the fact that both are biological renegades. The bat is the only mammalian species which rejected the common paths of mammalian life and took to the air. All his near relations live either in holes in the earth or in trees. Having departed from the ordinary conditions of mammalian existence, his queer habit of hanging head downwards is like a self-imposed penance for reversing the order of nature.

In like manner the snake is really a lizard who, after rejecting the archetypal pattern of locomotion, became a vertebrate centipede walking on the ends of its ribs. These significant departures from the morphological archetype are facts of science, but the impression produced by these creatures on the uninstructed popular mind is an immediate sense of something uncanny. If it could be shown that it is precisely those animals which have departed from the main morphological stream that tend to evoke sinister mythological projections, we should be justified in concluding that the psychological factor deciding these projections is the analogous renegade tendency in the human unconscious.

Whether or not this connection can, in fact, be demonstrated as a general principle does not affect the obvious symbolism of the present drawing.

In view of the patient's dream and the distinctly homosexual character of the face in this drawing, we may infer that the bat symbolizes a subliminal conception[1] of himself as a being singled out by fate to live an abnormal, solitary, and fundamentally antisocial existence. A very large number of individuals adapt themselves to a more or less overt homosexual way of life on the assumption that the main stream of instinctual energy, running from the ancestors to posterity, does not flow through their estate. They sense that the generative channel is blocked, and therefore they assume that the normal instinctive events cannot take place. They feel impelled to pursue eccentric goals and to excel in eccentric paths, as though some justification for their biological defection were required of them.

Nothing, perhaps, could more fitly represent a one-sided renegade-hypothesis than a hemiplegic bat. The normal position of a bat's leg in flight should be closely flexed to the body; we must therefore assume that the trailing leg seen in the picture is paralysed. The left ear and wing being affected in like manner, the bat discloses, by its very symptoms, its true significance as a sinister half-truth. If this half-truth should be accepted as valid for the further course of the patient's life it would mean a complete repression of the positive conception of himself envisaged in Drawing 2, and a definite choice to live on a lower level of consciousness than the one his psyche intends. In other words, he would have to keep himself unconscious of his real potentialities. Hence the hemiplegic bat is associated with a somnambulistic condition, and inasmuch as the logical sequel of accepting the renegade-hypothesis would be a more or less forcible repression of those functions which could create a stable, balanced and productive life, the creature which symbolizes

[1] Subliminal, because the patient is not conscious of any particular homosexual leaning.

this hypothesis must itself manifest a pathological one-sidedness.

Similarly, there is a good reason why the extended wing of the bat accurately covers the region of the head in which the trauma was located in Drawing 2. For the neurotic tendency will always make use of an actual lesion, or organic inferiority, as the *raison d'être* of the renegade-hypothesis. In other words, by accepting the homosexual personality as his destiny the patient's emotional injury would cease to be a problem; it would be completely covered by the hypothesis.

XI

So much for the idea. But what happens to the instinct if the renegade assumption is accepted? The monstrosity at the bottom of the picture provides a threefold answer to our question. The ogre's hand is eternally grasping, the ill-conditioned snake is eternally unsatisfied, and the rat is eternally outlawed. When the subject responded to the healing vision of regeneration in Drawing 2 he accepted totality as his goal. By accepting his vision he was thereby committed to the vital task of creating the self, the striving for his own being. On the other hand, his acquiescence in the renegade conception would mean a denial of the self, a choosing of death in place of life. He would be forced into a restless, dissatisfied pursuit of spiritual needs projected into objects; for what is unaccepted in oneself is sought vicariously in others. Under the ægis of the bat, therefore, the patient would be doomed to a psychological vampirism which would be all the more degrading because, at bottom, it would be a betrayal of ancestral values. Even if the destructive demon were only dimly sensed as something lurking in the underworld, that would be enough to undermine the sensitive springs of spontaneous feeling. A man of feeling would be warned not to come too near the person he loves lest the psychotic infection should reach out and destroy those having the clearest claim on his heart. This nemesis of the dæmonic personality is illustrated in Mary Shelley's macabre fantasy *Frankenstein*.

Repression of the monster, then, is no cure. For the

more an outlawed instinct is isolated in secrecy, the more one is doomed to share the outlaw's fate. Neither can it be extirpated and rooted out as an alien thing: for part of one's soul has become alienated, and therefore to root out the alien will would mean excising an essential part of one's nature.

Transformation is the only effective cure: the instinct must be converted from its allegiance to a false idea. This drawing is, in reality, a ruthless confession, for with this statement the patient admits and accepts the "Ugliest Man" in himself. There is nothing more to hide. The outlawed thing is brought into the light of consciousness, where it has to submit to the transforming power of the human communion.

* * * * *

The middle figure is a more concrete statement of the same confession. There are certain psychic facts which absolutely demand concrete expression. This jagged purple blot is thickly scored with penstrokes, as though the subject had been impelled to pour all his incommunicable torment into an actual pit. Indeed, he himself sensed it as the bottomless pit, a void in the centre of his being, absorbing his vital force as with an irresistible fascination.

The blot occupies the centre of the field, its two inverting streams symbolizing the morbid state of introversion which drags him ever nearer to the edge of the abyss. As the winged creature above represented perverted spirituality and the snake-monster below perverted sexuality, so the two river-systems represent the inverted orientation of these primordial functions of the soul.

So far as is known the first definite statement of the opposite principles of the human soul was the Zoroastrian conception of Ormuzd and Ahriman. As the God of Light Ormuzd was also conceived as the embodiment of everything that was fulfilled and manifest. Ahriman was the active power of darkness—not the mere absence of light, but a sucking void that drew things down into chaos, insatiable as the bottomless pit, and warring continually against the principle of light.

For the purpose of grasping the real nature of the conflict at the time of this drawing, this early conception of the dark power is far more cogent than the denaturalized conception of the Devil which has lingered on as a reminder of Puritan theocracy. It is vital to feel the concrete, active force of evil in this blot. All the power of malign fascination which has maimed the subject's life is centred at last in this black lake. It is not even the will to death, but the power that is pitted against life, the destroyer of value, the god-killer. In a sense this cold, insatiable, pitiless something is inconceivable, for it cannot be represented by any natural image.

We are told that a bottomless chasm once appeared in the forum at Rome. When soothsayers were consulted they declared that it could be closed only by throwing into it Rome's greatest treasure. Whereupon Mettius Curtius, a noble youth, mounted his charger and rode fully armed into the gulf.

All personal human needs can be satisfied. Only demons who borrow their power from the collective unconscious are insatiable. The Book of Proverbs names four of these elemental insatiables:

> " There are three things that are never satisfied,
> Yea, four things say not: It is enough;
> The grave; and the barren womb;
> The earth that is not filled with water;
> And the fire that saith not: It is enough."

The psychopathologist could name many more. The human thirst of the tired man, for instance, can be satisfied, but the demonic thirst of the dipsomaniac cannot be quenched. Therefore we speak of natural and unnatural appetites. If the dipsomaniac could stand and do battle or come to terms with his possessing demon his thirst would eventually become a natural appetite. But in that case he would also have a spiritual issue to face. In delirium tremens the victim is literally overrun by the spiritual forces and potentialities he has spent his life in evading.

A man with a demonic possession can cure himself only by psychological means, because the demon is a relentless spirit which cannot be appeased like a human appetite. What it demands, in effect, is an adequate human achievement.

This is the meaning of D. H. Lawrence's aphorism: " A man goes raging to woman only out of spiritual poverty."

In place of the sucking, insatiable void there must be the 'hall of the pillars of jade'[1] where the self is created. This slow work of creation originates also in that central place—Jung calls it the " virtual centre "—situated between the conscious and the unconscious.

* * * * *

The opposition between atavism and control assumes a less obvious but more integral character in this series. Compare, for instance, the representation of the conflict in the drawing of the flooded world (Drawing 15), with the present drawings. In the former the atavistic deluge was countered by intellectual aloofness and the geographer's lines of latitude and longitude; whereas in the latter the presence of the controlling will reveals itself exclusively in the fourfold grouping of the designs. In the first of the series (Drawing 19) this grouping appears in the four levels represented by the woman's head, the pitcher, the snake and the man's head below. It can also be seen in the four columns, the fourth column being represented by the weeping figure. In the second (Drawing 20) the statement of the essential opposition is found in the four and three of the calyx of the left-hand flower. Three as the dynamic number of creation and destruction is represented in the bracts, the knives, the rings and the candles; it also controls the design of the fourth drawing (22), while four as the principle of structural control governs the columnar design in 20 and 21, as well as the structure of the two plants in 20. The latter point is of peculiar interest, because the transformation from animal to tree was found to be (in Drawing 18) nature's own way of controlling a dangerous possibility. By comparing the fourfold grouping of the root-system of the brain-plant in Drawing 20 (the first branching on the left is somewhat obscured by the root-system of figure 1) with the disordered, chaotic lines of the roots of the same plant in No. 21, we can understand the extreme importance of control in this subject's psychology.

[1] *Vide* " The Secret of the Golden Flower."

We may also observe how control tends to dissolve as he approaches the deep affective roots of his problem. With this last comparison in mind, we might regard the faultless line and meticulous character of the patient's technique, and also his impeccable persona, as belonging to and instigated by the same fundamental need of control.

We observed the manifest efficacy of the quaternary symbol in the compass-sign with the sun's corona in Drawing 6; but its presence as a concealed principle was also discovered in the graded hierarchy of four cones on the left and the parallelogram of four cones on the right of Drawing 16. From that drawing we gained the impression that these ubiquitous signs of control were a deep psychical response to a lurking uneasiness or fear. In other words, schizophrenic defence is a complex formation directly rooted in the schizophrenic doubt.

CHAPTER VIII

SOLUTION OF THE COMPLEX: BIRTH OF THE LIVING SYMBOL

I

In the interval between the last drawing and the present one the patient had recommenced the analysis and had also communicated to me the fact of his early seduction, the repression of which throughout the years had helped to produce the state of emotional dissociation demonstrated in these drawings.

The fact of the confession cannot, of itself, explain the astonishing change which now took place. The patient had no difficulty in telling me the whole story; he even thought he had told me already. But in the almost laconic tones of his voice it was obvious that, although the fact itself was not repressed, he was insensitive to its emotional consequences. The strength of my immediate reaction doubtless had the effect of bringing the complex within the sphere of emotional realization; but its full impact was experienced only when the subject faced the necessity of telling his mother and his wife.

This painting was produced after the vital decision had been taken and just before the arrival of his mother, to whom he had cabled as soon as his mind was made up. He had already informed his wife; but it was significant that the confession to the wife seemed almost insignificant compared with the coming ordeal with the mother. The pact of secrecy which had guarded the seducer all through the years had usurped the place of the normal intimacy existing between mother and son, so now there were no faithful memories to support him.

II

DRAWING 23

The scene is under the sea. The blue depths are illumined by a candle which burns with a steady flame near the centre of the field. Attracted to the flame a shoal of small fish are seen swimming from the right into the orbit of light. These tiny fish are done with great delicacy. Some nearest the light bear a bright orange spot on their sides, as though reflecting the flame of the candle.

Circling the candle with leisurely power are two sharks, one of them lying north-west of the candle, the other south-east. Their position, equidistant from the candle in the centre, suggests a relation of polarity, and their curving motion suggests that they are circling slowly around the candle. The patient told me he had not intended them for sharks, but he agreed that sharks they undoubtedly were and suggested that their circling around the flame was a kind of dance.

* * * * *

Notwithstanding the irrational notion of a candle burning under the sea, this painting is the first natural expression of feeling the subject has yet achieved. There is no trace of symptomatic distortion or abstract symbolism; instead, the living denizens of the sea express an immediate sense of wonder. The concrete, almost tangible, quality of the imagery gives a peculiar reality to the irrational content of the mood. The mood is governed by a fantasy which assumes the undeniable texture of experience. What has been truly experienced carries with it a feeling of inevitability: it could not have been otherwise. In so far as we feel an event could have been different we have not fully experienced it. We remain partially unconvinced, even by our own experience. The experience upon which faith is established must be wholly convincing, otherwise we cannot fully believe in it. The experience may appear to come from without or from within, but the reality which it has for the soul depends primarily upon the efficacy or vitality of its essential content. For realization, as we have already seen, depends upon an organic unity of consciousness in which the emotions as well as the intelligence unreservedly participate.

In the present instance the richness of colour, the perfect economy of design, and the candid statement of the impossible denote a union of the rational and the irrational functions of the psyche resulting in a total moment of experience. Such a moment of experience is the only unshakable basis of faith. The idea of a candle burning in the midst of the sea, when asserted with such simple conviction, belongs to the same order of reality as Tertullian's *credo quia absurdum est.*

It would appear that complete assent of the mind is yielded only to the experience in which the rational and irrational elements of reality are harmoniously reconciled. We believe in spite of our reason, which means that the intrinsic quality of faith derives not from the pure light of reason, but from the reconciliation of the conscious and the unconscious in a living moment of realization. Essentially, therefore, faith is knowledge.

The steady flame of the candle represents a simple statement of spiritual fact. A light has been lit in the depths of the unconscious, and, because it burns in the midst of the sea, it is a light that cannot be quenched. This is no optimistic miracle, no mere wish-fulfilment. The subject is deeply sceptical of illusory enthusiasms. He has discovered something in himself that remains steady and unperturbed even when threatening clouds of emotion are approaching.

The significance of the candle as the germ of divinity derives from its emotional value as a phallic symbol, combined with the idea of light or cognition. Thus, in itself, the candle unites the rational with the irrational elements, symbolizing experiential knowledge or conative cognition. It is this power of uniting the conscious and the unconscious in a single significant expression which, as Jung has shown in *Psychological Types*, belongs uniquely to the reconciling symbol.

The unifying power of the living symbol comes from the fact that many vital tributaries from both sides have joined in its creation. In general, the candle is the archaic or original means of producing light; hence it was taken as the standard unit of measurement. In particular, it played a significant rôle in the bat dream recently discussed, where the candle stood for the light of inherited loyalties which the subject was trying to extinguish in a spirit of renegade revolt. It was also linked up to the homely rites peculiar to Christmas and birthday anniversaries. Advancing from this the subject connected the candle with the symbol of supplication and worship in the ritual of the Catholic Church. From one point of view, therefore, the candle is a farthing dip; from another it is a portion of the sun. But although the candle assembles a multitude of associations in itself, its value as a reconciling symbol resides in the fact that here it is *burning under the sea*.

A further significant connection can be traced to the extinguished candle in the last figure of Drawing 20. The reader will recall how the ambiguous dart which pointed the way down into the unconscious seemed to emanate from the smoke of the witch's candle, and how the putting-out of the candle synchronized with the self-destruction of the perverted intellectual function. Here again we find what was missing above appearing in a new connection below; in the present case the missing function undergoes a " deep-sea change " before it arises out of the depths.

The function extinguished in 20 was introspective intellect. We have watched throughout the series the desperate attempts of the intellect to control the activity of the unconscious, until at last, driven by inner necessity, the defences were surrendered and a natural balance between the opposites became possible.

III

According to the introverted systems of the East, this emptying of consciousness into the unconscious is the *conditio sine qua non* of psychological development. In Zen Buddhism, for example, there is a classical series of pictures called *The Ten Bulls*, representing both the process and the fruit of this purposeful introversion. The first half of the series is concerned with the problem of finding and coming to terms with the bull—that is, the dæmonic aspect of the libido. The second half is concerned with the gaining of enlightenment or wisdom through introversion, symbolized by the transformation into the tree. The immature ego is conceived as a boy, seen in the first picture with his cane and thin coil of rope, setting forth in search of the bull. In the second the boy sees the footprints of the bull in the sand and leaps forward to follow. In the third, catching sight of the bull in the distance, he dashes towards it like an arrow from a bow. In the fourth the boy has flung his rope around the bull's horns, and bull and boy are shewn whirling in space as though the battle of wills had lifted them both from the ground.

At this point the sagacity of the Eastern mind begins to feel its way towards the only possible solution. The boy is too weak to overpower the bull, and the bull cannot free his horns from the rope. So the boy says: " I know a place where there is good pasture and sweet water." The bull listens and is swayed. In the fifth picture boy and bull walk side by side, while the boy gazes with astonishment at his transformed and gentle companion. In the sixth, called the Homeward Way, the boy is riding on the bull's back, leaving him to find the path, he in the meantime playing on his pipe to beguile the way.

The Homeward Way is clearly intended for the introverting direction of the libido. The quest of the bull, ending in the struggle of wills, would correspond with the development of the *Yang* phase of the libido cycle. The moment in which the boy concedes the bull's standpoint and considers his vital needs corresponds to the seed of *Yin*, which begins to germinate only when the *Yang* phase has reached its natural term. From this point the *Yin* phase of introversion proceeds as naturally and inevitably towards the unconscious as the previous extraverting phase of *Yang* went out to gain the world.

In the seventh picture the bull is no longer seen, and the boy reclines on the ground watching the rising sun. In the eighth the introverting phase reaches its completion in a total emptying of consciousness into the unconscious. There remains nothing but an empty ring. The bull has gone, the boy too, and with them all passionate striving and personal lusts. This complete depersonalizing of consciousness is equivalent to the state of *Nirvana* of Indian philosophy. Only with the Zen conception this is not the end; a new phase of *Yang* begins on the suprapersonal level. The ninth picture shows an apple tree just coming into bloom.

This transformation of the bull into the apple tree is another classical example of the way in which nature persuades the wild dæmonic spirit into a more reasonable form, the same process, in fact, which converted the wild figure of Drawing 17 into the tree of 18. The yielding-up of the personal attitude of the ego is the indispensable preliminary to the development of the impersonal. In the East as in the West, we find the symbol of the tree expressing the way of spiritual growth as opposed to the biological phase of development.

In the last picture of *The Ten Bulls* we find a venerable sage, a spirit, carrying on his arm a basket of fruit. The boy stands, a diminutive figure, beside him, and seems to be pointing towards the basket of fruit. The text reads:

> " To seek the origin and return to the beginnings needs much labour:
> Strive to go straight downwards as if blind and deaf.
> In the middle of the temple I want to see nothing outside the temple.
> Water runs widely of itself and flowers grow red."

The essence of the analytical process is contained in this series of ten pictures. The goal of this introverted quest, as it is also the aim of analytical psychology, is the discovery of the original or true self. The false self is an acquired personality arising from perverted collective beliefs. Throughout Eastern thought this concept of the true self is linked up with the idea of a divine essence. Brahman is *Ananda* = bliss, or the *summum bonum*. Ryochi of the Japanese sage Nakai Toju is conceived as " God in us ": he dwells in each individual. In his *Psychological Types* Jung describes Ryochi as the " self-regulating function, the mediator and reconciler of the opposites Ri and Ki. It is in fullest harmony with the Indian idea of the " Ancient Wise One who dwelleth in thy heart." Or as Wang Yang Ming, the Chinese father of the Japanese philosophy, says: " In every heart there dwelleth a Sejin (sage), only man will not steadfastly believe it . . . therefore hath the whole remained buried."[1]

The living symbol gains its reconciling power not merely from a new combination of conscious and unconscious elements, but also, and above all, because it is an expression of the self. It possesses the power and command of a superordinated factor as well as a unique beauty of its own.

We might also express its power in terms of energy, as, for instance, the energy-content of the reconciling symbol is superior in all respects to the energy contained in the various partial systems falling within its orbit. From this point of view, the two sharks on the one hand, and the shoal of fish on the other, represent opposing tendencies which have been attracted by a symbol of superior energy-content, whose indwelling power reconciles them.

As the natural denizens of the sea fish symbolize the indigenous contents of the unconscious. At certain critical phases or points of transition the mythological depths of the unconscious are deeply stirred and are liable to assume a paramount significance. In the history of culture Spengler refers to periods that are determined mythologically, rather than by the process of history.[2] Mythological events cannot be judged historically, but only with the help of the psychic middle eye. It is remarkable, for instance, how often the symbol of the fish, the characteristic denizen of the unconscious, is found at the heart of the mythological event. I need only mention the essential fish-symbolism which accompanied the chief manifestation of Jesus to His disciples after the resurrection—*i.e.*, after His descent into the unconscious. The relative absence of the historical sense and of all historical data in regard to the life of Jesus, the most vital of all human events, tends to bear out Spengler's intuition.

The symbol of the fish, accompanied by the Fisher-King, is also found at the heart of the Grail legend, and again we note a corresponding absence of historicity in regard to the events concerned in this amazing legend. We might,

[1] *Psychological Types*, p. 269.
[2] *The Decline of the West.*

indeed, almost regard the appearance of the fish as a sign that a mythological event in human history is being recorded.

The fish leaps out of the river at the critical juncture in the Tobias myth. The complete ascendancy of the unconscious is graphically represented in the mythological motif of the swallowing of the hero by a whale or some other monster of the deep, as in the myth of Jonah, or in the modern instance of Ahab and Moby Dick.

Ea-Oannes, the Sumerian-Babylonian cultural deity, was represented in the form of a fish; every day he came up out of the sea to teach the people wisdom and the arts of civilization. Also Chidr, or el Khidir, the Verdant One, the living manifestation of Allah, appears at the moment in the journey of Moses and his servant when the fish which they left behind "pursued its course in a marvellous manner towards the sea."

Psychologically, as Jung has pointed out,[1] the fish is a libido-symbol, representing above all *the renewal of the libido* through introversion into the unconscious. That phase in which the historical level is suspended, or rather eclipsed, by the mythological events[2] would correspond, therefore, to the welling-up of the unconscious as a renewing stream of energy. Into the measured passage of time there suddenly breaks the timeless primordial image, bringing with it a sense of eternal significance. When we are in the stream of time every occurrence is threaded upon the string of causal continuity by which our normal waking intelligence is conditioned. But enveloped in the creative-mythological *dynamis* of the unconscious, we are in the presence of the "revolving pillar of fire"[3] which is the eternally existing core of all vital experience. So long as the living symbol occupies the mind the ordinary historical or objective process is to a large extent suspended. This is also true of the dream-state when, as

[1] *Psychology of the Unconscious*, p. 123. Kegan Paul, London.

[2] Jung describes this process of introversion into the unconscious, in which the ego-personality is dissolved in the stream of mythological images, as the night-journey under the sea.

[3] For the source of this figure I must refer the reader to *She*, the myth-story of Rider Haggard.

we know, the ordinary causal, spatial and temporal framework of waking consciousness is profoundly modified, if not wholly suspended.

* * * * *

IV

We have now to enquire whether an analogy reveals itself between the two kinds of fish in this painting and any two corresponding elements in preceding drawings. Regarding the living contents of this scene, for example, as elements in a symbolical pattern, we can distinguish a dynamic centre, two flowing curves, and a number of discrete points. This same pattern appeared before, though in a very immature, abstract form, in the vortical system on the right of Drawing 17. The elements of this system were traced back to the flowing lines and dynamic dots of Drawing 16. At all events the attempt to incorporate the two antipathetic elements of 16 into the vortical system of 17 produced energy in sufficient quantity to propel the anima across the schizophrenic gulf. We can therefore assume that these elements represent the dynamic idiom of the patient's psychology, much as the proton and the electron provide us with a means of conceiving the dynamics of the atom.

We are now in a position to discuss more closely the nature of these psychic elements. Our first hypothesis in regard to the flowing lines of 16 assumed the continuity of the mental process at two different levels. The dots, on the other hand, represented the energy-charge of an autonomous complex. In so far as a complex exists in an autonomous, dissociated state, its energy-content will be sensed as a hidden danger to the rational flow of conscious life, whereas the discharge of the complex into consciousness by means of a conscious act of realization produces a vigorous reinforcement of the conscious stream.

So much for Drawing 16. In the vortical system of 17 the two elements have become essentially modified owing to their mutual determination by a central dynamic nucleus, around which they revolve within a self-contained orbit and by which they appear to be controlled in some reciprocal activity. The drawing of the vortical system was very inadequate in 17. It was, as we said, rather like a nebula taking shape near the margin of apprehension; yet both in its structure and effect it pointed towards great subsequent potentiality.

In Drawing 18 we observed the idea of organic synthesis in the symbolism of the tree with its denizens, including a spider weaving its web—viz., the nebula under a new form. And later, in Drawing 21, we found the spider with its controlling web elevated to the position of ruling symbol. In this sequence we observe the vortical system beginning to assume the integrated structure of a *mandala*.

Bearing these symbolical antecedents in mind, we can begin to appreciate the feeling of fulfilment governing the dance of the fishes in the present painting. A further allusion to its emotional content is to be found in the specific character of the two kinds of fish. The shark belongs to the predatory, solitary, independent type which relies, like the eagle or the larger carnivora, on its strength, its speed of attack, and its aggressive equipment for successful survival. The shoal of small fish, on the other hand, belong to the type of gregarious, prolific, freely spawning creatures which form the natural prey of the former and which depend for their survival upon an almost incredible scale of reproduction. The former would represent the biological analogue of the introverted type, the latter of the extraverted.

William Blake, whose intuitive insight into the dynamic nature of the unconscious has never been understood, described the basic opposition in the very essence of being as the conflict between the Prolific and the Devouring. He says: " Thus one portion of being is the Prolific, the other the Devouring; to the devourer it seems as if the producer was in his chains; but it is not so, he only takes portions of existence and fancies that the whole. But the Prolific would cease to be Prolific unless the Devourer as a sea received the excess of his delights: Some will say Is not God alone the Prolific? I answer, God only Acts and Is in existing beings or Men." In a subsequent passage he says: "Religion is an endeavour to reconcile these two."[1]

In some of Blake's reflections he seems to be using this biological antithesis to describe two opposing types of men. At other times he is clearly thinking of the opposition as inherent in the very nature of being, as, for instance, in his idea that religion is an attempt to reconcile the conflict. All through his aphoristic writings Blake is fundamentally concerned with the opposition he feels between the rational conscious function—viz., Urizen, or heaven, and the dynamic unconscious—viz., the underworld or hell, the denizens of which he describes as the active creators of energy.

As a creative artist Blake is at heart a passionate partisan of the creative unconscious, and in so far as he conceived the Prolific-Devouring antithesis as an aspect of psychic duality, he must have identified the Prolific with unconscious creative activity, the Devouring with conscious intellect. From Blake's point of view science devours what nature creates.

To return to our material: in so far as we are justified in identifying the curving sweep of the two sharks in their circling dance around the flame with the flowing lines of Drawing 16 (which assumed a similar circular motion in the vortical system of 17), it would appear that our subject is also prompted to identify the devouring sharks with the principle of apprehension. By a parallel process of reasoning the identity of the shoal of small fish with the dynamic contents of the cones in 16, and with the dots in the right half of the vortical system of 17, equates the small fish with the prolific activity of the unconscious.

These thoughts may be helpful in our attempt to conceive the essential nature of the psychical dichotomy. Since the intellect is both tool and arbiter of all scientific enquiry, it is unavoidable that we should cherish a certain bias in favour of rational consciousness. But when it becomes a matter of life or death for dissociation to be healed, our intellectual bias has to go to the wall. For reconciliation of the opposites to become effective the conscious and unconscious elements

[1] *Marriage of Heaven and Hell.*

must be given full and equal value as reciprocal aspects of a single system.

Though fully accustomed to the use of such terms as grasping, seizing, apprehending, digesting, etc., as descriptive of conscious activity, we are none the less not a little startled when we find the most favoured servant of the mind represented as a predatory beast of prey. However, a little reflection reveals the truth of this characterization. It is patent, for instance, that the conscious function creates nothing of itself. Not only does it consume the energy provided by the unconscious, it also depends upon the amazing fertility of the autonomous psyche for every subjective image, every pregnant association, and every new idea.

Apart from our therapeutic programme an equal and reciprocal relation between the two opposing functions of the mind must entail a new kind of conscious attitude, one in which the prolific and the devouring aspects of being regain a true functional relativity in the observance of which neither presumes to be all-sufficient or to exclude its partner.

In the earlier drawings of this series we observed how the conflict between the two aspects of the mind assumed the symbolical form of the masculine versus the feminine, and we saw against what powerful resistance the anima had to contend before the validity of her principle was accepted and established. Civilization seems to have had a disturbing effect on the original balance of the psyche, somewhat analogous to its profound disturbance of the primordial balance between man and woman.

Among the indigenous food-gathering communities which have retained the original balance of nature observers have testified, in varying accents of surprise, to the excellent partnership prevailing between man and woman in all the essential functions of life. On the other hand, the whole history of civilized life reveals alternating social patterns in which either the matriarchal or the patriarchal principle has been uppermost, with a corresponding tendency to deterioration and suppression of the opposite principle. Thus the need to restore the pristine balance of nature becomes manifest throughout civilized psychology in manifold ways both within and without.

In the case of the subject of these drawings, since the pressure came from both sides, the need to create the living symbol which could bring long estranged opposites together in a common ritual dance was the essential necessity of his life. The same basic necessity in the soul of the Jewish people gave birth to the vision of the prophet Isaiah:

> " The wolf also shall dwell with the lamb,
> And the leopard shall lie down with the kid;
> And the calf and the young lion and the fatling together;
> And a little child shall lead them."

Actually, of course, no man sets out consciously to create the reconciling symbol. It is born out of deepest need; and with its birth a new conception of man has dawned. This flame burning in the midst of the sea is no product of the subject's conscious invention: rather is it an improvization deriving from an ancient mythological theme. The swallowing of the sun-hero by the great monster of the sea is the mythic form expressing the rebirth of consciousness out of the dark night of the unconscious. According to primitive ideas the life of the sun is eternally renewed through the impregnation of the maternal sea or monster by the dying sun, who therewith becomes the father of the new sun rising in the east. In the same way the libido is renewed through its descent into the maternal womb of the unconscious,[1] where the opposites which consciousness separated are eternally reconciled.

A graphic indication of this renewal lies here before our eyes. In the previous drawing we saw the inverted libido drawn into the dark central pit. It was the patient's own suggestion that the beautiful deep-blue wash of the sea in the present drawing might have originated from the dissolving of that viscous inky substance in the general unconscious. In other words, the healing power of confession is demonstrated as the flowing of the tormentingly personal into the

[1] In the present case this descent of the god-value into the unconscious is also concerned with the creation of a central power or control which takes the place of the former tyranny of consciousness.

impersonal, the isolated into the universal, the ethically impossible into the natural. The change from the opaque, angry ink of the former state into the translucent blue of the sea is a clear feeling-statement of the healing that has taken place.

V

DRAWING 24

A violent thunderstorm lashing a green sea. Again there is no sign of man nor any of his works. Out of a black-grey sky, charged with thunder, two lightning flashes break. Soon after it is discharged from the swollen cloud above, the one on the left divides into a complex skein of five or six lines. These consolidate again into a single line as the path approaches the sea. At the very end of its course it divides once more into a kind of delta before striking the surface of the sea.

The second flash, towards mid-heaven, is jagged in its course, and ends ineffectually in two forking branches. The left-hand branch finishes in a kind of three-fingered hand. Rain slants fiercely from heavy thunderclouds, and the wind whips spray from the crests of the waves. The wind is blowing the spray from left to right; yet the rain is slanting from right to left. Another contradictory feature of the storm is seen in the fact that the actual surface of the sea appears relatively calm.

Upon this tempestuous background two mythological figures are cast. A black horse, with flowing mane and tail, is seen galloping towards the right—*i.e.*, in the same direction as the scudding spray—and, directly in its path, a gigantic hand rises from the sea, apparently with the idea of catching the horse.

The whole scene is realistically executed, with the exception of the horse. Contrasted with the hand, in which the skilful use of light and shadow enhances the impression of superhuman power, the horse is flat and ghostly. Nowhere is light reflected from the surface of its body, and its hindquarters and legs appear dwarfed and somewhat out of scale. The painting of the leaden sky above is impressive.

* * * * *

This and the preceding painting are the only works in the series which are convincing as artistic products. Their eloquence has the ring of genuine emotion. The subjective problems of the artist are no longer interposed between the artistic conception and the observer. We are allowed full view, so to say, of the emotional event.

The drawings that went before were interesting because of their psychological content, and yet, however carefully they may have been executed no one could possibly mistake them for works of art, whereas in the case of the two paintings we are now considering, notwithstanding the symbolical nature of their content, no one would deny their genuine artistic quality.

I think the difference lies in this. Hitherto the subject has employed his artistic ability purely for the purpose of delineating his subjective problem. He has not been very concerned with the objective value of these delineations. In these two paintings, on the other hand, the soul of the artist is fully contained in the unity of the experience. There are no Hamlet-like soliloquies, no ironical commentary from the wings. Every function and every part is taken into service by the creative complex, and the result is the simplest possible statement of the emotional event.

The representation of the reconciling symbol—perhaps the most profound idea in the whole of philosophy—could scarcely be conceived more simply or naturally than in the last painting. It has the tangible quality of a natural truth; concrete, because the truth it contains has not yet been abstracted from its plastic vehicle. The idea of the present painting, though rich in prophecy for the tormented modern soul, is uttered with the same mythological simplicity. The primordial depths have been touched, whence the religious experience rises with its own peculiar power. Because the religious experience emerges autochthonously from the supra-personal depths of the unconscious, its symbolical expression tends naturally towards a cosmic mode of representation—a mode which manifests the universal and eternal nature of religious ideas.

Beside its obvious significance from the therapeutic standpoint, the transformation just witnessed, from more or less symptomatic products to convincing artistic creation, is also of considerable interest in respect to the general problem of the psychology of artistic production. It raises the question whether the modern artist, in his often unintelligible attempt to represent the unconscious, is not unwittingly seeking, in his own depths, that unity of experience which he has failed to find in the external world. If the hypothesis be conceded that the attainment of psychical wholeness is the desired precondition of valuable achievement, then the more or less obvious attempts at self-analysis observable in the works of many surrealist artists become at least psychologically intelligible.

* * * * *

With regard to the main content of this painting, the subject thought that the black horse had to do with panic, while he associated the hand with a passage vaguely remembered from the Bible concerned with " measuring the heavens with a span." The allusion is to the fortieth chapter of Isaiah, and it is probable that these famous passages were also linked up to the Messianic motif in his mind through their association with Handel's *Messiah*:

> " Comfort ye, comfort ye my people, saith your God. Speak ye comfortably to Jerusalem, and cry unto her, that her warfare is accomplished, that her iniquity is pardoned: for she hath received of the Lord's hand double for all her sins.
>
> " The voice of him that crieth in the wilderness, Prepare ye the way of the Lord, make straight in the desert a highway for our God. . . .
>
> " Who hath measured the waters in the hollow of His hand, and meted out heaven with the span ?"

The psychological significance of this association at this crucial time can be imagined. Even in the manner of its execution the power of this intervening hand emerging from the depths is incontestably real. Compared with this steadfast reality, the horse is the phantasm of a black mood—a nocturnal shape colliding with daylight reality. The spirit of panic is of the witch's brood; once loosed it knows no bounds. Hence the fullest power of control is needed.

I have already mentioned the reaction of the farm-hand who, when sheltering from a severe thunderstorm in a barn in the fen district, was overheard to say to his neighbour after a particularly violent crash: "Did you see the black horse in the sky?" The archaic image is far more expressive at such moments than the colourless response of artificially drilled affect. In folk-legends the storm-dæmon is frequently associated with a black horse. One thinks of the Walkyrie, the dæmonic daughters of Wotan, the sky-and-thunder deity of pagan Germany. The horses of the Walkyrie must surely have originated in driven storm-clouds.

The presence of contradictory forces and impulses, urging the subject in different directions, is indicated by the fact that the horse and the spray are driven in one direction, while the rain is slanting in another. Panic, as we know, is often bred from the clash of conflicting impulses.

The patient was torn by conflict and swept by fear at this juncture. At times he was undoubtedly tempted to run away from the ordeal. Never yet had he been able to stand firm through an emotional tempest. But in this moment a power stronger than himself took possession of him, and the uncontrollable mood was checked. Therewith he was forced to recognize a power in the centre of his being that was proof against fear. Later he connected this power with the candle burning in the midst of the sea. A voice out of the past wanted to call it "the hand of God"; but he preferred to leave it as it came—nameless. The one essential fact was its undeniable efficacy: his truth would stand whatever happened.

Whitehead has said that "religion is what a man does with his solitariness." This statement contains the philosopher's truth and implies the philosopher's doubt. But the touchstone of religious efficacy for men of every age has been the power that can overrule fear. Every rite, every object, every idea, every person through whose peculiar virtue his worst fears could be vanquished, has been given religious value by the questing soul of man. At the primitive level these things become endowed with magical attributes and are served by a magical fraternity. On a higher level we speak of religious symbols and sacraments in which the magico-religious feelings of the race are enshrined. Last of all we come to the individual religious experience which, carrying in its depths the same primordial idea of healing and atonement and yielding the same abundant efficacy, emerges redeemed from the magical twilight of man's infancy into the clear light of individual consciousness.

The lightning flash could be regarded symptomatically as a mere release of tension, but the impressive character of the experience precludes a purely symptomatic reading. Viewed symbolically, then, the flash on the left would correspond with a path of energy stretching between the two primordial elements — heaven and ocean. The division of this path begins near its source and attains its maximum degree of splitting in the course of its leftward curve. With the change of direction towards the right the lines tend to converge, and unity is again achieved as the energy-path nears its goal. The only other thing to note is the fact that the line divides again into four branches just before it reaches sea-level.

In contrast to this achieved electrical path the other flash to the right reveals a relatively long, unbroken course, then a sudden tangle or fraying of the flash, followed by an abrupt forking into two branches, both of which end in space. This would represent the unachieved path.

There is, of course, no obligation to regard every aspect of a work of art from the psychological point of view; but from our study of mythology we learn that cosmic happenings, accompanying a world-changing event on the human plane, are invariably symbolical in character. We also know that in the field of active fantasy a painting tends to be most revealing in those aspects which are not consciously intended.

Regarding these two types of electrical paths, therefore, as alternative paths, either of which is a feasible line for the subject's fate, we can recognize in the unachieved path in mid-heaven the intellectual hypothesis which left him, as it were, suspended in mid-air. This line would represent the attempt to control life solely from above, ignoring the instinctual grounding of the soul in the elementary human tasks and duties which relationship demands. The reader will recall, in our discussion of Drawing 20, how the subject was forced to confess the complete bankruptcy of the controlling intellect and how, in the same drawing, the root-systems of the two plants were left, as it were, naked in space instead of being earthed in the soil. A purely intellectual dissection of a vital system is liable to commit this error, inasmuch as it abstracts each system from its vital connections in order to bring it within the circumscribed field of the concept.

A comparison of the stem of the brain flower (the third figure in Drawing 20) with this forked lightning-flash reveals a certain kinship which, however, need not be followed too closely. In place of the schizophrenic thickening of the stem we find a tangle in the electrical path from which a secondary flash is given off in the reverse direction—a classical sign of resistance. The unity of the path over the greater part of its course corresponds to the subject's attempt to adapt to life on the basis of a single function.

The right-hand flash can be linked up, then, with the hypothesis that fails. The storm which is let loose is, of course, directly related to this failure, since the breakdown of a long-established psychological attitude is necessarily fraught with fear and peril.

The process of transition, in which a fundamental change of attitude is taking place, is frequently accompanied by dreams of storm and commotion. A reorientation of the vital attitude necessarily involves a great displacement of vital energy, and what is a storm of rain but a kinetic displacement of energy from a higher potential to a lower? From this energic standpoint it is not irrelevant that the artist has drawn his sheets of slanting rain in connection with the two lightning-flashes and principally in the immediate neighbourhood of the forking flash in mid-heaven.

In respect to the achieved electrical path on the left the most important thing to note is that the splitting into a number of separate paths is contained within the idea of one manifold channel. It is as though differentiation takes place within a unitary system whereby the single gives place to the manifold, which in turn becomes single again. By this means the electrical path is spread out over a fairly wide field without suffering loss of energy.

If we apply this analogy to the concept of psychological development we know that the libido achieves its maximum efficacy when it is differentiated along a number of specific functional paths. The state of unity precedes and succeeds the phase of differentiation; yet the primordial unity of the infantile stage is literally poles asunder from the integrated totality of psychological maturity, although both possess the efficacy of the single mind. In Plato's description of the World-Soul in the *Timæus*, we recognize the containing archetype of the embryonic monad or basal unity; yet its content is the complex totality of differentiated conscious experience. Translating this symbolism into psychological terms, the path of individuation proceeds from the state of the simple monad through the fullest differential education to that state of integration in which the original unity and simplicity of attitude is regained. This would be the story of the achieved path which the artist now discovers as an actually feasible path for his life's energy to follow.

The artist has added a detail to this achieved flash which bears the stamp of its psychological origin. This is the fourfold delta or foot with which the unified path is finally distributed. The fourfold reality-application of psychic energy, by means of the four main psychic functions, brings the idea of the achieved path into relation with the idea of all-round functional efficiency. Psychic energy must be conceived as making contact with the facts and situations of concrete existence through four main functional avenues. Without cultivated differentiation of function psychic energy would have no means of conversion from the potential to the actual.

But why, we may well ask, does the patient suddenly change his whole mode of expression? At one time he preferred pen and ink and tended towards small, frail and rather personal images such as flowers, candles, knives, insects, etc., in the representation of his psychological material.

Suddenly the scene is shifted into mid-ocean, and mythological and religious ideas are represented in a cosmic setting of storm and lightning. Not only so, but the subject unwittingly projects a certain aspect of his mental process into these cosmic events. Yet, in spite of this identification of the psychological with the cosmic, it must be conceded that the last two paintings are genuine artistic products, whereas the earlier drawings were often afflicted by a macabre subjectivity. With these two paintings before us we cannot but feel that the previous drawings were done by a man looking down the wrong end of a telescope.

The explanation is bound up with the fact that heretofore the subject had been isolated with his personal problem. His whole myth had the character of a deliberate understatement. His attitude was that of a man who conceives himself to be the singular exception in a world of normal individuals. There was little attempt to make his psychological representations intelligible, because he assumed them to be concerned solely with himself and his problem.

His acceptance of the fact that the imprisoned part of his soul was of vital concern to others besides himself had the effect of reversing the telescope which therewith revealed his psychological situation in universal terms. It is as though the dark personal affect pent up in the evil blot of Drawing 22 was suddenly released into the boundless sea of the general unconscious. From this point of view it is not too fantastic to imagine the opaque violet of the blot of 22 dissolved in the deep-blue wash of 23.

It would seem to be literally true that the solution of the hemmed-in individual problem is to be found through the immediate experience of the general unconscious, whereby the burden of personal shame is dissolved in a feeling of fundamental kinship with all mankind.

In spite of daring reports of rapid and apparently miraculous cures of psychoneurotics after a few " common-sense talks," I have to confess that I have never seen a lasting cure of long-standing dissociation without some such experience of the collective unconscious as we have witnessed in the present case. I cannot deny the accuracy of these reports;

but, if they are true, I would have to assume that there exist two distinct species of human beings: one in which the basic principles of spiritual reality govern the issue, and another in which they are strangely inoperative.

It is, as we have seen, perfectly possible to conceive of the psyche as a brain flower and the unconscious as its roots. But the truth is that there is no healing in this conception. It is merely an intellectual paraphrase of the anatomical viewpoint, and it is ineffectual just because it is inadequate to embrace the actual facts of psychic reality. It diminishes the psyche in order to gain power over it, whereas the storm, the rain, the lightning-flash, the black horse and the mighty hand present a mythologically realistic picture of a spiritual truth. The picture is true, simply because these symbols are adequate to the nature of the facts they represent. And the whole composition is beautiful and convincing because it is true.

It must not be assumed that a mere act of confession could work this sudden transformation; neither could a reluctant acceptance of the principle of restitution in regard to the two relationships which had been emotionally deprived. The healing effect came with the realization that relationship is a fundamental necessity of life, and that to deny the reality of this need means spiritual death.

The sphere of relatedness comes under the rule of Eros in the widest acceptance of this principle. But many men, with or without an unconscious homosexual disposition, are neurotically disabled from giving genuine service to this feminine principle of relatedness. There is even a tendency to disparage this other aspect of life, as though to be seriously concerned with one's vital human relationships were in some way effeminate. At all events the masculine overvaluation of the intellect and its achievement is particularly liable to appear as a compensatory development in just those cases where a real inferiority exists on the side of relatedness.

* * * * *

We can see this experience in its true proportions only when we remember how profoundly the subject had been occupied with the problem of control. From the point of view of his lifelong conflict, the black horse is the epitome of the whole atavistic tendency and the divine hand the most complete and perfect expression of integrated control. Naturally this conception of unshakable steadiness at the centre could not come to reality until conscious interference had ceased. Intellectual repression having failed, the way was clear for the power of the self to become manifest. The cosmic setting in which this manifestation takes place provides the clearest possible affirmation of the way in which the personal ego is dissolved in the direct experience of the unconscious. The general unconscious is experienced in this immediate fashion, however, only when the contents of the personal unconscious have first been analysed and cleared out of the way.

CHAPTER IX

THE SHADOW CASTING THE REALITY

DRAWING 25

THIS was done some little time after the vivid paintings of the previous chapter. It has little interest in itself but for one important particular emerging at the junction of the two worlds. It is studied and deliberate, hence a symptomatic rather than a symbolical product. The patient called it The Shadow casting the Reality.

Above is the flat silhouette of a nude feminine figure coloured in a drab bluish-grey. In her right hand she holds a long thin wand or staff. This is even in thickness throughout its length, and her arm rests upon it in a statuesque pose.

This upper figure is painted upon a square of pink distemper colour. To right and left of this square are two side-walls of reddish brown. The relation of these side-walls to the square end is determined by lines of perspective, so that one gets the impression that the female silhouette is painted upon the blank end-wall of a corridor.

At the level of the ankles the legs of this figure are continued downwards into those of a powerful, nude male figure of heroic proportions. This figure is painted on a background of chalky blue, and from the identity of posture of both figures, and from the fact that the male figure is in the reversed position and continuous with the first, we are evidently meant to conclude that the second is the reflection of the first.

In point of fact, however, the two are in vigorous contrast. For whereas the upper figure is feminine, two-dimensional, and painted in a drab monotone, the lower is masculine, muscular, three-dimensional, nearly twice as large as the first, and is painted in flesh tints under direct sunlight, though a faint mist impairs clear visibility of detail. The only thing that comes into brilliant focus is the tapering crimson staff which the man holds in his hand and which is intended to reflect the rather futile wand carried by the woman. In shape the man's staff resembles a billiard cue. It has clearly been painted with some care, in order to give it roundness and solidity. The rod is held in his left hand, his right being hidden behind his back. The head is slightly inclined to the right. The feet are absent from both figures.

* * * * *

The only occasion on which this drab, opaque colouring has been used before was in the cosmogonic fantasy of Drawing 13. We called it The Hour before Dawn, because it represented a conception of reality completely determined by collective or dæmonic unconscious forces. The freedom of individual consciousness had not yet dawned; it was therefore a world without light.

A similar lack of freedom is implied in the present picture, discernible in the dark constricting walls, the statuesque immobility of the figures, and, above all, in the omission of feet. Liberty of movement is the most elementary attribute of freedom, but where there are no feet there can be no movement. The passivity of the two-dimensional shadow-figure is emphasized by its obvious feminine outline and by its studied position in the middle of the square-end, like a figure enclosed in a frame.

Two important associations with previous drawings help to clarify the significance of this figure at the present juncture. In the first place its statuesque immobility and the feminine roll of hair at the back of the head bring to mind the line of "ideal" anima heads in Drawing 10. That the subject had the same feeling of determinism in regard to those heads was revealed by the fact that he described them as a "mental stammer."

The second association concerns the anima figure of Drawing 21, whose suspended position was due to the fact that she had not been given feet. The feet represent the instinctual "understanding" or standpoint. The foot is therefore intimately associated with sexuality. Both these attributes were concerned in our understanding of Drawing 9, in which a diminutive female figure was seen standing in the shoes of the subject. In that case not only was the anima deprived of her own independent standpoint, but she was confined within a mechanical system which completely occluded her upper half. It was as though the anima, imprisoned in a false intellectual conception, were revealing her plight by making the subject draw her standing in his shoes. Not only that, but the shoes were so arranged that left and right were perversely transposed.

Again, in Drawing 21 the maiming of the anima, both above and below, was clearly indicated, the absent feet and the skeletal hands suggesting that injury to the instinct below also entails a spiritual infirmity above. Sexuality and spirituality being interdependent dæmonic powers, when the roots are damaged the branches cannot remain unaffected.

All this is clearly suggested in the present picture. Creative spirituality lies dormant in the shape of the heroic or divine male figure, who seems to be waiting in the misty light of dawn for one last thing to be added. And this last thing, which could fire unknown potentiality from the unconscious, determined state, is the granting of an independent or other standpoint to the anima. The subject has confused the anima with his conscious ego, only because he has not been able to give the unconscious the value of origin or source. The needed differentiation of the primordial as distinct from the cultural standpoint has always been lacking.

In view of the continuity between the two figures, the effeminacy of the conscious personality would seem to be the cause which holds the unconscious potential from being realized. The situation is not unlike a frequent and most intractable marriage problem in which the husband complains that he could do great things if only his wife would give him freedom and independence, while the wife protests that her life would be fulfilled if only the husband would not project all his infantilism in her direction.

In both cases it is easy to see what is wrong, but how can the needed change come about? It is useless to say to a man:

"You are altogether too passive and effeminate, and you should not capitulate to your wife's tyrannical animus." He knows this already to saturation point. Neither was it feasible to say to this subject: "You must give your anima the value of an independent standpoint." He would have had no idea what to give her nor how to give it.

The situation is, as the drawing shows, an *impasse*; the two-dimensional figure is standing at the end of a *cul-de-sac*. Fortunately the way out is already suggested in the presence of the blood-red staff of desire in the hero's hand. The freeing of the self, the desire for one's own being, is instinct in this crimson staff. It is as much the staff of mastery and command as it is the symbol of desire. The baton, the sceptre, the sword, the staff, the mace—all these have sprung from the phallic root, but their significance is primarily concerned with mastery and control.

The *impasse* will be broken only when the subject longs for the creative man with such efficacy that the staff of mastery knows in whose hand it really belongs. Man cannot free woman, nor can woman free her man. Freedom is a value only to those that can desire it enough. And how could one desire it enough unless creation waited upon one's desiring? The anima will automatically be freed from her bondage to the ego, and therewith establish an independent feminine standpoint in the psyche, when the subject feels in his right hand the staff of desire which will lead him to the self.

As an alternative fate, instead of realizing his unconscious male potential in himself the subject might project this potential into another man, in which case a characteristic homosexual constellation would take the place of creative achievement. It is, of course, perfectly possible to demonstrate this drawing on the homosexual hypothesis, inasmuch as the feminine type of homosexual regularly shows this reversal—namely, the anima identified with the persona and the potential masculine character relegated to the unconscious. The danger is obviously present, and the success of the analysis will depend on whether the *impasse* can be overcome.

With this danger in mind we can appreciate that the identification of the anima with the shadow is by no means accidental in this drawing. The essential task of psychological maturity is the acceptance of the shadow-aspect of one's personality. Indeed, the anima can never manifest her positive capacity until the shadow has been accepted and assimilated. Civilized man has done the soul an injury in identifying himself exclusively with the ideal and rational aspects of his psychology, because he therewith unloads the unaccepted residue upon the anima. In this way he falls foul of his own soul, identifying her with a witch or demon instead of honouring her as a helpful ministering function. We shall see in the final chapter what great issues are involved in this honouring of the soul.

The importance of this painting at the present juncture has to do with the practical goal of the analytical procedure which is the transformation of attitude. The moment had come for a change that has been likened to that from the two-dimensional flat painting of primitive art to the three-dimensional perspective of the Renaissance. And what was it, after all, that Leonardo and his mighty contemporaries set going but that change in the whole intellectual and moral attitude with which European culture emerged from the Middle Ages into the modern world?

The subject has directly invited this analogy by contrasting his two-dimensional "shadow" with his three-dimensional "reality." The desire which could motivate this individual *renaissance* is symbolized by the rounded crimson staff.

The continuity of this symbol of desire runs in a clear sequence from the extinguished candle of Drawing 21 (where it was grouped with the sinister witch-face and the piebald intuitive shaft), through the unquenchable candle of 23 and the hand of mastery arising from the sea in 24, to the rod of desire and the fully personified hero-image of 25. The sinister laming of the creative trinity by the sexual seduction is suggested in 21; the symbolic development of the repressed instinct through identification with the archetype of the self is revealed in 23 and 24; and the emergence of the restored creative personality is prepared in 25. In this way the psyche creates the mature individuality with the symbolic material and restitutional activity generated by the emotional trauma.

CHAPTER X

THE BIRTH OF THE GOD

THE subject was not exalted or markedly inflated when he painted this final picture. But he did observe a certain liberation from his usual strict control, rather like the relaxation of tension from the effect of alcohol.

I

DRAWING 26

Against a sky of rich blue a Gothic cathedral with four towers is seen rising up into the heavens. The structure seems to be in the process of dissolution. Flying buttresses are like cascades of water. What was apparently the nave, to the right of the four towers, has all but melted away. The whole fabric has the airy lightness and butterfly colouring of something ephemeral and insubstantial. Slanting across the church from right to left are to be seen areas of thin white lines not unlike the slanting rain of Drawing 24. These areas are most conspicuous to the right of the unfinished fourth tower and to the left of the first spire.

In general the left-hand portion of the fabric (which is clearly the western façade) has a rather more solid appearance than the rest. The structure of the rose-window and the two western spires seems to be more intact than any other part of the building. One has the feeling that this part was the last to lose contact with the earth, an impression that is supported by the presence of three downward extensions from the angles of the nearest tower, one of which looks like a massive blade. These downward extensions resemble tent-pegs or roots that have been pulled violently out of the earth. Indications of similar roots are to be found to the right and left of these three.

In support of the idea that the fabric has recently been wrenched from its foundations, we find patches of angry cross-hatching in the intervals between the roots or pegs. These patches of violent lines are found nowhere else in the drawing, and it is obvious that they represent no part of the building. We must regard them, therefore, as areas of tension or disturbance, as though the tearing of the cathedral away from the solid earth was an idea which aroused considerable subjective resistance.

The structure of the fourth tower differs from the other three. It is quadrilateral throughout, while the other three taper to a spire. It has four rows of narrow arches with a stained-glass window on its western face. The top of the tower shows a jagged edge, as though it had either been broken off or had never been finished. At the top, on the right-hand face, there is a doubtful female figure in blue which might be an image of the Virgin. In the original this figure is naturally more visible than in the reproduction.

On the extreme right-hand edge of this tower a long crimson streak descends for about half the length of the tower, dissolving away in the remains of the nave. This crimson line is reminiscent of the tapering rod held by the hero-figure in the last painting.

The three spires are each surmounted by a cross. But in the case of the one nearest the observer, judging from the black pencil lines scored over the white painted cross, contradictory motives seem to have been at work.

The earth spread out below is an absolutely level plain, the horizon having been drawn with a ruler. Lines of latitude and longitude divide this plain into measured squares. In contrast to the unkempt lines of the flooded world of Drawing 15, all the longitudinal lines of the present painting converge with precision upon a single point just to the left of mid-horizon. The plain is barren; there is no object nor any sign of life as far as the eye can see.

Descending out of the dissolving cathedral, and poised with arms outstretched like wings over the barren, expectant earth, there is a naked human figure. Actually it is impossible to feel this figure to be falling. The beautiful poised body with extended feet like a diver, the clear single curve of the arms like the wings of a planing albatross, the vigilant, forward inclination of the head—in a word, the purposive carriage of the whole figure speaks of flight and of a judged descent.

Light falls strongly on this figure from above, casting a bird-like shadow on the ground beneath. Light and shade are vividly contrasted in this figure, as in the painting of the mighty hand in 24. Its shadow-aspect is towards the observer, the only thing which breaks the shadow being a white loin-cloth.

* * * * *

Our conclusion about this strange and rather beautiful painting must rest upon the question whether we are to regard it solely from the angle of the subject's individual problem, or whether it is possible also to view it in the light of a general prophecy. We can regard the dissolution of the cathedral as symptomatic of the disruptive, disintegrative tendency of the schizophrenic. But in that case we have to explain how it is that the whole conception gives one the impression of a meaningful, not to say inspired, content. We must also explain how a man, presumably in a dissolute mental condition, could measure the waiting earth with such meticulous precision and paint, in the centre of his picture, a figure so eloquent of poise and winged purpose. The picture is, in fact, a strange symbolical product which a hasty clinical judgment might easily misunderstand. Moreover, from a wider standpoint it possesses implications so significant for the modern soul that one is inclined to wonder whether the patient may not be representing an idea gathered mediumistically from the collective unconscious of our time.

Not to brush aside the pathological viewpoint altogether, it is extremely probable that a schizophrenic psychology would be unusually fitted to apprehend the early signs of disintegration in the general environment, and for this reason would be better able to prophesy the unconscious trend of events than those whose firm adhesion to existing forms and conditions renders them somewhat obtuse to the shape of things to come.

I have good evidence that the subject was himself unaware

of the meaning of what he had done. For his first idea about the picture was that it represented Christ upholding the Church. Although patently wide of the mark, his suggestion was none the less helpful, because it identified the descending figure with the divine Son of Man.

Here then are three vital elements: a dissolving cathedral ascending into the blue; a barren, expectant earth; and, descending from the dissolving cathedral to the waiting earth, a divine, naked man.

This is what the picture says. Now let us see how it is saying it. We have already noted the way in which the cathedral has been, as it were, torn from its roots, and we marked signs of resistance showing that the truth which enforced this idea was not easily obeyed. We observed also that the western end of the church seemed to be the last to leave its moorings, and that this end was the most substantial part of the fabric, whereas a rapid dissolution has done away with the eastern end where the altar should be. This may help to explain the fact that the descending Christ seems to have issued from the western end of the church.

Normally a cathedral is oriented towards the east, the point of the sun's rising. The west, being the end of the sun's journey, is associated with decline. As sun-hero, Christ must be conceived as originally entering the church from the east; now He leaves it by the western door. Having passed through the church, as though travelling the whole length of Christendom, He now descends as a new incarnation of the spirit upon the waiting earth.

When we come to an examination of the structure of the cathedral the first thing to arrest our attention is the presence of the four towers, arranged in the form of a square. Of these three are conventional spires, while the fourth belongs to an earlier style and period. The patient's association with this anachronism was that it was transitional between the Norman and the Perpendicular.

Examination of this tower in the original painting reveals an important difference in structural conception. Instead of the tapering spires with their dog-toothed edging, we have a square structure with at least four tiers of arches and with round or oval stained-glass windows. Several vivid points of colour—red, green, blue and white—are distributed over both faces of the tower in undesigned profusion; and at the top, on the right-hand face, there is the doubtful image of the Virgin. The broken, jagged lines at the top and the two irrelevant daubs of white are tangible signs of an unfinished or transitional conception. The cross-hatched white lines just to the right of its upper part, and the crimson streak already described, also suggest a concentration of libido in this odd fourth tower.

II

The conception of the four main psychic functions may not appear relevant to that of the Trinity. But when we consider that it is impossible for man to conceive of the nature of Deity, except through the natural and essential limitations of his own psyche, we have to admit that the concept of deity must, in one form or another, inevitably reflect the psyche which conceives it. From this standpoint it would appear almost incredible that the totality of God should be conceived in terms of three, when completeness necessarily demands a fourfold conception. The fact that it actually has been so conceived may have arisen from the basic dissociation in early Christian psychology resulting from repression of the feminine principle.

In overcoming and superseding the chthonic cult of the Magna Mater, the Early Christian Church swung over too far to the side of the masculine principle, the feminine being correspondingly repressed. So long as man saw woman only in relation to the fanaticized problem of sexuality, it was inevitable that the spiritual value of the human relationship should suffer, for many centuries, an almost complete eclipse. The Middle Ages, with its new ideal of chivalry and its ecstatic cult of the Virgin, brought back the long-repressed feminine values into Christian culture, albeit in a mystical form. The symbol of the Holy Grail expressed this new expression of the feminine principle in a deeply satisfying form—satisfying because the legendary material in which the symbol was enshrined, as indeed the vessel-symbol itself, found their way into the Christian stream from an older pre-Christian source.[1]

This exaltation of the feminine principle had a profound influence, not only on man's conception of woman, but also on woman's conception of herself. The number of women throughout Christendom who took the veil in order to keep their souls unspotted from the world is sufficient proof of the immense cultural authority given to the idea of Christian virginity.

Fear of the power of sexuality throughout human history can be measured by the terrific measures that have been used to repress it. In Western psychology the result has been to create a one-sided and rather sentimental insistence on the lofty superiority of the spiritual principle, together with a distinct tendency to identify sexuality with the Devil.

The conception of the Trinity necessarily reflected this titanic battle within the Christian soul. Milton voiced the feeling of Christendom when he acclaimed it as a victory of the powers of heaven, just as Homer extolled the sack of Troy as a triumph of Greek valour. Yet both Milton and Homer leave one with a sense of tragic loss for the glory of the vanquished. Lucifer, the light-bringer, was cast out of heaven for his rebellion against God. The fourth part of God became split off from the celestial remainder, with the result that the whole Christian world was rent by irreconcilable war between the sundered opposites. How could a man find lasting reconciliation between the light and dark forces within his own soul when unassuageable war had to be waged between God and His own rejected greatness? Or how could a man take the most crucial problem of his soul to a masculine divinity who was so abstracted from reality as to lack a feminine counterpart?

In the Catholic Church the deification of the Virgin must be regarded as an attempt to repair this breach and to re-establish the archetypal balance of a fourfold totality. The spontaneous tide of love and veneration which over-

[1] I refer the reader to Jessie L. Weston's admirable study *The Quest of the Holy Grail*. Compare also the magical cauldron or vessel of abundance in early Celtic myth.

flowed in the mediæval cult of the Virgin—and which still expresses the deepest longings of Catholic Christendom—bears witness to the deep need of the human psyche for the primordial condition of balance and harmony between the opposites.

A psychological appraisal of the great experiment of Christianity must seem presumptuous, or even blasphemous, to those who regard Christian teaching as the final revelation of God's will. But, apart from the question of the religious feeling which regards any such attempt as an impious encroachment on sacred ground, we are faced with the very real difficulty that we ourselves are part of the Christian tree, and that the very passion of the mind which asks forbidden questions has been nourished on Christian soil. However enlightened we believe ourselves to be, we cannot evade the fact that our emotional and cultural origins are fundamentally Christian.

In the picture we are discussing we have already observed tangible signs of stress in the attempt to get outside or above the Christian standpoint, notably in the marks of resistance about the uprooted base of the cathedral. If we are right in assuming this picture to be in the nature of a prophecy we have to conclude that the idea which lifted the cathedral into the air had sufficient power and universality to create a new cultural viewpoint, notwithstanding the whole weight of psychic inertia, with all its conservative tenacity, which holds the mind rooted to the past. But if the picture is informed with a world-changing idea we ought to find evidence of its presence in the painting.

This evidence is to be found, I believe, in the transition from the traditional cruciform plan of the cathedral to the idea of a square with four towers. We have already discussed the possible implications of the fourth tower, which, be it remembered, was described by the subject as "transitional." But apart from this the dissolution of the eastern portion of the structure, and the signs of histolysis pervading the part that is left, leave one with the impression that the structure enclosed by the four towers belongs to and expresses the emergent idea. We may observe a beautiful analogy to this appearance of the emergent form among the lepidoptera during the process of histolysis in the pupal phase. As soon as the transitional stage of pupation has begun, the head, proboscis, wing-cases and segmented abdomen of the butterfly are clearly visible in the pupa-case, long before the internal structure of the imago has been laid down.

In our attempt to make visible the emergent idea let us first enquire why the eastern part of the church had to be shed. The eastern end of a cathedral-plan corresponds, as everyone knows, to the upper end or T of the cross, whilst the nave, leading to the western door, represents the long upright. The original cross has four equal arms; it is the basic symbol of man. There would seem, by the way, to have been a reversion to this primordial type of cross at the top of the two western spires.

Comparing the Christian cross with this original archetype, we must assume that some partisan influence forced the three upper ends of the cross a long distance away from the lower end. Symbolically this distance would represent a dissociation of the three upper functions from the lower earth-function. The same upward tendency is also clearly manifest in the soaring aspiration of the Gothic church, with its high columns and pointed arches.

In the emergent form of our painting this symbolical dissociation is done away with, and the four functions or aspects of the cross are set in a new and yet older combination—namely, in the form of the square. The unfinished fourth tower has the appearance of having been recently added to the other three. This is the one associated with the feminine earth-principle.

Another historical aspect of this transition pertains to the fact that, in its origins, Christianity was a highly mystical religion coming from the East. In no sense can it be regarded as indigenous to our Western soil, whereas the cross, in its early primitive form of the sun-wheel, is found in all the indigenous cultures of the West.

In our painting there is a crescendo of value towards the west. The eastern part has practically dissolved away, but the structure is increasingly formed and lucid as we approach the western end. There is a profusion of libido-pointers in the vivid colours of the rose-window and in the points of colour scattered over the two towers of the western façade. The lines of force which slant across the building fall from east to west, and, finally, the birth of the Son of Man from the western end represents the climax of the westerly movement.

If these observations are correctly assembled and interpreted we must infer that the emergent form is an indigenous archetype which has reached its culminating power through a process of gradual evolution within the Christian framework. In other words, it represents a truth that has long been latent within the Christian tradition, but that only now becomes manifest.

In our efforts to discover the actual content of this idea we may derive assistance from our knowledge of the subject's pressing individual need. For although a truth may be projected into the heavenly sphere therewith claiming a certain universality, it is also deeply relevant to the life of the individual who utters it. Psychological development is, at bottom, intensely practical, and the truth we see is also the truth we need.

Briefly stated, the metamorphosis we have witnessed in the field of this patient's psychology is a transition from a partial persona-valuation to a conception of the self as a psychic totality. The persona in his case was a presentable façade which compensated a serious deficiency on the emotional side by an arbitrary superiority of the intellect. At bottom, he was never a true intellectual type. As the weapon of masculine power, the intellect is very often preferred by men whose inherent emotional weakness renders them psychologically vulnerable. Similarly, his almost ascetic self-control was not an expression of his original nature; rather was it a means of defence—based on the unconscious authority of Christian tradition—against atavistic emotional urgencies.

In this way the schizophrenic dissociation was unconsciously reinforced by the implicit authority of two traditional Christian ideals. On the one hand, the moral superiority of the masculine principle which excluded the feminine from the sacred nature of God; and on the other, the ascetic ideal which tended to prejudice woman as the inevitable sexual object, thus depriving her of full human dignity in the Christian community.

Naturally the Christian ideal was not intended to have this effect. Its aim was the overcoming of the lusts of the flesh, and woman was expected to participate in this campaign on equal terms with man. But the actual result of the crusade against the Devil was to raise the one sanctified form of sexual relationship to an idealized plane (which, by the way, it has never been able to sustain), and to condemn the instinct which asserted the freedom of love as belonging to the Devil. In this way the blessing of the Church came to be regarded as the vital factor in the launching of the human relationship. But the essential spirit of candour and integrity of feeling, without which the fundamental adaptation demanded by a vital human relationship cannot be achieved, was usually left to uninstructed individual discovery.

It was undoubtedly the existence of an inherent parallelism between the dissociation in the patient's own psyche and the vast historical dissociation in the Christian ideology which prompted this psychological answer to the Christian need.

In common with a multitude of serious men and women outside the Christian Church, the subject, though unaware of the fact, was deeply concerned with the religious problem. Sooner or later he was bound to realize that it was the power of his own truth which had destroyed his former masculine citadel and had forced him to accept and serve the irrational feminine principle as the vital need of his soul. But, since truth is not a local condition, nothing could stop him from turning this same light upon those general cultural foundations in which his previous attitude had been rooted. If his house has been proved defective, even dangerously one-sided, and he himself had no conscious hand in its design, then something must be amiss with the fundamental presuppositions determining its original structure.

When we really study this picture something of this unconscious logic forces its way into our consciousness. The picture has an unmistakably impersonal character containing no trace of the neurotic need for self-justification. It has none of the paranoid's " I am right and therefore all the world is wrong." A truth which can clarify an apparently hopeless situation and can bring proportion, harmony and colour into a world which before was futile, misshapen and meaningless is not something to be kept in a matchbox. It may have started as a candle burning under the sea; but even there, because it was set in the midst of the sea, it could never be taken as a purely domestic truth. A truth possessing the royal power of reconciling the apparently irreconcilable is effective above as well as below, in the greater as well as the smaller.

Approaching the picture from this standpoint it cannot be denied that a new truth is being born, and the picture is revealing the moment of its birth. The Mother Church is delivered of a Son who descends like a bird towards the waiting earth. But, before this deliverance could have come to pass, the mother must have been impregnated by a new idea. In a sense we have already recognized this symbolical advent in the transitional fourth tower which completes the archetypal square. The birth is proclaimed, and the character of the new conception can be inferred; but who can say what will be its effect ? Something with the power to prize a cathedral from the ground and to raise it up into the heavens must presumably possess incalculable potentiality. To venture more would be prophetic speculation.

III

It is possible, however, to bring into clearer visibility the elements of the new orientation suggested by this picture. We have discussed the historical psychological picture out of which the masculine Trinity developed, and we have discerned the truth that insistence on the superiority of the masculine over the feminine, or *vice versa*, springs from the vulnerability of the inferior function. When the insistence of superiority occurs in the individual it is a psychological bluff, but when it happens in a great collective movement, as can be seen in the totalitarian states of the present day, it must be regarded as a highly dangerous oscillation of the cultural pendulum. And here again the overcompensation of a feeling of inferiority is not far to seek.

Originally the symbol of the Trinity is rooted in the pattern of the human family. Osiris, Isis and Horus manifest this original form of the divine Trinity. Even in the Christian form the latent presence of the feminine principle is indicated by the presence of the dove, the symbol of Venus, Astarte, and other feminine deities of antiquity. Thus we see that the Trinity was, as the Creed says, originally " three persons," and that these represented the family, the basic unit of human society. As a collective symbol, therefore, guarding the integrity of familial and social institutions, and fostering the ancestral piety upon which civilized values rest, the Trinity represents the whole sanction of human feeling. It is only when we come to the problem of individuality that the question of the fourfold nature of God begins to trouble the mind. From the standpoint of society and the human family the conquest over the Devil, involving ferocious repression of sexuality, can be seen as a tragic necessity. But when we consider its effects within the individual soul we begin to understand why every collective or tribal deity has been represented, at one time or another, as a monster lusting for sacrificial victims.

Individuality and collectivity are a pair of opposites. Never has there been peace between them because each tends to make absolute claims. But the possibility of reconciling these two interdependent loyalties in a new conception of individuality has at last dawned, and the honour of this new psychological conception of man belongs to the present century, and chiefly to the post-war epoch. At the same time, the acceptance of the law of relativity, in the spiritual as well as in the spatial universe, has made it possible for men to think and to express ideas which were literally inconceivable so long as the mind was ruled by biological absolutes. Under the term " biological " I include the function of procreation, the gaining of food, and all the organized social activities and institutions which have for their aim the improvement or consolidation of external conditions of life. The psychological conception begins at the point where the biological province or phase ends. So long as biological aims and needs are paramount there are problems of adaptation, but there is not yet a problem of individuality.

Individuation, like everything else, begins in the unconscious, and often the first signs of the problem come to light in a feeling of futility and apathy in relation to just those biological aims which, only a short time before, seemed adequate and satisfying. At this juncture, when the claims of the self need to be distinguished from the surrounding welter of biologico-collective urgencies, the two directions are felt as mutually incompatible. But later, when individuality has been surely grounded upon the eternal granite of the self, the social task takes on a new complexion. An effective collaboration between the opposing but complementary aspects of life can then be achieved, though never without a thoroughgoing criticism of immature, fictitious goals.

The collective or dæmonic aspect of the soul naturally finds expression under the dynamic sign of the three, whereas the essence of individuality and conscious control demands the fourfold principle. The dæmonic aspect was seen and discussed in the three worlds of Drawing 13, while the quaternary principle has appeared wherever the control of consciousness demanded consolidation. Becoming versus being would be another view of the same antithesis. Becoming, being immature, stands under the dynamic sign three, while the problem of maturity or being demands the structural four. The necessitous, striving aspect of human fate in which birth, mating, death, food, sickness, procreation, familial and social claims, effortful progress, duty to others, to mankind, to the state, the whole field of ethical obedience—all these and many more would be embraced by the scope of the threefold symbol. But when we follow the introverted direction of the libido an entirely different criterion must prevail. The love problem, the relation to the soul, the deep moral issues, and, above all, obedience to the self—these can never be understood in their vital significance until the point is reached where being prevails over becoming. Both worlds represent essential aspects of human life, only they are governed by different principles.

Certain indications have suggested the idea that the transitional fourth tower represents the feminine principle, in contrast to the masculine, phallic nature of the other three spires. Assuming this supposition to be correct, we have a complete analogy to the psychological process of individuation, which depends, first and foremost, on the conversion of the anima from an autonomous, unconscious complex into an integrated function of consciousness.

It is impossible to say to what extent the autonomy or dissociation of the anima-complex has been due to the exclusion of the feminine principle from the divine realm. But it is significant, at a time when the problem of the unconscious begins to take on a certain reality, that the report of the commission appointed by Archbishop Davidson to " demonstrate the extent of existing agreement within the Church of England " should contain the unanimous view that sexuality should no longer be regarded as originally evil. Although this authoritative exoneration of the instinct is tardy and somewhat reluctant, it does imply that the problem of reconciling the opposites in human nature begins to be more important to the Church than its historical crusade against the Devil.

The truth of the fourfold structure of the psyche is by no means a mere academic fact, for it contains the whole difference between a well-balanced architectural design and a mere façade. Above all, therefore, it must possess revolutionary implications for a mind drilled on the parade-ground of persona ideals. As a latent truth it was tacitly accepted by the Catholic Church when the Virgin was given divine honour, thereby completing the fourfold nature of Deity.

The symbol that is born from the Mother Church in the present picture represents man as he actually is, the naked human being—no more and no less than the living truth. Being naked, he has perhaps divested himself of all the torturing doubts and presuppositions concerning his worthiness or unworthiness to inhabit a celestial kingdom, seeking rather his primordial birthright in the unreserved acceptance of his own nature. Therefore is he seen descending from the Church, his foster-mother, to the earth, his original mother. In the full acceptance of his own nature he honours the source of his being, while implicit in the idea of the two mothers is the symbol of renewal or rebirth.

* * * * *

In dealing with the symbol of transition we must not omit to mention the view, supported to some extent by astrological calculation, that the present is a transitional period, corresponding to the point in the zodiac between the constellations of the Fishes and Aquarius. On account of the precession of the equinox, it takes approximately two thousand years for the spring point (*i.e.*, the beginning of the zodiacal sign Aries) to move through a zodiacal constellation. This two-thousand-year span, or Platonic month, represents an astrological epoch. Christ was identified with the fish because the time of His birth approximately coincided with the entrance of the spring point into the constellation of the Fishes. Therefore He was called *Ichthus* (the fish), and in the carved inscriptions in the Roman catacombs He was alluded to with the symbol or sign of the fish.

Because of this synchronicity, and in view of the two-thousand-year cycle, it was prophesied by the astrologers that anti-Christ would appear at the end of the second millennium. The view is held by many that before the close of the present century the world-horoscope will fall under the rulership of the qualities and values that are, astrologically speaking, taken to belong to Aquarius. Already, therefore, it may be possible to conceive the character of the Aquarian man as in the embryonic or formative stage.

Aquarius is, of course, the water-carrier; it is represented by the figure of a man pouring water from a goatskin sack. The figure also embraces the idea of a cloud which, having gathered up its watery content from the earth and sea, is about to pour it forth as fertilizing rain. The Aquarian man has, too, been conceived as conserving and renewing certain virtues and values of preceding experience. The Aquarian man, conscious of his distance from primitive life, would nevertheless be aware of the essential value of that pristine experience. No longer carried along on the flood tide of affect, his task would rather be to consume his primitive impulses and from their distillation to scatter forth in a renewed form their innate heritage of wisdom. Conscious being would therefore be the goal of the Aquarian man, rather than that of biological becoming.[1]

The foregoing astrological analogy was suggested by the idea of the divine man, or sun-hero, entering the great Church of Christendom at the eastern end and passing out at the western, in the same way as the sun has figuratively passed through the constellation of the Fishes. Then, too, there is the waiting earth below, and the suggestion of cascades of water falling from the vessel which contains the Christian values. Moreover, the whole character of this prophetic conception, which projects the contemporary problem upon a cosmic background, seems to invite the long-range astrological view of human destiny. It might even be that the aridness of a scientifically explained and exploited universe, in which only those facts are credited which can be weighed, measured and numbered, is implied in the meticulously ruled lines covering the empty expanse below.

On the other hand, viewing the situation from the angle of subjective necessity we should compare these carefully ruled lines of longitude and latitude with the unkempt, ineffectual lines with which the patient tried, as it were, to hold the deluge in check in Drawing 15. And yet, from the general schizophrenic standpoint of control versus dissolution, the organization of the dissolving church by the fourfold principle contains so concrete an affirmation of central control that the ruled lines of the geographer below, although serving to enhance the idea of a parched, expectant earth, appear in comparison like a rather futile intellectual gesture.

[1] In the above description of the astrological process I have had valuable assistance from my friend John M. Thorburn.

CHAPTER XI

CHRISTIAN VERSUS PAGAN

I

I CONCLUDE this study with the discussion of a dream which the patient dreamed a few days after he had done the painting of the cathedral.

From the painting itself it was not easy to see what immediate relation the theme of the disintegrating cathedral had with the patient's personal life. In the dream this connection is clearly developed, though it could hardly be anticipated that the problem of instinctual inferiority would be found to reach right down into the historical foundations of Christendom.

The dream begins and ends with the problem of the intimate personal relationship. We can therefore assume that the whole drama, part historical and part mythical, which culminates in the collapse of the cathedral, is activated by the marriage-problem.

The structure of the dream is like a suspension-bridge. Between the personal prologue and epilogue there stretches a wide impersonal span in which the inherited determinants of the basic instinctual attitude come upon the scene.

It will be noted that the style of expression changes as the dream proceeds. There is a certain triviality in the opening scene with the dog. Then comes a superficial layer, equivalent to the subsoil, in which an enigmatic and decidedly puzzling mode of expression is employed. A deeper level is struck when we reach the period of the Holy Roman Empire, and at the same time the symbolical mode becomes correspondingly simpler. The scene in the cathedral is clear; it is dramatically felt and described, as though the subject were actually witnessing a world-changing event. In this part of the dream he is completely enfolded by the myth, and his attitude is as transparent as glass.

This change in attitude is significant, for it shows how the intellectual defences are gradually broken down by the rising flood of images, until the subject is finally carried off his feet, like a man submerged by a tidal wave.

The puzzling enigmatic style of the earlier part of the dream is characteristic of the attitude of opaque intellectual defence. It is symptomatic of the state in which no insight or understanding is permitted of the other part of the mind. The analysis of schizoid personalities is rendered decidedly more difficult on this account. Not only is the schizoid intellectual inclined to be humanly inaccessible, often due to a sceptical resistance and an inability to provide germane associative material; but the actual dream-content produced is often full of bewildering riddles and irrationalities, which serve to emphasize the patient's ironical detachment from the whole business.

This problem of the patient's attitude (which, in practice, is the decisive factor) can be effectively handled only by direct reference to the dreams. Many men pride themselves on their barbarous attitude to instinctive life both within and without, as though asserting a wholesome independence from nature's leading-strings. From one point of view, it is obvious that the activity of the unconscious, like other processes of nature, is independent of voluntary control or direction. This autonomy of the unconscious processes is, in fact, axiomatic. Yet we have to admit that domesticated plants and animals have undergone a definite modification of their original nature as a result of age-long subordination to conscious human purpose. In the same way we must regard the primordial human unconscious as to some extent contingent, in the mode of its activity, upon the coexisting conscious attitude, even though its essential nature remains independent.

An interesting parallelism between essential content and style of expression characterizes the dream we shall presently discuss. The essential content of the dream is like a stream issuing as a small jet from an underground spring. As it flows it gradually expands, gathering to itself other tributaries, until eventually it swells into a broad historical river, shaping its inevitable course towards the sea. As regards style, from a rather trivial personal note at the beginning, the dream falls into a rather dry enigmatic phase, and only when it gathers way from the historical momentum of the deeper levels does it sweep broadly and simply to its conclusion.

II

DREAM

" Sappho, our dachshund, is seated on a sofa, and I kneel in front, talking to her. I speak in French, because the maid is also present, hovering about in the background. I give Sappho a long list of good things she will have to eat (Coca-Cola is among them) and stroke her back. She turns into a cat, who snuggles up to my wife, purring. The cat squirms around, and my wife pushes her under the bedclothes.

* * * * *

" I now read about places where you can find cats when they are lost. The instructions are fully illustrated with pictures of commons. I read that: 'A common 60 feet long can be seen from all sides. It will be found to be almost always 23 feet high.' I see a picture confirming this. Further on I see that 'a common 25 feet long will have land sloping up from it, and will thus be 10 feet low.' (I have a vague idea that some of this literature is connected with archæological research; study of the ground-formation helping towards deducing what is buried below the surface, and also as a guide towards digging without damaging the remains.)

" I (and a very shadowy figure) are standing on the edge of a road. Across the road is a common. It really looks like an ordinary English village green, except that it has a ploughed furrow right across it. Also a curious ramshackle bus is driving over the grass, and passes out of sight. There is a notice, on the edge of the common, which says ' Edward II. furrow.' I am inclined to doubt the truth of this, although I am rather impressed. So I cross the road to investigate more closely. The sign now says: ' Sixty-six eyewitnesses say that the Angles traded by bus with the North.' I feel that the bus I just saw disappearing has some connection with the Angles, and that I too have been an eyewitness of the past.

* * * * *

"I am now in a dark and gloomy palace hall, and I am talking to Henry II. (of Germany). I don't pay much attention to him, as I am more interested in a curious suit in the corner. It is not a suit of armour, although it suggests one in the way it stands upright. It resembles more a rich burgher's dress of the sixteenth century. Henry tells me that it is the suit in which he intends to attack Schleswig. I notice that it is well stiffened with leather (somewhat like Japanese early nineteenth-century armour).

"There now follows a vague interlude. I have the impression that I left the palace, and then returned uninvited to make a further study of this armour. I look under a leather lapel and find a tiny gas-mask. (In *The Shape of Things to Come* H. G. Wells had the idea that costumes of the future would have many pockets for keeping tiny telephones, television sets, etc.) I hear Henry returning. He is talking to the Duke of Schleswig. I feel embarrassed and think of hiding, but there is only a small bench. It would be ignominious to be seen half under a bench, so I decide to be perfectly open. I call: 'Heinrich, mein frater!' But neither hears me, and they cross the hall into another room. A few minutes later the Duke returns alone. He goes to the front door and peeps through the grill. He seems to be in despair and I think that he is already a prisoner. I call to him and he looks round startled; but I am in deep shadow, so he cannot see me.

* * * * *

"I am now in a cathedral. Years have passed since the last scene, and Henry is an old man. I call him the 'dying Siegfried.' He is seated on a stool near the lectern. All the choir stalls are full, sunlight streams down and the whole scene is vividly coloured.

"A dragon is fighting with Siegfried's soul; the battle has

been raging up above for a long time. I catch a fleeting glimpse of a great green dragon, but my interest goes back to the old man. If he can start singing before the dragon wins he can save his soul. Siegfried takes his lyre and begins his song. Then the choir joins in. We all know that the dragon will be conquered and that the hero has won his last victory.

"Suddenly, behind me, out of the corner of my eye, I see a movement of someone or something leaving the church. Two dignitaries run past me to stop this shocking performance. I, too, run out to see what is the matter. Then I see that it is the stone steps themselves that are moving towards the door. Outside, the bottom of the walls is breaking up, and huge blocks of masonry are moving away from their foundations. The whole movement is slow and deliberate, like a glacier breaking up into the sea. We realize that the whole cathedral will soon crash down, and we run in panic. One of us yells to those inside, and then we stand at a distance to watch. People start streaming towards the door, but a wall crashes down on them. A few escape, but more towers and buttresses come thundering down. One column falls right across a group of girls, crushing them all. Finally, there is nothing left but a heap of ruins and a low cloud of dust. A few solitary survivors stand about.

* * * * *

"Then I am back in the cathedral again and Siegfried is about to start his song once more. I have a vaguely uncomfortable feeling that I have experienced all this before, that something will happen of even greater importance than Siegfried's song—but I cannot remember. Then Siegfried picks up his lyre, the song begins, and the choir joins in. We all know that Siegfried's soul will conquer the dragon. Behind me I suddenly catch sight of a strange stiff-looking man in what I take to be white armour. He walks very slowly, measuring his paces, first in one direction, then in another, but always coming nearer to the door. He starts to go out, and two dignitaries rush down to stop him. They have axes and strike him on the shoulder, but only chip off a small piece of stone.

" Then everything comes back to me. This man is only a statue, and it is the stonework of the cathedral which is beginning to move off. I run for the door, shouting a warning to all the people inside. But no more are saved than the first time. The scene repeats itself exactly, except that I now stand at a slightly greater distance. Blocks detach themselves, walls fall and people are crushed. Again a few escape, but when the dust settles I see that no more escaped than before.

* * * * *

" Then follows a short scene between my wife and myself. We are looking through a sample-book of cellulose lacquers. It contains the six colours used in the cathedral, and they had been brought from the North by the Angle bus-drivers. We say there must always be a small start towards building a new cathedral. Someone tells me that the Angle traders were very happy because they were high up in their buses and could see everything."

III

Analysis

In the rather intimate prologue to the dream proper we observe at once a sophisticated, trivial and rather effeminate attitude—an observation which serves as an index-finger, pointing to the heart of the dream-problem.

To begin with, the animal is a female and a dachshund—not the kind of dog a man would choose for a friend if his instinct were free. Then the dreamer's behaviour to the bitch seems to betray a certain feeling of shame. He even speaks to her in French, as though the presence of the maid made him conscious of something peculiar in his relation to the animal. The suggestion of pampered intimacy is borne out by the list of delicacies he promises her.

This whole scene—the pampered little bitch and the dreamer kneeling in front of her, talking to her intimately and persuasively in French—is far more suggestive of a man's attitude to a childish and exacting mistress than of his feeling for his dog. Apparently the dachshund is of the same opinion, since she forthwith changes into a cat. The cat can sustain the rôle of a spoiled and pampered pet better than a dog; for this reason it frequently symbolizes the egotistical, undeveloped, personal aspect of the anima in a man's dreams.

It is well to study carefully the opening statement of a dream: often it provides us with a key to its meaning. The dream is saying in rather pointed terms that the subject projects his anima upon his dachshund bitch. In other words, he has been content to leave his soul in exactly the same spoiled and pampered condition as in the scene depicted by the dream, as though it had no more purpose or significance than a petted animal.

World-wide prevalence of lycanthropic legends and stories concerning witches who are transformed into cats, foxes, hyenas, panthers, and even tigers, shows the empirical necessity of including a theriomorphic aspect in our conception of the soul. Even for highly sophisticated writers like George MacDonald and David Garnett the theme has still a certain potency. In *Lilith* George MacDonald portrays the ambiguity of the anima in the form of a blood-sucking, baby-killing woman who changes into a black panther for her baby-hunting forays, and a humane, angelic counterpart who transforms herself into a white panther in order to checkmate the evil designs of the first. The anima as god-dæmon could not be more graphically presented than in this fantasia of the unconscious.

In Garnett's *Lady into Fox*, on the other hand, there are no signs of the story having bubbled up out of the depths of the unconscious. The newly married wife, upon whom the husband pours a doting animal affection, simply becomes a fox and prefers to go to earth in the woods than sustain the husband's load of sophisticated indulgence. The husband goes in search of her and, having found her, allows his allegiance to the civilized world to be seduced by his renegade animal soul.

This remarkable story, which, as we said, reveals no trace of its mythological source, either in style or content, is very *apropos* for our study,[1] inasmuch as in both cases the object of a too doting and lavish affection is driven to transform herself into an animal, which thereupon gets lost. It is also the losing of the animal in both cases which forces the subject of the experience into a new attitude and a new fashion of life. The dachshund becomes a cat for the same reason that the lady becomes a fox. They simply cannot stand the enervating torpor of being idolized. Nature rebels, and the soul leaps out of the window.

The cat losing itself beneath the bedclothes or the fox running away to the woods, are these not modern variants of the flight of Eurydice, and was not Orpheus also punished by his soul for his too loving regard? Although so different from every angle, all three stories are essentially identical in the result achieved, in the fact that through the flight of the soul the subject of the story discovers the primordial roots of his nature.

Without penetrating into the personal life of our subject, it must be self-evident that the unconscious effect upon the wife of the projection of anima-libido on this level could easily become insupportable. Or on the other hand, being unconsciously constrained to fit in with this kind of projection, the wife might find herself playing the rôle of the pampered animal. Naturally this type of projection could only be taken up by an object who, to some extent, corresponded with its content. The tragedy is that once the projection is given and received, it is extremely difficult to break, inasmuch as the husband necessarily believes that his wife is as he sees her, while the wife cannot be different until she is sufficiently conscious both to discriminate and to disown the husband's projection. Myriads of marriages groan under these unconscious burdens, as though doomed by fate to perseverate the infantilisms of calf-love until the day of judgment, as, in point of fact, they are.

We can understand, therefore, why the cat becomes identified with the patient's wife, who, in fact, retained enough

[1] The theme of the lady changing into a fox is a classical motif in Chinese mythology. This agrees with the fact that the soul is a dualistic concept in Chinese thought, the celestial *Yang*-soul *hun* being balanced by a dark, dæmonic animal-soul *p'o*.

of the luxurious egotism of the spoiled child to absorb the pampering projection. Pushing the cat under the bedclothes is a metaphorical act of repression. It suggests that, by dint of projecting his erotic infantilism upon his wife, the patient contrives to remain unconscious of this undeveloped part of his nature.

The patient is both ambitious and gifted. But one essential is lacking, a realization that creative energy is not a product of the will but is born of an honourable relation to the soul. What is not honoured is relegated. Through infantile projections a man is liable to make his wife the custodian of his instinct, therewith divesting himself of all responsibility for his emotional life. This is how the cat gets lost.

* * * * *

The rest of the dream is concerned with the salvage of the lost instinct. First the subject reads a book of instructions dealing with places where lost cats are liable to be found. He is directed to the study of commons. And here we come to the puzzling phase of the two types of commons, to which we alluded above.

It is discouraging when a dream seems to lapse into nonsense; and yet, from a more resolute standpoint, we must admit that a dream which offers a book of instructions with illustrations, and takes particular pains to give the exact measurements of the thing it describes, must be referring to something quite definite.

The patient volunteered the idea that commons are symbolical of the original village communism. At one time he wanted to visit Russia because of his interest in the communistic experiment. The details of the two types of common were associated with a rather dull " treasure-hunt " organized at some French holiday resort. He remembered finding clues which told one to measure a certain distance from given landmarks. He was not amused, and somebody else found the treasure, which was a bottle of champagne.

The book of instructions was also associated with his father's archæological researches, in which as a boy he took a rather passive interest. His choice of history as one of his subjects at the university may have been associated with this latent interest. His association with the raised common "that was 60 feet long and 23 feet high" was a barrow or tumulus, while the corresponding association with the common that was "10 feet low" was a burial vault or pit. The one is raised up and plainly visible; the other, being sunk deep in the earth with nothing to mark it, is easily lost to human ken.

With regard to the numbers, the patient gave no associations by which any of the numbers could be related to significant facts in his personal history. But as a general association he remarked: "Sixty is an ancient 'round number' which still survives in our sixty minutes to an hour and sixty seconds to the minute."[1]

As to the commons, we are told that lost cats can be recovered in certain specified types of common which are confined by very precise boundaries. The dream has already depicted the patient's inadequate relation to his instinct leading to its loss under the bed-clothes. He lost the cat because, at bottom, he was ashamed of it. A function that one is ashamed of is neglected; it loses its dynamic functional relation with consciousness and accordingly slips away into the unconscious.

The first essential realization, therefore, is the obvious but disregarded truth that instinct is a common heritage. In a sense the whole of history is common land, the general cultural unconscious guaranteeing the validity of the instincts, just as common law protects basic human rights. Common land is free of privilege, belonging by natural right to everyone. In particular, just as dog and cat are domesticated animals, the commons also refer, not to the open wilderness, but rather to the ground owned in common by a community,

[1] Professor Zimmer has called my attention to the fact that sixty represents the neolithic number of totality appearing in the present French system of numerals (*soixante*, *soixante-dix*, etc.). The French took over the pre-Celtic system based upon sixty which prevailed in Northern France and Ireland before the Celtic immigration, crossing it with the decimal system, their common heritage with Greek, Latin and Sanskrit cultures. This archaism would be congenial to the patient's psychology because of the archæological tributary coming to him through his father.

ground used for grazing animals, village sports, and other domestic human purposes. The village green has been carefully guarded by ancient right from the encroachment of the individual proprietor. It is a limited piece of ground whose boundaries are clearly demarcated. In a society where individual property has achieved paramount consideration, the rights protecting common lands throughout the centuries bear witness to the power of the idea which the dream is emphasizing, the value of a common heritage.

Two types of commons are singled out for special attention, and the distinguishing feature of each type is its length. In dream-symbolism we know that long-bodied creatures, such as snakes, dragons, etc., represent things effective in time. The whole length of the creature symbolizes an effect or event, plus the whole time-perspective through which the event has been in preparation, or during which its effects will be realized. Thus to the primordial mind a powerful personality appears as a long snake.

In periods of historical transition certain individuals are thrown up embodying in an authoritative way the major tendency or direction of the racial unconscious. A man may be almost forced to become mediumistic to the unconscious. He begins to " speak with the tongues of men and angels "; or feels himself to have been singled out by fate to voice the " will of the Lord." These men cannot be judged as independent personalities, but as unwitting functions of history. It is said that the mother of L. Tarquinius, for instance (who became one of the greatest of early Roman kings), dreamed, during her pregnancy, that she gave birth to a python. The dream was interpreted as a sign that the child in her womb would be a mighty ruler. Christ is alluded to in a Gnostic writing as the Great Snake. It was prophesied in the early days of the Christian era that this snake would be two thousand years long. The Gnostics also created a god, Abraxas, consisting of a lion's head and a snake's body; it symbolized the idea of the summation of effect through time. Since it embraced everything that entered the sphere of reality and became effective, it was beyond good and evil. Abraxas was really a synthetic god, symbol of a philosophical point of view. This idea has been restated in modern terms by Bergson as the *durée créatrice.* In Gnostic symbolism every letter of the alphabet was identified with a specific number: the total of the numbers belonging to Abraxas was 365, the number of the celestial spheres in the Gnostic system.

Multitudes of examples could be given, but enough have been cited to show that the autonomous mind has a tendency to represent the dimension of time by the idea of extension: a long creature, a long road, a long object, etc. The very length of the present dream implies that it embraces an immense tract of time in its perspective.

According to the patient's associations, the former raised type of common is associated with the prehistoric barrow or tumulus. From this and the symbolical associations given above, we can conclude that the length of the common refers to length of time. Just as sixty, according to the patient's idea, is representative of a very ancient numerical system, it would also correspond, in the individual span of life, to the period of ripe age and long experience. Twenty-five, on the other hand, would correspond to the period of psychological puberty, when the individualism and self-sufficiency of youth are liable to prevail.

The neighbouring associations of tumulus and vault bring the idea of veneration for the dead into the picture. The cult of the dead was the main structural idea in early civilizing communities. We might even describe it as the piety of prehistoric man.

The cult of the ancestors maintains the feeling of racial continuity. The ancestral spirits are vehicles of tribal tradition: they inform the traditional command which prompts the living to undertake responsibility towards the future race. As long as tradition survives in the form of ancestral spirits, no historians are needed. But progressive detachment of individual consciousness from the tribal unconscious brings about a corresponding diminution of the sense of ancestral continuity. Consequently, the idea of chronicling events and the preservation of historical records can be regarded as a crucial landmark in the evolution of consciousness.

The whole meaning of the present dream rests upon our

appreciation of the fact that the deep unconscious is living history. The "Edward II. furrow" is the plainest possible statement of the effective continuity of the historical process within the psyche. Go back far enough in time, the dream seems to be saying, and you will discover a mysterious power in the idea of the common heritage—a power which raised great tumuli over the bones of the mighty dead, that the essential continuity of the spirit of the race should be safeguarded. This would be the long-range view of the instinctual inheritance associated with men of ripe age: in other words, the patriarchal vision. But when the unloving individualism of the new civilizing consciousness came pressing in, this piety of primordial man disappeared, and intellectual power began to triumph over instinctual submission. The dead were put away in deep hollows of the ground and the ancestral spirits were neglected. Thus the idea of the common inheritance of instinct began to fade from men's minds, for either a man was liable to be borne down by the solitary load of his individual fate or to become exalted by feelings of individual superiority.

Thoughts such as these might easily lead to archæological treasure-hunts in the deep historical levels, in order to find the forgotten birthright. These illustrations are particularly valuable apparently for purposes of archæological research, a study of the ground-information promising certain indications in regard to buried contents. Again we are reminded of Drawing 16, with its implicit analogies with the word-association method, by which it is possible, by following certain surface indications, to discover the existence of a buried complex and bring it gradually into the light. In this subtle way the dream draws the subject's present interest in psychological investigation into association with his father's interest in archæology, therewith again emphasizing the impersonal or ancestral nature of the salvage work he is engaged upon. Just as the trained eye of the archæologist takes note of any artificial disturbance of the normal contours of the earth, as indicating a place where ancient human relics might lie buried, so the observant psychologist singles out apparently accidental disturbances of consciousness which might point to the presence of a buried complex. And what is a buried complex but concealed value ?

Another factor becomes relevant from its association both with commons and with ancient burial grounds. The feeling that safeguards primitive societies from the evil consequences of individual ownership of land has nothing to do with long-sighted socialistic policy. It springs rather from the state of unconscious participation which unites the primitive, not only with all the other members of his clan, but also with the ancestral spirits inhabiting the earth, trees, rivers, stones and mountains of his native land. The inherent piety of the primitive mind is rooted in this feeling of the vigilant presence of ancestor spirits in everything common to the tribe. What has been called the animism of the primitive mind refers to a state in which the objective world is animated by projected contents of the ancestral unconscious: the primitive can be said to be enfolded completely within the timeless stream of tribal continuity. His almost complete lack of the historical sense is only a symptom of the fact that he is still one with his tribal myth. It is therefore probable that the irrational sense of guilt and responsibility that still clings to individual ownership of land may be rooted in this original piety which associated the idea of common inheritance with the ancestral spirits.

Assembling these various trains of thought, we conclude that, having forfeited the instinctual support of the unconscious because of a too limited and proprietary attitude to his soul, the patient was forced, somewhat unwillingly, to take part in this psychological treasure-hunt, in which he is persuaded to investigate the fundamental historical groundwork of our common inheritance. He had, in fact, to lose his soul before he could find it.

The relative significance of the two types of common is clear, and from the vantage-point now gained we can identify the raised burial ground with the earlier piety which clothed common things with veneration and pride because they housed the ancestral spirits, while the common that was 10 feet low would correspond to the opposite individualistic attitude, which regards just those things which are common to everybody as vulgar, cheap and common. Modern communities are so vast, and the mechanization of social life so elaborate, that only isolated patches of common land survive to remind us of simple communal decencies. But vulgarity of soul is not a product of size, speed or quantity; it is rather a symptom of the decadence of tradition. In primitive piety tradition is simply the way of the ancestors. Individualism, therefore, in so far as it leads to a contempt for tradition, a disregard of common duties, and a belittling of the common inheritance, is a dangerous impiety from the primordial standpoint.

We can therefore interpret the 60-foot common as the impersonal attitude to instinct and tradition (tradition, after all, being only the externalized form of the instinctual inheritance) which would be associated with the idea of a patriarch or headman of ripe experience. The 25-foot common, on the other hand, would represent the individualistic short-range vision of a youth simulating the ways of adult life. The one, viewing the historical process as the painful evolution of consciousness, would salve the values and gains of the past for the purpose of shaping the future, whilst the other might tend to view historical precedents merely as fetters designed to restrict his individual freedom. The contents of the cultural unconscious, described above as living history, might become visible from the elevated viewpoint of the first common, whereas they would be totally invisible from the depressed standpoint of the second. Hence the question of instinctual standpoint had to be made conscious before the historical content of the dream could be appreciated.

IV

The dreamer now finds himself on the edge of a road bordering a village green. With him is a shadow-self, his "dark brother." The shadow being the aspect of the personality that is turned towards the unconscious, it is almost invariably present in a dream which presents a new aspect of the unconscious. Sometimes this other personality takes an active, even a commanding rôle. Occasionally he acts as mentor and interpreter of the dream or fantasy events.

As an example of this rôle of psychopomp the angel-companion of Tobias occurs to the mind. In regard to the furrow, the patient had the idea of " ploughing a lonely furrow," but he could provide no specific association either for the village green or the omnibus. These are examples of common properties or archetypal contents of the collective unconscious.

In order to give an accurate empirical account of events observed in the psychical field, we must use terms with which we can discriminate the personal psychic property of the dreamer from the impersonal contents belonging to a whole community or even to a whole cultural group. Many of the contents of the present dream are general historical images to which the dreamer can lay no personal claim. The subject's inability to provide personal associations to these contents affords us an indication of their general source.

Across the village green there runs " a ploughed furrow." Allowing this statement to present itself realistically to our mind, we perceive at once that no one, not even a king, would dare to plough a furrow across the village green, unless it were perchance a ritual act. We are faced with a strange pair of incompatibles—a solitary, individualistic landmark trespassing upon the common amenities of a village green.

In opposition to the lonely furrow we have the curious ramshackle bus, which, like the furrow, is also being driven over the grass. Both the collective and the individual symbols are therefore found side by side upon the village green. As before, when the dreamer was given an illustrated book of instructions to help him in his investigation of commons, he is now assisted in this riddle of the furrow and the omnibus by certain invaluable clues. A notice-board on the edge of the common explains that the furrow is connected with Edward II. It is not clear why the dreamer should doubt the truth of this statement. We can only suppose that his doubt betrays an underlying personal identification with the maker of the furrow. For if it were not so, the information would leave him indifferent. But first doubting, then being impressed—this hesitation surely indicates the presence of an activated complex.

Investigating the sign more closely, the dreamer discovers

that it explains the nature of the bus: "Sixty-six eyewitnesses say that the Angles traded by bus with the North." Observe the archaic sixty-six and the enigmatic style of expression. The dreamer immediately accepts this incredible statement without a qualm, feeling that he too has been an eyewitness of the past. The notice-board thus deals impartially both with the individual and the collective aspects of the historical perspective, just as the book of instructions described the two types of common without bias.

We must now enquire why the dream-mind selects Edward II. to drive this symbolical furrow through history, and why the Angles should represent the open way; first, however, noting the movement from prehistory to historical time. Both the road and the furrow traverse historical time, as Watling Street traverses space. The Angles are not far from the further margin of history: but Edward II. stands in the centre of the historical arena—a solitary, somewhat pitiful figure whose individual traits are clearly visible.

The historian's portrait of Edward II. is that of an effeminate, indolent creature who in a time when ruthless courage and resolution were indispensable allowed a *laissez-aller* passivity to seduce him from the task of government. Too supine to resist, he was pushed from his throne by his treacherous wife Isabella and her lover Mortimer.

His father had been an able administrator but an oppressive ruler, whose conception of his kingly rôle rested upon a supreme contempt for the rights and liberties of his subjects. Yet the father died in his bed, respected by his barons and admired by all his contemporaries—the manifest ruler of a semi-barbarous feudal realm—while the son, who was correspondingly mild and equable, and to whom no act of injustice or oppression could be imputed, was deposed and murdered with the foulest cruelty in a prison. At a time when positive qualities were essential to life, unrelatedness and passivity proved merely suicidal.

Psychologically, these historical portraits are little better than shadows projected upon a wall. Nevertheless, reading between the lines, we may discern a sensitive youth, overshadowed by a brutal father, instinctively counteracting this influence by developing compensatory feminine qualities, the very qualities which had been fiercely repressed in his father's psychology. The son was fated to live the alternative hypothesis; but it proved inadequate for the rôle he had to play. Like Akhnaton of Egypt, in spirit a visionary forerunner of the Christian era,[1] Edward II. also stands out as a transitional experiment, a man singled out by fate to foreshadow the new cultural phase.

When times are settled and fundamental problems are laid to rest in a common faith, nature tends to reproduce the given historical pattern without attempting daring departures from type. But in times of transition the first outcrop of the new epoch appears in certain borderline personalities, as though, by virtue of a basic instability, they had been selected for experimental purposes. Such individuals are inevitably somewhat crippled from the standpoint of contemporary adaptation. Yet frequently their lives manifest, in an isolated individual framework, the germ of a cultural tendency which achieves general acceptance only in the course of the succeeding epoch.

The exalted rôle which a King has to play, and the massive expectations which constrain him to conform to the required pattern, lend a peculiar tragedy to these royal victims of the future.

Looking back along the highroad of history, we can see in the case of Edward II. that his reign was the hour before the dawn. In the epoch that followed the whole nation strode forward together as a single man in that amazing development of military spirit and knightly temper which made the name Crécy ring like a shout of triumph. The martial qualities of the common people created the English archer, who was able to teach the armoured knights of chivalry that a freely moving man with a bow was more formidable than steel-encased tradition.

The physical endurance and the intellectual vigour of the people which developed under Edward III. produced also a new conception of the relation of the subject to the monarch.

[1] For the full elaboration of this idea the reader is referred to the *Life and Times of Akhnaton*, by Arthur Weigall (Thornton Butterworth, Ltd.).

The burgher became resolved to maintain his free charter with his own practised arm, while the noble discovered that his security was dependent upon the liberty and welfare of the commons. Men began to think and the universities were filled with scholars. Miracles ceased in the presence of holy relics and dispensation for sin came to be despised. For the first time the laws were administered in the language of the nation.

Thus the " Edward II. furrow " runs back through five centuries, straight to the beginning of the course which brought the English people to its greatness and freedom.

The ploughed furrow across the common land of the village green can also be regarded as a symbol of the continuous cultivation of the soil to which a succession of yeomen and farmers have given their life's service. Herein lies the stability of a national culture—that it is prized, not as an ornament of the court, nor as a privilege of the ruling class, but as the very soil from which the spirit of a people is renewed, and in which their common freedom and natural loyalties are rooted. From this point of view, it is a significant fact that the furrow is identified with a King whose reign was marked by a tragic bankruptcy in the very fundamentals of effective government. So long as the sway of the ruler is absolute, individual character and enterprise find small scope. The defencelessness of the people of Britain, for example, after the collapse of Roman rule was due to a great extent to the enervating efficiency of the governing power which had left no responsibility or initiative to the people whom it had ruled and sheltered. Timidity and hesitation above, on the other hand, provokes the need for sturdy independence and reliability below.

On nearer scrutiny the subject learns from the historical sign-board that the cultural vista opened up by this furrow on the village green goes back another 800 years or more to the colonization of Britain by the Angles. He has even the impression that the bus just seen crossing the green was being run by the Angles. It is as though the idea of the common and the village green had brought a kind of time-telescope into action, inveigling first one and then another historical process into the field of consciousness. Whenever a cultural archetype has been activated in the unconscious, either by a particular place or by some critical event, this phenomenon of the time-telescope is liable to come into action. Not infrequently, when visiting a place rich with historical associations, such as the sun-temple at Stonehenge, for instance, or the chalice-well at Glastonbury, or the tombs of the Kings of Egypt, one's mind is liable to be invaded by images arising spontaneously from the unconscious. An instance of this phenomenon is recorded by two English ladies after visiting the Trianon at Versailles. They discovered that they had both walked into a ghostly historical scene which subsequently they were able to identify as the court of Marie Antoinette just before it was devoured by the guillotine.[1]

Sometimes the arousing of the primordial image is sensed as an enhancement of emotional participation, even to the point of mystical exaltation, or as a wave of irrational terror. But, to those mediumistic individuals whose conscious threshold offers little resistance to the unconscious, the activation of the archetype is liable to become directly manifest in living historical images or fantasies.

These general contents are alluded to in the dream as the remains beneath the " commons " which can be reached by digging. We may therefore conclude that the " Edward II. furrow " and the " Angles who traded with the North," as also the " ramshackle bus " which carried them, are general contents associated in the dreamer's mind with the historical archetype " village green."

The subject could remember nothing much concerning the Angles except that they played a large part in the conquest of Britain, and settled principally along the east coast from below the Wash to the Firth of Forth. Referring to an authority, however, he discovered that, unlike the Saxons who came over to Britain only in small companies, the Angles migrated in a body. It therefore seemed reasonable to suppose that the greater vigour and efficiency of their conquests were due to the fact that plunder was not their sole aim, but rather the desire to establish new homes for their wives and children.

[1] *An Adventure,* by C. Anne E. Moberly and Eleanor F. Jourdain. (Faber and Faber, Ltd.)

It is more than probable that the Angles spread to the northward, raiding and trading across the border into Scotland. That it fell to these people to give their name to England may possibly have been due to a real superiority either in purpose or character. It is, at all events, in keeping with historical data that the cultivator's furrow should reach back to the Angles, who transplanted their culture and their household gods upon English soil.

These facts are particularly relevant when we remember that the subject was early uprooted from his native soil and had never enjoyed a secure, established home. Frequent allusions to the tree in his drawings show how deeply his psychology needed to take root in a real earth and a real standpoint.

Everything in this first part of the dream seems to dwell upon the theme of participation in things that have always been held in common. The instinctual basis of life is a common burden and charge shared by all creatures. Out of this biological matrix there develops the idea of the common, the King's furrow, the King's highway, the village green, the omnibus (*i.e.*, the vehicle for everybody): these again lead on to the idea of trading and commerce between a more cultivated colonizing people and the indigenous clans of the North. The number of eyewitnesses also suggests a *consensus gentium* rather than individual testimony.

No particular associations were obtainable for the number 66. From the extraordinary frequency of the number 6 in apocalyptic metaphor, where a purely symbolical quantity is signified, we know it to be a relatively neutral number. This may derive from the fact that the numbers 1 to 5 possess definite personality for the primitive mind, corresponding to the number of digits on the hand, whereas the number 6, lying just outside the individualized group, begins that vague, indefinite conception of quantity which transcends the friendly, anatomical scale.

According to the same kind of primitive reasoning the " North " would be a vague, distant region of unknown people " away over there," accompanied by a gesture of indefinite scope. When we bear in mind that the patient's main problem and task is to open up a line of commerce with a *terra incognita* in his own psychology, and that this unknown potentiality is associated with an atavistic pull which both attracts and repels him, we can understand how this genial conception of a bus driven by an ' angel ' company, plying between the village green and a vague northern region, could carry a solid sense of comfort and reassurance. A place that is accessible to a ramshackle bus seen with one's own eyes can be neither too remote nor too dangerous. Then, too, the association with the first permanent settlers and colonizers after the Roman invasion brings his individual, subjective task into line with the main stream of native English culture. The dream almost seems to be arguing persuasively with the self-distrusting dreamer: " You remember how the Angles left their homeland and set sail over the sea to this unknown land, bringing with them their wives and all their belongings; how they had the courage to commit themselves irrevocably to the new experiment; and how they eventually conquered the land, planting their own culture and opening up trade and communication throughout the land. That was possible for them, and you come from the same stock. Very well then !" Remembering too that the primitive nature of the dream-mind delights in a childish play on words, we cannot ignore the traditional rôle of the angels to restore a man's belief in himself.

The atavistic pull is liable to find expression in unstable and restless moods, urging the schizophrenic subject to constant changes of direction. He becomes dissatisfied with his work, his marriage, the place he is in, etc. The lack of instinctive rootedness runs through every aspect of his life. This may result in a compulsive extraversion, steered not by objective purpose, but goaded rather by unconscious fear. Hence his need to settle down and to root his life, not in subjective doubts and fears, but in the common instinctive heritage of the race. There he could invoke the help of ancestral legions whose steadfast conservatism would be proof against the unquiet spirit.

So much for the general historical implications of the scene. But we have yet to discover why the dream notice-board should bring the " Edward II. furrow " into immediate connection with the " sixty-six eyewitnesses of the Angles who traded by bus with the North." On the strength of the patient's association with " the lonely furrow," coupled with the symptoms of affect which accompanied his reading of the sign, we may infer that he identifies himself in some way with Edward II. As a student of history he would presumably have reproduced the historian's two-dimensional portrait of the weak, effeminate King for examination purposes. But privily he must also have read between the lines, recognizing a psychological cousin perhaps in the lineaments of the King who was dispossessed of throne, manhood, and life by a woman boasting the aggressive, masculine character which he himself lacked. Behind the tragic fate of Edward he may have discerned the same reversal of masculine and feminine attributes which he himself depicted in the drawing of the effeminate figure counterbalanced by the powerful unconscious hero. We know that the unconscious attitude of a man often becomes externally visible in the rôle played by his wife. If he is too passive and indolent, his wife is forced into a compensatory aggressive rôle: if too isolated and aloof, she may tend to compensate his deficiency by a fussy exaggeration of her social function. In this way the law of compensation, which guards and conserves psychic equilibrium, also conditions the symbiotic relationship of husband and wife.

From this angle of judgment, the historian's portrait of Edward II. presents the characteristic features of anima-possession. Isabella becomes the symbol of the ruthless anima-demon, who, having seduced a man away from his human loyalties and tasks, inflates him into a friendless, counterfeit hero with extravagant power-fantasies. This description of anima-possession is not a mythological exaggeration ; it can be verified not only from the dream-records of patients, but also, in full daylight, in the most conspicuous figures upon the contemporary world-stage. On the other hand, the man who capitulates to a dæmonic anima-complex, for the sake of a lazy peace, is also quite liable to play the rôle of the helpless victim in relation to his wife, who is forced therewith to redress the balance by an exaggerated animus development.

Such a man will naturally tend to identify his anima-dæmon with woman in general, barricading himself in self-defence with elaborate fortifications against every feminine encroachment upon his private citadel. Thus he becomes more and more isolated from the humanizing influence of equal and candid relationship, and easily relapses into paranoiac moods of suspicion, adopting the traditional style of the meritorious but misunderstood victim.

In the case of our patient only the germ of this possible fate was visible to an observer. Yet even the germ was sufficiently potent to give the "Edward II. furrow" its peculiar significance for his psychology. The possibilities of dream-therapy are greatest during the early stages of a psychological infection, while the emotional situation is still plastic.

We have already had occasion to observe how the dock and the nettle grow side by side in the same psychical field. This homœopathic principle is illustrated in the dream notice-board, which first diagnoses the malady and then indicates its remedy on the selfsame village green. The disease is the lonely furrow which derives from the feeling that one is different, singular, apart, as though the arrows of fate in respect to oneself were especially tipped with poison. Hence the malady of the "Edward II. furrow" is rooted in resentment, and its solitariness is not accepted. The remedy is the feeling of kinship and the participation in a common venture and a common risk. This feeling is symbolized by the omnibus, the common vehicle crossing the common land which in its turn represents a common heritage. In other words, the cure of the separatism of the anima is through a ruthless scrutiny of anima-assumptions and the unreserved acceptance of the human pact. When the vital human relationship is kept real through frank communication of real contents, the relation to the anima undergoes a corresponding metamorphosis. Instead of a pitiless power-demon, the anima becomes a disciplined function of relationship.

The allusion to "the North" recalls the compass symbol of Drawing 6. After the insanity of Drawing 5, there was a spontaneous attempt to recover psychical equilibrium. We noted how the left arm of the nebulous figure reached across towards the northern pointer of the compass in this attempt. The North Pole is the natural point of orientation for all the dwellers in the northern hemisphere. Hence the symbolic north must indicate a corresponding polarity in the psychic world. The " trading of the Angles with the North " might allude, therefore, to a generally available method of orientation. Taking the four cardinal points of the psychological compass, intuition and sensation form the perpendicular arational line, thinking and feeling the rational horizon. According to this method of orientation, since the North corresponds to the function of intuition, " trading with the North " would symbolize the intuitive commerce with the unconscious which has been developing through the analysis.

Linking these two references together, we reach the conclusion that a generally available method of reorientation has been discovered, which is also a kind of intuitive traffic with the historical unconscious. Moreover, inasmuch as the Angles were the early colonizers of England, we must assume that the dream omnibus carries an analogy with that remote but crucial experiment. In other words, the task the subject is engaged upon is a pioneering work of general human significance.

The parallel with the modern analytical approach to the unconscious is indicated in three different ways, and the easy impersonal manner of its presentation is likely to have a positive effect upon the patient's conception of his task. Instead of regarding it as a specialized form of medical treatment for purely personal difficulties, the dream expands its significance in the most explicit terms, even suggesting that the angels are actively concerned in this new, yet very ancient, commerce. For it is well to remember that the interpretation of dreams was one of the first scientific attempts in the history of the mind, and that the enigmatic problem of individual fate has been from earliest times the seed-bed of philosophy.

Although science has been built on the foundations of these earlier quests and has superseded intuitive science with a massive accumulation of knowledge, the essential problem still remains. Analytical psychology is the first introverted attempt of modern science to deal with it. The ramshackle bus would seem, therefore, to be a whimsical device for uniting the archaic intuitive science of early civilizing genius with our most recent scientific discipline in one and the same symbol. We shall presently see how these same angel bus-drivers rejoice in the setting up of the neglected inferior function as the corner-stone of the new cathedral: as ever, it is this work of deliverance which invites angelic intervention.

V

We now come to the second part of the dream, where the dreamer becomes involved with two figures belonging to the epoch of the Holy Roman Empire.

Henry II. was crowned Emperor at Rome in 1013 and reigned till 1024. His reputation for devoutness earned him the title of ' the Saint '; partly, no doubt, because of his munificence to the Church, but also because of his ascetic piety. Kunigunde, his Queen, was equally pious, and, inasmuch as the imperial pair had mutually taken the vow of chastity, the marriage remained childless and presumably unconsummated.

The Duke of Schleswig appears to be fictitious. Schleswig is the northern part of Schleswig-Holstein, which was a borderline province of Prussia. Owing to the break-up of the Empire under Frederick III. (1439-1493) Schleswig-Holstein became united with Denmark. Before its conquest and absorption by the Holy Roman Empire it was presumably an independent kingdom. We could find no record of the conquest of this state by Henry II. There is, however, one relevant consideration in the fact that the Angles who migrated to Britain came very largely from the region known later as Schleswig.

These historical or quasi-historical figures are not, however, the centre of the subject's interest, which seems to be focused upon the curious suit the King intends to wear in his proposed attack upon Schleswig. The subject's uninvited return to the palace, in order to study this suit more closely, prompts us to do likewise. It is like armour, yet it is not armour. It bears a resemblance to the dress of a sixteenth-century burgher. It is stiffened with leather, suggesting nineteenth-century Japanese armour, and under the leathern lapel of the tunic a tiny gas-mask is concealed, therewith bringing it not only up to date, but into the future as well. For the gas-mask under the lapel is associated with Wells's conception of coming events.

In the presence of so remarkable a condensation of widely flung associations, we must assume that this suit symbolizes a defensive mechanism derived from a variety of sources. The behaviour of the subject in this part of the dream has a dual significance. First, his great interest in the leather suit tells us that the problem of protection and control is his main preoccupation. Secondly, his excited attempt to fraternize with the ascetic Emperor of the Holy Roman Empire informs us that his repression of instinct has tended to provoke somewhat grandiose power-fantasies.

The armour contains certain historical allusions which may afford us further clues. The style of a rich burgher of the sixteenth century suggests a man of property whose main concern would be to protect and maintain his possessions and his position; hence a conservative attitude. In the beginning of the nineteenth century Japan was still living in the feudal period. The power of the Emperor had decayed and the island was insulated from every contact with the outside world. The national spirit was none the less preserved, and the ancient military caste maintained a tradition of extreme severity, indicating a deep reserve of latent power. This Japanese association introduces the idea of an aristocratic tradition of discipline, capable of heroic self-sacrifice. The sixteenth century in Europe was a time when no citizen could feel very secure. Life and property were never really safe, either from attack or spoliation. Similarly, Japan in the early nineteenth century, having been cut off from all contact with the rest of the world, was peculiarly vulnerable to disturbing foreign influences. Both were periods in which a new evolutionary phase, instigated by necessity, was waiting upon the threshold of events.

The presence of the gas-mask brings these historical analogies, with a rather sinister implication, into the present. Again traditional culture is threatened; life and property are by no means guaranteed; and a phase of acute disturbance must be taken into account. The shape of things to come is not such as would readily persuade a man to a sublime faith in human destiny. Thus again the idea of self-preservation and control against the impact of atavistic conditions is implicit in this central symbol.

The personal aspect of the Aquarian transition should be mentioned here, though it may be no more than an idiom for expressing a certain aspect of destiny which cannot be grasped by other means. Certain people are undoubtedly lamed by the unconscious. This may be due in the main to a bad inheritance, or to adverse early conditions of one kind or another. But there are cases in which, though we ransack the lumber-rooms of the past never so thoroughly for the effective explanation, we are driven eventually to look in the opposite direction for the cause of the crippling.

Without losing our way in philosophical bypaths, we know, in practice, that we are determined by future events or possibilities as well as by the past. Determination by the future is, if anything, more potent, just because it is more indefinite.

Many psychoneurotics have the feeling very strongly (it is also quite common among borderline psychotics) that the shape of things to come has already laid its hand upon them. They feel that their adaptation to the here-and-now necessities and claims is, to some extent, undermined by the fact that their energies have been bespoken in preparation for a future condition.

If the world-transition, referred to above, from the zodiacal era of Pisces to that of Aquarius betokens a revolution in the fundamental premises of the European mind, as certain writers have predicted, it is reasonable to suppose that this event is more than liable to set its mark upon just those who are psychologically hampered in their adaptation to present-day reality. Where the necessity of the present fails, in other words, to grip our psychology and harness it to present claims, the approaching necessity of the future succeeds. To use an intuitive parable, the introverted schizoid type may be temperamentally fitted to sense the proximity of Niagara, whereas the well-adapted, extraverted oarsman may be so engrossed by his own magnificent efforts as to fail to observe the increasing force of the current.

In our judgment of a neurotic personality, it may be vital to ask ourselves the question, "Is it not possible that this individual has been lamed by the future, and if so, may not the direction of his cure lie in helping him to prepare the house for the future man in himself?"

From this point of view it is also important to discriminate the individual who has a neurosis from the neurotic personality. To have a neurosis can, as we have just seen, be almost a mark of honour, in so far as it traces for us the pathway of individuation. But to make the neurosis one's vocation means to resist the claims of the future as well as the present, and to live in a state of resentment against the past.

VI

We must now turn our attention to the historical personalities of the drama. We have internal evidence—in the fact, for instance, that the subject hails Henry as his brother—for assuming that the King represents a somewhat grandiose conception of his collective persona.

The persona is Jung's term for the outer character—in other words, the aspect of a personality that is formed by and adapted to the social environment. Hence it is a cultural formation, resting in the main upon the accepted traditional values of the society to which one belongs. Being answerable in all things to all men, hence embodying the collective ideal, the persona is frequently personified as a king.

In a young man, before individual character has been toughened by necessity, there is a very natural tendency to take shelter behind an unchallengeable persona. As a collectively guaranteed formula, the persona is a defensive mask, but its real power resides in the fact that it is rooted in sacred tradition. The gentleman ideal, for instance, which rules the Englishman's persona, is rooted in the tradition of knightly honour and fair dealing which came to its flower in the Arthurian legends. The sublime tonelessness of the so-called " Oxford voice " expresses the tradition of intellectual detachment from ordinary human emotions by which the civilized function of reason has achieved mastery over natural forces.

A good persona is therefore an implicit statement, not only of solidarity with one's civilized contemporaries, it is also an assertion of personal identification with certain traditional values. These positive aspects are clearly indicated in the historical associations appended to the suit of armour.

The sinister aspect of persona-identification is alluded to in the " gloomy palace hall," in the mediæval asceticism of the predatory King, and in the latter's ruthless attitude to the shadowy Duke of Schleswig.[1] In this aspect of the dream there is something dark and menacing which needs to be brought into the light. The very behaviour of the dreamer, first in his idea of hiding under a bench, then in his ineffectual and rather fulsome attempt to claim kinship with the King, bears witness to a shame-producing conflict of motives.

At first glance " Heinrich, mein frater " strikes one as a mere linguistic absurdity. But again we shall be well advised not to assume either an " accident " or a mere relapse to the fourth-form level of humour. There is a subtlety in this " mistake " which offers a clue to the discovery of the sinister motive. The mistake consists in the fact that the dreamer unconsciously mixes Latin and German in his inept greeting.

We know that the Holy Roman Empire was an attempt to weld together the Latin and Teutonic cultures in a grandiose dream of conquest. The sinister effect of this crusading power-fantasy on the spiritual life of Christendom will be discussed later when we come to the metamorphosis of the cathedral. At the moment we have only to observe that the disintegration of the Empire was inevitable, firstly, because it was an attempt to amalgamate by force essentially incompatible cultural components and, secondly, because this

[1] In view of this remarkable similarity of attitude to leaders of less powerful neighbouring states of the German ruler of the dream and that of the actual ruler of the Third Reich, it should be mentioned that this dream and the whole series of drawings appeared on the scene in the summer of 1935—some years therefore before Herr Hitler had perfected his ruthless political technique.

assertion of power by the Christian Church was diametrically opposed to the character and teachings of its Founder. Thus, in making his apparent mistake, the dreamer calls attention to the fact that he, like the Holy Roman Empire, contains two incompatible elements which refuse to be welded together. In calling the King his brother, the subject confesses to an inclination, similar to the King's, to repress his instinctive life under the guise of ambition and asceticism. From this point of view, we can regard the unfortunate Duke as personifying those un-Christianized pagan impulses which the saintly King so vigorously repressed in his own personal life.

The Duke of Schleswig is unknown to history, but he would seem to represent an independent pagan unit, about to be crushed and absorbed by a predatory Christian neighbour and host. The choice of this particular historical parallel at this juncture would argue that the problem of the persona is deeply rooted in a traditional attitude of power which prohibits the repressed antithesis from voicing a contrary standpoint in the open forum of consciousness. The persona becomes a harmful external crust or carapace only when it insists upon repressing native individual qualities, and therefore no longer represents the real nature of the subject. The paranoiac psychology of the dictator, whose absolute position is established upon the ruthless suppression of all opposition, exemplifies a law which is as universal and constant as the law of gravity. Repression generates insecurity, and the feeling of insecurity provokes further repression. Thus a vicious circle is established which eventually leads to revolution.

Although the operation of this law is transparently clear in the political sphere, it is not so obvious in the inner psychic economy, because of our inveterate habit of ascribing mental upheavals to external causes. When, for example, an individual collapses because his nature has rebelled against the tyranny of a single function which has repressed every other aspect of his personality, it is said, and believed, that he broke down under the strain of modern life. In a sense this is true, just as it might be said that the dictator's paranoia is due to the strain of autocratic rule. But in so far as we overlook the fact that the strain of external conditions is secondary to, and becomes insupportable because of, *the state of conflict within*, our explanation is both false and misleading.

The state of conflict is expressed in the dream (*a*) in the subjective feeling of gloom (the "gloomy palace hall"), (*b*) in the dreamer's attempt to ally himself with the superior or ruling function (King Henry), and (*c*) in the fact that he also calls to the inferior function (*i.e.*, the imprisoned Duke). Psychical conflict means that two incompatible standpoints are housed and are striving for mastery under the same roof. Every function naturally has its specific standpoint which the dream-mind personifies in a distinctive fashion.

Here, then, we have the Christian ascetic King and the independent pagan ruler appearing together in the rôles of the conqueror and his prisoner. The subject is caught, as it were, in the toils of this ancient conflict because he is himself both oppressor and victim. But if both are present and active in the mind, he cannot be a partisan of either without suffering dissociation or inner division. He calls to both, but with neither is his call effectual: the one cannot hear, the other cannot see who it is that calls.

The dream seems to be emphatic on the point that these historical antitheses exist in the mind independent of the ego, notwithstanding the fact that the latter automatically seeks to identify itself with the ruling function. Detachment from both sides provides the only possible solution. The manner of the solution is implied in the historical analogy given by the dream. For in point of fact, the hypothesis that diverse or dissociated elements can be permanently united in a system held together by repressive force was disproved by the breakup of the Holy Roman Empire. The eventual disintegration of the power-system, and subsequent regrouping of its independent functional units according to their natural affinities, would provide the most feasible basis for a solution.

The psyche develops a natural hierarchy of functional elements; but a state of equilibrium can be maintained in this hierarchy only in so far as the ego preserves an attitude of relativity or detachment—an attitude demanding self-discipline of a high order.

The reader will observe, from the nature of the dreamer's associations, that the suit of armour is, in no sense, an aggressive equipment. It is associated entirely with the ideas of self-preservation and self-discipline. Employed, therefore, by the all-powerful superior function for the purpose of repressing its inferior opposite, it would be altogether in the wrong hands. But if this symbol were adopted by the ego (*i.e.*, the dreamer) for the purpose of attaining self-discipline, and therewith restoring the natural balance of function, it would be employed under the right ægis and its traditional virtue preserved. Thus the dreamer's profound interest in the suit of armour becomes intelligible.

The ambivalency of this symbol is in keeping with the ambiguous behaviour of the dreamer throughout this part of the dream. And the rôle played by the dreamer is often, as we know, a valuable clue to our understanding of the dream. In the present instance a significant alteration of attitude is conspicuous in response to the successive phases of the dream-experience.

In the opening scene the dreamer's peculiar attitude to his dog offered a standpoint of criticism from which the whole historical drama could be viewed in its relevance to the dreamer's psychology. In the part concerned with the commons the dreamer is receptive rather than active. He is being instructed by visual demonstration, and he and the shadow are found standing side by side. All through this educational portion he is clear and positive in his attitude.

It is when we come to the gloomy palace hall that the dreamer begins to be dubious and complicated in his reactions. Evidently he is now seized by conflict, and it is this which provokes his interest in the suit of armour. The same curiosity forces him first into the position of intruder and eavesdropper and then, to disguise his embarrassment, into the compensatory heartiness of his " Heinrich, mein frater." This dual attitude of the dreamer illustrates perfectly the ambiguity of the persona-shadow situation. In his ignominious idea of hiding under the bench he personifies the feeling of inferiority, the fatalistic despair of the repressed inferior function. In his over-eager attempt to fraternize[1] with the powerful ruling function (which is identical with the persona) he personifies the craving for superiority.

There is a forced artificiality in both rôles which should warn the subject that they are essentially unreal. Perhaps the most ticklish and disagreeable point in psychotherapeutic education is when the analyst has to criticize the patient's persona, and prove to him that the rôle he is playing does not work. Whether it be the inaudible monotone of the patient neurotically bound to his inferiority, or the garrulous over-statement of the patient suffering from an inflated persona, both paralyse one's interest—the former lulling the mind to slumberous reverie, the latter filling the room with ineffectual noise. Both play a rôle which excludes any possibility of human intercourse, for how can one converse with a being whose real personality has been pushed on one side by a psychological intruder? We have to make known to the patient how completely his personality is falsified by these unconscious influences.

The same condition characterizes the animus-anima altercations of married couples. The familiar reproach, "Didn't you hear what I said?" or "Why can't you listen?" tells its own tale. It is an almost impossible feat to listen coherently to a woman in a hot animus-mood. It is as though the force of the accompanying affect obliterated the sense of the words uttered. In the case of a man with an anima-mood the alteration of personality not only makes intelligible communication difficult, but frequently the subject has a subsequent amnesia for what his anima has said.

By far the greatest source of misunderstanding between man and woman is due to personality distortion from the invasion of an autonomous complex, and in every case the pathological alteration or displacement of personality results from the autonomy of the complex.

This is exemplified in the dream by the almost complete absence of relatedness between the various personalities, and in the fact that the autonomous systems are represented

[1] Note the ingenious way in which the dreamer is made to divulge this motive in his "Heinrich, mein frater."

as historical ghosts. An autonomous complex pursues its way and goes through its paces, repeating its own special performance quite regardless of any human consideration. It is a kind of ghost haunting the corridors of the mind, and, like a ghost, it enters the sphere of the present from the still living past. It is elusive and hard to challenge like the ghost. Only analytical insight, with fair appraisal of its historical significance, can break through the intangible envelope and release the energy informing it.

We are now in a position to understand the crucial significance of the suit of armour which is not armour. It symbolizes the central attitude of control, compounded of responsible citizenship (sixteenth-century burgher), introverted self-discipline (nineteenth-century Japanese armour), and intuitive vigilance and foresight (the Shape of Things to Come). With these the autonomy of the historical ghosts can be effectively challenged and resolved. The need for this thoroughgoing preparation of the attitude of control will soon become apparent.

VII

We now enter the cathedral in which the moribund Henry is about to sing his death-song. The fact that the dreamer identifies him with the representative hero of pagan German mythology is of great interest. It informs us at the outset that we are concerned with the ever-recurring pagan-Christian conflict in the racial unconscious.

The whole scene is brilliant with sunlight and colour. We feel at once that the stage is set for the final act of the drama. It is like emerging from a dark tunnel or defile into a vast arena filled with an expectant throng. Again the dreamer reverts to his previous rôle of the passive witness.

Assuming that a logical continuity binds together every portion of the dream, there must be an emotional connection between the scene in the palace hall and this impressive finale. The connecting link will be found in the dream-reversion from Henry to Siegfried.

We have to remember that the Church, which was identical with the Holy Roman Empire, did not wait to persuade our barbarian Germanic forebears of the truth of Christianity. They were pitchforked into the Christian fold at the point of the sword, straight from the level of polydæmonism and nature-worship into a mystical Eastern religion, with which their own indigenous myth had nothing in common.

After millions of years of experimental research nature still practises the gradual method of evolution. The Church, however, attempted the shock tactics of totalitarian rule, in the belief that conquest was synonymous with conversion. It is the characteristic illusion of power-psychology, and although history has repeatedly proved it to be a false hypothesis, rulers, drunk with power, still pursue the same mirage with undiminished frenzy.[1]

From the evolutionary standpoint, we can understand why this policy inevitably created a dangerous dissociation between the repressed pagan levels of the unconscious and the massive Christian superstructure. Symptoms of this vast repression are not lacking in the subsequent history of Christendom. The break-up of the Holy Roman Empire was followed by the witch-madness, in which it is estimated that something like two million witches were burned throughout Europe in the space of a hundred years. Records of the trials of witches make it abundantly clear that the Church had to deal with a widespread renegade movement back to pagan practices. The allure of the repressed antithesis was sensed as a real danger, seducing men's minds from the security of Christendom. This much can be deduced from the ritual practised in the witches' Sabbath, which was a mixture of surviving pagan ritual and a satanic caricature of the Christian Mass.

The persecution of the Jews probably sprang from the same dissociation, inasmuch as the Jews were the people who refused to accept the divinity of Christ. Throughout the Middle Ages the Jews were forced to play the rôle of the scapegoat, upon whom the un-Christianized part of the Christian unconscious could be projected. It is highly significant, therefore, that this persecution should be revived again in its crudest form in the land which suffered most from the power-psychology of the Holy Roman Empire.

[1] This was written in 1938.

The following passage, quoted from an article by Jung, written in June, 1918, shows how an historical crisis can be predicted when its psychological antecedents are correctly seized:

"Das Christentum zerteilte den germanischen Barbaren in seine untere und obere Hälfte und so gelang es ihm—nämlich durch Verdrängung der dunkeln Seite—die helle Seite zu domestizieren und dafür die Kultur geschickt zu machen. Die untere Hälfte aber harrt der Erlosung und einer zweiten Domestikation. Bis dahin bleibt sie associiert mit den Resten der Vorzeit, mit dem kollektiven Unbewussten, was eine eigentümliche und steigende Belebung des kollektiven Unbewussten bedeuten muss. Je mehr die unbedingte Autorität der christlichen Weltanschauung sich verliert, desto vernehmlicher wird sich die 'blonde Bestie' in ihrem unterirdischen Gefängnis umdrehen und uns mit einem Ausbruch mit verheerenden Folgen bedrohen. . . ."[1]

Jung's prognostication, written in the last year of the war, is now tragically verified by events, though we cannot yet estimate the final consequences to Christendom of this latest eruption of paganism.

The basis of Jung's prognosis rests upon the principle that nothing dies until it is lived out. Many things have been superseded in the millennial rush of European civilization. They may have disappeared from view, but everything that has been swallowed is not necessarily done with. Vital affects which have their roots in the primordial psyche are never extinguished. They bide their time and reappear at the psychological moment.

The French Revolution, the terror in Russia, Germany and Spain show what can happen to civilized nations when

[1] *Schweizerland*, IV. Jahrgang, No. 9, p. 470, Juniheft, 1918: "Christianity divided German paganism into an upper and a lower portion, and succeeded—by dint of repressing the darker side—in domesticating the bright side and adapting it to civilized requirements. But the lower portion awaits deliverance and a second domestication. Meanwhile it remains associated with other relics of antiquity in the collective unconscious, necessarily involving a peculiar and increasing activation of the collective unconscious. The more the absolute authority of the Christian *Weltanschauung* wears thin, the more audibly can we hear the pacing to and fro of the 'blond beasts' in their subterranean dungeon, threatening us with an outburst which must surely have devastating consequences."

Christian forms decay and the archaic underworld breaks through. As the authority of the Church wanes the repressed pagan antithesis must surely come to the surface. The demoralization and disillusionment which followed the War were undoubtedly intensified by the dawning realization that our boasted civilization was not as Christian as we had believed.

Glancing back now to the previous scene, we recognize this same power-illusion—that conquest is synonymous with conversion—personified in the ascetic Henry II. and his proposed victim the Duke of Schleswig.

In the extraverted crusading fashion which the victorious Christian consciousness adopted towards its pagan origins, we catch a glimpse of a fundamental weakness, not of the religion of Christ, but of the traditional Christian Church. This inherent weakness is traceable to the fact that the Church fell a victim to that same illusion of power which Christ Himself overcame in His temptation by the Devil. Christ knew that conquest does not change the heart of man, and therefore He always spoke to the individual heart, and refused the way of collective power. Perhaps it was on this account that Judas Iscariot rejected Him.

The dissociation in the patient's psychology has been produced in complete accordance with the traditional pattern. The overweening claim to power by which the superior masculine function held the irrational feminine unconscious in rigid subjection was perfectly illustrated in the early drawings of this series. The first grim allusion to the repressive aspect of the ascetic tradition was seen in Drawing 8, in which the emaciated devil wore a friar's robe.

To go back to the source of the disease, the unconscious had to lay bare that greater dissociation between precept and practice which has afflicted the Church of Christendom, and which has given to our so-called Christian civilization its equivocal character in the eyes of Oriental and other non-Christian cultures. The one revealing truth which if generously realized could bring once again an invigorating breath of sanity into the body of Christendom is implicit in the whole development of the present dream. This is the fact that we are still pagan below, even though we may be sincerely Christian above.

In this final scene Henry, the ascetic Christian exemplar of the civilized persona, has become fused with the great pagan hero who is about to sing his death-song. Both must die. The conflict cannot be resolved by the victory of either side. There is a radical incompatibility between the pagan and the Christian characters which makes an organic combination of the two impossible. They will not unite; either one must displace and repress the other, or both must go and, in their going, generate a new soul.

We must now ask why both protagonists of this deep conflict are taken from Germanic myth and history, and why Siegfried, in particular, has been chosen to represent the pagan unconscious? The dreamer is not aware of having any specific German ancestry, although, naturally, we cannot exclude this possibility. The explanation which seemed most plausible to the subject himself had to do with the present situation in Germany. Abundant signs make it clear that the unlived pagan unconscious has broken through the Christian crust, and that this volcanic disturbance, as predicted by Jung, has shaken the whole world, setting in motion a great spiritual migration that is essentially hostile to the historical Christian philosophy. That Central European psychology is harking back to the Middle Ages can hardly be questioned. Not only is the atavistic momentum manifest in the persecution of the Jews and in the frank revival of pagan mythology and religion, but we are even invited to regard the Rome-Berlin axis as a modern attempt to repeat the power-fantasy of the Holy Roman Empire, albeit on a new ideological footing.

The Germanic hero Siegfried is also relevant to the present, inasmuch as his death was the signal for the collapse of Valhalla and the passing away of the old gods. The reign and authority of Wotan were undermined, not by alien powers of evil, but by his own double dealing and inner conflict. The spear of Wotan could no longer withstand the self-forged sword of the hero, whose mind was clear and who was therefore a stranger to fear.

Siegfried can hardly be expected to sing to a lyre. In this allusion there would seem to be a side-glance at Orpheus, the mythological forerunner of Christ. Though dissimilar in character, the two pagan heroes have this much in common: they were both initiated into the inner counsels of nature by means of music. The music of Orpheus was persuasive to animals and to all natural things; even trees and stones were moved by it. Siegfried, on the other hand, gained his immediate understanding of the songs of birds and of the living heart of nature through licking a drop of the dragon's blood which had fallen on his hand when he dealt the creature its death-blow. Orpheus had a positive artistry, a mastery of natural music. Siegfried, on the contrary, became sensitive to nature's music only after a magical initiation into her mysteries. Thus, in associating the lyre with Siegfried, the dream seems to combine the active and the passive attitude to nature.

These two attitudes are evidently concerned with the "great green dragon," with which the soul of Siegfried is engaged on the plane above. The very fact that Siegfried (rather than St. George) is selected to fight the dragon implies that Siegfried's way, that of courageously assimilating the peculiar virtue of the dragon, is to be preferred to the crusading Christian way of annihilation and rejection of the opposite principle. From the fact that Siegfried borrows the Orphic lyre for the singing of his death-song, and that the song gives his soul the victory, we infer that the music has an actively magical effect upon the dragon. Thus Siegfried borrows the artistry of Orpheus which is latent in the lyre, just as in the myth he borrowed the magical virtue of his father, Siegmund, when he forged the sword *Nothung*.

Doubtless an allusion to the *Götterdämmerung* motif is suggested in the transformation from Henry into Siegfried. Yet the central event of the dream is not the disintegration of the cathedral so much as the fight between the soul of Siegfried and the dragon. A correct understanding of this event should therefore give us the key to the whole drama.

In the description of this spiritual combat two important facts stand out: (1) the soul of Siegfried is conceived as the effective, dynamic aspect of the hero *on another plane*; (2) the dragon is not only renewed and verdant, but, like the Chinese dragon, has developed the power of flight. It is no longer a " loathly worm " cumbering the ground, but an effective celestial power.

Neither of these transformations accords with the traditional Christian view of spiritual reality. The battle, which is the climax of the dream, must therefore take place, not inside the cathedral but above it. No attempt is made to put the new wine into the old wine-skin.

VIII

In order fully to understand the nature and quality of the new wine we must enquire into its origins. First, let us compare the Christian with the pagan conception of the dragon. In the Book of Revelation (chapter xii.) the dragon is identified with Satan when he was vanquished and cast out of heaven:

> " And there was war in heaven: Michael and his angels fought against the dragon; and the dragon fought, and his angels, and prevailed not; neither was their place found any more in heaven.
>
> " And the great dragon was cast out, that old serpent, called the Devil, and Satan, which deceiveth the whole world: he was cast out into the earth, and his angels were cast out with him.
>
> " And I heard a loud voice saying in heaven, ' Now is come salvation, and strength, and the kingdom of our God, and the power of his Christ: for the accuser of our brethren is cast down, which accused them before our God day and night. And they overcame him by the blood of the Lamb, and by the word of their testimony; and they loved not their lives unto the death. Therefore rejoice, ye heavens, and ye that dwell in them. Woe to the inhabiters of the earth and of the sea ! for the devil is come down unto you, having great wrath, because he knoweth that he hath but a short time !' "

In the heroic Christian legends, of which St. George is the most famous example, the dragon is also conceived as the embodiment of evil which has to be utterly exterminated. But the attempt to cast out and exterminate the Devil was by no means a purely transcendental matter. Human nature itself was crucified and sundered by the belief in an absolutely irreconcilable opposition. Already in the time of St. Augustine we find fanatical persecution of the repressed instincts taking the place of genuine piety. Sins were tabulated into categories, and the penances prescribed were often unbelievably inhuman. The deadly sins, murder, adultery and apostasy, were not only unpardonable by the Church, but the sinner was actually excluded from divine compassion. Tertullian taught that even Christ could not plead for their forgiveness. Ten, twenty and even thirty years' penance could be prescribed for adultery, and lifelong penance for apostasy. While under penance a man might not marry or, if married, live with his wife. He was not allowed to undertake military service or go into business. He was literally cut off from the human community and treated like a leper. Even such lapses as eating on fast-days before the hour, or indulging in loose thoughts in church, or speaking lustful words, might be punished with seven years' penance, and three of them on bread and water!

The casting out of the Devil from heaven certainly brought woe to the inhabiters of the earth, as the prophet had predicted. Perhaps the most significant feature of this wholesale repression of the animal nature was the fact that cruelty was not even mentioned among the categories of sin. The savagery with which certain natural instincts were repressed was justified by the plea that the crushing of the instinct was a victory over the Devil. All the horrors and abominations of religious persecution, which have so often defiled the page of history, have been, and still are, justified on the same ground.

We can no longer close our eyes to the fact that the traditional Christian method of dealing with the dragon has entailed immeasurable cruelty to a countless multitude of human beings. Indeed, there is no man born of Christian stock who does not bear the mark of this agelong repression in his soul. We are all in some measure crippled by it.

There is no disloyalty to the source from which we come in this spiritual stocktaking. We have to know how we became estranged from our original nature and from the original source of our being. Our cultural home has not the deepest claim upon our loyalty. The real parent holds a closer tie than the godparent. It is from this deeper loyalty that we condemn the murderous attempt to crush out the fertile dragon element in human nature; and out of our condemnation emerge two vital truths. We can realize to-day, as never before, the enduring virtue of the primordial human soul and therefore, in a new way, the profound truth of the original Christian revelation. Both have marvellously survived the agelong ordeal of religious fanaticism and regimentation.

But if the Christian view of the dragon-element has had its day, whence comes the new redeeming conception? From the evidence of the dream it is patent that the dragon is not merely unconquered; it is actually rejuvenated. It dominates the scene. In its winged and verdant power the dragon of the dream is akin to the Chinese conception.

The earliest references to the dragon in Chinese literature show it to be a life-giving, beneficent source of power. In the *Yi King*, one of the greatest of the Chinese classics, the dragon is represented as the "god of thunder, who brings good crops when he appears in the ricefields (as rain) or in the sky (as dark and yellow clouds)." De Visser sums up the main conception of Old China with regard to the dragon as follows: "In those early days (just as at present) he was the god of water, thunder, clouds and rain, the harbinger of blessings, and the symbol of holy men. As the emperors are the holy beings on earth, the idea of the dragon as the symbol of imperial power is based upon this ancient conception."[1]

In the fifth appendix to the *Yi King*, which has been attributed to Confucius, we read in chapter x. that "*Khien* is the symbol of heaven and hence has the appellation father. *Khwan* is the symbol of earth and hence has the appellation mother. *Kan* shows a first application of *Khwan* to *Khien* . . . and hence is called the oldest son." In chapter xi. 17 it is stated that "*Kan* suggests the idea of thunder, of the dragon, of the union of the azure and the yellow (*i.e.*, heaven and earth), of development, of the eldest

[1] De Visser, *The Dragon in China and Japan*.

son." The philosopher Hwai Nan Tsze described the dragon as the "origin of all creatures that are winged, hairy, scaly and mailed." Thus the dragon also symbolizes the evolutionary impulse in living organisms. He also said: "Mankind cannot see the dragons rise; wind and rain assist them to ascend to a great height." Confucius is reported to have said: "As to the dragon, we cannot understand his riding on the wind and the clouds and his ascending to the sky. To-day I saw Lao-Tzü: is he not like the dragon?"[1]

In the *Li Ki* the unicorn, the tortoise, the phœnix and the dragon are called the four *ling*. De Visser translates this as "spiritual being." The dragon has more *ling* than any other creature. All flowing water, streams, rivers and also clouds are expressions of the dragon's power. Hence his dwelling is on high mountains where the streams take their source.

In confirmation of this naturalistic conception of the dragon-power I reproduce a Japanese Dragon-Tiger screen after a classical Chinese model (Fig. 10). Instead of a stylized, conventional figure, we see here a realistic body of draconian lightning, bursting from a dynamic concentration of cloud and wind and wave.

The dragon emerges from an inky cavern of cloud on the left side of the field. Forked lightning streams from its body at many points; the dragon is in fact the lightning. Storm-clouds throng the upper portion of the field, and waves of the sea, or of rivers, fill the lower part. From amidst the waves and the clouds clusters of bamboo-shoots appear, showing that the dragon is also the god of vegetation as well as a dæmon of the elements.

The most striking thing about the painting is the impressive power of the wind, which seems to come roaring out of the heavens. Three whirlwinds have been indicated by the artist: one beneath the dragon's foot, one at the bottom of the head-panel, and one, much fainter, in line with the extended head and neck. At the bottom of the screen plumes of spray are seen thrown up by the wind and waves.

From this evidence it is possible to trace the metamorphosis of the dragon from an elemental dæmon into a

[1] *Ibid.*, p. 65.

benign spiritual power. Though, in fact, the Chinese naturalistic conception which reduces the terrors of the moral conflict, in which the soul swings dizzily between salvation and perdition, to the play of natural forces—*Yang* and *Yin* expressing the same opposition within the soul as without—makes it difficult to discern where the elemental can be distinguished from the psychological.

With all these powerful attributes, and in the light of the Confucian appendix to the *Yi King*, the dragon emerges as an intuitive concept which embraces not only the energy generated between heaven and earth (*i.e.*, the energy of the whole process of nature), but also the primordial source of vital energy in the unconscious. In chapter iv. of appendix v. the author, having just said that the dragon is thunder, states that " thunder serves to put things in motion, wind to scatter them."

As far back as the idea of the dragon can be traced in ancient Chinese writings, we find the same beneficent elemental conception. From the beginning the Chinese seem to have favoured a dynamic rather than a moral conception of the universe. The specialization of the intellect never assumed so great an ascendancy as to pit reasoning man against unreasoning nature. Whereas the heroic attitude of the West tends to picture man in constant warfare with the destructive powers of nature, Chinese common sense prefers to convince the bull that a parallel movement is better in every way than mere opposition. In the West the dragon symbolizes the power of evil or the force of regression, for the Western mind is rooted in the idea that man's original nature is evil. In the East the dragon dwells on the highest mountains and is identified with clouds and flowing water, because the Eastern mind sees spiritual events as the interplay of natural elements. Hence the dragon, as symbol of the inexhaustible potential of natural energy, represents beneficent spiritual power. So long as it is conceived along Miltonesque lines as representing the power of hell, it has to be combated as evil. Yet if we only could regard the dragon as a superior power, it might possibly reveal to us the dæmonic aspect of God.

In thus representing the dragon as a superior power above the cathedral and above mankind the dream of our subject has clearly borrowed a living content from the East. What, then, of the soul of Siegfried?

In view of its comprehensive and somewhat dubious connotation, it behoves us to enquire into the meaning of the word "soul" as it appears in the dream-context. The pagan conception of the soul was very different from the Christian. If Siegfried had not displaced Henry the Saint, we might interpret the soul as a personification of that imperishable spiritual substance which has been delivered from the earth-bound condition. But, in so far as the dream states categorically that it is the soul of Siegfried, we have to consider how the idea of the soul was conceived in the historico-mythological stratum to which Siegfried rightly belongs.

It is by no means easy to wash away metaphysical contamination and reconstruct the pre-Christian Teuton conception of the soul. Rydberg, for example, expresses himself as follows:

> "Mythologists have simply assumed that the popular view of the Christian Church in regard to terrestrial man, conceiving him to consist of two factors, the perishable body and the imperishable soul, was the necessary condition for every belief in a life hereafter, and that the heathen Teutons accordingly also cherished this idea.
>
> "But this duality did not enter into the belief of our heathen fathers. Nor is it of such a kind that a man, having conceived a life hereafter, in this connection necessarily must conceive the soul as the simple, indissoluble spiritual factor of human nature. The division into two parts, *lif ok sala*, *likamr ok sala*, body and soul, came with Christianity, and there is every reason for assuming that, so far as the Scandinavian peoples are concerned, the very word soul, *sala, sal*, is, like the idea it represents, imported. In Old Norse literature the word occurs for the first time in Olaf Trygveson's contemporary Halfred, after he had been converted to Christianity.
>
> "The anthropological conception presented in Völuspa is as follows: Man consists of six elements—namely, to begin with the lower and coarser and to end with the highest and noblest:

(1) The earthly matter of which the body is formed.
(2) A formative, vegetative force.
(3) and (4) Loder's gifts.
(5) Honer's gifts.
(6) Odin's gifts.

Völuspa's words are: 'The gods found Ask and Embla (the first man and woman) on the earth with little power and without destiny. Spirit they had not; *odr* they had not, neither *la* nor *laeti*, nor the form of the gods. Odin gave them spirit, Honer gave *odr*, Loder gave *la* and the form of the gods.' "[1]

La means blood, and *læti*, united with *la*, means the way in which a conscious being moves and acts. *Odr* seems to have to do with inherited features and attributes. Loder also gives *litr goda*, the form of the gods.

"To understand this expression" (Rydberg writes) "we must bear in mind that the Teutons, like the Hellenes and Romans, conceived the gods in human form, and that the image which characterizes man was borne by the gods alone before man's creation, and originally belonged to the gods. To the hierologists and the skalds of the Teutons, as to those of the Greeks and Romans, man was created *in effigiem deorum*, and therefore had in his nature a divine image in the real sense of this word, a *litr goda*. Nor was this *litr goda* a mere abstraction to the Teutons, or an empty form, but a created *efni* dwelling in man, and giving shape and character to the earthly body which is visible to the eye. . . . Certain persons were regarded as able to separate their *litr* from its union with the other factors of their being, and to lend it, at least for a short time, to some other person in exchange for his."[2]

In spite of the fact that the *litr* could be, so to say, detached and occupy another position in space, the author is emphatic that the abstract conception of matter versus mind was alien to early Teuton thought. Every part of a man's being was material and actual, although some parts were of finer grain than others.

"Thus man has within him an inner body, made in the image of the gods, and consisting of a finer material, a body which is his *litr*, by virtue of which his coarser vehicle, formed from the earth, received that form by which it impresses itself on the minds of others."

[1] Rydberg, *Teuton Mythology*, p. 495. [2] *Ibid.*

In this form, when the coarser elements are left behind at death, the hero travels through the "deep dales," across the thorn-fields and subterranean rivers, and over the gold-clad *Gjallu*-bridge to Hades.

This conception of the *litr* has two features which are of great psychological interest. As the original form of the gods, borne by them before the creation of man, it corresponds to the Platonic archetype, the pre-existing Form. But besides being thus the general archetype of man, it is also and quite essentially a man's unique individuality, his essential self, that element by which he takes part in the divine nature.

To the unanalytical mind this union of the individual and the general in a single conception offers no difficulty. It is only when we begin to think about it that we encounter its inherent paradox. Jung's conception of individuality or self also embraces a similar duality in a single idea. He conceives it as an archetypal potential that is either created or left dormant by the individual according to the value given to it. From this point of view individuality is an inherited idea of universal potency as well as a unique individual achievement.

In Indian philosophy it is the self, not the soul, that is considered imperishable. The soul belongs to the realm of *maya* and can be distraught by illusory goals; but the self is Atman, "within the heart," and cannot be enslaved by error.

From this angle the battle that is being waged on the spiritual plane between the metamorphosed dragon and the *litr* of Siegfried can be viewed as the essential conflict of our time. In it we sense the birth-throes of a new conception of man. The hero is born when the time is ripe, and *Nothung* must remain buried deep in the trunk of the tree until the hero comes for whom it was prepared. When its blade was broken by Wotan's spear, the pieces awaited the coming of the hero who could forge them into the perfect sword. In the same way the Rhinegold was guarded by the dragon until the arrival of the hero, and was returned again to the Rhine at his death. Everything awaits the hero's coming: although the long-predicted event must come about, it can happen only when the hero wills it. Fafner, the unhappy, defrauded giant, was impaled upon the miser's fear of losing his hoard. Wotan himself was shadowed by the fear of Alberich's curse. Yet neither could be delivered or despatched except by the one "who was without fear."

In the manner of his death Socrates proved that as soon as individual consciousness had developed beyond the level of the earlier truth the gods, in their old form, had to go. Often the old god provides the weapon—*i.e.*, the idea—which brings about his own end. Wotan himself thrusts into the guardian tree the sword *Nothung*, by whose efficacy his spear of authority is finally shattered. The idea was first wielded by Siegmund, the father and forerunner of the hero, but in his hand it was not strong enough to cleave the spear of the god. It had to be reduced to powder, and its basic elements recreated into a new individual truth, before it could achieve the effective deed.

An historical example of this mythological theme is provided by the conquest of the Pharaonic ideal by the Christian revelation. In Egypt, as in other imperial civilizations of antiquity, the King was himself the god, and, because of his divine nature, he alone participated in the immortality of the sun. But the idea of immortality was vested only in him; the common people had no part in the divine nature.

This central idea of the Pharaonic religion was metaphorically reduced to powder. In other words, it sank into the unconscious, where it was recreated through combining with its opposite principle—namely, the natural communism of the human family—emerging again as the spirit of a new religion.

In the Christian revelation this royal idea became the Kingdom of Heaven, the individual truth which vanquished the Pharaonic ideal and undermined every throne that rested upon slavery. Democracy is rooted in the mystical truth that the soul of the slave is as good as the soul of Cæsar in the eyes of God.

The idea waits until the time is ripe for the hero to be born. It might even be said that the idea creates the individual needed to utter it.

But if the essence of our subject's dream is concerned with the birth of a new conception of man, why should this event be conceived as a battle ? At bottom, every birth is a battle between individuality and nature. This fact is expressed in the principle that every directional impulse gains its direction and momentum through the overcoming of a specific resistance. Everything that has ever been launched found its direction by overcoming a definite initial resistance. But for this opposition, energy would be dissipated and directional momentum lost. The principle is equally valid whether applied to the act of throwing a ball, to archery, golf, sailing, to the process of birth, or to the realization of a new truth.

In the realm of religious myth the resisting power is personified as the Devil: " that power which ever willeth evil while ever creating the good." The Devil is an archetypal content of the collective unconscious, personifying the archaic features of the self that have not been assimilated by consciousness. In unconscious fantasy the higher aspects of the self appear idealized, as, for example, Zarathustra in Nietzsche's psychology. This ideal figure is counterbalanced by the ugliest man, who stands in the path of the superman, demanding to be dealt with before the further goal can be realized.

As Jung points out in *Psychological Types*, the severance of the ideal from the archaic aspects of the self becomes extreme in Christian psychology in the figures of Christ and anti-Christ. The existence of this dangerous split in the Christian psyche helps to explain the desperate instability of our world.

In our analysis of the painting which constellated the present dream we discovered the archetype of individuality as a dynamic idea taking form out of the dissolution of the traditional structure, the cruciform shape giving place to the square bounded by the four towers. In the structural metamorphosis of the painting, the historical aspect of the conflict, suggested by the cathedral itself and by the presence of the transitional tower, contained no hint of the pagan struggle. Why should the inclusion of the inferior function entail, then, so vast an upheaval ? Why cannot the dragon eventually be assimilated by the Church, like every other heresy ?

As representative of the principle of evil the dragon cannot be assimilated by the Christian psyche. Some means must be found of resolving the absolute opposition of good and evil: as impossible for the ascetic King to resolve the conflict as for a knight of the Grail to regain the sacred Spear. Only the one who is detached from either side can be the deliverer. Siegfried is the ideal hero to play this rôle; for not only did he vanquish the dragon, but he himself assimilated its essential quality, therewith gaining an immediate understanding or pact with nature.

IX

On the side of the Devil we have also remarked an interesting metamorphosis, the result, presumably, of association with an impersonal dynamic conception of psychic conditions. Under this Oriental aspect the soul is seen as a field of natural forces.

This idea is not entirely new to the West. In his visionary attempt to resolve the Christian cleavage William Blake created a similar dynamic conception of the Devil. The following citations from *The Marriage of Heaven and Hell* reveal the poet's need to reject the downright antithesis of Christian orthodoxy in his longing to reconcile the opposites in his own nature. The chapter bears the title " The Voice of the Devil."

" All bibles, or sacred codes, have been the causes of the following errors:

(1) That Man has two real existing principles—viz., a body and a soul.

(2) That Energy, call'd Evil, is alone from the Body, and that Reason, call'd Good, is alone from the Soul.

(3) That God will torment Man in Eternity for following his Energies.

But the following contraries to these are true.

(1) Man has no body distinct from his Soul, for that call'd Body is a portion of the Soul discern'd by the five Senses, the chief inlets of Soul in this age.

(2) Energy is the only life, and is from the Body, and Reason is the bound, or outward circumference of Energy.

(3) Energy is Eternal Delight."

In the preceding chapter we read:

> " Without Contraries is no progression. Attraction and Repulsion, Reason and Energy, Love and Hate, are necessary to human existence.
>
> " From these Contraries spring what the religious call Good and Evil.
>
> " Good is the passive that obeys Reason; Evil is the active springing from Energy.
>
> " Good is Heaven. Evil is Hell."

Blake experienced the antitheses of his nature with such intensity that heaven and hell had to be reconciled. Creation he knew, from terrible inner experience, was impossible without conflict. He also knew that the energy which could create a new world sprang from the archaic roots of human nature. But from the very intensity of his acceptance of the dynamic aspect of life he was in danger of forfeiting those benefits of reason upon which, apart from everything else, intelligible communication depends. He adds a note at the end of the chapter quoted above showing where his quest for a solution had led him (namely, among the partisans of the repressed antithesis): " The reason Milton wrote in fetters when he wrote of Angels and God, and at liberty when of Devils and Hell, is because he was a true Poet and of the Devil's party without knowing it."[1]

It is interesting to observe the way in which the character of Satan develops throughout Blake's drawings. In a relatively early painting, representing the battle between Michael and Satan in heaven, the Devil is depicted as a vast spiny snake with a human head, but without wings. In subsequent drawings Satan is a god-like figure of immense power, sometimes with dragon-wings, as in " Satan exulting over Eve," and sometimes without, as in " Satan calling up his Legions."

Turning again to the battle in our dream, we are instructed on both occasions that the soul of Siegfried is able to vanquish the dragon in the moment when the hero begins his death-song. Yet the victory of the soul coincides with the spontaneous dissolution of the cathedral. This cannot mean

[1] William Blake, *Marriage of Heaven and Hell.*

victory in the traditional sense of extermination or repression of the dragon, for if this were intended the victory would reinforce the existing structure, not disintegrate it.

The song of the dying king-hero (accompanied by the choir) must be regarded, therefore, as a ritual act of deliverance, giving the sign for the passing of the old form and the heralding of the new. This conception—namely, the death of the old and the birth of the new—is confirmed by the brilliant light and colour which floods the cathedral. And we must not miss the significance of the human choir which heralds the symbolical event. It is as though the dream were saying, "Two thousand years ago the angelic choir heralded the birth of the divine Being who came to earth to save mankind. To-day the human choir heralds the birth of the redeeming Idea which ascends to heaven to heal the angels who have been cut off from the refreshing streams of new life." Life contains every attribute and every quality, but the Christian heaven was doomed to contain only ideal attributes, since their opposites, by contact with which the life of the spirit is renewed, were cast out into hell with Satan.

Blake called this pasteurized heaven Urizen, by which he designated the militant prejudice which would fain split the living texture of reality into a rational intelligible order identified with God, and an irrational, energic, unpredictable, disturbing element conceived of as alien to God's plan.

In this connection the former patient's dream comes to mind, wherein the snake accuses him of his sins before God.

The chief of these sins consisted in his identification of one woman with sex, another with spirit. This attempt to reduce emotional reality to labelled categories stultifies the possibility of creative adaptation. Moreover, the person who is so unfortunate as to become identified with one or other of the ideal attributes for which everyone professes veneration knows from bitter experience how utterly lifeless and boring a whole heaven of ideals must be. In the age of Victorian respectability collective ideals were publicly venerated as dignified figures in stone. It has been observed that people misguided enough to play an ideal rôle too successfully are liable to acquire the same statuesque dignity and to feel almost as cold to the touch.

Into this tepid upper zone, the green, rejuvenated dragon ascends out of the historical unconscious. But when the Devil was rejected from the idealized Christian conscious, he joined forces with other living elements of pre-Christian paganism in the unconscious. It is therefore entirely in harmony with psychological affinities that the revived dragon should form a constellation with the soul of Siegfried.

In the very moment when this dynamic event dominates the heavens the disintegration of the cathedral begins. The synchronicity of these two events in the dream reveals the operation of the irrational principle. There is no logical or rational connection between the fight in the heavens and the break-up of the cathedral. Yet they are essentially coincident events, in the sense that the same fateful constellation embraces both. This synchronicity is an aspect of causality to be understood emotionally or intrinsically; it is complementary to the principle of causality as conceived in the West. It is the modality of the natural mind and, as enshrined in the *Yi King*, is the root-principle of Chinese philosophy.

Another aspect of the spontaneous activity of the dragon is seen in the way the church disintegrates. There is no question of earthquake, or landslide, or even defect in structure. In a word, tbere is no rational material cause. From the dreamer's description, it is clear that the cathedral breaks up because certain individual stones assume independent activity. They behave like the energic elements within the atom which seem to possess their own peculiar freedom of movement. It is as though a complex and somewhat unstable molecule began to disintegrate, certain of its atomic constituents having elected to assume their original independence.

Throughout the course of this work we have frequently observed the operation of these two irrational principles in the products of the unconscious. If, indeed, we were asked to name the key-principles of autonomous mental activity, synchronicity and independence would have to be given as its most distinctive attributes. What I have termed dragon-effects in this work are manifestations of this kind of activity.

We could as well say that things begin to behave in the instinctual fashion. Unless we are free to assume that instinct works in this arational fashion, we must either overwork the theory of accidental coincidence or choose to ignore altogether this aspect of psychical reality. In either case we are precluded from any understanding of unconscious activity.

It has been observed that schizoid subjects (particularly in the case of men) are especially liable to rationalistic prejudice and one-sidedness. It is usually a defence mechanism, due to an instinctive fear of the archaic contents. The fear is justifiable, because the one-sidedness of his psychology renders the schizoid subject peculiarly liable to assaults from the dissociated other side. Hence the rational sceptic is not infrequently seduced into highly irrational conduct or superstitious belief, which he then proceeds to defend with as much vehemence as he had formerly used to condemn.

In so far as our subject had developed an intellectual position, designed to withstand every invasion from the unconscious, we might be justified in regarding these dragon-effects in the dream as the irruption of the irrational element of the unconscious into his traditional conscious edifice. We should be on perfectly safe ground if we took this limited view of the dream, and we could then regard the whole drama as a psycholeptic crisis with its characteristic feeling-symptom of the end of the world.

From the standpoint of scientific demonstration it would seem plausible to view this whole series of drawings as a personal, subjective record of a dissociated personality attempting to gain control over the unconscious. The further question as to whether, and how far, the individual problem was rooted in and therefore a part of the general collective background would come into consideration only when we were faced with material which could not conceivably be fitted into the personal framework.

The natives of Mount Elgon, who were entirely realistic in regard to their dreams, told us that when anyone had a "doctor" dream he took it to the headman, who would immediately summon the men of the tribe to a palaver. The ordinary personal dreams, on the other hand, were hardly noticed. Among primitives, therefore, the subjective valuation of the dreamer in respect to his dream is treated as seriously as, for instance, the excitement of a man coming in with a report of having seen the enemy on the war-path, or a rogue elephant near the village. Moreover, a psychiatric objection to the dream, on the ground that the subject is a pathological case, would have no weight at all among peoples whose survival depends upon their instinctual vigilance. In point of fact, the mediumistic function of the unstable personality is especially prized among primitive communities, and the authority and prestige of the *laibon* or *shaman* rest very largely upon his familiarity with the spirit-world and his ability to interpret dreams and augurs and other instinctual data.

X

A more cogent consideration supporting the hypothesis that the dream should be given a general as well as an individual significance consists in the fact that dreams of the break-up of a traditional structure occur with relative frequency in the dream-life of men and women of the present day. I have collected a number of such dreams, some from patients undergoing analytical treatment, others from friends and colleagues who are in no sense morbidly dissociated.

The following is the dream of a colleague who had idly overheard, in the conversation of two friends the day before, some allusion to the theme of a church collapsing. She has very kindly allowed me to make use of it.

" I was in a great cathedral built on an island in the estuary of a river (reminiscent of St. Michael's Mount or Mont St. Michel). I looked out of one of the windows, which was clear and very large, and saw the horizon swinging up and down. For an instant I thought we were on a violently rolling ship, then remembered it was a cathedral and realized that a great building, rocking in this way, must soon come crashing down. I started running to escape, and then thought, ' I must save the children,' and turned back. There were only a few people, also hurrying to escape, but there was a sense of more somewhere in the building. I found one child, dressed in white, and took it by the hand and ran. There were a few of us together.

" The bells of the cathedral were ringing a wild peal. I thought how the bell-ringers were staying at their posts in order to warn people. For the destruction which would come with the fall of the cathedral would spread beyond the building itself, and therefore the bell-ringers would inevitably be killed. There was something magnificent about the great rocking building and the clashing bells keeping to their tunes.

" We hurried on out of the cathedral, through the bishop's palace which touched it. This was a low, dark building; the corridors were absolutely dark. I had taken in my arms and was carrying a rather older child with a stiff hip, and had handed over the other child to someone else.

" I had a sense of the bishop—an old, old man—somewhere in the recesses of the palace. At last we came out at the far end of the palace and went straight off the island into water. We found ourselves in the water before we knew. It was shallow, a little over our knees, and dark. I saw it was full of dark reeds. We waded about a little, then turned back and for a time could not find the island, only more and more reedy water.

" Then we were on the island and walked up on to the top of the bishop's palace—now very low and covered with an enormous black tarpaulin. The palace was hummocky under it (like a temporary cover during reconstruction).

" We walked back and were in a hotel where the cathedral had been. The rooms were high and comfortless—rather sordid, even. There was a bar and a good many people about.

" A group of young girls came up to me. They had escaped on to the mainland, which I pictured as flat and salty and sandy. They had a donkey with them. They had gathered some succulent plants, some in flower, and had labelled them. These they brought and eagerly showed to me. One of the girls was one I had heard of the day before and whose photograph had been shown me. She was the daughter of an American millionaire who had volunteered as secretary to someone in the Grenfell Mission in Newfoundland."

I do not propose to analyse this dream, but merely to indicate certain significant points which demonstrate its general character. The personal aspect of the dream I am not at liberty to discuss.

The situation of the cathedral, on a raised island in the estuary of a river, suggests the point of emergence where the individual life-stream empties itself or becomes merged in the general unconscious. The allusion to Mont St. Michel relates the cathedral to something that has become insulated, or cut off from its original connections, like an island that has been gradually separated from the mainland by the invasion of the sea. The association with St. Michael may also be significant, since he was the leader of the heavenly hosts who overthrew Satan and his angels. In the Book of Daniel Michael is named as one of the chief " princes " of the host of heaven. The name therefore belongs to early Hebrew mythology and is probably connected with Marduk, the light-god of early Babylonian myth, who overthrew Tiamat and the forces of chaos and darkness.

The principle of the independent activity of the unconscious is implicit in the fact that there is no mention of any external cause, and that the rocking of the cathedral is felt as the movement of the sea.

The sense of general catastrophe is present in both dreams, but the impulse to rescue is stronger in the second. The heroism of the bell-ringers is paralleled by the steadfastness of the choir-singers in the previous dream. Both symbolize disciplined functions which remain steady in emergency, therewith transforming a catastrophic collapse into a victory of the human spirit. In both dreams the passing of the traditional form is accompanied by a sense of vivid beauty and magnificence, and in both we have the feeling of an inevitable, ordered process, notwithstanding the fact that it results in widespread destruction.

The child rescued by the dreamer symbolizes the emergent individuality or future potential, while the bishop, who is immensely old and associated by the dreamer with her father, represents the venerable spirit of the past, personified in the former dream by the moribund Christian King. The old man and the young girl are the familiar mythic pair symbolizing the backward and forward extension of the psychic continuity. Tobit and Sara, Simon Magus and Helen, Lao-Tzŭ and the dancing-girl, the ancient Keeper of the Fire and Ayesha—these and a hundred others embody the wisdom of age joining hands with the desire of youth. Through the mutual attraction of these opposites, the unbroken stream of psychic value is eternally safeguarded. The older child with the stiff hip, the low, dark buildings and the dark corridors seem to refer to the adverse effect of past influences on the present situation. The child with the stiff hip is associated with a relative of the dreamer who, as a girl, had tuberculous disease of the hip-joint, but was cured of it. Recently the possibility of pregnancy had arisen, and a surgeon had passed the pelvis as perfectly sound, finding no ground at all for guarding against pregnancy. Though these allusions have naturally an important bearing for the dreamer, they do not contradict the wider interpretation.

The emergence from the far end of the palace is analogous to the birth of the Son of Man from the west end of the cathedral in the final painting. It clearly refers to the moment of individual emergency or departure from the traditional container or pattern. Walking off the island into the water represents the instinctive search in the unconscious for something secure to take the place of the old order that is passing away. There may also be an allusion to the deluge here, and to Noah's human longing to find solid earth again. The dreamer associated the dark, reedy water with the film of the sinking of the *Panay*. The survivors took refuge in thick rushes, thereby escaping extermination. The reeds represent, therefore, a temporary asylum.

The return to the island reveals that the bishop's palace is undergoing reconstruction. The motif of reconstruction is found in the epilogue to our patient's dream, and in both cases the salving instinct is related to the feminine principle. The stronger emphasis on salvage and reconstruction in the second dream is probably due to the fact that a woman dreamed it.

The comfortless hotel with its sordid atmosphere is

peculiar to the second dream; this again is probably the woman's reaction to the extreme discomforts and uncertainty of life inseparable from a transitional period, the hotel being the classical symbol of transition.

The group of young girls who went scouting on the mainland represent an intuitive advance-guard, analogous to that of Joshua and his fellow-scouts in the land of Canaan, or to Noah's dove. The flat, sandy wilderness resembles the flat, expectant earth in the last painting. Its salty character might again refer to the idea of the deluge, for it is a land from which the sea has recently receded and it is not yet fit for cultivation. The donkey symbolizes the sagacity of the instinct in a critical situation, as in the case of Balaam's ass.

The gathering and labelling of the succulent plants is in keeping with the idea of exploring the possibilities of a new land, where experience has to be gained by the method of trial and error. The dreamer also associated the sending of new exotic plants to Kew to be named and, if possible, hybridized for the purpose of cultivation. Adam's work of naming the animals and plants here occurs to the mind. Again there is the suggestion of people being cast up on a new land, where everything relevant to food, shelter, and other vital needs is greeted with significant appraisal.

The reference to the girl who gave up her privileged security as a millionaire's daughter in order to volunteer for pioneering work on the outskirts of civilization accords with the whole feeling of the dream. Here is no rejection of the Christian tradition or of Western civilization; rather is it a realization that the old order had to go, in order to make room for the new, towards which the spirit of man is already migrating. People who have had this realization must either range themselves with the new order, resolved, with the dreamer, to salvage the essential values of the past, or succumb to a sense of hopeless despair.

A very remarkable " dream " of the same genre is the famous dream of Raskolnikov, in Dostoievsky's *Crime and Punishment*. Raskolnikov was a hero with whom the author obviously identified himself. Whether the dream was actually dreamed or merely invented by Dostoievsky is psychologically of small importance; in either case it has the self-evident character of prophetic fantasy.[1]

Raskolnikov dreamed that—

> " The whole world was condemned to a terrible new strange plague that had come to Europe from the depths of Asia. All were to be destroyed except a very few chosen. Some new sorts of microbes were attacking the bodies of men, but these microbes were endowed with intelligence and will. Men attacked by them became at once mad and furious. But never had men considered themselves so intellectual and so completely in possession of the truth as these sufferers, never had they considered their decisions, their scientific conclusions, their moral convictions so infallible. Whole villages, whole towns and peoples went mad from the infection. All were excited and did not understand one another. Each thought that he alone had the truth and was wretched looking at the others, beat himself on the breast, wept, and wrung his hands. They did not know how to judge and could not know whom to blame, whom to justify. Men killed each other in a sort of senseless spite. They gathered together in armies against one another, but even on the march the armies would begin attacking each other, the ranks would be broken and the soldiers would fall on each other, stabbing and cutting, biting and devouring each other. The alarm bell was ringing all day long in the towns; men rushed together, but why they were summoned and who was summoning them no one knew. The most ordinary trades were abandoned, because everyone proposed his own ideas, his own improvements, and they could not agree. The land too was abandoned. Men met in groups, agreed on something, swore to keep together, but at once began on something quite different from what they had proposed. They accused one another, fought and killed each other. There were conflagrations and famine. All men and all things were involved in destruction. The plague spread and moved further and further. Only a few men could be saved in the whole world. They were a pure, chosen people, destined to found a new race and a new life, to renew and purify the earth, but no one had seen these men, no one had heard their words and their voices."

In view of what has taken place in Russia during the present century (half a century after the above was written) it is impossible not to regard this dream as prophetic in an

[1] *Crime and Punishment* was written in 1866.

almost literal sense. That the purposeful microbes represent an archaic activation of the general unconscious, and that the infection described has spread to other European countries, is also beyond reasonable doubt. It is understandable that Dostoievsky's dream should have more of the end-of-the-world character than those of contemporary men and women. Apart from the fact that his genius was deeply rooted in a pathological constitution, the world in which Dostoievsky lived has long since actually come to an end. The confusion of purpose in the dream, the loss of moral values and sense of obligation, the killing and attacking without reason, the crazy individualism and suicidal unrelatedness—all these painfully familiar symptoms, whether appearing in the individual or in the State, belong to a condition in which consciousness is inundated by the unconscious. The decent landmarks of reasonable existence are submerged; in a word, there is a psychical deluge.

XI

Resuming the discussion of our patient's dream, we observe that, at the first sign of the traditional constituents leaving the church and assuming an independent freedom of action, an immediate conservative reaction takes place on the part of two dignitaries or custodians of the cathedral. (Note the word "dignitaries" and the ironical exaggeration of conventional outrage.)

Undifferentiated, static functions are frequently represented as twins or pairs by the dream-mind. Opposition being a product of consciousness, a not yet differentiated pair of opposites will necessarily appear in the unconscious as undistinguishable twins. From the standpoint of psychical equilibrium, we might also regard the action of the two dignitaries as an instantaneous response of the equilibriating function of the mind to impending catastrophe. This inference is borne out by certain clear indications of loss of control. Up to this point in the dream the dreamer has been composed, even somewhat detached, describing events from the individual angle of the first person singular. But as soon as he has recorded the deliberate movement of the collapse, "like a glacier sliding into the sea," he reverts to the collective "we," and his behaviour betrays obvious signs of panic. It is significant also to note the synchronicity of wholesale catastrophe with this psycholeptic reaction of the dreamer. Individuality is submerged beneath a tidal wave of general terror. *We* run, *we* yell, and *we* stand at a distance. *People* start streaming towards the door, a *group* of girls is crushed and a *few* survivors stand about.

Reversion to panic means annihilation of conscious values. It is imperative, therefore, that the dreamer be warned against this moral collapse. Hence the repetition of the whole scene. In dream language repetition means "Look out!" In the repetition of the scene a new feature is introduced; instead of the atomic elements of the traditional structure, a stone statue walks out. A statue being an attempt to immortalize an ideal quality, it is as though the historical soul of the Christian edifice had come to life and were migrating towards a new form. The form of a thing is maintained so long as it is decently wedded to its function. But as soon as the purpose it served is better expressed by a new form, its soul departs and the old form decays. Sentimental considerations may persuade us to embalm the dead, but the embalmed body has no soul. It no longer serves its original indwelling purpose, but only a secondary one imposed upon it by a pious posterity.

To the natural mind of a savage everything that functions is possessed of a soul. In a very real sense its function and purpose is the soul of a thing. The particles of wood and metal of which a boat consists will cohere together in a reliable and stable form just so long as it maintains its essential function. When it can no longer serve any useful purpose, it will soon decay, disrupt, or be destroyed, and the particles, now cohering in a disciplined firmness, will disband and be released from their service.

In this respect the psyche is like the boat, the indispensable vehicle of human purpose and communication. In its development from the primitive canoe to the 50,000-ton battleship the idea of the boat expands to the varying purposes of the civilized mind. But canoe and battleship both rely on the same fundamental principles for their successful adaptation. Just as the boat, with rudder, keel and sail, symbolizes the adapting purpose of man, so the psyche expresses the power of the idea. It is as much the creation as the vehicle of the idea. We marvel that men on a relatively primitive level of culture could make the temple at Stonehenge. But what is Stonehenge but an impressive statement of the power of the primordial image, prompting an equally impressive feat of practical intelligence?

The incident of the statue can be regarded, therefore, as an explanatory symbol of what is happening to the cathedral. For when an ideal is publicly venerated, or enshrined in a sacred edifice, it is usually a sign that men have discarded this virtue in the conduct of their lives. The enthronement of Reason in Notre Dame during the French Revolution, and the more recent example of the great palace at Geneva devoted to the ideal of Peace, occur straightway to the mind. Before virtue congeals into stone it is an essential, innate quality of the living being; but when it is taken from its natural soil and elevated to a higher sphere its virtue seems to depart from it. It has become a show-piece, garlanded with flowers at suitable intervals for educational or other less creditable purposes, but it no longer lives. Yet no spiritual quality can suffer death: it remains latent, like the sword *Nothung*, until it is needed by the heroic spirit of a new age.

From this point of view the self-moving stones and statues of the cathedral represent a resurrection of dead ideals, and the great church itself is seen as a great mausoleum, a fair monument to the heroic age of Christendom. This historical standpoint is actually alluded to in the dreamer's description of the scene. For first there is the impression of a man in white armour. Then the two dignitaries strike at the figure with axes, weapons more in keeping with the Inquisition or the Crusades than with the sober churchman of to-day.

What, then, is contained in the dynamic conception of the soul which could have such a revolutionary effect? Conceive how it would be if, instead of the soul-tormenting see-saw of salvation or perdition, the reciprocal play of opposites within the soul were accepted and understood in the same way as, for instance, the balancing interaction of heat and cold, light and darkness, sea and land, heaven and earth, male and female, conscious and unconscious, and so on. Under the protection of this truth the cruelty of the ideal absolute could no longer seize upon the soul.[1] To become reconciled again to nature's ways, the original mother; to gain therewith a sense of acceptance and certainty, all the more satisfying because no authority can intervene—this too is contained in the new truth.

The condition of inner necessity is the best possible safeguard against the risk of this dangerous truth falling into the wrong hands, inasmuch as only those who are moved by necessity are able to learn, and hold steadfastly to, the efficacy of the new way. The quality of the subjective experience is such that, when the solution is found, it is felt to be an individual relative truth. It is this realization which saves a man from the two worst pitfalls, collective propaganda on the one hand, and isolated individualism on the other.

* * * * *

We have come far from our original starting-point, following the dreamer's quest of his lost instinct. Like a hound on the scent, the dream-logic seemed to follow a trail, back through historical Christianity to the suppressed pagan antithesis. If this logic means anything at all, it means that the subject's inferior relation to the vital instinct is rooted in a general ancestral crime, and that this crime demands individual expiation.

The crime is laid at the door of the militant organization which strove to prove its absolute rightness and authority by asserting every other doctrine to be false. In its totalitarian efforts to suppress Mithraism and Gnosticism and every other possible rival in the religious field, the Church also disowned its own pagan roots through which it gained its deep mythological continuity with the past. An absolute claim to truth can be maintained only at the expense of all former truths.

[1] Arthur Waley in *The Way and its Power*, contrasting the moral dualism of Zoroastrianism with the natural dualism of *Yin* and *Yang*, writes (p. 112): " In Zoroastrianism darkness is essentially evil; the principle of light, essentially good. The fundamental conception of *yin* and *yang* is quite different. They are two interdependent and complementary facets of existence, and the aim of *yin-yang* philosophers was not the triumph of light, but the attainment in human life of perfect balance between the two principles."

Hence the very soil and matrix from which the new truth had emerged were disowned and rejected. In the human sphere such a rejection of the mother has always been regarded as the worst impiety. Is it, then, permissible for the gods to do things which even the most degraded among men would regard as outrageous? This was the defence of Socrates when charged with contaminating the Athenian youth with impious ideas. He dared to criticize the behaviour of the gods in the form in which tradition had handed them down—not the gods themselves, but rather the false conception of the gods which could no longer be revered.

An historical crime cannot be expiated by merely turning the tables. A totalitarian victory of the pagan antithesis, which is actually being attempted in Russia and Germany, could spell only worse disaster, inspired as it always is by resentment and fanaticism. Fanaticism must be cruel, because, as Jung has pointed out, it expresses the over-compensation of a hidden doubt.

The solution offered by the dream is based upon no absolute: rather does it sing the truth of relativity. In this solution the two protagonists of the pagan-Christian conflict are merged into one central figure whose voluntary death-song symbolizes an expiation of the ancient crime. In this symbolical renunciation of power the Church yields to a more humane conception of the religious impulse in man.

The truth of relativity is implied (1) in the choice of Siegfried as the celestial adversary of the dragon, inasmuch as Siegfried was himself changed and renewed by assimilating the dragon's virtue; (2) in the transformation of the dragon into a celestial power; and (3) in the independent activity of the individual stones and statues formerly held in subjection by the Christian absolute.

Relativity, in its application to human lives, fathers those truths to which the individual heart can respond. But only those who have retained the wild creature's instinct for discriminating the good from the poisonous can understand the saving value of a relative truth. Those who have lost this instinct, and with it a belief in the validity of their own thinking, must flock to the ideological absolute, which demands neither judgment, thought, nor feeling, but only blind submission.

The absolutist claim is necessarily collective in character, and, in so far as it is impelled by a millennial or utopian dream, it often assumes the proportions of a tidal wave, carrying all before it. Relative truth never develops this mass enthusiasm or frenzy. Its cogency rests in the agreement of the individual heart and head, not upon stupendous displays of unanimity.

Unanimity is demanded as a national necessity only when a certain common objective calls everyone to its service, as in the case of war, migration, or national consolidation, for in order to reach a distant objective leadership and collective submission are indispensable. Thus the absolutist claim is favoured during periods of transition or spiritual migration, when the biological archetype of the leader and the herd takes natural precedence over other instinct-patterns. Relative truth, on the other hand, corresponds to the phase of settlement, when the cultivation of individual vigilance, well-being and independence has a superior value to mere collective expansion. Collective migrations are always attended by grave risk, because of the irresistible momentum of the human flood, whether actual or spiritual, which has been set in motion. The setting up of an ideological absolute can be viewed, then, as an instinctive attempt to counter this risk. For the problem of archaism versus control is as urgent in the collective as in the individual psyche. It follows, therefore, that during the migratory phase individuation, with its preference for relative truths, must, to a large extent, be repressed.

If only it were possible to regard these opposing viewpoints, not as eternal statements of human enlightenment to be passionately defended to the last drop of blood, but as the necessary expressions of alternating phases in social evolution, the threatened catastrophe of civilization might be averted.

In point of fact the absolutist collective claim is never absolute, since individual freedom of mind cannot be annihilated. Beneath the collectivist crust we find the deathless human claim of individuality, which develops all the more passion and vigour because of suppression. The power of this idea is the eventual ruler of man's destiny. Every collective system or institution which has attempted in the past to crush out this indestructible idea has collapsed. Since it is the most potent thing in nature, only that political organization can have permanent validity which is grounded upon individuality as a basic fact.

XII

Our interpretation of the conflict between the soul of Siegfried and the rejuvenated dragon as a dynamic event introduces once again a Chinese parallel. In my possession I have a Chinese symbolical painting. It is painted on glass and represents the birth of the dragon from the pairs of opposites.[1]

The background consists of two mountains, the level of the one on the left being somewhat higher than that on the right. In the foreground two adversaries fight with swords; the one on the left is on foot, the one on the right mounted. The contestants are wearing masks symbolical of opposing passions. In the centre of the picture, below the level of the mountains and above that of the human adversaries, there is a dæmonic female deity seated on a piebald horse. In her arms she bears an infant, and from the top of the infant's head emerges a blood-coloured stream. This stream ascends and expands, becoming a fiery flood which fills the heavens. In the midst of this stream of fire is seen the newly born dragon.

This painting epitomizes the dynamic naturalistic conception of psychical events which pervades the Chinese philosophy of life. The opposing mountain masses represent the idea of opposition on the cosmic plane, the difference of potential between the two levels being clearly intended to indicate the basic condition under which energy is generated. The balance created by the opposing mountains above and by the human opposites below is an affirmation of the hermetic principle, " as above, so below." Nature within is the same as nature without, and energy generated within the soul is governed by the same laws as other natural processes.

The central figure on the piebald horse is a perfect example

[1] I regret that I am unable to reproduce this painting. Since writing the above it has been destroyed by fire.

of that principle which Jung has termed the *transcendent function.* The conflict of the opposites brings about a certain confluence of the two elements, whereby essential qualities of the one transcend across into the other and *vice versa.* This confluence is symbolized by the piebald horse. The dæmonic being who carries the child expresses the inevitable fact that, during the phase of conflict, the energy-process must be regarded as a power superordinated to conscious will and control. Regarded, therefore, as an aspect of cosmic energy conflict within the soul has a certain dæmonic or superhuman power which is indifferent alike to human good or evil and to personal happiness or misery.

The infant is the new beginning, the new idea, the new attitude or personality which is born of the conflict; it also reconciles the opposites. Strictly speaking, it is this product of the transcending opposites which Jung has termed the transcendent function. Again the issuc is stated in cosmic as well as human terms, the infant symbolizing the result on the personal, human level, while the dragon embodies its potential and invisible consequences. This identification of the infant with the dragon implies that every basic conflict is attended by an aura of incalculable effect. The visible result is only a partial statement of the issue.

From the examples I have given the reader will readily understand why allusions to Eastern ideas are liable to occur in a patient's material just at the critical juncture where the one thing needful is to be able to see things differently. These people are seriously seeking a more comprehensive view of themselves and of the universe than that provided by their own background. Naturally, only those who have felt cramped and stultified by the traditional view of the soul, which divided it arbitrarily into black and white, will be prompted to subject authoritative moral categories to psychological understanding. But once the sheep and the goats have escaped from their respective folds, they can never again be herded into authoritarian enclosures.

The problems of the soul are essentially remote from the authoritarian mentality, not because authority rests on historical precedent, but simply because it represents a collective principle that has to be enforced from above. Understanding, on the other hand, is only possible from below. A stable and reliable social order will be found eventually to rest on two reciprocal principles. The first is collective authority and discipline in all matters wherein conformity is indispensable, the second individual freedom of judgment in all matters which concern the life and health of the soul. Laws and statutes are as necessary for the one aspect of human existence as adult education and a wise and tolerant understanding of individual problems for the other.

* * * * *

The repetition of the final scene of the dream must be taken as the writing on the wall. Whatever the *Götterdämmerung* we have witnessed may portend for the world in general, we can now sum up what it means for the man who dreamed it. The self-moving activity of the stones and statues of the cathedral forms the essence of the message. The old order of authoritarian conformity is finished and the new dynamic conception of the soul has begun. If this dream means anything at all, it is saying that the one thing needful is to extend the range of consciousness beyond the traditional limits. The fact that the battle is waged outside and above the cathedral surely means that the issue cannot be grasped so long as the mind is narrowed by traditional blinkers. The subject has never belonged to the Church and is consciously no more concerned with the religious problem than was the former patient. Yet, in the creating of their individual myth, both subjects gravitated naturally towards the place where the god is born.

The birth of the god always signifies a deepening or intensification of consciousness through the release of libido from historical containers. But the break-up of the traditional container is a terrible event. From the fact that the subject was unaware of a religious problem, we know that the fundamental premises of his mind must have been taken for granted, just as we take for granted the structure of Westminster Abbey. The sudden independent activity of something believed to be as reliable as the earth itself is the most unnerving experience. It is like a betrayal of trust. Will the subject stand the test? Will he hold firm when he sees disruption all around him, carefully drilled functions claiming anarchic independence, and his whole intellectual fortress of control crashing metaphorically about his ears? As Christ predicted to Peter what his reaction would be when the real test came, so the dream depicts, twice over, how the subject will behave when his worst fears are aroused.

Whether the dream is held to refer to a widespread cataclysm in which he will be involved, or whether it portrays the disintegration of the traditional order in the subject's *Weltanschauung*, it is surely performing an essential psychological function. It is preparing the conscious attitude for a critical event. This is a vital function of the dream; it rests on the same common-sense principle as the training of the soldier, or the various forms of practice-drill which prepare people to meet terrifying emergencies in a reasonable spirit.

The spirit of reason in this case cannot be content with mere control of the atavistic tendency to panic. For if this were the case the careful historical preparation of the climax would have been pointless. The further aim of the dream is clearly to extend consciousness by means of the historical analogy. The dream-idiom is: as then, so now. In the first part of the dream, the relation between the common rights of the people and the power of the King formed an harmonious parallel. But in the second part the relation between Henry the Saint and his guest is rather that of the boa-constrictor to the animal in its coils. The Kings of the totalitarian Church allowed no freedom either in life or thought.

Fear of the atavistic relapse to paganism was the cause of the Church's cruelty and fanatical persecution, as of her attempt to gain absolute control within the soul. Henry the Saint seems to represent the high-water mark of ecclesiastical repression of the pagan without and the instinct within. Hence his metamorphosis into Siegfried would symbolize an essential yielding of the power-claim in favour of an enlightened acceptance of Nature and her laws. This voluntary surrender of the power-claim is perfectly expressed in the death-song of the King, accompanied by the disciplined choir.

In order to reach beyond the limits of the Church's jurisdiction, the subject has to accept responsibility for the historical totalitarian crime. There is no escape from the principle of maturity: Freedom of mind can be won only through accepting responsibility in full. All the injury he has inflicted upon his own nature has been done first of all by the Church to helpless men and women. And, like the Church, his tyrannizing was done ostensibly on principle, though actually in response to the same fear of atavism.

This does not mean to say that the subject was exceptionally arrogant in his intellectual control of the unconscious. But it does mean that he had an unusual capacity for consciousness, and that, if he could but understand what the dream was saying, he was singularly fitted to build the foundations of the more spacious Aquarian conception and to salvage a reborn instinct for his offspring, therewith helping to bring about the new order alluded to in the epilogue.

Little more needs to be said. The presence of this balanced design in the structure of the dream is evidence of the intrinsic power of the principle of psychic control, notwithstanding the manifest disintegration and panic. Regarding the scene of dissolution as part of this coherent structure, it must be taken, not as a prognostication of schizophrenic disintegration, but rather as the result of the shifting of libido-value from the old order to the new.

* * * * *

With immediate realism, the dream now confronts the subject with the problem suggested in Drawing 14. It is that of bringing his newly found truth into the realm of flesh-and-blood reality. The descent of the naked man (*i.e.*, man as he actually is) out of the dissolving church denoted the descent of the spirit into the flesh, or the new incarnation of the Idea. The dream and the painting are representations of the same event. One flows out of the other; hence the divine figure issuing from the cathedral belongs essentially to the content of the dream.

The age of faith which created the master-works of Gothic architecture no longer inspires stone and wood to become "fountains of praise." Lacking the millennial momentum, modern faith is more modest. Yet, if this visionary dream is to be believed, the angels are still taking a hand in the building of the new cathedral, though not visible to the eye.

The details of the epilogue are matter of fact. The lacquers are a familiar factor in the subject's daily occupation, the angels who bring them prefer bus-driving to chariots of fire, and the other human being in the dream is the woman to whom the subject is committed in marriage. Facts such as these need no elaboration. We see the god-value migrating from the great collective church (the ancestral spirit-house on the primitive level) to a new home, where it begins to create a new ideal of service.

No other interpretation of this epilogue will be found to make sense. But since the angels obviously prefer to work and travel incognito, it behoves us not to come too close to the new work. We must simply accept the fact that the god-value is moving from the sphere of the collective down into the individual relationship, and that this migration is actually sponsored and helped by the angels. Whatever we may think about it, it is certain that this event is pointing the way this life has to go.

Now that the solution has become visible, it is not hard to see why the vital human relationship should have become the site of the new cathedral. Uprooted from his background, the subject needed, more than anything, an instinctual tap-root to his life. As a borderline schizophrenic with the constant preoccupation of how to maintain reliable control, he needed to centralize his problem of emotional control in a secure relationship. Finally, because the disturbing symptoms appeared originally in the sphere of the marriage relationship, the healing extension of consciousness, which could bring his mature potentialities into effect, would be cultivated best in the same field.

This may also explain the statement that the six colours, representing the first beginnings of the new cathedral, have been brought from the North by the Angle bus-drivers. We know that the six colours refer to those the subject used in painting the last picture. Colours represent feeling-values, and it was just here that the subject was uncertain and negative. He tended to limit himself to line-drawing, because he doubted his competence with colours. His expression of feeling was handicapped in the same way. It is now clear that inhibition of feeling is necessarily bound up with repression of instinct. Whenever therefore libido is released from long-standing repression (*i.e.*, the birth of the god), the subjective experience is naturally expressed in terms of feeling.

The release of libido is represented as taking place on both planes. Above, the divine man is born out of the womb of the Church, while below the angels are depicted returning from the North, and rejoicing because they are high up in their buses and can see everything. The angels, in fact, are demonstrating in a very literal fashion that the attitude which accepts the instinctual inheritance as common to all mankind[1] affords the subject a more spacious range of individual consciousness. Therefore the birth of the god or the emergence of individuality as an effective power synchronises with the rediscovery of the instinct as the common birthright. But this rediscovery also entails a wider and deeper responsibility. It is as though the subject had first to release the whole of Christendom from an ancient incubus of shame before he could free his own instinct from its ignoble state. Such a labour lies clearly beyond human power; and so it falls to the angels to show the dreamer how to salve the threatened Christian values. Their remedy is symbolized by the ramshackle omnibus which, with fourth-dimensional facility, travels through historical time as easily as one may ride from Charing Cross to Bishopsgate. In this strange vehicle the deepest roots of individual freedom, the royal prerogative of man, are intertwined with that common inheritance of instinct which is free to all.

If the dream signifies that we have to learn to build psychical temples within the ancient field of the human relationship, it must also mean that a responsibility heretofore

[1] *Omnibus* means for all.

vested in God has returned to the human sphere. But, if the vessel of human destiny no longer sails under the guarantee of heaven, the individual man and woman must learn " to talk to their snake," and navigate their little craft as wisely as they can. The one thing, the only thing, which can heal the sufferings and dread of a tormented world is a deepening of individual consciousness. When the god-value descends into the human relationship, the relation becomes correspondingly vital and significant, but also more problematical. Marriage is a laboratory where consciousness can be generated, and consciousness is a force, perhaps, in the long run, the strongest force there is.

Drawing 27

The drawing which forms the frontispiece is also peculiarly fitted to bring this work to a close. Though not belonging to the series—it was drawn nearly three years after the analysis was finished—it none the less brings the series to a natural conclusion. It is a vision of the advent of the introverted principle to the Western world. In a remote legendary past the divine Boddhisatva was born from the lotus, filling the world with unimaginable radiance. Now again, among the high Alps in the midst of an anxious and troubled Europe, the same spirit calls man to be quiet and listen. Listen to what ?

In some notes kindly supplied with this drawing the subject tells of the way the drawing came to be. After a long spell of almost superhuman strain he had a great desire to escape to an isolated and remote hut in the mountains. As this thought came to him, immediately the summit of the mountain and the head of the Buddha appeared simultaneously in his mind's eye. With this there came an indescribable release of emotion and energy. The entire picture from start to finish took just under two hours of concentrated, almost feverish work. Reflecting upon his work, he had a feeling that he had written something whose words were familiar, but whose essential meaning escaped him.

A few days later he re-read *The Secret of the Golden Flower* and was very much struck by Wilhelm's description of the eight signs of the *Yi-King*. On a previous reading this had not interested him, and he had forgotten it. But now, realizing the psychological content of the trigrams, he felt that in some way he had embodied their essential spirit or meaning in the picture. The subject has a natural introverted interest in the older systems of the East; but he also thinks his inner ear may be peculiarly sensitive to Oriental suggestions from the unconscious on account of two hereditary factors. His grandfather held an official position in China and also explored Thibet, while his mother spent her early youth in Pekin. These facts are of great importance in our estimation of the subject's inherited unconscious disposition. Although no direct trace of Chinese influence was apparent in this series of drawings, he has made other fantasy productions where it was transparently present; and in general the subject's natural mood of introverted stoicism could easily have had its roots in China. The sense of release and commanding urgency which accompanied the making of this drawing also speak in favour of ancestral satisfaction, if one may be allowed to conceive the inherited unconscious in this way.

The subject began the drawing at the little mountain hut half-way up the mountain. This was the refuge for which he had longed. An immediate personal need seems, therefore, to have yielded the initial impulse of the drawing, though once under way, the impersonal, introverted principle took command of the drawing, and the full stature of a world-changing event began to emerge from the mist.

While he was doing this in Paris, his wife, in another part of Europe, painted a picture of a row of Alpine peaks whose slopes were obscured by a thick mist.[1] Below in the valley, issuing from beneath the blanket of fog, a winding stream appeared in much the same position in the field as the winged cobra of this drawing. Since both the subject and his wife were moved, quite independently, to represent the same theme in similar terms, we can assume an emotional identity between them. But in so far as the theme appears

[1] The fears of the wife obscured the creative value of the unconscious.

to be concerned with the new religious attitude, we are reminded of the prophecy contained in the dream-epilogue.

For the rest, the only points that need explanation are the winged snake, apparently blind, the little goat's head in the position of the navel, and the vertical exaggeration of the figure. In regard to the first, the subject tells me that the Alpine districts used to be fertile with legends about dragons. I have had no opportunity of following up this information, but, in view of the dragon's important rôle in the dream just discussed, the discovery of a dynamic pagan dragon-symbol in the middle of Europe would naturally have a peculiar significance for the subject.

With regard to the second, he tells me that he intended to draw a ram's head at the navel. This was suggested by the symbol of the ram governing the *Manipura chakra*—the navel centre—of the *Kundalini* system. " But," he adds, " somehow the ram came out as Aries the goat, in spite of more or less conscious intention to do otherwise."

All that might be germane to the third point is the subject's idea that the picture is " an attempt to reconcile the opposition between physical nature and spirit, or asceticism versus the instinct of the natural man, who wants to live in villages, close to the earth."

From these indications we obtain an insight into the unconscious conflict between East and West which the drawing as a whole seems to reconcile and unite. For example, the winged snake is associated with the dragon-legends of the Alps, which accords with our observation that in China the dragon is a celestial power as well as the dynamic mountain-spirit producing thunder- and rain-storms, lightning, clouds, and rivers. Compared with this developed conception, a blind cobra with almost embryonic wings would be like a tentative Western attempt, feeling its way towards a dynamic, naturalistic conception of the soul. The painting by the subject's wife, in which neither god nor dragon is yet manifest, but which depicts a river coming from behind the mist, is also in harmony with the Chinese point of view.

The snake issuing from the mouth of the Boddhisatva represents the idea of the Creative Logos descending upon the earth. In Drawing 25 this event was symbolized in Western cultural terms as the descent of the divine Man towards a barren, waiting earth. Here it is stated rather from the standpoint of the unconscious, as though so-called blind instinct became informed with the divine spirit and descended as a kind of contagion, as at the Feast of Pentecost. Thus the movement from the Western conception of the event of Drawing 25 to its present Eastern form involves perhaps the most important change of all, the depersonalization of the concept of deity.

With childish eagerness Christendom fastened upon the personality of Jesus, making Him into a marvel-producing God, while the spiritual principle, which, with a wealth of passionate imagery, He was inspired to make crystal-clear to his hearers, was relegated to a remote heaven. The plain fact has to be stated that Christ showed little interest in forming or founding a Church, but laboured with devoted passion to get people to see and experience the state He called the Kingdom of Heaven. Quite clearly this was to be achieved by becoming attuned to a governing vital principle. With the analogical method He instructed His hearers how to transform their attitude in accordance with this royal human principle, the efficacy of which He demonstrated abundantly in His life. Christ's Kingdom of Heaven was conceived, then, as an abstract principle similar to Tao.

In Lamaistic Buddhism disciples are warned against personifying spiritual principles as gods. All divine images are explained as an aspect of *maya*, which must eventually fall away and evaporate, for only then can the reality they contain be realized.

At this juncture we should be careful not to fall into the rationalistic fallacy of asserting that the gods, after all, are *nothing but* infantile fantasies. In one sense this is, of course, true, because in so far as we need to personify spiritual powers and principles at all we are still in the infantile condition. But this does not mean that when we cease to personify spiritual factors they are no longer real. The mental level of so-called scientific rationalism is in this respect equivalent to that of word-fetishism. To the primitive mind the word, and the thing designated by the word, are identical. To a tight, unimaginative mind the personification and the psychic factor designated by the personification are identical. It is natural, therefore, that an authoritative, rational explanation of the image should be credited with having done away with its content.

This peculiar blindness to spiritual facts is, after all, not peculiar to highly specialized minds: the migration of the god-value from the sacred images, where for generations it has been associated with sacred ritual and pious observance, must inevitably result in a widespread neglect or repudiation of spiritual values. Traditional vessels which no longer contain the living spirit soon fall into decay, and in the restless transitional period before the new symbol is born a troubling darkness and loss of faith must be anticipated.

All the illusions and tragic disillusionings of Christendom have resulted from the adolescent propensity to insist upon a concrete interpretation of a symbolical statement. The eagerness of religious enthusiasm is intolerant of impersonal interpretations. It gave rise to the absolute belief of the early Christians in the imminent destruction of the world, to the same expectation at the end of a thousand years, and to the constantly deferred anticipation of the Second Coming. From the standpoint of spiritual fact all the arguments concerning the historicity of Christ are equally beside the mark, since no one but a misanthropic specialist could mistake the vivid power of the Logos in the sayings and deeds attributed to the Jesus of the gospels. Truly to venerate the divine spirit which inspired Lao-Tzŭ, Confucius, Gotama, and Jesus, we must first release it from the burden of our adolescent expectations. These Immortals will be honoured to the end of time, not because they were gods, but because among men of their time they offered to the living spirit the most transparent vessel and the most authentic voice for the utterance of the redeeming truth.

But if the redeeming truth does not appear in the outer world, it should be sought in the inner with the light of introverted reason. To listen to the voice of introverted reason is our way of talking to the snake. When the author of these drawings, in his state of exhausted longing, turned within towards his own subject, he drew the Boddhisattva among the mountains he knows, and he made him equal and in a sense identical with the mountain. Moreover, as the high mountains are often concealed by clouds, so the self as the bearer of divinity is hard to discover behind the mists of illusion.

If the time has come for the West to leave behind its spiritual childhood and adolescence we shall not look for a new Saviour to come and redeem mankind, but learn instead the way by which the apparent blind drift and urgency of biological existence can be transformed through the discovery and service of the self. In the very making of this picture out of a harassed mood, the subject is following a practical and highly effective way. Everything one makes which is done with the motive of allowing the unknown to become manifest, or of making the unconscious conscious, is from this point of view a step towards spiritual maturity and responsibility.

Those, therefore, who are willing to listen to the voice of introverted reason will perceive in this descent of the winged dragon a very remarkable change from the representation of the same theme in Drawing 26. In the former drawing the birth was conceived as taking place from the church. Were this to be taken prophetically, it would be perfectly possible to cherish the notion of a Second Coming and to fall into the illusory expectation of concrete fulfilment. But the symbol of a winged serpent, by not lending itself to enthusiastic personification, challenges an act of reflection and interpretation, thus evoking an attitude of introversion. This is confirmed by the particular *mudra*, or gesture of the Buddha's hands, which denotes the idea of reflection and meditation as well as teaching or illustration.

* * * * *

Though in no sense invalidating its essential meaning, there is a detail in the subject's elucidation of the picture which throws an interesting sidelight on his individual problem. I refer to the goat's head which marks the position of the navel. This, as we discovered earlier, is the original centre of being, inasmuch as the first cells of the developing embryo are laid down at the umbilicus. The point of interest lies in the fact that the goat persisted in being represented in spite of the subject's intention to draw a ram. Not content with this, the subject proceeded to confuse the goat with Aries, the spring point of the Zodiac. Aries is, of course, the ram, with which the goat (*i.e.*, Capricorn) stands in the favourable relation of trine.

The persistence of the goat in coming thus uninvited into the picture, and the subsequent confusion with Aries in the subject's mind, are complex-indicators. On grounds of ancient Christian symbolism the ram and the goat are protagonists of the Christian-Pagan conflict, which was expressed in unmistakable imagery in the subject's own dream. A further allusion to the same problem may be discerned in his comment that the picture represented an attempt to reconcile "physical nature and spirit: asceticism versus the natural man, who wants to live in villages, close to the earth." The goat's head gives us the clue to this vast subterranean problem of the Western soul, but with the same aid we may also understand the strange, rather distorted proportions of the Buddha figure, suggesting a rather strained asceticism, rather than the serene poise of the God of the Lotus.

The goat wins his place in the central symbolical position because he represents the motive of opposition to, or departure from, the traditional pattern. From the point of view of the Christian sheepfold, the goat is the alluring renegade, seducing libido to the opposite principle. But how could the subject have discovered the mountain of introversion and the emotional release and fulfilment experienced in this drawing, if there had been no renegade goat to lead him into this strange country? Thus the goat is given the place of honour at the navel, and is even allotted the astrological place of honour normally occupied by Aries, the spring point of the Zodiac.

In saying that this drawing provides a fitting conclusion to the series, I had in mind the main psychological theme which runs like a silken thread throughout the series. I allude to the problem of archaic dynamism versus control. We saw how his frenzied intellectual efforts to enforce an arbitrary control over the unconscious led the subject inevitably to the *sacrificium intellectu* of Drawing 20, and how the solution emerged in the discovery of a totalized, central will which included both conscious and unconscious. The discovery of the supra-personal self is, as we have seen in both series, a world-changing event, and in this final drawing we see how the characteristic schizophrenic problem has prompted the subject to a deeply satisfying statement of the solution. The arch-symbol of archaic dynamism is transformed into the new aspect of the Creative Logos. The snake, the repudiated elder god of the Genesis myth, becomes the living expression of the introverting principle and the bearer of a new wisdom. Thus, instead of instigating an atavistic fall, this archaic ruler of the underworld becomes the fertilizing symbol of a new conscious discipline.

CONCLUSION

Before I bring this study to a close, the reader may wish to know something more about the two subjects who supplied the indispensable material for the investigation. Colleagues and general readers alike are liable to ask: " What results did you get ?" What am I to say ? As both subjects have participated in the making of it, they will also doubtless read the book, and they alone can say whether or not the work is adequate from the standpoint of the human document. In psychological matters this standpoint must claim priority, because a work that is humanly wrong cannot claim to be scientifically valid. Man is our study, and man is our judge.

Psychotherapy has a perfect right to be proud of its results. If the results of our work were not decisive I, for one, should be only too happy to dance on the grave of psychotherapy forthwith. Supposing, on the other hand, we approached either of the two men whose material we have studied with a naive " Are you cured ?" he would probably answer, " Cured of what ?" The schizoid individual is rarely, if ever, a disabled neurotic; neither does he suffer, as a rule, from distressing bodily symptoms. He is a man who has been singled out by fate to accept solitariness as the fundamental condition of his existence. The split in his own nature sunders him psychologically from his kind. What he needs, above all, is a means of understanding his own singularity, and a method by which he can look upon the strange opposition in himself and nature without fear or cynicism.

But let his understanding of himself be never so competent, the schizoid individual will always be solitary, even though he may not, perhaps, be noticeably cut off from his fellowmen. Solitariness is his fate, not because his nature is antisocial or misanthropic, but simply for the reason that the character of his inner experience is so different from that of the average man. The sense of kinship is rooted in common experience, and, if this is lacking, no amount of intelligible explanation can form the bridge which only coincident experience can provide.

With these subjects, therefore, it could never be a question of " a few common-sense talks " upon instinctual difficulties, nor would a merely mechanical drainage of the unconscious by reductive analysis meet the case.

The reader will have observed that, in both cases, the flow of unconscious events led straight to the religious problem. I would not go so far as to say that the religious question underlies every psychoneurotic disorder; but with regard to the borderline schizophrenic, the compulsion neurotic, and the greater number of obsessional cases, no cure is feasible, according to my experience, without a vital renewal of life, which is what religion is really concerned with.

In attempting to go with the wider implications of the material, I shall probably be reproached with unscientific methods. I have myself experienced the so-called scientific method of handling psychic material, and, in so far as this means the exclusion of every other criterion but that of the intellect, I must reject it as inadequate for the cure of souls. There is a vitality and an inherent, directing purpose in this so-called unconscious material which refuses to be reduced to elementary categories—not, at least, without offence to reason. It claims to be dealt with as an individual expression and understood with individual sympathy and discretion. My aim has been to hold this human claim in one hand and the claims of science in the other. From neither angle, therefore, will the work appear to be quite as it should be. From the human angle much has been said, and even underlined, which nice feeling and good taste would have omitted, while from the angle of science much has been asserted as psychologically probable for which adequate terms of reference are lacking. Yet in spite of the many intractable difficulties of demonstration, I am convinced that the investigation of the autonomous psyche and its products has an importance at the present time exceeding the claims of any other branch of knowledge.

On these grounds, therefore, I commend this work, with all its shortcomings, to the fair appraisal of reasonable minds, not forgetting Kant's humane definition of understanding: " the realization of a thing to the measure which is sufficient for our purpose."

INDEX

B

D

G

H

I

J

M

V

W

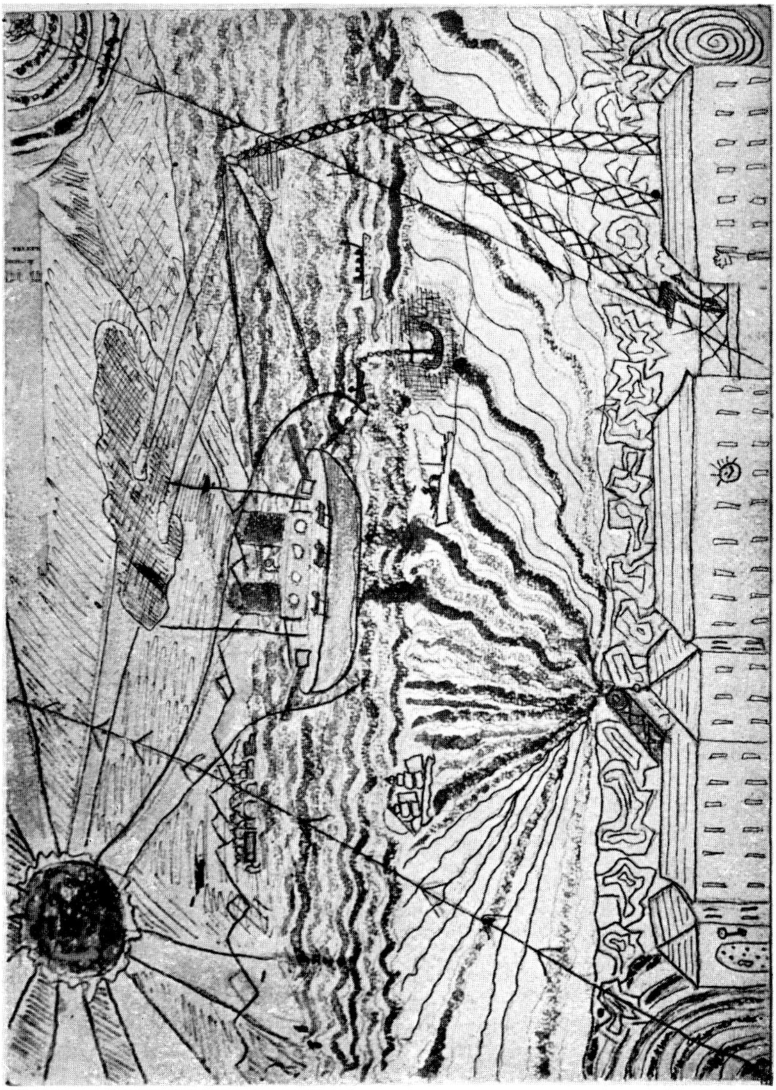

DRAWING I

DRAWING II

DRAWING III

DRAWING IV

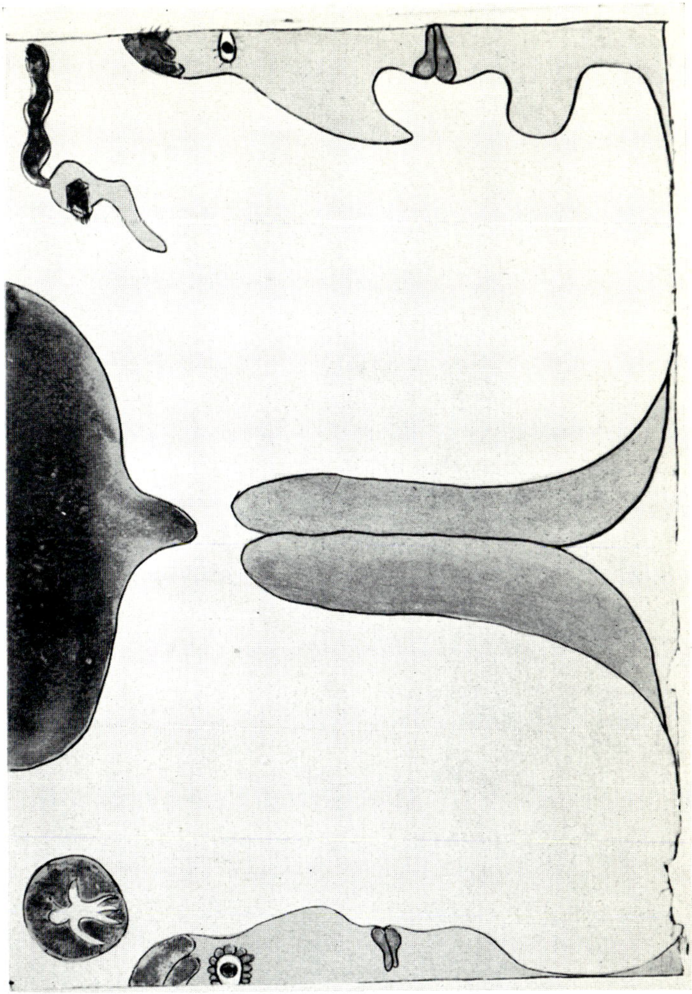

DRAWING V

DRAWING VI

DRAWING VII

DRAWING IX

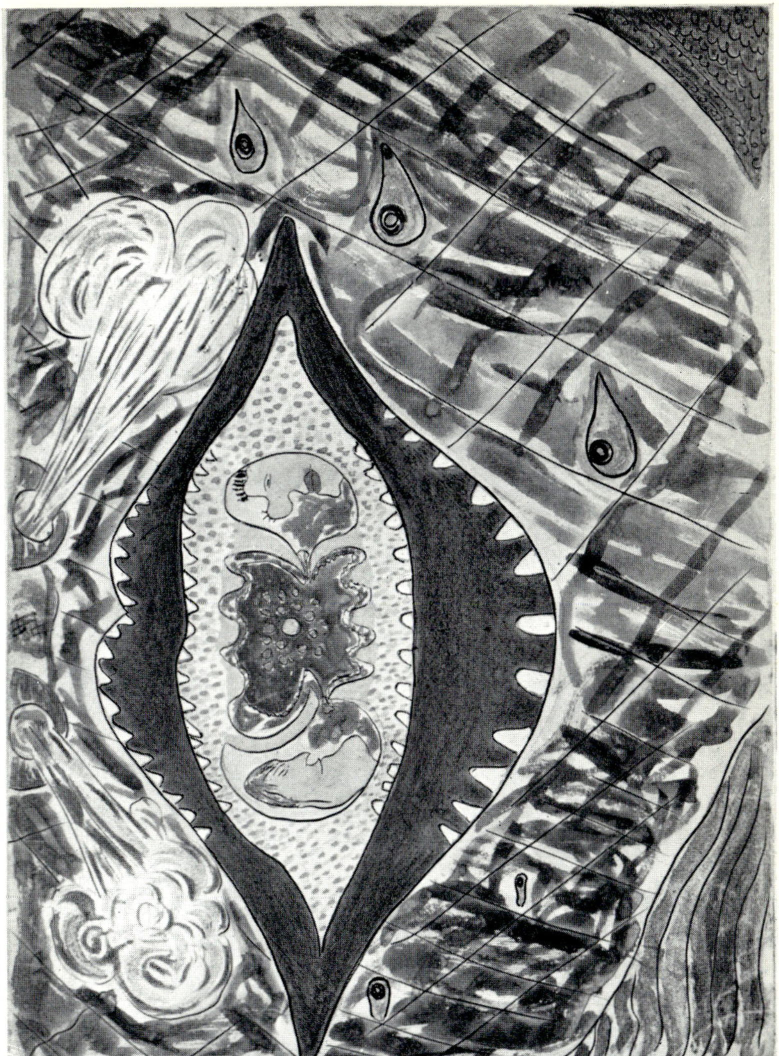

DRAWING VIII

DRAWING X

DRAWING XI

DRAWING XII

DRAWING XIII

DRAWING XIV

DRAWING XV

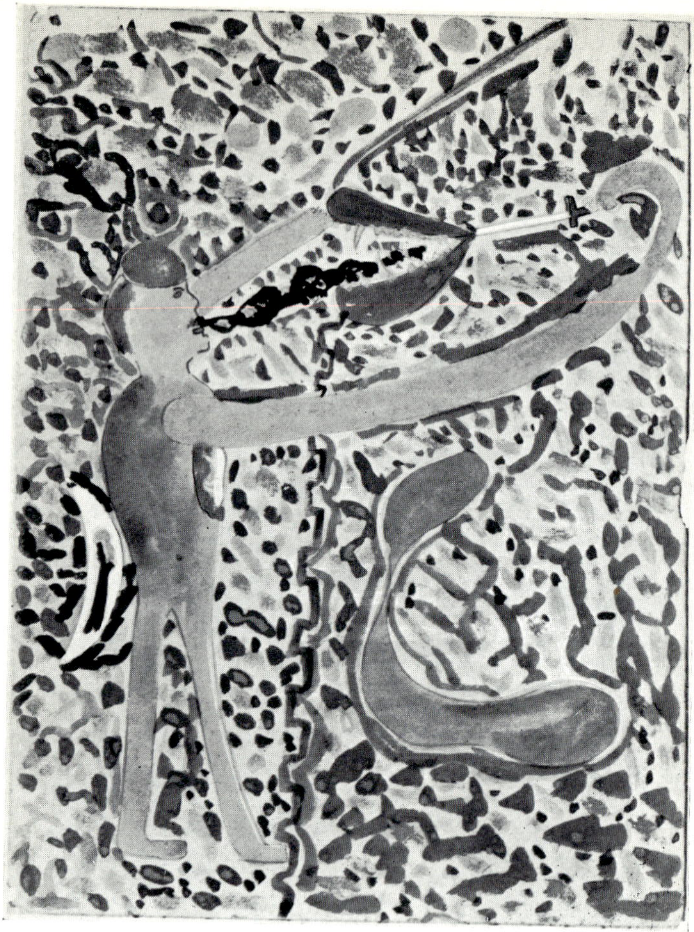

DRAWING XVI

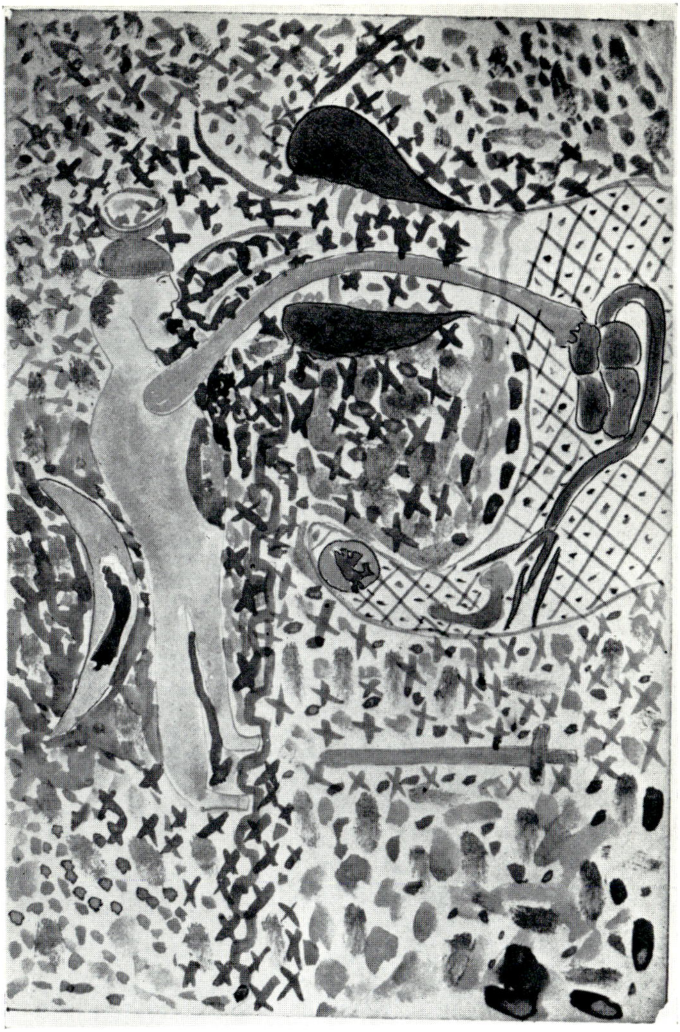

DRAWING XVII

DRAWING XVIII

DRAWING XIX

DRAWING XX

DRAWING XXI

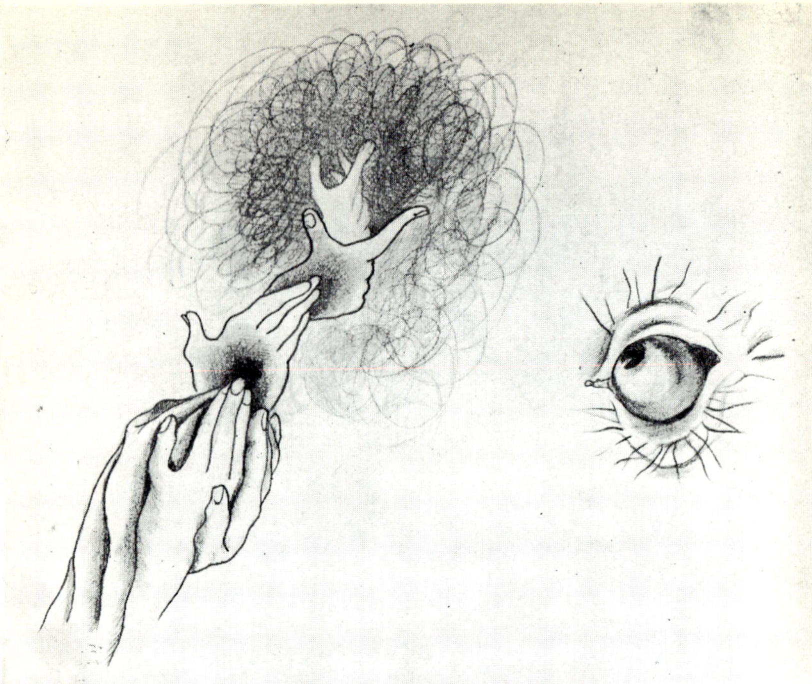

Drawing 1

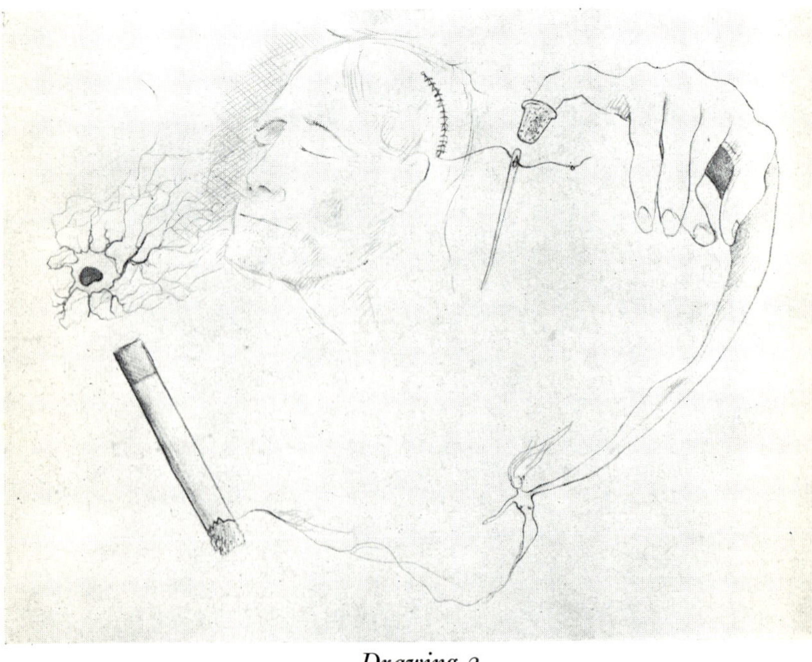

Drawing 2

Drawing 14

Drawing 13

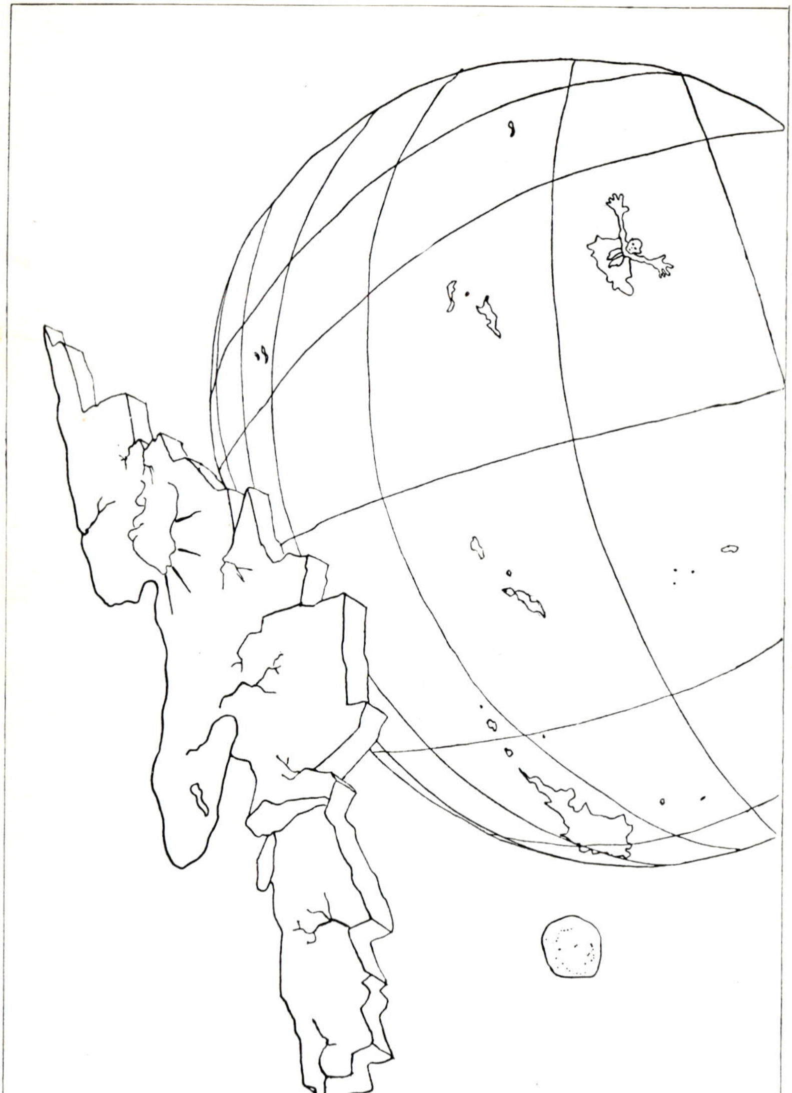

Drawing 15

Drawing 19

Drawing 20

Drawing 23

Drawing 24

Drawing 25

Drawing 26

Drawing 27

FIG I. A LAMAIST VAJRA-MANDALA

FIG 2. MULADHARA CHAKRA

FIG 3

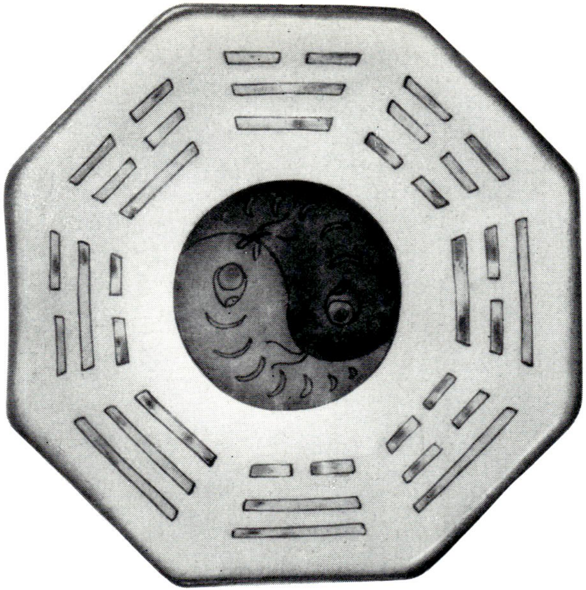

FIG 4. BOWL BEARING THE T'AI CH'I OR GREAT MONAD

FIG 5. HORRIFIC ASPECT

FIG 7
LE TEMPS ET
LES PLANTES

Paul Klee

FIG 8. PAYSAGE À LA LETTRE R

Paul Klee

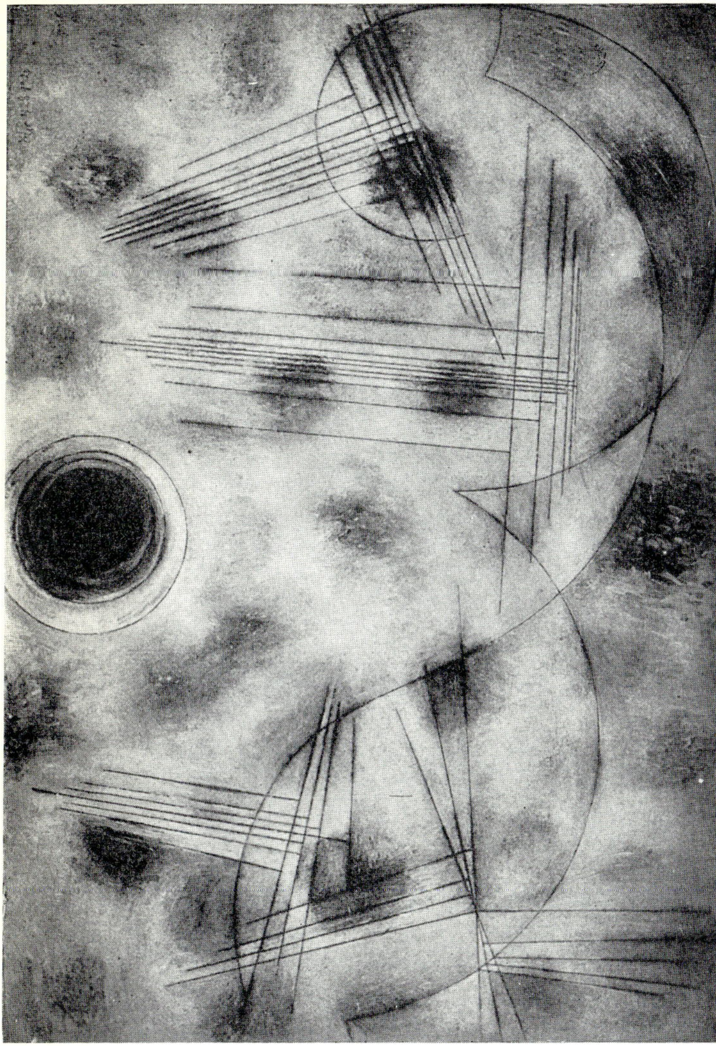

Paul Klee

FIG 9.
SONDES SUR
LES VAGUES

FIG 10. DRAGON TIGER SCREEN